# Protagonists of War

AVISOS DE FLANDES 18

Series Editor: Werner Thomas

# Protagonists of War

Spanish Army Commanders
and the Revolt
in the Low Countries

Raymond Fagel

LEUVEN UNIVERSITY PRESS

This publication is part of the project *Facing the Enemy. The Spanish army commanders during the first decade of the Dutch Revolt (1567-1577)* (with project number 360-52-170), NWO Free competition.

Published in 2021 by Leuven University Press / Presses Universitaires de Louvain / Universitaire Pers Leuven. Minderbroedersstraat 4, B-3000 Leuven (Belgium).

© Raymond Fagel, 2021
This book is published under a Creative Commons Attribution Non-Commercial Non-Derivative 4.0 Licence.

Further details about Creative Commons licences are available at http://creativecommons.org/licenses/ Attribution should include the following information: R. Fagel, *Protagonists of War: Spanish Army Commanders and the Revolt in the Low Countries*. Leuven, Leuven University Press.
(CC BY-NC-ND 4.0)

ISBN 978 94 6270 287 5 (Paperback)
ISBN 978 94 6166 403 7 (ePDF)
ISBN 978 94 6166 404 4 (ePUB)
https://doi.org/10.11116/9789461664037
D/2021/1869/28
NUR: 685

Layout and cover design: Friedemann bvba
Cover illustration: Left: Cristóbal de Mondragón. Painting by Abraham de Rycke (1591), private collection, Torre de Murga, Spain. Photo: Stadhuismuseum Zierikzee. Right: Sancho Dávila, anonymous painting, collection of the Marquis of Villanueva de Valdueza, Spain. Photo: Cuauhtli Gutiérrez López.

To Sam and Simon

# Table of Contents

**Abbreviations**   9

**Introduction**   11

**Words of gratitude**   25

**Chapter I: Captain Julián: the hero of the battlefield**   27

The myth of Captain Julián (**27**) – The hero of a duel (**31**) – In the service of the old Emperor (**37**) – In the service of the young King (**43**) – The Prince of Orange's dog (**49**) – The Duke of Alba's hangman (**60**) – Julián and the Prince of Orange (**66**) – Luctor et submergo (**74**) – ¡Adiós Julián! (**83**) – Fortune, fame and family (**92**) – The hero on stage (**103**) – A Spanish warrior (**110**)

**Chapter II: Sancho Dávila: the champion of Catholic Spain**   115

A Spanish hero (**115**) – A hero in the family (**116**) – An international soldier (1554-1567) (**122**) – Battling against the rebels (1568) (**127**) – The *castellano* of Antwerp (1568-1572) (**133**) – The relief of Middelburg (1572-1573) (**143**) – An Albista under Luis de Requesens (**155**) – The Battle of Mookerheyde (1574) (**159**) – The great mutiny (1574) (**164**) – The ongoing war (1574-1576) (**170**) – The Spanish Fury of Antwerp (1576) (**181**) – The Spanish Fury on stage (**184**) – His failed knighthood (**188**) – Last years in Portugal (1581-1583) (**192**) – Protagonist of a historical novel (2007) (**195**) – Friends and heretics (**196**)

**Chapter III: Cristóbal de Mondragón: the good Spaniard**   199

Eternal fame (**199**) – From soldier to captain (**202**) – The early years of the Revolt (**211**) – The search for a knighthood (**217**) – Goes: like Moses crossing the seas (**219**) – A commander in action (1572-1573) (**222**) – The siege of Middelburg: hunger and honour (**227**) – Orange and Mondragón (**234**) – The life of an Albista under Requesens (**236**) – Quarrelling around Breda (1575) (**241**) – The Red Sea opens again, and again (**244**) – The siege of Zierikzee

(1575-1576) (**247**) – The mutiny (**253**) – The siege of Ghent castle (**256**) – Life and death (1577-1596) (**257**) – Mondragón on the Dutch stage (**262**) – Victory of the good (**267**)

**Chapter IV: Francisco de Valdés: the exemplary soldier**     271

A Miles Christi (**271**) – A love story (**274**) – What a terrible man! (**280**) – The unknown Valdés (and the story of his wounds) (**283**) – The correspondence (**287**) – The first years in the Low Countries (1567-1572) (**289**) – From Sargento mayor to Maestre de campo (**294**) – The first siege of Leiden (1573-1574) (**300**) – The second siege of Leiden (1574) (**309**) – Mutiny (**320**) – Final years (**329**) – An exemplary soldier (**332**)

**General conclusion: episodic war narratives in comparison**     335

Chronicles, pamphlets and *relaciones* (**335**) – Friends and foes (**339**) – Before the outbreak of the Revolt (**341**) – A life in letters (**343**)

**Bibliography**     349

**Index**     377

# Abbreviations

| | |
|---|---|
| AA | Archivo de los Duques de Alba, Palacio de Liria, Madrid |
| AGS | Archivo General de Simancas |
| ARAB | Algemeen Rijksarchief van België, Brussels |
| AHN | Archivo Histórico Nacional, Madrid |
| ARCV | Archivo de la Real Chancillería de Valladolid |
| BL | British Library, London |
| BNE | Biblioteca Nacional de España, Madrid |
| BO | Correspondence of William of Orange (Briefwisseling van Willem van Oranje: http://resources.huygens.knaw.nl/wvo) |
| BZ | Archivo y Biblioteca Francisco de Zabálburu, Madrid |
| CD | *Colección de Documentos Inéditos para la Historia de España*, 112 vols. (Madrid 1842-1895) |
| CEF | Collection Edouard Favré, Geneva |
| CG | Correspondance de Granvelle, E. Poullet, Ch. Piot, *Correspondance du cardinal de Granvelle 1565-1586*, 12 vols. (Brussels 1877-1896) |
| CM | L.P. Gachard, ed., *Correspondance de Marguérite d'Autriche, duchesse de Parme, avec Philippe II* (Brussels 1867); J.S. Theissen, ed., *Correspondance française de Marguérite d'Autriche, duchesse de Parme, avec Philippe II* (Utrecht 1942) |
| CP | L.P. Gachard and J. Lefèvre, eds., *Correspondance de Philippe II* (Brussels, Ghent and Leipzig 1851-1960) |
| CSP | Calendar of State Papers |
| CT | L.P. Gachard, ed., *Correspondance de Guillaume le Taciturne*, III, (Brussels, Leipzig and Ghent 1851) |
| DBE | Diccionario Biográfico Electrónico, Real Academia de la Historia, http://dbe.rah.es/ |
| E | Sección Estado, AGS |
| EA | Duke of Alba, ed., *Epistolario del III duque de Alba*, 3 vols. (Madrid 1952) |
| IVDJ | Instituto Valencia de Don Juan, Madrid |
| NCD | *Nueva Colección de Documentos Inéditos para la Historia de España*, 6 vols. (Madrid 1892-1896) |
| RAH | Real Academia de la Historia, Madrid |
| RBM | Real Biblioteca, Madrid |
| UBL | University Library, Leiden |

# Introduction

This is a book on early modern war narratives. In order to reach a fuller understanding of war narratives in general and those on the Revolt in the Low Countries in particular, it is necessary to return to the stories as they came into being. How did people describe the events they participated in, witnessed or heard about? Episodic descriptions of war events and their protagonists can be found in letters and chronicles, but also in a wide variety of other sources, such as poems, theatre plays, engravings, songs and news pamphlets.

This is at the same time also a book about a small group of Spanish military commanders active in the Low Countries during the first decade of the Revolt (1567-1577). They are the authors of the letters, the protagonists people talked and wrote about; they were brave heroes in the stories of some, cruel oppressors in the stories of others. Starting from a nationalistic point of view, one could consider these opposites to be clearly divided between Spanish and Dutch sources. However, going back to the episodic narratives of the period itself, it will become evident that this is an unacceptable simplification of the dynamics of early modern society. The war narratives did not come into being as prefabricated building blocks of nineteenth-century nationalism. The Revolt was a civil war, not a clash between nations.[1]

The underlying idea of this book is that we must go back to studying the episodic narratives, the often very detailed anecdotes on the war's events and their protagonists.[2] Most of the chronicles and letters are very factual in nature, as Hayden White once noted with some disapproval: "These narratives do not conclude, they just terminate".[3] Though the terminology 'episodic narratives' has been used in the past to designate primitive forerunners of modern literature, in this book they are considered a timeless form of narrative, containing factual and detailed information without obvious or explicit hindsight as to its meaning.[4] By closely following the development of these episodic narratives we can try to understand the underlying assumptions. The stories change depending

---

[1] Van Nierop, *Verraad*.
[2] Fagel, 'Describir la guerra'; Idem, 'Introduction'.
[3] White, *Metahistory*, 5-6; Idem, 'Value'.
[4] Fineman, 'History'; Van Dijk, 'Episodes'; Fludernik, 'Towards'.

on the perspective of their authors, the period they were written in, the genre the texts belonged to, and the audience the authors were addressing. Episodic narratives constitute a main body of narrative that deserves closer attention within history writing. Most stories come into being as mere anecdotes, from the answer to simple questions like 'how was your day?' to the chains of anecdotes that are created when somebody tells his life story. This book looks at all the stories that were told at the time, and not just at those that have become part of the historical canon of either Spain or the Netherlands.

This focus on episodic narratives means that this book does not engage directly with other important and related fields within the study of war narratives. Judith Pollmann's pioneering research project on early modern memory and the Revolt in the Low Countries resulted in various relevant publications. Within this project, Jasper van der Steen studied the different narratives that were created in the Dutch Republic and in the so-called Spanish Netherlands.[5] German historians have especially considered ego-documents and autobiographical texts on the Thirty Years' War, while Yuval Harari wrote an insightful book on renaissance military memoirs.[6] In Spain, especially the literary side of war narratives has been studied, including theatre plays, epic poems and literary texts written by the military themselves.[7]

The episodic narratives on the Spanish commanders during the early phase of the Revolt in the Low Countries can also be used to counterbalance one of the most enduring master narratives of the early modern period, the so-called Black Legend of Spain.[8] Though very present in the Low Countries, this anti-Hispanic discourse can also be found in other societies that had to deal with a Spanish presence or the fear of such. During the period itself, the very negative image of the Spanish was already used as propaganda by those involved in the complaints and the subsequent rebellious movement that started around the time Philip II took over as Lord of the Low Countries from his father, Emperor Charles V. In order to smooth out the differences existing between the inhabitants of the Low Countries, the supposed opposition of all inhabitants to the

---

[5] Van der Steen, *Memory wars*; Van der Steen, 'North and south'; Pollmann, *Memory*; Erika Kuijpers, et al., *Memory*.

[6] Krusenstjern, *Selbstzeugnisse*; Harari, *Renaissance military memoirs*.

[7] Rodríguez Pérez, *Dutch Revolt*; García Hernán, *Cultura*; Martínez, *Front lines*; Murrin, *History*; Nievas Rojas, 'Nuevos datos'.

[8] García Cárcel, *Leyenda negra*; Pollmann, 'Natürliche Feindschaft'; Hillgarth, *Mirror*; De Schepper, 'Guerra de Flandes'; Martínez Luna, *Ondraaglijk juk*; Swart, 'Black Legend'.

Spanish was highlighted by rebel propaganda, creating at the same time an image of 'the' Spanish enemy. As early as 1569 Alonso de Ulloa wrote about the insulting books, full of cruel stories, published in Brussels against the Spaniards.[9]

During the Twelve Years' Truce (1609-1621), when discussion raged on the continuation of the war, this anti-Hispanic rhetoric became a dominant feature in many political texts. In the course of the seventeenth century this by then fully fledged enemy image was turned into the foundation narrative of the Dutch Republic, and as such it became the mainstream image of the Spanish, notwithstanding the fact that there could also be found – often occluded – praise for elements of Spanish culture within the Republic.[10] From the late eighteenth century on, modern nationalist cultural expressions again emphasised a clear and seemingly definitive dichotomy between the good inhabitants of the Low Countries and the evil Spaniards.

And although the inhabitants of the present Kingdom of the Netherlands no longer show hatred for the inhabitants of Spain and their culture, as soon as the discussion turns to the history of the Revolt and the Eighty Years' War the Spanish are again generally turned into the monsters they have been since the start of rebel propaganda. Every year during the festivities around the commemoration of the taking of the small Holland town of Brielle on 1 April 1572, the 'Spanish commander' is taken through the streets in a cage and the highlight of the celebrations is the hanging of the commander on top of a bulwark. Even though in 1572 there was no Spanish commander in Brielle.

In the Netherlands, this reaction is directly connected to the idea that the Spanish had once 'occupied' their country. The connection with the German occupation during World War II is easily made, and until the arrival of the Nazis in 1940 the Spanish army functioned as the national enemy number one.[11] In reality it had been a change of sovereign, from Charles V to Philip II, that supposedly turned Habsburg rule into a kind of Spanish domination.[12] After the start of the Revolt – taking the violent 1566 iconoclastic movement as its beginning – the arrival of a Spanish governor and Spanish soldiers, combined with an absent lord ruling from Spain, could easily and often willfully be misinterpreted as a Spanish occupation. In reality, Philip was the natural lord of the

---

[9] Ulloa, *Comentarios*, 18v.
[10] Rodríguez Pérez, *Literary Hispanophobia*.
[11] Lammers, *Vreemde overheersing*.
[12] Rodríguez-Salgado, *Changing face*.

Low Countries, making use of politicians and soldiers from his other domains, not only from Spain, but also from his other territories, like the Franche-Comté, Portugal and his Italian realms. At the time this seemed the logical thing to do for the monarch, – Spanish soldiers at this time had long served in Italy – but the criticism directed at using foreigners in his government and at his absence was also a logical reaction on the part of the inhabitants of the Low Countries. Philip II's inheritance of the Low Countries was troublesome from the very beginning.

The Spanish army in the Low Countries was brilliantly studied by Geoffrey Parker in 1972, and his standard work is still the point of departure for further research. No less brilliant are the much older articles written by the Belgian scholar Léon Van der Essen on the Spanish army in the Low Countries, and recently collected in a Spanish edition, with very clarifying introductions to his work and the Spanish army. Two of his articles on the government of the Duke of Alba and that of Luis de Requesens are especially useful for the subject. The 1933 anthology of Spanish war chronicles on the Revolt by Dutch hispanist Johan Brouwer is preceded by an elaborate and very original introduction. The practical sides of the Spanish army during the first decade of the Revolt (exactly the period of this book) were studied in 1979 by French military historian René Quatrefages. More recent contributions on the Spanish army in the Low Countries were published by Fernando González de León and Antonio José Rodríguez Hernández, though both authors focus mainly on the seventeenth century. As this book studies the narratives on the Spanish commanders, and not the history of the actual army, anybody interested in more information on the Spanish army in the Low Countries should consult the above studies.[13]

In Dutch historical literature on the Revolt the Spanish army is often considered as all the soldiers belonging to the royal army of the King of Spain. However, in this book its use is limited to the Spanish component of the royal army, that generally speaking was never much larger than 10,000 men, while the whole of the royal army could consist of more than 60,000 men, mostly Germans and Walloons, but also soldiers from England, Scotland, Italy, Portugal, and even Albania.

---

[13] Parker, *Army* (1972) and *Army* (2004); Parker, *Dutch Revolt*; Parker, *Spain*; Van der Essen, 'Kritisch onderzoek'; Idem, 'Kritische studie'; Van der Essen, *Ejército*; Brouwer, *Kronieken*; Quatrefages, *Tercios* (1979); Quatrefages. *Tercios* (1983); González de León, *Road* (1991); González de León, *Road* (2009); Rodríguez Hernández, *Tercios*.

## Four Spanish commanders

The Spanish military commanders in question are those who resonate most in the narratives of the time and held the most important positions during the first decade of the Revolt in the Low Countries. Sancho Dávila y Daza was the Governor of the Antwerp citadel and the commander of the Duke of Alba's personal guard; Cristóbal de Mondragón y Mercado was Governor of the castle in Ghent and a Colonel of Walloon troops. Julián Romero and Francisco de Valdés were both *Maestres de campo*, commanders of a Spanish infantry tercio, even reaching as high as being nominated *Maestres de campo general*, commanders of a whole army. None of these men belonged to the high nobility, and they were not even noble enough to put a 'Don' in front of their names.[14] The relatively low birth of some of the Spanish high command was exceptional in early modern Europe.

We find these four military commanders as the main protagonists in famous events such as the sacks of Mechelen, Antwerp, Zutphen and Naarden, the sieges of Mons, Middelburg, Haarlem, Leiden and Zierikzee, the battles of Dahlem, Heiligerlee, Jemmingen, the river Gete (near Jodoigne/Geldenaken), Quiévrain and Mookerheyde, and the infamous mutinies of 1574 and 1576. They were present at the executions of the Counts of Egmont and Horne, captured Marnix of Sint-Aldegonde, and almost got their hands on William of Orange during a nocturnal suprise attack on his army camp. These military commanders were also often responsible for their troops while being quartered in the cities and countryside of the Low Countries, causing major conflicts between the soldiers and the population. The continuous presence of Spanish troops during the first decade of the Revolt was an unprecedented event with foreign troops remaining under arms (and outstaying the welcome of the local inhabitants) for such a long period. Except for those staying in the fortresses, most military were lodged in private homes.

Two of these commanders, Julián Romero and Cristóbal de Mondragón, had been fighting in the Low Countries against the armies of the French kings for many years before the outbreak of the Revolt. Sancho Dávila and Francisco de Valdés, however, arrived in the Low Countries only in 1567 as members of the army of the Duke of Alba. Mondragón, Valdés and Dávila would all marry women from the Low Countries. Julián Romero was the exception. He had a wife and daughter in Madrid, but in Brussels he possessed a house where his three half-Netherlandish

---

[14] González de León, *Road* (2009) 64-65; Parker, *Army* (2004) 101.

children probably lived with their mother. Julián Romero was an exception also in that we cannot consider him a client of the Third Duke of Alba, Fernando Álvarez de Toledo, while the other three commanders clearly were the Duke's men. We shall see how this influenced their fates when Alba left the Low Countries and was replaced by the new Governor-general, Luis de Requesens.

The stories of Mondragón and Romero, in particular, make it possible to connect the history of the Revolt with that of the 1540s and 1550s, when Spanish soldiers were used by the sovereigns of the Low Countries to defend their territories against the troops of the French kings, taking us to the sieges of places like Saint-Dizier, Hesdin, Dinant, Lens, Saint-Quentin and Douai, all situated in the southern border region of the Low Countries. These anecdotes also connect the world of Emperor Charles V with that of his son, King Philip II, and show how Spanish influence gradually entered the lives of the inhabitants of the Low Countries as a result of the wars and the change of sovereign.

Studying the episodic narratives about these commanders makes it possible to compare how the Netherlandish and Spanish chronicles related the events and described their protagonists. However, it will become evident that there is no clear-cut division between the stories from Spain and those from the Low Countries. Stories change over time, but there existed a great variety of descriptions, far beyond a simple dichotomy between Netherlandish and Spanish sources. And these stories circulated in various forms throughout Europe, in German and Italian newsletters, as well as in chronicles from France and England.[15] Research shows that the difference between printed sources and manuscripts can also be an important explanation for diverging stories and images.[16]

In this book the chronicles and histories by Emanuel van Meteren and P.C. Hooft on the Dutch side, and Antonio Trillo and Bernardino de Mendoza on the Spanish side, have been used as a recurrent frame of the narratives on the commanders, but many other chronicles and histories have been used in the separate chapters, including those from other countries like France, Italy and England, as well as local chronicles.[17]

[15] Lamal, 'Orecchie'; Lamal, *News*.
[16] Álvarez Francés, 'Fabrication'; Fagel, Santiago Belmonte and Álvarez Francés, 'Eer en schuld'.
[17] Van Meteren, *Belgische oft Nederlandsche historie*; Van Meteren, *Historien*; Hooft, *Nederlandsche historien* (1642-1647); Hooft, *Nederlandse historiën* (2007); Mendoza, *Comentarios* (1948); Mendoza, *Comentarios* (2008); Trillo, *Historia*; Rodríguez Pérez, *Dutch Revolt*; Vermaseren, *Katholieke Nederlandse geschiedschrijving*; Van der Steen, *Memory wars*; Fernández Álvarez, 'Cuestión', 109-113; Groenveld, *Hooft*; Verduyn, *Emanuel*.

The availability of letters written by these same commanders makes it possible better to understand their experiences during the Revolt, but these sources also enable us to compare the manuscript letters with the published chronicles and other printed sources. It is unique to have letters written by the protagonists of the chronicles, and to be able to compare the descriptions in the letters with those in the more public sources, something that can hardly be achieved for earlier periods and other groups.

These letters have only incidentally been used for historical research. They often consist of loose strings of short paragraphs, each of them describing a different episode or anecdote, explaining events and the people involved. These letters served a very different purpose from the chronicles as they were written on the spur of the moment with concrete and often urgent intentions: asking for more money, extra soldiers or ammunition, outlining the strategic situation, or asking permission to leave the front. The archives of the Dukes of Alba at Liria Palace in Madrid, in particular, have provided many letters written by the commanders.

The four commanders also enable us to distance ourselves from the political points of view taken by the main political leaders of the period, such as King Philip II, William of Orange and the Duke of Alba, or by that of their political propaganda. Their views on the war will be used only when these are related to the functioning of our commanders. Giving a voice to the military commanders provides a perspective that differs from the traditional positions of both the royal government and the rebel leaders. They are not trying to defend their ideology, but write their letters as part of their military functions. The letters show that there was not one unchangeable and broadly shared Spanish outlook on the Revolt in the Low Countries.

Although the four chapters are clearly not genuine biographies of early modern individuals, the idea is that by collecting all possible information on the commanders and evaluating the documentation meticulously, we will be able to get as close to these people as the sources allow us to do. In this manner, the commanders become real people of flesh and blood, much more so than in the often very negative or very positive descriptions that are generally written about them.[18] In their letters the commanders offer insight into their political opinions and personal lives. These letters are often directed to people they knew personally, and there is no sharp division between their military office and what we consider nowadays as

---

[18] Brouwer and Limberger, *Hedendaagse biografieën*.

belonging to their private life. On all levels, professional and personal, these letters take us back to the actual war experiences. What was it like to be a Spanish soldier during the Revolt?[19]

Our point of departure is that these commanders are much more than just military men. They each have a personal life and their war effort is always related to their attempts to gain rewards and secure the future of their families and children. Being a military commander made having a private life a very complex matter, and the royal bureaucracy was so slow in rewarding its heroes that there was a constant flow of petitions from the commanders, functioning within a clientele system and fighting against the difficulty of residing far away from court for a very long period. They were not just defending God, King and country; the army was their only means of advancing personally in life. Especially for these men, who had little property of their own compared to the high nobility, royal favour was essential.

The Spanish officers' class from Romero's days has been described by Raffaele Puddu as a group of traditional knights of the cross who, as a kind of Don Quixotes *avant la lettre* were fighting for God, the King and honour. Puddu has constructed this devotional picture based on the study of treatises on the perfect soldier, literary sources such as plays, and artistic representations. Using Lope de Vega's plays and the El Greco portrait, Puddu describes Julián Romero as a brave but mostly obedient and pious soldier.[20] This image, however, reflects more a literary ideal than the real lives of these commanders.

The fact that both Sancho Dávila and Cristóbal de Mondragón were never awarded a knighthood in one of the religious chivalric orders in Spain because of doubts about their ancestry also demonstrates the rigidity of Spanish societies' ideas on purity of blood. On the other hand, in the case of Julián Romero it was said that he had received a knighthood without his ancestry being evaluated, this in close connection with another debate in the period around 1600: the position of professional military commanders of low birth in comparison to the traditional role of the high nobility. In the seventeenth century in particular this became an important issue.[21]

The stories of the four commanders will be followed up to the present day, showing that their *Nachleben* has taken very different forms. Theatre plays on these commanders were essential in structuring their present

---

[19] Smith, *Embattled self*, 13.
[20] Puddu, *Soldato*, 154-156; González de León, 'Doctors', 62.
[21] González de León, *Road* (2009) 7.

*Introduction*

image, often with important changes in the eighteenth century. The fact that nowadays Francisco de Valdés is better known in the Netherlands than Julián Romero has nothing to do with their lives (or with their image in the seventeenth century) but everything to do with the way Valdés's image was moulded from the eighteenth century onwards. In Spain, however, Julián Romero and Sancho Dávila have been the protagonists of recent biographies and historical novels, while a recent series on military commanders describes Mondragón, Dávila and Romero, but omits Francisco de Valdés, who in Spain is mostly known only for his military treatise.[22]

These four commanders belong to a larger group of commanders that has been studied during the research project entitled *Facing the enemy. Spanish army commanders during the first decade of the Dutch Revolt*.[23] Gaspar de Robles and Francisco Verdugo, both governors of Frisia, are two of the other important commanders during this period, and Portuguese-born Gaspar de Robles is a protagonist within the research of Beatriz Santiago Belmonte and Leonor Álvarez Francés.[24] Both Verdugo and Robles had lived in the Low Countries for many years before the outbreak of the Revolt, and they had both married women from the nobility of the Low Countries and commanded Walloon and German soldiers. Verdugo is famous for his treatise on his government of Frisia, while Robles even has a statue in Frisia, erected during the early modern period, and recently he received a great deal of local attention, even resulting in an opera. However, though there are some very thrilling anecdotes to be found on these two commanders, there is much less material when compared to that on the other four.

The same holds for Alonso López Gallo, Governor of Culemborg and Colonel of Walloon troops, and his collaegue, Francisco de Montesdoca, from Maastricht, Maestres de campo Sancho de Londoño, Alonso de Ulloa, Gonzalo de Bracamonte, Fernando de Toledo (Alba's nephew and brother-in-law) and Rodrigo de Toledo, Governor Jerónimo de Salinas of Ghent castle, and cavalry generals such as Alonso de Vargas, Juan de Mendoza Sarmiento (murdered in Antwerp on 3 January 1574) and

---

[22] De las Heras, *Julián*; Esparza, *Memorias*; Martín García, *Sancho*; Martínez Ruiz, *Castellano*; Martínez Laínez, *Ocaso*.

[23] NWO Research project *Facing the enemy. The Spanish army commanders during the first decade of the Dutch Revolt, 1567-1577*, Free Competition, NWO 360-52-170 (2014-2019).

[24] Álvarez Francés, 'Robles'; Van Soest, 'Español'; Sevenster, *Stenen man*; Fagel, 'Imagen'; Fagel, 'Francisco Verdugo'; Van den Broek, *Voor God*.

Fernando de Toledo (Alba's natural son).[25] Other military officers who can be found as protagonists of war narratives during this decade include famous captains like Rodrigo Zapata, Lope de Acuña, Lope de Figueroa, Bernardino de Mendoza and Hernando Pacheco.[26] Of course, there is also Don Fadrique de Toledo, the Duke's son and heir, but his presence in the Low Countries would deserve a more elaborated biography than is possible within this context, also because his status places him in between the commanders and the governing policy makers.[27]

This book is an invitation to return to the sources of early modern Europe. When we leave the nationalist histories of the nineteenth and twentieth centuries behind, and look further than the canonised images they have left us, there arises an enormous richness of stories and opinions, not fitting simple nationalist agendas, showing a Europe that was continuously at war, but also a Europe in which frontiers and language barriers were easy to cross. The first decade of the Revolt in the Low Countries was both a civil war and a European conflict, with protagonists from very different parts of the continent, but also with commentators writing from many different angles. By focussing on four Spanish commanders and rewriting the history of their participation in the Revolt and of the narrativisation of their deeds and experiences, it is possible to create new stories about an old conflict or, better, to give old stories a new life.

In *La famosa comedia de Don Juan de Austria en Flandes* (1604), nowadays attributed to playwright Alonso Remón, we encounter three of the four protagonists of this book. Both Cristóbal de Mondragón and Sancho Dávila have speaking roles, while Julián Romero can be found only once on stage: "salen Julián Romero y Mondragón, y todos los soldados que puedan, y Sancho Dávila".[28] It is unclear how the audience would actually know one of the commanders was the famous Julián Romero. Was he recognisable to them by his physique, or was he announced as such?[29] His use as a cameo in this play is clear proof of his fame, but, of

---

[25] Cabañas Agrela, 'Alonso de Vargas'; García Hernán, 'Sancho de Londoño'; García Hernán, 'Don Sancho'; Caunedo del Potro, 'Disgregación', 88, 94 (Jerónimo de Soria y Salinas was the son of Burgos merchant Diego de Soria and Catalina de Salinas); de Jonge, 'Culemborg'; (on López Gallo). On Salinas: *Van Vaernewijck, Beroerlicke tijden*. Juan de Mendoza Sarmiento is also known as Juan de Mendoza Noroña.
[26] Landía Pascual, 'Hernando de Toledo'; Fernández Conti and Labrador Arroyo, 'Entre Douro'; Mazzocchi, 'Lope de Acuña'; Cabañas Agrela, *Don Bernardino*.
[27] Cabañas Agrela, 'Fadrique'; Martínez Hernández, 'Desafío'.
[28] Remón, 'Famosa comedia', 409-410, 427-428, 431.
[29] Romero also had a non-speaking role in a 1934 Dutch film about William of Orange.

course, the same holds true for Mondragón and Dávila. Francisco de Valdés may be considered less famous in the literary world of Golden Age Spain, but we can also find him as an experienced commander in Lope de Vega's *El asalto de Mastrique por el Príncipe de Parma*, together with Cristóbal de Mondragón.[30] And there are more Spanish plays that use these commanders as protagonists – Julián Romero even being the eponymous hero of two of them – or mention their names as examples of famous commanders.[31] The only other Spanish commander of this period with a life on stage is Captain Lope de Figueroa, who was indeed already famous during the first decade of the Revolt in the Low Countries – for example during the Battle of Jemmingen – but who was not yet playing an important role as a military commander.[32]

Francisco de Valdés and Cristóbal de Mondragón will also gain fame on the stage of the Low Countries, while Sancho Dávila even makes it to the English stage, though with a mutilated name as Sancto Danila.[33] Julián Romero also reached the stage in the Low Countries, but mostly as a minor figure, although he had the honour of being assasinated in his tent by Dutch national heroine Kenau of Haarlem, as a form of poetic justice.[34] In 2013 he was back as the main villain in a Dutch historical novel.[35]

Due to the availability of sources and the character of the narratives, not all the chapters are entirely comparable. The first chapter on Julián Romero focusses mainly on chronicles, as the volume of his correspondence for the period between 1567 and 1577 is limited. As the archives of the Dukes of Alba are the main source of the commanders' letters, they are much more abundant for the other three commanders, who were more closely connected to the then Duke. Like Romero, Mondragón also features very often in the chronicles of the time, much more than the other two. Valdés, who is known mainly only for his treatise and his presence around the siege of Leiden, is much less prominent in the chronicles.

My research on these commanders also has a convoluted – and already quite long – history. I started by writing a study in Dutch on Julián Romero which forms the basis of the present chapter by way of an adapted, expanded and updated translation. This somewhat larger chapter

---

[30] Lope de Vega, 'Famosa tragicomedia'.
[31] Lope de Vega, 'Comedia famosa'; Cañizares, *Comedia famosa*.
[32] Escudero Baztán, 'Construcción'; Belloso Martín, *Antemuralla*.
[33] Greg, ed., *Larum*.
[34] Meijer-Drees, 'Vaderlandse heldinnen'; Hessen, *Beleegering*; Van der Eembd, *Haerlemse*.
[35] Van de Wal, *In naam*.

also delves more into the historical context of the period, explaining the most important events and actors involved. Perhaps we can consider as the centrepiece of Romero's chapter his possibly questionable behaviour as commander at the cruel punishment of the small town of Naarden in 1572.

The research on Sancho Dávila is completely new for this book, although the events around the infamous Spanish Fury of Antwerp (1576), of which he was the main protagonist, in particular have been the subject of several smaller contributions. The Fury is clearly the centrepiece of this chapter. Both Julián and Sancho were famous in their time and have also received much attention from historians, especially in Spain. These two chapters analyse the fame of two of the greatest heroes of the Spanish army of the sixteenth century: 'Él de las hazañas' (Julián: the man of great deeds) and 'El rayo de la guerra' (Sancho: the Lighting Bolt of the war), names that were already in use during the early modern period.

Cristóbal de Mondragón was also famous in his own time (in part because of his very long career), whereas Francisco de Valdés was much less well known. However, these two commanders are important protagonists within Dutch culture. A first draft of this book's chapter on Cristóbal de Mondragón had already been written when the plan for an exhibition on this commander in the Stadhuismuseum Zierikzee in 2020 came up. As a result, more specific research has been done on the local sources and circumstances around the siege of Zierikzee in 1576, turning it into the centrepiece of that chapter. Francisco de Valdés is a local celebrity of Leiden, the location of my university. Every year since 1997, we have co-organised a lecture on the 1574 siege of Leiden with the 'Association for the celebration and conmemoration of the siege and the liberation of the city on the third of October 1574', the *Drie Octobervereeniging*. In 2017 the draft of my chapter on Francisco de Valdés, already partially written, was turned into the lecture for the twentieth anniversary of the series, with an accompanying small publication in Dutch, and this subsequently became the extended basis of the current book chapter on Valdés in which the siege of Leiden is clearly the main event.[36]

Despite these internal differences, all four chapters delve into the same questions regarding the episodic narratives written about and by these commanders in an attempt to offer more insight into the construction and deconstruction of narratives, but also hopefully to recreate their life stories in order better to understand the similarities and differences that

---

[36] Fagel, *Leids beleg*; Idem, *Spaanse belegeraar*.

can be found among Spanish commanders active during the first decade of the Revolt in the Low Countries.

The different character of Francisco de Valdés also becomes evident when one focuses on the pictorial heritage on these commanders. Apart from some engravings, the only painting we have of Valdés is by the nineteenth-century Dutch history painter Simon Opzoomer, now in the collecction of the Rijksmuseum in Amsterdam, and is related to the story of his love for a woman from the Low Countries. The other three commanders were painted during or directly after their lives, showing the importance attached to them at the time, and these painings remained – at least for some time – in the hands of their heirs. Such was the case of the painting of Julián, now in the Prado museum in Madrid, which had been owned by descendants of his sister. The portraits of Sancho Dávila and his wife are still in the possession of his noble descendants, and the same holds for the portrait of Cristóbal de Mondragón. These last two portraits have recently been photographed as part of the research project on the Spanish commanders, and I would like to express my gratitude to their owners for allowing the photographing of these portraits.

All quotations have been translated into English, and for those that come from literary and archival sources, the original text is provided in the annotation.

# Words of gratitude

This book could not have existed without the NWO project *Facing the enemy*, in which I have worked closely with Beatriz Santiago Belmonte, Leonor Álvarez Francés and Jeroen Duindam. I especially thank Leonor and Beatriz for our collaboration, The project also included a conference in Leiden on war narratives in May 2018, and I would like to thank all participants. There were many more meetings within the project, in which we were able to discuss our ideas with well-known specialists like Geoffrey Parker, Gustaaf Janssens, Enrique Martínez Ruiz, Fernando Bouza, Alicia Esteban Estríngana and Santiago Martínez Hernández. We were also able to present our findings at meetings in Mechelen, Brugge, Amsterdam, Leiden, Groningen, Zierikzee, Wedde, Utrecht, Florence, Madrid and Santander.

A special word of gratitude goes to José Manuel Calderón Ortega, who helped us out with the letters in the ducal archive at the Liria Palace in Madrid, to Judith Pollmann and the other members of the redaction committee of the Three October Lecture in Leiden, to Albert Scheffers and all collaborators involved in the exhibition on Mondragón in Zierikzee, and to my brother Roland for editing the Dutch book on Julián Romero. And, of course, I would like to thank all archivists, librarians and historians who have assisted me throughout these years, including non-academic specialists on the Spanish army like Juan Luis Sánchez and Carlos Valenzuela.

My good friend Máximo García Fernández from the University of Valladolid has helped me ever since I arrived in Valladolid for the first time when working on my PhD. In Madrid, Bernardo García García of the Complutense and of the Fundación Carlos de Amberes is another indispensable friend. My wife Yolanda is the third Spanish pillar of my research, always ready to help out with her knowledge on the early modern period and the Revolt in the Low Countries. Without her it would have been a very different book. However, I would like to dedicate this book to our children, Simon (Simon Manuel) and Sam (Samuel Antonio), our own Hispano-Flemish heroes.

Julián Romero as knight of the Order of Santiago. Painting attributed to El Greco, Museo del Prado, Spain. © Photographic Archive Museo Nacional del Prado

CHAPTER I

# Captain Julián: the hero of the battlefield[1]

## The myth of Captain Julián

Captain Julián was already an international celebrity in his lifetime. A legendary duel, fought in the summer of 1546 at the royal court at Fontainebleau in the presence of the French royal family and the envoy of the English King, first made the name of this hitherto completely anonymous soldier a famous 'nom de guerre'. And this would not be all. In 1557 he was one of the most important Spanish heroes at the heroic struggle for Saint-Quentin between the French and the army of King Philip II. Between 1567 and 1577 he served as commander (*Maestre de campo*) of a regiment (*tercio*) of Spanish infantry troops sent to suppress the Revolt in the Low Countries.

We find the name of Captain Julián very frequently in chronicles and correspondence from his own time, both in Spanish and Netherlandish sources, and remarkably he is generally referred to as simply "Captain Julián" even after he had already been promoted to Maestre de campo. Cardinal Granvelle,[2] Governess Margaret of Parma, and even King Philip II all tended to refer to him in their letters solely by his first name. When he was nominated as the new Maestre de campo of the tercio of Sicily, the Viceroy knew the King would perfectly understand whom he meant by "Maestre de campo Julián".[3] We can find the same pattern in sources of a more literary nature. In the famous epic on the heroic deeds of the Spanish army, the *Araucana* (1578) by Alonso de Ercilla, he is simply mentioned as "el fuerte Iulián", "the strong Julián".[4]

The same occurred in Netherlandish literary sources as, even for his sworn enemies, the protestant Beggars, his first name was sufficient. In the famous Beggar song 'the safe-conduct to hell' he is scornfully called "our best friend captain Julian", with the verses wishing him to "the peat-

---

[1] This chapter is a reworked version of *Kapitein Julián. De Spaanse held van de Nederlandse Opstand* (Hilversum 2011). Some of the contents have been previously published in Spanish: Fagel, 'Julián'; Fagel, 'Describir'.
[2] Antoine Perrenot de Granvelle became a cardinal in 1561.
[3] CM III (1942) 359; Marichalar, *Julián*, 17; CD XXX, 109.
[4] Ercilla, *Araucana*, 515, 522.

cellar".⁵ It was not uncommon for Spanish military men to be addressed simply by their first name, but with Julián Romero the omission of his family name occurred much more frequently. Apparently, he had developed into a special character when he was still a captain and "Captain Julián" turned into a fixed form of identification.

There is no doubt that Julián himself contributed to a large extent to the creation of his own myth. He must have been an incredibly captivating and gifted storyteller. The famous French author Brantôme (a combination of war correspondent and chronicler of court life) declared that he hung on every word during their walk through the Sicilian harbour of Messina (in August 1565), where the French knight Brantôme had joined the Spanish army to support the liberation of Malta from Ottoman occupation. A few years later he travelled to Lorraine specifically to admire the Spanish army on its passage from Italy to the Low Countries, with Julián as Maestre de campo of the tercio of Sicily. Brantôme praised his eloquence "in the style of soldiers": never had he heard a soldier speak so well.⁶

Romero's fame lived on during the seventeenth century. Historian P.C. Hooft uses him regularly as a speaking protagonist in his *Nederlandse Historiën*, the unparellelled and magisterial epic on the Revolt, though he is not always as reliable as we would wish. It seems that Hooft uses Romero as a literary figure, who stands out as the prototype of the Spanish military man in the Low Countries, and possibly ascribes to him deeds that may have been the work of others. He even puts dialogues into his mouth to vivify his accounts. The Julián as created by Hooft is a dubious character: a brave warrior, but at the same time a typical Spaniard full of vanity and hypocrisy.

Spanish playwright Lope de Vega considered Julián to be the greatest Spanish hero of his time: "the brave Julián Romero, the bravest Spaniard born in our times". He may have even dedicated a whole comedy to him, simply called the *Comedia famosa de Julián Romero*, but there is uncertainty about the attribution. We also find Julián in two other plays by Lope de Vega: "the brave Romero, of whose rare virtues the books are full".⁷ In *El Buscón* (ca. 1605-1608), the picaresque novel by Francisco de Quevedo, Julián Romero is quoted as an exemplary military

---

⁵ *Nederlandsche geschiedzangen* II, 205.
⁶ Morand, *Monplaisir*, 32-33.
⁷ 'Al bravo Julián Romero, El más valiente español que ha nacido en nuestro tiempo'. Vega y Carpio, *Aldehuela*, 115-116. Idem, *Comedia*. See the last section of this chapter.

hero.⁸ The Julián of seventeenth-century Spanish literature is the perfect soldier who has worked his way up, without any help from a noble birth and without moaning for rewards for his deeds. This reputation has to this day remained alive in Spain, where he is still remembered as "Él de las hazañas" (the man of the heroic enterprises).⁹ This honorific title can also be found on the portrait of Romero attributed to El Greco, where we see him together with his namesake, a twelfth-century saintly bishop and protector of the city of Cuenca, highly esteemed by King Philip II.¹⁰

His remarkable image led to the publication of a voluminous biography in 1952. The author, Antonio Marichalar (1893-1973), Marquis of Montesa, was a complex character: the eternal bachelor, an intellectual dandy surrounded by beautiful and elegant women, a supporter of the Republic in the 1930s, and afterwards a mixture of liberal and conservative. Initially, he tried to enter the international literary avant-garde. His first attempts at writing were received with benevolence by literary masters such as Miguel de Unamuno and José Ortega y Gasset, and Marichalar became the international ambassador of the Spanish literary generation of 1927. He even published an article in T.S. Eliot's leading journal, *Criterion*. However, after the Spanish Civil War he decided to switch from literature to history.¹¹ His sizeable book on Romero, of more than five hundred pages, is one of the most prominent fruits of his historical labour.¹² The book is very well documented, and dedicated to Flandrina, the daughter of William of Orange, "who embraced the Catholic faith and died with the odour of sanctity surrounding her, as abbess of the convent of the Holy Cross in Poitiers". Though in part outdated – for example because the sources in Dutch on Romero were not accessible to Marichalar – this biography still remains, after more than half a century, the single most important source of knowledge about Julián Romero. The book is rich in style and vocabulary, perhaps even baroque: the passage on Romero's death is a true masterpiece of the art of literary and historical description, and in 1952 a critic called it one of the most beautiful fragments from the Spanish literature of its time.¹³

8   A sonnet on Julián by Diego Jiménez de Ayllón (1530-1590) starts with: 'temido vuestro brazo fue y espada' and also mentions William of Orange as his adversary. Díaz, 'Julián'; Ximénez de Ayllón, *Sonetos*.
9   Briones Moreno, *Julián*; Losada, 'Julián'; Heras, *Julián*.
10  The attribution to El Greco is considered dubious, but is still under discussion: Díaz, 'Julián'.
11  Ródenas de Moya, 'Presentación'; Idem, 'Antonio'.
12  Marichalar, *Julián*.
13  Marichalar, *Julián*, 442-445; Mayalde, 'Antonio', 179; Marichalar, 'Muerte'.

*Protagonists of War*

In the work of Geoffrey Parker, without any doubt the single most important contemporary historian on the Spanish army in the Low Countries, Captain Julián plays little more than a modest supporting role. In *The Dutch Revolt* he is not even mentioned at all. In *The Army of Flanders and the Spanish Road* he is mentioned twice, first in the same sentence as Cristóbal de Mondragón and Francisco Verdugo as examples of career soldiers from the gentry, and on another occasion related to the rewarding of the Spanish military. In the reworked edition of this book, from 2004, Parker adds to this how Captain Julián Romero had lost in battle an eye, an arm and a leg (a correct list of injuries, though he failed to mention the loss of an ear).[14] Parker now also mentions the existence of his portrait, and he points out that these three Spanish commanders – the other two being Sancho Dávila and Francisco de Valdés – were officers who, notwithstanding their service of several decades, still had not earned the right to put the title Don in front of their names. That's it. Also in recent works on the Revolt Captain Julián does not play a significant role.[15] His limited fame amongst historians may be caused by the fact that he did not leave any treatises or chronicles, unlike his comrades-in-arms Sancho de Londoño, Francisco de Valdés, Francisco Verdugo and Bernardino de Mendoza.[16]

How does the Julián from the sixteenth-century chronicles compare to the later hero of Hooft and Lope de Vega? How do Netherlandish and Spanish authors differ from each other? There is even an English Julián. The hero of the 1546 tournament was characterised by Hume in 1896 as a "swashbuckler". Another English historian, Walsh, described him in 1937 as a "romantic and resourceful fire-eater".[17] The French Julián is mainly the Julián from Brantôme: not only an excellent soldier, but also a very gifted storyteller.

We have fewer letters from Romero himself, when compared to those from Sancho Dávila, Cristóbal de Mondragón and Francisco de Valdés, but it is still possible to characterise his specific style as testimonies of a very eloquent soldier and somebody who had worked his way up from the lowest echelons of the army to the highest attainable level of

---

[14] Parker, *Army* (2004) 101-103, 142.
[15] Parker, *Army* (1972) 118-120; Parker, *Dutch Revolt*; De Graaf, *Oorlog* 171, 178, 212, 277; Más Chao, 'Soldado'. The publication of Fagel's *Kapitein* did lead to a more frequent mentioning of Julián Romero: Van der Ham, *Tachtig*, 113; Van der Lem, *Revolt*; Noordervliet, *Door met de strijd*.
[16] For example: González de León, 'Doctors', 64-65.
[17] Walsh, *Philip II*, 195; Hume, 'Julian'.

commander. His letters are very direct, untainted by any rhetorical or humanist education: he writes as somebody who has learned everything through practice. Though the letters offer the image the hero wanted to show of himself, we also see him struggling with his difficult life in the Spanish military during the Revolt in the Low Countries. In short, there are sufficient sources available for one to produce a sketch that shows him as a military man of flesh and blood, within the context of the continuously changing practices of early modern warfare.

Was Julián the best soldier of his time, as Lope de Vega considered him? Maybe not. "Without downplaying anybody, he is the best soldier His Majesty has in his service", wrote Alba's secretary, Juan de Albornoz. However, he was not refering to Julián but to his eternal rival Sancho Dávila, 'the Lighting Bolt of the war', who will be studied in the second chapter.[18]

## The hero of a duel

Julián Romero was born around 1520 in the village of Torrejoncillo del Rey, situated in the hills close to the city of Cuenca in what nowadays is the region of Castilla-La Mancha.[19] He was the son of mason and builder Pedro de Ibarrola and Juana Romero. The family lived near the village where Juana had been born and where Pedro had moved to from his native region of Biscay. As all inhabitants of Biscay were considered free burghers, Pedro was counted among the *hidalgos*. Besides fiscal advantages, this gave him the right to bear a sword and possess a coat of arms. As the story goes, father Pedro is supposed to have died from fatal wounds suffered in a bullfight, a truly fitting death for this father of a ferocious Spanish hero. His mother remarried.[20]

Around Christmas 1534 young Julián decided to join the army. We do not know why he did so. Perhaps he had been impressed by the 1528 visit of Charles V who, with his no doubt very impressive court,

---

[18] Albornoz to Gabriel de Zayas, Brussels, 5 August 1571, EA II, 701; Alba to Philip II, Brussels, 23 May 1572, Idem III, 119. On Albornoz: Hortal Muñoz, *Asuntos*, 109; Huisman, 'Serviele secretaris'.

[19] Julián is also celebrated as a native of Huélamo. In August 2018 the Asociación cultural Julián Romero in Huélamo organised a series of events around the military commander. Also a statue has been erected and the village's *plaza mayor* is named after Julián Romero. www.aosciacionjulianromero.es, accessed 3 July 2019. Heras, *Julián*, 57, 70.

[20] Juana Romero married Miguel de Sicilia, from the village of Poyatos (Cuenca). Martínez Laínez, *Ocaso I*, 192.

had spent the night in Julián's small village.[21] The first ten years of his military career remain completely obscure, until he appears in 1545 in a Spanish chronicle as a mercenary of the King of England. However, his first decade as a soldier can be reconstructed. Around 1534, Charles V was gathering troops to join his large expedition fleet against the pirate base of Tunis, ruled by the feared Barbarossa. In a play about his life Julián is described as a member of this international naval expedition that resulted in a much acclaimed victory by the Emperor. Young Julián could have been one of the boys we find on the famous tapestries by Willem de Pannemaker from Brussels, based on the cartoons by Jan Cornelisz. Vermeyen from Beverwijk, working at Charles's court in Spain.

It is more than likely that Julián subsequently remained with the Spanish troops in Piedmont and that he joined the Emperor's international army when he went to the Low Countries in 1543. Thousands of Spaniards were used in the wars against the Duke of Guelders and the King of France. It was in these years that the Duchy of Guelders finally fell into Habsburg possession. The small city of Düren was completely destroyed during the hostilities; the city went up in flames, and all soldiers and inhabitants without exception were mercilessly killed. At the time this was an unusual form of retribution, and the Duke of Alba in 1572 could perfectly recall the treatment of Düren, even though he had not been present. The harsh treatment of Düren forced the whole of the Duchy of Guelders to surrender unconditionally, and the Duke of Alba expected the same to happen after the ruthless treatment of Zutphen in 1572.[22] In November 1544 the Spanish troops were dismissed; they had to board ships near Bruges that would take them back home. The presence of these Spanish soldiers in the Low Countries caused conflicts with the local population, and there are stories reporting plundering and violence.[23]

Several ships arrived in the port of Plymouth, and around seven hundred Spanish soldiers entered the service of the English King, Henry VIII. In itself this was not a new phenomenon: King Henry had often used Spanish troops against the *Auld Alliance* of France and Scotland. In a chronicle on this period, Julián is one of the main protagonists of the story. He finally rises from obscurity as a mercenary in foreign military service.[24] In April 1545 Julián went to Newcastle, together with some one thousand other Spaniards under the command of Pedro Gamboa, to

---

[21] Briones Moreno, *Julián*, 38; Martínez Ruiz, *Soldados*, 969-970.
[22] Fagel, 'Duke'.
[23] Fagel, *Hispano-Vlaamse wereld*, 389-396.
[24] *Crónica del Rey*; Hume, 'Julian' and Idem, 'Mercenarios'.

fight the Scots. Gamboa was a famous captain who had left home because of a murder he had committed. In 1550 he would himself die at the hand of a murderer. His light cavalry of Spanish and Italian horsemen, armed with arquebuses, played a key role in the war against the Scots. The presence of so many foreign soldiers caused problems in Newcastle. A British chronicler remarked about the foreign garrison

> It was a sad sight to see the ungodly beastly lives they led defiling and corrupting the purity of the girls and women of the town and country until the men of the town rose against them and killed them when any one of them was caught astray.[25]

Julián survived the vengeance of the population and became a captain under Gamboa. Together they fought the French in 1546, being active in the region between Boulogne-sur-Mer and Calais, fortified towns that had remained in English hands for more than a century after the end of the Hundred Years' War.[26] Here Gamboa came into conflict with another Spanish captain, Cristóbal de Mora, who, after many years in English service, had defected to the French, taking with him some men and sixty brand new muskets.[27] As soon as Henry VIII and Francis I had signed a peace treaty on 7 June 1546, Mora decided to challenge Gamboa to a duel. However, it was Julián who accepted the challenge on behalf of his commander, "either for some reason of disparity of age or rank between the two, or else out of mere hot-headed combativeness on the part of Julian".[28]

Near the royal palace at Fontainebleau a closed space was prepared for the duel, and people came from afar to watch. The overwhelming interest even created a run on post horses, and the English envoy made it only just in time. Both Kings were closely involved with the duel, as it also concerned their own honour. Francis I and the future Henry II of France were personally present at the duel which took place on 15 July 1546. The French King even served as judge. This is also the story

---

[25] Phillips, *Anglo-Scots war*, 52-58.
[26] Romero's fame as a captain in England is mentioned in the evidence from 1560 of a witness who had seen a letter from Gamboa to Pedro Gaytán. Briones Moreno, *Julián*, 31.
[27] Fagel, 'Spanish side-changers'.
[28] Hume, 'Julian', 83; CSP, *Foreign and domestic, of the reign of Henry VIII*, XXI, I, n. 1148, 1212, 1257-1259, 1367 and II, 199; Millar, *Tudor mercenaries*, 169-170. See also Wriothesley, *Chronicle*, I, 173-174, who speaks of 'Julian, an Italian'; Julián Romero, *El barba azul de los reyes* (Paris); Heras, *Julián*, 78-80.

as Julián personally told it to Brantôme when they saw each other in Sicily. The famous Dutch Hispanist Johan Brouwer dedicated four pages to this legendary duel in his book on Spanish military chronicles related to the Revolt in the Low Countries.[29]

Both gamecocks were to fight on horseback, each with a sword, a foil and a dagger. They each had two holes in the back of their armour, each the size of two fists. This way Mora hoped to stab his opponent in the back, as he had a faster horse at his disposal. It turned out to be a very unchivalric encounter, though Mora did throw away his sword after Julián had lost his. Mora's tactic did not work, so he decided to kill Julián's horse. At that point Julián also lost his foil, leaving him with no more than a dagger. For three hours Mora circled around Julián, who was hiding behind his dead horse, but Mora was unable to hurt him. Mora continuously shouted to Julián to surrender, but the latter did not utter a word. Dusk had started to fall when Julián cut his spurs and he was able to hurt Mora's horse. Mora, now on foot, still had his spurs. Julián ran towards him and they fell to the ground. When Julián was able to cut the straps of his opponent's helmet with his dagger, Mora surrendered.

According to the story, during the duel Mora taunted Julián three times, "no te quiero, segnor Juliano" ("I don't like you, segnor Juliano"), hoping that he would leave his shelter behind his horse. Brantôme states that this Spanish sentence became a popular phrase at the French court every time somebody tried to avoid a confrontation. Brantôme got his story not only directly from Julián, but also from accounts he had heard from much older French noblemen who had been present at the duel. They informed him that the duel had been considered more a joke, a "risée et mocquerie". At the time, duelling was a noble occupation, even though non-noble military were taking over this custom during the sixteenth century. The opposition between the nobility and officers of low birth can also be found in the Spanish plays of the seventeenth century. But this particular victory had turned Julián into a kind of European cult hero and had given him mighty protectors at both courts.[30] Also the people back home in Torrejoncillo heard about the duel.[31]

There was no disdain or contempt for his low birth directly after the duel. King Francis I and the Dauphin, both fanatical lovers of the manly

---

[29] Brouwer, *Kronieken*, 31-34; Brantôme, *Oeuvres*, XIII, 104, 109; Millar, *Tudor mercenaries*, 169-170.
[30] Brantôme, *Oeuvres*, XIII, 111-112; Kiernan, *Duel*. In the *Crónica del Rey*, 179, Mora uttered: 'Julian, rindete, que yo no te quiero matar'.
[31] Briones Moreno, *Julián*, 28.

competition for honour, received Julián in the royal palace. Francis I had challenged his rival, Emperor Charles V, to a duel in 1528, while the Dauphin, after he had become King Henry II of France, would even die from injuries suffered during a tournament, when the lance of the captain of his Scottish guards pierced his eye. Directly after the duel Julián received three portions of meat, served by the King's own men, watched from nearby by many courtiers. He was also given a heavy gold chain and an expensive golden cloth. Queen Eleanor, Charles V's eldest sister, received the hero as well, and her ladies-in-waiting arranged for the appropriate entertainment that same evening, although unfortunately we do not know its specific character.[32] Julián would also have been awed by the beautiful Renaissance hall that had been finished at Fontainebleau shortly before his visit. Once the soldier returned to England, Henry VIII received him with great honour and granted him a life-long pension of six hundred ducats, though in practice it would be paid for only a few years.

Without a war going on Julián remained unemployed, hanging around London with fellow Spanish officers and, according to Hume, "quarrelling, gaming, and swaggering". It seems he enjoyed his unexpected fame a little too much and became seriously in debt, to the point of being afraid of walking the streets. When he was on the brink of being incarcerated for his debts, Julián is said to have started raging against the English King and his Protestantisation of the Church. However, not one witness was found who was willing to testify to Julián saying that he would fight the heretics with a pike on his shoulders. But he had also insulted King Henry and his Royal Council, stating "that he preferred serving somebody else for four ducats than remaining here and earning a treasure".[33] He had to face a charge before the Royal Council and only because of his very influential friends was his punishment limited to a severe reprimand. The story is proof of his privileged position, but also of his turbulent, not to say impetuous, character. And of his failure to resist the pernicious idleness of peacetime.

Fortunately for him, war was never far away. After the death of Henry VIII in 1547, his successor, the young King Edward VI, was persuaded by his principal advisor Edward Seymour, the Duke of Somerset and Lord Protector, to start a new war against Scotland. Somerset intended to capture the Scottish Princess Mary to make her marry Edward. His military strategy consisted of the construction of an English pale in

---

[32] *CSP, Foreign and domestic, of the reign of Henry VIII*, XXI, I, n. 1298. Henry Knyvet to Henry VIII, 17 July 1546.
[33] *Crónica del Rey*, 198.

Scotland, like the one in Ireland. Control over this territory had to be provided by means of new fortresses, built according to the new style of the *Trace Italienne*, consisting of low earthen walls with angled corners, capable of resisting cannon fire. Somerset had learned about the new style from the French fortresses during the struggle around Boulogne.[34] The French had imported the technique from Italy. Unfortunately, there are very few remains left of these fortresses, like the one on the Eyemouth Peninsula.[35]

During this new war Julián served under Peter Mewtys, commander of six hundred Spanish and Italian harquebusiers. It was a cruel war. At the siege of Thornton the defenders did not surrender directly, giving the attackers the right to kill them all. The garrison even pleaded to be executed by hanging. However, the Lord Protector decided to spare their lives. So, long before the massacres of Naarden and Haarlem, Julián had already experienced different ways of treating stubborn defenders in sieges like Düren and Thornton. The heroes of the war against the Scots were the horsemen of Pedro de Gamboa, armed with arquebuses. At the Battle of Pinkie, on 10 September 1547 (since then called Black Saturday), the Scots suffered a tremendous defeat. In the shadow of Gamboa we find Julián playing an important role during the battle, and he was also involved in the burning of nearby Leith.[36] The Spanish chronicle of this period states that Julián received a knighthood after the battle, but Hume has not found any documentary evidence of that. We do know that on 28 September Gamboa and a few other Spaniards were knighted for their bravery. The first mention of Julián as a knight dates from 31 January 1549.

In 1548 many Spaniards in the border area deserted, as they did not want to live in their simple shelters made of peat and branches, unlike the English soldiers who seemingly accepted these mean conditions. The Spaniards wanted at least a tent, but preferably a real house. Another problem was the delay in their payments, which in some cases had fallen behind by seven months. Some of the Spaniards were prompted by these dire circumstances to solve the problem by trying to sell a fortress back to the Scots in order to obtain the money owed to them. We do not know whether Julián was involved in the plan. In the Spring of 1549, fresh Scottish and French troops threatened Julián's regiment near the border

---

[34] Phillips, *Anglo-Scots wars*, 178.
[35] Merriman and Summerson, 'Scottish border'.
[36] Hume, 'Julian', 90; Phillips, *Anglo-Scots wars*.

in Jedburgh, but he succeeded in retreating safely to England.[37] By that time he commanded a unit of 177 men, the equivalent of an infantry banner in the Spanish army. Julián and his men were also used to ending the farmers' revolts taking place in England, and he may even have been active in Ireland, as somebody stated in 1574 that he had known Romero when he had still been a poor captain in Ireland.[38] By this time, the plan to create an English pale in Scotland had failed completely. Somerset fell into disgrace and lost his head on the block. Boulogne was sold to the French and peace was signed. Julián, now a military man in his early thirties, well known in England, and in some ways famous even for his deeds in Fontainebleau, would return to the Continent. In French court circles 'segnor Juliano' was the subject of a familiar saying.

## In the service of the old Emperor

In 1552 Julián entered the service of Charles V for a second time, on the brink of a new series of wars between the Habsburgs and France. The fighting would be interrupted by a brief ceasefire in 1556 and then continue until the Peace of Câteau-Cambrésis in 1559 put an end to this very long and intensely violent war. In 1553 imperial troops totally wiped Thérouanne and Hesdin from the face of the earth, while a year later the French ravaged Binche, Mariemont, Bouvignes and Dinant.

The resumption of the war drew more Spanish troops to the Low Countries. Charles V had originally planned to bring six thousand fresh Spanish soldiers by sea, but experience had taught him that inexperienced soldiers from Spain did not survive well in the Low Countries. Besides, the arrival of such a large number of Spanish soldiers would raise suspicion and anxiety among the inhabitants. Therefore, the new recruits were sent to Italy, and experienced soldiers had to reach the Low Countries from Italy overland. It was a system that would be maintained during the years of the Revolt, and has been described as 'the Spanish Road'.[39]

In order to assist at the Siege of Metz in the Summer of 1552, 5,600 Spanish troops had already crossed the Alps via the Brenner Pass.[40] The famed siege ended in a major failure, and Charles V's immense army had to remain in the north for the Winter. Some three thousand Spaniards lived for three months in Cambrai, accumulating large debts to the

---

[37] Phillips, *Anglo-Scots wars*, 221, 244; CSP, *Privy Council*, II, n. 286, 451, 462, 683, 693.
[38] CSP, *Foreign*, X, n. 1302. Anonymous letter to Captain Windebank, January 1574.
[39] Parker, *Army* (2004).
[40] Fagel, *Hispano-Vlaamse wereld*, 399-401; Zeller, *Siège*.

inhabitants and finally even starting a mutiny. They chased their officers from the city and chose their own leader, as would happen in subsequent mutinies during the Revolt. Other Spaniards even decided to go over to the French, becoming spies in Brussels. Chronicler Louis Brésin, originally from that region, complained about the terrible behaviour of the Spanish soldiers. The inhabitants could not walk the streets in safety, and they had lost control over their own homes.[41] Finally, these troops agreed to march against Thérouanne.

This almost one-thousand-year-old city, see of the Bishop, would become the first victim of the renewed war between France and the Habsburgs. The bishopric fell under the French Crown, and as such it remained a hostile enclave within the County of Artois, which had been completely severed from France in 1526. There is a description of the fighting written by the father of one of Julián's most loyal servants, Cristóbal Vázquez de Ávila. According to his own father, young Cristóbal, aged around eleven at the time, had been present at the attack at such an early age.[42] Cristóbal's presence is the only clue to Julián's involvement in the attack. Charles V had united an enormous army, though we must always be careful not to take the numbers given by the chroniclers too literally. Brésin speaks of 1,500 Spanish light horsemen and twenty-four banners of Spanish infantry. Even if we assume the banners were no larger than two hundred men, there must have been more than six thousand Spaniards around Thérouanne. Spanish historian Sepúlveda even mentions a total of 7,500 Spaniards within an army of thirty thousand. On 11 June 1553 a first massive attack by the Spaniards did not succeed in penetrating the city's still mainly medieval fortifications. In the end, the city fell into imperial hands by 20 June, to be completely erased from the face of the earth: the destruction included the thirteenth-century gothic cathedral, two parish churches and several abbeys and convents.[43] Not one single building remained standing, not even the most modest constructions, so as to make it impossible for the Bishop, a French nominee, to return to his see. The attackers succeeded wonderfully in their scheme. There would never be another Bishop of Thérouanne, thus ending a long list of bishops that went as far back as the seventh century.

---

[41] Brésin, *Chroniques*, 207.
[42] Vázquez de Ávila, 'Nuevas'.
[43] Marichalar, *Julián*, 79; Fagel, *Hispano-Vlaamse wereld*, 401-402; Archivo Histórico Provincial de Madrid, protocolos n. 500, f. 1543; Delmaire, 'Thérouanne'.

The small fortified city of Hesdin in Artois would change overlord seven times between 1477 and 1553. A Spaniard in the army camp in front of Hesdin wrote to his wife in Zamora that there were too few Spanish soldiers in the huge imperial army which was made up of thirty thousand infantry and ten thousand cavalry, "It is detrimental that there are no more than 4,000 Spaniards; if we were to have another 4,000, or even 1,000 fewer, they alone would suffice to give battle".[44] History seems to have proven this bragging letter-writer right, as the odds for success on the battlefield changed with the arrival of another three hundred Spanish arquebusiers. It is very possible that the sources are referring to the 330 Spanish arquebusiers under Julián's command that were active around Saint-Omer a little earlier. The attack on the citadel of Hesdin lasted an impressive sixty hours, killing some seventy Spaniards. Hesdin was completely dismantled and abandoned. A few miles further on a new citadel was built. Given the name of 'Nouvel-Hesdin', it followed the design of the new Italian art of fortification.[45]

Romero's last feat of arms under Emperor Charles V was the defence of Dinant in 1554.[46] This city belonged to the Prince-Bishopric of Liège, at the time an imperial ally, as the governing Prince-Bishop was George of Austria, a natural son of Emperor Maximilian I, Charles's grandfather. Julián was ordered to support the defenders against the French siege. He succeeded in resisting the French attacks four times, but by 11 July capitulation had become inevitable. In 1610 a witness, who was over a hundred years old, still remembered the fighting. He described a deceptive trick by 'Julien Omere' who deluded the French into believing that the castle had already been abandoned. When the French arrived at the top of the castle and shouted victory, "chasteau gaigné", the defenders appeared from their hiding places shouting "Espaigne" and thus fending off another attack.[47] From this period there are also a few letters of praise from Granvelle to Captain Julián Romero in which he specifically thanked the Spanish captain for his deeds and for the information he had provided on the enemy.[48] The fact that Julián corresponded directly with the influential royal minister proves that he was already much more than a simple captain. And he would have agreed wholeheartedly with this

---

[44] 'Es el daño que en todos no avra mas de 4.000 españoles; y si huviera otros tantos, y aun mill menos, bastarían ellos solos para dar la batalla', Ocampo, 'Sucesos', 98r.
[45] Delmaire, 'Thérouanne'.
[46] Baes, 'Guerre', 191-196; Idem, 'Episode', 331.
[47] 'Documents inédits', 200.
[48] Marichalar, *Julián*, 82-84; RBM, Manuscript 2193.

judgement, as his behaviour in Dinant shows. The *Connétable de France* leading the Siege of Dinant, Anne de Montmorency, offered the defenders an honourable retreat: they had to abandon the artillery but could take with them their luggage, swords and daggers. Other weapons had to be left behind. Julián complained about the offer during the negotiations with the Connétable during a long speech we can find written down in the works of Brantôme:[49]

> My Lord, if it be true, that there are no better judges of any art than the artist himself, and since there's no lord or captain that has better handled, or more practised arms than your Excellency, I hope you will this day favour the cause of arms to the utmost of your power, with regard to us Spanish soldiers, by treating us not as vanquish'ed men, but according to our valour and courage; which, for my own particular, I chose, some years ago, at Fontainbleau in presence of King Francis, to trust to the doubtful chance of single combat, rather than suffer any deshonour or affront; cherishing my honour more than my blood, or my life, which I have always chearfully employed in so many thousand dangers, passing and repassing so many seas and lands, purely to gain glory and renown; where in fortune, a friend to the brave and the bold, has so much favour'd me, that I can reckon myself among those who have gain'd something by their efforts and their prowess, which is to me the Summum Bonum, the supreme happiness in which I hug and applaud myself; arms being the superstructure of all I have and the foundation of all I have not; and the preservation and keeping of those arms more dear to me than all things. If I must lose them, may the whole world despise me; and if such a misfortune shou'd happen, en we shou'd be forc'd to abandon them, we rather chuse, every man of us, like men in despair, if the oars fail us, to help ourselves with the sails, and fight till we die…

Julián more or less demanded to be allowed to leave without leaving any weapons behind. These haughty words spoken by Julián were not well received by Montmorency. He was surprised that the defeated tried to impose a new kind of law of war on the victors. If Julián did not surrender the castle very soon the French would attack, and if he did not die by the sword he would be hanged. The stubborn Spaniard still did not give up, and tried to organise an honourable retreat just for himself and twelve

---

[49] Brantôme, *Oeuvres*, XIII, 103-106; Idem, *Spanish rhodomontades*, 70-72.

of his men. Clever Montmorency, however, had informed the defenders in the meantime that their commander had already surrendered, so they followed what they erroneously believed to be his example. French chronicler François de Rabutin characterised Julián's behaviour towards Montmorency as "la façon espagnolle, faisant grandes exclamations".[50]

Julián was captured by Jean d'Estrée, Henry II's artillery master. The ensuing negotiations on the liberation of prisoners seemed endless and laborious, finally resulting in a five-year truce, agreed on in the Abbey of Vaucelles (in Hainaut) on 6 February 1556. All prisoners could be bought free for the price of their yearly income. Commissioners went out to collect the necessary information. Only the three most important prisoners were excluded from the deal, among them the son of the Connétable and the Duke of Aarschot.[51] It would take a long time for Romero to regain his freedom. Only by October 1556, more than two years after the fall of Dinant, did his release seem imminent. As D'Estrée still had to pay 4,000 écus for the liberation of his own son, he offered to pay a further 2,000 together with the liberation of "ledict conte d'Arc, Juliain et Rogrofz". Habsburg ambassador Simon Renard expressly pointed out to his new King, Philip II, the value of the count, a 'gentilhomme' of the court, and it seems that Julián was nothing more than small change. The letter shows, however, that Philip II needed no more than his first name to know with whom he was dealing. By this time, Charles V had abdicated in Brussels and been succeeded by his son, Philip II, born in Valladolid in 1527.

Philibert of Savoy, Governor-general of the Low Countries, informed Renard two weeks later that he wanted to hold on to the 4,000 écus for Estrée's son, and with it the three men, but "however, if this is not in any way possible, you should stop precisely at three thousand".[52] We do not know exactly when Julián was liberated, but in the Summer of 1557 he was again active in the resumed war against the French.

It is possible that Romero did not await the end of the complicated bargaining. According to one story, D'Estrée had wanted to take him to Laon, and during that journey Julián succeeded in escaping with the assistance of a beautiful twenty-five-year-old woman from Bouvignes who had fallen for his charms. Together they returned to Bouvignes,

---

[50] 'Documents inédits', 197; Paradin, *Histoire*, 771-772.
[51] Cloulas, *Henri II*, 415; Baumgartner, *Henry II*, 174-176, 180; Verhofstad, *Regering*, 11-14.
[52] Weiss, *Papiers*, IV, 735-748.

completely burned down by the French, and to her husband.⁵³ It is possible that the woman in question herself told this to the anonymous chronicler who wrote down the story, but more evidence concerning this anecdote is yet to be found. When the Duke of Aarschot, Philip of Croÿ, escaped from the castle of Vincennes on 10 May 1556, the French complained of this deed, as the Duke had broken his word of honour by escaping.⁵⁴ A possible escape by Julián would thus surely also have been considered a not very honorable deed, although, of course, the words of a high nobleman had a much greater value than those of a simple Spanish captain. At the time, there was also another story going around. Julián's servant Pierre, born in the Flemish village of Laleu, "a man of good spirit, well trained in Spanish, French, English, German, and Flemish", had gone to Renard to collect money for his own liberation and in order to do so he carried letters addressed to two Spaniards. Six months later Julián's servant was under close watch as he was suspected of espionage "that you know he practises over there in detriment to the service of the King".⁵⁵

Even without taking his escape and his spying servant into consideration, it is clear that Julián was again an ambiguous hero in Dinant. His honour seems to have been greater than his sense of reality. However, the anecdote featuring Montmorency and Julián again added to his fame. He did receive a critical remark from chronicler Prudencio de Sandoval in his famous history of Charles V. According to the Spanish historian, the fall of Dinant had been caused by Julián's incompetence; "seldom do bravery and prudence reside within the same person, although later this captain demonstrated that he possessed them both, as he was one of the famous men of our time".⁵⁶ There exists another Spanish description of the fighting around Dinant in which Julián serves as a classical Spanish hero who courageously entered the city after a bloody confrontation. He lost 170 men, who were killed, wounded or had been taken prisoner. However, the remaining 170 succeeded in entering the city and killed and wounded some 2,500 enemies. In this story, even the enemies praised his bravery. During the siege another seventy of his men died, leaving

---

[53] *Chroniques Liégeois*, 442; Austrian State Archives, Vienna, WSA, P.A.-99, box 37, f. 305; 'Documents inédits', 200; Brantôme, Œuvres, XIII, 106-109; Montaigne, *Essais*, I, 6, 'L'heure des parlements dangereuses'.
[54] Weiss, *Papiers*, IV, 564.
[55] Weiss, *Papiers*, IV, 515-518, 634-637.
[56] Sandoval, *Historia*, 436.

only some one hundred men out of the original 340.⁵⁷ Julián did not spare the lives of the men under his command, unlike the cautious Duke of Alba during the Revolt in the Low Countries. Honour and bravery suited Julián better than wisdom and caution.

## In the service of the young King

Hostilities in the frontier region between France and the Low Countries started again after January 1557, as the ceasefire of Vaucelles had lasted less than a year. There were attacks from both sides. French Admiral Gaspar de Coligny tried in vain to occupy the city of Douai, while the army of the new King Philip II launched an unsuccessful attack on Rocroi. After Coligny had taken the small Artesian town of Lens and burned it to the ground, the Governor-general of the Low Countries, Philibert of Savoy, began a large counter-offensive. On 2 August his troops appeared before the walls of the strategically situated Saint-Quentin. The siege would last until 27 August, but the famous battle took place on 10 August, Saint Lawrence's Day. In the library of the royal palace in El Escorial, dedicated to the same saint and directly related to the battle, there is an extensive manuscript on the battle and the siege of Saint-Quentin. The first Spaniard to be mentioned in this text is Captain Julián. He was one of the two people that had been able to convince the King to attack Saint-Quentin. It shows that although he was merely a captain of a banner of some 170 soldiers, he played an important role as a military advisor. Julián was also directly involved in the first attack on the town's outskirts, and after taking possession of this suburb he received the order to organise its defence. His position is indicated in a popular engraving of the siege which even includes his name. In the manuscript text Julián happily offers to defend the Duke of Savoy's position against the whole army of the King of France. We recognise his already well-known rhetorical use of grand gestures.⁵⁸ From his outpost Julián successfully bombarded the town, but sometimes this went wrong, as on the day a cannonball landed in their own trenches, killing five Spaniards. He would suffer a leg wound while commanding a joint attack by Spanish and English troops, and it seems obvious that his long career in English service had made him especially qualified for this command.

[57] Marichalar, *Julián*, 87; 'Relación de la toma'.
[58] Fagel, 'Esplendor'; Mesa and García Pinto, *Batalla, 1557*, 25-26.

The Battle of Saint-Quentin was the result of a French attempt to get a large relief army into the town. However, the plan was discovered, and the Duke's cavalry succeeded in destroying a large part of the French army, taking many prisoners. Count Lamoral of Egmont, the commander of 1,200 light horsemen from Spain, Italy and the Low Countries, played a heroic part in the battle, and this would add greatly to his fame as a military hero. Among the prisoners was the Spanish Captain Carvajal, who was fighting on the side of the French. Carvajal had fled from the Habsburg army under suspicion of sodomy, but Julián defended him as they had been good friends in the past. Admiral Coligny and Connétable Montmorency were also taken prisoner, which meant that Julián could again meet the man who had defeated him at Dinant.

The storming of Saint-Quentin led to the brutal sacking of the town, with King Philip trying to protect only the possessions of the Church. In the manuscript Julián is clearly seen as one of the most important heroes of Saint-Quentin, his name being connected with one of the greatest victories of the Habsburg army in the sixteenth century. Though being a simple captain of a banner of infantry soldiers, he was already functioning as an important military commander. In 1560 news of his deeds in Saint-Quentin also reached his home village of Torrejoncillo.[59]

In recent years, the battle and siege of Saint-Quentin have inspired two Spanish historical novels. In 2005 Juan Carlos Losado decided to take the Count of Egmont as his main protagonist, while in 2019 José Javier Esparza put a martial Julián Romero on the front cover.[60] Losado devotes several pages to a biographical description of Julián as "one of the most famous adventurers of the sixteenth century", also calling him a mythical figure. The author, however, refuses to accept Romero's role in the decision-making process around Saint-Quentin: "cosa absolutamente imposible", but at the same time he is much too positive about his behaviour: "never were any unworthy deeds known of him, nor attempts to take somebody else's property or commit cruelty against civilians". The novelist also offers us a very romantic picture of his *Nachleben*: "during many years, thousands of blind men and comedians recited romances and songs around all villages praising his heroic deeds".[61] Esparza takes even more liberty with the historical facts and figures on Romero. The captain resides in Brussels with a woman from Ghent he met in a tavern, and they have two children, Juliana (true!) and Guzmán. There is now also a black

---

[59] Briones Moreno, *Julián*, 28.
[60] Losada, *San Quintín*; Esparza, *San Quintín*.
[61] Losada, *San Quintín*, 116-119, 165.

servant. The decision to attack Saint-Quentin is completely Romero's initiative. He is even depicted as asking the King's permission to speak, boldly saying, "San Quintín, mi señor". After the town's surrender, the King comes to his tent and calls him Maestre de campo. The actions of both the captain and the King in this novel are completely unhistorical.[62]

After Saint-Quentin we find Romero in Guînes, a small fortified town that had been in English hands since 1352. And again he was fighting alongside the English against the French. Philip had sent him with a few dozen Spaniards to protect this strategically important town. After a brave defence – we even have a description of the fighting in Romero's own hand – he had to yield the town to the French.[63] In the following period we find Julián involved in the taking of Ham and the Battle of Gravelines. During this last battle, Egmont was again one of the acclaimed heroes. We do not know whether Julián was involved in the violent confrontations between Spanish troops and the inhabitants of the city of Arras in 1558, when several Spaniards were killed during an affray.[64] His heroic deeds during the war gained Romero a royal reward. On 10 July, Philip II and secretary Francisco de Eraso signed a document that made him a knight of the Order of Santiago, receiving the income that belonged to Jerez de los Caballeros in Estremadura. It was a huge honour for a military man of low birth like Romero. In the seventeenth century the story went that Philip II had given Romero the knighthood without the normal necessity of checking for possible ancestors of new-Christian blood, that is to say, of Jewish or Islamic origin. Playwrights were keen to make use of this idea: a King who rewarded bravery with the status of a knight, regardless of birth.

After the signing in 1559 of the Peace of Câteau-Cambrésis, King Philip decided to leave 3,200 Spanish soldiers to defend the Low Countries, as history had taught him that peace with France could be very brief. Captains Pedro de Mendoza and Julián Romero would command the sixteen banners of Spaniards, but in order to avoid complaints about these foreign troops Mendoza would officially serve under Egmont and Julián under William of Orange. In the preserved correspondence between Julián and Orange we can read about the difficult position these Spanish troops found themselves in: problems with discipline, the hatred of the local population, problems with the payment of wages, and the complicated organisation of their return to Spain. Soldiers who misbehaved

[62] Esparza, *San Quintín*, 13-15, 89, 293.
[63] Biblioteca de El Escorial, Ms. III-23, f. 240; Marichalar, *Julián*, 111-112.
[64] Verhofstad, *Regering*, 35.

were severely punished, but Romero also complained about the local population: "the inhabitants of these villages are so bad that they don't want to bring us anything".⁶⁵ During this period Romero spent most of his time in Damvillers in the Duchy of Luxembourg, as he had in 1559 been appointed governor of its citadel. In 1561 he served for a short while as governor of the citadel of Douai, but by then he was already on his way to Spain.⁶⁶ It had been decided to withdraw the Spanish troops from the Low Countries, mainly because of the complaints from the Estates, but first they had to be paid their overdue wages which by that time amounted to three years' back pay.⁶⁷

The letters exchanged between Romero and Orange demonstrate the existence of a clientele relationship between the two men, as Julián was clearly writing as the submissive client of a high nobleman. When Julián wanted to take his leave of his patron the Prince, Orange had just left for Germany, but not without leaving a valuable chain with one of his noblemen who had to hand it over to Julián. In a letter Julián thanked the Prince for the gift, kissing his hands a thousand times, a well-known Spanish expression of gratitude. In a more general expression he also wrote that it had not been at all necessary as he would keep serving the Prince in the same manner, with or without gifts.⁶⁸

On 22 October 1560, Romero was already in Zeeland, prepared to board ship with his soldiers. From there he wrote another short note to Orange to ask him to take into his service a Spanish soldier who for specific reasons could not return to Spain: "although I know it hurts your lordship to give it to him as he is a foreigner, I dare to ask you, being such a servant of your lordship".⁶⁹

Both Spanish captains were praised by Governess Margaret of Parma for their exemplary behaviour. They had remained on their ships to speed up the departure, even though life on board had been very uncomfortable. Her praise may have been influenced by the fact that Charles de Tisnacq in Toledo had heard that Romero was not very well at the time:

---

⁶⁵ 'Los paysanos de estos villages son tan malinos que no quieren traer nada', Romero to Orange, Damvillers, 28 November 1559, BO.
⁶⁶ In 1571 there was still a court case going on before the Council of Malines regarding a loan given to Julián when his troops were living in Alternach (Luxembourg). De Smidt, *Chronologische lijsten*, VI, 293-294.
⁶⁷ AGS, Contaduría Mayor de Cuentas, IIa época, 75, Philip II to Romero, 17 July 1559.
⁶⁸ BO; Postma, *Viglius*, 185-189.
⁶⁹ 'Aunque yo se que se le ara de mal a Vuestra Señoría de darsela por ser estranjero me atrebo yo siendo tan serbidor e Vuestra Señoría', Romero to Orange, Middelburg, 24 October 1560, BO. See also CP I, 192-193.

"I understand that captain Julian who is at Cádiz (Cales) has fallen into a frenzy of fantasy and melancholy (as one says), I hope God will give him enlightenment".[70] Was his depression the result of the long wait in the harbour? We already know from ten years earlier in London that periods of waiting and forced idleness were a greater threat to Romero's health than the worst conditions of war.

Whatever the precise circumstances, in January 1561 Romero arrived in Lisbon, and from there he travelled to Toledo, and further in the direction of Malaga, to board ship with three banners of soldiers that he had taken with him from the Low Countries. He then stayed until at least January 1562 in the fortress of La Goleta near Tunis, the same region where his military career may have started in 1535. The region was confronted with a new struggle between Spain and the Ottoman sultan. During these Mediterranean years Romero sometimes wrote letters to Orange, for example about personal information such as the wound to his leg: – "I have been very close to death" – and about a visit by the Prince's servants to Julián's house in Brussels where his natural children lived with their mother.[71] On that subject he had also written to Granvelle from Lisbon and Toledo. He had asked Granvelle to take care of his family in the Low Countries. His companion was pregnant again, and he feared he would not be able to return to the Low Countries before the child was born. If that happened Granvelle was to appoint godparents for the child. A few weeks later it became clear that he would indeed not be able to make it in time for the birth of his third Netherlandish child: "I am going so far away that I cannot make it".[72]

In another letter to Orange, he again recommended another Spanish friend, asking for him to be given a place among the Prince's troops. He also informed Orange about the peace with the King of Tunis, whom he did not trust at all. On 8 October 1562 he wrote to Orange from Madrid, the last letter we have from this period. He had by then stayed for eight

---

[70] CM, 38, 81-82, 131, 335-340, 369-374, 395-396, 399. 'Jentens que le capitaine Julian qui estoit a Cales seroit tombé en frenesie et de fantazie ou melancolie (come se dit), dieu luy veulle donner allegement', Tisnacq to Margaret of Parma, Toledo, 7 January 1561. ARAB, Audience 240, 25. I thank Liesbeth Geevers for this reference.

[71] 'He estado muy çerca de morirme', BO, Romero to Orange, Malaga, 17 April 1561.

[72] 'Yo voi tan lexos que no lo podré hazer', Romero to Granvelle, Toledo, 10 February 1561, RBM, II/ 2275, 70; Idem, Lisbon 24 January 1561, Idem, II/ 2291, 290r-v. I thank Liesbeth Geevers for the references; Geevers (2008). Also: Romero to Granvelle, 8 January 1561, Idem, II/2291, 283r-v, and Idem, Lisbon, 23 February 1561, Idem, II/2291, 302r-v; Juan de Mendoza to Granvelle, Flushing (Vlissingen), 8 December 1560, Idem, II/2249, 83r-84v.

days at the royal court in Madrid, to meet Philip II – who had arrived there a year previously – and to ask him for financial compensation for his deeds. Romero called it with a certain sense of understatement "asking to get food" ("dar de comer").[73] Mondragón would use the same phrase in one of his letters. It shows that the mythical military hero perfectly realised that in order to receive new sources of income one had to go to the King in person. During this period he also visited his relatives in the villages around Cuenca.[74]

By this time Julián's career was quite successful. The King showed his confidence in him by sending him with a thousand men to Ibiza in 1563 to organise the fortifications. At that time the island found itself in the firing line between Philip II and the Ottomans, who were contesting the hegemony of the Mediterranean.[75] He cannot have remained long on the island as we find him on 30 July 1564 getting married in Madrid to María Gaytán, the only daughter of Captain Pedro Gaytán and the rich Catalina de Vitoria y Zárate.[76] In 1565 Julián also became *comendador* in the Order of Santiago for Mures and Benazuza. In a few years, the captain had earned great respect and had risen to a considerable social and financial position.

His star would rise even higher. In the same year, 1565, he was sent to Sicily to support García de Toledo, the Viceroy of Sicily, with the relief of Malta, which was being besieged by Ottoman troops. When, on 12 August, Melchor de Robles, the Maestre de campo of the tercio of Sicily, died after being shot when he was looking over the parapet without his helmet on, Julián was appointed his successor.[77] In the correspondence between the Viceroy and Philip II on the new appointment, the first spoke about "Maestre de campo Julián", while the King simply referred to "Julián".[78] On 25 August 1565 six thousand Spanish soldiers left Syracuse, 1,700 from the tercio of Lombardy under the command of Sancho de Londoño, 2,800 from the tercio of Sicily under Julián, and more than a thousand from the tercio of Sardinia with their Maestre de campo, Gonzalo de Bracamonte.[79] These men must have been roughly

---

[73] Romero to Orange, Madrid, 8 October 1562, BO.
[74] Marichalar *Julián*, 128-130.
[75] ARAB, audience, Tisnacq to Margaret of Parma, Madrid, 9 April 1563. I thank Liesbeth Geevers for the reference; Marichalar, *Julián*, 140.
[76] In or before 1560 Pedro Gaytán had received a letter from England written by Gamboa. Briones Moreno, *Julián*, 31.
[77] Fagel, 'Imagen'; Crowley, *Empires*, 179.
[78] CD XXX, 72, 109, 173.
[79] Balbi, *Siege*, 170.

the same ones that the Duke of Alba would take with him to the Low Countries two years later, in 1567. In this sense, the relief of Malta served as the overture to the conflict in the Low Countries. Romero spent most of his time waiting in Messina harbour, and in the end a direct confrontation with the Ottoman forces was avoided, as they retreated after the Spaniards had landed on Malta.

During this period he also met Brantôme. When Romero arrived in Messina with the Spanish galleys he heard about the presence of several French knights who wanted to join the fight against the Ottomans. As "très-courtois cavallier", Julián went to salute them, and as Brantôme was the only one who spoke decent Spanish, they entered into a conversation Brantôme may have forgotten in his writings that Romero must have spoken French as well! Julián inquired about the wellbeing of the *connétable,* and he recounted his adventures to the Frenchman. He did this particularly well, "with the most beautiful words of the world, better spoken than I have ever heard, as is he very eloquent *à la soldade*".[80] The walk around the port of Messina is a key moment in Julián's history: here merge together the real Romero of flesh and blood and the fictional hero of the chronicles. Here merge his extraordinary deeds on the battlefield and his remarkable and bold soldier's tales. At the same time, a fairytale was unfolding: the soldier from humble origins had made it all the way to the top, becoming commander of one of the four large Spanish tercios in Italy.

## The Prince of Orange's dog

The joy over the relief of Malta was still being savoured in Philip II's chambers when the first news letters about the iconoclastic fury in the Low Countries started piling up on his desk. In this sense, the war against the Protestants seamlessly followed the crusade against the Ottomans. And the King would also make use of some of the same Spanish soldiers. The iconoclastic fury brought the Low Countries back to the centre of his attention, and Philip II must have remembered his years in the north and the endless and harsh wars against the French. Soldiers like Julián Romero had also experienced those wars.

The Spanish and Italian soldiers who would leave for the Low Countries in 1567 were placed under the command of the Duke of Alba, a high nobleman born in 1507 and the most experienced general in the King's service. He had fought all over Europe and had frequently been in the Low

---

[80] Brantôme, *Oeuvres,* XIII, 109-110.

Countries, though strangely enough he had never actively participated in the great battles against France and the Duchy of Guelders.[81] Julián and Alba most certainly knew each other, but there were no close ties between them, such as those we shall witness later with Francisco de Valdés, Cristóbal de Mondragón and, most of all, Sancho Dávila. Through the Viceroy of Sicily, García de Toledo, who had been involved in Julián's appointment as Maestre de campo, there was a connection with the Alba family, as García was a cousin of the Duke.

Julián had already become a famous hero before travelling with the Duke of Alba to the Low Countries. His great fame was the result of his duel at Fontainebleau and his heroic deeds in the wars against the French. Everybody knew who Captain Julián was, at the courts of France and England, but also in Brussels and Madrid. And they must all have had quite similar ideas about the man, as a brave and dashing soldier who had earned his promotions by his sword. It is this image we shall also find later on in seventeenth-century plays. It must have given Romero special status within Alba's large army: he was more than just the commander of a tercio; he was an authentic Spanish war hero.

The Revolt in the Low Countries offered the opportunity for new heroic deeds, but Julián and his myth became stuck between the conflicting parties. At the beginning of the conflict, the inhabitants of the Low Countries still had respect for the hero of Saint-Quentin, but later on he was turned into the personification of the much-feared Spanish soldier, as we see, for example, in the *Nederlandse Historiën*, written in the seventeenth century by Calvinist author P.C. Hooft. He became the focus of war propaganda on both sides, a war hero for one and a war criminal for the other. His image also became much more defined. Already in 1567 it was clear that Julián was above all a man skilled in the practical sides of warfare, but who could get into trouble for his obstinate actions. During the struggle in the Low Countries, Romero became caught in the snake-pit of Habsburg politics. As we have many more sources for this period of his life, we see even more clearly how Julián was more than just the unselfish hero that authors would make him from the seventeenth century on.

The army that arrived in the Low Countries under Alba's command consisted of four Spanish infantry tercios. Romero headed the tercio of Sicily, Sancho de Londoño was the Maestre de campo of the tercio of Lombardy, Gonzalo de Bracamonte Dávila was commander of the

---

[81] Fagel, 'Duke of Alba'.

tercio of Sardinia, and finally Alonso de Ulloa led the tercio of Naples. Furthermore, the Italian Giovanluigi (Chiappino) Vitelli served as Maestre de campo general of the infantry and as artillery general, while Fernando de Toledo, Alba's natural son, served as general of the cavalry. This army of ten thousand men consisted of 8,795 infantry soldiers, divided among 49 banners, and some 1,200 horsemen.[82] On 16 June, Romero wrote from Livorno to Juan de Albornoz, the Duke of Alba's personal secretary, discussing payment for the troops.[83] Two days later, the troops departed from Asti, and after a successful journey along the 'Spanish Road' they arrived on 3 August in Thionville, the frontier town of the Low Countries. On 21 August Alba entered the city of Brussels, with Romero most certainly among his followers. The journey on foot had taken the army past Savoy and Lorraine, and Brantôme, who out of curiosity had gone to watch them, said the common soldiers looked like captains and the musketeers even resembled princes.[84]

In order to keep all Spanish soldiers close to him, Alba decided to quarter them in Ghent (tercio of Naples), Lier (tercio of Lombardy), Enghien (tercio of Sardinia) and Brussels (tercio of Sicily), while the cavalry would remain in the vicinity of Diest. Romero's tercio consisted of ten banners, 1,641 men when they left Lombardy, and, as said, they remained in Brussels, where he possibly still had his own house where his children lived, perhaps even still with their mother. The youngest child had survived the risky first years of his life, and this now six-year-old saw his Spanish father for the first time, even though this father was now also lawfully married in Spain. It seems that Romero sincerely tried to keep the peace between the inhabitants of Brussels and the soldiers, and when they left the city he also tried to treat the population honourably. In a letter to secretary Albornoz he informed him that his tercio had spent 6,000 ducats on food, weapons, pharmacists, doctors and the washing of shirts. Most of it had been directly paid back to the inhabitants with the payments worth almost 8,500 the soldiers had received. The burghers were very satisfied, though there was still a debt of some 5,000 ducats for goods bought by the Spanish soldiers. Romero was also very strict

[82] Quatrefages, *Tercios españoles* (1979) 83-84; Mendoza, *Comentarios* (1948) 404; Parker, *Dutch Revolt*, 102-104.
[83] Marichalar, *Julián*, 166-167; AA, C.48/194.
[84] Brantôme, *Œuvres complètes*, I, 28-29: 'Qu'on les prenoit plustost pour capitaines que soldats... Et eussiez dict que c'estoient des princes, tant ils estoient rogues et marchoient arrogamment et de belle grace'. Brantôme, *Oeuvres*, XIII, 116; 'Jusques à leurs courtisannes, qui en parures, paroissoient princesses'; 'Their very whores were as fine as princesses'. Brantôme, *Spanish Rhodomontades*, 79.

regarding soldiers violating the rules. Just before he left Brussels, several thieves and murderers among his men were convicted and sentenced to death or were sent to the galleys.[85]

On 9 September, Count Lamoral of Egmont was arrested in Brussels for his role in the disturbances during the past years. The night before his arrest, a masked Spaniard is said to have visited his palace in order to warn him about his impending apprehension. Egmont's widow, Sabine of Bayern, later said she thought it had been Julián Romero who had come to warn his old comrade-in-arms.[86] What we do know for sure is that Romero again played a role during the last day of Egmont's life, on 5 June 1568. Together with Captain Salinas he commanded a large Spanish force that had to safeguard the place of execution, the Grand Place of Brussels. Though most sources indeed put Romero on the spot, close to the scaffold, some authors, such as Emanuel van Meteren and P.C. Hooft, make his role even bigger. In the former's version the Count asked Romero "if there was no mercy, and he shrugged his shoulders and responded with a no". Hooft copied this part but added "with a no, as if he pitied him". These authors connected the event in 1567 with the old military relationship between Romero and Egmont they were clearly aware of. Van Meteren also mentions in his work Julián's important role at Saint-Quentin where he and Egmont had gained fame and honour.[87]

A Spanish manuscript newsletter reports another short discussion between Egmont and Julián, which took place just before the walk to the scaffold: "He [Egmont] begged Julián to cut the collar of his doublet and his shirt, so the executioner would not find any resistance". After this was done the count asked to be allowed to close a button of the long robe he was wearing in order not to have an open neck. He promised

---

[85] Marichalar, *Julián*, 178-179, 189-190; Romero to Albornoz, Brussels, 30 October 1567; Romero to Alba, 28 June 1568; Romero to Albornoz, Rhey [Rheden], 3 July 1568, AA, C.48/195-197. Later in Mechelen (Malines) Romero punished a soldier who had stabbed another Spaniard to death, Mechelen 1569, Archief van de Spaans-Nederlandse regering te Brussel, 1567-1576, Dutch National Archives, The Hague, 11, n. 60.

[86] Motley, *Rise*, I, 347.

[87] Van Meteren, *Belgische oft Nederlandsche historie* (1599) 10v, 43v; Hooft, *Nederlandsche historien* (1642-1647), book V, 182. Van Vaernewyck, *Van die beroerlicke tijden*, IV, 107, also includes a dialogue between the Maestre de campo (Romero?) and Egmont, with the commander asking Alba to pardon Egmont when the count was already standing on the scaffold. Op. cit. Rittersma, *Mytho-poetics*, 56. This might well reflect the same situation recounted by Hooft and Van Meteren. Ulloa, *Comentarios*, 25r, mentions Alonso de Ulloa as the Maestre de campo present at the scene.

to undo it as soon as he reached the scaffold. When Romero told him he could not do this because his hands would be tied, Egmont begged him to leave his hands untied, giving his word as a knight that he would remain calm.[88] As most descriptions of the execution describe the count as having his hands free, it seems the Spanish did decide to honour the count's last request.[89] Almost ten years after the count's execution, Romero's presence at the scene was still remembered. Spanish councillor Gerónimo de Roda told Philip II in a letter about the rumour that Julián had removed the heads of Egmont and the Count of Horne after their executions and had disposed of them somewhere.[90]

During this period Julián was also involved in several military encounters with the rebels. Strangely enough, Spanish military commander, diplomat, and chronicler Bernardino de Mendoza does mention Romero in his work, but without casting him as an oustanding hero. Hooft, on the other hand, again turns Romero into an important character, both at the siege of Mons in Hainaut and at the Battle of Jemmingen (Jemgum) in East Frisia. He was also a member of Alba's army which afterwards pursued Orange and his troops until the rebellious nobleman had no more money left to pay his soldiers and had to disband his army. The most memorable deed we can find took place around Sint-Truiden, when Romero's arm was wounded by an arquebus shot, and he had to recover in Maastricht. We could say that this first phase of the Revolt passed without great heroic deeds on Romero's part. He simply did his job as a commander of one of the Spanish tercios.[91]

However, we do find our very familiar Julián – the legendary Spanish storyteller – in an anecdote from Granvelle's confidant, Maximilien Morillon. According to Morillon, Romero had brought some two hundred oxen and cows back from East Frisia after the Battle of Jemmingen. He had heard this personally from Romero himself, and he seemed as impressed by Captain Julián's rousing soldier's stories as Brantôme had

---

[88] 'Y rogo a Julian que le cortase el quello del jubón y de la camisa para que el verdugo no hallase ynpedimiento y así se hizo'. Copia de nuevas de Flandes, BNM, Mss. 12622, Antonio Barahona; Rittersma, *Mytho-poetics*, 57-58.
[89] Rittersma, *Mytho-poetics*, 357, 381.
[90] Gerónimo de Roda to Philip II, Brussels, 18 May 1576, CP IV, 141-142. A rumour existed that Philip II had asked Romero to send the heads of the two Counts to Spain. Briones Moreno, 87.
[91] Mendoza, *Comentarios* (1948) 410, 424-425, 433-434, 459-461, 470; Van Meteren, *Belgische oft Nederlandsche historie* (1599) 44v; Hooft, *Nederlandsche historien* (1642-1647) book V, 187 and book VII, 269; CD XXXI, 21-22; Trillo, *Historia* (2008) 79; Kervyn de Lettenhove, *Relations politiques*, V (1886) 182.

been. The anecdote also gives us an insight into the daily reality of war, with the stealing of cattle as a legitimate action:

> It was beautiful to hear him speak about the indeed miraculous defeat … this captain told that nine men could chase six hundred, and maintaining that no one from our camp ever saw the face of an enemy, except when they fell over dead.[92]

From December 1568 Romero was quartered in Mechelen with five banners of his tercio, and together with Captain Osorio he lived in the house of the Lord of Berlo in the Grain Market. The city paid for twelve pieces of tapestry and ten beds with bedding. His troops also received money, housing and other supplies from the local population. Though Romero made the city pay less than Alba had wanted him to do, relations with the burghers must have been complicated. For example, there were complaints about the behaviour of one Captain Juan de Salazar. In an anti-Spanish pamphlet dated long after their stay in the city, the author cited the behaviour of the soldiers of the tercio of Sicily in Mechelen as a main reason for the later refusal to let royal troops into the city. The Spaniards had

> more from premeditated cruelty and evil plans than from anything else, spoiled the furniture of the mentioned burghers, broken and taken it, and by provoking and shouting in all kinds of ways, even threatening, throwing and chasing them out of their houses, and even murderously killing them.

They had also "raped some honest women and young daughters, violated and brought to shame", even committing nasty deeds with girls from the ages of six and seven. According to the pamphlet, the soldiers were hardly punished for their deeds, and unfortunately we do not know whether Julián in Mechelen had deviated from his normal behaviour by failing to treat harshly any misconduct by his soldiers.[93]

Most sources agree that Julián left the Low Countries in 1570 with the fleet that would take Anne of Austria to Spain. Emperor Maximilian II's daughter boarded ship in Zeeland on 25 September 1570 to marry Philip II, her father's cousin but also her own mother's brother. The Duke of

---

[92] Morillon to Granvelle, 23 August 1568, CG III, 335.
[93] CG III, 24, 433, 447; Van Doren, *Inventaire*, IV, 210-214; 'Waerachtige beschryvinge',142. The 'beschryvinge' was first published in Mechelen in 1581; Azevedo Coutinho, *Korte chronycke*, III, s.f., December 1568; Romero to Alba, 2 August 1569, AA, C/48, 198.

Alba gave Romero a letter of recommendation to take with him in order to secure royal favour: "I do not wish to explain… everything Maestre de campo Julián Romero has served His Majesty and the Emperor, our lord who rests in peace, as this is known to everybody (todo el mundo)".[94] Again we find a reference to the international fame Julián had already achieved. The Revolt in the Low Countries had been crushed and Alba could spare his important officer for some time.

During his journey to Spain Julián again became part of a new myth. According to rumours Philip II was organising an invasion of Ireland and Romero played a part in the story. We find this idea in the correspondence of the English ambassadors, though Alba wrote that he did not believe a word of it.[95] But it was true that one Thomas Stukeley had landed in Spain and had invited the King to invade Ireland. He would need one thousand Spanish troops, but if the King gave him Julián as their commander five hundred would be sufficient. It shows that his name and fame had not been forgotten by the English.[96] At the time Romero was also mentioned as the possible leader of an expedition to the New World.[97]

In Spain, Romero was ordered to organise a new regiment consisting of six banners, with 1,600 soldiers in total, that would travel to the Low Countries with the new Governor-general, Juan de la Cerda, the Duke of Medinaceli. It appears that the English had feared that this armada would sail in the direction of Ireland. The new soldiers had to be experienced, as Romero was asked not to hire "boys or useless men". The boarding of the ships in Laredo went far from smoothly, and Romero had also to be urged regularly to be prepared for sailing. The Royal Council even investigated whether he should be punished for abandoning his troops without permission. According to several witnesses, he had gone to Biscay, where he was received in his father's ancestral region with celebrations and bullfights to honour their famous local hero. Directly after reaching Spain he must have travelled to Madrid, as his daughter would be baptised

---

[94] Alba to Diego de Espinosa, Brussels, 24 February 1570, EA II, 345.
[95] Alba to Francés de Álava, Brussels, 7 March 1571, EA II; Guerau de Spes to Philip II, London, 14 March 1571, CD XC, 439; Francis Walsingham to William Cecil, 25 February 1571 and Henry Cobham to Lord Burghley, 18 April 1571, CSP, *Foreign*, IX, n. 1578 and 1663.
[96] CSP, *Ireland, Tudor Period*, III, n. 20; Cf. García Hernán, *Ireland*, 36, 66-67 who states that Romero did work as a military instructor in Ireland. Parker, *Felipe II*, 554.
[97] Consulta of the Council of the Indies to Philip II, 13 June 1571, IVDJ, Envío 23, c.36, 446.

in the church of San Ginés on 29 May 1571.⁹⁸ This last date raises the suspicion that Romero might have travelled from the Low Countries ahead of the royal party, not having waited for the new Queen Anne of Austria who embarked on 25 September 1570. Between her arrival in Santander in early October (on 4 or 7 October) and the baptism of Julián's daughter less than eight months had elapsed.

The first letters on the troops' embarcation date from April 1571, but in December Julián was still waiting to board ship, hopefully within a few days.⁹⁹ Finally, Alba's designated successor as Governor-general would sail only on 30 April 1572 and arrive in the Low Countries on 10 June.¹⁰⁰ On board were 1,263 soldiers, of whom 179 were destined for Romero's own tercio of Sicily.¹⁰¹ This meant not only that Romero had to wait more than a year before sailing again from Spain, but also that the royal policy regarding the Low Countries had come to a complete standstill for over a year, and with serious consequences. On 1 April the Sea Beggars had taken the small town of Brielle, starting the second military phase of the Revolt. The ships bringing Medinaceli and Romero were received at Flushing (which already had joined the rebellion) with hostile cannon fire.

Several reasons can be given for the resumption of the Revolt, but it is clear that the Duke of Alba's government was at least partially responsible for the dissatisfaction of many inhabitants of the Low Countries. The Tenth Penny, a tax on merchandise, had been introduced without the agreement of the Estates-General, and the quartering of foreign soldiers had already lasted for five years. Though they had been sent to defend the inhabitants of the Low Countries against the rebels, these much-criticised Spanish soldiers had become an important cause of the continuation of the very Revolt they had been suppressing.¹⁰²

In a long letter to royal secretary Gabriel de Zayas, closely connected to the Duke of Alba, Julián extensively described the journey and the welcome they had received in the Low Countries, apologising for his verbose letter.¹⁰³ Even ten sheets of paper had not been enough. It was

---

[98] De Wolf, 'Burocracia', 105; CD XXXV, 407, 413, 450, 469-470, 530-544, 558-570 and Idem XXXVI, 38, 45; Marichalar, *Julián*, 201, 206; Heras, *Julián*, 191.
[99] Romero to Zayas, Laredo, 5 December 1571, AGS, E. 547, 19.
[100] Medinaceli to Romero, Laredo, 3 April 1572, AGS, E. 547, 18.
[101] Marichalar, Julián, 238; Quatrefages, *Tercios* (1983) 154; Phillips and Rahn Phillips, 'Spanish wool', 320,
[102] Rooze-Stouthamer, *Opmaat*, 101-111.
[103] Romero to Zayas, 24 June 1572, CD LXXV, 55, 59-62; Hortal Muñoz, *Asuntos*, 100.

also a very frank letter in which he expressed his concern about the situation. He had been gone for almost two years and much had changed during that time. During the fleet's difficult arrival, navigating between dangerous sandbanks and enemies, he had also received a wound to his leg. They were received first in Ghent and afterwards in Brussels and, according to Romero, their welcome had been very enthusiastic:

> It is certain, and frightening, the joy and the receptions that were held in all territories to celebrate the arrival of the Count of Medina[celi] as they think that their remedy has now arrived… All the roads we passed through and all the cities were so full of people who wanted to see us that it is impossible to believe.

This joy was not the result of a great love for the Spaniards:

> The detestation they have for the name of the house of Alba is so great that it is impossible to believe, and neither can it be put into words or be exaggerated. Your honour knows how the people in this land are, that if they have been convinced of something, they all follow suit.

This combination of gullibility and stubbornness as characteristics of the inhabitants of the Low Countries can be found in many Spanish chronicles on the Revolt.[104] Julián understood the essence of the problem:

> How bad are the Tenth Penny and the one who invented it, as it is the origin of all this, and this they [the inhabitants of the Low Contries] said out loud in public; and it was very negligent to invent this Penny without having prepared the troops and without everything secured; it was said on the streets that people already knew about this revolt for six months, and even the children spoke of it.

Almost directly after his arrival Julián travelled from Brussels to Mons in Hainaut to join the besiegers of this city, as on 24 May Mons had joined the Revolt. According to Welsh soldier and chronicler Roger Williams, Julián led the failed attacks on a breach in the city walls and "escaped with great danger". During the battle at nearby Quiévrain, Julián once again excelled. The royal army succeeded in intercepting

---

[104] Rodríguez Pérez, *Tachtigjarige Oorlog*, 63-64; Idem, *Dutch Revolt*, 70-72.

a relief army of six thousand Frenchmen.[105] Together with a group of some two hundred arquebusiers he was the first to make contact with the enemy; Romero was clearly not a commander who watched battles from a distance. Notwithstanding, he wanted to become more than just a fighter. A few weeks after Quiévrain he reminded the King in a letter of his earlier request to become an official member of the Council of War. The always very cautious King Philip back in Spain had given him his usual answer, replying that he would look into it. Romero had been allowed occasionally to join the Council's meetings, but now he desired a proper seat, which would allow him really to give his opinions on the war. For the time being, he could only offer his opinions in his letters, like the one to Zayas of 3 August:

> Holland is still as much in ruins as before, and Frisia is in no better state, and Zeeland even worse. But this means nothing compared to Mons, that feels like it has pierced my heart, because if we can fill this hole at the frontier, everything else is like thin air. Even though we will have to sweat if we have to camp there during this winter, as this will have to be with skates on.[106]

His hopes were soon to be fulfilled. That very same night the Massacre of Saint Bartholomew's Eve took place in Paris and with it in one blow the threat of Protestant support for the rebels from France disappeared. There was, however, still a large relief army of some twenty thousand men on the way to Mons, headed by the Prince of Orange. On 11 September the two armies were camped very near to each other and Julián was sent to attack the army camp in the middle of the night. According to Hooft, Julián had with him some three thousand men during this *camisade*, all wearing white shirts so as to be able to recognise each other in the dark:

---

[105] 'Relaçion breve del buen suçeso que el felicisimo exérçito del rey nuestro señor ubo con los herejes que venian de Françia al Socorro de Mons en Henao', 17 July 1572, BL, Add. 28.387, f. 90.

[106] Williams, *Memoriën*, 71-72; Williams, *Actions*, 47; Romero to Philip II, camp outside Mons, 31 July 1572; Romero to Zayas, camp outside Mons, 23 August 1572, CD LXXV, 67-68, 87-88; AGS, E. 549, 105 and Idem, 552, 31. See also Romero to Zayas, camp outside Mons, 22 September 1572, Idem, 104-106; AGS, E. 549, 151 and Idem, 552, 39. In January 1573, Zayas sent a newsletter from Holland to Juan de Borja, but originally it had been a letter or report from Romero to Zayas: Rodríguez-Salgado, '"Do not reveal"'; AGS, E. 391, 133, Juan de Borja to Zayas, Lisbon, 22 January 1573.

> Subsequently, Julián thrusts himself in with no less violence and after knocking down all the guards he encounters on his way he reaches the place of arms in front of the prince's tent, so swiftly that even those of the guard had not been alarmed before seeing their own soldiers fleeing with the enemy close behind them. Afterwards, the prince often called himself lucky for the loyalty of a dog that had started to whine through the noise, then had jumped upon his face and had scratched him awake, before any of his followers had woken up. And ever since, until the day he died, he always kept the offspring of this dog as his watchdog, while his servants also had to take care of several of these dogs. Without the vigilance of this animal, he would have been taken prisoner.[107]

Hooft is here following the description by Roger Williams, who in early 1574 would enter into Julián's service. This Welsh adventurer had since 1572 served with William of Orange, together with the English company of Thomas Morgan, but when these men returned to England after a conflict Williams decided to stay and joined Romero's troops. The Spanish commander was not just an enemy, as Romero had been fighting in Saint-Quentin together with Williams's old protector, Count Pembroke. The Spanish commander highly praised the deceased English Count, creating a connection between Romero and Williams. The fact that Hooft often makes use of Williams's chronicle may partly explain why Romero is such a prominent protagonist in Hooft's work. The Dutch author seems to have chosen him as a Spanish protagonist in order to give his *Historiën* colour and life. Williams, of course, also knew the Prince of Orange personally, and he had often heard the story of the dog that saved his life from Orange himself.

According to chronicler Bernardino de Mendoza, the Spaniards stayed for over an hour in the enemy camp and left behind some three hundred dead rebels, as well as sixty men from their own ranks. However, in his chronicle we do not read anything about the dog or the possibility of capturing Orange. It seems the Spanish had not realised at the time how close they had been to capturing their most dangerous enemy.[108]

---

[107] Hooft, *Nederlandse historiën* (2007) 126; Hooft, *Nederlandsche historien* (1642-1647), book VII, 274.
[108] Williams, *Memoriën*, 77-78, 157-158; Van der Lem, *Opstand*, 84-85; Mendoza, *Comentarios* (1948) 469; Siebelink, 'Ik bleef krabben', 16.

Two days later Alba applauded this nocturnal massacre of the enemy in a letter to the King. The Duke of Medinaceli did the same, and in his words we hear even more praise for Julián:

> Maestre de campo Julián acted in such a manner that Your Majesty has with him a marvellous soldier and a great executor of war, that even if he would let me wait again in Laredo – and I don't say hours but ten years – I would forgive him and would share my cape with him.

Philip II replied to Medinaceli with great praise for Romero, and a large reward seemed to be only a question of time:

> Although the will and intentions with which Julián Romero serves me are more than enough proven by his deeds, your approval and that of the Duke will put him even more into my consideration.[109]

## The Duke of Alba's hangman

At the surrender of Mons on 19 September 1572, Romero was one of the royal officers who organised the free departure from the city of the defeated and very ill Louis of Nassau, Orange's brother, and his men. He assured Louis that the treaty they had signed would not be violated.[110] From Mons, Romero went with Alba's army in the direction of the Duchy of Brabant, to punish cities that had opened their gates to the rebel troops. The Sack of Mechelen is the first of a series of atrocities committed by the royal army in the Low Countries; Zutphen and Naarden would soon follow. This would create an even worse image of the Spanish soldiers: they were described as a gang of cruel murderers whose hideous crimes did not even spare women and children. We can find this image in chronicles and pamphlets, but also in the famous Beggar songs: "Hear what the Spaniards did to the small children. They pierced them with their lances, cut them with their swords and ripped them to pieces while still alive".[111] These descriptions were influenced by the fixed clichés

---

[109] Alba to Philip II, camp outside Mons, 13 September 1572, EA III, 208; Medinaceli to Philip II, camp outside Mons, 16 September 1572, and Philip II to Medinaceli, El Escorial, 29 October 1572, CD XXXVI, 107-118.
[110] Nuyens, *Geschiedenis* II, 89-90; Herwerden, *Lodewijk*, 173.
[111] Spaanse fury te Maastricht, *Nederlandsche geschiedzangen*, II (1864) 173.

on violent plundering, but also fitted the reputation in Europe of the Spaniards as a cruel people. Protestant authors, in particular, had widely published on the character of the Spanish Inquisition in the decades up to the Revolt. This negative image of the Spaniards would continue to grow, and at the beginning of the twentieth century Julián Juderías and others would call it a true 'Black Legend' of Spanish cruelty, pointing, for example, to the important role of the *Apology* (1580) by William of Orange and his ghost writers.[112]

On the other hand, Spaniards defended their actions based on the current laws of war, as explained, for example, by Francisco de Vitoria of Salamanca University. The Duke of Alba and his son Fadrique made use of their own system for the punishment of rebellious cities, distinguishing six different situations. It seems that they acted according to these ideas. Under the laws of war it was seen as normal for defenders of a place that did not surrender before the placing of artillery to be left at the mercy of the besiegers. As the Spaniards also saw them as people rebelling against a lawful sovereign, severe punishment could also be defended from that angle. Spanish authors were, however, divided on the influence of religion on the severity of the punishment. For example, the influential Francisco de Vitoria did not think religious wars were justified.[113]

In many of the chronicles, like those by Trillo, Mendoza and Van Meteren, Julián did not play a specific role during these punishments. However, in the seventeenth century Hooft would again turn Julián into one of the main protagonists. He describes how he took possession of Mechelen with his troops, and how he did the same in Naarden and Haarlem. Hooft also tells the story about the only three houses in Mechelen that were left standing, one of which belonged to Jan van Brançion, an old friend of Romero's. Hopefully his famous garden was spared as well![114] A description of the plundering of Mechelen written almost directly after the events seems to praise the Spanish commander for his behaviour, but this praise was ambiguous. When Spanish soldiers were ravaging a large hospital, Romero went into action:

> He chased out the mentioned soldiers and all the others who were there, searching even in the beds of the nuns, but this helped the poor burghers little because this Julián kept all the furniture

---

[112] See the introduction.
[113] Arnade, *Beggars*, 212-259; Parker, 'Etiquette'; Van der Essen, 'Kritisch onderzoek'; Soen, 'Más allá', 47; Charles, *Sac*.
[114] Van Gelder, *Tussen hof*, 23.

he could find for himself, estimated to represent a large sum of money.[115]

We can read about Romero's role in the three-day plundering of Mechelen in the letters from Morillon to Granvelle. According to Morillon, Romero had in Mechelen amassed more than one hundred thousand écus and his troops had treated the population as if they were dogs. We have already seen that Morillon and Romero knew each other. Morillon was Vicar-general of the archdiocese of Mechelen, of which Granvelle was the Archbishop, while Romero had been quartered in the city for some eighteen months and had friends in the city.[116] In the eyes of the Catholic royalist Morillon, Romero had changed within a few years from a sympathetic and tough hero fighting on the side of good (still in 1568) into a cruel oppressor and exploiter. His revised view on this Spanish commander might be taken as an example of that of many of the faithful Catholic subjects of Philip II in the Low Countries during these years.

Though Julián must have been involved in the storming and sacking of Zutphen in the Duchy of Guelders under Don Fadrique, the mostly very brief descriptions do not attribute an active role to him. However, in the subsequent siege and sacking of the town of Naarden in the County of Holland he is the main protagonist of several anecdotes. The Duke of Alba had remained in Nijmegen due to his gout, making Julián one of the most experienced advisors of the relatively young – and inexperienced – Don Fadrique. The signs had not been good for little Naarden. At Mechelen and Zutphen the royal policy makers had noticed that the severe punishment of one town led to the surrender of many more. And though Naarden sided with the rebels, the garrison was too small and its walls not very strong. Naarden was also the first city in the County of Holland on the army's route and thus very well situated to serve as a deterrent example. As noted, Julián is missing from the descriptions of Naarden by Spanish chroniclers like Trillo and Mendoza, but also from those by Van Meteren, Roger Williams or Walter Morgan.[117]

In Hooft's work we find Romero again as a protagonist. When the burghers of Naarden realised their hopeless situation, they sent a group of seven negotiators to the besiegers in order to discuss a surrender. This delegation met Romero on their way, and the Spanish commander told

---

[115] 'Plundering', 413.
[116] Hooft, *Nederlandsche historien* (1642-1647) VII, 277-278; Morillon to Granvelle, 18 October 1572, 1 November 1572, 30 November 1572, CG IV, 467-468, 493, 519.
[117] Morgan, *Expedition*.

them he could speak on behalf of Don Fadrique: "Here then, they hand over the keys, and pray to be forgiven. Julián at first answered very kindly but unclearly to their petition".[118] He subsequently gave his word that the burghers and garrison would be spared and confirmed this by three times shaking the hand of one of the representatives of Naarden, Hendrik Wou, who spoke French very well. Out of respect or inexperience, so Hooft argues, the delegation forgot to ask Romero for written confirmation of the treaty. Romero was received in the town with twenty-eight men who were offered a banquet, followed by another four hundred Spaniards who were also given food and drink. Subsequently, the male inhabitants were ordered to go to the town hall where they were all massacred, followed by the sacking and burning down of the town.

We can already find Hooft's story in the work of Pieter Bor, but without many of the details. He does not mention the twenty-eight nor the four hundred soldiers and the banquet. It is also unclear what language was spoken between Julián and the negotiators, as in Bor's account he had spoken with Wou in Spanish. In later editions of Van Meteren's chronicle this version was included.[119]

The treacherous part played by Julián was thus not Hooft's invention. Three local texts also mention him. The 'Cort verhael van de moort...' by Pieter Aertsz. was included by Gysius in the 1626 edition of his history of the Revolt, while a pamphlet called *Moort-dadich verhael...* also originated with the Aertsz family. Lambertus Hortensius, Principal of the Latin school, wrote his Latin description shortly after the events.[120] Like alderman Gerrit Pieter Aertsz., Hortensius was a member of the delegation that went to discuss the town's surrender and an eyewitness to the meeting with Romero. After the fatal ending, both Aertsz. and Hortensius had a specific interest in negating any doubts about the possible failure of their delegation.

The texts emphasise the problems around Romero's promise. In Hortensius, Romero expressed himself at first very unclearly – and almost threateningly: "Now, he said, give me the keys to the gate. There you will be informed on how we think about pardon and grace". He repeated those words again, and at the gate he indeed received the keys to the town. According to Hortensius, Romero expressed himself "calmly but not very clearly". This phrase may have led to Hooft's formulation, as

---

[118] Hooft, *Nederlandsche historien* (1642-1647) VII, 288-289.
[119] Bor, *Nederlantsche oorloghen*, 150-152; Van Meteren, *Historien der Nederlanden* (1646); Boomsma, 'Beeldenstorm'.
[120] *Moort-dadich verhael*; Aertsz, 'Cort verhael', 484; Hortensius, 'Over de opkomst'.

Hooft certainly made use of Hortensius. The Principal states that only after insisting for quite some time, did Romero promise that all lives and goods would be spared, to be confirmed by the triple handshake between Wou and Romero. However, we do not read anything about the arguments they used to obtain such an obliging promise from the strict Spanish commander. The idea of sparing rebellious but powerless Naarden and its inhabitants without any clear reason does not fit Alba's policy, the current laws of war or the power relations of the moment. The negotiators from Naarden, of course, were aware of this. Pieter Aertsz. adds another element to the description of the meeting. According to him, Romero had first demanded that in order to leave the burghers at peace one or two hundred Spaniards had to be allowed to enter the town and take as much with them as they could carry, and moreover all burghers and soldiers had to take a new oath of loyalty to the King. This proposition fits much better the power relations between the large army and the inhabitants of Naarden, and it also coincides with Romero's well-known interest in material gain.

The author of the pamphlet does not mention any obscurities and spends many words on defending the idea that there was a real treaty: "the aforementioned delegates were of the opinion that by such deeds those of Naarden were sufficiently secured against any violence from the enemy towards their life and goods". The problem, as Hooft also indicated, was that the delegation had not asked Romero for a written statement. The texts mostly try to prove, on the contrary, that the members of the delegation had not made any errors, which means that we have to take care in judging Romero's behaviour and in accepting any harsh accusations levelled at him. These texts are written with a clear purpose, and accusing Romero of false promises could clearly have been a good solution. Did the triple handshake really mean that Romero promised to spare everybody without getting anything in return? Both his emphasis on his military honour and his lust for material gain would seem to contradict this idea.

The reliability of the local texts is also partly nullified by a very extensive and incredibly 'atrocity marrative' of the Spanish crimes regarding women, children and old people in these texts.[121] A 70-year-old man was stabbed with a dagger in his neck, after which the soldiers drank his blood from their hands. These stories are full of the gruesome clichés related to plundering: many heads and hands are chopped off,

---

[121] Pollmann, *Memory*, 162.

a pregnant woman is raped four times and afterwards the unborn child is cut out of her womb and deposited in a bag, nuns are raped, heavily pregnant women are hung by their breasts, a smith sees his legs cut off with his own axes, centenarians are killed and the Spanish even steal an infant's nappies. In the pamphlet, Hortensius's son is stabbed to death in the presence of his father and his heart is cut out "and as some say, subsequently cooked and eaten". Hortensius himself, in total control of his feelings, noted, "Before my very eyes, five people were killed in my house and on my yard, and among them, one who as my kin, was not strange to me".

The treacherous breaking of his word as recorded by Dutch authors is refuted by the Spanish authors, as in their descriptions there are no negotiations. Less than three weeks after the events, Alba mentioned Romero's presence in Naarden and, according to Alba, the Spaniards were able to get over the walls during an attack, after which they "cut the throats of burghers and soldiers without letting anybody escape". The famous Belgian historian Léon van der Essen, who studied the historial sources from both sides, concluded that negotiations were taking place during which some defenders started shooting. The Spanish immediately attacked. Dutch sources do mention the shooting incident and the subsequent attack, but state that this concerned an earlier round of negotiations. Morillon wrote to Granvelle on 9 December, a mere eight days after the massacre, on the events at Naarden:[122]

> While the burghers took their keys to Don Fadrique, their excuses were not accepted, as Don Fadrique wanted to see if they would still be as brave the next day. In the morning our men entered the town without any resistance from the burghers. As soon as they had entered, Captain Julián made the burghers enter the town hall where they were all cut to pieces. After it had been sacked, fire was put to the four corners of the town. Everything was turned into ashes, and many children and pregnant women were burned. These people never do anything else and they have great pleasure in human blood and in making many widows and orphans. It was a nice merchant town, as large as Vilvoorde. It made other towns not very willing to surrender. However, this lord said he had heard that those of Leiden had taken their keys to Don Fadrique....

[122] Alba to Philip II, Nijmegen, 19 December 1572, EA III, 261; Van der Essen, 'Kritisch onderzoek', 29-31; Morillon to Granvelle, Brussels, 9 December 1572, CG IV, 525-526.

So Morillon does not mention the storming of the walls we find in the Spanish sources, but he also fails to mention the false promises from the Dutch texts. The delegation from Naarden had offered the town's surrender, but Don Fadrique used his power to postpone his final decision until after his troops had entered. Morillon wrote only one week after the events, and as a royalist – but at the same time also a declared enemy of the Spanish military – he may be the most reliable source for the time being. At the same time, the stories about the treacherous Julián cannot be completely dismissed. But do they really coincide with the image we have of this Spanish commander?

## Julián and the Prince of Orange

Morillon was right in his idea that Naarden's fate kept the other cities in Holland from surrendering. After Naarden the royal army continued towards Haarlem, which indeed refused to surrender. On 9 December, the army arrived before the fortress at Spaarndam. Again, Julián was present at the front, and, confirming his well-known reputation for bravery and self-confidence, he declared that he would take the fortress that very same day. With four hundred arquebusiers he crossed the ice and dared the defenders to enter into combat by shooting at them. During the batttle he had already shouted that the attackers were going to win. In Spanish chronicles Julián receives the laurels of victory, though his fellow Maestre de campo, Gonzalo de Bracamonte, also received (somewhat less) praise. There were some two hundred dead enemies against thirty casualties, dead or wounded, in the royal camp. Romero's glory, however, seems to fade in Hooft's description, where Catholic spies informed Romero about a path across the ice, 'the inside path' by which one could attack the enemy from the rear. Gone is the heroism and again the smell of treason returns to the story.[123] In a letter from Don Fadrique to his father, Romero is the main executor of Don Fadrique's plans. But Don Fadrique does ask his father for a good reward for the brave Julián, describing how the commander and his men had been standing up to their knees in water. Julián's lame leg led Don Fadrique to offer a small linguistic joke: "What a good leg is his, to go about in this manner" ("Qué buen

---

[123] Trillo, *Historia*, 167-188; Mendoza, *Comentarios* (1948) 478; Van Meteren, *Belgische oft Nederlandsche historie* (1599) 63r; Hooft, *Nederlandsche historien* (1642-1647) VII, 295-296; CD LXXV, 142-145; Claude de Mondoucet to Charles IX, 17 December 1572, *Lettres et négociations*, 125-126.

pie el suyo para andar de esta manera").[124] In a letter of February 1573, Alba received orders from Philip II to inform Romero that his King was very grateful for his brave deeds at Spaarndam.[125]

The siege of Haarlem would drag on for many months. During it Romero wrote a long letter to Alba in which the experienced soldier expressed his amazement at the uniqueness of the siege:[126]

> What happens here is worth travelling a hundred miles to see and it is not to be written down, as it has never been seen by anybody who has been born, and there are no descriptions possible of what has happened here; with only one word the whole world would be silenced.

He also gives examples of the very special nature of the conflict:

> The method they have to inform others is by taking two or three pigeons, and when they arrive at their fleet, they write what they have to write, tie it to a pigeon and let it fly. Then it goes to its home ground and in this way they receive their messages.

He was also full of admiration for their great capacity to jump across the many canals:

> They have a large number of poles for jumping, very light and thick, larger than pikes, and ending with an iron point just like a pike. At the bottom there is a piece of wood like a small plate to take care that the pole does not sink into the mud from the canals, and in this way they jump.

He also noticed their tactic of throwing water over the attackers, to force them to stand up to their knees in water, and also the speed with which they repaired their defence works: "You have to start bombarding at dawn, and then start the assault after dinner, and not leave it for the next day, as in one night they would make it even stronger than before". This admiration for the adversary we also find in the work of Bernardino de Mendoza who emphasises their control of the water. Mendoza also

---

[124] Don Fadrique to Alba, 11 December 1572, CD LXXV, 91-97.
[125] Philip II to Alba, Madrid, 4 February 1573, CP II, 310.
[126] Romero to Alba, army camp at Haarlem, 25 May 1573, CD LXXV, 237. Also Kooij, *Spaanse ooggetuigen*.

mentions the jumping pole, along with the stories of peasant women who went to the market on skates, with baskets full of eggs on their heads, pulling sledges full of produce.[127]

Apparently, Romero was in charge of daily affairs during the siege of Haarlem, and he must have often stayed in Fadrique's headquarters at the House of Cleves, though he may have resided at one of the monasteries outside the city.[128] The anonymous captain who gives us this information affirmed in a letter of February 1573 that he had already known Romero for twenty-four years. So maybe he had even fought alongside him during the wars against the French. His opinion of the commander is ambiguous: "I have never seen him as a politician, and he certainly is not, though as a soldier nobody is better than him, and few just as good".[129] The anonymous captain added that among the people rumour had it that the Prince of Orange had been captured at Delft, and if this were true then Romero's lack of governmental experience would no longer be an obstacle. It was not to be. The collaboration with Don Fadrique also did not go perfectly smoothly. Romero and some other high officers criticised Alba's son when he ignored their advice and ordered the storming of a small breach in the city walls. When Romero saw that the soldiers did not stand a chance because their pikes could not reach the enemy, he personally went to the front line to get the men back, during which he was shot in the eye. Though this act of bravery can be found in many of the accounts of the siege, there is also another version in which he was shot "standing in the trenches watching the assault".[130] The French ambassador turns the same story completely around in a letter to Charles IX. According to him, Romero wanted to reserve the glory of the taking of Haarlem all to himself and for that reason he himself had ordered the attack. The attack was unsuccessful and cost the lives of more than two hundred men, among them "the best men and almost all the officers".[131]

The story of Julián's eye reached the King through a letter by the Duke of Alba:

---

[127] Rodríguez Pérez, *Tachtigjarige Oorlog*, 59-60; Idem, *Dutch Revolt*, 66-67.
[128] Martínez Laínez, *Ocaso*, I, 161.
[129] An anonymous captain to his friend, 5 February 1573, CD LXXV, 178.
[130] CD LXXV, 160-161.
[131] Mendoza, *Comentarios* (1948) 479-480; Hooft, *Nederlandsche historien* (1642-1647) VII, 298; Don Fadrique to Alba, 9 April 1573, CP II, 327-328; Mondoucet to Charles IX, 26 December 1572, *Lettres et négociations*, 135.

> He was shot by an arquebus in his right eye, and they say he will not die of it, but I miss him very much, as Don Fadrique is very lonely as he has nobody with him to help him out, and Julián does that very well and is a man of much service.[132]

The French ambassador came to the same conclusion and stated that the success of the siege was now in danger, "as there is nobody in whom the Spaniards have more faith". Don Fadrique acknowledged Romero's importance for the outcome of the siege and insisted that Romero recover from his wound in Fadrique's own very comfortable house in Amsterdam. If Romero refused to obey, he would burn down Romero's residence in Amsterdam. The wounded commander received all kinds of gifts, including a jar of jam from Albornoz, Alba's personal secretary. In a letter Romero asked Albornoz to hurry in sending another jar as the first one was already half empty. He was so well taken care of that after a fast recovery he was back in action by February.[133]

The anonymous captain mentioned above puts Romero's heroic deeds in a different perspective. Julián lost one eye, so he stated, but high officers in the end all recovered from their injuries, while the poor soldiers almost always died when they received an injury, that is, if they had not already died of hunger. The lengthy siege of Haarlem was a disaster for the royal army, ending in a pyrric victory on 12 July 1573.[134]

Close to the end of the siege, Julián is supposed to have won another major battle, the battle at the Manpad, at least if we credit the evidence of his friend, Captain Esteban Illán, who described that fourteen hundred corpses were lying around the war theatre: "and I promise your honour that Julián did as he usually does". His letter offers us the opportunity to sense the optimistic and bellicose atmosphere in Romero's camp, three days before the surrender of the city. Captain Illán hoped that in his next letter to Albornoz he could inform him of the surrender of Haarlem and of the killing of all heretics.[135]

After the surrender of Haarlem, Julián was the first commander to enter the city, and he was also directly involved in the execution of part

---

[132] Alba to Philip II, Nijmegen, 8 January 1573, EA III, 274; Idem, 287, Romero to Albornoz, Amsterdam, 13 January 1573, CD LXX, 175, AGS, E. 552, 104; Romero to Albornoz, Amsterdam, 1 January 1573, BNM, Manuscript 18762, f. 93.

[133] Monducet to Charles IX, 4 January 1573, *Lettres et négociations*, 139 and Idem, 26 December 1572, Idem, 135; Philip II to Romero, Madrid, 10 February 1573, AGS, E. 554, 19.

[134] CD LXXV, 161-167, 178.

[135] Illán to Albornoz, army camp before Haarlem, 9 July 1573, Marichalar, *Julián*, 283.

of the garrison. The English and Germans were free to leave, but the Scots, Brabanders, Flemings and Walloons were executed, at first by the sword, but afterwards also by throwing them tied into the river Spaarne. Among the civil population only a small group of leaders was executed, and Romero promised to protect the inhabitants from his troops. Trillo mentions the figure of three thousand deaths, "men who with so much arrogance said that Haarlem was to be the grave of the Spaniards". Strangely enough, Hooft mentions only nine hundred excutions, but he uses his low estimate to attack the Spanish chroniclers for their higher numbers, "as if one could gain honour with the killing of prisoners". Romero's actions at Haarlem would survive for centuries. In a play from 1739 the famous Haarlem widow, Kenau, goes to the Spanish army camp and stabs Romero to death in front of his tent.[136] In real life, Romero's life was truly in danger in Haarlem, albeit not through the dramatic deed of a bold national heroine, but at the hands of his own men. They had not been paid for a long time, and after the city's surrender they decided to start a mutiny. William of Orange wrote to his brother Louis that Julián had to run and climb a breach in the wall in order to escape from the mutineers. It would not be the last time. According to the French ambassador, the mutineers had willingly let Romero go free.[137]

At the siege of Alkmaar, Romero was again among the most prominent commanders and the bravest warriors, even if information is scarce. Eyewitness Nanning van Foreest mentions him only once as a Spanish colonel in the headquarters at Oudorp, but without labelling him an important commander.[138] Spanish chronicles generally do not pay much attention to this siege, as it ended in a quick retreat. Alkmaar had worked hard at improving its defences after going over to the rebel side in June 1572, but when the royal army arrived only four new bulwarks had been ready. Therefore, all artillery fire and storming took place at the old walls on the north side of the city. The size of the royal army is unclear. Numbers reach as high as sixteen thousand and as low as 6,500. The last number comes from the declaration of a Spaniard taken prisoner. On 18 September the major attack took place, costing the lives of many Spanish soldiers. Though Bor and Hooft mention some one thousand deaths,

---

[136] Trillo, *Historia*, 207-208; Hooft, *Nederlandsche historien* (1642-1647) VIII, 325; Verwer, *Memoriaelboeck*, 1-112; Meijer-Drees, 'Vaderlandse heldinnen', 76.

[137] Orange to Louis of Nassau, Dordrecht, 10 August 1573, *Archives*, IV, 180; Mondoucet to Charles IX, 30 July 1573, *Lettres et négociations* (1891) 346-347, and Idem, 3 August 1573, Idem, 348.

[138] Van Foreest, *Kort verhaal*, 51-101.

modern historians consider two hundred more likely. The chronicles report that Romero once left the war council on horseback, and he gave a good example of an old warhorse when the soldiers did not want to fight and he, "with his sword in his hand", threw the enemy from the trenches. There is also a rather bizarre anecdote that tells how Julián during the storming of the walls got stuck in a bridge made of barrels, from which perilous situation he could barely be liberated.[139]

On 8 October 1573, the royal army retreated from Alkmaar. It went south in order to organise a broad siege ring around Leiden. Julián travelled through the dunes past Noordwijk and Katwijk towards The Hague. From there he continued to the Duchy of Brabant, where he would be busy reorganising the Spanish tercios under the new Governor-general, Luis de Requesens. Philip II had ordered him to remain in the Low Countries to serve under the new Governor-general, and Romero had accepted, though he had "very much wished to go to Spain and had put much effort into this". He was allowed to send Esteban Yllán in his place, taking his letter to the King.[140]

He played only a minor role at the famous siege of Leiden. He arrived almost at the end after fellow commander Francisco Valdés had asked for reinforcements (31 August 1574). Requesens approved of the idea, stating that even if Romero went merely on his own, this would be very beneficial. The Governor-general clearly showed his appreciation for the old hero. But when Romero and his men arrived around Leiden, it seems that Valdés thought the city would fall soon, and he did not really need him any more. According to Trillo, Julián got the impression that Valdés could finish it on his own and did not want to share the honour of the impending victory with somebody else. Romero therefore left Leiden after just one week.[141] Valdés would not gain any fame at Leiden, and Romero had left in time to avoid being part of the honourless retreat on 3 October 1574. The incident shows the difficult relationship between the two high officers. The conflict will also be discussed in the chapter on Valdés.

---

[139] Mendoza, *Comentarios* (1948) 499-500; CP II, 428; Cabrera de Córdoba, *Historia*, II, 659-660; Wortel, 'Vesting', 52, 55; Schulten, 'Beleg', 71-80.

[140] 'Desseado mucho yr en Spaña y hecho para ello mucha instancia'. Philip II to Romero, Madrid, 21 October 1573, AGS, E. 554, 47; Requesens to Philip II, Brussels, 10 December 1573, AGS, E. 554, 165; Romero to Philip II, Antwerp, 27 December 1573, AGS, E. 555, 128.

[141] Trillo, *Historia*, 254; Requesens to Romero, 2 September 1574, NCD V, 159-160.

On 4 November 1573 Romero's troops captured Philip Marnix of Sint-Aldegonde, one of Orange's main advisors, in the vicinity of Maassluis. Marnix's apprehension led to a short-lived revival of the correspondence between the Spanish commander and William of Orange.[142] Marnix informed Orange that he was well taken care of and called it "our fortune" that he had fallen into Romero's hands and not into those of one of the other Spaniards. From Delft, Orange informed his brothers that Marnix had been taken as a prisoner to The Hague:

> He was grateful for the good treatment he received. The said Romero has written me [William of Orange] three or four times letters full of courteous and honourful offers, to which he had responded in equal terms.[143]

The exchanged letters were friendly and polite, with Orange ending his letters with words like "be it that the affairs end good or bad, you will always find in me your affectionate servant". Though Orange feared – and with reason – that Marnix would not survive were he to fall into Alba's hands, he did not accept an exchange of Marnix for stadtholder Boussu[144] as proposed by Romero, calling it "so out of reason and proportion". As Requesens did not accept other proposals for an exchange of prisoners, the negotiations would drag on for quite some time. It is clear that Marnix was saved because the royal government really wanted to get Boussu back. After he had been taken to the citadel in Utrecht he was finally exchanged for Cristóbal de Mondragón in October 1574.[145]

However, Julián wanted more than just exchanging prisoners. He wanted to use Marnix to force Orange into a personal meeting with him about peace. Orange rejected the proposal. The idea was that such

---

[142] Van Schelven, *Marnix*, 78.

[143] Fruin, 'Prins Willem', 349; 'Duquel il se loue assez pour le gratieux traictement qu'il en reçoit. Le dit Romero m'a escript troys ou quatre fois des lettres palines de courtoisies et honestes offres, ausquelles luy ay respondu en pareilz termes'. Orange to his brothers, Delft, 13 November 1573, *Archives*, IV, 237-238.

[144] Maximilian de Hennin, Count of Boussu (1542-1578).

[145] 'Soit que les affaires viègnent bien ou mal, trouverez en moy tousjours ung serviteur et bien affectionné vostre'; 'Sy hors de propos et raison'. BO, Marnix to Orange, 7 November 1573, CT III, 776 and letters Orange to Romero, Delft, 7, 8, 9 and 10 November 1573, CT III, 81-87 and in Spanish translation: AGS, E. 557, 161-164; Requesens to Romero, 30 June 1574 and 5 October 1574, NCD III, 202-203 and Idem, V, 351-352; *Marnixi epistulae*, 206-226; Rijkse, 'Marnix', 182; Mondoucet to Charles IX, 11 December 1573, *Lettres et négociations*, 61-63.

a meeting should not be based only on the old friendship between the two men, but also their shared disgust about the cruelties of the current war. Julián wished to return to the days of the "bonne guerre", the good war, and Orange agreed: "It would be very good to see all those cruelties and inhumanities end that were not used before".[146] We find the same idea in another letter from the Prince: "good war, that like before, has always been practised between all the others nations, stopping all the cruelties so unworthy of christians".[147] In a 'good war' the church and the clergy were spared, there existed respect for the civil population, honourable and just rules would be used during negotiations, and no cruel methods would be used during a siege. The leader of the Revolt and the Duke's hangman from Naarden and Haarlem agreed with each other that the character of the war in the Low Countries had unfortunately deteriorated from that of previous wars, wars in which they had been fighting on the same side.

Julián's initiative was not well received by Requesens, who even complained to the King about Romero and had copies made of the correspondence that were sent to Madrid.[148] The Governor-general still respected him as a military hero, but at the political level Romero was more and more seen as a liability. Romero had even informed the French ambassador about his letters to Orange, who subsequently informed the French King:

> This Julián says to me that he is sure the prince [Orange] would be satisfied with a pension in Germany of thirty or forty thousand écus a year if his son [Philip William] – who is in Spain – would be returned his goods and inheritance, and in the same manner dealing with the other noblemen.

The ambassador even wrote that Julián planned to go to Madrid in January to speak to the King.[149] The journey never took place. Requesens would never have permitted it.

---

[146] 'J'eusse esté très-aise de veoir cesser touttes les cruaultez et inhumanitez cy-devant non usitées'.

[147] 'Bonne guerre, ainsy que, par-cy-devant, entre toutes aultres nations at tousjours esté practiqué, faisant cesser touttes cruaultez tant indignes de chrestiens'.

[148] Baes, 'Guerre', 187-188; Requesens to Philip II, Antwerp, 30 December 1573, CP II, 451; 'Romero requires earnestly to talk with him'. Thomas Morgan to Lord Burghley, 1 November 1573, CSP, *Foreign* X, n. 1221.

[149] Mondoucet to Charles IX, 11 December 1573, *Lettres et négociations* (1892) 60-63.

## Luctor et submergo

In early 1574 Julián was involved in an attempt to relieve the besieged city of Middelburg in Zeeland. Sancho Dávila would command a fleet of large vessels, while Romero would head a fleet consisting of many smaller ships for the transportation of troops. The complete failure of the expedition, near Reimerswaal and Bergen-op-Zoom, has turned into one of the most notorious episodes in his career. Already at the start the signs pointed to disaster, as the ceremonial shots with which the fleet saluted the Governor-general who was present caused the loss of one ship as fire broke out. In the continuation, Romero had to confront enemy attacks, the negative behaviour of Dutch sailors in his service, and the always dangerous sandbanks of Zeeland. Julián was defeated on 29 January and had to abandon ship.[150]

Van Meteren described him as an "old experienced man of war" and tells us that "the admiral Julián Romero crept from a gun port and got away in a small boat". Hooft makes the story even longer, again using Roger Williams as his source, as Williams was himself involved in the events. Romero "jumped out of a gun port, and with the men he reached land, either in a rowing boat or by swimming". Requesens stood waiting for him on the quay in Bergen-op-Zoom – in the rain – and Julián told his governor, "quite insolently" according to Hooft, "that he was a soldier and not a boatman, and perfectly capable of making within a wink of time a disgrace of any other fleet".[151] A Beggar's song relates how "capitein Juliaen de Romero" would have addressed his men before the struggle against the heretics, with an image of the Virgin Mary in his hand, followed by the distribution of wine. One of the wonderful tapestries from Zeeland from the late sixteenth century pictures Romero's defeat at Reimerswaal.[152]

Spanish chroniclers try to conceal the failure of their hero. As Romero lost eight hundred men and the rebels some one thousand, Trillo even turns the battle into a royal victory. Pedro Cornejo added the presence of many spies, who had informed the enemy about the fleet. Mendoza's chronicle may have been the source for Hooft's famous quotation from Romero: "Your excellence knows perfectly well that I am not a

---

[150] Requesens to Philip II, Antwerp, 18 January 1574, CP III; Requesens to Romero, 9 and 17 January 1574, NCD I, 29-30, 52-53.

[151] Van Meteren, *Belgische oft Nederlandsche historie* (1599) 67v-68r; Hooft, *Nederlandsche historien* (1642-1647) IX, 345-347; Williams, *Memoriën*, 158-163.

[152] *Nederlandsche geschiedzangen*, II, 110; Van Swigchem and Ploos van Amstel, *Zes unieke wandtapijten*, 72; Heyning, *Tapijten*; De Graaf, *Oorlog*, 212.

sailor, but a soldier, so do not give me more war fleets, because even if you gave me a hundred fleets, it may be feared I would lose all of them". However, Hooft stops here, while Mendoza's story continues, and he relates how subsequently Romero was received as a brave hero by Requesens. It shows how Captain Julián's fame easily protected him against the negative images surrounding the disaster.[153]

In reality, the situation was completely different. In a letter to the King Requesens accused Romero of gross errors and even described his actions as a "grandisimo disparate". One did not need to be a sailor in order to navigate for three hours following very precise instructions. Morillon also attacked the Spanish commander now turned admiral: "a very big error of captain Julián to have been so reckless" and "the said captain Julián has followed them very badly". Granvelle showed both sides of Romero:

> Julián has proved himself to be brave on land, but in his short time on water to attack the enemies, he made maritime errors, as he went against the wind and against the tide, while the smoke of the artillery was hiding his enemies, who at close range shot at his men, and it is said, I do not know if it is true, that on this journey he did not show his usual valour.

Philip II, however, supported his hero and asked Requesens to comfort him.[154] But still, Romero's image at the courts of Madrid and Brussels had certainly been damaged by this incident as well as by his controversial attempt to negotiate directly with William of Orange. He was still a brave hero, but the limits of his capabilities became more and more evident. The best example to demonstrate this change can be found in a letter from Requesens to his brother. The paragraph in question was written in cipher for security reasons and the Governor-general was less careful in his wording than in the official correspondence:

> The Duke has very good reasons for stating that his best soldiers here are Sancho Dávila and Mondragón, and certainly it is like this, although…

---

[153] Trillo, *Historia*, 223-224; Mendoza, *Comentarios* (1948), 503-504; Cornejo, *Sumario*, 194.
[154] Requesens to Philip II, Antwerp, 13 February 1574, CP III, 15-16; Morillon to Granvelle, Brussels, 1 February 1574, CG V, 18-19; Granvelle to Juan de Zúñiga, Idem, V, 60; Philip II to Requesens, Madrid, 31 March 1574, CP III, 46; Granvelle to Juan de Zúñiga, 25 February 1574, NCD I, 239-240 ('La poca ventura que ha tenido Julián Romero').

And here the cipher starts:

> Julián is the best man in the execution of war, but only when he is serving his general and does not have to make decisions on his own, because if he has to be guided by his own head he is worth nothing, and so he has done more than one hundred thousand things wrong for me, even without counting that of the sea, and I fear that he will keep delivering the same number of errors in the future. And as he does not remedy the chaos amongst his soldiers, they hate him worse than the devil, because he dishonours them and they hate going with him anywhere and even then they keep on playing dirty tricks on him.[155]

Romero went into the field again, in Holland, but now he had to obey the moderate policy of Requesens, who explained this in a letter to the commander:

> And so it is necessary that most of all Your Honour must be careful in avoiding that the Spaniards, the Swiss, nor the others nations, will hurt the local people, and instead make sure that they are being treated well, so that their example will make other places surrender, something they will not do when they see that the treatment is bad.

Together with Sancho Dávila he received the power to offer pardon to places that surrendered without consulting Requesens. He also worked on the contruction of fortressses near Zevenbergen, Geertruidenberg and the Langstraat to block the entrance into Brabant from the north. According to Romero, these works were not sufficient to close the frontier, but Requesens was already satisfied with the fact that in this way the enemy cavalry could no longer enter, as they caused most of the damage. Julián gained military honour during the reconquest of Zevenbergen in the spring of 1574 and during the successful attack on the castle of

---

[155] 'El duque tiene muy gran razones en decir que los mejores soldados que aquí ay son Sancho de Avila y Mondragon que cierto es assi y aunque... Julian lo es para las execuciones, es para las que haze delante de su general donde no le queda a el ninguna resolución que tomar, pero en qualquier cosa que se haya de guiar por su cabeça no vale nada y ansy me ha hecho cien mil borrones sin el de la mar y temo que ha de hazer otros tantos y con no remediar los desordenes de sus soldados le quieren ellos peor que al diablo por que les deshonrra y van de muy mala gana con el a nada y con todo esto no pueden dexar de cometersele muchas cosas'. Requesens to Juan de Zúñiga, 14 April 1574, IVDJ, Envío 67, caja 90, 211.

Loevestein. A spy had reported on the very small number of soldiers defending the castle, most of whom were sick. The Spaniards, however, succeeded in exposing him as a double agent, after which Romero was able to take the castle. At Zaltbommel he was less successful. That place wanted to surrender only to a negotiator from the Low Countries, 'de par deça', and when the rebels broke the dykes Julián had to give up the siege.[156] In March 1574 he was also occupied with an important transport from Holland to Nijmegen, accompanying ten cartloads of money.[157]

His own soldiers were also a danger to the commander. After Sancho Dávila's huge victory on 14 April 1574 during the Battle of Mookerheyde, an enormous mutiny broke out that also infected the garrison in Antwerp. Mutiny was most probably the main problem of the royal army in the Low Countries, as the soldiers' pay always lagged many months behind. Spanish troops had the habit of mutinying after a victory, and this meant that the army commanders could never really take advantage of a victory.[158] Angry mutineers tried to take Romero prisoner as they considered him their worst enemy, being the only commander who diametrically opposed them. He had to hide on the roof of merchant Jacob Hoefnagel's house, close to the building of the Antwerp exchange. He stayed there with some ten to twelve other captains. In the end, Julián succeeded in leaving the city, but without taking any food with him. When he arrived in Brussels, the gates to the city remained closed, "about which he was very angry", but finally he was allowed to enter. The mutineers refused to serve under Romero, and he severely criticised them: "He says as many negative things about the Spanish soldiers as they say of him; he says they are cowards, that they badly serve His Majesty and that he will inform His Majesty of this".[159] Requesens ordered him to act with force against the mutineers and explain to them that "the hands of the King are so long, that when they escape from these states, he will get them in the end".[160] Thirty-five soldiers from his own tercio tried to flee to France,

---

[156] Trillo, *Historia*, 253; Requesens to Romero, 2 April 1574, 8 April 1574, 20 July 1574, 26 July 1574, 27 July 1574, 4 August 1574, 5 October 1574, NCD II, 75-76, 124-16; Idem IV, 53-54, 156, 162-163, 242; Idem V, 347-348; CP III, 14, 42, 48-49; Soen, *Geen pardon*, 261-262; Mondoucet to Charles IX, 1 April 1574, *Lettres et négociations* (1892) 159.

[157] Document 8 March 1574, IVDJ, Envío 68, caja 92, 195; NCD I, 324-327.

[158] Parker, 'Mutiny'.

[159] 'Dict autant de mal des soldatz Espaignolz comme eulx font de luy; il dict qu'ilz sont couardz; qu'ilz servent très mal Sa Majesté, et qu'il le ferat ainsi entendre à Sadicte Majesté'.

[160] 'Las manos del rey son tan largas, que cuando se escaparan de las destos estados les alcanzarán donde quiera'. Ibid.

but they were apprehended at the frontier. Thirteen of them died during the following skirmish, and several others were beheaded.[161] Julián's role during the reorganisation of the tercios also did not help his popularity. He was famous for his very strict punishments: "he is the best man in disciplining", and for that reason "the soldiers really don't like him".[162] We may conclude that Romero did not answer to the clichéd image of a rough warhorse carried on the shoulders of his soldiers. That image perhaps much better fits the Duke of Alba who, notwithstanding his fame as the Iron Duke, always operated with great care.

Around this time Julián really had had enough of the war in the Low Countries, and he wanted to hand in his resignation as a commander. On 18 June 1574 the French ambassador informed the Queen Mother, Catherine de Medici, that Romero's natural son had died crossing a river (Maas or Waal). But there was more to it. In a very long letter, dated 2 August 1574, Romero informed Requesens that he did not agree with the planned reorganisation of the army.[163] According to Romero, there were not enough Spanish soldiers to fill twenty-four banners. Even if they limited the number to twelve, there still would not be enough Spaniards to reach the usual size of two hundred for each banner.

If the reorganisation were to go ahead, Francisco de Valdés, who had given up the siege of Leiden, and Fernando de Toledo y Enríquez would both receive as many troops under their command as Romero, and this he could not accept, "because it would be against God's will that Valdés, who has been a captain for only eight years, nor Don Fernando, who was born when I already was a captain, would be equal in commands and companies".[164] For Romero, with his decades of army service, such a situation was completely unthinkable, though he also defended his own position in these same letters as being poor and without any support besides that of God. Don Fernando de Toledo y Enríquez comes in for special criticism. This cousin of the Duke of Alba also happened to be

---

[161] Van der Essen, 'Kritische studie', 6-7; Martínez Ruiz, 'Gran motín', 649; González de León, *Road* (2009) 110.

[162] 'Es el que mejor la disciplina'; 'Le quieren tan mal los soldados'. Requesens to Philip II, 12 June 1574, AGS, E. 558, 33.

[163] Romero to Requesens, 2 August 1574, IVDJ, envío 68, caja 92, 187; Marichalar, *Julián*, 343-345. AGS, E. 560, 120 contains: Romero to Requesens, army camp, 2 August 1574; Requesens to Romero, Antwerp, 5 August 1574; Romero to Requesens, 7 and 8 August 1574.

[164] 'Porque nunca Dios quiera que pueda decir Valdés, que no ha ocho años que es capitán, ni don Hernando, que cuando él nació lo era yo, hayamos de vivir a las parejas en cargos y compañías'.

the Duke's brother-in-law. Romero refused to become a kind of assistant to Don Fernando, who would remain in Bois-le-Duc or Brussels because of his health, while Romero would have to campaign, day and night, doing God knows what. If things went well Don Fernando would share the honour, and if things went badly Julián would receive all the blame: "I am fed up with undergoing these things. I can't do it any more".[165] Every time the King was told that his deeds had been executed by some "Pedro or Sancho", while he refused to sing his own praises in his letters to the King. Don Fernando should be sent to the field and Romero would go home. He hoped Requesens would answer this long and conflicted letter, "because I am a friend of clarity".[166]

The discussion between Requesens, Philip II and Romero turned into a never-ending story. Notwithstanding Romero's threat to leave the Low Countries even without official permission, he kept serving his King.[167] It becomes clear that Romero had few remaining friends either at the court in Brussels or among the high officers in the army. Relations with the Maestre de campo general, Chiappino Vitelli, also worsened, as the result of Romero being present at the beating of a family member of Vitelli's, who in turn was punished for ordering the beating of a Spanish soldier.[168] Romero lived at odds with Sancho Dávila and other high officers nominated by the Duke of Alba, such as Francisco de Valdés. The focal point of his hatred, however, was the already-mentioned Don Fernando de Toledo y Enríquez. His nomination as Maestre de campo of the tercio of Lombardy in 1569 was a textbook case of nepotism, as he had never before occupied an important military position. The relatively young cousin and brother-in-law of the Duke of Alba was born around 1530. It is important to realise that we are not talking here about Alba's natural son, Fernando de Toledo, who functioned as captain-general of the cavalry and was seen as a very capable commander. Romero's statement that he was already functioning as a captain when Don Fernando was still being weaned in the cradle is greatly exaggerated: his favourite bête noire was only ten years younger than himself. However, Don Fernando's complete lack of military experience must have influenced Romero's judgement.

Peace negotiations at Breda in the spring of 1575 led to a new episode in the relationship between Romero and William of Orange. The rebel side demanded certain hostages: Frédéric Perrenot (Lord of Champagney,

---

[165] 'Estoy harto de sufrir estas cosas que ya no puedo más'.
[166] 'Porque soy amigo de la claridad'.
[167] See the section on his family and his rewards.
[168] Marichalar, *Julián*, 334.

Cardinal Granvelle's brother), Cristóbal de Mondragón, Sancho Dávila and Romero, or at least two of these men. Requesens kept producing excuses for not sending Romero as a hostage and sent him on an inspection tour of the garrisons of Utrecht, Guelders, Holland and Overijssel, with an order to discover and punish all possible abuses.[169] Requesens informed the rebels that Romero was in Friesland "ou là-entour", that he was the only available commander and as such indispensable, and that he was lying ill in his bed in Holland. The last excuse at least was true in May 1575, when he almost died of fever and bloodletting. Maybe this is also the reason why he was not present at the marriage of his natural daughter, Juliana, born in the Low Countries, to Captain Damián de Morales. Many important guests were invited, even Requesens, and Bernardino de Mendoza informed Juan de Albornoz, Alba's secretary, about the celebration in a letter.[170]

The rebels persevered in demanding Romero as a hostage and stated their unwillingness "to enter into any communication before Julián's departure to render himself as hostage". Romero himself was anxious to participate, as he was convinced the rebels wanted his presence because of "the urgent request of the Prince of Orange to speak to him because of their ancient acquaintance".[171] From Dordrecht, Orange sent him a passport, and in the accompanying letter he mentioned "the desire I have since long… to meet you".[172] Requesens did not trust this old friendship between Romero and the Prince, as we have seen before. The Governor-general believed in the commander's good intentions, but did not want to use him as a negotiator, as "the prince is rhetorically much better schooled than him".[173] After several months, Requesens broke off the negotiations on 13 July 1575. But still in September, Morillon was gossiping from Brussels to Granvelle about Romero, who was said to have bragged about secret state affairs to impress a young woman from the Low Countries, "Julián has written letters to the daughter of the amman [Antwerp's main bailiff] then in this town, telling everything that was happening and that

---

[169] González de León, *Road* (2009) 109.
[170] Mendoza to Albornoz, Antwerp, 9 May 1575, Cabañas Agrela, 'Agentes', 489-490. I thank Máximo García Fernández (Valladolid) and Antonio Sánchez Jiménez (Neuchâtel) for their help with this letter.
[171] 'La mucha instancia del Príncipe d'Oranges de hablarle claramente, por el conoscimiento antiguo'. Requesens to Philip II, Antwerp, 7 April 1575, CP III, 279, 300-301.
[172] 'Le desir mesmes que jay eu de long temps…de vous veoir'. BO 1844, Orange to Romero, Dordrecht, 9 March 1575,
[173] Requesens to Philip II, Antwerp, 7 April 1575, CP III, 279, 300-301, 591-611, 617, 639-640, 707, 729; BO 1844, Orange to Romero, Dordrecht, 9 March 1575.

he went to Dordrecht and that he would be received with open arms as an honoured guest". Though the precise meaning of these letters remains very obscure, Morillon was clear about his judgement: "Letters like these should be bought at all expenses to be sent to the King, so he can see how he is being served". Biographer Marichalar, himself a gallant even in his advanced years, stated he would have liked to know more about the mysterious relationship between Julián and this young flamenca, the daughter of Antwerp's main bailiff, Adrian van Oss, Lord of Heembeke.[174] However, the letters have still to be discovered.

Directly after the negotiations had been cancelled, Requesens started a new offensive in order to divide the rebellious territories into two parts. Oudewater was taken and Zierikzee was besieged. Julián was during this time active in the south of Holland. On 1 October he informed Requesens from Schoonhoven that he hoped within twenty-four hours to attack IJsselmonde, an island of great strategic importance (nowadays Ridderkerk lies more or less in the middle of this former island; a large part of it now belongs to the city of Rotterdam). However, rain and storm made it impossible to use either ships or artillery. Romero did not fear the enemy, but he had to wait until the weather got better. On 7 October he wrote to his Governor-general from Krimpen aan de IJssel. The weather had brightened, and he had by that time collected a fleet of seven large ships, nine peat-boats and fifty smaller boats; these last could not carry more than seven to ten men. Romero wanted to act directly and land on the island, but at the Council of War it became clear that most officers wanted to wait for more ships, or even until the first frost, when it would be possible to advance over the ice. Romero was suspicious and thought that the Count of Megen, Charles of Brimeu, resented him receiving the glory of a victory. Megen's brother-in-law, the Lord of Hierges, was at the time the general commander of the whole expedition army in the County of Holland. Julián now asked Requesens to be removed from Holland, as he felt he was hampering everybody: Hierges, Megen and Fernando would be capable of doing the job themselves.[175] Of course, this was probably the complete opposite of what Romero really thought.

---

[174] Morillon to Granvelle, Brussels, 24 September 1575, CG V, 397; Marichalar, *Julián*, 384.

[175] Requesens to Philip II, Mons, 21 September 1575, CP III, 366; Marichalar, *Julián*, 373-378; Romero to Requesens, Schoonhoven, 1 October 1575, IVDJ, envío 68, n. 192; Romero to Requesens, Krimpen aan de IJssel, 7 October 1575, AGS, E. 564, 125. See also: 'Utrechtsche kroniek', 245-247: Julián had spoken to the German troops 'as if they were dogs' (alsoff zy honden waren geweest); Utrechts Archief, Raad Dagelijks Boek, 114v, 17 October 1575.

In a letter of 9 October Romero informed Requesens that he had received information from an enemy captain taken prisoner, not only about their troops, but also on the residence of William of Orange. The rebel leader had moved from Dordrecht to Rotterdam where he had received the English Queen's ambassador. In exchange for sending four thousand English soldiers the Queen would receive the Low Countries, so Romero had learned from this prisoner. Elizabeth I, however, was not at all interested and even informed Philip II in 1575 that she had been asked several times to govern Holland and Zeeland but had never entered into any negotiations. He should consider her his best friend. In the meantime Megen had arrived from Utrecht with extra ships and so there was no reason left to postpone the attack on IJsselmonde any longer. However, at midnight the soldiers started a mutiny with the intention of frustrating the invasion plans. Julián quoted the mutineers literally in his letter:

> And the language they used was as follows: 'the scoundrel of a Maestre de campo has to leave from here, and he must not think he can take us to stay the winter on that island. If we take it, we will plunder and burn it so it will be impossible to make us remain there'. One hour before daybreak they quietened down, as it was their only intention to get rid of me and make clear that they were not going to attack the island, and that they should be allowed to continue stealing and plundering as they had done this summer. And because I do not agree, even if they go to the Low Country, to take and steal, they say I am the worst person in the world.[176]

Romero and Megen decided to halt any action for the time being. In this way they at least obliged the enemy troops to remain in the vicinity so that they could not be sent to help with the relief of Zierikzee. Again Romero informed Requesens that he wanted to leave as soon as possible. He had problems with everybody. It was not his war any more.

---

[176] Marichalar, *Julián*, 379-381; 'Y el lenguaje que hablaban era: 'Vaya de aquí el bellaco del Maestre de campo, y no piense que nos ha de llevar a invernar a la isla; y si la tomamos sepa que la hemos de saquear y quemar por que no haya ocasión de alojarnos en ella'. Una hora antes del día se apaciguaron, porque su intención no era otra sino de echarme a mí de aquí y dar a entender que no querían acometer la isla, y que la habían de dejar robar y campaña franca, como la han tenido este verano. Y porque yo no los consciento, aunque pasan en el País Bajo, traer ni robar, dicen que soy el más mal hombre que hay en el mundo'. Romero to Requesens, Krimpen, 7 October 1575, AGS, E. 564, 127; Cf. Wernham, *Making*, 49-50.

## ¡Adiós Julián!

The King's affairs in the Low Countries kept deteriorating. In September 1575 Philip II even announced a formal state bankruptcy.[177] There was no more money to be expected from Spain to pay for the soldiers. The death of Governor-general Luis de Requesens on 5 March 1575 had left a complete power vacuum in the Low Countries. The new governor, Don Juan de Austria (the natural son of Charles V and Barbara Blomberg), would arrive in Luxembourg only by early November.[178]

Julián informed the King in a letter of 6 March of Requesens' death, probably one of many letters on the subject that must have arrived on his desk, full of detail about the governor's illness ("a lump that grew on the top of his left shoulder") and death. He clearly understood that his attempts to receive permission to go to Spain would come to a temporary halt as he knew his duties: "I write to my wife begging her to be patient for now".[179]

In the meantime, the Council of State was governing the country. Julián regularly participated in the meetings, though he was not formally a member.[180] The dominant Spanish councillor was Gerónimo de Roda, who had also been in charge of the Council of Troubles for some time, and had functioned as a kind of prime minister during Requesens' government.[181] However, his real power was very limited. The elite from the Low Countries started to grumble, the soldiers started mutinying, and in the meantime the struggle against the rebels continued.

Julián only just succeeded in pacifying a mutiny in Mol by paying the troops, but this concerned only a small group of mutineers.[182] He was also involved in an attack on the County of Zeeland in April and May. He was ordered to go to Roosendaal to cross from there to the island of Tholen. However, the expedition to Zeeland was commanded by Sancho

---

[177] Carlos Morales, *Felipe II*, 131-200; Drelichman and Voth, *Lending*.
[178] Santiago Belmonte, 'Year'; Janssens, *Brabant*, 267-324.
[179] 'Un arbunco que la nascio en la punta de la espalda yzquierda'; 'Escrivo a my mujer rogándole que por agora tenga paciencia'. Romero to Philip II, Brussels, 6 and 10 March 1576, AGS, E. 567, 2, 6; Philip II to Romero, Madrid, 24 March 1576, AGS, E. 569, 93 and Idem, Madrid, 3 April 1576, Idem 569, 107. Also Philip II to Romero, Madrid, 28 February 1576, AGS, E. 569, 106.
[180] CP IV, e.g. 477-494.
[181] Versele, 'Jerónimo'.
[182] Council of State to Philip II, Brussels, 31 March 1576, CP IV, 10, 21; Idem, 182, 211-212; Daniel Rogers to Walsingham, 1 April 1576, CSP, *Foreign*, XI, n. 716; Requesens to Romero, February 1576, CEF XXX, 397.

Dávila and Cristóbal de Mondragón, and much more on these events can be found in the chapters on these two commanders. After the capture of Zierikzee by Mondragón on 2 July 1576, Spanish troops present there also started a mutiny: they would move to Aalst and enter that city on 25 July. On 15 July, Romero had already left Brussels together with the Count of Mansfelt in an attempt to pacify the mutineers, but without much success.[183]

People in Brabant and Flanders now started to resist the Spanish troops and the temporary government. Some of the burghers of Brussels took up arms and started to control the city in which the Council of State had its meetings. After armed men had entered Roda's house, the Count of Mansfelt warned Roda about Romero. Roda should avoid being seen walking in the streets with the commander, as then they would probably both be shot. Romero was hated in Brussels, a city where he had lived for many years and had even owned a house long before the outbreak of the Revolt. One afternoon Romero was standing in front of the door to his own house – maybe even still the very same house – when passing city guards shouted at him, calling him a traitor and a villain. According to Roda, Julián kept admirably calm at this humiliation.[184] Supposedly for their safety, Roda, Cavalry General Alonso de Vargas and Romero were taken to the palace, where they would remain secluded for weeks. The three Spaniards considered it an imprisonment. Finally, Vargas and Romero left on 11 August in the direction of Aalst in a new attempt to negotiate with the mutineers.[185]

On 4 September all members of the Council of State were confined to the palace, again supposedly for their own safety. By that time, the Estates-General of the Low Countries had been hastily united – without Philip II's permission – and they started negotiating with the rebels. These actions left Philip II without any control of the government in the Low Countries. The Duke of Aarschot, who had been a loyal nobleman of the King, complained about Romero's misconduct in Leuven and its countryside, and this complaint perfectly served the anti-Spanish camp.[186] It all led to a declaration from the Estates-General that outlawed all Spanish soldiers in the Low Countries, not only the mutinying soldiers, but also the loyal Spanish troops. The division in the government is also evident from the fact that though Philip II continued to demand that

---

[183] CP IV, 252, 270-271, 575-576.
[184] Roda to Philip II, Brussels, 27 July 1576, CP IV, 265.
[185] CP IV, 280, 301-303, 309, 312-313, 315, 339, 350; CD XXXI, 993, 99-100, 116.
[186] CP IV, 378-379.

Spanish troops obey the Council of State, the King approved of the military actions organised on their own account by Vargas and Romero.[187]

Julián had the opportunity to gain even more military fame. Hooft relates the story of a battle that took place on 14 September between Romero's troops and a large group of local burghers, students and other young people near Vissenaken, in the vicinity of Tienen. They had gone to fight, "attracted by curiosity, or by the hope of sharing in the spoils, as it was thought that those from the estates were sure to win". However, the untrained rabble did not stand a chance: "The Spanish warrior, well trained by his lengthy practice, pretended to hesitate, but only in order to suddenly start the attack". The rebellious burghers were caught in a trap and more than two thousand died on the battlefield.[188] Poet Pedro de Padilla (1540 – after 1599), a good friend of Miguel de Cervantes, is probably referring to this battle in his 1583 *Romancero*: "because Julián Romero, this Spaniard without equal, with some of his men, went out to meet them, killing eight hundred and capturing a captain, the best they had, a natural from Leuven".[189] This *Romancero* contains several poems dedicated to the Revolt in the Low Countries, including three on the death of the Counts of Egmont and Horne, in which Egmont is even called "the father of the fatherland".[190]

On 17 October Romero left Lier with both his infantry and cavalry. The next day, near Walem, in the vicinity of Antwerp, they entered into combat against four banners of Walloons from Mondragón's regiment who had now entered the service of the Estates-General, of course, without their Spanish colonel. According to a letter from Roda written on the very same day, more than five hundred of the enemy were killed during this confrontation between two sides that until very recently had served on the same side. For Julián this victory may have had a black edge, as some sources tell how his new son-in-law, Damián de Morales, lost his life there, though other sources state that Morales would be severely wounded during the Spanish Fury a month later.[191]

---

[187] Philip II to Roda, El Pardo, 17 October 1576, CP IV, 428-429.
[188] Hooft, *Nederlandsche historien* (1642-1647) XI, 459.
[189] 'Porque Julián Romero, aquel español sin par, con algunos de los suyos saliéndoles á encontrar, les mató ochocientos hombres, y les prendió un capitan, el mejor que ellos tenian, de Lobayna natural'. Padilla, *Romancero*, romance 21. Also romance 15.
[190] Padilla, *Romancero*, romance 4.
[191] Roda to Philip II, Antwerp citadel, 18 October 1576, CP IV, 438-439; *Mémoires anonymes* I (1859) 229; Génard (1876) 588.

Based in fortified Lier, Romero would organise more successful expeditions, which can be followed in Mendoza's chronicle, with the author himself commanding the cavalry. The most famous action took place on 2 November. Romero then apprehended Florent, Lord of Floyon, a son of the Count of Berlaymont.[192] What most sources do not report is that during this period Julián refused to send a relief force to the besieged garrison at Ghent castle. This decision brought him into conflict with Gerónimo de Roda and – not for the first time – with Sancho Dávila in the Antwerp citadel. Champagney refers in a letter from this period to the mutual hatred between Romero and the officers who had been appointed by Alba, like Sancho Dávila:

> I would also like to inform you that I understand that there exists some jealousy between Maestre de campo Julián Romero and those who are in the castle over here. So much that the said Maestre de campo did not want to move from Lier in order to help Ghent out. And this is no wonder, as Roda, though he pretended the contrary, never was a friend of Romero, as he has already shown a long time ago with several things during the lifetime of the Grand Commander [Requesens] and afterwards. And all those who are at the castle are creations of the Duke of Alba and they hate Romero as much as possible.[193]

Nevertheless, Romero also did not belong to the confirmed anti-Alba camp. In the spring of 1576 the Duke had written him a letter, and Julián had been very happy that Alba had not forgotten him. The letter shows that during the previous years there had not been an intense correspondence between the two. But now that Romero knew that Alba appreciated his letters, he promised to keep him informed on the events in the Low Countries. In the letter he said there was nothing much to tell, but he did mention the fact that people in the Low Countries rejoiced over the arrival of Don Juan de Austria as the new Governor-general of the Low Countries, and offered more information on the military developments. The letter was, however, in the first place intended as a letter of recommendation for Captain Diego de Felices, who also carried it in person. Romero kept his promise to the Duke, and two weeks later he informed Alba again on the developments in the Low Countries,

---

[192] Roda to Philip II, Antwerp, 6 November 1576; *Mémoires de Frédéric Perrenot*, 196; Lom, *Beschryving*, 53-57.
[193] Champagney to Aarschot, Antwerp, 29 September 1576, Génard, 'Furie', 211-213,

and this letter was followed another nine days later by a new one. Now – prematurely – he predicted that Zierikzee would soon surrender. In this period Julián also corresponded with Don Fadrique and with Alba's secretaries, Juan de Albornoz and Esteban de Ibarra.[194]

Notwithstanding these few letters, there really is no evidence to turn Romero into an Albista, a loyal follower of Alba, as argued by military historian Fernando González de León. For one thing, such a judgement would not correspond with the often virulent hatred between Romero and some of the real Albistas residing in the Low Countries. One of Romero's letters to Alba is signed with the very obligatory "your very affectionate servant" ("*su muy afisionado servidor*"), but generally his tone is less high-flown. This contrasts with the way real Albistas signed their letters to the Duke, such as Maestre de campo Gonzalo de Bracamonte who called himself a "personal servant and creation" ("criado y hechura") of the Duke.[195] We shall find the same wording in letters from other Albistas like Sancho Dávila and Cristóbal de Mondragón. There is no evidence that Romero saw himself as a personal servant of Alba, and González de León's idea that Romero was aware of the existence of a "school of Alba" also lacks evidence in the sources.[196] Julián had on the contrary been capable of building a military career for himself without the Duke's guidance.

Finally, Don Juan de Austria arrived in Luxembourg on 3 November 1576, one day before Spanish and German troops would invade Antwerp at the beginning of the so-called 'Spanish Fury', a struggle over the control of this very important city. One day later, at eleven in the morning, Romero entered Antwerp's citadel. He took charge of one of the squadrons, attacking the city on the side of the gate of Saint George and Kipdorp. Though the defenders had twice as many soldiers, they could not hold out against the experienced Spanish tercios. It remains difficult to unravel the truth about the number of atrocities committed during the fighting and the subsequent pillaging. It seems plausible that violence was mostly used as a tool to amass as much spoil as possible.[197] Much more on the Spanish Fury can be found in the chapter on Sancho Dávila.

---

[194] Marichalar, *Julián*, 397-403; Romero to Alba, Mechelen, 13 April 1576 and Brussels, 27 April 1576 and 5 May 1576; Romero to Juan de Albornoz, Brussels, 5 May 1576, AA, C/48, 201-204; Romero to Philip II, Brussels, 13 April 1576, AGS E., 567, 123.
[195] AA, C/30, 115.
[196] González de León, *Road* (2009) 56, 112.
[197] Pollmann, *Memory*, 160; Pollmann and Kuijpers, 'Why remember terror?'.

According to several authors, it was Julián who captured the young Count Philip of Egmont, the son of his old comrade-in-arms, Lamoral. Biographer Marichalar states that Romero's daughter in Madrid possessed the banner of the Count of 'Agamont'.[198] On the third day of the sack, Romero refused to sell flour for the provision of the poor, supposedly because he could not control his soldiers, but in reality he sold the flour later that same day, most surely for a higher price. Other documents state that he received money to save the cathedral and that the city honoured him with gifts of wine after the ending of the violence. He may even have taken "valuable silks, hangings and fustians" belonging to the English courtier Christopher Hatton. Julián did not like wild pillaging by his troops, but he never said no to money or gifts.[199]

The evidence suggests that Romero had not been an advocate of the wild pillaging. When Sancho Dávila was accused of being the leader of the Spanish Fury, Romero had no problems in presenting evidence as a witness against him. He described how two years earlier he had overheard Sancho stating that he intended to attack the city with his men in order for them to get their hands on the inhabitants' rich possessions. At that time, Julián had quarrelled with Sancho and had even threatened to take up arms against him. The Governor of Antwerp, the Lord of Champagney, had foreseen the confrontation between Sancho Dávila and the city. He had already asked several times to have Sancho replaced by Romero as Governor of the citadel because of Romero's "particular fidelity towards the service of the King, and the love he has for his people".[200]

On 8 November the Estates-General signed an agreement with William of Orange which is known under the name of the 'Pacification of Ghent'. This was followed on 9 January 1577 by the 'Union of Brussels', an agreement with broader support that focussed in particular on the departure of all Spanish troops. There were even those who wanted the death penalty for the main Spanish officials and military officers; Roda, Vargas, Dávila and Romero were explicitly mentioned. The hero of Saint-Quentin had been turned into a war criminal who deserved to die on the scaffold.[201]

---

[198] Marichalar, *Julián*, 417-418.

[199] Génard, 'Furie', 460-466, 479, 535, 539, 702-703; Rooms, 'Nieuwe visie', 50-54. Though the author speaks of a Captain Johan Romero, this probably refers to Julián: Doran, *Elizabeth*, 156.

[200] Frédéric Perrenot, Lord of Champagney, to Philip II, Brussels, 30 November 1576, CP V, 73-75; *Mémoires de Frédéric Perrenot*, 83; Champagney to Requesens, London, 10 March 1576, Idem, 388; De Schepper, 'Frederik', 235.

[201] CSP, *Foreign*, XI, n. 1037 and 1123, November 1576.

In a letter to Don Juan dated 14 December 1576 Romero warned the new Governor-general not to put too much trust in the politicians from the Low Countries, but at the same time he stated that "there is nobody in the world who more desires peace and tranquility for these states than I do". His analysis of the situation was firmly based on the fact that "I know the people of this country well because I have been dealing with them for thirty-five years".[202] On 27 January the Estates-General and Don Juan reached an agreement leading to the Eternal Edict, signed on 12 February, in which Don Juan promised to uphold the provisions of the Pacification of Ghent. Two weeks later Romero announced these provisions to his troops stationed in Lier.[203] On 21 March he left this Brabantine town, and on 28 April all Spanish troops were ordered by Don Juan to leave the Low Countries through Maastricht, in the direction of Italy, with Julián Romero among them.

In the Beggar song 't safeguard to Hell' ('t vrijgeleit na der Hellen'), the author mentions several royal commanders by name: Vargas, Vitelli, Roda and Robles, but also two only by their first names, "Sancio" for Sancho Dávila and, of course, "our best friend, Captain Julián, who always did his best". On Julián and Sancho the song continues:

> It would be a pity if both of them remained outside
> It would be best to lock them in the peat-cellar
> Because it would be a pity, even though Julián is half blind
> That he would not be under hellish government
> Said Lucifer with all of his council
> If you do not believe it, it doesn't matter[204]

They wished Julián would go to hell, though the story of his blind eye did give him a more humane appearance: a blind eye that had become part of Romero's imagery in the Low Countries. On an engraving dated 1578 on the death of Don Juan and the humiliation of the Duke of Alba

---

[202] 'No ay ninguno en el mundo que tanto desea la paz y quietud destos estados como yo'; 'Yo conozco bien a la gente deste pays porque a treynta y cinco años que los e tratado'. Romero to Don Juan, Liège, 14 December 1576, AGS, E. 569, 193.

[203] Spanish Council of State to the Bishop of Liège, 28 February 1577, CSP, *Foreign*, XI, n. 1320.

[204] 'T Waer jammer dat zy beyde bleven daer buyten, men salse beste inden peck-kelder sluiten, want 't waer jammer, al is Juliaen half blent, dat hy niet en waer onder 't helsche regiment, sprack Lucifer met alle zijnen raet, diet niet en gelooft, doet goet noch quaet'. *Nederlandsche geschiedzangen*, II, 205; also just as Julián in 'Een nieu liedeken op de wijse Swinters, somers even groen...', Idem, 171.

we find Romero lying under a horse with the name 'Iuliani', written beside him.²⁰⁵ His departure gave Hooft a last chance to use his brave but unsympathetic protagonist. The Council of War had decided to appoint nobleman and commander Alonso de Vargas as the Maestro de campo general of the whole army that was ready to leave, but "Julián Romero, out of swollen Spanish pride, refused to stand below somebody, who according to him had been his soldier". However, Hooft forgets to mention that many more Spanish officers refused to serve under Vargas. Again he used Romero as the personification of the Spanish commanders. And Juan de Escobedo, secretary to Don Juan, had indeed written to Philip II that Julián would be the best man to lead the troops out of the Low Countries.²⁰⁶

At the time of the demobilisation the Spanish treasury owed the infantry soldiers twenty-three months' worth of wages, and the cavalry even 73 months' worth. In the end the Estates-General and Don Juan together paid about one third of the total debt. This was acceptable and enough for the 5,300 Spanish veterans to leave the Low Countries as rich men, with money in their pockets, with the rich spoils of war, and with the some two thousand male and female servants who had made life easier for them.²⁰⁷

On 10 August Don Juan would recall the Spanish troops back to the Low Countries, even without waiting for his royal half brother's approval. In his power struggle against the Estates he had made use of armed intervention and now he urgently needed reinforcements. At first, Francisco de Valdés – not much appreciated by Julián – was chosen as the new Maestro de campo general of the army that had to return from Italy to the Low Countries. However, once the decision to return was final, Julian was proposed as the general commander of the army. The King affirmed his preference for Julián, but if he had already gone to Spain somebody else had to be nominated. Again, Julián was not allowed to go home. Valdés felt passed over, and complained about the injustice done to somebody with thirty-nine years' military service.²⁰⁸ Julián, who had left La Mancha in 1534 as a child, now finally had become the highest

---

²⁰⁵ Horst, *Opstand*, 253.
²⁰⁶ Hooft, *Nederlandsche historien* (1642-1647) XII, 502; Escobedo to Philip II, Antwerp, 21 March 1577, CD L, 334; Don Juan to Philip II, Leuven, 7 April 1577, CP V; Quatrefages, *Tercios* (1983) 145-146.
²⁰⁷ Parker, *Army* (2004) 151, 192-193.
²⁰⁸ Quatrefages, *Tercios* (1983) 415-416; Philip II to the Marquis of Mondéjar, 31 August 1577, IVDJ, Envío 47, c. 61, 17.

commander of a large Spanish army. He had reached the top. It also turned out to be his final adventure. While still in Italy, just starting the journey to the Low Countries, he suffered a stroke on 13 October 1577, falling dead off his horse. His biographer, Marichalar, described his final act in a paragraph that in 1952 was called by a literary critic one of the most beautiful fragments of contemporary literature:

> He took the Flemish Road, satisfied with his rewards. He did not feel the heaviness of his weapons, the iron did not wear him out. He went with joy and satisfaction. And he felt, again, as if somebody firmly pressed his waist, the arm of a girl that had jumped on the back of his horse, making him feel both determined and excited, as in the old days. The pressure grips and holds him, shaken and in love, alarmed. It does not let loose, whatever happens. But he goes on happily, slowly riding down the long road. His heart is bouncing in his armour and doesn't fit any more within his breast. There is no space left between his breast and his back to quietly keep breathing. The pressure grows stronger. Julián starts to realise he is suffocating, at the same time as his vision is blurring. The dust is hiding the multitude of pikes and flags marching in front of him. The sun shines on the steel of the Maestre de campo. Julián's armour is blinking with his sweat. And then with a shock he falls off his horse, as if struck by lightning. Death had said: enough. Julián, collapsed and defeated, eats the dust, with his face between the hooves of the horse. The animal made a strange movement when it felt the sudden fall. [209]

---

[209] 'Y emprende el camino de Flandes, pensando su contento y su desagravio. No le pesan las armas; los hierros no le cansan. Va lleno de júbilo, satisfecho. Y siente, otra vez, cual si le apretara el costillar, el brazo de una moza que le hubiera saltado a la grupa, entre resuelta y azorada, como antaño. La presión se le agarra, estremecida, amorosa, asustadiza; no le soltaré ya, haga lo que haga. Pero él va alegre; cabalga al trote corto, camino largo. El corazón le salta en la armadura; no le cabe en el pecho. No le queda ya sitio ahí, entre peto y espaldar, para latir a sus anchas. Insiste la presión, cada vez más ceñida. Julián empieza a sospechar que se sofoca, al tiempo que la vista se le nubla, y en el polvo se borra el tropel de las picas y banderas que marchan delante. Destella el sol en los aceros del maestre de campo. Julián brilla, sudoroso. Y de súbito, cae del caballo abajo, como fulminado. La muerte ha dicho: basta. Julián, desplomado, vencido, muerde el polvo; el rostro entre los cascos del caballo; el animal ha hecho un extraño al sentir el brusco restregón del batacazo.' Marichalar, *Julián*, 442-445; Mayalde, 'Antonio', 179.

We also find reflections on his death in the chronicles. Martin Antonio del Río stated:

> With this news the rebels were no less satisfied than the King's men were sad, because there was nobody more ideal for the war in the Low Countries than Julián Romero, who with his long experience knew all the roads, passages, villages and towns, but, more importantly, had always been feared by his enemies.[210]

Granvelle was less impressed. In a letter to Philip II he merely expressed his hope that the commander's death would not delay the transportation of the troops.[211] His remark demonstrates how the once very friendly relationship between the Cardinal and the captain had not survived the Revolt in the Low Countries.

## Fortune, fame and family

Was it lucrative to be a Spanish hero for decades during the international wars of Charles V and Philip II? Julián did not possess a vast patrimony like the Duke of Alba, who could invest large sums of his own fortune in the wars in the Low Countries. After his duel at Fontainebleau Captain Julián must have reached a certain level of wealth for the first time, receiving precious gifts from the French King and an annual allowance from the King of England, Henry VIII, who also paid him for his military service. However, a few years later he had spent so much in London that he even feared being arrested for defaulting on his debts.

On 10 July 1558 Philip II signed in Brussels a document in which Captain Julián was appointed a knight of the Order of Santiago, with the income from Jerez de los Caballeros (Badajoz) that went with it. This was a very high honour for a soldier from a humble background. González de León, as mentioned earlier, thinks it probable that Romero had Jewish ancestry, making this appointment even more special. However, there is no evidence at all to be found in the sources that points to a Jewish background. Just as González de León tries to count Romero among the Albistas, he also tries to use the hypothesis of a Jewish background to strengthen his point that the Duke of Alba did not bother about the origins of his commanders.[212] The problems Sancho Dávila and Cristóbal

---

[210] Del Río, *Crónica*, 182.
[211] Granvelle to Philip II, Rome, 31 October 1577, CG VI, 282.
[212] Fernández Izquierdo, 'Órdenes'; González de León, *Road* (1991) 47-48, does not mention this idea but Idem, *Road* (2009) 65, does.

de Mondragón would have with the religious military orders may be used as evidence that the Order had not been able to find fault with Romero. Notwithstanding, at the beginning of the seventeenth century questions were raised about the ancestry of Romero's Madrilean wife, but this issue did not affect Romero during his lifetime.

The inquiry into the origins of a new knight was designed to find out whether the candidate had *limpieza de sangre*, that is to say, showed no trace of Jewish or Moorish ancestry. Such inquiries, first written down in the Toledo regulations of 1449, were in 1558 in use at several religious and academic institutions. The aim was to exclude the descendants of converted Jews (marranos) and later also of converted Muslims (moriscos). As a simple soldier, Romero had no doubt earned his knighthood of the Order of Santiago with his heroic deeds around Saint-Quentin. In the documentation preserved at the Archivo Histórico Nacional in Madrid we can read that his leg had been injured in the attack on Saint-Quentin and he now had a limp. Some twenty witnesses, from Torrejoncillo and Huélamo in the vicinity of Cuenca and from Murélaga (Aulesti) in Biscay, were questioned in 1559 and 1560; most did not know him personally or had not seen him for more than thirty years. When he left he had still been very young. But this was no problem, as the inquisitors were mainly interested in his parents and his grandparents.[213]

Later, the story circulated that there had never been an inquiry into Romero. We find this idea, for example, in the work of historian Luis Cabrera de Córdoba (1559-1623), the author of a prestigious biography of King Philip II. According to Cabrera, Philip had decided to omit the very strict official inquiry (*las pruebas*) because the King valued brave deeds above nobility.[214] Playwright José de Cañizares would take this idea – giving the habit of the order without *pruebas* – as the theme of his play on the commander's life. The story of the inquiry, however, explains more about the preoccupations and mentality of the seventeenth century than about Julián's actual life.[215]

Shortly after his knighthood had come through, in 1562, Julián was again nagging the King about more rewards. In 1564 he married the rich María Gaytán, a member of the Madrilean elite and in possession of a house on the Calle Mayor of the brand new capital. María was the daughter of Captain Pedro Gaytán and the rich heiress Catalina de Vitoria

---

[213] AHN, Consejo de Órdenes, Santiago, expediente 7213; Idem, Inquisición de Toledo 349, 2, n. 1223.
[214] Cabrera de Córdoba, *Historia*, II, 818.
[215] Porreño, *Dichos*, 103, 111.

y Zárate, who had inherited the so-called 'houses of Gibaja', situated at the end of the Calle Mayor, close to the Gate of Guadalajara and in front of the house of the Tassis family, who controlled the postal services between Madrid and the rest of Europe. The family also owned property in the nearby village of Vallecas.[216] On 30 July 1564 Julián married María in the church of San Ginés, the church where future playwright Lope de Vega had been baptised two years earlier. Priest Juan de Lodeña performed the marriage ceremony in the presence of priest Francisco de Santana and Luisa Méndez as witnesses. Also present was Romero's Biscayan servant, Juan Pérez de Goitia Jubero, who would follow him to Ibiza. Though Julián would spend little time at home during his marriage, the marriage did produce a daughter, Francisca, who was baptised on 29 May 1571 in the same church of San Ginés.

On 15 May 1565, Romero was appointed Comendador of the Order of Santiago for Mures and Benazuza (San Lúcar de Barrameda) with an annual income of 139,387 maravedís. This new royal favour may be related to his nomination as Maestre de campo of the tercio of Sicily in that very same year. On 21 April 1571 he received a new position within the Order: he had to renounce his earlier possessions, but now he received the Encomienda of Peñausende (Zamora), worth 313,621 maravedís. He was in Madrid at that time, and it is likely that the new honour was a result of a personal request to the King.[217]

During the Revolt in the Low Countries Julián received income from the battles and the pillages, including those of Mechelen and Jemmingen. After the victory at Haarlem, Philip II promised the commander a reward of seven thousand escudos (some 2.4 million maravedís), but due to the troublesome circumstances he would receive only part of the money. In comparison, the monthly salary of a commander was about 80 escudos, Alba as Captain-general of the army was due to receive 1,200 escudos a month, while Captain Lope de Figueroa was rewarded with 2,500 escudos for his share in the victory at Jemmingen.[218]

Romero repeatedly complained about the fact that he was never offered a fixed residence, in the form of a governorship of a citadel in Italy or the Low Countries. His lawful wife María had always stated that she did not want to leave Spain for an existence of wandering from army camp to army camp, and Romero kept hoping he could send for his wife and daughter to join him. The lonely hero missed his family. He had never

---

[216] Marichalar, *Julián*, 131-133.
[217] Marichalar, *Julián*, 206-210.
[218] Marichalar, *Julián*, 425; Quatrefages, *Tercios* (1983) 312-313, 321.

been stationed in one place for long. In 1559 he had been governor of Damvillers for a short period, followed in 1561 by that of Douai, but then he had to leave the Low Countries. In the 1560s he temporarily governed La Goleta in North Africa and the Ibiza citadel. In 1569 Alba wanted to reward Romero with the government of the fortress of Hesdin, but the function was still in the hands of Antoine de Helfault and Philip did not want to intervene. A year later it was decided that Helfault would receive Saint-Omer, so Julián could receive Hesdin, but in April 1572 he was still complaining about the delay in the appointment. In the end nothing materialised.[219] In 1573 Alba was occupied with asking Philip II to reward Romero with the governorship of Alessandria della Paglia in Lombardy, stating that "you do not know and cannot know even half of what he is worth and how much he has served".[220] Again, nothing materialised.

In December 1573 Alba – preparing for his journey home – asked Philip II to be allowed to take Romero with him to Spain as he had already served for forty years and he was "one of the men of his level with most services rendered".[221] However, Requesens, Alba's successor in the Low Countries, advised the King not to let him go home because of his long experience and the services he still could provide. Romero remained, but he sent his Captain, Esteban Illán, to Spain to organise his affairs, taking letters with him, as well as the banners that he had taken from the enemy and that his daughter was to receive for safekeeping.[222] In his letter to Philip II he promised to follow the King's instructions, but he also told him that he was urgently needed in Spain. He also started to use his bad health as an argument: "already my legs, arms, and eyes are failing me".[223]

Under Requesens' government, Romero kept pushing for higher rewards. And though the Governor-general promised to do his utmost, it all came to nothing. Julián now started to threaten that if his income were not raised he would leave the Low Countries even without permission. This was an open violation of the usual language of servitude to the sovereign.

---

[219] Alba to Philip II, 31 January 1569, 24 February 1570, 19 October 1571, 2 April 1572, EA II, 274, 333, 757 and Idem III, 73; CD XXXV, 419; Idem XXX, 436; CP III, 138.
[220] Alba to Philip II, Utrecht, 29 July 1573, Marichalar, *Julián*, 285-286.
[221] Alba to Philip II, Brussels, 15 December 1573, CD LXXV, 256-257.
[222] Marichalar, *Julián*, 267; Philip II to Requesens, 10 February 1574, AGS, E. 561, 17.
[223] Romero to Philip II, Antwerp, 27 December 1573, CD LXXV, 257-258, AGS, E. 555, 128. See also: Philip II to Alba, Madrid, 17 July 1569, CD XXXVIII, 168.

> It is true that it hurts me that Your Majesty is handing rewards to others who were still sucking milk when I started to serve, while I am being forgotten. But I attribute this to my lack of luck (*poca ventura*) and that God wants to keep me wanting. I was born naked and I have lived an honourable life, and this consolation makes me forget everything else.[224]

Requesens had to inform his King about his commander's moods:

> When I came here, I found the Maestre de campo Julián ready to leave for those kingdoms, as I have written at the time to Your Majesty. I have done everything possible to make him stay, and have continuously offered him presents and honoured him. And though this has given him much satisfaction, and he also should be satisfied with the rewards Your Majesty has given him, the world at the moment is such that very few are satisfied, and the other day he wrote me the letter that goes with this one, making it perfectly clear he is not waiting any longer than September, and after that he is not serving anywhere without being able to take his wife.[225]

Even then appointment to the governorship of Hesdin was still being discussed, but the office remained occupied by someone else. Requesens suggested that the King write a letter to Romero

> telling him how sorry he is for the death of his son, who was killed one of these days by arrtillery fire – and he certainly was a high spirited and courageous boy – and offering some reward to marry off the daughter he has over here, who is of age to do so, and providing him with the means to take his wife to these estates.

Philip indeed wrote a letter in which he offered his condolences on the death of Romero's son and promised to support the marriage of his daughter from the Low Countries, but there was nothing in the letter about a possible solution to his wife's situation. Interestingly, in the draft of the letter, Romero's description mentioned his "worth and courage" ("valor y buen animo"), but this was struck through and replaced by the much more elaborate "good intentions, diligence and determination"

---

[224] Requesens to Romero, 24 June 1574, NCD III, 98-99; Romero to Requesens, Workum, 21 June 1574, CD LXXV, 265, AGS, E. 558, 89.
[225] Requesens to Philip II, 2 July 1574, NCD III, 214-220. See also AGS, E. 560, 151.

("voluntad, diligencia y determinacion"). Several weeks later Romero wrote again to Requesens, boldly stating that only his own death could stop him from leaving the Low Countries soon. His lamentation offers an insight into his life as a soldier in the service of the Habsburgs:

> This Christmas I have already been serving Your Majesty for forty years, and all that time I have never left the war nor the posts that were given to me, and in the war I have lost three brothers, an arm, a leg, an eye and an ear… and now, lately, a son I had set my eyes on.[226]

We do not know who his brothers were. Julián mentions them in this letter for the first time and we need to keep in mind that he was using his mother's last name, while his older brother used the last name of his father, Pedro de Ibarrola. In sixteenth-century Spain second sons often took their mother's last name. The family of Julián's sister Catalina, who married Pedro Miota, also kept using the name Romero. Her grandson, Julián de Miota Romero, was an important silk trader in Granada, who also held public office and supported the Corpus Christi festivities. The Count Duke of Olivares offered him a knighthood of Santiago, allowing him to follow in the footsteps of his famous ancestor.[227] In 1691 Pedro Melchor de Miota Romero would become the first Marquis of Lugros, with his residence in Alcalá la Real. The portrait of Julián Romero attributed to El Greco was sold by one of his descendants in 1890. After changing hands several times, it entered the Prado Museum in 1927.[228]

Romero also complained about the fact that he had not spent more than a year in total with his wife in the nine years of their marriage to date. He had also spent most of her dowry in the Low Countries, some eight thousand ducats (three million maravedís). He further had one daughter in Spain and one in the Low Countries, and no money

---

[226] Romero to Requesens, 21 July 1574, CD LXXV, 262-264. See also: Requesens to Philip II, Antwerp, 19 August 1574, NCD V, 77-79 and Idem IV (1894) 335; Romero to Requesens, 7 August 1574, Idem V, 82-85; Van der Essen, 'Croisade', 76-77; Philip II to Romero, 18 August 1564, AGS, E. 561, 106. Requesens described the death of Romero's son in a letter to Vitelli: 'De la muerte del hijo del Maese de campo Julián me pesó en el alma, así por el sentimiento de su padre como porque era el más bonito mozo del mundo'. Requesens to Vitelli, 24 June 1574, NCD III, 95-97. A journalist headed his article on Romero as follows: Cervera, 'Sir Julián de Romero. El temido "mediohombre" de los tercios de Flandes'.

[227] Casey, *Family*, 46-47.

[228] Díaz, 'Julián'.

to marry either of them off. He reminded Requesens that his most urgent desire was to obtain a post somewhere he could take his wife, as "without her there is no place in the world I shall move to". In his role as an intermediary, Requesens tried to satisfy both Romero and the King. He answered Romero in friendly tones that he had already been waiting for more than two months for a reply from the King. He informed the King that he had written to Romero with the necessary mildness, but also that he had much criticised Alonso de Sotomayor, Romero's good friend and confidant, who had also been the one to take Romero's letter to the Governor-general:

> I explained to him the lack of reason Julián had for complaining about Your Majesty and that you were desiring to reward him on top of what he already had received. And that I also had helped and honoured him after my arrival here, of which he should not only not complain, but instead be very satisfied. I also explained to him what he risked in leaving the field without my licence and that I then would do what I have to do. And certainly, if he did it, I would make him stay a few months in Vilvoorde [the prison]…

> As Your Majesty can see in another letter he wrote to me, he has decided to remain as Maestre de campo only until the end of September and then leave for Spain. I think he wants me to give him the patent of General and a very large payment for expenses and a pay increase, and that all five tercios of the infantry were to be joined in his one. I very much hope that Your Majesty will decide to reward him before the time limit he has given, as I have requested these last months, because, in the end, he has served for many years and still can continue to do so, and if he were to commit the foolishness he is hinting at, then it is impossible to use him according to our wish. But getting angry like this (*alterarse*) is a terrible way of obtaining what he wants.[229]

Philip II kept calm with Romero, "having so few Spaniards with his history and experience in this army", and suggested rewarding him with the encomienda of Paracuellos de Jarama (Madrid), which had become available in March 1574. However, he had to relinquish Peñausende which could then go to somebody else. Though the new encomienda

---

[229] Requesens to Philip II, Antwerp, 19 August 1574; Requesens to Romero, 5 August 1574; Romero to Requesens, 7 August 1574, NCD V, 77-79, 82-85, Idem IV, 335. The verb 'alterarse' was also used to describe the actions of mutineers.

would have an income of 711,246 maravedís, Julián refused to accept the honour, leaving Philip II astonished, as we see in the comments in the margins of a letter: "I was shocked that they had not accepted [Alonso de Vargas, too, did not accept his new appointment], at least Julián". The King wanted full reports on his desk as soon as possible.[230] We can only speculate as to Romero's motives for this refusal. Maybe he considered the offer too low and, of course, it still did not make it possible for him to be united with his family in Madrid. Later that same year he repeated his wish to be able to go home for four or five months in order to arrange family matters. He hoped now was a good time, as he had been trying to get permission for a journey home since the siege of Haarlem.[231]

As mentioned before, the Lord of Champagney tried to get him promoted in 1576 as the new governor of Antwerp's citadel, while in that very same year there was also discussion about the governorship of Alessandria. As there was no war in Lombardy, Romero promised to remain in the Low Countries if he became the new governor of Alessandria. It remains unclear what this would have meant for his wife and daughter. The new Governor-general, Don Juan, also tried to help the old Spanish hero. On 11 May 1577 he wrote an enthusiastic recommendation for him, emphasising not only his valour and his deeds, but also the blood that he had shed during the wars. Furthermore, he had played an important role during the departure of the Spanish troops. His age, his wounds and his deeds gave him the right to ask for a fitting reward. By rewarding Romero well, argued Don Juan, the King would also improve the morale of the Spanish soldiers. In his own hand Don Juan added for his brother that he considered it unnecessary to write more, as the King had himself been present at several of Romero's deeds, and in the case of such a special soldier all the rest spoke for itself.[232]

On 3 May 1577 Philip had already thought of another possibility, offering Alessandria to Sancho Dávila, then Romero would receive the fortress of Cremona in Lombardy. If Sancho did not accept the offer, Romero would receive Alessandria and Cremona would go to Cristóbal de Mondragón. Rewarding the military commanders clearly was a

---

[230] 'Haviendo tan pocos españoles de su antiguedad y experiencia en esse exercito'; 'Espántome de que no hayan acetado, a lo menos Julián'. Philip II to Requesens, 24 September 1574, AGS, E. 561, 113; Marichalar, *Julián*, 369-370; Secretary Gaztelu to Philip II, Madrid, 19 March 1575 and 10 May 1575.

[231] Marichalar, *Julián*, 385-386; Romero to Philip II, Brussels, 26 November 1575, AGS, E. 564, 48-49.

[232] Don Juan to Philip II, Brussels, 11 May 1577; Marichalar, *Julián*, 435-436; AGS, E. 1246.

complicated puzzle for the royal bureaucracy. Dávila did not refuse directly, but he asked for permission to come to Spain first and explain his services to the King in person. Romero did not want to decide without first seeing his wife. When he received news of his appointment as the new Maestro de campo general of the whole army that would return to the Low Countries, he accepted Cremona and wrote back that he felt fitter than ever.[233] Felled by a stroke on 13 October 1577 en route to the Low Countries as the new Maestro de campo general of the army he would never see his wife and his daughter or his native country again, and he would also never again see his family back in the Low Countries.

His natural daughter Juliana from Brussels, residing in Alessandria and recently married to Captain Villalba, received Romero's belongings, and he was buried in the church of San Giacomo della Vittoria in Alessandria. Forty years later, Governor Pedro de Toledo of Milan erected a plaque conmemorating Julián's burial in the church, recalling his "many wounds received over there [the Low Countries] during the rebellion".[234] The Governor was the son of García de Toledo, who had been Viceroy of Sicily when Julián had been appointed Maestro de campo of the tercio of Sicily.

His lawful wife made sure that she and her daughter – as the only heirs – would receive all Julián's belongings, including his clothes, weapons, books and papers.[235] After his death, royal secretary Mateo Vázquez explained to the King that it is was necessary to pay Romero's widow all that she rightly deserved. Julián still had to be paid 5,200 ducats (1,950,000 maravedís) of overdue wages. Vázquez not only gave a humane reason for his advice, but he also explained that this would have a positive effect on the spirit of the Spanish soldiers in the Low Countries and elsewhere in the world.[236] This means that the men fighting in the Spanish army were all watching what would happen to the family of a deceased hero: if the King did not pay his debts even to such an eminent soldier, the men would certainly lose their faith in him. Though the Council of Castile proposed a yearly pension of five or six hundred ducats for the widow and a dowry for the daughter of some four to five thousand ducats, in the end it was decided that Maria – who would die on 16 April 1612 –

---

[233] Requesens to Philip II, Brussels, February 1576, CP III, 448; Philip II to the Marquis of Ayamonte, Aranjuez, 3-4 May 1577 and the Marquis to Philip II, Vegeven, 5 July 1577, CD XXXI, 154-158; Marichalar, *Julián*, 436-441; AGS, E. 1246.
[234] Díaz, 'Julián'.
[235] Marichalar, *Julián*, 450, 459-461.
[236] Saltillo, 'Servidores', 120-122.

would annually receive one hundred thousand maravedís (267 ducats) and daughter Francisca would receive a dowry of three thousand ducats.

Is it right to say that Julián and his family were well rewarded for his services? Julián himself was never satisfied, but this is also the result of our sources consisting mainly of letters written to complain about his position. His greatest problem was the fact that he never received a fixed residence that would enable him to send for his wife. But there were also different views on the matter. An anonymous captain informs us that he had known Romero as a poor captain in Ireland and that in 1574 he was worth two thousand [ducats, pounds?] and receiving an annual pension of a thousand ducats. When in 1578 Sancho Dávila complained about his poor income, he used the recently deceased Romero as an example of somebody who had received many rewards during his career. Dávila was envious of the captain's salary Romero had received beginning in 1558, without the need to stay in one place,[237] strangely enough something Romero would have liked as he had always been looking for a fixed residence. We shall see that as governor of the citadel Sancho was tied to Antwerp for many years. But perhaps it was also the fact that Romero did receive a habit of a religious Order and Sancho did not, as we shall also see later, that may have been at the root of Sancho's bitter complaint.

Romero's daughter Francisca contracted a good marriage with nobleman Don Alonso de Avalos y Guzmán, a courtier of the King. His father had been a member of the Council of Archduke Albert, the son of the Emperor who was to govern the Low Countries together with Isabel, the daughter of King Philip II. His mother was the sister of Albert's 'sumiller de corps' and of a captain in the Spanish army in the Low Countries. After the death of this nobleman from Toledo on 13 December 1611, Francisca dedicated herself to the foundation of a convent in order to keep alive the memory of her glorious father, a man she had hardly known. It was to be a convent of the Franciscans of the third order in what was then called the Calle Cantarranas in Madrid, dedicated to San Ildefonso, and in part paid for by the sale of her parental home in the Calle Mayor. Here all the banners that Julián had sent to Spain – among them those of Egmont and Orange – were to be kept, together with the famous painting of Julián that would be placed in sight of the main altar.[238]

---

[237] CSP, *Foreign*, X, n. 1302, CD XXXI, 161-162.
[238] González Dávila, *Teatro*, 290; León Pinelo, *Anales*, 192; Philip II to Francisca Romero, CP (1960) 257; Williams, 'Philip III', 754.

Francisca would become the first prioress, but she had not really entered the monastic order. In her house, built against the convent, she would continue to receive visitors. This caused much criticism, and for this reason the foundation was later taken over by another noble family, leading to the disappearance of Captain Julián's memorabilia. A daughter of playwright Lope de Vega had entered this convent in 1622, which means that the daughter of the 'Fenix' of Spanish literature and the daughter of the great war hero must have known each other.

Francisca also supported a convent in Toledo, the city where her deceased husband had his roots in the same parish as El Greco. In a 1662 history of this religious order Julián was described as somebody who "through his valour, heroic deeds and military experience had risen from the pike to the baton of *Maestre de campo general*". The same work also mentions that Francisca had given the convent a shroud of Christ that her father had been presented with by the Duke of Savoy.[239]

In 1629 Francisca bought the jurisdiction of a village in the vicinity of Toledo, Cobeja de la Sagra, where her husband had already owned much property. She changed the village's name to 'Cobeja de Julián Romero' in a new attempt to preserve her famous father's memory. After Francisca had died in 1643 leaving no issue, the village lost the additional name, and we can now find it back on the map of Spain, ingloriously and simply named 'Cobeja'.[240]

From his relationship with a woman living in Brussels, whose name we do not know, Julián had three children. Two had already been born by 1560 and the other one was born after his father had left the Low Countries. One of them was the son who died in combat in 1574 and there was a daughter, Juliana, who married Captain Damián de Morales in 1575. Morales would die about a year later. Juliana was remarried soon afterwards to Captain Pedro de Villalba, but he died not much later in the Andalusian town of Baza, leaving Juliana with a son. According to the transcription of the original text on his tomb in Antwerp, this Julián Romero de Villalba would die a soldier at Hulst in 1595, aged 38.[241] A birth date around 1557, however, is not realistic, and he may not have been much older than 20. The actual siege of Hulst took place in 1596. On the tomb it was recorded that he was a grandson of Julián Romero de Ibarrola.

[239] *Chronica*, 16, op. cit. Díaz, 'Julián'; Heras, *Julián*, 254.
[240] Marichalar, *Julián*, 502-509.
[241] Simons, *Over 't kasteel*, I, 66.

As Juliana had no money left after travelling from Italy and the death of her husband, she decided to look for help from María Gaytán and the King. In 1580 she received a small annual income of thirty thousand maravedís for the rest of her life. Later she also looked for support from her half sister, Francisca. In May 1601 Juliana married Captain Francisco del Arco.[242] Unfortunately he died within three months of the marriage at the siege of Oostende. Juliana, who herself died after 1613, had thus been married successively to three Spanish captains and four times the war had made her grieve. Romero's third child born in the Low Countries was called Pedro de Ibarrola, using the last name of Julián's father. He studied at Alcalá de Henares and became a priest. He was also one of the heirs of his half sister Francisca. As a priest he even occupied himself with the court cases related to the convent. Pedro died around 1643 in Spain, at a very advanced age.[243]

Despite his daughter's attempts to keep the hero's memory alive through the founding of a convent, the conservation of banners and the change of a village's name, it is the chronicles, the plays and the painting ascribed to El Greco, that today remain witnesses to Julián Romero's glory and fame.

## The hero on stage

The Spanish authors of the Golden Age wrote many *comedias* with the war as their central theme or using it as an element in the background. These plays were an excellent way to put military heroes on stage and to narrate their great deeds. In this way the images of the war could reach a large audience that came to the theatres (*corrales*) to be entertained, but at the same time the public was confronted with a certain vision of the war. It would be wrong to think that all the plays served as royal propaganda, but it was surely difficult to put a very critical play into the repertoire. Drama had to conform to society: in this case, a monarchy with a strong nobility. Most authors also lived and worked in Madrid, making it difficult for them to feel totally free from the influence of the Habsburg court.[244]

---

[242] Francisco del Arco came from Borja in Aragon. Martínez Laínez, O*caso*, I, 172.
[243] Marichalar, Julián, 474-479.
[244] García Hernán, *Cultura*, 113-114, 175; Rodríguez Pérez, *Tachtigjarige Oorlog*; Sánchez Jiménez, 'Comedias'.

*Protagonists of War*

One of the many plays attributed to Lope de Vega was simply called *Comedia famosa de Julián Romero*. Biographer Marichalar connects this play with the period in which Lope's daughter Marcela and Francisca Romero were both attached to the same convent, that is to say between 1622 and 1629. He assumes the play was commissioned by Julián's family to honour his memory. However, the attribution to Lope de Vega has been questioned and, based on stylististic elements, it has to be said that if it were Lope's play then it would have to be an early work, dating from the 1597-1604 period. In that case it cannot be connected to the convent.[245]

However, there is a way to connect the two arguments. The play clearly consists of older material that was re-used for the occasion. Lope wrote hundreds of plays of which we now still have some four hundred left to us, but there are those who claim that he may have written over 1,500 plays. This indicates a very fast production, using and re-using texts and supported by collaborators, even though we know little of his actual writing practices. The publication history of Lope's work is also open to question. In the beginning Lope was not even involved in it. He wrote the plays to be performed and the idea to publish them all developed only later. We cannot completely exclude the possibility that in the years 1622-1629 a play on Romero was put on the stage, commissioned by his heir, and partly composed of older materials.[246]

For example, the play begins in a very strange way. A young sexton from Cuenca named Beltrán was completely enthralled by a captain who was looking for new recruits. After following him all morning, the captain became impressed by the brave, but also impudent sexton who, after several missing verses, is suddenly called Julián Romero. When the recruits are joining the banner of Don Fernando de Acuña, Julián can no longer be stopped:

> That sound upsets my heart. By God! Who does not get excited by a drum? What should I do? I have to stop. I have to be a soldier and not a priest. And if I shall be succesful in war and when everything is mixed up, I can even become a commander....
>
> Aquel son me alborota el corazón. Valgate Dios, tapatán! Quién hay que no se alborote de una caja? Qué he de hacer? No puedo

---

[245] Vega y Carpio, 'Comedia'; Marichalar, *Julián*, 489-501; García Hernán, *Cultura*, 63; Morley and Bruerton, *Cronología*, 488; Rennert, *Life*, 190.
[246] Arellano, *Historia*, 171; Rozas, *Obra*.

> más, yo he de ser soldado, y no sacerdote! Y en la guerra, si el pie stampo una vez y me acomodo, cuando corra turbio todo puedo ser Maese de Campo….

In the end he joins as the servant of a drummer. A humbler beginning is almost impossible to imagine, especially for somebody who would become a general in the Spanish army. His first war directly concerned one of the most famous expeditions in the sixteenth century: the attack on Tunis, defended in 1535 by the feared Barbarossa. Among the protagonists we find the already mentioned Acuña as his captain. This was not a coincidence, as Fernando de Acuña was not only a soldier, but also one of the most famous poets of the sixteenth century. Another protagonist in the play was García de Toledo, who was also very important in Romero's real life as the Viceroy who was involved in his appointment as the new Maestro de campo of the tercio of Sicily.

Almost immediately Julián shows his usual bravery in the play when he informs Don García that he himself is worth two hundred men, volunteering to lead a reconnaissance mission of the enemy positions. Don García asks Fernando de Acuña who this Romero is and the captain replies that "he came as a servant to Italy, my lord; he is a brave man, his father was a nobleman from Biscay".[247] That day Julián became a real soldier and showed his courage:

> as he had jumped into a boat, with only a sword and a dagger as his weapons. He was hurt by a bullet and a thousand arrows flying at him, but he still succeeded in capturing and killing their captain.
>
> Porque habiéndose arrojado dentro de una galeota, herido de una pelota y de mil flechas pasado, llevando una espada sola y una daga, acometió al arráez y lo mató.

Already made a sergeant, he fights in the front line. Arquebusiers sound behind the scenes, and Romero appears somewhere high up with a banner in his hand, shouting "¡Viva nuestro Emperador! ¡Viva España!". Don Pedro de Toledo, the Viceroy of Naples, wants to thank Romero for his heroic deeds by appointing him governor of the fortress they have won, but Romero refuses and tells the Viceroy he wants to go with him to England:

---

[247] 'A Italia vino por mochillero, señor; es hombre de gran valor, su padre era vizcaíno hijodalgo'.

> This war has ended and what is there left for me to do in a faraway corner of Africa? I want to go to England if there is any fighting to do, because I only thrive where there is a war.
>
> Ya esta guerra se ha acabado y aquí no la puede haber pues yo, qué tengo de hacer en Africa arrinconado? Quiero ir a Ingalaterra si allá se va a pelear, que yo no puedo medrar sino donde hubiere guerra.

The long English episode in the play around Mary Tudor's succession to the throne and her marriage to Philip II has little to do with Julián's life and could be the result of recycling old material for a work written on command. Philip II's journey to England to marry Mary Tudor was a well-known event at the time, and the material could perfectly well have been used for another work. The idea that Pedro de Toledo and his two tercios went to England in order to conquer the country seems to be a prediction about the famous story of the *Armada Invencible* in 1588. In England Julián kills five men who were planning an attempt on Philip's life, but the local judge wants to convict Julián for these murders. He is already standing on the top step of the gallows with the rope around his neck when King Philip saves him and appoints him captain of his personal guard. [248]

In the third act, Philip II sends Julián to Charles V in the Low Countries, asking his father to reward the captain for his services. The insolent and daring Julián asks the Emperor to give him the governorship of Douai, precisely at a time when the town is threatened by a large French army under the Admiral of France (Gaspard de Coligny). In real life, Romero did become governor of Douai for a short period, but there is nothing known about his involvement in defending the city against Coligny. According to old stories, the French attack on Douai failed because of the shouting of an old woman, not the heroic deeds of a brave Spanish hero. The story in the play seems to relate more to Julián's adventures at Dinant where it was the Connétable (Anne de Montmorency) who was involved in the attack and not the French Admiral.

Romero arrives in Douai too late to be able to enter the city, and he decides to go to the French Admiral and tell him he wants to serve under his command. He tells him he is fleeing after killing a secretary of the Emperor. The Admiral sends him together with a Frenchman as messengers to the city in order to inform the defenders that there will be

---

[248] Marichalar, *Julián*, 99.

no relief army from the Emperor and that they had better surrender. At that point Romero reveals his duplicity: he informs the defenders – with the Frenchman present – that he has deceived the Admiral and that there is indeed a relief army on its way. He threatens to imprison the Frenchman but lets him go free in the end. This way he can tell the Admiral that an army is on its way. After the Frenchman has left, Romero explains to the defenders that now the Admiral has to choose between leaving the siege and reorganising his army. This gives Romero time and space for the ultimate stratagem. While the enemy regroups, the defenders leave the city through a secret gate and spread themselves in small groups walking around with drums and torches to give the impression of an approaching army. The women have to stand on the wall and make lots of noise, showing that the defenders are already aware of the relief army. After the French army retreats for fear of the relief forces, Romero and his men go after it and destroy it.

The most important difference from the events at Dinant is, of course, that there Romero was defeated, though the defeat would bring him fame. In the play the Emperor wants to reward him immediately after the victory, indeed offering him the governorship of Douai, but he refuses again. He does not want to govern what is safe, and instead asks for the governorship of Saint-Quentin that is still in French possession, led by the Connétable. How different was Romero's reality, always looking for a fixed residence in order to be united with his wife, but always ordered to continue in the army because of his combat qualities.

In the play, still before the Battle of Saint-Quentin, the King wants to offer him the possessions belonging to the Order of Santiago in Yeste (Albacete), in spite of the resistance of those in the Order, and with Julián refusing to pay for the inquiry into his ancestry. In reality his first appointment to a knighthood of the Order of Santiago took place in 1558, thus after the victory at the Battle of Saint-Quentin. In the play Romero claims he is of noble origin, but that he has no possessions other than his wages. He also describes at this point how he rose from being a drummer's servant to the rank of captain. According to him, no inquiry was necessary, as everybody was aware of his career. When asked about the origins of his father, he answers:

> The arquebus is my father, and this [his fist, a sword?] is my mother. See if I have enough seniority on my mother's side. I am a son of the one who made the pedigrees on earth and the trunk of mine I hold in my right arm.

> El arcabuz es mi padre, y ésta [a sword?] mi madre; mirad si tengo harta antigüedad por la parte de mi madre. Hijo soy de quien ha hecho los linajes de la tierra, y el tronco del mío se encierra en este brazo derecho.

The noble knights who criticise his appointment are beaten by him in combat. It is clear that the play's author is playing with the discussion in his own time about the importance of professional soldiers in relation to the nobility.[249] He has Romero say to the defeated noblemen whom he forces to leave dishonourably without their weapons, "today my pedigree starts and you are ending yours".[250]

The last scene of the play shows the attack on Saint-Quentin with Romero as commander of thirty banners – though in reality he commanded three. In the play a spy informs the King that behind the weakest part of the wall there is a church dedicated to the 'Spanish' saint, San Lorenzo. The pious King refuses to attack at first, but Julián convinces the King that Spanish saints are willing to sacrifice their church if only the King promises to offer them a new and better church, a clear reference to the building of the palace and monastery of El Escorial. Then the trumpets sound, the drums beat and the attack starts. Besides Romero we also find the Count of Egmont and the Prince of Orange fighting in the front line, together with the commanders of the Spanish tercios at Saint-Quentin, Cáceres and Navarrete. Of course, in the play it is Romero who captures the French commander. In reality, Julián did play an important role at Saint-Quentin as he was one of the two advisors who had persuaded the royal army to move against Saint-Quentin. The Admiral and the Connétable, however, were taken prisoner not during the attack on the city but during the previous battle.[251]

It is remarkable that the author chose to focus on the events taking place before the Revolt in the Low Countries. It demonstrates that Romero had earned his fame during these earlier years and was clearly still well known in the seventeenth century. In another play by Lope de Vega, dating from around 1612-1614, we do find Romero active during the Revolt. In *La Aldehuela y el gran prior de Castilla* he is referred to as "the courageous Julián Romero, the most valiant Spaniard born in our time" ("Al bravo Julián Romero, el más valiente español, que ha nacido en nuestro tiempo"). In the play he liberates the son of the Duke of Alba

---

[249] González de León, *Road* (2009) 373-375; García Hernán, *Cultura*, 142.
[250] 'Hoy empiezo mi linaje y vos el vuestro acabáis'.
[251] Fagel, 'Esplendor'.

from a siege.[252] In another play which used to be attributed to Lope de Vega, *Don Juan de Austria en Flandes*, dated 1604, he stands on stage as a silent extra, without any specific function.[253] Lope's friend and pupil, Juan Pérez de Montalbán (1602-1638), used the story of the habit of the Order of Santiago to produce the characteristic image of a brave soldier of low descent. When some noblemen ask Philip II that they be given a habit the King answers that he prefers to give it to Romero, as he has already earned it through his deeds. One of them answers that Romero has not requested a place in the Order, to which the King replies that this is even more reason to give it to him. He is a soldier who earned the cross [of Santiago] through his deeds.[254]

The famous satirist Francisco de Quevedo mentions him in his picaresque novel, *El Buscón,* as the perfect image of a military hero: "I swear to God, better than García de Paredes, Julián Romero, and other good men".[255] In this early work, dating from the first years of the seventeenth century, Romero is mentioned in the same breath as one of the greatest heroes from the Italian wars of the beginning of the sixteenth century, Paredes, the Samson of Estremadura. It shows that both men were considered in the early seventeenth century to be well-known military heroes. In 1600 Lope de Vega also wrote a play on Paredes.[256]

A play by José de Cañizares (1676-1750), a follower of the great playwrights of the Golden Age, was published in 1768 as the Comedia famosa, *Ponerse avito sin pruebas y guapo Julián Romero*,[257] though the play may have been performed as early as the beginning of the eighteenth century. At that time, the play was dismissed by the critics. Modern literary scholars nowadays have a growing interest in the author's critical treatment of the nobility. The title of the work is based on the fact that Romero received a habit without the inquiry into his ancestry. At the same time he is characterised as a *galán*, a beautiful young hero. The stage directions that go with the first act state that he has to be dressed as follows: 'with a sword, shield, shoulder belt and in a short soldier's jacket'.[258] However in the second act he appears with the baton of a captain, after having served for six years in the army, gaining his merited promotion:

---

[252] Vega y Carpio, *Aldehuela*, 115-116, 133, 135, 139, 141; Morley and Bruerton, *Cronología*, 412-413.
[253] Remón, *Famosa comedia*.
[254] Pérez de Montalbán, *Segundo Séneca*, 8; García Hernán, *Cultura*, 141.
[255] 'Voto a Dios!, ni lo que García de Paredes, Julián Romero y otros hombres de bien'.
[256] Quevedo, *Buscón*, 155; Sánchez Jiménez, *Sansón*.
[257] Cañizares, *Comedia*; Fernández Gómez, 'sobre la comedia'.
[258] 'Con espada, y broquel, charpa, y casaquilla hueca'.

> I left the Low Countries overwhelmed, and today my victories and the cheers of my bravery resonate in the bronze statue of Fame in the whole of Spain, as I am already a great leader.
>
> A Flandes dexo aturdida, y los victores, y aplausos de mi valor, en el bronce de la Fama resonando en España estarán oy, porque ya soy un gran cabo.

In this play he is depicted as an ambitious warrior who returns to Spain to fight alongside Don Juan de Austria against the rebellious moriscos in Granada. According to Cañizares, Romero was a native of Antequera in Andalusia. We can find this erroneous place of birth also on the painting that has been attributed to El Greco. The most interesting element is the discussion on the Order of Santiago and the encomienda of Alaejos (Valladolid) with the King, who utters, "Julián Romero, who does no know what fear is, and whom I know, respect and esteem for his brave undertakings". In the end the King ends the dialogue with Julián by confirming his appointment: "I care more about shed blood than about hereditary blood".[259]

## A Spanish warrior

Captain Julián's eventful life, with that colourful collection of stories and anecdotes, offers the opportunity to look at several neglected sides of the Revolt in the Low Countries. In seventeenth-century literature, in the Low Countries as in Spain, he seems the perfect personification of a Spanish soldier. Hooft turned him into a warrior with an exagerrated sense of pride and honour and a tendency towards hypocrisy, perfectly fitting the clichéd image of the Spanish character. Because of Hooft, Romero is especially known as the hangman of Naarden. Lope de Vega, on the other hand, turned him into the perfect model of a hero who had worked his way up the ladder and who could be used as a mirror for the much less heroic nobility of the seventeenth century. These noblemen received their military commissions based on pedigree, and not – as in the days of the Duke of Alba – based on merit.[260] Lope de Vega's Julián was a brave and pious hero, perfectly fitting the image Raffaele Puddu presents us with: a hero fighting for God, the King and Honour. However, all these images say more about the image of the Spanish military in

---

[259] 'Julián Romero, pues vos, que no sabeis lo que es miedo, y à quien por vuestras hazañas, conozco, estimo, y aprecio'; 'Yo atiendo mas à la sangre vertida, que à la heredada'.
[260] González de León, *Road* (2009).

the seventeenth century than serve to bring us closer to Julián and his comrades-in-arms.

In the chronicles on the Revolt in the Low Countries from the sixteenth century, Romero is mostly visible as a commander endlessly involved in skirmishes and battles, invariably present in the front line. There he is the great Spanish hero, bellicose, courageous and full of bravery. French author Brantôme offers the key to a much livelier image of Julián. This chronicler of court society and international military beau monde agrees with the image of Romero as a brave soldier, but adds two new elements to his image: his almost exaggerated sense of honour and the tendency to speak enthusiastically about his own heroic exploits. Besides a sharp sword, he also possessed a sharp tongue to serve as his weapon.

The warrior he was kept calling for attention and craved more recognition. He tried to fulfil a political role during the Revolt in the Low Countries, befitting his military rank and his status as a war hero, but Requesens, in particular, considered him unfit for such a role. He generally wrote clearly and simply. The idea that he could bring an end to the Revolt through a good conversation with William of Orange – however attractive it may sound – offers proof of his lack of political insight and – to be cautious – a certain level of inflated ego. He also collided with representatives of the high nobility, such as Fernando de Toledo, the cousin and brother-in-law of the Duke of Alba, who had reached his position in the army solely through his family relations. Romero was far from liked by many of his colleagues. And though even the mention of his name could strike fear into the hearts of the enemy, his own soldiers also feared his harsh and strict measures. However, this did not stop chroniclers to describe him as a commander loved by his soldiers.[261]

His constant pleas for more influence, but also for a higher financial reward and a fixed position as governor of a fortress, found their way to Philip II's desk. The King treated the hero of Saint-Quentin with respect, but his promises often did not materialise. The fact that Romero threatened to leave the Low Countries even without official permission shows that he did not blindly obey and follow the King's orders. Spanish soldiers fought to serve God and their King, and to gain honour, but they were no strangers to worldly desires. They remained professional soldiers. In the end, Julián and his family were well rewarded for his career, especially considering the wedding between his legitimate daughter, Francisca, and a high nobleman. He never really knew a normal family life, as during his

---

[261] Herrera y Tordesillas, *Historia*, II, 162.

lifetime he served in the army almost continuously, notwithstanding his many pleas for a long leave in Spain. And maybe he was most at home in an army camp or near the enemy. His natural children born in the Low Countries and their mother may have seen more of him than his wife and his legitimate daughter. But we do not know much about his family. During the wars against the French – think of Saint-Quentin – he was also a hero for the people in the Low Countries, and he maintained warm personal relations with some of the most influential men at court, such as Cardinal Granvelle, the Count of Egmont and, of course, the Prince of Orange. His involvement in Egmont's execution in Brussels, the nocturnal raid in which he almost succeeded in taking Orange prisoner, and the correspondence with the Prince about the good old style of war, 'la bonne guerre', are examples that show again and again that the Revolt created a split with the time before, but also that the Revolt cannot be fully understood without including this earlier period. During the Revolt, Romero's image developed from that of a much respected military man – for example in the eyes of Granvelle's confidant, Morillon – to that of a much hated and feared war criminal who deserved the death penalty.

Liberated from all the dominant clichéd images of the seventeenth century an image appears of a unique figure who had in his own time already grown to the level of an internationally renowned hero. But he was most of all a human hero: hard and merciless, craving honour and financial gain, but also somebody who had worked his way to the top and who tried to survive in very difficult circumstances. He could moan and whine, about money, office and honour and respect, but at the same time he could tell fantastic stories about his own exploits. And this last characteristic of Julián's had charmed French author Brantôme in 1565, when walking in Sicily. That encounter, on the eve of the Revolt, perhaps offers the most clarifying insight into the true Julián: a tough and experienced warhorse who could vividly narrate his adventures: somebody you can hate, but also somebody who at the same time can put a smile on your face. In the end, even in the bloody songs of the Beggars we can detect a certain sense of affection: he was a much feared and sometimes ruthless enemy – half-blind Julián – but also an enemy whose sometimes very humane traits could not be denied.

Detail from Sancho Dávila, anonymous painting, collection of the Marquis of Villanueva de Valdueza, Spain. Photo: Cuauhtli Gutiérrez López.

Chapter II

# Sancho Dávila: the champion of Catholic Spain

**A Spanish hero**

Within Spain, Sancho Dávila (sometimes written as D'Avila) is undoubtedly the most famous military commander of the first phase of the Revolt, and perhaps even of the whole early modern history of the Spanish army. His fame started with the very positive judgement offered by the Duke of Alba and his secretary, Juan de Albornoz, in his own time: "without downplaying anybody, he is the best soldier His Majesty has in his service".[1] A first biography of Sancho was published as early as 1713, written by his direct descendant, Gerónimo Manuel Dávila y San Vitores. The title of his book, *El rayo de la guerra* (the Lighting Bolt of the War), acknowledges his fame as an extraordinary military hero. In 1857 another of the commander's descendants, Manuel Pando Fernández de Pineda, Marquis of Miraflores, and "holder of the house and goods of that famous military leader", deemed it necessary to write another biography, and this nobleman was also involved in the publication of sources about Sancho in the influential national series *Colección de Documentos Inéditos para la Historia de España*. In 2010, finally, a new and annotated biography of the commander was published, this time by a specialist in the history of Ávila, Gonzalo Martín García. In between, historian Enrique Martínez Ruiz published several articles on this commander between 1968 and 1976, while in 2007 he also produced a historical novel with Sancho as its protagonist, to which we shall turn at the end of the chapter.[2] Sancho's noble descendants still live on the country estate in the vicinity of Ávila where the commander may have been born, proud of its heritage and cherishing the portraits of their famous ancestor.

---

[1] Albornoz to Gabriel de Zayas, Brussels, 5 August 1571, EA II, 701; Alba to Philip II, Brussels, 23 May 1572; Idem, III, 119; Fagel, 'Mejor soldado'.
[2] Dávila y San-Vitores, *Rayo*; CD XXX y XXXI; Martín García, *Sancho*; Martínez Ruiz, 'Sancho Dávila en las campañas'; Idem, 'Sancho Dávila y la anexión'; Idem, *Castellano*; Pando Fernández de Pinedo, *Vida*; Martínez Laínez, *Ocaso*, II, 187-210.

In contrast to this overwhelming attention to Sancho Dávila in Spain, he remains a mere footnote in the history books of the Low Countries and, if mentioned at all, usually solely in relation to the famous Battle of Mookerheyde in 1574 and the infamous Spanish Fury of Antwerp in 1576.[3] There are no specific articles or books published in the Netherlands or Belgium that use Sancho Dávila as their main protagonist. The only Dutch or Belgian biographical dictionary paying attention to him is that of 1852 by Van der Aa, who erroneously has him die during the siege of Maastricht in 1579.[4] As we saw in the previous chapter, he is once mentioned as *Sancio* in a Beggar's song, "Sancio, the drummer (*trommelslager*), who would make them all dance".[5] The use of just his first name may be considered evidence of his fame in the Low Countries during his lifetime, as was the case with Julián Romero. In general, Dutch anti-Hispanic texts have a tendency to emphasise the low birth of the Spanish commanders but, as we shall see, in the specific case of Sancho this was certainly not true. Interestingly enough, the seventeenth-century play about Julián does describe how this commander started off as the servant of a drummer, showing that rising high from low birth could also be considered very positively.

In this chapter we will try to understand these two diverging historiographical traditions and to connect them as much as possible, looking for a middle ground that gets us as close to Sancho Dávila as possible. We are aided in this task by the availability of a wide array of publications on his life and deeds, and a large body of preserved letters from him, which makes possible a chapter that is built less on chronicles and more on historiography and correspondence than the previous chapter on Julián Romero.

## A hero in the family

Nobleman and politician Gerónimo Manuel Dávila y San Vitores stated on the title page of his 1713 biography of the commander that he was Sancho's great-great-grandson, dedicating his book to King Philip V, a direct descendant of King Philip II through the female line, but above all the first Spanish King from the Bourbon dynasty. In the short preface to the book he explains that he was a servant of the last Habsburg King, Charles II, but now he was poor: "I do not have anything to eat, or

---

[3] Van der Lem, *Opstand*, 100.
[4] Van der Aa, *Biographisch woordenboek*, I, 439-441; Van der Lem, 'Sancho'.
[5] *Nederlandsche geschiedzangen*, II, 205.

anything to do good with". Using Sancho as the perfect example of a good royal servant he hoped to obtain royal favour from the new Bourbon King, "that Your Majesty makes amends and supports me".[6] Though the subject of the book is war, the author makes clear he hates "our wars, that have put us into so much danger", referring to the violent Wars of Spanish Succession between the followers of the Habsburg and Bourbon pretenders (1700-1714). From the licences and privileges we learn that the book was already under official scrutiny from August 1710, but it was three years before the official royal corrector gave his final approval to the edition. By that time the war was coming to a close. In 1710 the outcome of the succession wars was not yet clear, giving Sancho's biography a role in the complicated political landscape during these chaotic years. Was Gerónimo perhaps changing loyalty at the time and did he need the help of his famous ancestor in order to succeed, or was he merely a poor nobleman trying to survive in dangerous times?

The author also frames his work as destined specifically for Catholic readers, introducing the famous locally born Saint Teresa of Ávila, "my defending counsel and relative" and a declared enemy of heretics. In this way the author connects the wars in which Sancho participated with fighting heresy in general. An engraving of Teresa can be found at the end of the book, balancing the engraving of Sancho at the beginning. In 1713 it was not yet public knowledge that the female patron saint of Spain came from a *converso* family, and the author would probably have omitted this family relationship had he known.[7] Together, Teresa and Sancho symbolise the struggle against heretics, the saint armed with her books and Sancho with his sword.[8] The tone of the whole book is extremely anti-Protestant, always connecting the historical stories about Sancho with the political situation of his own time.

According to Gerónimo, Sancho's father, Antón Vázquez, had gone to Worms in 1521 to meet Charles V on behalf of the rebellious Castilian Comuneros. In his book Gerónimo tries to defend the Comuneros as people looking for the "good government of these realms", but he has to admit that the Emperor had him briefly incarcerated.[9] Sancho was born on 21 September 1523 out of Antón's marriage with Ana Daza.[10] The fact that we actually know his date of birth already shows his relatively

---

[6] Dávila y San-Vitores, *Rayo*, dedication.
[7] Saint Teresa was the daughter of Beatriz Dávila y Ahumada.
[8] Dávila y San-Vitores, *Rayo*, 2.
[9] Dávila y San-Vitores, *Rayo*, 348-349.
[10] Dávila y San-Vitores, *Rayo*, 2.

high birth compared to those of commanders like Romero, Valdés and Mondragón. Young Sancho is supposed to have played with wooden swords, and he became angry when they were taken away from him, at least according to a side note in the margin of the book quoting 'D. Fernando Davila, notice of his father'. However, the son of Antón Vázquez Dávila and Ana Daza, from a gentry family (*hidalgos*), first followed the path of the religious orders until an astrologer in Rome put him onto the military path, at least according to his first biographer. In 1569 Sancho would marry Catalina Gallo, the daughter of Juan López Gallo, Lord of Male, and Catalina Pardo. With Catalina Sancho had a son, Fernando, born in 1570 in the citadel of Antwerp, but she died soon afterwards. According to Gerónimo, Sancho never remarried, "nourished in the war he was holding on his shoulders". However, we shall see that he did in fact remarry.

His son, Fernando Dávila, would become a page to Philip II, marrying twice in Ávila, first to Teresa de Toledo, with whom he had a young son, Sancho, who died at an early age, and a daughter, Catalina, who entered a convent; and secondly to Luisa de Guevara, with whom he had many children, among them his successor, also named Sancho. This Sancho became a knight of the Order of Alcántara and a governor of the province of Zacatecas in New Spain. In Ávila he married his cousin, Francisca del Peso y Guevara. Their son, again called Sancho, and also a knight of Alcántara, served both Philip IV and Charles II, and married three times. His first marriage was to Francisca de San Vitores from Burgos, who was related through her mother to the famous Maluenda merchant family. Besides the author of the 1713 biography they also had another son called Sancho Joseph, who became a Jesuit, and a son, Antonio, who died a captain during the war of Messina. Gerónimo ends his biography with a long genealogy of all the branches of his family, turning the biography of his most famous ancestor into a family memorial. His uncle on his mother's side, Diego Luis de San Vitores, the last family member he mentions in his book, was an important but controversial Jesuit missionary in Guam, who died there in 1672.[11]

Using Sancho's service memorial ('memorial de sus servicios'), Gerónimo stated that Sancho had been one of the ten Spanish soldiers who crossed the river Elbe in 1547 by swimming with their swords in their mouths, leading up to the famous Battle of Mühlberg.[12] We will later see that an identical story is told about Cristóbal de Mondragón. The same source

[11] Risco, *Apostle*.
[12] Dávila y San-Vitores, *Rayo*, 5.

puts him in the city of Africa (Mahdia) in 1550 and with the fleet that accompanied Prince Philip to England to marry Queen Mary Tudor. Subsequently, Sancho, by then an infantry captain, served the Duke of Alba during the wars in Italy. We find in this book the complete transcription of the official appointment, dated 15 July 1561. Here the story does not follow a strict chronological line, as the author continues with the disastrous attack on Djerba in 1560, during which Sancho, together with his commander Álvaro de Sande, was supposedly taken prisoner by the Ottomans.[13] We find a wonderful description of this last story in the fourth Turkish letter of the Flemish humanist and ambassador Boesbeeck who became friendly with Álvaro de Sande at the Ottoman court in Istanbul. Boesbeeck took care of the commander's release, and together they travelled back to Emperor Ferdinand. However, Sancho is never mentioned in the story.[14] Enrique Martínez Ruiz makes both Sancho and Álvaro de Sande row in the Ottoman galleys after their capture, and though not very probable, this detail does make for an interesting orientalist image.[15]

After inspecting the fortresses in Valencia, he was appointed governor of the important Italian castle of Pavia, as evidenced by a document of 24 December 1562.[16] Using the work of Gil González,[17] the biography describes a duel between Sancho and monsieur de Molve, "a knight of disproportionate height". Molve used a two-handed sword, while Sancho was armed with a simple sword and a shield. Gerónimo still possessed Molve's arms as evidence of Sancho's victory, which resulted in Molve's death. We find a more exaggerated description of this heroic deed in a manual on weaponry:

> He gave death to a giant in Moncalvo in single combat, though with unequal arms, as the giant fought with an enormous two-handed sword, and Sancho Dávila with his usual sword and his shield, of which Sancho Dávila came out victorious, like David to Goliath.[18]

---

[13] Dávila y San-Vitores, *Rayo*, 17.
[14] Huussen, *Leven;* Von Martels, *Augerius*.
[15] Martínez Ruiz, 'Sancho Dávila y la anexión', 9.
[16] Pando Fernández de Pinedo, *Vida*, 118.
[17] González Dávila, *Teatro*, II, 302-303.
[18] Lorenz de Rada, *Libro segundo*, 19-20.

Though clearly Sancho's first biographer, Gerónimo was not the first family member to take Sancho's history to the printing press. Somewhere between 1629 and 1637, Sancho's grandson, Sancho Dávila y Guevara, prepared a printed version of the *Memorial de los servicios del General Sancho Davila*.[19] He considered that both his grandfather and his father had not been sufficiently rewarded for their services to the crown, and now asked for "the government of New-Biscay, or the government (corregimiento) of Zacatecas, any other government, or a similar function comparable to such important services". Grandfather Sancho was highly praised as "an oracle" in matters of war and a defender of the faith. In order to achieve its goals, the document offers a series of quotations from letters by Philip II and official dignitaries from between 1568 and 1575, as well as a short paragraph on his earlier deeds, here quoted in full:

> He served in the expedition to Germany, found himself in Africa and in the war in Lombardy. He accompanied Philip II during his journey to England, who gave him the title of captain and he served with him in the wars of Piedmont, Naples and the taking of Africa.[20]

This published memorial may have been the document Gerónimo used in his book, but there is as yet no mention of the Battle of Mühlberg. The memorial shows that the 1713 biography followed up on an earlier printed document, already asking for advancement for the author based on his ancestor's deeds, and making use of official letters to prove his valour. In 1637 Sancho was indeed appointed the new governor of the rich mining city and region of Zacatecas (Mexico). Being the descendant of a hero was a valuable part of one's inheritance.

In 1857 Manuel Pando Fernández de Pineda, Marquis of Miraflores (1792-1872) and also a descendant of Sancho, decided to follow the lead with a new biography. This high nobleman was an important royalist and conservative politician, ambassador to Paris, London and Rome, cabinet minister in various governments, and twice even briefly

---

[19] Dávila y Guevara, *Memorial*. The document mentions the date of 20 June 1629, but the author is called a knight of the Order of Alcántara and his entry took place only in 1636. In 1637 Sancho was appointed corregidor of Zacatecas, placing the document between 1629 and 1637, but probably closer to the latter year. Muñoz Altea, *Blasones*, 362.

[20] The lines quoted here have been erased in the copy of the memorial preserved in the Royal Historical Academy of Spain, together with the erroneous changing of grandson in the title to great-grandson.

Prime Minister of Spain.[21] In 1850 he had become a member of the Real Academia de la Historia. In his introduction the author highlights an interesting combination of three important developments from the sixteenth century: religious reform, the Jesuits and communism. Before the sixteenth century there was "a clear supremacy in the hands of kings", but then a new society, defined by the "disturbing flag of free choice", had come into being.[22] The aristocratic author pleads for a larger place in society for the Jesuits as "a useful means for a prudent and wise religious and conservative restoration, so needed in the world, fortifying the few solid elements the states possess to fight the threatening monster of socialism".[23] Thomas More was a socialist, and as far as anabaptism was concerned it was nothing more than "communism lifted to the level of religion".[24] The fight against heresy addressed in Gerónimo's book in 1713 was continued by Don Manuel in 1857, albeit with the Jesuits and not Saint Teresa of Ávila as religious champions.

The Enlightenment and the French Revolution are both explained by the author through this growing influence of communism. The Paris revolution of 1848 figures, of course, as the worst moment in history: "really mournful was the spectacle that France presented in 1848".[25] The anti-revolutionary aristocrat wished to demonstrate the sterility of revolutions in history, turning the directly following biography on Sancho Dávila and his activities during the Revolt in the Low Countries into an exemplary story of the continuing struggle against communism by a defender of the old order. However, it is important to remark that the Marquis had in his youth fought against the domination of the French imperial forces in Spain and had been both a refugee in and an ambassador to Paris. It takes the Marquis almost a hundred pages to start the actual biography of his ancestor. On the period up to Sancho's departure to the Low Countries no new information is offered compared to Gerónimo's in 1713, and he attempts to hide Sancho's father's Comunero past, instead highlighting that Sancho's father had served the king against the French at Fuenterrabía in 1521.[26]

---

[21] Valle de Juan, 'Manuel Pando'; Pando y Fernández de Pinedo, *Vida política* (1865).
[22] Pando y Fernández de Pinedo, *Vida*, 7-9.
[23] Pando y Fernández de Pinedo, *Vida*, 54.
[24] Pando y Fernández de Pinedo, *Vida*, 62-63.
[25] Pando y Fernández de Pinedo, *Vida*, 92.
[26] Pando y Fernández de Pinedo, *Vida*, 97-98.

The 2010 biography, on the other hand, calls Sancho the son of a Comunero immediately on the first page of the presentation by the provincial president of Ávila, and their revolt makes up one of the nine chapters of the book.[27] In twenty-first-century Castile, Comuneros are regarded more as patriots *avant la lettre* than as rebels.[28] The commemoration of the defeat of the Comuneros at Vilallar on 23 April 1521 has since 1986 even become the national holiday of the autonomous Spanish region of Castilla y León. With the information from this new biography we get a better grasp on the family of the future commander. The marriage of Antón Vázquez Dávila and Ana Daza produced three children: Beatriz, who became a nun, Tomás and Sancho. In 1534 Charles V stayed in Ávila for five days, and this visit may have had an influence on young Tomás and Sancho. Their father died in the 1530s, but we may presume that by that time Sancho had heard his father's stories of his two important journeys to the Low Countries in 1517 and 1521. Little would he have known that he would go there himself in 1559 and again in 1567. After his father's death, his mother looked for support from her uncle, Pedro Daza, the important arch-dean of the cathedral. Sancho's brother Tomás would participate in the failed 1541 expedition to Algiers, and a few years later Sancho probably went to Rome, although the 1713 biography is the only evidence of the astrologist's prophecy turning a man of the cloth into a soldier.[29] If so, did Sancho indeed at first follow a clerical career because of his influential uncle, or did he possess a religious vocation which may have influenced his outlook on Protestantism in later days?

## An international soldier (1554-1567)

Sancho's first moment of fame – if we leave out the duel with the giant – is the crossing of the river Elbe as one of ten Spanish arquebusiers who swam the span. His 1713 biographer Gerónimo was sure his forefather had been one of them, and the 2010 biographer follows this lead: "It is possible. We do not have data or motives to doubt the truthfulness of the information".[30] However, the most recent biographer is mistaken. The fact that the same story has also been fabricated around Cristóbal de Mondragón makes it already less probable, but neither man is mentioned

---

[27] Martín García, *Sancho*, 7.
[28] Martín García, *Sancho*, 37-41.
[29] Martín García, *Sancho*, 47, makes use of the preserved testament of Ana Daza. Idem, 64, 69-70, 73-74.
[30] Martín García, *Sancho*, 84.

in a chronicle written by a witness to the events who lists all the eleven (!) Spaniards who actually performed the hazardous crossing.[31] This shows that biographers have a tendency to enrich the unknown part of their protagonists' life with heroic moments.

In the case of Sancho Dávila this means that we do not have any reliable evidence of his presence during the wars in Germany, and considering the fact that the first Italian period is also solely based on one quotation from Gerónimo in 1713, we are left completely without reliable evidence about his military life for this early period. What to do with the 2010 affirmation that Sancho in Germany "participated in many skirmishes, ambushes and suprise actions ordered by the Duke [of Alba?]"?[32] Apart from Gerónimo's biography we have only a short description by Antonio de Cianca, and this might well have been a main source for the biographer:

> One of the valiant and prudent soldiers that the Spanish nation has had, as is well proven by his deeds and exploits, from the war Emperor Charles V, our lord of good memory, fought against the rebel princes and their allies in Germany, where he became a soldier, and afterwards in the conquest and the destruction of the city of Africa, and from there to the wars in Lombardy, Piedmont and the Roman countryside, where he became a captain of Spanish infantry.[33]

The next military stop in the 1713 biography was the expedition to the city of Africa (Mahdia). And, again, the 2010 biography does not offer any additional documentation. Of course, Gerónimo was his descendant and he quotes a memorial of his services, but the fact that the Mühlberg story does not hold good makes us wonder about all the other information on Sancho's early career. This reservation also extends to his participation in Philip II's journey to England in 1554.[34] This last unproven fact coincides with the theatre play on Romero in which – and once more unproven – he was said to have participated in the English journey. It seems that Philip II's English expedition was another good story to use both in memorials and plays.

---

[31] Bernabé del Busto, 'Quadernos'; Idem, *Geschichte*, 179.
[32] Martín García, *Sancho*, 83.
[33] Cianca, *Historia* book III, 40.
[34] The soldiers in the fleet did not disembark in England, but went straight back. Martínez Ruiz, 'Sancho', 646.

The first documentary proof Martín García provides dates from 1559, when the Duke of Alba recommended Sancho Dávila to Philip II:

> [...] Captain Sancho Dávila, carrier of this letter, has served Your Majesty for many years in all the journeys that have presented themselves, and, as from five years, with an infantry company, proving himself as a good soldier on the occasions that have arisen [...].[35]

The letter proves that he was an infantry captain from around 1554, at that time under Maestre de campo Sancho de Londoño of the tercio of Lombardy, and that he had been fighting in many other expeditions before that date. As Philip II lived at the time in the Low Countries, Sancho must have travelled there in 1559. But the document does not place him directly at famous historical events like those in Mühlberg, Africa and England. And we must also question his presence in Djerba, as even here his last biographer is quite negative:

> However, it is not clear that Sancho Dávila was at Djerba [los Djelves] nor that he was one of the captured men. This is only affirmed by Gerónimo Dávila, who is always inclined to sing the praises of his ancestor, and by father Juan de Mariana in his *Historia General de España*. And we do not have any other source of information that can prove this.[36]

After Alba's letter from 1559, the next piece of documentary evidence can be found in a royal letter from June 1561, with Philip II already back in Spain.[37] The letter proves that Dávila had been serving with his company in Naples during the government of the Duke of Alba in Italy. There is nothing to be found on Djerba. In June 1561 Sancho was probably in Spain, as Martín García has found him present at a procession in April of that year in his home town. He may have used his stay to secure payment of his wages at court. According to seventeenth-century local historian

---

[35] 'El capitán Sancho Dávila, llevador desta, ha servido a Vuestra Magestad muchos años en todas las jornadas que se han ofresçido y, de çinco acá, con una compañía de infantería y señalándose como buen soldado en las ocasiones que han ocurrido [...]. Alba to Philip II, Milan, 10 May 1559, AGS, E. 1210, quoted in Martín García, *Sancho*, 81.
[36] Martín García, *Sancho*, 91; Juan de Mariana, 'Historia general', II, 394.
[37] Philip II to the Marquis of Pescara, Madrid, June 1561, AGS, E. 1212, quoted by Martín García, *Sancho*, 90.

González Dávila, he had returned to Spain, having "decided to lay down his arms", but at court the Duke of Alba convinced him "to return to [military] service".[38] The next document is his new appointment to infantry captain of 15 July 1561, already published in full by Gerónimo in 1713. He was to earn 50,000 maravedíes a year.[39]

In this new office Sancho's first task was the control of the fortresses on the Valencian coast and the construction of a new fortress in Bernia, a task comparable to Julián Romero working on Ibiza during those same years. We know of these activities from letters written by Sancho to the Duke of Alba in 1562.[40] For the first time we hear from Sancho directly, making it possible to offer a better picture of his career from this moment onwards. For the period up to 1562, the first almost forty years of his life, we have nothing but second-hand stories and a few scattered pieces of documentary evidence that have been preserved. The history of this early period was fabricated mainly after he had become an important military commander. Connecting him to important events in history including royal visits and crucial heroic battles may have been part of the myth-making process of a military hero. In part the same process took place around Julián Romero. However, in both cases it seems probable that they had acquired experience both in Italy and the northern territories of the Habsburgs.

After asking the Duke of Alba for a new posting in a letter from June 1562, he was nominated as the new governor of the fortress of Pavia, a wonderful promotion, most surely the result of the Duke's protection. On 17 February 1563 Sancho was back in Madrid where he swore an oath as an infantry captain, before travelling to Italy to occupy his post.[41] In 1566 his cousin, Rodrigo Orejón, became his lieutenant in the fortress, and he stayed there quietly for a few years between 1563 and 1567. Martín García found only one letter that showed some tension when the city guards and the soldiers from the castle had been fighting, using arquebuses and pistols. In October 1566 he informed the Duke of Alba that he was bored and begged for action:

> When Your Excellency favoured me by giving me the government of this castle of Pavia, I did not think this was to stay behind,

---

[38] Martín García, *Sancho*, 91-92, 99.
[39] Martín García, *Sancho*, 100.
[40] Martín García, *Sancho*, 101.
[41] CD XXX, 433-435; CD XXXI, 15-18; Martín García, *Sancho*, 103-104; AGS, E. 1130, 93.

> but I saw it as an intermediate period until an opportunity or journey presented itself in which I could be employed similar to my services, as these have always been, thank God, with so much caution as suits a soldier worthy to be called a servant [*criado*] of Your Excellency.[42]

Sancho wanted to join the Duke of Alba on the expedition he was preparing:

> This has made me dare to ask Your Excellency, understanding that there will be a journey on which Your Grace will go, to employ me in his service and go with him, as the whole world understands that I am a servant [*criado*] of Your Excellency and it would give me great shame if I were to remain stuck over here.[43]

We hear the voice of a commander who wants to be part of the action. Until then his career had been succesful but not extraordinary, he having become an infantry captain around the age of thirty and having got his tenure as governor of an important fortress in Italy when he was not even forty. But still, until then there had not been much evidence to suggest that he would become a famous early modern military commander, least of all a national hero. Brantôme wrote that people were surprised that the Duke took Dávila with him as he was not yet considered an important captain.[44] When looking back at his departure in 1567 for the Low Countries, he was described by the famous poet, Pedro de Padilla, in 1583 as "a highly esteemed man, fortunate and valiant".[45] Baltasar Vargas, who published his *Breve relación en octava rima* on Alba's journey

---

[42] 'Quando Vuestra Excelencia me hizo merced en que se me diese la tenençia deste castillo de Pavia no pensé yo que fuera para quedar atrasado sino en un ínterin (hasta) que se ofreciese ocasión o jornada en que poder ser empleado conforme a mis serviçios, questos an sido siempre, bendito Dios, con tanto cuidado como conviene a un soldado que se piensa valer en ser llamado criado de Vuestra Excelencia'. Dávila to Alba, Pavia, 24 October 1566, AA, 433/24, quoted in Martín García, *Sancho*, 106.

[43] 'Esto me a atrevido a significar a Vuestra Excelencia, entendiendo que se haze jornada en que Su Merced va, para que me emplee en que yo pueda servir y pasar adelante, pues todo el mundo entiende ser yo criado de Vuestra Excelencia y es me gran vergüença quedarme aquí estancado'. Idem. According to Maltby, Alba did not accept to go to the Low Countries until 29 November. Maltby, *Alba*, 134.

[44] Brantôme, *Oeuvres completes*, I, 150-151; Cornejo, *Sumario*, 103.

[45] 'Hombre de muy grande estima, dichoso como esforçado'. Padilla, *Romancero*, 31. The original was published in Madrid in 1583.

to the Low Countries in Antwerp in 1568, in his epic poem called him a good soldier, "always loved by the general [Alba]".[46]

## Battling against the rebels (1568)

The Duke of Alba asked Sancho to raise a company of light cavalry that could serve as his personal guard, and it was in this capacity that he left Italy for the Low Countries in 1567, with one hundred lancers and fifty men armed with arquebuses. We can presume Sancho stayed close to Alba during these first years, in part because we do not have any correspondence between Sancho and the Duke until 1569. His company was at first lodged in a village five miles outside Brussels, as in general cavalry regiments remained in the countryside for reasons of provision and accommodation.[47]

The first episode Sancho played a part in concerns the imprisonment of the Count of Egmont on 9 September 1567, very shortly after the arrival of Alba and his troops in Brussels. It is one of the most dramatic moments in the early history of the Revolt. Egmont was invited to Alba's residence to discuss the defence works of Thionville and Luxembourg with other noblemen, but then at the end of the meeting Sancho Dávila told Egmont very politely to hand him his sword and he was then taken prisoner. However, in Hogenberg's engraving of the event it seems that Alba approached Egmont himself.[48] Chronicler Mendoza tells that Alba:

> had ordered that the Count of Egmont and the Count of Horne were to leave through two different doors; at one door there was Sancho Dávila, captain of the Duke's guards, with orders to apprehend the Count of Egmont, and at the other door captain Jerónimo de Salinas, governor and castellano of Puerto Herculis, to apprehend the Count of Horne.[49]

Hooft, of course, made the most of this dramatic moment:

> And then, with the closure of the meeting, Egmont, leaving the room, was told that the Prior [Fernando de Toledo] was waiting for him to continue the game. Then he turned around through a

[46] 'Siempre del general [Alba] ha sido amado'. Vargas, *Breve relación*, 68.
[47] Martín García, *Sancho*, 115; Dávila to Albornoz, Milan, 23 May 1567, AA, 433/26; CD XXX, 435-436.
[48] Vandormael and Goosens, *Slachtoffer*, 146-148; CP, I, 573; Nievas Rojas, 'Nuevos datos'.
[49] Mendoza, *Comentarios* (1948), 408.

certain room, where he was met by Sancho Dávila, who, as captain of the ducal guard, and by order of the King, took away his weapon, taking him prisoner. The count, not understanding what was happening to him, wanted everything that was said repeated. Then, finding it hard to separate himself from his sword, he stated that it had so often loyally served the King. However, he had to hand it in and remain there, complaining about the force and violence used, and referring to the freedom of the Order [Golden Fleece] and the laws of the country, stating that he did not need to remain. However, the Spaniard's ears remained deaf to his complaints.[50]

In a letter written from Brussels and sent on 11 September we find another description of the event that had taken place only two days earlier:

When they were all standing, they said to Egmont that the Prior [Fernando de Toledo] had asked if he wanted to play piquet, and going towards the room of the Prior, Sancho Dávila, the captain of the guards of Your Excellency, approached him, telling him that he was arrested by His Majesty and that he had to enter the room. On entering, he told him to hand over his sword, which he did much against his will, saying that with it he had always served Your Majesty, defending these lands.[51]

The story we find in Hooft's history reflects the same dialogue as the Spanish letter written only two days after the event. An interesting new detail is the name of the game they were presumably going to play, 'los cientos', also called piquet, a fashionable card game of probably Spanish origin that had reached England in 1554 with the wedding of Philip II and Mary Tudor, and that can already be found in Rabelais' work.[52]

Sancho would in 1568 be involved in various battles and skirmishes, including three major battles: the Battle of Dahlem, the Battle of Jemmingen and the Battle of the river Gete. He would also be hurt in

---

[50] Hooft, *Historiën* (1972), 163.
[51] 'Y asi estando todos en pie dixieron al de Agamon que el prior [Fernando de Toledo] dezia si queria jugar a los çientos y yendo asi al aposento del prior llego a el Sancho Dabila capitan de la guardia de Su Excelencia diziendo que fuese preso por su Magestad y que entrase a aquel aposento y al entrar del le dixo y dexe la espada, la qual se le hizo muy mal de dexar diziendo que con ella abia servido sienpre a su Magestad y defendido estos estados'. Ochoa de Arizpe to Pedro de Acuña, Brussels, 11 September 1567, RBM, Gondomar Collection, II, 2212, doc. 6.
[52] https://en.wikipedia.org/wiki/Piquet (accessed 20 May 2019); Vandormael and Goosens, *Slachtoffer*, 47-52.

one of the lesser battles taking place between the armies of William of Orange and the Duke of Alba.

We find Sancho with his guards at Maastricht on 23 April 1568, and in the following days he was involved in the fighting near Roermond under Maestre de campo Sancho de Londoño. In Londoño's description of the events, Dávila clearly stood out, together with some others like Francisco de Valdés. Near Dahlem he attacked the enemy, "and though the country was filled with fences, ditches and woodland, Sancho's attack made their cavalry abandon the battle and start running". Alba sent Londoño's letter with one of his own to Philip II, and the King congratulated Sancho on his brave behaviour, writing, "I will keep this in mind for when the occasion comes to reward you". This important letter containing a royal promise was preserved in the family archive.[53] In another letter, to paymaster Castellanos in Antwerp, written in June 1568 while the promised royal reward had not yet arrived, Sancho spoke of "the success that God has given to me in Dahlem against those heretics and rebels", further emphasising the fact that he had not received royal rewards for the last twenty-five years.[54] Sancho was ordered by Alba to take the most important prisoners to Brussels, but he had to hang all others in the vicinity of Maastricht, gruesome details that show the harshness of early modern warfare.[55]

He would also be present at the Battle of Jemmingen on 21 July of that same year, together with other Spanish army commanders like Julián Romero. And again he could be found among those who had done particularly well "up front only he [Lope de Figueroa] and Sancho Dávila, who were in the vanguard of all the army".[56] As in Dahlem, the

---

[53] Londoño to the Duke of Alburquerque, Roermond, 26 April 1568, CD XXX, 438-443; Idem, CD XXXVII, 234-239; Alba to Philip II, Brussels, 29 April 1568, CD XXXVII, 240-244; Alba to Alburquerque, 3 May 1568, EA I; Philip II to Dávila, Aranjuez, 22 May 1568, Martín García, *Sancho*, 127; Pando Fernández de Pinedo, *Vida*, 128-129; Dávila y San Vitores, *Rayo*, 39; Dávila y Guevara, *Memorial*. In a letter from Philip II to Alba (minuta) Philip ordered Alba to congratulate Londoño, Count Heberstein, and Dávila 'De lo bien que se hubieron aquel dia'. Philip II to Alba, Aranjuez, 23 May 1568, CD XXXVII, 261-262.

[54] 'El subçesso que Dios fue servido de darme en Dalem contra aquellos herejes y rebeldes de Su Magestad'. Dávila to Castellanos, Brussels, 21 June 1568, BL, Add. 28.386, f. 152.

[55] Alba to Philip II, Brussels, 10 May 1568, CD XXXVII, 249-250. See on Sancho's actions at Roermond and Dahlem Padilla, *Romancero*, 37-38.

[56] Alba to Philip II, Jemmingen, 22 July 1568, CD XXX, 443-450; Report on the Battle of Jemmingen, 21 July 1568, CD XXXI, 19-24; Fagel, Santiago Belmonte and Álvarez Francés, 'Eer en schuld'.

enemy ran away and many were killed. And, again, a victory was a good moment for Sancho to ask for rewards. Again he spoke of a large victory given to them by God. About his own activities at Jemmingen he was rather modest: "I only shall say that I did in this day like in all others where I have participated, as much as possible". However, and probably supported by the victory at Dahlem, he was less modest about deserving a good reward: "a reward worthy of my services, that if I was not confident that I really deserved it, I would not dare to put it in this way".[57]

Bernardino de Mendoza's chronicle also shows Sancho as the most active commander at Dahlem and describes how he had the honour of taking the most important prisoners to Brussels. Just before the Battle of Jemmingen, Sancho caught up with some enemies, "taking one with his own hands". However, his further role during the battle was minimal. During the Battle of the river Gete on 20 October he is mentioned as leading four hundred cavalry, but nothing more is said of him. It is surprising that this last battle is little known in the historical literature of the Low Countries, though Mendoza claims that some three thousand enemies were killed, counted by the villagers that had buried them.[58] Chronicler Antonio Trillo also highlights Sancho's cavalry attack at Dahlem, but leaves him out of the stories of Jemmingen and the river Gete.[59]

Another Spanish chronicler, Pedro Cornejo, turned Sancho into the great hero of Dahlem, and even as one of the main heroes of his book:

> This was the first time Sancho's valour was made known in these states, for his qualities as a commander and for his spirit, courage and his fortune in fighting and defeating the enemy, elements that in our days very seldom are found together in one man, but all came together in this knight, as you shall see in the continuation of this history.[60]

Dutch Protestant historian Emanuel van Meteren mentions Sancho as leading commander at Dahlem, but clearly does not see him as a hero; "continuing his victory he did a lot of evil in the land of Julich and its vicinity". Van Meteren tells that just before the Battle of Jemmingen Sancho went on a reconnaissance mission with thirty horsemen and later on he engaged in combat with Louis of Nassau and his army,

---

[57] 'Solo dire que yo he hecho en esta jornada, como en las demas donde me he hallado, quanto me ha sido possible'; 'La que mis serviçios mereçen, que sino estuviese confiado de que la tengo muy mereçida no me atreveria a representallo desta suerte'. Dávila to Alba [?], Hieme [?], 23 July 1568. BL, Add. 28.386, f. 162.

[58] Mendoza, *Comentarios* (1948), 411-413, 423-427, 436.

[59] Trillo, *Historia*, 60-61.

[60] Cornejo, *Sumario*, 113; Ulloa, *Comentarios*, 19r, 33v.

commanding 1,400 horsemen.⁶¹ Historian P.C. Hooft also mentions Sancho at Dahlem as one of two outstanding commanders and states how they captured the Lords of both Villers and Huy,⁶² who were then taken to Brussels. At Jemmingen, Hooft mentions Sancho but clearly gives prominence to Julián Romero, while at the Battle of the river Gete he is not mentioned at all.⁶³

There is a clear difference in his importance and role during these three main battles, depending on the sources. The Spanish letters and accounts from 1568 place him in a prominent light, while some of the Spanish chroniclers pay less attention to him, as a secondary figure, and the Dutch even less. However, the hero of Dahlem is one of the favourite soldiers of chronicler Pedro Cornejo, publishing between the events themselves and the chronicles of Mendoza and Trillo. It proves that his fame as a good commander of horsemen on the field of battle was constructed during this year. In an account of all the Spaniards who had served well during this first campaign he was, strangely enough, mentioned for his participation at Jemmingen, and not for the victory at Dahlem.⁶⁴

Following Orange's army in the direction of France, Sancho stayed with the Duke of Alba's army. Near Binche the troops engaged by the end of 1568 with some of the enemy infantry, "whom they slaughtered close to a village, although not without danger for captain Sancho Dávila, who was hurt in his thigh by a halberd".⁶⁵ According to the Marquis of Miraflores, after having "his thigh pierced by a halberd and his face splashed with his own blood" he shouted to his soldiers, "this blood that stains my face is blood that bleeds from my own face because of the shame of seeing you flee". In the 1713 biography we already find the same story with beside it in the margin "noticias de su padre", indicating that this was perhaps a family story that was passed down from generation to generation.⁶⁶

While chronicler Bernardino de Mendoza does not make much of the encounter in which Sancho received his wound, there is a different version of this story that has turned the event into a real battle. The 'Battle of Le Quesnoy (1568)' has its own page on *Wikipedia* in which Sancho

---

⁶¹ Van Meteren, *Belgische ofte Nederlandsche historie* (1599), 42r, 44v.
⁶² Jean de Montigny, Lord of Villers, and Philip of Namur, were both beheaded in Brussels.
⁶³ Hooft, *Nederlandsche historiën* (1972), 176, 187, 198.
⁶⁴ CD XXXVII, 365; Martínez Ruiz, 'Sancho Dávila en las campañas', 105-142.
⁶⁵ Mendoza, *Comentarios*, 439; Martín García, *Sancho*, 130.
⁶⁶ Pando y Fernández de Pinedo, *Vida*, 135-136; Dávila y San Vitores, *Rayo*, 58. Both early biographies situate his injury during the Battle of the river Gete.

stars among the wounded. During this victory of the Prince of Orange on 12 November, "the Spanish commander Sancho D'Avila, along with his officers Francois de Tolede and Ruy de Lopez, was wounded, and the son of the Duke of Alva Don Rufille Henriques died in the action".[67] In Mendoza's chronicle there were two confrontations: Sancho received his injury during an earlier confrontation, followed by the fighting in which Ruy López de Ávalos, captain of light cavalry, died, and Francisco de Toledo, a brother to the Count of Orgaz, was wounded.[68] Trillo also distinguishes two different encounters but does not mention Sancho. In the second he describes the death of Ruy López de Ávalos in more detail.[69] Dutch chronicler Van Meteren mentions the battle won by Orange near Cambrésis on 12 November, "where many noblemen were killed or taken prisoner", mentioning the son of the Marquis of Olivares, Don Juan de [Tallen] and Don Ruffin Henricus.[70]

Perhaps the connection between Sancho's injury and this encounter on 12 November originates with the Italian seventeenth-century historian Famiano Strada, who combined two events that had in reality occurred a day apart:

> They arrived around Quesnoy, and as Alba was following him from a close distance, it occurred that in a more than normal skirmish, he dispersed some Spanish and High German banners, and Sancho Dávila, with César Dávalos, who in vain tried to keep their men together, were seriously hurt, serving at least partially as revenge for his [Orange's] earlier defeat.[71]

In particular, the detail of their attempt to keep the troops together coincides with Sancho shouting to his troops in his biography. But who invented the story that the Duke of Alba's son had died in the fighting, a fictitious story that was already circulating in 1680 and was subsequently forgotten, but that has fairly recently made its reappearance on *Wikipedia*?

---

[67] https://en.wikipedia.org/wiki/Battle_of_Le_Quesnoy_(1568), (accessed 11 April 2019). The page quotes Aubery du Maurier, *Mémoires*, and De Thou, *Histoire universelle*. Aubery stated: 'Le Prince defit entierement dix-huit compagnies de gens de pied, & trois cens chevaux, & fit presque tous les chefs prisonniers; Dom Rufille Henriques, fils du Duc d'Albe, étant demeuré mort sur la place'. Aubery, *Mémoires*, 37; http://www.marceltettero.nl/Spanje/Avila/Avila.htm, (accessed 11 April 2019).
[68] Mendoza, *Comentarios* (1948) 439.
[69] Trillo, *Historia*, 80.
[70] Van Meteren, *Belgische oft Nederlandsche historie* (1599) 45v.
[71] Strada, *De thien eerste boecken*, 491-492; Reijner, *Italiaanse geschiedschrijvers*.

## The *castellano* of Antwerp (1568-1572)

Alba was well aware of Sancho's skills as governor of the citadel of Pavia as well as of his abilities as a good commander in the field, and therefore promoted him around May 1568 to captain of Antwerp and governor (*castellano*) of its citadel which was under construction, as can be understood from a letter from Morillon, Granvelle's confidant in the Low Countries. At this time, Morillon still saw this nomination as "la préservation de la ville", putting his faith in the Spanish commander as he had also done with Romero, and probably reflecting the general opinion of Catholic Netherlanders at the time.[72] However, a modern American historian described Sancho at this same point in his book anachronistically as "of all his race the most hated in Antwerp".[73]

Beginning on 1 January 1569, there has been preserved a whole series of letters from Antwerp from Sancho to the Duke and to Albornoz, the Duke's secretary. In a letter to the Duke he thanked him again for his new position, "whether it is a good or a bad life to be governor of the citadel, I put myself completely in the hands of Your Excellency".[74] One Spanish soldier poet even dedicated to the new *castellano* a sonnet which was published in Antwerp in 1569 together with sonnets praising other military commanders: "fame moves in a swift and fast flight, lifting your name up to heaven".[75]

The Duke of Alba had visited Antwerp for the first time by the end of October 1567, with, according to local chronicler Godevaert van Haecht, three hundred Spanish horsemen. Sancho must have been among them. The burghers complained about the new taxes that were needed for the construction of the citadel, although Alba tried to defend his decision by

---

[72] Morillon to Granvelle, Brussels, 23 May 1568, CG III, 233. See also Alba to Philip II, Brussels, 31 January 1569, EA II, 174; CD XXX, 436.

[73] Wegg, *Decline*, 137; Ochoa de Arizpe, Camp outside Maastricht, 20 September 1568, RBM, Gondomar, II/2212, doc. 12; Boone, 'From cuckoo's egg'.

[74] 'Ni si es buena vida o mala ser alcaide, sino en todo remitirme a la voluntad y orden de Vuestra Excelencia'. Dávila to Albornoz, 1 February 1569, AA, C33/28; Dávila to Alba, Antwerp, 6 February 1569, AA, C33/32, quoted in Martín García, *Sancho*, 136. Gabriele Serbelloni to Philip II, Brussels, 19 February 1569 (*CP* II, 64) explained he had been replaced as governor of the Antwerp citadel by Dávila.

[75] 'La fama con veloz y presto vuelo, levanta el nombre vuestro hasta el cielo'. Ximénez Ayllón, *Sonetos*, sonnet 16,

stating that once it was finished the soldiers could live in the citadel and would no longer be quartered in the inhabitants' houses.[76] In September 1568 six hundred Spanish soldiers came to stay in the citadel. Van Haecht describes how in October four out of nine banners left again, but soon afterwards another six hundred new Spaniards arrived; "these were lodged in the city, though there was enough room in the castle. And all arrived naked, and were dressed here as noblemen (*jonkers*)". By the end of October most of these Spaniards did move to the citadel, as their beds and mattresses had arrived. Some of the officers took with them much household equipment from the houses they had stayed in and when the burghers complained, they just said "it is all ours" ("'t hoort al ons"). By early December another 250 Spaniards had arrived in the city, "skinny and naked wretches" ("hamels"). The cold winter meant that some Spaniards froze to death "as they are not accostumed to such cold".[77] On 29 January 1569, most of the Spanish soldiers again left the citadel with only two Spanish banners remaining in Antwerp.

Van Haecht never mentions Sancho's appointment or any other news about the new governor in his chronicle. Painter Godevaert van Haecht was born in Antwerp in 1546, and except for a long stay in Paris between April 1570 and September 1571 he seems to have remained in the city. It makes him an excellent eyewitness to most of the events up to 1574, especially since his work resembles loose notes penned directly after the events themselves.[78] For a young man of some twenty-three years the appointment of the new *castellano,* however, was not worth mentioning. The Duke of Alba absorbed all his attention, as in May 1569 the citadel prepared for a visit by the Duke, "and the castle walls all around were filled with cannons, as he would come to inspect it, and there existed differences between the masters of the castle as how to finish it". The Duke arrived on 27 May "and in the castle cannons were fired and also the Spaniards fired besides their weapons some rockets; on the 28th day he drove around the castle, and during this triumphal ride he was almost hit with a wooden cannonball".[79]

Meanwhile, Sancho used his experience with the citadel of Milan, where he had resided for some time, to evaluate what was needed in Antwerp. So it was not only the Italian architects who brought with them

---

[76] On the costs of the citadel: Brulez, 'Gewicht', 394.
[77] Van Haecht, *Kroniek*, I, 238, 241; II, 41, 52, 54, 59, 62.
[78] Van Haecht, *Kroniek*, introduction, xvii-xviii. During his absence his brother continued the manuscript.
[79] Van Haecht, *Kroniek*, II, 76, 90-91.

their experience of the Italian citadels, as Sancho also understood what was necessary for a citadel to function properly. A detailed comparison found among his letters to Albornoz explains that he needed a doctor and a surgeon, but also an auditor, "very necessary, and there is no castle that does not have one".[80] He was an experienced Spanish commander well versed in the art of war as it was practised in Renaissance Italy.

One can even study the contruction works on the citadel using these letters, as when in April 1569 it is stated that "the bullwarks are already high, and we have to put the arms of Your Majesty and the Duke, my lord, on them".[81] However, the final touch would come much later. In a letter of 18 March 1571 to Prior Fernando de Toledo, Alba's natural son, whom Sancho clearly considered as a close patron and protector, he described "the statue that has to be put here in this citadel of the Duke my lord; it is said that it is the best thing in the world and with God's help, by Easter we can install it here".[82] The infamous statue, made out of the cannons won at Jemmingen, would be placed in the citadel's main square in May of that year.[83]

Until this moment in his story, the local chronicler had not yet mentioned Sancho, who had been in Antwerp at least from February 1569. It will finally be in August that he writes:

> Also in this time, the governor of the Antwerp castle named *Sanxo Daver* was a bridegroom, as he married the daughter of a Spaniard in Bruges, and as one heard, the father was a banker. There was a very pompous celebration, even though he had been just a drummer. It was heard that the Duke of Alba had given him a present of 2,000 crowns; and around the 15th day he called for a tournament in Antwerp, as he wanted to return home to the castle by that time, and for this reason, by the first of the month the preparations started to prepare the lodgings for the Spanish lords that would come to the tournament.[84]

---

[80] 'Es muy necesario y no ay castillo que no le tenga'. Dávila to Albornoz, Milan, 23 May 1567 to 29 May 1567, AA, C33/25-27; Idem, Antwerp, 10 February 1569, AA, C33/38.
[81] 'Los baluartes ban ya altos, abiéndose de poner en ellos las armas de Su Magestad y las del Duque, mi señor'. Dávila to Albornoz, Antwerp citadel, 21 April 1569, AA, C33/47, quoted in Martín García, *Sancho*, 137. Soly, 'Bouw'.
[82] 'La statua que se a de poner aqui en esta çiudadela del Duque mi señor dizen que a salido la mejor cosa del mundo y para Pasqua con la ayuda de Dios la pondremos aquí'. Dávila to Hernando de Toledo, Antwerp citadel, 18 March 1571, AA, C33/42.
[83] Mulcahy, 'Manifestation', 163-165; Horst, 'Duke', 133-135.
[84] Van Haecht, *Kroniek*, II, 97.

Again we find in this description the idea that the Spanish commanders were of low birth, it calling Sancho somebody who had started off as a 'drummer', a description that was also used for Sancho in a Beggar's song and for Julián in a play by Lope de Vega. This second mention of Sancho as a drummer may indicate that this image of Sancho had spread through the Low Countries. The preparations for the wedding can be found in several of Sancho's letters, for example on the question whether to celebrate the wedding in Bruges or in Antwerp. Sancho was marrying Catalina Gallo, the daughter of Juan López Gallo, one of the great Spanish financiers from Bruges, who served as a financial factor for Philip II from 1557, and baron of Male from 1560.[85] Juan López Gallo was the son of Spanish merchant Luis López Gallo Vega who had by the end of the fifteenth century already possessed a house in Bruges. Juan had married Catalina Pardo Garrido, the daughter of Silvester Pardo and Josine López, also very important members of the Spanish merchant colony in Bruges. A grandson of Silvester's, Juan Pardo, Lord of Frémicourt, would become Mayor of Bruges in 1574.[86]

Barbara, a sister of Sancho's future bride, would marry Alonso López Gallo, born in Burgos in 1533 and Governor of Culemborg and Colonel of Walloon troops during the Revolt. Barbara was Alonso's niece and Alonso was definitely not Juan's son, as has often been suggested in the historical literature.[87] In 1567 Alonso had still been a servant of Governess Margaret of Parma, and in that capacity he had gone to Spain in February to inform the King on matters she did not want to put down on paper.[88] Barbara and Catalina had a brother also named Juan López Gallo (who died in 1616) who married Anne of Aspremont, a daughter of Cristóbal de Mondragón's wife from her earlier marriage. It shows the close relations between Sancho Dávila from Ávila, Cristóbal de Mondragón from Medina del Campo and Alonso López Gallo from Burgos, but also their strong connection to the Spanish merchant colonies of Bruges and Antwerp.

Also involved in the marriage plans was Spanish merchant Hernando de Frías from Antwerp, who seemed to act as an intermediary and whose house in Antwerp might have been used for the celebrations.[89] After

---

[85] Fagel, *Hispano-Vlaamse wereld*, 404; Maréchal, 'Portretten'; Geevers, 'Hoe toegankelijk'.
[86] Fagel, *Hispano-Vlaamse wereld*, 107-108.
[87] Dávila Jalón, *Nobiliario*, 77, 307. They returned to Spain in 1580. Alonso died in 1596 and Barbara in 1629. Their son, Gregorio Gallo y López, was born in Culemborg, but taken to Burgos 'al pecho de su madre'.
[88] Margaret of Parma to Philip II, Brussels, 16 February 1567, CP I, 510.
[89] Dávila to Albornoz, Antwerp, 22, 23 June and 21 July 1569, AA, C33/48-50. Sancho is mentioned in a letter from Hernando de Frías Cevallos to Simón Ruiz, Antwerp, 7

Alba's embargo on English goods in December 1568, the Duke had sold everything for a reasonable price to the same Frías.[90] In 1573 Frías helped Sancho to send objects to Spain: small square cloths with heraldic symbols (reposteros) and handkerchiefs (pañuelos).[91] In 1574 Frías was praised by Requesens in a letter to Philip II for his financial capability: "whose services were so praised by the Duke of Alba, that many times he had said to me that this man had been the single cause why these states had not been lost". In 1573 Frías bought a large hôtel in Antwerp which he gave to the Jesuits for their first college in the city.[92] Interestingly, the Duke of Alba was a declared enemy of the Jesuits, while Requesens was much more supportive of the order.[93]

On 14 January 1569 Prior Fernando de Toledo visited Antwerp where he was very well received by the Spanish and Italian merchants, the city government, the captains of the German troops in the city and the captains of the ten Spanish banners in the fortress. He went to visit the citadel on the 16th "and then they fired all the cannons with blanks, but the community (*gemeynte*) did not celebrate his arrival very much".[94] Again, on 11 August 1569, Fernando returned to Antwerp for Sancho's tournament, described by Van Haecht in great detail, in an exception to most of his very concise entries, thus showing the importance he gave to these events. The young man must have been impressed by the glamour of the celebrations, albeit at the same time very critical of the participants and reflecting the dissatisfaction of the people:

> And they demanded that around the 15th day the golden rooms around the market square and the rooms of the largest guilds had to be opened, to dress and serve all those who came to the tournament. When those of the city had turned this down, they demanded the building of the silversmiths.
>
> And on the 13th day the bride of the castellan came sailing from Bruges to Antwerp with the cities' barge, and a banquet was held

---

July 1568, Vázquez de Prada, *Lettres marchandes*, II, 49.

[90] Other references to Frías: Dávila to Juan Moreno, Saeftinghe, 14 March, AA, C/33, 74 and Dávila to Albornoz, Antwerp, 30 March 1573, AA, C/33, 75; Dávila y San-Vitores, *Rayo*, 97; Letters to Frias also in EA III. Albornoz to Lixalde on Frías, Utrecht, June 1573, EA III, 483. Vázquez de Prada, *Lettres marchandes*, I, 216-217.

[91] Dávila to Juan Moreno, Breda, 6 October 1573, AA, C/33, 104.

[92] Requesens to Philip II, 16 March 1574, NCD I, 376-377.

[93] Goris, 'Alva', 290-301; Maltby, *Alba*, 213-214.

[94] Van Haecht, *Kroniek*, II, 75.

on the quay. There were shots fired from the castle as if a queen had arrived and when a cannon burst, it left a Spaniard dead. The bride entered through the back gate of the monastery of Saint Michael, forced open by the Spaniards because Colonel Count Albrecht Ladron, who had to safeguard the city with his German soldiers, had refused to give them the keys….

On the 15th day in the morning, it started to rain again, and the same happened in the afternoon, ruining their celebrations and making them very angry. On the market square there were buried more than 330 small barrels with gunpowder, tied with iron strips and covered with wood and sand. … At four o' clock it was fair weather again and the gentlemen came out to play, covered in silk and velvet, with feathers and other ornaments, but all on foot. Their small lances were as strong as glass as not to hurt each other, and the people did nothing else but mock them for not jousting on horseback.

On the 17th they arrived on horseback on the Meir, tilting at the ring, and in the end a man sat down on a wooden horse, gaining money by breaking up to two hundred lances on his armour. By then they had changed their dress, again very richly. There were also some brawls between their followers and the common people ('den gemeyn volke').

On the 18th after noon they tilted again at the ring inside the castle, but before noon it had rained again as heavy as the day before, with thunder and lightning. That night the corner of one of the walls of the castle collapsed.[95]

There seems to have been a very good relationship between Sancho and Prior Fernando de Toledo, both belonging to the circle of the Duke of Alba, but perhaps also because of their functions within the cavalry. Fernando often visited Antwerp, and his presence at the wedding festivities must have been very important for Sancho. And Fernando would return more often to enjoy himself in the city, as in February 1570 the Antwerp chronicler noted, "And it is known that the son of the Duke of Alba, now present in Antwerp, called the Grand Prior, lost ten thousand guilders in one night".[96] In a letter from March 1571 to Fernando, Sancho reminds him of their good times together:

---

[95] All earlier quotations are also from Van Haecht, *Kroniek*, II, 99-100.
[96] Van Haecht, *Kroniek*, II, 122.

> Of this city, I only have to tell Your Excellency that every day the absence and solitude that Your Excellency is making to the ladies is felt more strongly, be it widows, married ones or those still to be married. They are very pretty and have celebrated Carnival lacking in parties and people. The game has been stopped completely, as the players have neither credit nor money. That is a great loss for me as well, as there is no money for the construction of the citadel and it is a great pity that such an important work cannot be finished.[97]

Also in 1569, Alba tried to convince Philip II to reward Sancho with a place in one of the knightly orders in Spain:

> I have written to Your Majesty several times about how much Sancho Dávila, castellan of Antwerp, has served here, and how much he deserves to be rewarded. For this I beg Your Majesty to reward me by sending him a habit, for I would appreciate it as much as if Your Majesty would hand it to myself.[98]

Only a few months later Alba received a positive answer from the King:

> For what Your Majesty has done regarding the habit of Sancho Dávila, I kiss his feet many times, and I can affirm to Your Majesty that he is one of the men of most service of all those he has in his estates.[99]

In a next letter he thanked the King on Sancho's behalf: "Sancho Dávila is grateful for the habit he has been given".[100] It is uncertain whether Alba knew it had not been a simple decision for the King. In his letter to Alba informing him of Sancho's habit the King had simply stated that "based on the services rendered by Sancho Dávila and your mediation,

---

[97] 'Desta billa no tengo que avisar a Vuestra Excelencia sino que cada dia se siente mas la falta y soledad que Vuestra Excelencia haze las damas asy biudas como casadas y por casar, estan muy hermosas y an pasado el carnabal echando menos mas fiestas y conpania. El juego a faltado de todo punto y los jugadores el credito y el dinero, que es arta soledad para my porque tambien falta el dinero para la fabrica desta çiudadela que es la mayor lastima cosa tan prinçipal que no se acabe'. Dávila to Hernando de Toledo, Antwerp citadel, 18 March 1571, AA, C33/42.
[98] Alba to Philip II, Brussels, 11 December 1569, CD XXXVIII, 254-255; see also Zayas to Alba, Madrid, 6 April 1569, *Idem*, 63.
[99] Alba to Philip II, Brussels, 24 February 1570, EA II.
[100] Alba to Philip II, 29 February 1570, CD XXX, 437.

I have approved giving him the habit of Santiago, as you asked me to". However, the minutes [draft] of the King's letter had another sentence in between the lines, which had been struck out: "Although it was the idea to close the door to the habits for some time, but for things you want and request so wholehartedly, I could do nothing else than keep the door open".[101] Also in 1570, he finally received payment for his years as an infantry captain, covering the period from its beginning on 15 July 1561 up to 1568, totalling perhaps 350,000 maravedíes.[102]

By 1570 Sancho Dávila had become a very important Spanish officer in the Low Countries, highly esteemed by the Duke of Alba, in part because of his decisive role in several battles against the rebels in 1568; he stood in close relation to the Duke's son, Fernando; he was the official commander of Alba's personal guard and *castellano* of the important citadel of Antwerp; the King had agreed to nominate him to become a knight of the order of Santiago; he had recently received a large payment for his office as infantry captain; and on top of all that he had married the daughter of a very rich Spanish merchant from Bruges, and the celebrations of his marriage had been the talk of the town. In 1570 he even had a son, an heir, called Fernando, surely in honour of the Duke and/or his natural son.[103] Could life get any better?

However, below the surface matters were not all that perfect. The knighthood still had to be approved by the order itself; relations between the Spanish troops and the burghers of Antwerp continued to worsen; there were people who wanted to take Antwerp citadel away from him; and, on top of everything, he was soon to lose his wife.

The local chronicler often reports on problems between the Spanish troops and the inhabitants of the city, now clearly criticising the behaviour of the Spaniards. For example:

> On 4 April [1570] a Spaniard who was standing watch on the walls of the castle shot dead a burgher who, according to him, was walking too close to him. And recently, a Spaniard was kicked in the city for what he had said, and his companion escaped and ran to the castle shouting "Spani, Spani"; and a group of soldiers came out of the castle ready to enter the city, but then they wisely decided to remain.[104]

---

[101] Philip II to Alba, Talavera, 22 January 1570, CD XXX, 436-437. See also CD XXXI, 24.
[102] CD XXXI, 17-18; Martín García, *Sancho*, 143; AGS, Contaduría del sueldo, 2ª época, legajo 38.
[103] Martín García, *Sancho*, 143.
[104] Van Haecht, *Kroniek*, II, 125-126.

At another time they entered the city's gardens:

> At the end of this month, on the day of Saint John the Baptist, very early, some two hundred Spaniards had left the castle, breaking with their feet and swords, all the trees, fruits and herbs, standing around the castle in the Markgravelei ruining all the gardens and shelters, and dragging the trees behind the roads.[105]

Was this last action perhaps related to the bonfires the Spanish build even today to celebrate the feast of Saint John the Baptist? In any case, it seems the chronicler did not understand their behaviour. The only other possible explanation could be that they wanted to have a better view from the citadel. But the idea of a celebration is plausible, as also on the day of Saint James we find the Spanish celebrating their national saint.

Remarkably, we also have reports by Sancho of the difficult relations with the inhabitants of Antwerp: "Yesterday those of the city came to talk to me about the order to bring the keys for the night to the castle and the discomfort that this would entail for them". They also complained about the new taxes and they wanted to give the keys to only two gates close to the citadel as two other water gates had to be opened every night "for cleaning the city". Sancho hoped Albornoz would send an order to obey him "because they come up with more than a hundred thousand things, like those in Aragon".[106] In this quotation we see that complaints of the Antwerp mayors were being compared to the complaints of the officials of Aragon about their privileges. Sancho clearly did not welcome too much influence on his government from below.

It is possible that Sancho's difficult relationship with the inhabitants may have been the reason for the Duke of Medinaceli, who had come to take over the government from Alba, suggesting that Sancho relinquish his post as *castellano* of Antwerp, "to take the castle of Antwerp away from Sancho Dávila and give it to another knight".[107] When he heard of this plan, Alba was furious and called it "una monstruosidad". The

---

[105] June 1570, Van Haecht, *Kroniek*, II, 128-129.

[106] 'Ayer benieron los de la villa a ablarme sobre la orden que tenian de traer aquy las llaves de noche y las descomodidades que les ara'; 'para la limpieza de la ciudad'; 'porque dan çien mil ocasiones como los de Aragon'. Dávila to Albornoz, Antwerp, 7 March 1571, AA, C33/41. Discussion on the keys to the city also in Requesens to Dávila, 8 June 1574, NCD II, 348-349.

[107] Alba to Zayas, Brussels, 7 June 1571, CD XXX, 451-452; EA II, 618. Medinaceli wanted to put Juan de Mendoza Sarmiento in his place as castellan of Antwerp. Zayas to Doctor Velasco, Madrid, 14 August 1571, CD XXXV, 405 and also Idem, 412-413.

Duke's letter shows how strongly he defended his own men: "it would be such a great insult that I would not know where to hide for the people not to see me". Alba understood Medinaceli was attempting to remove the men he himself had put in important places. He praised Sancho for all his services, and especially for the victory at Dahlem, one of his claims to fame up to 1571. The Duke's anger is visible even through his rather dramatic formulation: "He [Sancho] is resting from his works and from the sweat and all the blood that he has shed, as he is such a man that if he were at the very end of the world, one should throw out the Duke [Medinaceli] and beg on our knees to His Majesty that he would make him come over here". Alba had seen him fight "a million times". Fortunately for Sancho, Medinaceli never really took over the government from Alba. And although Philip II had decided at some point to follow Medinaceli's idea, this plan did not actually materialise at the time.[108] Sancho would remain as *castellano* of Antwerp until 1577.

His most important setback, however, was the death of his wife in this period, leaving him with a new-born child, just as would happen to his friend and colleague Cristóbal de Mondragón. Young Fernando – "he was a beautiful child" – would be raised in Bruges in his deceased wife's rich family. However, death struck again, as we find Sancho in October 1571 writing about the death of his father-in-law, Juan López Gallo.[109] He had been to Male where he had also found Alonso López Gallo, one of the heirs. Most of Juan's belongings, however, went to his eldest son. In the same letter Sancho expressed his wish to go home: "I desire to go to Spain as I have written to Your Honour, and now more than ever". These last three tiny words ("y ahora mas") are the only evidence of his personal feelings about his pitiful situation. His sentiments had changed, though the professional soldier was not spilling too many words on the subject.

After the death of his wife and his father-in-law, relations with the Spanish merchants continued, as with the already mentioned Juan Pardo, a cousin of his wife Catalina and at the time an important member of the Bruges government as its first alderman. In December 1571 Sancho wanted to put this in-law forward as the new commissioner of Bruges

---

[108] Las cosas que Su Magestad ha mandado que se digan al presidente Hopperus, AGS, E. 567, quoted in Martín García, *Sancho*, 216-217.

[109] 'El niño queda vonito'; 'Deseo de yr a Spaña como tengo escrito a vuestra merced y ahora mas'. Dávila to Albornoz, Antwerp citadel, 11 October 1571, AA, C33/52; Martín García, *Sancho*, 143. Juan López Gallo died on 4 October 1571. 'Los que estamos en este castillo y yo comemos y para tanto no puede bastar la hazienda de mi hijo'. Dávila to unknown [Albornoz?], Antwerp, 27 June 1573, AA, C/33, 93.

within the four Estates of Flanders, and for this he needed a letter from Alba.[110] As has been said, in 1574 Juan Pardo would become Mayor of Bruges. Based in Antwerp, Sancho was perfectly situated to connect to the rich Spanish merchant families of Antwerp and Bruges.[111]

## The relief of Middelburg (1572-1573)

After the taking of Brielle by the rebels on 1 April 1572, the Revolt entered its second phase. When Spanish troops tried to enter Flushing to defend the town against the rebels, the inhabitants started firing at their ships and took one Spanish captain, Hernando Pacheco, prisoner. The city had changed sides. In early May, the town of Veere also joined the Revolt.[112]

Around midnight on 6 May a fleet left Bergen-op-Zoom's harbour with some 540 Spanish troops and seven hundred Walloons. The leader of the expedition was Sancho Dávila. It seems that Fadrique de Toledo, who himself was present in the harbour, did not agree with his father regarding Sancho's appointment: "I harbour doubts about his old age and experience in warfare".[113] This seems a strange remark. The commander was 48 years old at the time and very experienced. It may reflect a troublesome relationship between the Duke's son, Fadrique, and Sancho, while we have already seen that Sancho seems to have been very close to the Duke's natural son, Fernando. Sancho, however, speaks highly of Fadrique's military capabilities in a letter to Albornoz: "señor Fadrique is such a good warrior".[114]

The expedition has been recently described in detail by Clasien Rooze-Stouthamer. After disembarking the troops headed for the besieged Middelburg. The Walloons went first, with the Spaniards behind them, as they feared the burghers might not want to let Spanish troops in. Even Sancho himself was dressed as a Walloon. They succeeded in defeating the small rebel army around Middelburg and afterwards they also managed

---

[110] Fagel, *Hispano-Vlaamse wereld*, 107; Dávila to Albornoz, Antwerp citadel, 4 December 1571, AA, C33/54.

[111] A Jerónimo Pardo was one of the major contractors of the Antwerp citadel. Quatrefages, T*ercios* (1979) 58.

[112] Rooze-Stouthamer, *Opmaat*, 101-129.

[113] 'Je me doubte pour son ancien eage et experience au fait de guerre…'. Fadrique de Toledo to Philip of Lannoy, ARAB, Audientie, 486, f. 34, quoted in Rooze-Stouthamer, *Opmaat*, 139.

[114] 'Señor don Fadrique pues es tan bien guerrero'. Dávila to Albornoz, Antwerp, 16 July 1573, AA, C/33, 100.

to conquer the port town of Arnemuiden (Ramua in Spanish sources) after a fierce confrontation resulting in many deaths.[115] Cornejo even mentions the fact that Sancho had wished to continue towards Flushing, but his plans were thwarted by the governor of Zeeland.[116]

In a very long letter Alba informed the King of the "cosas de Holanda y Gelanda", giving the main credit for the expedition's organisation to his son Fadrique. The Duke also wrote about the Walloons and the Spanish troops and how they went "so alike as if they were from the same nation", probably referring to their clothing. According to the Duke, when they had all landed successfully at ten o'clock in the evening, Sancho told the troops that "nobody was to be disobedient in sacking or doing anything else", threatening them with death. Alba informed the King about the plan to put the Walloons in the van "so that those of Middelburg will not be disturbed by seeing Spaniards". However, in this version, the Spanish were essential to the fighting: "slaughtering a large number of them". The Duke also used this letter to praise his beloved Sancho:

> I do not want to leave unsaid to Your Majesty that in all his estates he does not have a better soldier than Sancho Dávila, and as good, only very few… Besides actual fighting, like nobody has ever done, he has good fortune ("fortuna") and therefore I took him out of Antwerp castle for this.

Of course, it all revolved around remuneration: "to reward him and to thank him, for winning a battle over here and serving as he did in the expedition to Frisia [Jemmingen] in which he played a major role, as until now he has not been given any reward".[117] Does this mean that the earlier promises had not materialised yet, or is the Duke exagerrating Sancho's needs?

In a Spanish account from the same day it was clearly Sancho's decision to put the Walloons in the van, and this story can also be found in other reports of the event. One of these even mentioned Sancho as the principal actor in its heading. In this version Sancho also hides the Spaniards including himself "in Walloon dress". On the fighting near Ramua we read about "slaughtering an enormous number of enemies".[118]

---

[115] Rooze-Stouthamer, *Opmaat*, 138-141.
[116] Cornejo, *Sumario*, 150.
[117] Alba to Philip II, Brussels, 23 May 1572, EA III, 112-120.
[118] CD XXXI, 24-29. See also CD LXXV, 44-46 and 50-53 (relación de lo sucedido en Valchrem, por Sancho de Avila, en 6 de mayo de 1572). For another account see AGS, E. 552-599.

The 1713 biographer uses the histories and chronicles of Bentivoglio, Trillo and Mendoza to create a completely different story, including a long speech by Sancho just after landing on the island of Walcheren: "We are going to attack sailors and fishermen, who hardly know the names of the weapons".[119] This narrative, mostly based on Trillo, is almost the complete opposite of the Spanish accounts. In this version Sancho wants to fight and he puts his Spanish troops in the van, and does not warn them to refrain from plunder. Trillo even adds that around Arnemuiden four hundred of the enemy were killed against only twenty wounded on the royal side. The fact that Trillo speaks of German troops fighting together with the Spaniards demonstrates his poor knowledge of the events.[120] We therefore see that the relief of Middelburg has two very different narrative traditions within the Spanish sources: we have the aggressive commander from Trillo and the 1713 biography, and the smart and tactical commander from the reports and Alba's letter. Maybe we should put more faith in the texts written directly after the events which were not meant for publication.

To this can be added that, according to the author of the 1713 biography entitled *El rayo de la guerra*, it is precisely the very quick relief of Middelburg that gave Sancho the reputation of the Lighting Bolt of the war.[121] Poet Pedro de Padilla, describing Sancho's actions in Arnemuiden, specifies that "he massacred three companies of the enemy".[122] Interestingly enough, the victory over Arnemuiden had a very different impact on English public opinion:

> They go about the streets greatly lamenting that in Arnemuiden not only were the men killed after surrendering, but also all the women and children, and this is what the English believe, saying that we are tyrants.[123]

A Spanish manuscript chronicle however explicitly contradicts this version: "in less than one hour more than five hundred rebels died and nobody

---

[119] Dávila y San-Vitores, *Rayo*, 66-69; Quatrefages, *Tercios españoles* (1979), 107, gives part of Sancho's speech from Bentivoglio: 'En el valor militar consistirá el vencer, o el perder…quien ay aquí de nosotros que no aya visto, o hecho alguna acción señalada en tan antigua milicia como la nuestra'. More examples of speeches by Mondragón and Dávila are in Quatrefages, *Idem*, 108-109.

[120] Trillo, *Historia*, 105-106. 800 dead rebels in Arquellada, *Sumario*, 274.

[121] Dávila y San-Vitores, *Rayo*, 68; Martínez Ruiz, 'Sancho', 647.

[122] 'En ellas tres compañías, de enemigos degollava'. Padilla, *Romancero*, 59.

[123] Antonio de Guaras to Alba, London, 18 May 1572, CD XCI, 20.

*Protagonists of War*

was left alive, except the women, children and the clerics who remained in the church".[124] Is this manuscript trying to counter the circulating negative views on the events at Arnemuiden?

A few of Sancho's letters from Arnemuiden are preserved, and they can contribute to reconstructing the situation. The writer says he is not very satisfied with his new place of residence, calling it "a very unhealthy place". Hitherto he had had little experience in the wetter parts of the Low Countries. Sancho shows himself in these letters as a man drawing a clear distinction between good and evil. The Lord of Beauvoir (Babues in his letters), Philip of Lannoy, was highly praised: "he is such a good nobleman, has rendered important services and has upheld this island, and I am very pleased to be his soldier".[125] On the other hand, his opinion of the rebels was quite the opposite: "it is rabble, they use the same type of boats as the indians". On Fadrique he writes positively though quite reservedly to Albornoz: "I think his presence here would be of much relevance", but the comments on Fernando de Toledo seem more personal and might again relate to their shared banquets. Regarding himself he informs Albornoz that "my feet are feeling a little better, as I have not been able to walk for I do not know how many days". The Lighting Bolt of the war had hardly been able to stand on his feet during the events that gave him his heroic nickname. He was by then almost turning fifty.

After this first expedition to Zeeland Sancho returned to his citadel in Antwerp, at least as from early July 1572. He was busy organising the citadel, asking for more men and more artillery. It is striking that from this moment onwards the enemy is almost systematically called "the heretics", unlike by other commanders like Mondragón and Valdés, who generally speak in a more neutral tone of 'the enemy'.[126]

---

[124] 'En menos de una hora murieron de los reveldes mas de 500 y a nadie se perdono la vida. Salvo a las mugeres, niños y a ciertos clerigos que estavan en la iglesia'. 'Libro de las cosas', 22r.

[125] 'Tierra mal sana'; 'Es tan buen caballero y a servido tan prinçipalmente y sustentado esta isla que yo me huelgo mucho de ser su soldado'. Dávila to Alba, Arnemuiden, 16 May 1572, AA, C33/57; Dávila to Albornoz, Arnemuiden, 13 May 1572, AA, C33/55; Dávila to Albornoz, Arnemuiden, 16 May 1572, AA, C33/56.

[126] 'Es una canalla, como indios sirvense destos bersos de nabios'; 'Creo su persona seria de mucha inportançia aquí'; 'Al señor don Hernando tiene aquí tantos papagayos, monos, y perçelanas si bienen de las Indias o honbres que les sirvan con ellas que podra hacer un banquete con las lenguas'; 'Voi sintiendo un puco de mejoria en los pies que no he podido andar no se quantos dias'. Dávila to Alba, Antwerp citadel, 4, 6 and 7 July 1572 and Dávila to Albornoz, 5 July, AA, C/33, 58-61. Granvelle's confidant, Morillon, reported in August that some time before Dávila had had a conflict with those in the city government. Morillon to Granvelle, Brussels, 17 August 1572, CG IV, 375-376.

Antonio Trillo describes that around that time Alba ordered Sancho to help out the besieged city of Goes in Zeeland. In his name Sancho sent his Antwerp Sargento Mayor, Francisco de Salvatierra, with gunpowder and rope for fuses. It was a very difficult undertaking as enemy ships had the island closed off, and "not even a bird could pass". Salvatierra, however, told Sancho he would enter or die, to which Sancho answered, as was quoted literally in the chronicle, "it is not about entering or dying, but about entering or not going". One morning before the end of July, Salvatierra left Bergen-op-Zoom disguised as a fisherman with two sailors and a servant, with the ammunition hidden under straw and fishing nets. Their expedition in disguise proved successful.[127]

Sancho then left with the army for Mons in Hainaut, where the army besieged the city which had taken sides with the rebels led by Count Louis of Nassau. Here again Sancho played a key role as a good practical commander. In the vicinity of Jemappes, Sancho ordered that nobody fire until the enemy was at close range, so no shots would be lost.[128] However, in Trillo's description of the siege of Mons Sancho's role was limited to this brief appearance.

In October 1572 it was Sancho himself who successfully liberated Goes from the siege by the rebels, together with the Colonels Cristóbal de Mondragón and Arrieta. This is the famous crossing through the water that will be discussed in the chapter on Cristóbal de Mondragón. In Sancho's letter to the Duke he described the situation just before the action:

> The Sergeant Major of Colonel Mondragón and a soldier from the castle over here went on a reconnaissance mission, reporting that it was possible to execute the crossing, and for this reason Colonel Mondragón was now leaving in order to arrive at seven in the morning at the crossing where according to the information during low tide it was possible to walk in three hours up to the dykes, taking with him all his men and those of Colonel Arrieta and a company of Germans and a hundred Spaniards coming from elsewhere and from the castle over here, with more than twenty measures [quintales] of gunpowder in three hundred leather bags. Information about the outcome will be sent to Your Excellency

---

[127] Trillo, *Historia*, 119.
[128] Martín García, *Sancho*, 151-152; Trillo, *Historia*, 131, 140; Mendoza, *Comentarios* (1948) 467.

> and if it turns out as hoped, Your Excellency may decide whether they have to go ahead or if they have to return after liberating the island.[129]

Though Mondragón was really the main protagonist of the expedition to relieve Goes, Sancho also received some of the praise. Alba and Albornoz sent him letters of congratulation. Alba even seems to put him before Mondragón; "so much satisfaction as was to be expected with you as the one guiding the relief of Goes".[130] Albornoz showed in his letter that he completely understood Sancho's feelings: "the affairs are going so well that with the help of God, we will soon be able to see each other in Madrid".[131] Within the realm of literature, Sancho is also the central figure in the verses by Pedro de Padilla, and in one other story Sancho plays a specific role at the critical moment when two hundred Walloon soldiers refused to enter the water: "if he had had a gallows at his disposal, he would singlehandedly have hanged these cowards himself".[132] The precise origin of this very cruel quotation, however, remains unclear, but it is certain that the crossing episode had become a fruitful narrative that entered the people's imagination through literature.

That Sancho may have had a strong personality and harsh character can be discerned through other sources. We know that Jean de Hangest, Lord of Genlis, had been taken prisoner at the Battle of Quiévrain on 17 July 1572, and by January 1573 he was in Antwerp in Sancho's custody. In a letter Dávila described how this French Huguenot leader, who had already served Orange in 1568, had bribed a musician in an attempt to escape, and now Sancho wanted to execute this musician for treason, "leaving his head as an example on the scaffold of the castle square". Sancho also wanted Genlis dead, and if he could not be executed for trying to escape, "it is possible to burn him as a heretic, and this

---

[129] 'A rreconozer el sargento mayor del coronel Mondragon y un soldado de aquí del castillo, los quales dizen se puede muy bien pasar para lo qual parte a la ora el coronel Mondragon para estar mañana a las 7 horas en el paso que según la informazion con la baja marea sera camino de 3 horas asta los diques, lleva consigo toda su gente y la del coronel Arrieta y una compania de alemanes y 100 españoles de los que vinieron de fuera y de los de aquí del castillo, llevan mas de 20 quintales de polvora en 300 bolsas de cuero, del subceso se dara aviso a vuestra excelencia y si es bueno como se desea vuestra excelencia mandara aviso si an de pasar adelante o si dejado el socorro en la ysla se bolveran'. Dávila to Alba, Antwerp citadel, 19 October 1572, AA, C/33, 62.
[130] Alba to Dávila, Nijmegen, 27 October 1572, EA, III, 236-237.
[131] Albornoz to Dávila, Nijmegen, 27 October 1572, EA, III, 238.
[132] Rooze-Stouthamer, *Opmaat*, 205-206. See the chapter on Mondragón.

would be of great service to God and to His Majesty".¹³³ Though Sancho wrote that he wanted to send him to the famous prison of Vilvoorde, history has it that he died secretly strangled in his prison cell in Antwerp citadel.¹³⁴ The author of the 1713 biography must have known this dark story as he specifically added about Genlis "that he afterwards died of a disease".¹³⁵ Though existing literature generally does not connect Sancho to this deed, there is no doubt that he must have been the one giving the order. And, given his letter, he must have had no remorse in doing so. However, in July 1573 Sancho had still been unsure about Genlis's future:

> After orders came to take away Genlis's irons, I am left totally confused by the copy of the letter that states not to lengthen his stay in prison ... I think of letting him go, Your Honour should tell me what to do. If the Duke wants him to be put in another room with a guard at his cost, I do not refute that if this is what one wants to give him, this would not be a sad prison, being alone without anybody else, and more, he deserves it, although he says he has returned to being a christian and many other nice words.¹³⁶

Because he was based in Antwerp, the conflict in Zeeland, and especially the preparation of an armada, took up a large part of Sancho's attention.¹³⁷ While Albornoz had his doubts "whether it was convenient to risk this armada", Sancho wrote to him with a firm "if one does not risk, one is not to gain much". In another letter he elaborated on his views:

> If one does not fight, it is impossible to know whose would be the victory, and being the affair of the relief of Walcheren so very important, even though there would be a great risk of losing this

---

¹³³ 'Dexar la cabeça por exemplo en la horca de la plaza del castillo'; 'Se puede quemar por ereje y se hara gran servicio a dios y a su Magestad'. Dávila to Albornoz, Antwerp, 11-17 January 1573, AA, C/33, 64

¹³⁴ Regt, 'Jan van Hangest-Genlis'; Trim, 'Huguenots', 162.

¹³⁵ Dávila y San-Vitores, *Rayo*, 73.

¹³⁶ 'Despues que vino horden para quitar los grillos a Janli, me mata con la copia de la carta diziendo que no se la alarga la prision ... estoy por soltarle, vuestra merced me embie que dezir, si quiere el duque que se le mete en otro aposento con guardia a su costa, yo no niego que si a el le quieren regalar que no es triste prision la que tiene que estar solo sin anima, mas el la mereze aunque dize que se a buelto cristiano y muchas otras buenas palabras'. Dávila to Albornoz, Antwerp, 16 July 1573, AA, C/33, 100.

¹³⁷ For example: Dávila to Albornoz, Antwerp, 31 January 1573, AA, C/33, 68 and Dávila to Alba, Antwerp, 13 January 1573, Idem C/33, 69.

armada, I think that, if one does not try to relieve them, it is as if the armada were lost anyway.[138]

We appreciate the precision in his preparations. He also suggests that it would be good to reward the sailors who wanted to serve in the fleet. In the end he seemed satisfied because though there were not enough sailors available, there were very good Netherlandish and Spanish seamen to serve in the expedition.[139] In another letter he notes that many sailors did not wish to serve and tried to make others do the same.[140] On 14 March Sancho was staying in Saeftinghe, from where he wrote a letter about the problems the ships were facing with getting through.[141]

In April a new fleet had been prepared, "as this relief has to be done because it is so important… I have great faith in God that we will succeed".[142] But this did not mean that he put his trust solely in God. To Alba he explained why he thought they were going to be successful: "Our ships are provided with good weapons and cannons, with good sailors and with many of our warriors".[143] On 12 April Sancho and Mondragón met to discuss the organisation of the troops for the expedition.[144] Four days later everybody was ready; "the people have embarked and we shall leave with the afternoon tide". He really hoped he could do this good service to God and King.[145] On April 17 he was indeed on board a ship,

---

[138] 'Si conviene aventurar esta armada'; 'Si no se aventura mucho no se gana mucho'; 'Si no se conbate, no se puede saber cuya avia de ser la vitoria, y siendo el negoçio de socorrer a Balquem (Walcheren) de tan grande ymportançia, aunque sea de tan grande arrisco el aventurar esta armada, me pareçe que, si no se socorre, la armada es como perdida'. Dávila to Albornoz, Antwerp, 3 February 1573, AA, C/33, 70; Dávila to Alba, Antwerp, 3 February 1573, AA, C/33, 71.

[139] Dávila to Alba, Antwerp, 3 February 1573, AA, C/33, 71.

[140] Dávila to Albornoz, Antwerp, 6 February 1573, AA, C/33, 72. See also: Dávila to Albornoz, Antwerp, 1 and 3 April 1573, AA, C/33, 76-77. According to Granvelle, the sailors did not want to serve 'por el mal tractamento que les hazen Sancho Dávila and Juan Moreno'. Granvelle to Abbé Sagante, Naples, 11 and 15 June 1573, CG IV, 570.

[141] Dávila to Juan Moreno, Saeftinghe (Safetin), 14 March 1573, AA, C/33, 74.

[142] 'Pues este socorro se ha de azer por ymportar tanto… tengo grande esperança en dios del buen subçeso'. Dávila to Albornoz, Antwerp, 9 April 1573, AA, C/33, 83.

[143] 'Llevamos muy bien armados y artillados nuestros navios y con buenos marineros y muchos nuestros guerreros'. Dávila to Alba, Antwerp, 11 April, 1573, AA, C/33, 84.

[144] Dávila to Albornoz, Antwerp, 12 April 1573, AA, C/33, 86.

[145] 'La gente esta embarcada y con la marea de la tarde partiremos'. Dávila to Albornoz, Antwerp, 16 April 1573, AA, C/33, 87.

but it was difficult to navigate, mostly because of the wind: "for the enormous winds… my greatest fear is having the ships colliding, God may guide us".[146]

These expeditions are also described in Trillo's chronicle, and here Sancho clearly appears as the protagonist of the action. One problem was the shallowness of the water, and on another occasion a thick fog prevented Sancho from seeing the enemy fleet. Trillo also describes the intense fighting and the fact that a cannon killed four soldiers, "taking the head of Colonel Arrieta". However, besides the elements, the enemy fleet was also too strong. Trillo presents us with the heroic commander Sancho, who ordered "that everybody follow him and that they either die or destroy the enemy and pass", but also with the experienced commander who was "well aware of what was needed".[147] Alba also defended Sancho in a letter to the King: "he fought for almost three hours with the enemies, and though they had more men, if the wind and the sea had not been against him, he would have passed with the ships of his armada".[148] Alba also wrote to Dávila after receiving the good news, "I have heard about the good results Your Honour had during his journey, and I never doubt that you will always have the same results with everything that Your Honour will undertake".[149]

In April, Sancho's expeditions even reminded the Duke of an event five years earlier: "for having occured in April, and almost on the same day you broke the heads of the rebels at Dahlem".[150] One Spanish unpublished chronicle mentions that by accident Sancho's ship caught fire "and Sancho and sixty soldiers returned home with burned hands and faces".[151] However, this story cannot be found in other chronicles of the period. It could be that these kinds of stories were considered less suitable for publication, since they sometimes presented these heroes in too vulnerable a position. In May the Duke complained about the lack

---

[146] 'Por el grandisimo viento… el mayor temor que tengo es esto del tocar, dios nos guie'. Dávila to Albornoz, on board in Herden, 17 April 1573, AA, C/33, 88; Idem, on board, 18 April 1573, AA, C/33, 89-90.

[147] Trillo, *Historia*, 191-195; Mendoza, *Comentarios* (1948) 493-495; Van Meteren, *Belgische* (1599) 66r. See also the 'Libro de las cosas', 39r.

[148] Alba to Philip II, Nijmegen, 18 March 1573, EA, III.

[149] Alba to Dávila, Nijmegen, 23 April 1573, EA, III, 366.

[150] Alba to Dávila, Nijmegen, 23 April 1573, EA, III, 366. See Idem, 367; 'Libro de las cosas', 40v.

[151] 'Y salio quemado Sancho de Avila con 60 soldados en las caras y manos'. 'Libro de las cosas', 41v.

of letters from Dávila, but then good news must have reached him, as he showed his great satisfaction: "el Duque está contentísimo".[152]

It is in the letters of this period that Sancho consistently started to use the word 'herejes' (heretics) as his most common name for the enemy, although 'rebeldes' is also used.[153] We do not find this early confessionalisation of the conflict in the letters from the other commanders in this book, though Mondragón also used the word 'heretics' around the time he was in Antwerp with Sancho. It is remarkable that Sancho also uses the word 'amigo' more often than the other commanders,[154] suggesting that Sancho was apparently a man who divided the world into friends and foes. However, it is also possible that Sancho possessed a more religious outlook on the conflict, maybe related to the fact that he may have started his career with a religious vocation. This would fit the image the two biographers from his family wished to present, clearly depicting him as a Catholic hero fighting heresy, together with the Jesuits and the inspiring Teresa de Ávila.

One of the friends who appeared in the letters of this period was Antonio del Río, again a member of the Spanish merchant elite in the Low Countries, writing to him from Bruges on matters related to the war in Zeeland.[155] Sancho tried to help him become the new commissioner of the confiscated goods. He started by pleading with Albornoz that "I do not have the wherewithal to pay those who show me their friendship", and that only favours from the secretary could help him out. Del Río was "a person who merited so much and whose wishes were so deserved… a trustworthy person". This he further explains by stating that "though he is Spanish, he understands the language of this country". Hernando de Frías, who would also plead for his appointment, was also a friend of

---

[152] Albornoz to Dávila, Nijmegen, 11 May 1573, EA III, 392. See also Alba to the Duke of Savoye, Nijmegen, 6 May 1573, EA III, 388, and Alba to Dávila, Nijmegen, 10 and 18 June, 1573, EA III, 433-434, 444. Mondoucet to the French King, Nijmegen, 3 May 1573, Mondoucet, *Lettres*, I, 252. About the relative success of the expedition, see CP II, 356.

[153] Dávila to Alba, Antwerp, 3 February 1573, AA, C/33, 71. For example also in Dávila to Albornoz, Antwerp, 4 April 1573, AA, C/33, 78, and Dávila to Albornoz, Antwerp, 9 April 1573, AA, C/33, 83.

[154] For example, Dávila to Albornoz, Antwerp, 1 April 1573, AA, C/33, 76. 'El buen amigo el coronel Mondragón'. Dávila to Albornoz, Antwerp, 15 November 1573, AA, C/33, 107.

[155] Dávila to Albornoz, Antwerp, 5 April 1573, AA, C/33, 79. Albornoz to Dávila, Nijmegen, 9 April 1573, EA, III, 320.

Del Río's, "amigo suyo".¹⁵⁶ Antonio del Río, Lord of Cleydael, would in 1573 indeed become the new commissioner of the confiscations. In later years, rebels would destroy his castle and he would lose everything, going to Spain where he died in 1586 as councillor to Philip II. His son, Martín Antonio del Río, would occupy important positions in the Habsburg government. He would later become a Jesuit and author a chronicle on the Revolt. Martín Antonio was also a friend of Justus Lipsius and connected to humanists in the Low Countries.¹⁵⁷

In June there was a female visitor in the citadel, simply called doña Juana in the letters to secretary Albornoz:¹⁵⁸

> My lady doña Juana has stayed in the house of Fernando de Sevilla, so well attended by his wife and his children as possible. The day before yesterday she came to the castle at lunchtime without informing both me and Mondragón though we were serving the table. I asked her to stay in this house anywhere she wanted, as there are sufficient rooms. However, she decided to go to a house over here in the citadel, situated above the gate by the river. I think she will feel very alone there, though she has with her Hernández [?] who is so elegant and beautiful that it is a pleasure seeing her. Thank God that my lady doña Juana is recovering her health.¹⁵⁹

---

¹⁵⁶ 'Yo no tengo con que pagar a los que me hacen amistad'; 'Persona que mereze tanto y sus prentensiones tan justas.... Un hombre de confiança'; 'Aunque es español se le entiende la lengua deste país'. Dávila to Albornoz, Antwerp, 7 July 1573, AA, C/33, 97.

¹⁵⁷ Fagel, 'Es buen católico', 303; Del Río, *Crónica*.

¹⁵⁸ Dávila to unknown [Albornoz], Antwerp, 27 June 1573, AA, C/33, 93. Earlier references to her: Dávila to Albornoz, Antwerp citadel, 21 November 1571, AA, C/33, 53: 'Damas españolas son rrecatadas... damas y en tierra agena es cosa lleballes la condicion'.

¹⁵⁹ 'Mi señora doña Juana ha estado en casa de Fernando de Sevilla tan acariciada y regalada y de su mujer y hijas quanto es posible. Antier se bino aquí al castillo a ora de comer sin hazernos saber nada a Mondragón y a mi que estan al servicio a la tabla. Yo le suplique se quedase en esta casa pues ay artos aposentos de la manera que los quisiese, no a querido sino yrse a una casa que esta aquí en la ciudadela sobre la puerta del rio. Creo estará muy sola aunque tiene consigo a Hernandez que esta tan galana y hermosa que es una envidia de verla. Parezeme bendito dios que mi señora doña Juana ba recobrandose de salud'. Dávila to unknown [Albornoz?], Antwerp, 27 June 1573, AA, C/33, 93. Fernando de Sevilla was an important Andalusian merchant in Antwerp, born in the Low Countries. He had contacts with Alba but was also a friend of the Protestant merchants Marcos Pérez and Martín López. According to Jerónimo de Curiel, Sevilla sympathised with the Calvinists. Vázquez de Prada, *Lettres marchandes*, I, 226.

On the feast of Santiago [25 July] doña Juana was still around: "my lady Juana is alternating good and bad days".[160] Sancho was writing here to Albornoz about Albornoz's own sister and the wife of Sancho's cousin, Rodrigo Orejón, his lieutenant in 1566 and during the Revolt the *castellano* of the important citadel of Valenciennes. Juana Albornoz had lived in Antwerp since 1571 and had fallen ill there. She refused to use the medicine prescribed by the famous humanist Benito Arias Montano and did not keep to her bed. By the end of August she had left for Spain, to die that very same year in Valencia.[161] Not only did Sancho have his network of Spanish military commanders and Spanish merchants, but he even had his contacts in the Duke's intimate circle through his personal secretary.

The news that Haarlem had been won by the royal army in July 1573 makes Sancho dream about the complete surrender of the County of Holland: "Haarlem is now ours, with God's help, with more time and money, all of Holland will be ours.... I wish this war to be over now". [162] It is possible that Alba then asked Dávila to join him in Utrecht, as suggested by a letter from the Duke.[163] From a letter by Albornoz, written in September from Amsterdam, it seems Dávila was indeed with him at that time.[164]

In October 1573 we find Dávila in the city of Breda, where he had arrived with troops and artillery on 5 October.[165] However, he returned to Antwerp before the end of the month. In between, Sancho was involved in the attack on the castle of Oosterhout and the town of Geertruidenberg. The eighty defenders of the castle tried to flee during the night, but at dawn Sancho's cavalry reached them "and cut them all to pieces, without anybody escaping". During the fighting at Geertuidenberg "a good horse on which Sancho Dávila was fighting was wounded and died".[166] It seems obvious that Sancho was not a commander

---

[160] 'Mi senóra Juana esta como suele un dia buena y otro malo'. Dávila to Albornoz, Antwerp, 25 July 1573, AA, C/33, 102.
[161] Huisman, 'Serviele secretaris', 23-24.
[162] 'Arlen ya por nosotros, plegue a dios con mas costa y tiempo lo seamos de toda Olanda... Deseo ber ya acavada esta guerra'. Dávila to Albornoz, Antwerp, 16 July 1573, AA, C/33, 100.
[163] Alba to Dávila, Utrecht, 27 July 1573, Pando Fernández de Pinedo, *Vida*, 155.
[164] Albornoz to Juan Moreno, Amsterdam, 15 September 1573, EA, III, 521-522.
[165] Dávila to Juan Moreno, Breda, 6 October 1573, AA, C/33, 104; Dávila to Alba, Breda, 12 October 1573, AA, C/33, 105.
[166] Trillo, *Historia*, 217.

who passively looked on at the fighting from a distance. A good friend to have, but a terrible enemy to fear, especially for those he considered to be rebellious heretics.

## An Albista under Luis de Requesens (1574)

By the end of the year the Duke of Alba was leaving the Low Countries and Luis de Requesens (1528-1576), Grand Commander [Comendador Mayor] of the Order of Santiago, would take over as the new Governor-general. He was the son of Juan de Zúñiga, former tutor to the young Philip II. It was the last opportunity for the military commanders to secure benefices from the old Duke and hopefully a passport to return with him to Spain, while at the same time the Duke himself was busy trying to convince them to remain in the Low Countries. In early December 1573 Alba wrote a long letter to Philip II in which he criticised the King for his treatment of Sancho, "who is very dissatisfied seeing that after so many years of service, Your Majesty has not given him any rewards, not even ordered to write to him". Alba is clear in his opinion of Sancho: "Your Majesty has in these estates not one soldier like this one".[167] Again the question is whether the Duke was exaggerating Sancho's needs in order to support his demands.

Sancho accompanied the Duke all the way to Namur in the south, and on 23 December he wrote a letter to Albornoz, who almost certainly was also present in the same city, beginning directly with an open and frank "the rewards Your Honour has to make me in Spain, with God's help".[168] As the governorship of Antwerp was a very difficult position, complicated by the officials of the city government and the presence of many heretics, if the King wanted him to continue "he has to give me a very good reward of a continuous rent and raise my salary". He seemed to understand that a knightly order would be a difficult reward to achieve, also suggesting the governorship of the castle of Milan,[169] but otherwise leaving it to Albornoz to consider what was best for him. Sancho then reminded him of all the actions in which he had risked his own life:

---

[167] Alba to Philip II, Brussels, 2 December 1573, EA, III, 563.

[168] Alba was present in Namur at least between 22 and 26 December, EA, III, 567-569; 'La merçed que vuestra merced me ha de haçer en España con ayuda de dios'; Me ha de haçer mui buena merçed de rrenta perpetua y creçerme el sueldo'. Dávila to Albornoz, Namur, 23 December 1573, AA, C/33, 108.

[169] He must have asked Albornoz earlier for this post in Milan. The Duke's secretary, however, had informed Dávila that he had not received news that the former castellano had died. Albornoz to Dávila, Amsterdam, 22 October 1573, EA III, 534.

> en la rrota de Dalem (Dahlem)
> y la de Frisa del conde Ludovico (Jemmingen)
> y en la escaramuça de la Yasa (river Gete; in Walloon: Djaçe)
> y en el socorro de Guelandia (Zelanda)
> de Bergas (Bergen-op-Zoom)
> y en los de Anberes (Antwerp)
> a Balquem (Walcheren)
> y en la escaramuça sobre Mos (Mons)
> y en la rrota de la corneta de herreruelos sobre Santibitinbergue (Geertruidenberg)
> y la toma del castillo de Hostraat (Oosterhout; not Hoogstraten).

And, of course, he had also served when his life had not been in danger, as he had been a soldier for thirty years. And he wanted to have permission to go to Spain.[170] Did Sancho in Namur still try to join the Duke in his return to Spain? It is more than likely. Alba had to write explicitly to Requesens to inform his successor that he had sent Dávila back from Namur to serve the new governor.[171]

Sancho was indeed right about the influence the change of governor would have on his career. For example, already by the end of January he was complaining that everybody else had received letters from Albornoz except him, though "nobody would be more happy with your letters than I would".[172] But of course he now received letters from Requesens.[173]

During Requesens's first months in office another naval attempt was undertaken to lift the siege of Middelburg, with Sancho as the admiral of one of the relief fleets, the other one under Julián Romero. However, hardly any of Sancho's letters from this period are preserved and more attention to this expedition has already been given in the chapter on Julián Romero. In a letter Requesens explained why he had chosen Sancho:

---

[170] See also 'No quiero sino yrme a España, y si su merced no me hiçiere mas merçed que pagarme mi sueldo me yre mui contento'. Dávila to Alba, Maastricht, 26 March 1574, AA, C/33, 110.

[171] Alba to Requesens, Namur, 22 December 1573, EA, III, 567; Dávila to Albornoz, Antwerp, 22 January 1574, AA, C/33, 113.

[172] 'Nadie ternia mas contento con sus cartas que yo'. Dávila to Albornoz, Maastricht, 31 March 1574, AA, C/33, 111.

[173] 29 letters from Requesens to Sancho between 27 January and 25 July 1574, NCD I-IV.

"although he is not a sailor, he is a smart soldier with much courage and he has gone several times on these armadas".[174]

The day before boarding his ship for this naval expedition, hoping to help out the besieged Cristóbal de Mondragón, Sancho was realistic about his own chances: "I don't think we can relieve them, but we can divert the enemies by going to fight against them close to Flushing, so the ships that are loaded here can go from Bergen-op-Zoom to take the relief goods".[175] He even feared for his life and used a well-known expression to hide his emotions, thus revealing his philosophy: "a jug that often goes to the well will break its handle or spill the water".[176] He also hoped his return to Spain was getting closer: "if this war ends, and I think this will be soon, with God's help, because if they do not surrender to us, I think soon by force we will surrender to them".[177] It is interesting to see that one of the most martial of all Spanish commanders in the Low Countries could imagine defeat. Julián's expedition resulted in disaster, and this also forced Sancho to return to Antwerp, but not without losing his main ship which got stuck in the sand.[178]

The new government literally knocked at his door, as councillor Gerónimo de Roda came to visit him to discuss Albornoz's position. Sancho directly explained to Roda "la amistad" he had with Albornoz. It seems that the conversation dealt with accusations of theft, but Sancho defended his old friend as a good servant of the King. He accused others of "finding faults in everything from the past". In Spain Albornoz was imprisoned, but in the end all charges of corruption were dropped.[179] He would inform Requesens about "the truth and the dirty tricks". At this time Sancho was still very positive about the new governor:

---

[174] Dávila to Albornoz, Antwerp, 14 January 1574, AA, C/33, 109. 'Aunque no sea marinero, es muy cuerdo soldado y de mucho ánimo y ha ido algunas veces en estas armadas'. Requesens to Francisco Montesdoca, January 1574, AGS, E. 557, 57, quoted in Martín García, *Sancho*, 168-169.

[175] 'No me pareze que podremos meter socorro sino devertir los enemigos yendo a pelear con ellos junto a Fregelingas para que carguen aca con algunos navios para que los que ban por Verghas puedan hazer el socorro'. Dávila to Albornoz, Antwerp, 22 January 1574, AA, C/33, 113.

[176] Idem, 'Cantarillo que muchas vezes ba a la fuente, se rompe el asa o se vierte'.

[177] Idem, 'Si esta guerra se acava que creo sera presto con ayuda de dios porque si ellos no se rinden a nosotros presto creo sera fuerza nos rindamos a ellos'.

[178] Morillon to Granvelle, Brussels, 1 February 1574, CG V, 20.

[179] Parker, 'Corruption', 153-154, 158.

> The lord Comendador Mayor [Requesens] rewards me much and I almost think he wants to reward me even more in secret, as he understands that there are many who do not like me. Until now he shows great worship for the affairs of the Duke [Alba].[180]

Sancho also reflected on the future: "if the King would not give more to my children than to me; if God gives me glory this would mean more than anything". Does the use of the plural form regarding his progeny imply that young Fernando had siblings, as Sancho could never have lied about this to somebody like Albornoz who knew him so well? Furthermore, as we have seen, they were even family, as Sancho's cousin, Rodrigo Orejón, the *castellano* of Valenciennes, was Albornoz's brother-in-law.[181] Or is he simply speaking in general terms and maybe thinking of future offspring?

At the beginning of March 1574 Sancho headed for the surroundings of Maastricht. Trillo informs us in his chronicle that Sancho had been appointed Captain-general of the whole army that would be gathered there to stop the new invasion from Germany. According to the French ambassador, a first attack by Sancho on the enemy camp had ended in disaster, with three captains dead and between three and four hundred dead soldiers.[182] Trillo, however, attempts to portray Sancho as victorious during these confrontations.[183] By the end of March Sancho was still stationed in Maastricht, where he happened to be involved in an 'encamisada' in the village of Meerssen, "killing more than four hundred men". He even gave an evaluation of his own position in a letter:

---

[180] 'Poner defeto en todo lo pasado'; 'La verdad y bellequeria'; 'El señor comendador mayor me haçe mucha merçed y casi conosco que tiene boluntad de haçer mas en lo secreto si no que le debe de pareçer que debe de aver muchos que me quieren mal, muestra asta aora tener en gran beneración las cosas del duque'. Dávila to Albornoz, Antwerp, 14 January 1574, AA, C/33, 109.

[181] 'Si no diere mas el rrey a mis hijos que a mi si dios me da gloria bale mas que todo'. Dávila to Albornoz, Antwerp, 22 January 1574, AA, C/33, 113. Juana de Albornoz had married Rodrigo Orejón, and she came to Antwerp in 1571 with her mother, Elvira. Elvira resided in a convent in Antwerp. Huisman, 'Serviele secretaris', 23-24; Morillon to Granvelle, Brussels, 25 May 1572, CG IV, 228.

[182] Mondoucet to the French King, Antwerp, 15 March 1574, Mondoucet, *Lettres* II, 146; Requesens to Gaspar Gómez, 5 March 1574, NCD I, 294. According to Bernardino de Mendoza, who was present at Maastricht, Sancho had already arrived on 3 March 1574. Mendoza, *Comentarios* (1948) 507.

[183] Trillo, *Historia*, 230-231.

> In affairs of such importance I wanted to govern myself as a captain of Venetians, because it is certain that all of us here seem to be men of republics, because although I am the eldest here, until now there is not a better one.[184]

Sancho knew with certainty that a battle was approaching: "we could go and attack these heretics and I thought that with God's help we could break them... our soldiers are good-spirited and the heretics are very fearful". [185] The same martial tone can be detected in Trillo's chronicle: "General Sancho Dávila always had a great desire to battle with the Count of Nassau". Here, the reality of the letters coincides perfectly with the tone of the chronicler. Even Requesens lost his mostly reserved tone: "it was a good occasion to break the heads of these villains", further speaking of "breaking these heretics".[186] Maybe Requesens knew that Sancho had a preference for the word 'heretics', and used it accordingly.

## The Battle of Mookerheyde (1574)

Bernardino de Mendoza, captain of light cavalry, belonged to Sancho's impressive army that had to thwart the invasion from Germany under Count Louis of Nassau, together with Maestres de campo like Gonzalo de Bracamonte and Fernando de Toledo, and other experienced commanders such as Cristóbal de Mondragón.[187] Maestre de campo Francisco de Valdés was still on his way from Leiden. The royal army crossed the Maas looking for the enemy. Eyewitness and participant Bernardino de Mendoza has left us a detailed description of the events, in which Sancho clearly comes to the fore as the main commander of the army taking all the important decisions, and Bernardino himself, present in the third person, as one of the main protagonists of the battle in his role as commander of the cavalry. On 14 April the rebel army lost 2,500 men, "according to what

---

[184] 'En cosas de tanto peso yo me querria gobernar de mi parte como capitan de beneçianos porque çierto los que aquí estamos pareçemos honbres de rrepublica porque aunque yo estoi aquí como mas viejo asta aora no ai otra majoria declarada'. Dávila to Alba, Maastricht, 26 March 1574, AA, C/33, 110.

[185] 'Se podria salir a estos herejes y que me pareçia que con ayuda de dios los rromperiamos... Los soldados nuestros entiendo que estan con mui buen animo y los herejes mui medrosos'. Dávila to Albornoz, Maastricht, 31 March 1574, AA, C/33, 111.

[186] Requesens to Dávila, 29 March and 5 April 1574, NCD II, 60-62, 101-103. Also letters from 12 April, Idem, 154-155.

[187] Requesens to Vitelli, 5 April 1574, NCD II, 99-101; Requesens to Dávila, 5 April 1574, Idem, 101-103.

the villagers said, without counting those who remained at the battlefield and those who drowned".[188] The royal army took some thirty banners, with only about forty deaths and over a hundred wounded. Interestingly, Bernardino in his chronicle praised Louis of Nassau and the other enemy commanders as "valiant noblemen (caballeros)" and as "good soldiers and captains".[189] The tone of the learned nobleman Mendoza's chronicle is again quite different from Trillo's much more aggressive texts.[190]

Trillo calls him "the very brave Sancho Dávila", and his excellent tactics were "extremely prudent (prudentíssima), ... copying the ancient Romans. In this Sancho Dávila there was so much valour and military prudence that among all the nations he was seen as a very important captain".[191] In Trillo's chronicle, Sancho decided that some German prisoners were not to be killed but instead gave them some money after making them swear they would not serve Orange for the next two years. Compared to the mostly strategic comments on the battle from Mendoza, we find more small details in Trillo's description, like the story of a wounded soldier asking a barber to cut off his arm, offering him his own dagger. They buried the arm and after six hours of bleeding he was cured. In Trillo's history the ordinary soldiers were also heroes.

The Battle of Mookerheyde was international front-page news, and many pamphlets on the events in German, Spanish, French and Italian flew off the printing presses.[192] In the French version Sancho even made it into the title of the publication, while in the others only the defeated Louis of Nassau was prominently mentioned. While both the Italian and the French texts agree on the number of deaths on the rebel side (five thousand infantry and 1,500 cavalry) and on the fact that Louis had escaped alive, information which was not at all accurate, they differ greatly in style. The pamphlet in French is strongly religious and dedicates most pages to voicing a Catholic vision of the situation in the Low Countries. Sancho is praised as "accort et vaillant", and the text even precisely records the places where Louis was hit (ribs; thigh). This text was written in Antwerp on 18 April 1574. On the other hand,

---

[188] Mendoza, *Comentarios* (1948) 509-513.
[189] Mendoza, *Comentarios*, 512.
[190] Rodríguez Pérez, *Dutch Revolt*, 70.
[191] Trillo, *Historia*, 237-244. See also Padilla, *Romancero*, 91-92; Cornejo, *Sumario*, 198; Herrera y Tordesillas, *Historia*, I, 573.
[192] *Relación*; *Discours*; *Vera relatione*; French translation of the Spanish account: CP III, 51-53; *Newe Zeitung*.

the Italian pamphlet is much more military in its content, mentioning the names of all important commanders, including Mondragón and Bernardino de Mendoza. Nothing special is mentioned about Sancho, and Requesens is seen as the great victor. This text was written in Brussels on 17 April. The title of the Spanish pamphlet reveals that it is closely related to the Italian one.[193] Finally, the short German *Newe Zeitung* was clearly supporting Louis of Nassau, mentioning nine hundred deaths, but adding that this was "without [counting] the women and the small children, that were pierced by the Spaniards who miserably killed them in the relief train of the army".[194]

Looking at other sorts of sources we encounter different echoes. The French secretary of Louis of Nassau, for instance, described Sancho as a "bon cappitain" who at the battle "was resolved to prefer dying to failing".[195] The tone of a published pamphlet and a letter could therefore strongly diverge in their message, even if they came from the same side of the conflict: a valiant enemy did not fit the pamphlet, but emphasising the cruel deeds of the Spaniards did. Interestingly, a more nuanced military author such as Mendoza found it unproblematic to praise Louis of Nassau in his published chronicle.

The victory of Mookerheyde has in subsequent centuries generated an important memory culture in both Spain and the Netherlands. Many of the banners, among them the banner of Count Louis of Nassau, would end up in the central chapel of the church of John the Baptist in Ávila, where Sancho and his descendants would be buried, and some of these banners remained there until the War of the Spanish Succession (1700-1714). The mast of Louis of Nassau's banner was still in the possession of the Marquis of Miraflores when he wrote his book in 1857, together with parts of his armour and paintings of Sancho and his family members.[196] Both the paintings and a piece of the mast of Nassau's banner still remain in the possession of Sancho's descendants.[197] Among the spoils of war, there was also William of Orange's command baton, which he had given to his brother Louis. This baton entered the estate of Luis de Requesens and has recently been discovered among the Jesuits of San Cugat, who in 2017 handed it over to the King of the Netherlands, to be displayed

---

[193] See also: Mondoucet to the French King, Brussels, 17 April 1574, Mondoucet, *Lettres*, II, 171-177.
[194] L'Agarge, *Blokkade*, 27.
[195] Huguerye, *Mémoires*, I, 220, 232.
[196] Pando Fernández de Pinedo, *Vida*, 172.
[197] Fagel, *Cristóbal*, 50.

in the Dutch National Military Museum, though the baton remains the property of the regional government of Catalonia.[198]

In the nineteenth century a fierce debate on the commemoration of the Battle of Mookerheyde emerged in the Low Countries. It was the period of Catholic emancipation, and several Catholic authors from the eastern regions of the country refused to see the battle according to the Protestant and Hollandocentric vision of the war in which the Nassau brothers were considered national heroes defending the patria. Local historians, such as Catholic priest Meulleners, disagreed in their articles with the views of eminent academic professors such as Robert Fruin and P.J. Blok. In 1891 a commemorative plaque was unveiled, attached to the wall of a Protestant church in Heumen, a village within the province of Gelderland, as those from the adjacent province of Limburg did not want to participate in the celebrations. Maastricht city archivist and historian H.H.E. Wouters attempted to bridge the divide during a speech in Mook at the 1974 commemoration, but there is still even today a large gap between the understanding of the war in the often Catholic regions of the south-eastern parts of the country and the dominant Hollandocentric and Protestant master narrative, a historiographical dichotomy that also resurfaced during the commemorations of the beginning of the Eighty Years' War in 2018.[199]

In the context of historical reevaluation an educational programme for schoolchildren has recently been developed to provide a better understanding of the Battle of Mookerheyde. In this manner Dutch children may learn about Sancho's 'trick', leaving his trumpeters and drummers on a small island in the river. At night they started making lots of noise, depriving the rebel troops of sleep, but also leaving them unaware of the real location of the royal troops. In Mendoza's words, "soldiers that everywhere and all the time were restlessly sounding the call to arms, both on the river in small boats and on the other side".[200] Gasparus de L'Agarge, possibly the chaplain of the Lord of Hierges, has left a description of the battle in which he highlights the great deeds of his lord, but also mentions the remarkable noise-making, as the Spaniards were "cunning as ever".[201]

---

[198] Punt and Sloot, *Willem*, 154-156.

[199] Meulleners, 'Slag'; Blok, 'Slag; Wouters, 'Beschouwingen'; Van der Ham, *80 jaar*; Documentary series '80 jaar oorlog. De geboorte van Nederland 1568-1648' (NTR 2018).

[200] https://www.huystemoock.nl/nl/verhalen-2/lespakket-slag-op-de-mookerheide (accessed 16 April 2019); Mendoza, *Comentarios* (1948) 510.

[201] L'Agarge, B*lokkade*, 21.

Close to the scene of the battle (in Bisselt) there are roads called Mendozaweg, Mondragonweg and Avilaweg, named after three of the Spanish commanders involved in the battle. Nonetheless, Sancho remains quite unknown within the Dutch context. A Dutch author who recently wrote a long article on the battle failed even to mention Sancho's name, as Mookerheyde is mostly seen in Dutch historiography as the battle of the Nassau brothers. However, there is also a recently published Dutch historical novel on Mookerheyde in which Sancho is described as a very experienced commander who was a hero and celebrity in his own country because of his victories. According to this book, Sancho had not dared to start the battle until he knew reinforcements were on their way, and he outsmarted Louis of Nassau on the battlefield.[202] Such positive descriptions of a Spanish commander against the backdrop of the Revolt in the Low Countries are not obvious for most Dutch authors, since the Black Legend narrative still plays a role in perpetuating historical stereotypes.

The victory at Mookerheyde would, however, become a bittersweet one, as the soldiers would start a mutiny directly afterwards. In the long letter Sancho sent to Requesens on 14 April he still told him just about the victory, describing the heroic deeds of his men and of the most important officers. He also reported on the death and wounded: "We have only a few dead and wounded men, though it still weights heavily for concerning such good soldiers".[203] Three days later, Requesens forwarded this letter to the King together with one of his own: "I hope this [victory] offers the occasion and the start of a different way of managing the affairs of these states, completely different from the way it has been proceding until now".[204] Requesens expressed his hope for a decisive change, and he had wished to continue attacking the enemy. However, then the tone of Requesens's letter changed completely, as he had to inform the King that "the Spaniards present at this battle have done what they had said they would do, that is starting a mutiny, only a few hours after the victory".[205]

Requesens's letter to Philip II was successful as the King would reward Sancho with an annual income of two thousand florins from the confiscated goods. He would also be sent the official papers of his

---

[202] 't Hart, 'Slag'; Nicolasen, *Geuzendochter*, 108, 112, 140-143, 148, 200.
[203] Dávila to Requesens, Hemes [Heumen], 14 April 1574, CD XXX, 453-455; AGS E. 557, 120; González de León, *Road* (2009) 1-2.
[204] Requesens to Philip II, Brussels, 17 April 1574, CD XXX, 455-460.
[205] Requesens to Maestre de campo Fernando de Toledo, 22 April 1574, NCD II, 176-177.

position as *castellano* of Antwerp citadel as he would now finally receive this office in full possession.[206] Royal secretary Zayas also congratulated him on the victory a few days later.[207] Sancho had to wait much longer for a letter of congratulation from Alba, as it took the Duke until July of that year to write to him. As an excuse he used his indispositions, which had been manifold and very heavy, but he noted that he always loved reading his letters and that his happiness was great regarding the Battle of Mookerheyde:

> I may say that I have raised you all at my breast, and especially Your Honour as we have been walking together for many years in this office, and so they have congratulated me for your exploits, and for a good reason, as nobody deserves this more than me.[208]

## The great mutiny (1574)

The story of the mutiny would overshadow Sancho's heroic victory at Mookerheyde. Mendoza informs us how Sancho spoke to the mutineers directly the morning after the mutiny:

> Sancho Dávila addressed them, saying what an ugly thing they were trying to do, and that they should see that with it they obscured the honour that their nation had received the day before and that they cut the thread of the victories and exploits that were expected of them, eradicating the rebels from the states.[209]

The mutiny took the glory of the victory away: "I am shocked that they so voluntarily wish to lose the fruits and the honour of the victory", wrote

---

[206] Philip II to Dávila, Aranjuez, 12 May 1574, quoted in Pando Fernández de Pinedo, *Vida*, 173; Dávila, *Memorial*. Philip II to Requesens, Aranjuez, 12 June 1574, Dávila, *Memorial*; Domingo de Zavala, Antwerp, 24 January 1575, Dávila, *Memorial*. Already on 10 April, four days before the battle, it was clear that the soldiers were close to mutiny: Requesens to Dávila, 10 April 1574 and Requesens to Gonzalo de Bracamonte, 10 April 1574, NCD II, 139-143; Requesens to Dávila, 20 April 1574, NCD II, 173.

[207] Zayas to Dávila, Madrid, 20 May 1574, Dávila, *Memorial*.

[208] 'Puedo decir que os he criado á mis pechos, y especialmente vuestra merced que ha tantos años que andamos juntos en este oficio, y asi me han dado la enhorabuena de vuestros sucesos, y con mucha razon, pues á nadie se le puede dar mejor que á mí'. Alba to Dávila, Cerrada, 18 August 1574, quoted in Pando Fernández de Pinedo, *Vida*, 176-177.

[209] Mendoza, *Comentarios* (1948) 513; Trillo, *Historia*, 244-245.

Requesens to Sancho.²¹⁰ Requesens explained that he had always paid his troops well, but now there was no money left: "I am Spanish, and I love and appraise my nation so much, as all those who were born in Spain, and the more I suffer for giving others a reason for undervaluing us". He would forgive the mutineers without any punishment, and even offered "his silver and the jewels from his house, leaving me with nothing, and I would even hand them my own person".

On 22 April Sancho arrived from Mookerheyde at Antwerp's city gate with a company of cavalry. Those of the city let only Sancho's servants enter and not the soldiers, until they had received orders from Governor Champagney to let them in. However, before Champagney arrived, Sancho had already entered with all of his men through the citadel, which had its own outside gate, "sounding the trumpets and dragging along the banners they had won at Mookerheyde".²¹¹ Champagney and Dávila found themselves now clearly on two opposing sides, though both serving the interests of the King: "it was heard that there had been a conflict or hate between the castellan and Champagney, and it is to be feared that the burghers will have to suffer the consequences".²¹² Morillon also informed Granvelle of another story that was going round Antwerp: "it is said that Sancho Dávila had promised to allow them [the mutineers] to enter [the city of Antwerp] and to pay them after they had beaten the enemy".²¹³ Also, according to Antwerp chronicler Van Haecht, Sancho had promised the soldiers before the battle that they would be paid in full.²¹⁴ Months later, Morillon would even turn Sancho into the cause of everything: "Sancho Dávila, the real source of the mutiny, having personally brought the soldiers to Antwerp".²¹⁵

At the end of April Dávila wrote a letter about Mookerheyde to his old master, the Duke of Alba, but it was all about the mutiny. He explained how the mutineers had entered the city of Antwerp and "stuck to the wall until the junction with the castle". Dávila was critical of the mutineers in his letter to Alba since they had entered while Requesens was in the city, but he remarked that he still thought they were behaving decently: "until now they have not created more disorder". Because Requesens

---

²¹⁰ Requesens to Dávila, Brussels, 20 April 1574, CD XXX, 460-464, AGS E. 557, 127.
²¹¹ Champagney to Philip II (copy), 28 April 1574, CD XXX, 465-484.
²¹² Van Haecht, *Kroniek*, II, 295-296.
²¹³ Morillon to Granvelle, Brussels, 1-3 May 1574, CG V, 82. The same idea can be found in a rebel song on the mutiny in which Sancho is called Seignor Daniel. *Nederlandsche geschiedzangen*, II, 121, 123.
²¹⁴ Van Haecht, *Kroniek*, II, 294.
²¹⁵ Morillon to Granvelle, Brussels, 19 July 1574, CG V, 160.

did not have enough experienced men around him, "it is not possible he [Requesens] is without confusion".²¹⁶ No doubt he was accusing Champagney, but he did not mention him explicitly.

The very same day he wrote a much longer, and much more personal, letter to Albornoz, now directly attacking Champagney and criticising Requesens's strategy: "He is so inclined to comply with Champagney that even the other day when he came from Brussels, though I [Sancho] had not kissed his hands after the journey [Mookerheyde] I did not succeed in doing so, and at the quay where he disembarked he did not speak a word to me, but only slightly removed his hat".²¹⁷ This moment must have certainly hurt Sancho. The hero of Mookerheyde had just returned from his victory and his Governor-general did not receive him with the necessary honours: "the lord Commander [Requesens] knows how he [Champagney] really is, but for some reason he has to treat him with kid gloves".²¹⁸ In a letter to Champagney Requesens, however, made clear that refusing Dávila entry into the city had been a huge mistake and that the men responsible had to be punished.²¹⁹ It shows the difficult position Requesens was in, trying to placate both Champagney and Sancho Dávila.

Champagney wanted to use force against the mutineers, while Sancho tried to avoid any violence: "he [Champagney] wanted to take some cannons from the armada and put them on the wall against the soldiers. To this I replied that it would not be a bad thing to remove the cannons that were facing the Prince [Orange] and put them facing the Spaniards". This is the most sarcastic remark to be found in Sancho's correspondence with Albornoz. Sancho also told Alba's secretary the story about Champagney refusing him entry to the city.²²⁰ And while he still

---

²¹⁶ 'Pegados a la muralla hasta la junta del castillo'; 'Hasta agora no ayan echo mas deshorden'; 'no puede dejar de allarse en algunas confusiones'. Dávila to Alba, Antwerp citadel, 26 April 1574, AA, C/33, 112; Morillon to Granvelle, Brussels, 1-3 May 1574, CG V, 83.

²¹⁷ 'Es tan amigo de complaçer a Champani que aun esotro dia quando vino de Bruselas no le aviendo besado las manos despues de la jornada llegando a besarselas. Alli al pasage donde se desembarcava no me hablo palabra sino solo quitarse un poco el sombrero'. Dávila to Albornoz, Antwerp, 26 April 1574, AA, C/33, 114.

²¹⁸ Idem, 'el señor Comendador [Requesens] le conoçe y le tiene por el que es, sino que debe de ir con contemplaçiones con el por algunos respetos'.

²¹⁹ Requesens to Champagney, 22 April 1574, NCD II, 178-179.

²²⁰ 'Queria [Champagney] sacar unas pieças de larmada para ponerlas contra los soldados en la muralla a esto yo le respondi que no seria malo quitar las pieças que estavan contra el prinçipe y ponerlas contra los españoles'. Dávila to Albornoz, Antwerp, 26 April 1574, AA, C/33, 114. Requesens also defended the use of violence from the citadel against the mutineers: 'Si no quisieren reducirse, los ha de tratar el castillo como á enemigos'. Requesens to Dávila, 23 April 1574, NCD II, 191-192.

hoped the mutineers would remain calm, for himself his objectives were clear: "to go to Spain".[221]

Champagney wrote a long letter in French (in cipher) to Requesens in which he tried to convince the Governor-general of his side of the story.[222] He stated that regarding Sancho "I have no particular feeling", though he was not a friend of his. But he had learned that Sancho had written letters against an important figure, "subtly to sow dissension". But he had calmed everything down in order not to fuel the "hate and enmity between the nations". He even said that if the highly placed Netherlanders knew of Sancho's letters, they would all try to kill Sancho "even if he possessed a hundred lives".

After this general characterisation of the situation, Champagney entered into more detail. Sancho had already promised his men before the battle that they could enter Antwerp afterwards, "where they would be paid by the burghers", a story also to be found with Van Haecht and Morillon. Sancho had also taken no action against the mutineers. Champagney wanted only to return to Antwerp with enough soldiers of his own, "otherwise I would merely serve as the subject of mockery and laughter, for both Sancho Dávila and his fellows, and as object of their growing insults". He had always been a friend of the Spaniards, but only of those who feared both God and King.

Matters got even worse in Antwerp, and in the words of Requesens, "this mutiny of those from the castle has been the worst evil in the world". Requesens would later even blame the mutineers for losing the Low Countries, as quoted in a famous letter by Hernando Delgadillo:

> He [Requesens] insisted that it was not the Prince of Orange who had made them lose the Low Countries, but the soldiers born in Valladolid and Toledo, because the mutineers had driven money out of Antwerp and destroyed all credit and reputation, and he believed that within eight days His Majesty would not have anything left here…He continued for almost three hours.[223]

The situation was now out of control. The mutineers even tried to kill Francisco de Valdés and Julián Romero during the course of the mutiny. In a long letter, Requesens, who had preferred to wait to write to the

---

[221] 'Yrme a España'. Dávila to Albornoz, Antwerp, 26 April 1574, AA, C/33, 114.
[222] Champagney to Requesens, castle Cantecroy (Mortsel), 30 May 1574, NCD II, 304-316.
[223] Hernando Delgadillo to Albornoz, 9 July 1574, AA, 33/156, quoted and translated by Parker, *Army* (2004) 157.

King until after the mutiny was over, had no choice but to inform the King while the mutiny was still in full swing.[224]

Requesens's brother, Juan de Zúñiga, discussed Sancho's position in a letter to his brother:

> Regarding Sancho Dávila there has to be taken much consideration, as he is such a good soldier, and Your Excellency has so few who can really help out, that there has to be great care taken not to stain him with being the one behind the mutiny.[225]

Juan could not believe that Sancho was the instigator of the mutiny, but he did agree that Sancho had not done enough to stop the mutineers. A good option would be to take him with the army that summer and then send him to Spain on some commission. The King could then use him somewhere else: "he is so hated by those of these lands that it would cause much damage if he were to stay". Juan also discussed with his brother the possibility of giving Sancho the command of the light cavalry and Alonso de Vargas the Antwerp citadel, but Juan thought the citadel would be better for Gaspar de Robles or Cristóbal Mondragón "as they are such good soldiers and so accepted by those of these lands". The command of an infantry tercio for Sancho would be unfair compared to his governorship of Antwerp citadel, because "with his reputation he could not accept it".[226]

Requesens explained the situation to the King: "[Champagney] serves with such disgust and controversy that it is impossible to reconcile both him and Sancho Dávila, although I have tried my very best with both of them, and it will create great inconveniences".[227] Little would Requesens know that after his death the conflict between these two men would escalate severely, leading up to the Spanish Fury. The Governor-general clearly supported Sancho, "the soldier with the most services that Your Majesty has in these estates", but he still thought it better to use Sancho somewhere else because of the 'general opinion' that he had played a role in the entry of the mutineers into Antwerp.

---

[224] Requesens to Philip II, Antwerp, 15 May 1574, CD XXX, 484-496.
[225] Juan de Zúñiga to Requesens, 5 June 1574, NCD II, 325-331.
[226] Juan de Zúñiga to Requesens, 10 July 1574, NCD III, 327-332. Comparable arguments in Granvelle to Juan de Zúñiga, Naples, 9 June 1574, NCD II, 352-355. See also Juan de Zúñiga to Requesens, 17 July 1574, NCD IV, 25-26.
[227] Requesens to Philip II, 19 August 1574, NCD V, 62-81.

Morillon offers the most terrible description of the mutiny in his letters to Granvelle. The Spanish mutineers awakened the inhabitants at night screaming as if they were going to kill everybody, and in this way an infinity of pregnant women aborted or gave birth before their time, and many old people died or were sick with fear, "and more than two or three thousand women went to [the County of] Flanders". All the foreign merchants, Portuguese, German and English, were leaving the city as they wanted security "and they don't want to trust a barbarian castellan, saying that the castle, that should protect them is the origin of the danger". Together with barbaric castellan Sancho as the main cause of the disaster, Mondragón is also attacked by Morillon: "And it is certain that Sancho Dávila and Mondragón, through their imprudence (*témérité*) and insolence (*oultrecuidance*), have caused the robbing of this city". It is clear to Morillon that "if the said Sancho Dávila remains in the castle, it is everybody's opinion that the merchants will abandon the city". He even feared Sancho would become the new governor of the whole city, as this would cause its complete ruin, "as he is not a politician, but brutal and superb as a lion, he would prefer to tyrannise, something the people in the long run will not support". The inhabitants would then even welcome the enemy into the city. At a more general level he blamed the Duke of Alba who had permitted the soldiers to do what they wanted, and "all those who have had offices under him are frauds and robbers, getting pleasure out of destroying the country". They should send them all to Italy and bring back "better disciplined soldiers".[228] In a letter somewhat later, Morillon defined his views on the situation in a one-liner: "Sancho d'Avila, who on his own is the source and cause of all our trouble".[229]

The fact that the Spanish soldiers from the citadel had not fired on the mutineers when they were getting in also meant that there were people who wished to have Sancho removed as castellan and his place taken by somebody from the Duchy of Brabant. This story also reached the French court.[230] But it may even have been the case that Sancho never actually received the official patent of castellan. In a letter written several months after Sancho's victory at Mookerheyde in 1574, the King told

---

[228] Morillon to Granvelle, Brussels, 1-3 May 1574, CG V, 84-88. Champagney also points out the possibility of the merchants leaving Antwerp: Champagney to Requesens, 20 May 1574, NCD II, 304-316.

[229] Morillon to Granvelle, Brussels, 1 June 1574, CG V, 100. Also Idem, 14 June 1574, CG V, 139

[230] Mondoucet to the Queen regent, Antwerp, 18 August 1574, Mondoucet, *Lettres*, II, 292; France, *Histoire*, 528.

Governor-general Requesens that "I have decided that he may receive the office of castellan of Antwerp as his property, though for the moment it seems to me more convenient not to send him the official papers, out of respect for the pretentions of those from Brabant against giving offices to foreigners, but you can say it to him from my part, although he has to keep silent about it until the right time comes". The mutiny made the whole situation too complicated: "the papers will be sent when the time is ripe and the present problems are gone, most of all those with the Estates of Brabant".[231] It would take two months and the money of the Antwerp burghers to end the mutiny.[232] However, the enmity between Champagney and Sancho did not come to a halt, and Sancho's position as castellan remained a disputed one.

## The ongoing war (1574-1576)

Sancho remained in Antwerp after the mutiny had ended. However, it was clear that the tide had turned, perfectly demonstrated by the fact that Requesens had removed Alba's statue from the citadel's central square and placed it in a room in the citadel. Sancho wanted to know from the Duke how to send it to Spain as it was "a pity to destroy it". The plinth, which was very heavy, could be buried in a bulwark for the time being. A few days later, Sancho suggested the statue could go to Alba's palace in Alba de Tormes or to La Abadía, now calling it "such a lovely piece".[233] The idea that it was sent to Spain also circulated in the Low Countries.[234]

Requesens had informed Sancho that the King had decided to reward him with an income of a thousand escudos, but the commander was not satisfied as he had hoped for more. His deeds at Mookerheyde, his new and most important claim to fame, in his eyes justified his higher expectations. However, he did acknowledge that Requesens had given him many favours and gifts "out of respect for the Duke my lord" and had also invited him to meetings of his war council on the expedition to

---

[231] Philip II to Requesens, Madrid 10 August 1574, quoted in Pando Fernández de Pinedo, *Vida*, 174-176; Dávila, *Memorial*.

[232] More details on these events are in Martín Garcia, *Sancho*, 179-187; Martínez Ruiz, 'Gran motín'.

[233] 'Lastima deshazerla'; 'Por ser pesada'; 'Tan linda pieza'. Dávila to Albornoz, Antwerp citadel, 16 and 20 June 1574, AA, C/33, 115 and 118. Requesens to Dávila, Antwerp, 4 June 1574, quoted in Pando Fernández de Pinedo, *Vida*, 184-185. Juan de Zúñiga supported taking away the statue: Juan de Zúñiga to Requesens, 10 July 1574, NCD III, 327-332.

[234] Pollmann and Stensland, 'Alba's reputation', 319; Smolderen, 'Statue'.

support Zeeland. His main wish was to receive a licence to go to Spain: "I don't want a castle nor more rewards than that what they have to pay me", and even more poetically, "I am already [too] old to always eat kisses". But his patron could not help him: "I cannot become accustomed to the fact that the Duke my lord lacks the power to support me".[235]

Morillon reports on a party in the Antwerp citadel when Requesens came to visit on 19 August:

> In general it was taken badly that instead of chasing out Sancho Dávila, as according to everybody's opinion he rightly deserved, His Excellency [Requesens] went to have dinner with him at the castle… Where there was a great feast, with the most beautiful ladies of Antwerp, leaving their husbands at home. There was nobody from the Low Countries at the party.[236]

Notwithstanding the ladies from Antwerp, Sancho regretted the fact that he had lost most of his friends in the Low Countries: "it makes me sad to see so many people and friends leave these estates", using a famous quotation to underline this idea: "it seems that one might use the words of Carvajal, that the wind is removing strands of my hair, two at a time".[237] In the chapter on Mondragón we will see somebody quoting this same saying.

Again we find traces of Sancho's special relationship with merchant Hernando de Frías: "He has given his friends all the sorrow in the world as we received news that he had been killed in France". Only later did they learn he was held prisoner. Sancho showed how he valued his friendship wih Frías: if he did not have the money for his ransom, his friends would give it to him. "Until now I have not heard that he has been set free and

---

[235] 'Por respeto del duque mi señor'; no quiero castillo ni merçed mas de que me paguen'; ya estoi biejo para comer siempre besos'; 'No me puedo acostumbrar de que el duque mi señor no tenga mas fuerça para valerme'. Dávila to Albornoz, Antwerp, 16 June and 28 October 1574, AA, C/33, 115 and 121; Dávila to Alba, Antwerp, 20 June 1574, AA, C/33, 116; Dávila to Albornoz, Antwerp, 1 January 1575, AA, C/33, 126. Requesens to Philip II, 8 June 1574, NCD II, 344-348; 'Aunque no son [Mondragón and Sancho] del todo marineros, han navegado algunas veces estos canales'.

[236] Morillon to Granvelle, 5 September 1574, CG V, 200. See also Idem, 6 September 1574, CG V, 212.

[237] 'Harto me pesa e ver yr tanta gente y amigos destos estados'; 'Pareçe que se podria decir lo de Carabajal, estos cabellicos dos a dos me los lleba el ayre'. Dávila to Albornoz, Antwerp, 22 January 1575, AA, C/33, 127. The saying refers to the conquistador Francisco de Carvajal, the 'demon of the Andes'. Other references to 'amigos' are in Dávila to Albornoz, Ouwerkerk, 4 May 1576, AA, C/33, 135.

returned home, something I wish with whole my heart (*en estremo*)".²³⁸ In another letter to Albornoz he was even more explicit: "he is the best friend we have… he is so passionate for what is important for us… one of the most honourable men I have ever met".²³⁹ His frequent use of 'amigos' in this period is again matched by a similar use of 'herejes' when he speaks of the rebels.²⁴⁰

In June 1574, Sancho suddenly speaks of a second marriage, although it is difficult to judge whether he really meant what he was writing:

> I have decided to get married and it has been accorded to take place within ten to twelve days; they say the lady is not very beautiful, as I have not looked at her very well; she will be virtuous as she also has no possessions; God will approve and separate us from sin.²⁴¹

By August 1574 they were already marrried, but again Sancho was not lucky with the health of his new wife: "the lady Violante is so sick and so thin that the only thing to say is that she has to remain in bed without moving for eight or nine months".²⁴² Was she pregnant? The next year he had to give Albornoz the sad news: "God has been served by taking the lady Violante to heaven at the time I stayed at the islands of Zierikzee, and although I already for a long time held her for dead, I have felt it, and am feeling it, as one might imagine".²⁴³ In June 1576 Alba would

---

²³⁸ 'A nos dado toda la pena del mundo a sus amigos porque tubimos nueba que le avian muerto en França'; 'aunque el no tuviera dineros para rrescatarse no le faltaran de sus amigos, asta ahora no entendido que sea libre y esta en su casa que lo deseo en estremo'. Dávila to Albornoz, Antwerp, 28 October 1574, AA, C/33, 121.

²³⁹ 'Que es el mayor amigo que tenemos… es tan apasionado por lo que nos toca… uno de los honrados hombres que jamas he tratado'. Dávila to Albornoz, Antwerp citadel, 20 June 1574, AA, C/33, 118. See also Idem, 10 August 1574, Idem, 119.

²⁴⁰ Dávila to Albornoz, Brussels, 14 December 1574, AA, C/33, 124. Gonzalo de Bracamonte as an 'amigo' of Dávila: Requesens to Dávila, 29 March 1574, NCD II, 60-62.

²⁴¹ 'He rresolvido de casarme y esta acordado de que sea dentro de 10 o 12 dias, dicen que la dama no es mui hermosa que yo no la he visto muy bien, sera virtuosa que tampoco tiene hazienda, dios nos de buena dicha y nos aparte de pecado'. Dávila to Albornoz, Antwerp, 20 June 1574, AA, C/33, 117. The bride would receive an income of 400 escudos for life if he died without her having children.

²⁴² 'La doña Biolante esta tan mala y tan flaca que no se puede mas deçir estase en una cama sin poderse menear 8 o 9 meses…'. Dávila to Albornoz, Antwerp citadel, 10 August 1574, 4 and 19 December 1575, AA, C/33, 119 and 131-132.

²⁴³ 'A sido dios servido estando yo en las yslas de Ziricsea de llevarse a doña Violante al çielo, que aunque a muchos dias que yo la tenia por muerta lo he sentido y lo siento como se puede pensar'. Dávila to Albornoz, Antwerp, 21 April 1576, AA, C/33, 134.

send his condolences to Dávila: "it has hurt me in my soul to hear about the death of lady Violante".[244] He had married hoping for more children: "if God would give me children, good brothers and sisters (*hermanos*) for the one I have".[245]

The inheritance of his son, 'Hernandico' (Fernando), was partly in the hands of Hernando de Frías, but he was also thinking of involving the Fugger bankers by getting them to invest part of the money.[246] Around this time Requesens calculated Sancho's annual income at around seven to eight thousand escudos.[247] Sancho also considered buying property in Spain: "I really wish to buy a small hacienda in Spain, good and cheap". However, he found the prices of the estates in the neighbourhood of Ávila too high, but also blamed his representative at home: "the haciendas in Spain seem very expensive to me, or he does not know how to buy cheap". In 1577 Sancho would pay eighteen thousand ducats for the Dehesa de Villagarcía, in the vicinity of Ávila.[248]

In his letters Sancho complained about the behaviour of the rebels, the Spanish mutineers, and the inhabitants of the Low Countries: "the news from La Goleta and other failed exploits related to the affairs of His Majesty, seems to be celebrated in public". A victory would change all that; "it seems they value us little now, but then [after a victory] they would value us more and they would show us more friendship and they would support us more than they do now".[249] He was a clear opponent of peace talks as he thought the rebels had to be punished, as "in any other

---

[244] Alba to Dávila, 10 June 1576, EA, III, 613.

[245] 'Si dios me diese hijos dexar buenos hermanos al que tengo'. Dávila to Albornoz, Antwerp, 21 April 1576, AA, C/33, 134.

[246] Dávila to Albornoz, Antwerp citadel, 10 August 1574 and 4 and 19 December 1575, AA, C/33, 119, 131-132.

[247] 3,000 from his first wife or his son of less than four years old, 150 escudos a month for the Antwerp citadel, and more than that sum in relation to other smaller incomes, and 1,000 escudos a year on the Low Countries given by the King. Requesens to the Count of Monteagudo, 7 July 1574, NCD III, 291-293.

[248] 'Yo deseo bien comprar una haçendilla en España buena y barata'; 'me hacen muy caras las haciendas de España o el no sabe comprar barato'. Dávila to Albornoz, Antwerp, 19 December 1575, AA, C/33, 132; Martín García, *Sancho*, 237, 241.

[249] 'De las nuebas de la Goleta y qualquiera otro mal suçeso que benga cosa que toque a Su Magestad pareçe que se alegran en publico'; 'Que pareçe que nos estiman agora en poco, nos tendrian en mucho y nos mostrarian mas amistad y nos harian mas asistençia de la que hazen'. Dávila to Albornoz, Antwerp, 28 October 1574, AA, C/33, 121; Dávila to Albornoz, Antwerp citadel, 10 August 1574, AA, C/33, 119; Dávila to Alba, Antwerp citadel, 22 January 1575, AA, C/33, 128; Van Haecht, *Kroniek*, II, 318-319.

way both these estates and the reputation would be lost".²⁵⁰ Morillon knew of Sancho's opinions, and saw no difference from Mondragón's: "Sancho Dávila and Mondragón tell His Excellency [Requesens] that he should not listen nor negotiate with the enemies of our faith".²⁵¹ This quotation supports the idea of Sancho having a more outspoken religious opinion, but it does not fit the balanced image of Mondragón (chapter III). However, it is not the first time Morillon considered that the two men held the same opinions.

It is important to remark that Sancho was not just commenting on events but also taking action. In December 1574 the army commanders were again planning an expedition to Zeeland. Sancho would take one fleet from Bergen-op-Zoom, but he was not very confident of success because of the lack of good sailors. He thought the best option would be for the King to send an armada from Spain because then they would have good and loyal sailors at their disposal. Together with good soldiers this would solve their problems.²⁵² Describing another naval expedition, Morillon reported that Admiral Sancho took a Vice-admiral from the Low Countries with him, so this man could be blamed if things went wrong. Sancho could then excuse himself, saying that "he was not as good on sea as he was on land", a phrase that reminds us of the debate on Julián's behaviour at Reimerswaal.²⁵³ In October, Morillon blamed Sancho and Mondragón for initiating such a "hazardous expedition" only for "greasing their own hands".²⁵⁴

In early December 1575 Sancho returned to Antwerp after another expedition to Zeeland. The letter to Albornoz is full of words of defeat, though they had won in the end: "we lost many friends… they did us much damage…. they killed many of our good men… they made us retreat… the affairs of these islands had not been very prosperous".²⁵⁵ Finally the royal army –Mondragón was also involved – succeeded in gaining the small fortress of Bommenede: "on Sunday morning… we

---

[250] 'De qualquiera otra manera se pierden estos estados y la reputaçion'. Dávila to Alba, Antwerp citadel, 22 January 1575, AA, C/33, 128.
[251] Morillon to Granvelle, Brussels, 11 July 1575, *CG* V, 336.
[252] Dávila to Albornoz, Antwerp, 30 December 1574, AA, C/33, 125; Dávila to Alba, Antwerp citadel, 22 January 1575, AA, C/33, 128. Pí Corrales, *España*.
[253] Morillon to Granvelle, Brussels, 18 September 1575, CG V, 391.
[254] Morillon to Granvelle, Brussels, 9 October 1575, CG V, 409-410.
[255] 'Nos costo artos amigos… nos hiçieron mucho daño… nos mataron mucha gente y buena…. Nos hiçiron retirar… el no aver suçedido mui mas prosperamente estas cosas destas yslas'. Dávila to Albornoz, Antwerp citadel, 4 December 1575, AA, C/33, 131.

started the assault and took the town, slaughtering all those inside". Requesens spoke of seven hundred defenders killed, but he also wrote to the King about their own high losses:

> There are so many wounded Spaniards, and some banners are left without healthy soldiers, and others with only three or four, and with twenty at the most. But the majority of the wounds are from pikes and stones, and they will heal rapidly, although there are also many men wounded by arquebus shots, of which they will die.[256]

The many casualties may have led Sancho Dávila to criticise Requesens' policy, at least if we are to believe Morillon:

> They [Sancho and Juan Osorio] have decided to go and complain to the King, and if ever there was a reason to bring down this Catalan Comendador Mayor. The said Sancho Dávila is ready to break with him; and I heard this from none other than [Pedro] Castillo.[257]

By now we know Morillon hated Sancho and that he would be glad to write down any negative rumour he overheard, but it is remarkable to note the use of Requesens' Catalan origins as an argument that may have been used against him. However, there are no traces of this idea in Sancho's own correspondence. The source of the rumour Morillon mentions, Pedro del Castillo, was the son of a Spanish merchant from Bruges, working for the central government.[258]

After Bommenede, the next attack was aimed at Zierikzee, a siege most closely related to Cristóbal de Mondragón, so most details of this siege can be found in the chapter on Mondragón. Requesens, who was present in Zeeland, had wanted to attack the city directly, but Sancho and Mondragón convinced him that the troops could not stand another assault. At the beginning of the siege the Governor-general still hoped the city could be won in a month. He was very wrong, and would not live to see its surrender. Dávila describes how the rebels tried to enter Zierikzee with large support fleets.[259] On 3 March 1576 he wrote a letter

---

[256] Requesens to Philip II, Sint Annaland, 4 November 1575, CD XXXI, 31-39. 'El castellano de Amberes, en la isla se alojar', Padilla, *Romancero*, 99.
[257] Morillon to Granvelle, Brussels, 6-7 November 1575, CG V, 421. Juan Osorio also participated in the expedition to Zeeland with Sancho Dávila and Cristóbal de Mondragón.
[258] Fagel, 'Cardinal Granvelle'.
[259] Dávila to Albornoz, Antwerp citadel, 19 December 1575, AA, C/33, 132.

to Requesens asking for provisions, but only six days later he had to write a letter to the King about Requesens's death: "a day after I returned from the island of Zierikzee I heard about the death of the Comendador Mayor [Requesens]".[260]

He heard about Violante's death when he returned from Zierikzee in April 1576, and on that journey he had also been in danger when his ship had to cut anchor during a storm to end up on "a beach where we did not lose men or artillery, but we did lose the limited amount of clothes I had with me".[261] In England, Lord Burghley would receive the same news also by late April: "Sancho Dávila, who was driven to save himself by wading up to his neck in water, is come sick to Antwerp to make the funeral of his wife".[262] Morillon, as always, added a pinch of anti-Hispanism to the story: Sancho had almost drowned because he had gone against the winds and the tides, "according to the nature of these people who do not follow any advice".[263]

In that same letter from Dávila there is a very detailed description of the fighting to stop the rebel fleet from reaching Zierikzee, with both losses and gains. If the town surrendered "they [the rebels] would have to give up all the islands of these canals of Holland". He even hoped that the important fleet of Zierikzee would then join the royal side. Sancho had meanwhile returned to Antwerp to ask the Council of State which had taken over after Requesens's death to provide the means to end the siege. By early May it was clear that they would take Zierikzee, "although they remain obstinate even though we know they have little food left, though more than we would have liked".[264]

Requesens' sudden death created a power vacuum in the Low Countries.[265] In his letter of 9 March 1576 Sancho directly asked the King for a replacement.[266] It would, however, take more than a month for the news to arrive from the King that everyone had to obey the Council

---

[260] Dávila to Requesens, Antwerp, 3 March 1576, CD XXXI, 40-41 and Dávila to Philip II, Brussels, 9 March 1576, Idem, 42-43.

[261] 'Una playa donde no se perdio la gente ny artilleria aunque la poca ropa que yo llevaba'. Dávila to Albornoz, Antwerp, 21 April 1576, AA, C/33, 134; Morillon to Granvelle, Brussels, 7/8 April 1576, CG VI, 51.

[262] CSP, *foreign, Elizabeth 1558-1589*, XI, 317 and 233.

[263] Morillon to Granvelle, Brussels, 7/8 April 1576, CG VI, 51.

[264] 'Tienen por perdidas todas las yslas destos canales de Holanda'; 'Aunque estan todavia obstinados no obstante que se entiende tienen poca comida pero no tan poca como querriamos'. Dávila to Albornoz, Ouwerkerk, 4 May 1576, AA, C/33, 135.

[265] The following is partly based on Santiago Belmonte, 'Year'.

[266] Dávila to Philip II, Brussels, 9 March 1576, AGS, E. 567, 26.

of State until a new Governor-general had been appointed, confirming what the Council had already done directly after Requesens's death. It meant that Sancho and the other Spanish commanders now had to obey the Council of State, dominated by the nobility of the Low Countries and controlled by the Duke of Aarschot. Gerónimo de Roda was the only Spanish member of the council, and Aarschot clearly tried to remove the Spaniards from the decision-making process.

The same tension can be detected from a letter by Granvelle's confidant, Morillon, who stated that "Sancho Dávila and all those of the nation hate the Lord of Lalaing", referring to Philip of Lalaing (1533-1582), Count of Lalaing and Governor of Hainaut.[267] 'Nation' here clearly means the Spanish nation, a term used increasingly with this meaning in the context of the conflict in 1576. A crystal clear example of a euphemism.

After Zierikzee's surrender to Mondragón, Spanish troops started a mutiny, and on 25 July they took the Flemish town of Aalst. The situation came to a head in Brussels, where the inhabitants attacked the Spaniards present in the city, starting a popular rebellion. The Council of State found itself in a difficult position and decided to outlaw the Spanish mutineers and give the States of Brabant permission to raise troops for their protection. During these chaotic months, Sancho maintained a close correspondence with the Council of State. The Council considered the popular rebellion a result of the mutiny, but Sancho did not agree and saw the popular rebellion as the real problem, and in part sympathised with the mutineers. "We know such a great movement is not caused by the mutiny of the Spaniards, because it had started much before, when already things were happening and words were overheard".[268] He also felt that the members of the Council of State were being controlled by the burghers of Brussels, especially after Gerónimo de Roda, Alonso de Vargas and Julián Romero had been locked up within the palace by the rebelling inhabitants. This measure also implied that Sancho no longer trusted the Council of State's decisions.[269] As early as in May 1576, Morillon stated that the Spanish commanders had acted against the wishes of the Council of State: "Sancho Dávila and Mondragón do not obey at all, but the said Council does not wish to complain, so it does not seem like they hold a grudge against the nation".[270]

---

[267] Morillon to Granvelle, Brussels, 19 March 1976, CG VI, 31.
[268] Dávila, Antwerp, 16 August 1576, CD XXXI, 129.
[269] This is in short Santiago Belmonte's argument, 'Year'. CD XXXI, 72-111.
[270] Morillon to Granvelle, Brussels, 21 May 1576, CG VI, 77-78; Council of State to Philip II, Brussels, 12/14 August 1576, CP IV, 301.

Again, all faults were to be found with the Spaniards, described again as 'la nation'.

Sancho turned himself into the representative of the Spanish military commanders in the Low Countries, "seeing this country so revolted (*alterado*) and already some Spaniards have been killed", and also understanding how little could be done to pacify it all, with the Council arrested and imprisoned in that city.[271] According to Sancho, the burghers of Brussels controlled the situation and they were responsible for outlawing the mutineers:

> They felt so arrogant and brave that they asked the lords of the Council… that they should declare the said Spaniards that had entered Aalst as disobedient rebels and enemies of His Majesty and of the country… and they pressed so hard that against their wish they made them publish a general placard in this sense.[272]

When the Council wrote that the mutineers wished to head for the Antwerp citadel, he denied this: "I have not heard such news", and he confirmed to them that "I do not intend to host any soldiers suspected of mutiny".[273] A day earlier a group of high commanders, among them Sancho, had written an ultimatum to the Brussels government, stating that they wanted the arrested members of the Council to be set free, or otherwise they would go into action. Santiago Belmonte is right in describing this ultimatum as an 'act of treason', as Philip II's explicit orders had been to obey the Council of State. The military were now following their own policy. Roda wrote to the King during these days saying that he supported Sancho's policy, but that nobody was to know, because he feared for his life if they did.[274]

As the arrival of the newly appointed Governor-general, Don Juan de Austria, was taking too long according to Sancho, he wrote to the King to emphasise the urgency of his arrival.[275] In his next letter he set out his ideas on the best royal policy:

---

[271] Dávila to the Council of State, Antwerp, 1 August 1576, CD XXXI, 81-82; Notes of the Council of State, 3 and 6 August 1576, CP IV, 513, 523.

[272] Dávila to the Duke of Brunswick, the Duke of Cleves, The Bishop of Liège and the Archbishop of Cambrai, Antwerp, 1 August 1576, CD XXXI, 109.

[273] Dávila to the Council, Antwerp, 6 August 1576, CD XXXI, 90.

[274] Roda to Philip II, Brussels, 7 August 1576, CP IV, 290; Roda to Philip II, Antwerp, 30 August 1576, CP IV, 339; AGS, E. 567, 30.

[275] Dávila to Philip II, 15 August 1576, AGS, E. 567, 95.

There should be sent as many Spanish soldiers as possible, gather German companies and all those coming from the country, for the war of Holland and Zeeland… The magistates and abbots should be deprived of most of their rents and taxes (*gavelas*), leaving them very little… It would be convenient to build castles in all the important cities… break down the walls of some of the cities and punish them, as all this and more is what they deserve.[276]

On 30 August Orange's men were let into the city of Brussels, and on 4 September all the members of the Council of State were arrested, a 'coup d'état' that provided the subject for one of Hogenberg's engravings. The Estates of Brabant and the united Estates-General would now take over, with the fast-growing influence of the rebels under William of Orange.[277] A day later, the Council of State sent a representative to the King, carrying instructions to put the blame for the crisis on Sancho Dávila and asking the King for an exemplary punishment. They spoke of "the braveries (*bravades*) of Sancho Dávila and his followers". On 11 September the King wrote to Roda and told him that he was satisfied with Sancho's actions, but Sancho had to obey the Council of State in everything, "showing his complete submission and obedience".[278] All parties involved, including the King, were playing tricks, hiding their true ideas on the matter. For many Netherlanders Sancho had become one of their main enemies.

On 22 September 1576 the decree against the mutineers was extended to include all Spanish military in the Low Countries. Sancho found himself in a hostile country, completely at war. And still the new Governor-general had not arrived. Morillon blamed Sancho and Roda for the rebellion, caused by their "pride and violence", a vision he shared with Granvelle.[279] In the evening of 14 July 1576 Champagney had already placed guards in the streets leading to the Antwerp citadel, and Roda considered that if Sancho did nothing to stop this "it would be like the citadel was being

---

[276] 'Embiasse mucha gente Española, toda la que se pudiese y que se hiziesen Alemanes y que todos biniesen del pays tomando por azesorio [?] la guerra de Holanda y Gelanda … los magistrados y abades quitandoles todas sus rentas y gavelas y dejandoles dellas muy pocas… convernia hazer castillos en todas las villas principales … derrocar las murallas a algunas de las villas y castigarlas pues todo esto y mas parece que lo merezen'. Dávila to Philip II, Brussels, 16 August 1576, AGS, E. 567, 100.

[277] Janssens, *Brabant*, 293-296,

[278] Instruction of the Council of State to Rassenghien, Brussels, 31 August 1576 and Philip II to Roda, El Escorial, 11 September 1576, CP IV, 342, 344, 367; AGS, E. 569, 118.

[279] Morillon to Granvelle, Saint-Amand, 15 September 1576, CG VI, 129; Granvelle to the Prior of Bellefontaine, Rome, 6 December 1576, CG VI, 179-180.

besieged".[280] This was written several months before the attack on the city from the citadel on 4 November, showing that the situation was already extremely tense during the summer.[281]

On 26 September troops gathered against Ghent citadel, where Mondragón's wife and his lieutenant resided, and on 20 October an open rebellion against royal commander Francisco de Montesdoca in Maastricht ended in the sacking of the city by royal troops. On 12 September the King had written a short letter to Sancho urging him to obey Gerónimo de Roda, responding in this way to Sancho's letters written between 29 July and 17 August.[282] However, the letter would not have arrived before the end of September or early October. In the chronicle by Antonio de Herrera y Tordesillas, published in 1601, Julián Romero had adverted Sancho that the Estates-General wanted to besiege the Antwerp citadel, 'but he [Sancho] did not believe it, because the Count of Eberstain had given his word that he would keep the city on the side of the King'.[283] Unfortunately, we lack further proof of this early warning by his fellow commander.

On 3 November 1576, on the very eve of the Spanish Fury in Antwerp, Morillon described the difficult situation Sancho Dávila found himself in: William of Orange had promised to deliver the citadel of Antwerp to the Estates-General within six weeks after the first cannon shots. However, Morillon hoped they would act without Orange's help. He also thought Roda and Sancho would not simply wait for what was to happen: "I do not think that Sancho, however reckless he may be, nor Roda, will remain waiting". In an intercepted letter to the castellan of Valenciennes, his cousin Rodrigo, Sancho had written that he could not come to his rescue and that "the stubborness of the mutineers from Aalst will be their common ruin".[284] Those in the citadel of Antwerp found themselves in the same hopeless situation; "as the castle is a world of merchants, paymasters and others from the nation that have retreated to the said castle of Antwerp, all fearsome people who will make the soldiers lose heart".[285]

---

[280] Roda to Philip II, Brussels, 15 July 1576, CP IV, 254.
[281] Champagney to Philip II, Antwerp, 10 August 1576, CP IV, 292.
[282] Philip II to Dávila, El Escorial, 12 September 1576 (AGS, E. 569, 23-24) and Idem, El Pardo, 17 October 1576, CD XXXI, 136-137.
[283] Herrera y Tordesillas, *Historia*, II, 94; Kagan, *Clio*, 144-149.
[284] Morillon to Granvelle, Saint-Amand, 3 November 1576, CG VI, 153-154.
[285] Idem.

In the same letter Morillon also reported on the arrival of the Marquis of Havré, Charles-Philip of Croy (1549-1613), in Antwerp with five hundred horse and twenty-one infantry banners as a result of an agreement between Champagney and the Estates-General. Havré was Aarschot's half-brother.[286] The always well-informed Morillon added "that it is said that the Lord of Havré has the government of the castle and of the city and that monseigneur de Champagney has the admiralty". Thus, according to Granvelle's confidant, Dávila's job as castellan had already been given away. Morillon also reported in the same letter that Julián Romero was trying to convince the mutineers of Aalst to join them "to occupy the city with the help of six companies under Count Hannibal". The mutineers, however, had gone to plunder in Geraardsbergen.[287] Although staying in Saint-Amand in Hainaut, Morillon already understood how both sides in Antwerp were preparing for battle.

## The Spanish Fury of Antwerp (1576)[288]

The most frequently used sources on the Spanish Fury of Antwerp in 1576 are a series of engravings by Frans Hogenberg and the description given by the Englishman George Gascoigne in his *The Spoyle of Antwerpe* (1576). The engravings were later re-used in a combination engraving showing the city of Antwerp in the middle with six other scenes draped around it.[289] Although Gascoigne's work has until recently been considered an example of early modern autobiography, it turns out to be mostly a translation and elaboration of a pamphlet in Dutch written by an eyewitness who clearly hated the Spanish presence:

> *The true description of the taking of Antwerp and of the inhuman and very gruesome murder, fire, sack, and the unheard violation of women and girls by the Spanish and their adherents, on November 4, 1576, and several days therafter, written by one who had been present himself.*[290]

---

[286] De Schepper, 'Markies', 34.
[287] Morillon to Granvelle, Saint-Amand, 3 November 1576, CG VI, 156-157. Count Hannibal was Jacob Hannibal of Altemps (1530-1587).
[288] The Spanish Fury of Antwerp has already been treated more extensively in: Fagel, 'Furia'; Idem, 'Gascoigne's *The Spoyle*; Idem, 'Imagen', Idem, 'Origins'; Idem, lecture 'The Spanish Fury of Antwerp revisited (1576)' at the Sixteenth-Century Conference, Bruges, 19 August 2016; Idem, lecture 'The Spanish Fury of 1576: the story behind the images', Rijksmuseum Amsterdam, 16 September 2016.
[289] Rijksmuseum RP-P-OB-76.862.
[290] *Warachtige beschrijvinghe*, Leiden University Library, Thyspf. 258.

Though recent historiography tends to describe the Fury as the result of a mutiny, in reality it was a battle in the city, in which the mutineers did play a role, but where the decision to attack on 4 November 1576 was made by Sancho Dávila and royal councilor Gerónimo de Roda. In line with the interpretation of the Fury as a mutiny, both the recent historiography and the Hogenberg engravings play down the presence of troops defending the city, turning it into an act of blind violence against innocent burghers by mutinying Spanish soldiers. Sancho was the main commander in the citadel, and he accordingly plays an important part in the narratives on the Fury. Génard, who published an extensive volume on the sources of the events, stated in 1876, "For Sancho Dávila was reserved the shame of being the general commander of this troop of barbarians".[291]

On 9 November, only days after the Fury, the newly arrived governor of the Low Countries, Don Juan de Austria, wrote a strongly worded letter to Sancho Dávila:

> Señor Sancho Dávila, the revolt that has taken place in Antwerp has given me great pain and it would be worse if I knew it has happened because of you or because of the Spanish soldiers there present.[292]

Sancho answered the letter on 14 November, but informed Don Juan at the same time that Gerónimo de Roda had already written to him in order to explain the situation in a more elaborate manner. However, Sancho did not refrain completely from giving explanations to the new Governor-general. He clarified how the citadels in both Ghent and Valenciennes had been under attack and that they had now succeeded in avoiding the same fate in Antwerp. It had been a kind of pre-emptive strike:[293]

> When you will be informed, you will understand that our people had been forced to act for their own health and safety and that they had always tried to avoid it.[294]

---

[291] Génard, 'Furie', 461; CD XXXI, 140; Reijner, 'Lode', discusses Italian historiography on the events.
[292] Don Juan to Sancho Dávila, 9 November 1576, CD XXXI, 138.
[293] Fagel, 'Origins'.
[294] Sancho Dávila to Don Juan, 14 November 1576, CD XXXI, 141

Sancho accused the city government of collaboration with William of Orange, while they themselves had only acted in the best interests of the King.

Unfortunately, the letter from Gerónimo de Roda to Don Juan that Sancho mentioned is not extant, but we do have a letter from the royal councilor to his King written on 6 November, with the plundering still ongoing.[295] Roda informed the King that the city government had let in German troops paid by the Estates-General and that they had built entrenchments against the citadel, even installing artillery pieces. The troops from the citadel had attacked these entrenchments before the mutineers' arrival, an event described by chronicler Antonio Trillo but also to be found in an anonymous English pamphlet, *An historical discourse or rather a tragicall historie of the citie of Antwerpe* (1586). According to Trillo, this easy victory gave the Spanish troops in the citadel the idea that an overall attack on the city might be feasible.[296] These data make clear that the violence started before the mutineers' arrival, but also that Roda and Sancho did not use the presence of the mutineers to free themselves of any guilt regarding the excessive violence used by the troops.

Another aspect of the letter from Roda is his definition of the event as a victory in a battle, and his statement that the main commanders, including Sancho, Julián Romero and Francisco de Valdés, should be rewarded by the King for their actions. The victory had been 'sanglante' and much damage had been done, but it was a very important one, as from now on the Low Countries would take the citadel more into their consideration.[297]

There was another aspect that contributed to the events: the festering personal conflict between Sancho Dávila and Governor Champagney. As mentioned before, Luis de Requesens had been perfectly aware of the situation, but clearly sided with Sancho:

> Sancho Dávila, without offending anybody, is the best soldier the King has at his disposal in the Low Countries and you can only blame him for his violent passion towards Champagney, while Champagney possesses a terrible hatred towards the whole Spanish nation and everything that is decided and done in Brussels and Madrid.[298]

---

[295] Perrenot, *Mémoires*, 195-201.
[296] Trillo, *Historia*, 298; Lancaster, 'Larum', 461-462.
[297] Roda to Philip II, Antwerp citadel, 6 November 1576, CP V, 15; AGS, E. 566, 57.
[298] Perrenot, *Mémoires*, xxv-xxxii-xxxiii.

The personal conflict between Champagney and Dávila dated from at least 1574 when the Spanish soldiers had celebrated their victory at Mookerheyde in the streets of Antwerp, with lots of noise, shouting and trumpets. Champagney also related in his memoirs that Sancho had been waiting for a good opportunity to rob the city of its riches, and this had almost led to a duel between Sancho and Julián. We find the same idea in a letter to the King.[299]

The 1713 biography connected the attack with honour because of the victory over a strong enemy, but tried to minimise the plundering: "by ordering not to take anything out of the city, part of the damage could be resolved, and the goods returned to their owners at a low price".[300] Sancho's biographer in 1857 decided to minimise the space given to the Fury, not even half a page, and concluded without quoting any sources that Sancho had tried to avoid the sacking of the city, probably based on the 1713 text.[301] The entry in Spain's new biographical dictionary also does not pay much attention to this event and states that it was the result of problems between the Council in Brussels and Sancho, and that the action was undertaken to punish the city for supporting William of Orange, and as a way of paying for the troops.[302] If this last argument had been true Sancho would actively have favoured the sacking. The 2010 biographer is the first to dedicate a whole chapter to the Fury, called 'el saqueo de Amberes'.[303] The author claims that the defenders of the city started using their artillery against the citadel, turning Sancho's attack into a reaction, but the only moment in this text when Sancho is actually given any protagonism is when he asked the mutineers to join them. There is no reflection whatsoever on Sancho's role in the events.

**The Spanish Fury on stage**

The Antwerp Fury has inspired plays in both Spain and England, studied by Ann Mackenzie in 1982 in an elucidating comparative article. There is doubt about the authorship of *El saco de Amberes* as both Pedro Calderón de la Barca and Francisco Rojas Zorrilla have been mentioned, while *A Larum for London* has remained anonymous. Both plays have recently

---

[299] Perrenot, *Mémoires*, 39-40, 83; Champagney to Philip II, Brussels, 30 November 1576, CP V, 73-75.
[300] Dávila y San-Vitores, *Rayo*, 203.
[301] Pando Fernández de Pinedo, *Vida*, 216-217.
[302] Martínez Ruiz, 'Sancho Dávila', 647.
[303] Martín García, *Sancho*, 207-215.

attracted scholarly interest and recent editons of both are available.[304]

In *A Larum for London* Sancho is one of the main protagonists, albeit under the name of Sancto Danila, clearly the result of bad copying. He is the first to enter the stage after the prologue. And it is directly made clear that Sancho started the violence and why:

> The plot already is determin'd of, and say Cornelius [commander of German infantry] doe but keepe his word; these swilling Epicures shall taste of death, whilst we survive to rifle their rich coffers.... if men ever had a fit occasion to inrich themselves, and fill the vast world with our eechoing fame, now is that instant put into our hands.[305]

The anonymous author of the play has no interest in possible political or military reasons behind Sancho's motivation to attack the city. The only other argument mentioned is the fact that the inhabitants had permitted Orange's fleet to anchor. Interestingly, the element of helping the Prince of Orange can also be found in the surviving correspondence. The element of mutiny is not used and the mutinying troops arriving from Aalst are not described in any special way.

The strength of the play lies in Sancho's characterisation as a violent and very cruel man. When he found out that an old man had hidden his daughter in a convent, he ordered his troops to fetch her: "welcome faire sweet, mine armes shall be thy throane". Sometime later, when the fighting needed his full attention, he decided without remorse to kill her with his own pistol, "rather tan another shall inioy, what Danila held esteemed in his eye, heere it began, and heere my love shall dye".[306] The scene may have been based on a story in Gascoigne's *Spoyle*, where two soldiers raped a girl after getting her out of her hiding place in a convent.[307] Danila also stars in the last scene, just before the epilogue, when entering the city victoriously with drums, banners and soldiers:

> Her streetes lye thwackt with slaughtered carcasses,
> her houses that before were stuft with pride,
> are left as naked as the wilderness:
> Oh in remorse of humaine clemency,

---

[304] Mackenzie, 'Study'; Idem, 'Saco; Rodríguez Pérez, 'Amotinado'; Idem, 'Muiters'; Truan, *Saco*; Lancaster, *Larum*.
[305] Greg, *Larum* (1913) lines 20-23, 63-65.
[306] Greg, *Larum*, lines 1023, 1075-1079.
[307] Mackenzie, 'Study', 289.

> My heart (me thinkes) could sigh, my eyes shed teares,
> To call to minde and see their misery:
> But they were wanton and lascivious,
> Too much addicted to their private lust:
> And that concludes their martirdoome was iust.[308]

Just for one moment it seems Sancho was capable of pity, but he remains a perfect example of the Spanish soldier as described in texts belonging to the discourse of the Black Legend: cruel, bloodthirsty and merciless. There is nothing authentic about his depiction, and not even his name was rendered correctly.

For its part the Spanish *comedia* offers a completely different version of events. The play is set before the actual Fury takes place, with Sancho again as one of the main protagonists. This loyal servant to the crown appears on stage trying to convince the mutineers to stop their mutiny and come to his rescue: "Return, return, Spaniard, for our nation… to move the hardness of these rebel souls, returning to save us".[309]

In the end, Sancho will succeed in convincing the mutineers and they will arrive at the gates of Antwerp citadel, staging a dialogue between Sancho and *electo* Juan de Navarrete, the leader of the mutineers:

> Sancho: ¿Quién llama?  
> Navarrete: Los de Alost.  
> Sancho: ¿Y con qué intento?  
> (¿si acaso les ha animado  
> lo que anoche les previne?)  
> ¿Venís a que se amotine  
> la gente que me ha quedado?  
> Navarrete: No es de tan infame ley,  
> la acción que nos ha movido  
> Sancho: ¿Pues que es lo que os a traído?  
> Navarrete: Ganalle a Amberes al Rey,  
> pues con hecho tan valiente,  
> nuestra misma afrenta cessa.[310]

> Who is calling?  
> Those of Aalst.  
> With what intention?  
> Maybe you are encouraged  
> what he told them last night.  
> Have you come to make mutineers  
> out of the people that are left to me?  
> There is no bad intention  
> behind the reason for our arrival.  
> So then, why have you come?  
> To win Antwerp for the King  
> because with such a brave endeavour  
> we can make up for our affront.

In the play it is clearly stated that it was Sancho who decided to open the gates for the mutineers: first, those from the outside to the citadel and

---

[308] Greg, *Larum*, lines 1610-1625.
[309] 'Bolved, volved, Español, por vuestra nación… para mover la dureza, destos animos rebeldes, porque a socorrer me buelvan'. Truan, *Saco*, II, 670-671; III, 220-226.
[310] Truan, *Saco*, III, 578-591.

then those from the citadel to the city. "I want to point out, that by my order they have opened it [the gate of the citadel towards the city]". And we also find him, almost at the end of the play, participating personally in the attack: "slashing several", as the author summarised the action.[311]

Related to this episode, there exists a famous quotation, spoken by *electo* Navarrete, the leader of the mutineers: "we shall eat in Antwerp or dine with Jesus Christ".[312] The quotation assigns some of the protagonism to the *electo*, but it seems that the valour of the mutineers is what is being emphasised here. We can find a variation of the quotation in the chronicle of Bernardino de Mendoza who relates how the Spanish mutineers were let into Antwerp citadel on 4 November 1576, at eight in the morning:

> And Sancho Dávila and the other commanders asked them if they wanted to rest for a while and eat, but they, coming with green leaves and hope of success for their good spirit, responded that there were determined to eat in paradise or dine in the city of Antwerp'.[313]

Why the order of elements has been changed remains unclear, but it is undeniable that the playwright clearly knew his chronicles. This remark can also be found in the previously mentioned anti-Spanish Netherlandish pamphlet on the Fury and in later Protestant histories of the events: "they swore an oath not to eat, nor drink or rest before they could do the same quietly and easily within the city of Antwerp".[314] It looks as if the rather general quotation of the pamphlet later became embellished with a religious point in more elaborated texts. *Electo* Navarrete died during the first attack on the defence line, and even in Hooft's history the author no longer differentiated between mutineers and other soldiers.

*El Saco de Amberes* is a very interesting play as it turns mutineers into heroes fighting for King and country.[315] One could even describe it as a nationalistic play. Sancho's role is paramount, since he had succeeded in converting the mutineers again into active and loyal soldiers. As they had not yet been paid, they were allowed to fight under their own banners and under their own *electo*. In that sense, of course, there were Spanish

---

[311] 'Ya advierto, que por mi orden lo han abierto'; acuchillando a algunos'. Truan, *Saco*, III, lines 636-637, after line 674.
[312] 'Vamos a comer a Amberes o a cenar con Iesu Christo'. Truan, *Saco*, III, 563-564.
[313] Mendoza, *Comentarios* (1948) 549.
[314] *Warachtige beschrijvinghe*; Hooft, *Alle de gedrukte werken* IV, 469-470; Brantôme, *Oeuvres compléts*, I (1839) 150-151.
[315] Rodríguez Pérez, 'Amotinado'.

mutineers during the Spanish Fury, but it was not a mutiny that got out of hand; it was a battle within the city, against a large army of defenders with different parties involved. In the military sense it was a victorious assault by Sancho's troops. Even the Netherlandish pamphlet considered it a work of God, "because otherwise it would have been impossible that so few soldiers would have been capable of gaining a city with so many inhabitants and with so many soldiers".[316]

## His failed knighthood

The Perpetual Edict issued on 17 February 1577 included the surrender of the citadels to people born in the Low Countries and the departure of all Spanish troops. The King had already given his new Governor-general the right to take Antwerp from Sancho, as can be found in a letter to Dávila from 6 November 1576, written when the Spanish Fury was already taking place, but, of course, without the King being aware of it: "if I order you to give up the government of this citadel, you have to do it without any doubts and without any difficulties".[317] It was an order, though still politely formulated. In January 1577, Philip's tone was much harsher: "though for duplicated letters I have ordered and commanded you to hand over the said castle".[318]

Don Juan informed the King that Sancho was very unhappy as the citadel had been given to him as compensation for his services, and Sancho considered the King should take this away only if he were to receive greater compensation.[319] The worst was that he would have to hand the keys to his castle over to the Duke of Aarschot, his enemy from the Council of State.[320] According to chronicler Cabrera de Córdoba, he could not make himself give the keys to Aarschot, so he left and delegated this difficult job to his lieutenant, Martín del Hoyo.[321]

---

[316] *Warachtige beschrijvinghe*.

[317] 'Si os ordenáre que dejeis el cargo de esa ciudadela, lo hareis sin poner en ello duda, ni dificultad alguna'. Philip II to Dávila, Madrid, 6 November 1576, quoted in Pando Fernández de Pinedo, *Vida*, 222-223; AGS, E. 569, 22.

[318] 'Aunque por cartas duplicadas os he ordenado y mandado que entregueis el dicho castillo'. Philip II (secretary Antonio Pérez) to Dávila, Madrid, 31 January 1577, quoted in Pando Fernández de Pinedo, *Vida*, 224-225.

[319] Don Juan to Philip II, Marche, 2 January 1577, CP V, 135.

[320] Juan de Austria to Dávila, Leuven, 3 March 1577, quoted in Pando Fernández de Pinedo, *Vida*, 226-227.

[321] Martín García, *Sancho*, 219; Cornejo, *Sumario*, 284.

On 28 April 1577 most Spanish troops left the Low Countries by way of Maastricht, "with money in their pocket, plunder, and booty in their bags, and the firm promise of more to come". The 5,300 soldiers had two thousand servants, but needed provisions for twenty thousand.[322] There had been a discussion about who would function as commander of these troops. Was it to be Alonso de Vargas, Sancho Dávila, Julián Romero or Francisco de Valdés? In the end the Count of Mansfelt led the expedition to Italy. However, the commanders were very unhappy that they had to give up their positions without knowing what they would get in return.[323] According to Italian historian Bentivoglio, Sancho had boldly stated on his departure from the Low Countries that they would be back soon: "Your Highness forces us to leave the Low Countries, but remember, very soon he will find himself forced to recall us".[324]

In May 1577 Philip II was thinking how to reward the commanders who had returned from the Low Countries, as we have already seen in the chapter on Julián. The citadel of Alessandria was for Sancho, but if he did not want it the citadel would go to Romero, and this would also have repercussions for Mondragón. But the King kept changing his mind, and Sancho was not satisfied with the offer: "it will not be solved until he [Sancho] can kiss the hands of Your Majesty and explain to him his services and some other pretentions he has". According to the Marquis of Ayamonte, Governor-general of Milan and (like Requesens) a member of the important Zúñiga family, Romero and Sancho did not behave as they should, but "soldiers that comply by fighting can be excused for their lack of courtesy".[325] Sancho did indeed go to court, as is proven by a letter from September asking the King for compensation for his services.[326] Though he had not fulfilled all requirements, as some payments depended on his being present at court, the royal council decided to give him what he asked for because of all his services. One royal secretary added in the margin of the document, "this has consequences for others and it should not be done with those who have been absent,

---

[322] Parker, *Army* (2004) 79, 193; Parker, *Dutch Revolt*, 181.
[323] Don Juan to Philip II, Leuven, 7 April 1577, CP V, 299.
[324] Quoted in Quatrefages, *Tercios* (1979), 273.
[325] Quatrefages, *Tercios* (1979) 44-45; Philip II to the Marquis of Ayamonte, Aranjuez, 3 and 4 May 1577, CD XXXI, 154-156. Philip II to Dávila, Aranjuez, 3 May 1577, Idem, 156-157; Ayamonte to Philip II, Vigevano, 5 July 1577, Idem, 157-158; Ayamonte to secretary Antonio Pérez, Vigevano, 8 July 1577, Idem, 159-160.
[326] Dávila to Philip II, Madrid, 4 September 1577, CD XXXI, 160-161.

and especially with those that have good salaries like his". Sancho was also appointed Captain-general of the coast of Granada.[327]

But he did not attain his main objective, a knighthood of the order of Santiago, promised to him by the King in 1570, but still under scrutiny.[328] The council of the military orders did not limit itself to meekly following Philip II's wishes, since when dealing with military commanders it did investigate their noble status and their purity of blood.[329] At the time of the first request, the council had found a problem with a great-grandmother of Sancho. In 1578 the case was still being debated between the president of the council, the King and the Duke of Alba. Finally, Alba understood that Sancho was not going to be handed a habit, though he still suggested the possibility of asking the pope for a dispensation. The debate continued, and when the pope seemed willing to provide Sancho with a dispensation, the president of the order did not accept this option: "to give a habit to a converso, and to such a well-known personality… would be the knife and the end of the orders".[330] The Marquis of Aguilar tried to convince the King to intervene in this case:

> As it is a matter of honour, it seems to me not unreasonable, because without it he cannot serve His Majesty, and His Majesty would then lose a great captain and soldier, who has been succesful in all affairs he was involved in.

The Marquis also sent a memorial of Sancho's with his letter in which Sancho pleaded his case with the King, threatening to leave his offices:

> Without this contentment and satisfaction, my spirit would not be enough for me to continue serving Your Majesty in this function, nor in any other related to war, because he would understand that my sword and chance (*ventura*) would fail me in everything.

Sancho also tried to frame the situation as an insult to the King's powers: "I cannot believe that Your Majesty is not powerful enough to honour those who serve him, and lift men up from the dust of the earth, because these are the powers and the greatness of kings". Seemingly Philip II did

---

[327] CD XXXI, 161-166.
[328] AHN, Ordenes militares, Santiago 8581.
[329] Fernández Izquierdo, *Orden*, 215.
[330] Fernández Izquierdo, *Orden*, 215-218.

not send a reply to the commander on the matter.³³¹ However, on 20 October 1579 Sancho received his patent as Maestre de campo general of the army that had to enter Portugal.³³²

In 1580 his old friend Fernando de Toledo, the Duke's natural son and Prior of the Order of San Juan, did his best to help Sancho, asking for approbation of his habit:

> And even if Sancho Dávila was not my friend, I would do the same for any other person whom I would see in the same manner, because he is the most desparate man on earth, because his honour cannot walk around the world as it should, and it would be so easy to resolve it.

Even his old 'amigo' could not help him out, and Sancho would die in 1583 without having received his habit and without having regained his honour.³³³ In 1636 Sancho's grandson, Sancho Dávila Guevara, would finally receive a habit of the order of Alcántara, just before travelling to America in the service of the King. In a document of the Council of the Indies we see that the grandson earned his new positions in large part through his famous grandfather, whose years in the Low Countries were summarised as follows:

> He went to Flanders as captain of cavalry and the Duke's guards, where he apprehended the Count of Egmont, destoyed the rebels at Dahlem, slaughtering more than five thousand; in Frisia he defeated Count Louis, offering valuable services during this war, destroying the Prince of Orange, killing and capturing in Tienen (Tirlemont) the best men of the army – and where he was shot in his thigh; he saved Middelburg, slaughtered the heretics who had besieged it, won Arnemuiden and four hundred ships worth many millions. During the nocturnal attack (*encamisada*) on Arnemuiden, under his command and that of others, they used ladders to climb the walls, and in Moncalvo he killed in a duel a knight who was almost a giant arriving with a double-handed sword and Sancho with his sword and shield. He discovered the

---

[331] Marquis del Aguilar to secretary Juan Delgado, Madrid, 24 August 1579 and Memorial de Sancho Dávila, CD XXXI, 166-169; Philip II to Dávila, San Lorenzo de El Escorial, 19 September and 4 October 1579, Idem, 169-172.
[332] CD XXXI, 173-175.
[333] Dávila to Philip II, Lisbon, 8 April 1583, CD XXXI, 555.

treason of Roermond, pacified the mutiny in Antwerp, conquered the islands of Zierikzee, Duiveland and Philipsland.[334]

In the seventeenth century the rules of the orders regarding purity of blood were clearly less stringent than in the later years of Philip II but, of course, the candidates' past also became less easy to control, as with the passing of time it became more difficult to find evidence of a converso background. A comparable situation occurred with the possible knighthood for Cristóbal de Mondragón.

Martín García in his 2010 biography does address Sancho's converso background, asking the question "and why not a habit of the Order of Santiago?", suggesting that Sancho had already harboured doubts about the origins of his two grandmothers from Salamanca and Segovia. The documentation from the council of the orders points to the family of his mother, Ana Daza, the daughter of Rodrigo Orejón and Andresa del Espinar. Andresa was thought to be a descendant in the third degree of conversos from Segovia.[335] In 1857, the Marquis of Miraflores completely avoided writing about the possible converso background of his ancestor, not even mentioning the debate about the habit. Gerónimo Manuel Dávila y San-Vitores also did not mention a converso background, neither did he refer to the negated knighthood. While Gerónimo filled many pages of his book with genealogical information on his own family, there is nothing to be found about Sancho's mother's side.[336]

## Last years in Portugal (1581-1583)

Sancho played an instrumental role not ony in the Low Countries, but also in Portugal. As *Maestre de campo general* of the army he helped the

---

[334] 'Pasó a Flandes por capitán de cavallos y de la guardia del duque de Alba, donde prendió al conde de Agmon, desbarató los reveldes en Dalen pasando a cuchillo más de 5,000; en Frissa venció al conde Ludobico haçiendo en esta guerra notables serviçios, desbarató al prínçipe Dorange, degollando y prendiendo en Tylimon la gente más luçida del exérçito y a él le dieron un balaço en un muslo, socorrió a Middelburg, degolló los herejes que la tenían cercada, ganó a Ramua y 400 navíos y urcas que valían muchos millones. En la encamisada de Ramua, haviéndose encomendado a él y a otros, un escala para arrimarla y en Moncalvo mató de solo a solo un cavallero que era medio xigante viniendo con montante y Sancho Dávila con espada y rodela. Descubrió la trayçión de Roremunda, apaciguó el motín de Amberes, conquistó las islas de Zirqueça, Duvelanda y Filispidan'. Archivo General de Indias, Indiferente 111, 202, quoted in Martín García, *Sancho*, 285-287.

[335] Martín García, *Sancho*, 10, 46, 139, 143.

[336] Pando Fernández de Pinedo, *Vida*; Dávila y San-Vitores, *Rayo*.

Duke of Alba to pacify Portugal and facilitate Philip II's access to the Portuguese throne. The Duke, as leader of the whole expedition, had requested Sancho's presence from the beginning.[337] His final enterprise has also turned him into one of the protagonists of a play attributed to Lope de Vega, *La defensa en la verdad*:[338]

| | |
|---|---|
| Y assi el Español monarca | And so the Spanish monarch |
| Para hazañas tan grandes, | For exploits so great, |
| Embió al rayo de Flandes, | Sent the lighting bolt of Flanders |
| Al cuchillo de la parca, | The knife of death |
| Al mas valiente Español | The most valiant Spaniard |
| Que al furioso mar se obliga; | Who forced the furious sea |
| Que con la sangre enemiga | With the blood of the enemies |
| Puso rojo todo el sol. | Turned the sun red |
| Sancho de Avila en efeto | Sancho Dávila indeed |
| Que en la docta escuela la aprende | Who in the learned school was taught |
| Del gran Duque de Alva a Ostende, | By the great Duke of Alba, with Oostende |
| Y Mastrique en el aprieto. | And Maastricht in distress |
| Mayor de Sancho temblaron, | Fearing Sancho so much |
| Al fin a su nombre ygual. | And in the end even his name. |

During this last expedition Sancho again worked together with his friend, Prior Fernando de Toledo.[339] The expedition offered new possibilities for asking for royal rewards, reminding the King of the more than thirty-eight years he had served as a soldier: "I hope.... if I don't die, to receive many rewards and honours from your hand".[340] He also reminded the King of the fact that the rewards he had been promised after the Battle of Mookerheyde had still not been paid. Now he wanted an office and an estate in Portugal that had become vacant, not for himself, but "to leave to my son". In March 1581 he was still waiting for his financial reward from Mookerheyde and by then he suggested he be given another estate in Portugal.[341]

---

[337] Valladares, 'Alba'.
[338] Vosters, *Nederlanden*, 261-262; Vega y Carpio, *Defensa*.
[339] Fernando de Toledo to Zayas, Setubal, 19 July 1580, CD XXXI, 207-213. Many letters to and from Sancho in CD XXXI.
[340] Dávila to Philip II, Quinta da Gaya [Gaia?], 29 August 1580, CD XXXI, 217-218.
[341] Dávila to Zayas, Porto, 18 March 1581, CD XXXI, 559-560; Dávila to Juan Delgado, Puerto de Santa María, 19 December 1581, CD XXXV, 339-342; AGS, GM 120, 86.

Sancho also complained in his letter that he had never in his life received a good ransom from a rich prisoner:

> Though I had taken one during the victory at Dahlem who would give me five thousand escudos, but the Duke cut off his head and did not give me anything in return; and another very rich German during the battle of Mookerheyde, but the Comendador Mayor [Requesens] asked to exchange him for Luis Ponce, the son of Andrés Ponce, who had been taken prisoner by the Count of Nassau, a brother of the Prince of Orange, and I also handed him over.[342]

In April 1583 Sancho was still desperately engaged in trying to obtain his promised habit: "I beg that you find it at your service to issue an order to give me an encomiendo with the habit that would honour me… And if possible to enjoy it during my lifetime, and it seems it is high time, as I am already around sixty years of age".[343] And he was right, as he died on 8 June of that year:

> A horse had kicked Sancho Dávila and he did not make much of it. At first he was cured with the use of incantations; after three days the wound closed with medicines; by then he already had fever; they bled him three times and he was purged, and as the remedies were started late, he died on the ninth day.[344]

His executors were Alonso López Gallo, Antonio del Río and Luis de Barrrientos (of the royal war council in Portugal), who wrote a letter describing Sancho as indeed "a great soldier with friends and enemies (*soldado de gran opinion con amigos y enemigos*)", the image we can also deduce from his own letters, dividing the world into excellent friends and despicable enemies.[345]

His body was taken to the church of Saint John the Baptist in Ávila. In his will he expressed his wish to have a chapel for himself and that his first wife's body be brought there from the Low Countries. His young son, Fernando, would receive an inheritance worth some sixty thousand

---

[342] Dávila to Zayas, Barcelos, 3 August 1581, CD XXXI, 474-477.
[343] Dávila to Philip II, Lisbon, 8 April 1583, CD XXXI, 553-555.
[344] According to Brantôme, Sancho had died at the siege of Maastricht (1579). Brantôme, *Oeuvres completes*, I, 151.
[345] Barrientos to secretary Juan Delgado, Lisbon, 10 June 1583, CD XXXI, 556.

ducats.³⁴⁶ In the end Sancho had accumulated a handsome fortune during the more than forty years he had served as a soldier. His descendants did well, obtaining a habit, and in 2019 Marquis Alonso Álvarez de Toledo is still guarding the family inheritance, including the paintings of Sancho and his wife Catalina.

## Protagonist of a historical novel (2007)

Enrique Martínez Ruiz, in 2007 still an active full professor of Early Modern History at the Complutense University of Madrid, published that year a lengthy historical novel on Sancho Dávila. Though this military specialist and authority on the history of Sancho Dávila knew better, it was decided for commercial reasons to call the book *El castellano de Flandes*, instead of the correct but less attractive *El castellano de Amberes*. The subtitle shows the importance the author assigns to his protagonist: 'the man who kept Philip II's empire standing' (*el hombre que mantuvo en pie el imperio de Felipe II*).³⁴⁷ The novel portrays Sancho's eventful life from his native Ávila, passing through all the important places of his career in the Low Countries, including Dahlem, Mookerheyde and Bommenede. However, it takes the author more than half of the more than six hundred pages to arrive in the Low Countries.

Elaborating on a well-known and emotionally charged historical moment, Martínez Ruiz offers us a moment of intimacy between Sancho and Egmont after his arrest: "their looks crossed each other; and in that of his one could see a reproach (*las miradas se cruzaron; en la de aquél había un reproche*)". The scene resembles the emotional moment between Egmont and Julián Romero just before the count's execution in Brussels that we can find in several chonicles. Furthermore, the author devotes much attention to the description of his wounds and to the peculiarities of military life at the time, using original sources. A fictitious love story with Agnes, a woman from the Low Countries with blue eyes, is also added to the plot.³⁴⁸ It is noteworthy that his two real-life marriages were omitted from the novel. Almost at the end of the book a chapter entitled "Apocalipsis en Amberes" describes the Spanish Fury. After the attack on the city had started, Sancho rushed to Agnes's house, only to find her tortured and brutally killed by soldiers looking for money. It makes him finally understand the position of the victims, after all those

---

³⁴⁶ Martín García, *Sancho*, 276-278.
³⁴⁷ Martínez Ruiz, *Castellano*.
³⁴⁸ Martínez Ruiz, *Castellano*, 356, 393, 397.

violent years: "For me, nothing will ever be the same and I fear that I will turn into a man who hates his destiny" ("*Para mí ya nada será igual y me temo que me convertiré en un hombre que abomina de su destino*").[349]

## Friends and heretics

When considering the texts written by Sancho Dávila and those that have been written about him, two interrelated elements come very much to the fore, in contrast to the other commanders studied in this book. There is the fact that in his correspondence Sancho much more frequently uses the word 'heretics', turning the rebellion in the Low Countries into a religious conflict. This 'confessionalisation' of the Revolt by the Spanish commander may have been the reflection of a more profound religious sentiment. As the biographers have it, he started his life in search of a religious career, perhaps under the guidance and protection of his uncle, the arch-dean. But at the same time he seems to have always had a martial heart, which may have been the genetic inheritance from his early deceased and combative Comunero father. It may well have been that Sancho, more than the other commanders, was a soldier with a religious heart. This possibility must then be combined with the problems with the laws of purity of blood that prevented him from acquiring the habit of one of the religious knightly orders. For a Spanish soldier with a converso background religion may have been a more important issue since it also intersected with his very own personal life and career, but this question is imposible to answer with the available sources.

Nevertheless, in the same letters in which we encounter the frequent use of 'heretics', we also find the recurring use of 'friends'. Compared to the others, Sancho writes much more about his friends. Particularly strong friendships are those with the rich merchant Hernando de Frías and with Fernando de Toledo, Alba's natural son. One of his executors, Luis de Barrientos, when reflecting on Sancho's life, called him "a great soldier with friends and enemies". This chimes perfectly with the idea one gets from reading his letters. If this were the case, we would then have to be cautious in interpreting his use of 'heretics' too narrowly as a purely religious statement. It can certainly be a way of expressing the dichotomy between friends and foes, preferring a clearly negative word for the enemies to a more neutral one. Maybe his feud with the Lord of Champagney is also a case in point.

---

[349] Martínez Ruiz, *Castellano*, 603-604, 612-613, 620.

However, for the moment it might be best to interpret both these elements at work within this Spanish commander, combining his martial and religious background with his personal character which tended to divide the world in a Manichean dichotomy. Sancho functioned for ten years without any disruption in the Low Countries, a region where there was a religious divide he had not experienced in his earlier life in Ávila and in Italy. And over time, the Low Countries became more and more hostile to Spanish commanders, magnifying even more the influence of both his character and his background.

At the same time we should not overlook the fact that Sancho was also a professional and experienced soldier who craved recognition and the rewards that corresponded to his accomplishments, a need that was connected with the idea of building an inheritance to leave for his only son. Despite the difficult negotiations, he was actually very successful because, notwithstanding all the complaining in his letters, he did amass a small fortune during his military career. Furthermore, he also passed on another legacy: his memory and fame. Already starting with his grandson, his descendants used the memory of the great deeds of their ancestor to promote themselves, continuing at least until the Marquis of Miraflores in the nineteenth century. Having such a great hero in the family was beneficial without any doubt. His descendants who took up the pen to write his biography also framed him as a 'Catholic' hero, combining this image of a war hero with that of a hero defending Catholicism against heresy, which could also be useful in the Spain they were living in. At least judging from his own letters, using 'heretics' so frequently, Sancho may have felt himself indeed a champion of Catholicism, in a more pronounced way than the other commanders.

Dutch historiography has not paid much attention to this great Spanish military figure. He was clearly famous, and much hated, in the Low Countries during his lifetime, maybe even as the drummer turned commander, but his fame was lost after his death. Though difficult to prove, it might well be the fact that he was so close to the Duke of Alba, and so close to the negative characterisation of the Iron Duke, that Dutch historiography did not need to create a separate protagonist. It was easier to emphasise the much more famous Duke of Alba as the symbol of Spanish and Catholic cruelty. In that sense Sancho's image was overshadowed by that of his master.

Cristóbal de Mondragón. Painting by Abraham de Rycke (1591), private collection, Torre de Murga, Spain. Photo: Stadhuismuseum Zierikzee.

# Chapter III
# Cristóbal de Mondragón: the good Spaniard

## Eternal fame

An eighteenth-century chronicler from the town of Zierikzee in Zeeland described the Spanish commander Cristóbal de Mondragón as an exceptional person: "Mondragón possessed a noble heart, that was able to value even the merits of an enemy". In his chronicle from 1795 he elaborated further on this idea in a footnote:

> We admire this virtue in a Spaniard of those days. Thumb freely through the patriotic (*Vaderlandsche*) histories of those centuries; I doubt if you will be able to find a second Mondragón; whose decent (*braaf*) behaviour, compared to the wickedness, perjury and inhuman cruelties of other Spanish commanders, stands out even more.[1]

Mondragón is the exception to the rule, the only virtuous Spaniard. His presence allows the author to denounce all other Spaniards as extremely cruel. For this reason, praising Mondragón still belongs to the Black Legend of Spain, the narrative tradition among mostly Protestant authors that describes the Spanish as a people cruel by nature. The comparison between Mondragón and the Duke of Alba in particular has often been made, as we can read in a Beggar's song on the surrender of Zierikzee in 1576: "they keep their body and leave; Mondragón has received them with mercy, he did better than the Duke of Alba, when Haarlem had surrendered".[2] The merciless third Duke of Alba, Fernando Álvarez de Toledo, can be considered the dark shadow of the noble Mondragón.

---

[1] De Kanter, *Chronijk*, 152-153. This chapter was partly translated and reworked for a Dutch book: Fagel, *Cristóbal*.

[2] 'Behouden lijf en leven; Mondragon heeft s' in genade ontfaen, hy heeft beter als duc d'Alf gedaen, doen Haerlem worde opgegeven'. *Nederlandsche geschiedgezangen* (1864) 161.

This positive image of Mondragón still exists in Zierikzee today. On a gate in the city's harbour, the Noordhavenpoort, we find a metal pole described as Mondragón's sword, left behind after the Spanish commander had taken Zierikzee in 1576 in the name of King Philip II. The newspaper *Zeeuwsch Dagblad* on 6 May 1960 wrote a little disrespectfully about "an iron bar that is called: Mondragón's sword".[3] Not free of sarcasm, the journalist described what, according to him, had happened after Mondragón had hastily left Zierikzee in 1576: "Then, in all consternation, he must have forgotten his sword that then was planted 'for eternal memory' on top of this gate". The French novelist Victor Hugo visited Zierikzee in 1867 and his coachman showed him the sword and explained the story when they drove under the gate, and even then the author understood how exceptional it was that the conquered honoured the sword of the conquerer.[4] When in 2017 the sword suddenly disappeared from its towering position, it was front-page news in the local media. After several weeks it became known that the theft was a publicity stunt for a new hotel in the city called Mondragón that opened its doors in 2020. The hotel is in the same building that had housed a restaurant and cinema with that name between 1947 and 2001.[5] Near the harbour, the house where the commander had stayed, called 'De Mossele', was also a place of rememberance. Mondragón's fame in Zierikzee even led in 2002 to the creation of a tourist route called the path of Mondragón, 'het Mondragónpad', with a leaflet and a map available for visitors to the island.[6]

Mondragón is a local hero not only in Zierikzee. In Groenlo, a town he successfully defended against Maurice of Nassau in 1595, there is a street that bears his name, and we find the same in Maastricht, where he was one of the commanders who in 1579 successfully besieged the city under the command of the Prince of Parma, Alexander Farnese. His sword seems to possess a special commemorative power, as in the past a church tower in the city of Luxembourg perhaps also had his sword on top of it. In 1926, the colleagues of the young Francisco Franco Bahamonde had two copies of the sword made as a gift for the celebration of his appointment to General. One of the swords was destined for the Spanish

---

[3] *Zeeuwsch Dagblad*, 6 May 1960, 3.
[4] Hugo, *Oeuvres complètes*, II, 532; Uil, 'Degen'.
[5] 'Zwaard van Mondragon op havenpoort'; 'Zwaard van Mondragon moet zo snel mogelijk terug'; 'Verdwijning'.
[6] Visser and Hoogenraad, *Mondragónpad*; Blokker, *Waar is de Tachtigjarige Oorlog*, 62-63; Steegmans, 'Erfenis'.

national military museum; the other was handed to the man who would later become Spain's dictator. These copies could be made because the commander's descendants were then, and still are, in possession of a sword belonging to their illustrious ancestor.[7] The Kunsthistorisches Museum in Vienna possesses a cuirass and a helmet that belonged to him; the cuirass was included in the 1948 exhibition in Delft conmemorating the peace of Münster and in the 2020 exhibition on Mondragón in Zierikzee.

His fame in Spain may have been enhanced by the very fine biography on Mondragón published in 1905 by Ángel Salcedo Ruiz (1859-1921), though he modestly called it 'notes for his biography'. It has remained the reference work on his life to this day. The author, an auditor for the Spanish army, was also a well-versed conservative journalist and an editor of *La ilustración Católica*. He published widely, including in 1903 a book on Prior Don Fernando de Toledo, the natural son of the Duke of Alba, active in the Low Countries during the Revolt and, as we have seen, closely connected to Sancho Dávila.[8] A few years later, in 1912, the famous Spanish history painter, Ricardo de Medrazo y Garreta, made a portrait of the old general, now held in the national war museum in Toledo. So, at the beginning of the twentieth century it seemed he was well on his way to becoming a national Spanish hero.

However, nowadays, to many people Spanish commander Cristóbal de Mondragón is not much more than a local hero from the remote times of Philip II. In his home town of Medina del Campo, situated on the Castilian meseta, a historical re-enactment group called 'Tercio compañía de Cristóbal de Mondragón y de Mercado' has been present at many local and regional festivities since 2013.[9] This interest in the history of the early modern Spanish infantry can be explained both by a growing general interest in the history of the Spanish tercios and by a renewed awareness of the region's history related to the sixteenth century. At the time this region, and even more so the commercial city of Medina del Campo, was at the very heart of the Habsburg empire of Charles V and Philip II. Of course, there can also be found a more ancient local tradition conmemorating this historical commander, as he was already included in a manuscript on 'Medinenses ilustres' dating from the early seventeenth century.[10]

---

[7] Martínez Laínez, *El ocaso*, I, 86.
[8] Velasco Sánchez, 'Ángel Salcedo'.
[9] https://terciocristobaldemondragon.wordpress.com/.
[10] Salcedo Ruiz, *El coronel*, 8-9.

The main question in this chapter is how Mondragón became such a hero in Spain, while at the same time earning a positive reputation as an honourable old officer in the Low Countries, though in general Spanish commanders are seen there as the enemy. Somebody capable of gaining the hearts of both the Spaniards and the Netherlanders must have been a remarkable person. It is this idea that stands out in this chapter on the narratives and the memories of Cristóbal de Mondragón.

**From soldier to captain**

We know very little of Mondragón's early life, more or less the first fifty years of his life, until the beginning of the Revolt in the Low Countries. The same applies to the other Spanish commanders in this book. The first parts of their careers has been mostly reconstructed afterwards, when they had already become important military men. Though historians have been looking for more information, there are often relatively few documents for the earlier years. We may presume that Cristóbal was born around 1514, though there are also authors who have placed his birth in 1504. We do know for certain that he died in Antwerp on 4 January 1596. By that time he must have been around eighty-one years of age and still in office as a military commander. His extremely long career has made such an impression that a Spanish chronicler from the seventeenth century stated that he had been more than a hundred years old at the time of his death. We shall frequently encounter this image of the ancient Mondragón. Johan Brouwer, the most exiting Hispanist ever working in the Netherlands, defined him for this reason as a figure of almost Homeric proportions.[11]

Biographer Salcedo Ruiz collected a great deal of information on Mondragón's early life. His father, Martín, was born in Medina del Campo, of Basque origin like Romero's father, while his mother, Mencía de Mercado, came from an important family in that city. An official document from 1574 claims he was sixty then, which provides us with a year of birth around 1514. In his mother's last will and testament from 1545 we read that besides Cristóbal there were only two sisters still alive at the time: Magdalena, married to Diego González del Castillo, and Catalina, the wife of Francisco de Herrera Daza, both burghers of Medina. In 1545 we can also find a Martín de Beamonte, the son of his

---

[11] Brouwer, *Kronieken*, 30; Vosters, *Nederlanden*, 421; Villalobos y Benavides, 'Comentarios', 110-111.

deceased brother, Juan, three children (Antonio, Martín and Bernardina) of his deceased sister, Maria, who had been married to Juan de Alamos, and two children (Isabel and Fernando) of his deceased brother, Alonso, and his wife, Teresa de Cárdenas.[12]

The young Cristóbal is said to have entered the army in 1532 and, as he claimed himself, he participated in Charles V's famous attack on Tunis in 1535, organised to break the maritime power of Barbarossa, whose fleet was making the Mediterranean unsafe for Spanish and Italian ships. Most probably he then spent time in the garrisons of Italy before travelling to the northern territories of the Habsburgs. The earliest documentary proof is a payment in 1543 and his appearance on a list of wounded soldiers after the attack on Saint-Dizier on 15 July 1544, during the Habsburg-Valois wars. He was serving as a soldier in the tercio of Lombardy under Maestre de campo Luis Pérez de Vargas, who was also wounded at Saint-Dizier.[13] The Spanish soldier had become involved in the wars between Emperor Charles V and the French King Francis I, participating in a military campaign of the Emperor, who at the same time was also King of Spain and Lord of the Low Countries. He was part of an international army and as a Spaniard he had to serve the dynastic aspirations of his sovereign. At that time, there were some ten thousand Spanish soldiers present in the north of Europe, about as many as would come to the Low Countries with the Duke of Alba in 1567.[14]

Some years later he was supporting his King during the struggle against the German Lutheran princes. The most important battle occurred near Mühlberg, on 24 April 1547, also famous for a painting by Titian of Charles V on horseback. According to Mondragón's biographer, he would be promoted after the battle to *alférez*, comparable in rank to a lieutenant. He was said to have been one of the heroes who swam across the river Elbe and had made it possible for the Duke of Alba's army to reach the other bank of the river.[15] The story of Mondragón's act of heroism has

---

[12] Salcedo Ruiz, *El coronel*, 11, 27. Last will of Mencía de Mercado, Medina del Campo, 23 March 1545, AHN, Ordenes, Reprobados Santiago, 8bis; ARCV, Pleitos civiles, Pérez Alonso, caja 1033, 3 (1552-1555) and Idem, Registro de ejecutorias, caja 830, 64 (31 May 1555); Atienza and Barredo de Valenzuela, 'Los Mondragón'.

[13] Bermúdez de Castro, 'El tercio', 61; Rozet, 'L'invasion', 343. I thank Juan Luis Sánchez Martín and Carlos Valenzuela for these references. Parker, *Emperor*, 301-303; AGS, Contaduría Mayor de Cuentas, 1ª época, 1049. F. 150. In 1543, Mondragón served under Captain Jerónimo de Guijosa.

[14] Fagel, *Hispano-Vlaamse wereld*, 389-392.

[15] Salcedo Ruiz, *El coronel*, 37.

recently been retold by the modern Spanish author, Arturo Pérez-Reverte, famous for his series of novels on infantry captain Alatriste:

> He is completely exhausted, damns the Germans and all their bloody mess; and while he curses as a heretic and takes his sword in between his teeth, he starts swimming at a ford in the river, under a rain of arquebus shots. He shows he has balls and reaches the other bank, fighting and foaming with anger, and killing five of them.[16]

We see how Pérez-Reverte turns him into a typical masculine hero, including by using a quite vulgar colloquial idiom in order to recreate what he sees as the world of the tercios. According to this story, Mondragón was the first of a group of Spanish soldiers who swam across the river Elbe, and that made it possible for Charles V's army to cross the river after them. He calls Mondragón in the same text "the best soldier of the best regiment of the Spanish infantry". This last phrase strongly recalls the title of an article of 1936 by a Spanish general in which the same story is told in a more restrained style:

> Suddenly, a soldier takes off his clothes, holds his sword with his teeth, throws himself into the water and swims under a hail of projectiles. On the other riverbank he starts to fight with the enemies and kills five. After him, his captain and nine other soldiers have jumped in, and they arrived in time to help out the one who was fighting desperately; it was Mondragón.[17]

We frequently find this story repeated, for example in the leaflet on the Mondragón path, but is it true?[18] In his famous history of the wars in the Low Countries, Italian historian and Jesuit Famiano Strada asserted about Mondragón, "they say he was one of those ten Spanish men who with admirable bravery, crossed the Elbe swimming with the swords in their mouths".[19] And Strada was right to be careful in his wording. Chronicler Bernabé del Busto had been present at the battle and in his

---

[16] 'Se le va la pinza y empieza a ciscarse en los Alemanes y en todos sus muertos; y jurando en arameo se pone la espada entre los dientes, echa a nadar por el vado bajo una lluvia de arcabuzazo, llega a la orilla con dos cojones, arremete contra los alemanes echando espumarajos, y mata a cinco'. Pérez-Reverte, 'Una historia'.
[17] Bermúdez de Castro, 'El tercio', 61.
[18] Fuente, 'Cristóbal'; Cervera, 'El viejo'; Visser and Hoogenraad, *Mondragónpad*, 3.
[19] Salcedo Ruiz, *El coronel*, 37.

work he mentions the names of all Spanish swimmers, and Mondragón's is not among them.[20] The same holds for Sancho Dávila, indicating that famous acts of heroism were often attributed a posteriori to important commanders. Somewhere along the line the rumour had turned into fact, maybe through the work of General Bermúdez, who on 19 July 1936 published his article on Mondragón, two days before the outbreak of the Spanish Civil War. He was most probably looking for real Spanish heroes who could serve as examples during this new clash with the heretics.

We also know now that Mondragón obtained his promotion to *alférez* even before the Battle of Mühlberg. In the files of a civil trial between Cristóbal and his sister Catalina that went on for years, concerning the possession of several houses in Medina del Campo, we find an authorisation written by Cristóbal, at the time "alférez of the company of lancers of captain Juan Navarro and citizen of the city of Medina del Campo". The document had been issued on 5 June 1546 in the Emperor's army camp in the vicinity of 'Tanbergue' (Tännisberg?).[21]

From 1552 on there are finally more reliable sources available on Mondragón's life. He was around thirty-eight years of age at the time and would participate in the bloody wars between Charles V and Henry II, the new King of France. We may presume that he had remained in the north after 1544, although it cannot be ruled out that he returned to Spain for some time. On 22 July 1552 he received an order from the Duke of Alba to organise his own hundred horsemen, "good soldiers and well provided with weapons". In November of that same year his dissatisfied troops tried to overwhelm the city of Douai in the south of the Low Countries. Mondragón succeeded, however, in calming his men down and taking them peacefully back to Marchiennes, thus avoiding a violent confrontation between the local population and the foreign troops in the service of the sovereign.[22] It is the first time we really witness his conciliatory abilities.

---

[20] Busto, 'Quadernos'. The names can also be found in the German translation, *Geschichte).*, 179. I thank Juan Luis Sánchez (Madrid) for the reference, and Carlos Valenzuela for providing me with a copy of the manuscript. Mondragón is missing from Lope de Vega, 'El valiente Céspedes', 55. Part of the description of the swimming is, however, taken from his work. Bermúdez de Castro, 'El tercio', 58-61.
[21] Lawsuit of Cristóbal de Mondragón against Catalina de Mondragón and Francisco de Herrera Daça, ARCV, Pleitos civiles, Pérez Alonso (F), caja 1033,3.
[22] Alba to *alférez* Mondragón, Brixinon, 22 July 1552, EA I; *Chroniques de Douai*, II, 146-147; Ocampo, 'Sucesos'.

In a declaration used in the above-mentioned trial with his sister Catalina, Cristóbal declared on 11 August 1553 that he was captain of a company of light horse, residing at the court of Emperor Charles V in Brussels. Catalina argued that her brother had given her some houses out of their father's inheritance, but Cristóbal contradicted her by saying that "he could never have given her these houses, because they are the largest part of his possessions and he had no other income to live on". He wanted to rent out some of theses houses.[23] In 1554 he wrote two letters to important figures in the Habsburg army.[24] After more than twenty years under arms and some ten years active in the border area between France, Germany and the Low Countries, he was well on his way to becoming an important officer in the Emperor's army.

After Philip II had in 1555 taken over the government from his father, the war between the Lord of the Low Countries and the King of France was resumed. On 24 May 1557 a French army attacked the city of Lens where Mondragón was serving as governor. The French admiral's troops sacked and burned most of the city. Mondragón was taken prisoner, just as Julián Romero had been a few years earlier after Dinant had fallen into the hands of the French. His imprisonment may explain why we never hear anything about Mondragón being present at the famous Battle of Saint-Quentin on 10 August of that same year. The army of Philip II – Netherlanders, Germans, Englishmen, Italians, Spaniards – at Saint-Quentin inflicted a devastating defeat on the French. Because of his imprisonment, Mondragón missed out on one of the greatest moments in the military history of the sixteenth century.

However, we do find him again in October of that year as captain of a company of Walloon soldiers. This suggests that he may have received his freedom somewhere in between. The fact that he was able, and allowed, to command French-speaking soldiers from the Low Countries shows that he was considered a very well-integrated Spaniard.

In a letter to Philip II he stated, "having been taken prisoner at Lens and escaping from the Bastille in Paris to inform Your Majesty in Brussels what was happening in France". The document verifies the story by Juan López Osorio from the early seventeenth century in which Mondragón escaped by jumping from a tower.[25] We may thus imagine Mondragón

---

[23] See above. The houses were situated on the square behind the church of Saint Antolín, next to the church of Our Lady of Saint Julián.

[24] Mondragón to Luis de Ávila y Zúñiga, Soble [?], 7 July 1554; Mondragón to the Duke of Savoy, Floresse, 8 July 1554. ARAB, Audience 1667, 1804/1; Ocampo, 'Sucesos'.

[25] *CSP and manuscripts, relating to English affairs*, VI, 2, 1126; *Chroniques de Douai*, II,

jumping from a tower of such an emblematic building as the Bastille in Paris and running to freedom. At that time the Bastille was already in use as a prison, as it would still be more than 230 years later, on 14 July 1789. This fact-based anecdote of a hitherto unknown story can, we hope, fill the void left by the most probably untrue story about Mondragón's famous swim over the river Elbe.

After the signing of the peace treaty with France at Câteau-Cambrésis in 1559, Mondragón received a financial reward "for his good services to the Emperor and Philip II". Most of the Spanish troops left the Low Countries, but some three thousand soldiers remained to safeguard the country against the French threat, half of them under the command of Julián Romero.[26] Mondragón also travelled to Spain in 1560, but only to return again by the end of the year.

He used his stay in Spain to collect letters of recommendation, among them one from the Count of Feria, Gómez Suárez de Figueroa. The Count even called him 'my friend (*mi amigo*)' and described in the short letter to Granvelle (and indirectly to the Governess-general, Margaret of Parma) how Cristóbal was left without a royal income after 1559 and he hoped Margaret would take him into her service. He was indeed appointed the new military governor of Damvillers in Luxembourg, replacing his colleague, Julián Romero. Damvillers was a modern fortress that had to safeguard the Low Countries from attacks by the French. But the letter also refers to his impending wedding, "as he is returning to that country to get married".[27]

The Duke of Alba also gave him a short letter of recommendation intended for Granvelle, showing that Mondragón had visited the Duke in October.[28] The fact that he had letters from these two high noblemen is remarkable, as they belonged to rival factions at the Spanish court, playing a power game to obtain the best positions and the greatest influence. Feria had been considered to be Alba's 'enemy for life' ever

---

153. The chronicle stated that Mondragón would later die in Douai and would be buried at the Franciscan monastery in the city; Fagel, *Kapitein Julián*, 23-24. According to Salcedo Ruiz, *El coronel*, 39-40, Cristóbal was taken prisoner in 1558. The capture of Mondragón is in Hooft, *Histoorien*, I, 11. Fagel, 'Esplendor', 150; 'Haviendo sido preso en Lence y escapandose de la Bastilla de Paris a dar abiso a Bruselas a Vuestra Magestad de lo que en Franzia se hacia'. Mondragón to Philip II, Santander, 21 October 1570. AGS, E. 545, 92.

[26] Salcedo Ruiz, *El coronel*, 40; Marichalar, *Julián*, 124.
[27] 'Que se buelve a casar a esse pais'. Feria to Granvelle, Toledo, 10 November 1560, RBM, Granvelle collection II/2249, 27r.
[28] Alba to Granvelle, 2 October 1560, RBM, Granvelle collection II/2291, 271r-271v.

since 1541, and he was clearly associated with the Eboli faction.[29] On 28 October 1560 Mondragón wrote a letter from his home town, Medina del Campo, directly to Granvelle, evidence of the existence of a personal relationship between the captain and Granvelle, but probably simply used to accompany the recommendation letter by the Duke of Alba.[30] Mondragón also brought with him letters from Martín Alonso de los Ríos to give to Granvelle for the same purpose. Los Ríos counted Mondragón amongst his friends, "such honourable knights, so brave and so wise". He had also given Mondragón a bottle of balm for Granvelle, and he promised to send him more products from the Indies and the Canary Islands.[31]

Three letters from 1564, written to the Duke of Alba, offer some insight into his life during these years, still written from his residence in Damvillers. Alba was clearly his patron, as he himself stated in February, using the classical terms that went with such a patronage relationship: "I have always held myself, and still do, as a servant of Your Excellency and I am your creation".[32] He reminded the Duke how he had come to Alba de Tormes to ask him for permission to marry in the Low Countries. This must have been in October 1560. However, in the same letter he now had to inform the Duke that "Our Lord has been served by taking last Thursday my wife during childbirth". He was now free for new duties and stated that "it is my desire to die serving": the words of a client putting his destiny in the hands of his protector.

Such patronage ties were always of an unequal nature, and poor Mondragón did not get a swift reply to his letter. The Duke took his time in answering, and two months later Mondragón had to write him a reminder. He needed Alba's support, as he now had a daughter and during his many years outside his 'patria' in the service of the King he had spent most of his patrimony. He hoped the Duke could help to

---

[29] Maltby, *Alba*, 46, 72.

[30] Mondragón to Granvelle, Medina del Campo, 28 October 1560, RBM, Granvelle collection II/2291, 276r-277r.

[31] 'Tan honrrados cavalleros y tan balientes y tan cuerdos'. Martín Alonso de los Ríos to Granvelle, Toledo, 9 November 1560, RBM, Granvelle collection II/2249, 26r-26v; idem, 30 September 1560, II/2291, 278r-278v. Martín Alonso de Córdoba y de los Ríos (died 1569) was an ambassador and an admiral, commander of the Order of Calatrava, Rivarola y Pineda, *Monarquía*, II, 368.

[32] 'Como siempre me aya tenido y tengo por uno de los criados de vuestra excelencia y sea su hechura'; 'Nuestro señor [fue] servido de que el jueves pasado de un parto me llevo a mi mujer'; 'Mi deseo es morir sirviendo'. Mondragón to Alba, Damvillers, 5 February 1564, AA, C44, 171.

convert his lifelong payment from 1559 into one that would continue also during his daughter's lifetime, securing her future in this way, a not unreasonable precaution for somebody in such a dangerous profession. A third letter, from October, shows his desperation. He now wanted to go to Spain to meet the Duke and inform the King personally of his situation and of the situation in the Low Countries. He needed a licence to leave his government for only six to eight months, just as fellow commander Gaspar de Robles had received earlier. He also claimed some 'greedy men' were after his governorship of Damvillers. He further repeated his hopes of converting the payment for his daughter "of such tender age".[33]

He was a widower, aged around fifty, with a newborn baby, the fruit of his marriage to Catherine du Hem from Douai, the city where we find Mondragón already active in 1552. Catherine was the daughter of Robert du Hem, Lord of Auby, and Jeanne (Jenne) de Haussy.[34] His daughter, Margarita, would later marry his nephew, Alonso. Mondragón was now ready for new military duties, but he clearly needed the support of his patron. Without direct assistance at court, he could not expect to be heard. The only alternative would be to go to Spain himself, but, for that, one first needed permission, and this again required mediation.

However, in 1565 Philip's ambassador to England, Guzmán de Silva, spoke to him in Brussels during his visit to the Low Countries. He is introduced in the ambassador's letter to King Philip as the Governor of Antwerp, "a very diligent man, who has much experience in the affairs of these lands". It is not very plausible that Mondragón functioned as Governor of Antwerp at the time – as this would be against the

---

[33] 'golosos'; 'de tan tierna edad'. Mondragón to Alba, Damvillers, 11 April 1564 and 19 October 1564, AA, C44, 172-173.

[34] Testament of Jenne de Haussy, Registre aux testamens de l'hostel de la ville de Douai, 216v-220v, 19 January 1581. She wanted to be buried in the church of the Franciscans in Douai next to her deceased husband and her daughter, Catherine. Roquefort, Glossaire, III, 156; *Souvenirs de la Flandre wallone,* 38. Catherine had at least one sister, Françoise (married to Artus Le Baron, Lord of Brunémont), and a brother, Nicolas, who lived in 1615 in Gravelines, serving the Habsburgs. Perhaps he was the Captain Dohein [?], brother-in-law to Mondragón, who asked to receive the bailage of La Motte, in the Nieppe forest. Gerónimo de Roda to Philip II, Brussels, 1 July 1576, CP IV, 220. During Queen Anne's voyage to Spain in 1570 one of the eight Walloon banners under Mondragón was headed by a Captain Du Hem. Cotereau, 'Voyage', 574. Jeanne (Jenne) de Haussy was the daughter of Maurand de Haussy, Lord of Remerchicourt, and Jeanne de Lalaing, daughter of Médiador de Lalaing, écuyer d'écurie of Maximilian I and Philip the Handsome. The Spanish Wikipedia page on Cristóbal de Mondragón mentions a certain Catalina de Hens as his first wife, and wrongly puts the second marriage to Guillemette in 1572. Wikipedia.org.

privileges – and he was most surely still the governor of Damvillers. The further description seems, however, to fit the character. When asked, Mondragón understood that the high nobles could indeed be a threat to the government of Philip II, but he did not think this very plausible.[35]

Mondragón would remarry: Guillemette de Châtelet (Chastelet) from the Duchy of Lorraine would become his second wife. An old genealogist of the Châtelet family stated that the marriage between Mondragón and Guillemette took place in 1560, but this does not correlate with the story about the death of his wife in 1564. In 1558 Guillemette had become the widow of Gerard d'Aspremont, Lord of Marchéville, Vatronville and Ambly. She was the daughter of Claude de Châtelet and Hélène de Roucy, and the sister of Claude de Châtelet, Lord of Bulgnéville. Guillemette was heir to the lordships of Aulnou, Lagrange, Parfonru, Allaumont, Tigeville, Saint-Aignan and Rabuecourt. Most territories from the Châtelet-Aspremont family were part of the Duchy of Lorraine. From her marriage to d'Aspremont, Guillemette had several daughters, one of whom would marry the important Spanish entrepreneur Juan López Gallo from Bruges. Two of Gallo's sisters would marry the Spanish military commanders Sancho Dávila and Alonso López Gallo, himself a nephew of the entrepreneur. Mondragón is described in the sources as 'chevalier seigneur' of Remerchicourt (Remicourt), Lus (Luz) and Gussainville. We know Remerchicourt came through his first wife, Catherine, and Gussainville probably through his second wife, Guillemette, as it can be found belonging to the Aspremont family.[36]

Mondragón had by then become a member of a noble family living in the frontier region between France, Lorraine and the Low Countries, and the government of Damvillers in the Duchy of Luxembourg fitted perfectly with the families' domains. It was a mere thirty-three kilometres between his government and his seigneurie of Gussainville.[37] Mondragón

---

[35] Geevers, *Gevallen vazallen*, 142; Guzmán de Silva to Philip II, Brussels, 28 November 1565, CD LXXXIX, 241.

[36] Archives départementales CG54, Inventory B 438, Aspremont, 49. https://fr.geneawiki.com/index.php/Maison_du_Ch%C3%A2telet, accessed 26-10-2018; Calmet, *Histoire* généalogique, clxxvi, ccxc, 158, 176, 184; Moréri, *Grand dictionnaire*, 562.

[37] An unexpected insight into the life of his Walloon soldiers in 1564 can be found in Dehaisnes, *Inventaire sommaire*, III, 129: 'George, batard de Malberg, de la compagnie de Christophe de Mondragon, gouverneur de Dampvillers, qui "le jour de Caresme" estant allé en masque porter quelque mommechance, a se prit de querelle avec Aymot Belpois, soldat de la même compagnie, et le blessa mortellement d'un coup d'épée, frappé à l'aventure'.

combined service to his Habsburg sovereign with his own family interests. By the time revolt broke out in the Low Countries he had probably been living for more than twenty years in French-speaking territory. He must have been perfectly integrated and well versed in the language and the culture of his new home. This is surely part of the explanation for the positive opinion people in the Low Countries would have of him. However, at the same time he remained a true Albista, somebody who had to thank the Duke of Alba for every step in his career.[38]

**The early years of the Revolt**

The arrival of the Duke of Alba and his army in the Low Countries in 1567 would be of utmost importance to the life of the well-integrated Mondragón. In 1568 Mondragón corresponded with the Duke from his home in Damvillers. He informed his patron about developments in France, but above all he insisted in partaking in the military expeditions of the new Governor-general of the Low Countries; "though Your Excellency has a complete army at his disposal, he does not have anybody with the same affection and service to His Majesty and Your Excellency as me". He described his position in Damvillers as a kind of banishment: "to find myself in this corner, governing four villagers and a hundred soldiers".[39] His soldier's blood craved military action, but the Revolt also offered possibilities for the advancement of his own career, especially now that his own protector was handing out the jobs.

It is unclear whether he participated in the military campaigns in Frisia and Brabant in 1568 as has been suggested.[40] With his Walloon troops he was mostly used to control castles, fortresses and cities, and during this period he was also promoted to Colonel of these same Walloon troops. It must have been very welcome for Alba to have at his disposal a loyal servant well versed in French and the culture of the

---

[38] Within the Brussels political scene, he seems to have been regarded – together with Gaspar de Robles – as a client of Tomás de Armenteros, Margaret of Parma's influential Spanish secretary. Derks, 'Madama's minister', 64; Weiss, *Papiers*, VIII, 518-519.

[39] 'Aunque su excelencia tenga un exercito entero, en todo el no tiene persona con mas afizion al serbizio de su Magestad y de su excelencia que yo'; 'Verme aquí en este rrincon gobernando quaro billanos y zien soldados'. Mondragón to Albornoz, Damvillers, 25 January 1568; Mondragón to Alba, Damvillers, 25 January 1568 and 27 June 1568, AA, C44, 174-176. Already in 1565 Mondragón sent information about the border region to the ambassador in France. Philip II to Francés de Álava, Madrid, 22 December 1565, Rodríguez and Rodríguez, eds., *Don Francés*, 30-31.

[40] Cabañas Agrela, 'Cristóbal', 551.

Low Countries. For example, in November 1568 Alba sent him with six hundred arquebusiers to the city of Huy in the Prince-bishopric of Liège.[41] This neutral power needed to be treated with care, and who could do this better than Mondragón?

However, soon he also became active in Dutch-speaking territories. At least from 31 January 1569 he acted as governor of the city of Deventer, as he wrote a letter that same day describing his difficult arrival in the city: "It had not been without hard work, as for fifty years never such a quantity of water was seen flooding the river banks".[42] He also had to fight to get control of the keys to the city. But his largest problem concerned the fact that the Duke still had to send him the official papers proving both his governorship of Deventer and his appointment as Colonel of the Walloons.[43]

Local sources from Deventer on his government are very critical. For them, he was just one of the cruel Spanish oppressors from a long list. It is interesting that the sources wrote his name as 'Mons. Dragon', dividing his last name in two, resulting in the usual French abbreviation for a lord and the French word for dragon, 'Monseigneur Dragon'. Monseigneur Dragon prohibited the burial of a Protestant councillor in the city's church, and he put a schoolmaster in jail under suspicion of reading prohibited books to his pupils. When the schoolmaster escaped the city prison, Mondragón sent the two burgomasters responsible to prison in Brussels. Furthermore, Fadrique de Toledo visited the city during his government with plans to build a fortress within the city, another issue that must have aroused ample criticism. His government of Deventer may have continued until August 1570, when he and his men were replaced by Captain Pacheco and four regiments of Spanish soldiers. It is this Pacheco who would later be killed by the rebels at Flushing. All this means that within the local historiography of Deventer the positive image of Mondragón is not to be found.[44]

---

[41] Mendoza, *Comentarios*, 434, 438-440; Alba to Mondragón, 4 November 1568, EA II. Alba to Philip II, Camp outside Liège, 6 November 1568, CD 37, 502-504.

[42] 'No a sido sin arto trabajo porque a zinquenta años que no san visto tantas aguas debordadas desta ribera'. Mondragón to Albornoz, Deventer, 31 January 1569, AA, C44, 177. Already on 17 December 1568 Alba is busy sending Mondragón's six ensigns to Deventer. EA II.

[43] Mondragón to Albornoz, Deventer, 31 January 1569 and 9 February 1569, AA, C44, 177-179.

[44] Mondragón to Alba, Deventer, 5 July 1569. Nationaal Archief, The Hague, Archief van de Spaans-Nederlandse regering te Brussel, 1567-1576, inv. 1.01.01.13, document 11, 413; Holthuis, *Frontierstad*, 27; Reitsma, *Centrifugal*, 100; Moonen, *Korte chronyke*, 109-113.

While in Deventer, he also had to defend his rights to Damvillers where he had put his nephew as his lieutenant, "twenty-five years of age and a responsible and nice man".[45] In the same letter he explained to Alba's secretary, Albornoz, that they should not take the government of Damvillers away from him, because if he were to be left without any income "I can retire to the house closest to Damvillers of those my wife has in the vicinity of the town". He was even trying to get his hands on the government of Tournai.[46] Mondragón wanted to be involved in the military action, but at the same time he was busy trying to augment his income and influence in the southern border region. In October 1569 he had to go with his troops from Deventer to help fellow commander Gaspar de Robles defend the coast of Groningen against a possible rebel fleet.[47]

The journey of the future queen, Anne of Austria, to Spain presented a golden opportunity to improve his position. This daughter of Emperor Maximilian II and Philip's own sister, Mary, had to travel in 1570 from the Low Countries to Spain in order to marry her uncle the King. Mondragón was designated to secure the transport over the sea with 1,600 Walloon soldiers.[48] He hoped he could finally go home, and maybe even present his situation to the King in person. However, a letter from Philip II prohibited him from visiting the royal court and he had to remain with his troops. The King did promise to look at Mondragón's memorial, which Captain Arrieta had given him. This is typical behaviour for King Philip, preferring paperwork to personally meeting the people who were defending his interests. The Colonel was very sad that he was not allowed to visit the King in person: "For me it is a great pity to have arrived here and not kiss the hands of Your Majesty".[49] Beside asking for rewards for his loyal captains, he wanted for himself the confiscated goods in Artois of two noblemen, monsieur de Noyelles and monsieur

---

[45] 'De beynte y zinco años onbre responsable y querido'. Mondragón to Albornoz, Deventer, 6 May 1569, AA, C44, 181.

[46] 'Yo me podria retirar a la casa mas zerca de los que mi mujer tienen en torno de Danbileres'. Mondragón to Albornoz, Deventer, 4 June 1569, AA, C44, 183.

[47] Mondragón to Alba, Deventer, 16 October 1569, 23 October 1569, and 3 November 1569, AA, C44, 187-189; De Meij, *Watergeuzen*, 235.

[48] Cotereau, 'Voyage', 574. The eight banners of the Walloons were commanded by Mondragón, Haro, Verdugo, Gile le Vilain, Ariette, Henry de Tseraerts, Gustin and Du Hem; Wyts, 'Voyages'; Wyts, 'Itinera', f. 2r-3r.

[49] 'Es para mi gran lastima aver llegado aqui y no besar las manos de Vuestra Magestad'. Mondragón to Felipe II, Santander, 21 October 1570, AGS, E. 545, 91-92 (memorial); Salcedo Ruiz, *El coronel*, 51-61; Felipe II a Mondragón, Madrid, 15 October 1570, AGS, E. 554, 190; Idem, El Escorial, 2 November 1570; Alba to Philip II, Brussels, 23 March 1571, Alba, EA II, 545, on his good services during the queen's journey.

de Longastre.⁵⁰ Longastre had his goods close to Dourlens and Noyelles in the vicinity of Amiens, close to his wife's properties. Again we see him building his own little empire in the south of the Low Countries. The memorial Mondragón sent to Philip II describes his merits and the ideas he had on compensation, including his participation at Tunis and his escape from the Bastille:

> Cristóbal de Mondragón, Colonel of the Walloon infantry and Governor of Damvillers, says he came from the Low Countries in 1564 to inform Your Majesty about the disturbances that had started at that time and Your Majesty ordered him to return directly. He has served the Emperor, of glorious memory, since the expedition to Tunis, without ever failing in any of the armies and expeditions that have presented themselves, as is well known, and after having been taken prisoner at Lens and escaping from the Bastille of Paris, he came to inform Your Majesty in Brussels about what was happening in France, and since then he has not stopped serving, also in the fortunate journey of the Queen our lady, arriving in these kingdoms, as Your Majesty will read in a letter the Duke of Alba has given at the departure, requesting Your Majesty that as reward for his services you should order to give him the confiscated goods of monseigneur de Noyelles and monseigneur de Longastre, leaving Your Majesty the three hundred escudos rent on the new tax on wool that he had been given, and requesting the reward will be for him, his children, and heirs.⁵¹

---

⁵⁰ George de Montigny, Lord of Noyelles-sur-Selles. Governor of the garrison in Leiden during the first siege in 1574 but sent away because of his bad conduct. Charles de Houchin, Lord of Longastre. Lottin, 'Nobles'. For Longastre and Noyelles, see also Mondragón to Philip II, Antwerp, 24 January 1571, AGS, E. 547, 117.

⁵¹ 'Christoval de Mondragon, coronel de infanteria valona y governador de Dampvillers, dize que el anno de 64 vino de Flandes a dar aviso a Vuestra Magestad de las alteraciones que entonzes se empeçavan y Vuestra Magestad le mando tornar espresamente y atento que ha que sirve desde la jornada de Tunes a su Magestad Cesarea de gloriosa memoria sin jamas faltar en ninguno de los exercitos y jornadas que se an ofrescido como es notorio y despues haviendo sido preso en Lence y escapandose de la bastilla de Paris, vino a dar abiso a Bruselas a Vuestra Magestad de lo que en Francia se hazia y de alli, asta agora no a dexado de servir y en el felicissimo viaje de la reyna nuestra señora biniendo en estos reynos como Vuestra Magestad vera por una carta que el duque de Alva le dio a la partida, supplica a Vuestra Magestad en remuneracion de sus servicios sea servido mandar hazelle merzed de la hazienda confiscada de Mos. de Noyela y de la de Mos. de Longater y dexara a Vuestra Magestad los trezientos scudos de renta que Vuestra Magestad le hize merzed sobre el nuevo inpuesto de las lanas, y supplica a Vuestra Magestad sea la merzed que se le iziere para el, sus hijos y herederos'. Mondragón to Philip II, Santander, 21 October 1571, AGS, E. 545, 91-92.

Mondragón was back in Antwerp in January 1571, when he wrote to the King to inform him about the successful but "very difficult and dangerous" journey, but again it was all about getting a reward for his many years of service. The *juro* bonds of three hundred ducats that belonged to his patent as captain of cavalry were all he had been given.[52] If he could get the confiscated goods of the two noblemen, then he could give the *juro* to his daughter whose fortune he had spent serving the King: "I have children and for many years I am eating their possessions".[53] Were there more children, or was he talking about the children from Guillemette's first marriage?

In 1571 his position was regularly debated. The King proposed to give him the frontier fortress of Mariembourg instead of Damvillers, but this fell through. Alba also thought of "the most elegant fortress" of Thionville, but he was not able to remove the present governor. The government of Utrecht was another possibility as this would give him a deserved higher income, "because this is one of the old soldiers who know this country".[54] As Philip did not want to decide before receiving a memorial with all information on the commander, Alba sent one to Spain in October, repeating his wish to give Utrecht to Mondragón:

> As his services deserve it…Your Majesty had few men like him in all his estates, nor anybody who has done better in everything that was assigned to him until now.[55]

The memorial convinced the King who would react much later saying that he agreed, though he would have preferred him at the frontier and not so much in the interior of the country.[56] However, in the end, it all came to nothing.

---

[52] Rojo Vega, '1572'. Hernando's will was dated 23 December 1572, and in it we find information on the payment of the *juro* of 300 ducats. The last time it was paid was 1569. Hernando was a nephew of Cristóbal and the son of Magdalena de Mondragón.

[53] 'Tan trabajoso y peligroso'; 'tengo hijos y que a muchos annos que les como sus aziendas'. Mondragón to Philip II, Antwerp, 24 January 1571, AGS, E. 547, 117; CD XXXV, 402-403. Other letters in this period: Mondragón to Albornoz, Nieuwkerke, 29 January 1571 and Mondragón to Hernando de Toledo, Antwerp, 21 February 1571, AA, C44, 190-191; Mondragón to Philip II, Brussels, 18 March 1571, AGS, E. 547, 118; CD XXXV, 403-404.

[54] Philip II to Alba, El Escorial, 4 July 1570, CP II, 138; Alba to Philip II, Antwerp, 13 July 1571, EA II, 669.

[55] Alba to Philip II, Brussels, 19 October 1571, EA II, 755.

[56] Salcedo Ruiz, *El coronel*, 66; CP I. Letter from Alba to Philip II, 13 July 1572.

*Protagonists of War*

On 1 December 1571 he was back in Damvillers where he stayed for the rest of the year. He wrote to Albornoz to complain about the many things required in Damvillers and the need for improving its defences with new artillery and soldiers. If this was not possible, it would be even better "to tear down the walls and turn it into a village". Again he was looking for a more important office: "I am hanging by my hair, and in order to leave here I would gladly do this even without waiting for compensation".[57] In the meantime he informed Albornoz about what was happening across the border in France: for example, reporting on the growing influence of the Calvinists in Metz. He also included several documents with his letters, including some 'nouvelles de France'.

Alba did start to make use of Mondragón again, as we can find him in Zevenbergen, near Breda, reporting in January 1572 that "those of the sea are menacing us with visiting and killing us".[58] It shows that the Spanish commanders were well aware of what was coming. On 1 April 1572 those of the sea, the Sea Beggars, took the small town of Brielle, and with it started the second phase of the Revolt in the Low Countries. Everything became much more violent.

Around early October 1572, three regiments of Walloons under Mondragón sacked the small town of Dendermonde, "looking for booty like the others".[59] Fortunately for the commander, this dark episode has not blackened his name in the history books. At the same time, the English had also turned their sights on Mondragón, but they did not know how to place him: "the leader of the soldyers was the coronell of this towne named monsr. Mondragon, a Spanyerde's sonne, but borne in Artoys".[60] For this English letter-writer Mondragón must have appeared to be a native of the Low Countries. By that time, he had probably been active for already some thirty years in the French-speaking world.

Also another negative description did not have much lasting influence on the commander's image. Around the same time, the Antwerp Protestant chronicler, Godevaert van Haecht, recorded several episodes between

---

[57] Derocarle las murallas y hazer della un villaje'; 'Yo estoy aqui colgado de los cabelos y para salir de aqui muy de buena gana le haría sin aguardar otra recompensa'. Mondragón to Albornoz, Damvillers, 1 December 1571, 2 December 1571 and 27 December 1571, AA, C44, 192-194.

[58] 'Estos de la mar nos amenazan a visitar y pasarnos por delante'. Mondragón to Albornoz, Zevenbergen, 23 January 1572, AA, C44, 195.

[59] Mondoucet to the French King, Brussels, 8 October 1572, Didier, *Lettres*, I, 59. See also CG IV, 457. The plundering took place on 4 October.

[60] Thomas Brune to Lord Burghley, Antwerp, 19 October 1572, Kervyn de Lettenhove, *Relations politiques*, VI (Brussels 1888) 553-555.

1572 and 1574 in which Mondragón was involved. It seems he had his soldiers shoot at burghers who were walking too close to the city gates, he had evacuated his own wife for reasons of safety, and he had wanted to execute a high city official because he had wounded one of his soldiers.[61] But the most striking element of Van Haecht's stories is that he calls him 'Lap ooge' (the man with an eye patch).[62] The only other mention of this specific hallmark can be found in one of the Beggar's songs: "in the square of Middelburg, we find with one eye, monseigneur Dragon alone".[63] Furthermore, on his portrait, painted much later, we do find the remnants of a wound close to his eye. The fact that both textual mentions are related to 1574 makes it probable he had worn an eye patch at least for some time. He had more luck than Julián who had lost his eye at the siege of Haarlem.

## The search for a knighthood

Mondragón was certainly not born in Artois as the son of a Spanish father, as he was a native of the Castilian trading town of Medina del Campo. But there was indeed something the matter with his family tree. When Mondragón went to Spain with Anne of Austria in 1570, he used the opportunity to travel to his home town.[64] Besides a family visit, it was his intention to collect the necessary family papers needed for an appplication to the Christian knightly order of Santiago. For such orders it was compulsory to deliver proof of a perfect, old Christian genealogy, without any Jewish or Islamic ancestors. Mondragón's timing, however, was terrible. In one of the most dramatic chapters of the biography, Salcedo Ruiz relates how just before his arrival the Inquisition had come to town to put a *sambenito* in the church of Medina, a plaque commemorating the execution of a certain Zalamea. People in Medina said that Mondragón's mother was a descendant of this convicted and burned converso. In 1591 a witness during the investigation related to the entry of Mondragón's son-in-law, Alonso, into the order, remembered that in the city rumours went around that "the Mondragóns had lost their honour".[65] The family succeeded in moving the plaque to a

---

[61] Haecht, *Kroniek*, II, 211, 213 (2 September 1572).
[62] Haecht, *Kroniek* II, 286 (19 February 1574).
[63] 'Int Middelburghsche pleyn, met één ooghe bevonden, Monsieur Dragon alleyn'. *Nederlandsche geschiedzangen*, II (Amsterdam 1864) 115.
[64] Salcedo Ruiz, *El coronel*, 51.
[65] Salcedo Ruiz, *El coronel*, 57.

higher position on the wall above the entrance, but the damage had already been done.[66] One of the witnesses of 1591, Sebastián de Caraballo, declared:

> That colonel Cristóbal came to Medina in the year 70 to collect the proof (*hacer probanza*) needed for receiving a habit for his services. But important people had to disappoint him, telling him that on the side of his father everything was good, but that on the side of his mother he had the case of Zalamea. And he thanked them for telling him the truth, and returned to the Low Countries.[67]

In the archives we can find a collection of documents on the case, including testimonies of witnesses, but it remains unclear whether Mondragón's mother really was a descendant of the said Zalamea.[68] These kinds of inquiries into the origins of families in order to enter the nobility or in this case to enter into a religious knightly order are notoriously difficult to understand, as witnesses did not necessarily tell the truth. In any case, the situation in Medina made it impossible for Mondragón to enter the order of Santiago.

Becoming a *caballero* of one of the knightly orders was the ideal reward for Spanish military commanders, as there was no need to reside in any particular place and there was always a handsome income attached. We have seen that a commander like Julián Romero did obtain his knighthood of the order of Santiago, while Mondragón's close associate, Sancho Dávila, never succeeded in entering. In 1649 Juan de la Barrera y Mondragón, his great-grandson, finally succeeded in getting the Zalamea story off the table, and it was taken for granted that Zalamea was a Portuguese Jew who had come to Medina and that there was no relationship with the Mondragón family.[69] Again, much the same happened with the descendants of Sancho Dávila.

For Cristóbal the visit to Medina in 1570 must have delivered a severe blow. One of the most important routes to receiving a substantial royal reward for his services had been cut off. And the King had not even wanted to receive him at court. He had to continue fighting and continue

---

[66] Salcedo Ruiz, *El coronel*, 18, 23, 31, 51, 57-59.
[67] Salcedo Ruiz, *El coronel*, 59.
[68] AHN, Ordenes, reprobados Santiago, Exp. 8bis (1625); Expendientillos N. 819 (1623-1629).
[69] Salcedo Ruiz, *El coronel*, 57-58. Juan de la Barrera y Mondragón was the son of Alonso de la Barrera y Montalvo and Catalina de Mondragón y Castillo, granddaughter of Cristóbal. Atienza and Barredo de Valenzuela, 'Mondragón', 325.

moaning about rewards. Until this time he was an important commander of Walloon soldiers, a loyal servant of the King with a good knowledge of the language (French) and the culture of the Low Countries, through marriage related to the local nobility and protected by the Duke of Alba. But he was not yet a real celebrity.

## Goes: Like Moses crossing the seas

In 1572 Mondragón became more and more involved in the war on the islands of Zeeland. His troops were active in a successful attack on the island of Walcheren, followed by a failed attempt to free the city of Goes on the island of Zuid-Beveland. Sancho Dávila functionned as admiral of the fleet, while Mondragón had the command of some two thousand Walloons from the garrisons of Lier and Antwerp. The fleet was stopped by the rebels, and Mondragón barely saved himself when his galley sank. With the help of some Netherlandish seamen from the region, a new plan was developed: crossing the water around the island of Goes on foot at low tide from the coast of Brabant near Calfven (between Woensdrecht and Ossendrecht). After long deliberations, the troops started off on their hazardous crosssing on 20 October 1572.[70]

The crossing to Goes is Mondragón's most famous undertaking and a story present in many chronicles of the time. Spanish chroniclers describe the daring undertaking, with in addition to the Walloons another five hundred Germans and only some one hundred Spaniards. In the morning, the water "was very cold", we learn, but nevertheless the soldiers, entered full of joy:

> Seeing the so very honourable grey hairs of Colonel Cristóbal de Mondragón, with the water coming up to his waist, and up to his knees in the mud, even more tiresome than the water… The infinite number of shells caused a great nuisance, as the soldiers had gone into the water with bare feet and legs, the shells had ripped open the soles of their feet.[71]

The reference to Mondragón's age is clear. According to Mendoza, Mondragón was even the first to enter the water: "not withstanding his age and showing as always his heart and bravery". The soldiers had to swim during the crossing, carrying their packs high up their very long

---

[70] Rooze-Stouthamer, *Opmaat*, 137-141, 204-206.
[71] Trillo, *Historia*, 154-162; Mendoza, *Comentarios*, 473-474. Also Cornejo, *Sumario*, 175-176.

pikes. Once on the island, the attack was brutal: "this day there was but little compassion, and no man was forgiven", and Trillo informs us of more than 2,500 dead rebels. Instead, the more balanced Mendoza accentuates the great wisdom of Mondragón's decision to leave the island again as soon as possible after the relief of Goes in order not to be surrounded by the enemy.

The Dutch Protestant chronicler Van Meteren also pays attention to the story, calling Mondragón an "old and experienced Spanish man of war". The seventeenth-century Protestant writer and historian, P.C. Hooft, does not mention the commander's age, though the title of his story, 'Mondragón's stoutness relieves Goes', does show his high esteem for the Spaniard.[72] However, in his book he never aludes to Mondragón's old age, an element he could easily have made use of for dramatic purposes. By this time, Mondragón was about fifty-eight years old, the same age at which Emperor Charles V had died in Yuste. In 1572, the old and grey Duke of Alba was about sixty-five years of age. Hooft described the crossing as follows:

> And walking further, with sometimes the water up to their knees, and sometimes up to their navels, they reached the other side after more than four hours; not losing more than nine soldiers, who had not kept to the path, and drowned in the currents.

Spanish novelist and writer Arturo Pérez-Reverte dedicated a short article to the liberation of Goes, comparing the event to a sports match and Mondragón to a Spanish sporting hero.[73] He hispanises the event, turning our Colonel of Walloon troops into a Maestre de campo with 2,500 Spanish 'viejos tercios', experienced infantry soldiers, and calling the Germans and Walloons no more than support troops: "seventeen kilometres at night, splashing in the dark, wet up to their beards, their bare feet hurt by the stones and the gravel, worn out by the slimy mud". Mondragón speaks to his 'compañeros', telling them that he will set a good example and go in first, then they must cross rapidly and silently, and once on the other side they "were not going to leave one damned heretic alive": Mondragón's words as imagined by the modern Spanish writer, Pérez-Reverte, clearly play with the story using vulgar and

---

[72] Van Meteren, *Historie*, 61v; Hooft (1972), *Histoorien*, VII, 281-282.
[73] 'Diecisiete kilómetros de noche, chapoteando a oscuras, mojados hasta la barba, heridos los pies descalzos en las piedras y cascajos, fatigados por lo pegadizo del fango'; 'No iban a dejar un puto hereje vivo'. Aruro Pérez Reverte, 'Cuartos'.

colloquial language, and the supposed hatred of Protestants amongst the Spanish troops.[74]

In his letter, the Duke of Alba much more subtly compared Mondragón's action to Moses crossing the Red Sea.[75] Philip II would reward him with the confiscated goods of rebel leader Arend van Dorp, in Philip's letter expressively described as meant "for the shoes he wasted on the passage to Goes". It seems that the King had not understood that they had gone bare foot. In 1574, Mondragón still had to ask for payment of the promised reward. The same Arend van Dorp would defend Zierikzee against Mondragón in 1576.[76] Alba's secretary, Albornoz, wrote to Philip's secretary, Zayas, about "the good old Mondragón" and about "one of the strangest solutions ever thought of by a man: using the low tide to cross the arm of a sea and go from the mainland to an island".[77]

Mondragón was also perfectly aware himself that this was a very important military achievement. On 21 October he wrote a letter from Goes, the only one preserved in the archives of the Duke of Alba on his crossing:

> In the letters I wrote to Your Excellency on Monday and Tuesday, Your Honour will see what has happened to me, a miracle to pass where we passed. God has been served in rendering us his spirit and by giving what Your Excellency had wished for so hard....[78]

Unfortunately we have only this short message in which he calls it a wonder, but we lack the earlier two letters in which he must have explained the events in much more detail. Were these letters taken to be used to write a memorial of the events, or were they even considered directly as such? He also wanted Albornoz to forward the letter he had written to his wife.

Mondragón also sent a painting of the 'relief of Goes' ('*socorro de Dargus*') to the Duke of Alba, who was very pleased with it and wrote

---

[74] Pérez-Reverte made use of the works of Fernández Duro and Bentivoglio for his description.
[75] Alba to Philip II, 19 November 1572, EA III, 244-245.
[76] Mondragón to Albornoz, Antwerp, 17 September 1574, AA, C44, 255.
[77] Albornoz to Zayas, Nijmegen, 5 November 1572, CP II, 290. Salcedo Ruiz, *El coronel*, 71-72. Related to a later crossing, chronicler Juan de Arquellada speaks of 'rios que pasaban por debaxo del agua de la mar'. Arquellada, *Sumario*, 283.
[78] 'Por la del lunes y la del martes que escrito a su Excelencia bera vuestra merced lo que me a suzedido que a sido un milagro poder pasar donde pasamos. Dios a sido serbido de darnos su animo que se aya serbido con lo que su Excelencia tanto deseaba....'. Mondragón to Albornoz, Goes, 21 October 1572, AA, C44, 208.

back to him, "I think about ordering to have a larger painting made, because I can assure you that it is such a special and memorable enterprise as has been done in the last thousand years".[79] Requesens referred to the crossing in a letter to the commander in August 1574 when he had to ask Mondragón to send troops to Goes: "Nobody could have done better than you, because with so much personal valour you opened up the way".[80] The crossing also inspired military poet Pedro de Padilla, but in his verses Sancho Dávila seems to be more prominent than Mondragón. Emphasis is again put on his age:

> And Colonel Mondragón, though his age was not a problem, to put himself in such a great endeavour as the one that presented itself over there, was the first to enter the water, stepping in with his old feet.[81]

## A commander in action (1572-1573)

Mondragón's more than forty letters preserved from the period between June 1572 and July 1573 can be used to put the heroic and less heroic deeds described in the chronicles in historical perspective. During this period he would mostly be writing from the cities of Antwerp and Bergen-op-Zoom, with the exception of an occasional letter from Goes, Woudrichem or Breda. He was occupied with organising his garrison troops in places like Geertruidenberg, Bergen-op-Zoom, Breda, Reimerswaal, Arnemuiden, Goes and Weert. There were all kind of problems to solve: in Geertruidenberg the burgomasters wanted to get rid of the garrison; in Weert there was a soldier who had stolen weapons; and he also had to expell all unreliable Frenchmen from his Walloon troops. And then he had to listen to the Governor of Antwerp, Champagney, as if he were the Duke of Alba.[82]

---

[79] Alba to Mondragón, Nijmegen, 23 April 1573, EA III, 363.
[80] Requesens to Mondragón, 5 August 1575, NCD IV, 255-256.
[81] Salcedo Ruiz, *El coronel*, 187-190; 'Y el coronel Mondragón, aunque su edad no sufria, ponerse á tan gran trabajo, como el que allí se ofrecía, fué el primero que en el agua, los ancianos pies ponía'. Padilla, *Romancero*, Romance XV.
[82] Mondragón to Alba, Antwerp, 30 June 1572 and 3 July 1572, AA, C44, 198-199; See also EA III, 158; Mondragón to Albornoz and Idem to Alba, Antwerp, 6 July 1572, AA, C44, 204-205; Mondragón to Albornoz, Antwerp, 8 July 1572, AA, C44, 206; Mondragón to Alba, Antwerp, 21 July 1573, AA, C44, 233.

Mondragón was also involved in military actions that have not received much attention from the chroniclers, defending both the borders of the Maas and the islands of Zeeland, "always full of privateers". On New Year's Day he had to stop the rebels from Gorinchem (Gorcum) from burning down the nearby town of Woudrichem, and in March he participated in a failed naval mission to the island of Walcheren in Zeeland, together with Sancho Dávila. He wrote to Dávila about his men's fears: "because of the fear they have in their bodies, every small boat seems to them a huge vessel". In his letters we can almost hear the cannons roar: "they fired more than two hundred cannon shots at us, because for four hours they were doing nothing else".[83]

In April there was a new attempt to free Walcheren, Dávila and Mondragón again working closely together. In the letters we find him using the word 'herejes' (heretics) but also 'protestantes', terminology rarely used by the other Spanish commanders. Although he had high hopes for a victory by Dávila, matters got worse, and from a spy he heared that "the heretics that have disembarked at Middelburg had received orders from the Prince not to move until they would take the city or make it surrender; this is crazy!"[84]

On 8 May Mondragón did gain a major victory in the vicinity of Tholen from where he sent to Alba his 'relation of the events and the victory that God has given to us against the traitors'.[85] This time, the commander was positively surprised by his men: "it was more remarkable than all war deeds I have seen afterwards, as they went in the water, halfway up to their thighs in order to attack the fortress from the back". When an enemy ship wanted to surrender, Mondragón's troops attacked it during the negotiations, killing more than a hundred men. But most of the enemies drowned: "they threw themselves in the water in a way

---

[83] 'Siempre lleno de cosarios'; 'Segun el myedo questos tienen en el cuerpo cada charrúa les parecerá una hulca'; 'Nos tiraron mas de ducyentos pelotasos porque duro quatro horas que no hyzyeron otra cosa'. Mondragón to Alba, Woudrichem [Worcum], 2 January 1573, AA, C44, 209; Idem, Bergen-op-Zoom, 12 March 1573 and 13 March 1573, and to Dávila and Albornoz, 13 March 1573 and 16 March 1573, AA, C44, 210-213; Mondragón to Alba, Antwerp, 21 July 1573, AA, C44, 233.

[84] 'Los herejes que an desanbarcado a Medyalburque tyenen horden del principe que no se mueban hasta tomar o hacer rendyr la villa, ello es disparate'. Mondragón to Juan Moreno, Bergen-op-Zoom, 21 April 1573; Idem, 18 April 1573, and to Alba, 19 April 1573, AA, C44, 221-222, 225.

[85] 'Relacyon del suceso y vitoria que dyos nos a dado contra estos traydores'; 'hasta la mytad del muslo para tomar las espaldas a su fuerte'. Mondragón to Alba, Tholen, 8 May 1573, AGS, E. 556, 184.

that never there was a lagoon or a coastal area so full with cormorants, as one could consider the heads of those who were drowning". The Duke of Alba responded very enthusiastically: "even from the grave I expect you to give so many victories to Your Majesty for many years to come".[86] We can find news about this event in both English and French sources. In an English newsletter we read how "mounser Dragon, who was the chefe captayne ther' killed 1,100 and drove the rest into the sea where they all drowned, so that of 1500 ther escaped none alyve". The French ambassador also informed his King that "Colonel Mondragón had his horse killed from underneath him", and talked about seven to eight hundred dead, "the others barely saved their lives in their ships". A few days later he downplayed the news, explaining that, "the defeat excecuted by Mondragón was not as big as first had been made public".[87] Again it is clear that besides the victory itself, it was very important how the victory entered the public realm, even in countries like France and England.

The letters from Mondragón during this period offer some insight into his personal thoughts. When he had to recommend a replacement for the deceased captain Haro, we encounter him in a reflective mood: "it hurts me much not being able to bury him and honour him in death as I have done during his lifetime".[88] We also find another personal note as he refers to his age: "old men should take a small break when possible", and he even realised, describing Haro's death, that "little by little we are all coming to our end".[89] After falling ill he had to take to his bed for several weeks, and from his bed in Bergen-op-Zoom he still heard the

---

[86] 'Fue una cosa mas notable de ver que yo e visto despues cosas de guerra'; 'Se echavan en lagua de manera que no se a visto jamas laguna ny marina cargada de cuervos marinos como se veya las cavesas de los que se ivan ahogando'; Y aun desde la sepultura espero habéis, señor, de dar muchas victorias a Su Magestad de aquí a muchos años'. Albornoz to Juan Moreno, Nijmegen, 11 May 1573, EA III, 393; Alba to Philip II, Nijmegen, 13 May 1573, EA III, 397. Alba to Mondragón, Nijmegen, no date, Idem, 409. Another victory against the rebels on 8 May 1573. Vloten, *Middelburgs beleg*, 58-59.

[87] News from Antwerp, 15 March 1573, Kervyn de Lettenhove, *Relations politiques*, VI, 680-681. Also as Monsieur Dragon in: *Mémoires anonymes*, 114-116. Monducet to the French King, Nijmegen, 7 May 1573; Idem, 12 May 1573; 15 May 1573, Didier, *Lettres* I, 259, 264, 266. See also: Alba to Philip II, Nijmegen, 13 May 1573, CP II, 357, mentioning not only 700 dead rebels but also the capture of three or four important commanders from the rebels who had previously served the royal army. Also in 1582 his horse was shot dead underneath him. Vázquez, 'Sucesos', 72, 371.

[88] 'Pesome mucho de no poder enterrarle y honrrarle en la muerte como lo e hecho en la vida'. Mondragón to Alba and to Dávila, Breda, 10 April 1573, AA, C44, 216-217.

[89] 'Tomar los viejos un poco de reposo quando puedan'; 'Poco a poco nos vamos acavando todos'. Mondragón to Albornoz, Breda, 20 April 1573, AA, C44, 218.

noise of the artillery: "I eat my own fingers out of curiosity to know what it is".[90] After his recovery he took the liberty of asking Albornoz to give him a holiday of some four to five months "to free myself of my many tasks, more than ever in my life, and as the cure [of the Revolt] has been long and the costs very high, there is no estate that can endure this. If Your Honour wants me to eat, than he has to send me what I need for it".[91] He not only needed free time, he also needed financial compensation for his work, and he dared to make these complaints so openly only to Alba's secretary, Albornoz.

In the letters we find more evidence of the good relationship between Mondragón and Albornoz, for example by his starting a letter with wishing him a good New Year.[92] Because of the comprehensive character of the information in Mondragón's letters, Albornoz generally sent copies of his letters to Don Fadrique and sometimes even to the King, even when the letters were badly written:

> It is not only now that I am very fortunate with Your Honour for hiding my blunders and those of my secretary, who is as bad at Spanish as I am; Your Honour had always accepted me for being his servant and him for coming from Lorraine. I am very thankful for sending the letter to His Majesty, because though it is badly written, it has been well worked'.[93]

After some thirty years in the north, Mondragón's own command of Spanish had much deteriorated and his secretary was a French speaker.

When a conflict occured between Mondragón and nobleman Don Gabriel de Mendoza, the secretary ordered the latter to show respect to the former: "for his services and grey hair he deserves every respect, and it is with reason that if Your Honour wants to be obeyed and respected by

---

[90] 'Me como las manos por saver ques'. Mondragón a Albornoz, Bergen-op-Zoom, 23 May 1573, AA, C44, 227.

[91] 'Para quytarme de trapaxos los quales no e tenido tantas a my vida y como la cura a sido larga y los gastos grandes no ay hacyenda que la sufra, sy vuestra merced sera servydo que coma, mande me enbyar de que'. Mondragón to Albornoz, Antwerp, 15 July 1573 and Idem, Bergen-op-Zoom, 3 July 1573, AA, C44, 229 and 232

[92] 'Y tan buenas Pascuas y año de Dios a vuestra merced'. Albornoz to Mondragón, Nijmegen, 11 May 1573, EA III, 392.

[93] 'No es de aora estar yo muy contento de la merced que siempre me a hecho en cubrir mis gasafatones y lo de my secretario que tan mal romançado es como yo, sufre nos vuestra merced a my por ser su servydor y a el por ser de Lorena. No tengo poca merced lo que me a hecho en enbyar la carta a su Magestad que aunque va mal escrito va bien obrada'. Mondragón to Albornoz, Bergen-op-Zoom, 23 May 1573, AA, C44, 227.

his soldiers, you have to respect the people who deserve obedience for so many reasons".[94] Here, old age and experience were valued above a noble title. It seems the 'shameless' Don Gabriel did not want to abandon the castle of Ghent, while Mondragón wanted to leave the castle in the hands of his nephew, Antonio de Alamos. In his letters we find a Mondragón very angry at nobleman Mendoza.[95] The fact that Spanish commanders like Mondragón were not of high birth did play an important role in such a hierarchical society.

But perhaps the best evidence of the good working relationship between Albornoz and Mondragón is the assasination plan directed against Antoine Olivier, "the painter who had executed the treason of Mons". This double agent had betrayed the Duke of Alba and had seemingly fled to England, and now there was a price on his head: four thousand guilders alive and two thousand dead. Albornoz stated that "it is very important to bring down this villain".[96] Mondragón had to select from his regiment two Walloons who could go to London and pass for men from Lorraine or France, in order to kill him.[97] However, Olivier had gone to Holland, where he would die during the fighting. In the same letter, Albornoz informed the commander of the enquiry into the goods of 'that heretic' that should go Mondragón's way.[98] Also, Albornoz was satisfied with the horses Mondragón had sent him, and he would also accept the dapple-grey horse if it was any good: "Your Honour is generally bad at selling; you are better in fighting than in merchandising and horse dealing". This last sentence again shows the high level of trust between the two men. For Mondragón this relationship was of vital importance. The secretary could personally influence the Duke, and Alba was not only the Governor-general of the Low Countries and the Captain-general of the army, he was also Mondragón's old patron and protector. As in the case of Sancho Dávila, Albornoz played a key role as intermediary between the commanders and the Duke.

---

[94] Albornoz to Gabriel de Mendoza, Utrecht, 27 July 1573, EA III, 470.
[95] Mondragón to Alba, Antwerp, 27 July 1573, AA, C44, 237. see also: Mondragón to Albornoz, Antwerp, 22 July and 27 July 1573, AA, C44, 234, 236.
[96] Simonneau, 'Antoine Olivier'. News of his death during a fight on the dykes close to Amsterdam in a letter from Alba to Philip II from 13 May 1573, EA III, 396: 'Aquel bellaco traidor del Oliver… Con todo esto le mandé poner en cuatro palos'.
[97] Albornoz to Mondragón, Nijmegen, 9 April 1573, EA III, 323.
[98] Possibly Arend Van Dorp.

## The siege of Middelburg: hunger and honour

The surrender of Mondragón after the siege of Middelburg by the rebels may be regarded as one of the most heroic and honourable defeats within the history of the Revolt in the Low Countries. However, these events have lost the fame and glory they once possessed; especially outside Zeeland the siege of Middelburg does not belong to the canonical highlights of the Revolt. In Middelburg, the siege was commemorated in 1924 with a plethora of events, including an open-air play in which Mondragón figured as one of the main protagonists. The play's author was the well-known Middelburg poet, P.C. Boutens. After the famous crossing to Goes in 1572, the heroic defence and the honourable surrender of Middelburg is Mondragón's second claim to fame. At the same time, the events in Middelburg can be considered a mirror for the siege of Zierikzee in 1576, when it was Mondragón who would lead the siege. The positive image of the commander in the Low Countries is closely connected to this Zeeland triptych.

There are three interconnected narratives to analyse regarding this period: the starvation during his government of Middelburg, his honourable surrender, and his promises to William of Orange. During this period Mondragón acted as Governor and Captain-general of the County of Zeeland, at first as temporary replacement for the Lord of Beauvoir. Already in July 1573 Alba had proposed that Philip II appoint Mondragón as the new governor of the island of Walcheren, explaining "that for sure he is going to perform his duties very well, as there is no man in these estates like him who is always doing what he has to do".[99]

In his first letter from Vrouwenpolder, the commander described his arrival on the island of Walcheren as a disaster. Too many provisions got lost during disembarcation, and quite a few ships were lost. There was discussion about who was to lead the expedition, with the choice between Sancho Dávila and Mondragón on one side and the former Governor of Zeeland, Philippe de Lannoy, Lord of Beauvoir, on the other. The command of the royal army was clearly undermined by the factional struggle between Spanish and Netherlandish commanders, not only here but, for example, also during the siege of Leiden in 1574.[100] Mondragón did not trust the collaborators of Beauvoir, who included someone who had been sent to the galleys by Alba and someone he described as a 'breaker of churches'. Other sources state that Mondragón

---

[99] Alba to Philip II, Nijmegen, 7 July 1573, CD LXXV, 230-236.
[100] Fagel, *Spaanse belegeraar*.

had accused Beauvoir of handing secret information to the enemy. This ended in Beauvoir's entry in Van der Aa's biographical dictionary of 1851 as a short but very dramatic scene: "He took it so badly, that he got ill and died of sadness".[101]

Already within the walls of Middelburg, Mondragón found out there was no money to pay the troops and only bread and water to feed them. The commander also did not receive any messages from court, and on 8 September he still wondered whether Alba had heard of his arrival on Walcheren. And then there were the enemies who had ships everywhere. He tried to build a small fortress near the harbour to protect the few ships they had left. According to Mondragón, the royal government of Walcheren had completely failed. They had not even worked on the dykes that protected the island: "this island is in very bad condition and if it is not remedied this year it will be in great danger of being lost, as the dykes are completely ruined, and if you don't see it, you don't believe it".[102] The always precarious situation in Zeeland had deteriorated because of the famous flood on All Saints Day 1570, when large parts of the coastal area of the Low Countries had been flooded.[103] This may have been the largest inundation disaster in the Netherlands and Belgium in modern history, and its consequences played a major role during the first years of the Revolt. Zeeland was more dominated by water than ever.

Hunger would become the other great enemy during the siege by the rebels, and both Spanish and Dutch chronicles testify to this. Spanish chronicler Antonio Trillo said:

> Colonel Mondragón saw that there was no hope of relief, and that he and his Walloons had eaten the horses, and even the mice, and that the only food they had on most days was toasted linseed, fried with the grease of whales, and even this had finished, and with these forced needs and excessive hunger, some soldiers had

---

[101] Van der Aa, *Biographisch* woordenboek, XI, 150-151.

[102] 'Rumpedor de yglesyas'; 'Esta isla la qual queda muy mal y sy no se remedya esta anno ella quedara en gran peligro de perderse porque los diques son enteramente ruynados y no lo pudyera creer sy no lo vyera'. Mondragón to Albornoz, Vrouwenpolder, 25 August 1573; Mondragón to Juan Moreno, Vrouwenpolder, 25 August 1573, Middelburg, 28 August 1573 and 31 August 1573; Mondragón to Albornoz and Francisco de Lixalde, Middelburg, 2 September 1573 and Mondragón to Albornoz, Middelburg, 8 September 1573 and 24 October 1573, AA, C44, 241-248.

[103] Buisman, *Duizend jaar*, 642-654.

fallen dead and others were left without strength, as they could expect nothing else than that all would die in that city.[104]

Chronicler Bernardino de Mendoza mentions the eating of cats and dogs and the skins of all available animals.[105] English Protestant soldier Thomas Morgan, fighting in Zeeland, informs us that Mondragón's troops in Middelburg had mutinied "for theis causes: they have not any other vitaile then bisket, cheese and brackyshe water".[106] A letter from Augsburg by an Italian Protestant suggests that this was reason for Mondragón to intervene: "the inhabitants of Middelburg have been in dire straits since their commander Captain Mondragon has deprived them of victuals which he has distributed to the soldiers ravaged by hunger".[107] The claim that Mondragón had taken the provisions from the inhabitants to give to his soldiers can also be found in a letter from the French ambassador to his King. He refused to surrender the city, stubbornly "saying that he would prefer to have his soldiers eat each other than to surrender".[108] Here we have the image of a harsh commander, harsh on the inhabitants entrusted to him, and harsh on his own soldiers. But do these images fit the commander's behaviour?

Mondragón already described the terrible situation in an early letter from 8 September: "The soldiers fall ill... they can count our bites... we get tired of the drinking, as there is not a seed of grain, nor any hop, to make beer...". Beer was much safer to drink than water, which most of the time was heavily polluted. He needed a metaphor to cope with the situation: "I wish we could sustain ourselves like chameleons, so we would not have a lack of food".[109] A chameleon feeds, according to modern advice, on insects like crickets, cockroaches and worms.

---

[104] Trillo, *Historia*, 226.
[105] Mendoza, *Comentarios*, 503-505.
[106] Thomas Morgan to Lord Burghley, Flushing, 12 September 1573, Kervyn de Lettenhove, *Relations politiques*, VI, 809-810.
[107] Pietro Bizari to Jean de Vulcob [French ambassador in Vienna], Augsburg, 15 October 1573, Kuin, ed., *Correspondence*, 31.
[108] Mondoucet to the French King, Antwerp, 4 January 1574, Didier, *Lettres* II, 85.
[109] 'Los soldados cayen malos... nos puedan contar los bocados... la bevida nos fatigarya porque no ay un grano de cevada ny de houblon con que poder hacer cervesa'. 'Yo querria que nos pudyesemos sustentar como camaleones que no tendriamos falta de mantenimiento'; 'Mire vuestra merced la pena que esto podra dar à un coraçon de piedra'. Mondragón to Albornoz, Middelburg, 8 September 1573, AA, C44, 247.

On 15 December 1573 Spanish officer Diego Carreño Maldonado cried out for help to one of Alba's secretaries. They had eaten all the dogs, cats and horses. Nothing was left. The soldiers deserted and went over to the other side:

> I cannot stop singing with a certain falsetto when a man walks around the walls, the same song Carvajal sang in Peru.[110] My Walloons, o mother, the wind takes them two by two, and I beg God, that I become a captain of Alaraves,[111] and not of them, because their insolences are so enormous and the fact that they do not know how to suffer is more torture than engaging with the enemies.[112]

The inhabitants were starving, even the rich ones, and every day four to six men and women died of pure hunger: "Look Your Honour, the pity this could give to a heart of stone". Time was running out, and if a relief armada did not arrive in time all would be lost. They had just enough provisions for ten to twelve days.

Carreño Maldonado also decribed how they had sent inhabitants away to have fewer mouths to feed. However, William of Orange sent them back to Middelburg after having taken everything from them, warning Mondragón to stop sending people to him: "and if by this you [Mondragón and his men] would be the cause of their death… In our hands, you will not only be treated as soldiers, but as cruel and inhuman murderers of subjects of His Majesty".[113]

That very same day Mondragón also sent a letter to Requesens, adding that he was willing to die in the service of God and his Majesty, but

---

[110] A reference to Francisco de Carvajal (1464-1548), 'el demonio de los Andes', singing at the Battle of Jaquijahuana of 9 April 1548: 'estos mis cabellicos, maire, uno a uno se los lleva el aire'. https://es.wikipedia.org/wiki/Francisco_de_Carvajal.

[111] Refering to a Moorish, Arabian origin.

[112] 'Y no puedo dexar de cantar con un çierto falsete quando el hombre anda rondando las murallas, lo que cantava Caravajel en el Peru. Estos mis Walones madre, dos à dos me los lleva el ayre, y plega à Dios que antes me vea yo capitan de Alaraves que no dellos, porque son tan grandes sus insolençias y su no saber sufrir que es mayor tormento que el acabar con los enemigos'. Diego Carreño Maldonado to Esteban de Ibarra, Middelburg, 15 December 1573, Vul. 104, UBL.

[113] 'Et que ainsi soyez [Mondragón and his men] cause de leur mort…en noz mains, serez traictez non-seulement comme soldats, ains comme cruels et inhumains meurdriers des subjectz de Sa Majesté'. Orange to Mondragón and his officers, Flushing, 2 January 1574, BO, 3096. A Spanish translation is in CEF, Collection Edouard Favré, Genève, vol. 60, 77.

also that he should send a replacement as commander of the Walloons, because "my bad health means I can no longer stand my work nor the air of this island".[114] In one and the same letter we find both the heroic Mondragón and a complaining and old Mondragón. He was both at the same time.

In January the rebels intercepted a letter from Mondragón to Requesens in which he mentioned that they had only five to six days' provision left, giving the attackers a very clear insight into the desperate situation in the city. The rebels also took some passports that had text on the back that could be read only when held close to a fire as it had probably been written with onion juice. Communciation was now almost impossible. When writing to Philip II on 13 February, Requesens said that the last letter he had received from Mondragón was dated 19 January.[115]

By that time, one of two relief fleets had been destroyed on 29 January 1574, under Julián Romero as its admiral. He had been given the command of a fleet with smaller transport ships while Sancho Dávila had commanded the armada with larger ships.[116] At that point it became totally clear to everyone that Middelburg had to surrender, and Mondragón was preparing to hand the city over to the rebels. Fortunately we have a collection of documents on the matter, starting with a remonstration by Mondragón from 4 February 1574.[117] It is a beautifully written collection of documents that must have served to be presented to the crown, and with it Mondragón no doubt defended himself against any possible accusations relating to his handling of the siege and surrender of Middelburg. Both the description of his deeds and the description of the suffering may have been influenced by these intentions.

He had asked all his officers to discuss the difficult situation and the shortage of food. Their rations of bread had gradually become smaller, later on mixed with oats. They had also received some money to buy apples and mussels. Mondragón proposed holding on for two more weeks,

---

[114] 'De mas de mi salud no darme lugar a poder sufrir el trabajo y los ayres desta isla'. Mondragón to Requesens, Middelburg, 15 December 1573, Vul. 104, UBL.

[115] Vloten, *Middelburgs beleg*, 96-97; Le Petit, *Grande chronique*, 271; Requesens to Philip II, Antwerp, 13 February 1574, CP III, 17; Requesens to Mondragón, 16 January 1574, NCD II, 48-49.

[116] Fagel, *Kapitein Julián*, 57-59. The fleet carried 300 men to replace Mondragón's missing troops. Requesens to Philip II, Antwerp, 25 January 1574, CP III, 13. See also the chapter on Julián Romero in this book.

[117] 'Remonstración hecha por el coronel Mondragón a los 4 de hebrero de 1574 a su regimiento en Meddelburgck', Middelburg, 4 February 1574, AGS, E. 557, 77. Another copy is in Zabálburu, Colección Altamira, 96, D1, D61/1-8. See also NCD V (1894) 191-213.

but the officers first wanted to talk to their soldiers: "it was not in the service of His Majesty to have them die of hunger, so they preferred to be employed in some occasion where they could die and end their lives as soldiers with weapons in their hands".[118] Eight days later there was food left for only six more days. The inhabitants of the city asked to be protected, but they had already counted 568 people who had died of hunger between Christmas and 12 February alone. This number was incorrectly copied by Mendoza as 1568, and in a Dutch theatre play it would be rounded off as 1600.[119]

A day later Mondragón announced that he was starting negotiations with William of Orange. Alba had written to him that if they had to surrender it had to be "in a way the enemies would benefit very little from the city".[120] Mondragón then asked the officers if they were willing to die and ruin the city, but they said they were not willing to do so. The situation was such that when the soldiers heard Orange would let them go free, they were planning to walk out even without an official capitulation. For anyone who read this document it must have been clear that Mondragón had tried everything that was within his power, but that he had no other option than to surrender. The document ends with a special paragraph that shows the horror of this siege:

> They have consumed 1800 sacks of linseed that have fed the soldiers and the burghers, because the small quantity of bread they were given was not enough, and they employed it in waffles, that have caused them so much feebleness and weakness that the burghers and the soldiers died of eating these waffles, for this seed goes completely against nature, as has been seen in many occasions in Middelburg in which they have opened the human bodies, proving that their stomachs were not capable of digesting this food, finding the entrails burned by it.[121]

---

[118] 'No hera servicio de su Magestad hazerlos morir de hambre que querrian antes que les empleassen en alguna ocassion donde pudiessen morir y acabar como soldados con las armas en las manos'.

[119] Mendoza, *Comentarios*, 504-505; Claerbout, *'t beleg*, 10.

[120] 'De manera que los enemigos sacarian bien poco frutto de esa villa'.

[121] 'Hanse consumido en linaça 1800 sacos de que los soldados y burgeses se han mantenido porque con el poco pan que se les dava, no bastava para su entretenimiento y en vafres empleavan parte de su socorro, que les han causado tanta debilidad y flaqueza que burgeses y soldados han venido a morir de los dichos wafres, por ser aquella simiente enteramente contraria a la natura, como se ha visto por muchas esperiencias que se han hecho en la dicha Mediamburg abriendo cuerpos humanos, y hallar que el estomago no avia podido en ninguna manera digistir aquella vianda y hallar las entranas quemadas dello'.

The eating of linseed is often mentioned in connection with the siege of Middelburg, but nowhere so expressively as in this document.[122] The eating of waffles of linseed would earn the inhabitants of the city the name of 'waffle-eaters' for centuries to come.[123] The terrible description of Mondragón seems to coincide with modern knowledge about the eating of linseed. It is considered very healthy in small quantities, and it depends on the way the food is prepared. The modern advice is to eat no more than 45 grammes a day. The inhabitants must have eaten much more and maybe also not properly prepared, and in that case the human body may even start producing cyanide, a deadly poison. It is a terrifying story that should be told along with the well-known history of the suffering of the inhabitants of Leiden during that same year. Within Dutch history the stories from the County of Holland are clearly dominant in comparison to those from other regions, such as the County of Zeeland. However, in the case of Middelburg the besieged were the royalist Catholics and the attackers the Protestant rebels under their leader William of Orange.

There is an even more gruesome story, that hopefully does not correspond to reality. Maximilien Morillon, Granvelle's confidant in the Low Countries and by this time no friend of the Spanish military, lists in a letter to the Cardinal the prices of grain in besieged Middelburg, and then continues with one simple phrase: "The Spanish soldiers have eaten children and for this Mondragón had them executed".[124] The story can be connected to a similar anecdote in Van Haecht's chronicle on Antwerp. One of the burgomasters of Middelburg had in December 1573 gone to Antwerp to inform the new Governor-general (Requesens) about the situation. The food they had received was not enough by far for the two thousand soldiers and the inhabitants. And all other seeds, cats, horses and dogs had already been eaten. There were many women still in the city and "the rumour was that often children were lost, and it was feared the soldiers had eaten them". Mondragón did not want to surrender the city and wanted to hold on until the last man standing. A few days later the chronicler came with more news: "there was so little space in the city, and it was said that monseigneur Mondragón as commander had locked up moaning women in cellars to let them die there". He is supposed to have said, "as long as there are people to be

---

[122] For example in the play by Joos Claerbout, 't beleg, 11, 28-29.
[123] http://www.verhalenbank.nl/items/show/39216.
[124] Morillon to Granvelle, Brussels, 26 January 1574, CG V, 12.

eaten, there is no famine". Again we hear the story of the children: "and often children got lost, and it was feared that they were eaten by the soldiers", but the chronicler ends his text with a reasonable "but I think they were secretly brought out of the city".[125] But still, there are clearly narratives to be found in which Mondragón plays a very negative role, including in the letter mentioned earlier from the French ambassador. However, strangely enough, the honourable surrender of Middelburg would in fact be very positive for the image of the Spanish commander.[126] Though the Middelburg poet, P.C. Boutens, did not participate in the glorification of the Spanish enemy when he wrote the text of the staged open-air play commemorating the siege in 1924:

> Never the Spanish devil Mondragón
> surrenders himself on pardon!
> His desperation makes him risk everything
> and the city goes through hell! [127]

## Orange and Mondragón

On 18 February 1574, Mondragón capitulated at last. Chroniclers Trillo and Mendoza considered the surrender honourable as he was a very experienced and trustworthy captain and the troops could leave the city honourably with their weapons and their banners before enemy ships took them to Terneuzen. In the chronicles Requesens received Mondragón with all honours, and we know indeed that Philip II had asked his Governor-general to offer the utmost consolation to the defeated commander, as in the case of Romero.[128] Mondragón had been able to leave as a free man because he had promised Orange to do everything in his power to free Philip Marnix of Sint-Aldegonde and some other rebel prisoners. If he did not succeed, he would put himself again into the hands of William of Orange. According to Morillon, the commander would indeed try to reach Orange without permission, but he was apprehended on Requesens's

---

[125] Van Haecht, *Kroniek*, II, 273 (18 December 1573) and 274-275 (20 December 1573).
[126] Vloten, *Middelburgs beleg*, 29.
[127] 'Nooit geeft de Spaansche duivel Mondragon, zich over op pardon! Eer zet zijn wanhoop alles op het spel, verkeert de stad in hel!'. Boutens, *Middelburg's overgang*, 14.
[128] Requesens to Philip II, Antwerp, 24 February 1574, CP III, 24-27; copies of the capitulation documents are also in CEF, vol. 60, 77 and NCD II, 191-216; Philip II to Requesens, Madrid, 13 March 1574, CP III.

orders to prevent that from happening.[129] Knowing Morillon, this story was not given as evidence of Mondragón's sense of honour, but to show he did not obey his Governor-general. The treaty between the Prince and the Spanish commander was printed in Delft in the same year, with a combined Dutch and French text, so everybody could read the promises made by Mondragón.[130]

The negotiations on the capitulation had thus brought Mondragón into close contact with William of Orange. Morillon did not trust Orange at all and wrote to Granvelle, "if he falls into their hands, he will be mistreated like all the good Catholics who have lived in peril for so long in this city". In another letter his fears were even greater: "If they catch him, it will cost him his life or the major part of his possessions, that he himself has estimated before at a hundred thousand écus, that he wanted to give in marriage to his only daughter". News from Antwerp seemed at first to confirm his fears, but William of Orange decided to treat him humanely, "and so the Captain Mondragón only says wonderful things about him [Orange]".[131]

The gentlemen's agreement between Mondragón and Orange led to a series of at least eleven letters written by Orange to Mondragón, dated between 16 February and 5 September 1574.[132] In April Orange summoned him to Geertruidenberg as his prisoner if he did not succeed in liberating Marnix of Sint-Aldegonde and the others, signing the letter "vostre bien bon amy à vous faire service, Guillen de Nassau".[133] The friendly tone slowly changed into a more formal one, as Mondragón was continously begging for more time. Orange ordered him in stricter terms to follow his word as a 'gentilhomme d'honneur'. And in May he wrote, "for my part I am happy that at least this serves as an example for you right now, and for posterity, that one should not so easily trust the servants of Philip, even those who among the Spaniards have the reputation of being the most sincere and

---

[129] Morillon to Granvelle, Brussels, 1 June 1574, CG V, 102.
[130] *Tractaet van accoordt.*
[131] Morillon to Granvelle, Brussels, 1, 15, 23/25, and 24/27 February 1574, CG V, 19, 31-32, 41, 47.
[132] BO, accessed 21 November 2018: Orange to Mondragón:16 February 1574, Flushing (3113); 17 February 74, Flushing (9049); 19 February 1574 (11159); 23 April 1574, Zaltbommel (10352); 3 May 1574, Dordrecht (10353); 5 May 1574, Dordrecht (3150); 17 May 1574, Dordrecht (3164); ca. 20 May 1574 (3166); c. 23 May 1574 (3168); 24 July 1574, Rotterdam (3185); 5 September 1574, Rotterdam (2369).
[133] BO: Orange to Mondragón, Zaltbommel, 23 April 1574.

virtuous".[134] He was clearly playing with the image of Mondragón as the exceptionally good Spaniard. It proves Mondragón was already considered as such in 1574. Orange's chancellor used the situation even as a reason not to trust any Spaniard: "he openly says that his master wil not negotiate with Spaniards, as Mondragón has not kept his word, after he and his followers had been treated so well, though they could have died of hunger".[135] Requesens's correspondence makes it possible to look at the discussion from the other side. The Governor-general did not want to lose Mondragón, but at the same time he tried to reach a good deal with William of Orange without offering too many prisoners in return.[136] In the end, Marnix of Sint-Aldegonde would be freed in exchange.[137]

## The life of an Albista under Requesens

We have already seen that Requesens and Mondragón did not agree on everything.[138] The commander remained a creature of the Duke of Alba, to whom and to whose secretary, Albornoz, he continued writing. These letters no longer reflect the direct hierarchy within the royal army in the Low Countries, but show the clientèle relationship between a patron from the high nobility in Spain and his client. Mondragón kept asking for favours from his old patron, maybe not completely understanding that Alba's position at court had severely weakened. In return he could offer information, so he included copies of papers and of the capitulation treaty in his letters to Alba. After the defeat at Middelburg he wanted to go home, and Alba was his best way out as he wanted to return to his service:

---

[134] 'De ma part je suis joyeulx qu'au moins ceste exemple servira presentement a vous et a la posterite pour nestre desireulx et faciles a se fier aux promesses et serviteurs de Philippe la mesmes qui entre les Espaignolz auront reputation destre les plus sinceres et virtueux'. BO: Orange to Mondragón, ca. 20 May 1574 and Idem, ca. 23 May 1574.

[135] Morillon to Granvelle, Brussels, 19 July 1574, CG V, 163.

[136] Requesens to Mondragón, 12 April 1574, NCD II, 154; Requesens to Dávila, 12 April 1574, Idem, 154-155; Requesens to Champagney, 7 July 1574, NCD III, 280-283; Requesens to Mondragón, 29 and 31 July; 2 and 15 August 1574, NCD IV, 185-186; 211-212; 228-229; 367-368; Requesens to Francisco Hernández Dávila, 31 July and 13 August 1574, NCD IV, 210-213; 334-335; Requesens to Lannoy, 31 July 1574, NCD IV, 213-214.

[137] Schelven, *Marnix*, 88.

[138] 14 letters from Requesens to Mondragón between 16 January and 4 October 1574, NCD I-V.

You know how I have served and the age I have, and combined with my lack of health, I need another function for the future and some payment for the thirty-eight years of service that Your Majesty could reward me for with honour, because I deserve this for the age and experience I have in following Your Excellency and being your soldier.[139]

Two weeks later, on 14 April 1574, Mondragón was active at the famous Battle of Mookerheyde, won by Sancho Dávila against an invasion force coming from Germany and organised by William of Orange and his brothers. Chronicler Trillo stated that Mondragón fought "with determination to die or be victorious", but all we hear of his participation is the order to unite his troops from the garrisons of Brussels, Leuven and Tienen. By the end of April 1574 he was ordered to divide his more than two thousand Walloons among garrisons in places like Bergen-op-Zoom and Breda, and on the only two islands of Zeeland left to Philip II, Zuid-Beveland and Tholen.[140] A list of 14 January 1575 shows that he was by then supposed to have 3,600 men in eighteen Walloon companies, but in reality there were only some 2,520 men available.[141]

After the victory at Mookerheyde, an enormous mutiny broke out under the royal troops, as we saw in the chapter on Sancho Dávila. Unfortunately we have no letters from Mondragón for this period, but we do know Mondragón was in Antwerp when the city was harrassed by the mutineers during the early days of May. Morillon blaimed both him and Sancho Dávila for the situation.[142] He clearly saw both commanders acting as one and criticised their actions: "Sancho Dávila and Mondragón have procured that His Excellency [Requesens] should not listen to the enemies of our faith".[143] This seems to contradict the image we have of Mondragón from Middelburg and his contacts with William of

---

[139] 'Save como yo e servydo y la edad que tengo y poca salud que se me va juntando para poder mejor servir de aqui adelante y tener algun pago de treynta y ocho annos de servicio me podria su magestad honrrar y hacer merced pues la edad y espiriençia que tengo de aver siguido a vuestra excelencia y sido su soldado lo mereza'. Mondragón to Alba, Antwerp, 1 April 1574, AA, C44, 249. His health was discussed by Requesens in a letter to Sancho Dávila: Requesens to Dávila, 29 March 1574, NCD II, 60-62. On 2 April 'se hallase en disposición para hallarse en Mastrique'. Requesens to Mondragón, 2 April 1574, NCD II, 76.

[140] Trillo, *Historia*, 238; Report from 14 April 1574, CP III, 52; Requesens to Philip II, Antwerp, 30 April 1574, CP III, 64.

[141] CP III, 246. Another list of his men on 2 August 1574: NCD IV, 230-237.

[142] Morillon to Granvelle, Brussels, 13 May 1574, CG V, 85, 89.

[143] Morillon to Granvelle, Brussels, 11 July 1575, CG V, 336.

Orange. Later, both commanders were held responsible for the failed expedition to Zeeland and accused of being interested only in their own profit.[144]

After the expedition to Mookerheyde and the mutiny of 1574, Mondragón resumed contact with Alba and his secretary. He was very pleased to hear that Alba and his wife had arrived in Madrid, so the Duke could ask for favours from the King in person. Mondragón was crying out from Brussels, "Your Excellency knows that there is no soldier who more rightly deserves the favours of His Majesty than me".[145] He asked the Duke for a licence to come to Spain in order to ask the King in person to grant him favours to help his daughter, "if it was not for the rewards I pretend Your Majesty shall give me, it would be as if she had had no father, and I would be forced to send her to my Lady the Duchess".[146] He was clearly threatening the Duke of Alba. Mondragón did not get a quick response from his patron, who most probably had enough to deal with regarding his own precarious position at court. The Duke's enemies had succeeded in convincing the King that the deteriorating situation in the Low Countries was the result of Alba's harsh policy, and on top of this there was also a conflict with the King about the marriage of Don Fadrique.[147]

Two months later, Mondragón wrote another letter, now in an even more aggressive and demanding tone: "I cannot stop bothering Your Excellency".[148] He stated that the Duke had probably not received his letters, because otherwise he certainly would have answered them. Again he described himself as the best soldier of the King, but he was left out while others "even received many rewards while sleeping".[149] His plea for a personal visit to the King, his old age and his daughter all returned in this letter: "don't wait for me getting even older than I am now, and if I did not have children, I would be satisfied to die poor".[150] He suggested another idea to the Duke. What if the King were to grant him permission

---

[144] Morillon to Granvelle, Brussels, 9 October 1575, CG V, 409-410.
[145] 'Vuestra excelencia save despues que me conoce ningun soldado merece mejor que yo que su rey le favoresca'. Mondragón to Alba, Brussels, 1 July 1574, AA, C44, 252.
[146] 'La qual sy no fuere con la merced que pretendo Su Magestad me haga no podra alavarse de aver tenido padre, y sera me fuerza de embiarla a mi señora la duquesa'.
[147] Martínez Hernández, 'Desafío'.
[148] 'No puedo dexar de importunar a vuestra excelencia'. Mondragón to Alba, Antwerp, 1 September 1574, AA, C44, 253.
[149] 'Questandose dormiendo les hace mucha merced'.
[150] 'No espere a que sea mas viejo de lo que soy y sy no tubiese hijos conhorteria me de morir povre'.

to retire to the castle of Ghent, given to him by Alba but still without receiving the income because the confirmation of the governorship had not yet been given. He had taken over on 4 December 1572, replacing the deceased Jerónimo de Salinas. As the official patent was issued on 23 August 1574, it was in fact on its way when Mondragón was writing this letter.[151]

The letter to Albornoz was even more agressive: "I have very good reasons to complain about Your Honour".[152] He had not heard from him since they had left the Low Countries and he had doubts about their 'amistad'. He also not included any news: "I don't write about the news because others do so of which Your Honour is satisfied".[153] Refusing to serve as a source of news and information shows the depths of his anger. If Alba did not do what a patron had to do, then the client would also stop playing his part. One week after writing these letters, Mondragón received a letter from the Duke dated 16 August. He wrote that Requesens had promised to grant him permission to go to Spain if the royal permission did not arrive within two months. However, the very experienced commander knew that nothing was sure, "as here something new could occur, that would stop them from giving me my licence".[154] Again we have letters to both Alba and Albornoz on the same day. He started his letter to Albornoz with the image of a dream: "I would be satisfied to sit together on the new chairs Your Honour says he has in his house, to tell Your Honour about my work and how I found the situation after leaving [the island of] Walcheren".[155] He is again more outspoken to the secretary: "It is very urgent to make the journey".[156] He also blaimed Requesens for not granting permission to go to Spain, but he knew those in command were unaware of his deeds and he had always been a servant (*criado*) of the Duke of Alba. Letters in November repeated the same issues, adding a description of how Requesens had left him isolated in between dykes and fortresses, "where I think my services are going to be

---

[151] CP III, 182.
[152] 'Muy gran rason tengo de quexarme de vuestra merced'. Mondragón to Albornoz, Antwerp, 1 September 1574, AA, C44, 258.
[153] 'No scrivo nuevas porque otras las escrivan de que vuestra merced se holgar'.
[154] 'Porque aca se podria ofrecer cosa con que no se me diese la licençia'. Mondragón to Alba, Antwerp, 17 September 1574, AA, C44, 254.
[155] 'Yo me contentara de que sentados en las sillas que vuestra merced dice en su casa pudiera yo dar quenta a vuestra merced de mis travajos y de las cosas que halle quando saly de Valqueren'. Mondragón to Albornoz, Antwerp, 17 September 1574, AA, C44, 255.
[156] 'Tengo arta necessidad de hacer la jornada'.

buried".¹⁵⁷ With his old patron not listening to him, his old friend Albornoz not responding, and his new Governor-general unaware of his services rendered, Mondragón felt completely lost, abandoned and isolated.

When he had to write a letter of recommendation to Albornoz for an Italian captain going to court, Mondragón completely broke down: "I have little hope left that if I had died, or would die tomorrow, that Your Majesty would remember my services, nor anybody else, because my deeds from before the arrival of the Comendador Mayor [Requesens] are worth nothing".¹⁵⁸ He felt betrayed, having thought that with Philip II knowing him so well and with Alba and Albornoz as an "alarm on my behalf" at court, things would go his way.¹⁵⁹ He had heard Philip II wanted to reward him, but without granting permission to go to Spain.

He then took things one step further: "If Your Majesty does not decide, then I think I have to take my licence myself, without it being given to me, and I could venture returning to my home".¹⁶⁰ If he was not allowed to go to Spain, he would leave the war on his own account. This was his last resort, hinting at desertion. Other commanders had the same problems when looking for compensation for their deeds, and Julián Romero, too, had to threaten to leave the Low Countries without permission in order to get things moving.

His anger seems to have worked. Besides the patent for the castle of Ghent from 23 August 1574, he was also suggested –along with Gaspar de Robles – as a good possible replacement for Sancho Dávila as governor of Antwerp citadel. Juan de Zúñiga, Requesens's brother, argued that both he and Robles "were such good soldiers and so accepted by those of the country".¹⁶¹ Again we find proof of the positive image of Mondragón held by people of the Low Countries in his own time. In May 1575 Mondragón would write to the King that he was very happy with the large reward of ten thousand guilders in a single payment to use as dowry for his daughter. Now he was ready to remain in the service of the King "hasta la muerte", as he phrased it himself. Little did he know

---

¹⁵⁷ 'Donde creo mis serviçios han de ser enterrados'. Mondragón to Alba and to Albornoz, Heusden, 4 November 1574, AA, C44, 256-257.

¹⁵⁸ 'Poca esperança me queda sy oviera muerto o sy muriesse mañana que su magestad se acordasse de mis serviçios ny nadie, pues que no valen nada los hechos hasta la venida del señor comendador mayor'. Mondragón to Albornoz, Breda, 10 February 1575, AA, C44, 259.

¹⁵⁹ 'Despertador de mi parte'.

¹⁶⁰ 'Sy Su Magestad no se resuelve creo avre de tomar liçencia sin que me la den, lo que podre aventurar sera bolverme a mi casa'.

¹⁶¹ Juan de Zúñiga to Requesens, 10 July 1574, NCD III, 327-332.

then that this would mean another twenty years of service, as in 1575 he was already writing about his old age and his grey hair.[162]

## Quarrelling around Breda (1575)

By this time, peace negotiations were taking place in Breda in February and March 1575 and again in July and August. Mondragón was, like Julián Romero, among the hostages sent to the rebels during the talks.[163] For Mondragón it meant meeting William of Orange again, of which meeting we have evidence in the chronicle by Trillo and in a letter from Requesens to the King, itself based on a letter the Governor-general had received directly from Mondragón. Mondragón and Orange met two or three times and had several conversations.

Spanish chronicler Antonio Trillo informs us amply on their meeting in Dordrecht:

> The Prince of Orange, present in Dordrecht, was very depressed and confused, because Cristóbal de Mondragón had confronted him one day in public, saying to him that he should not miss the opportunity, because by signing the peace he would save his soul, his honour and his possessions. He would also be remembered as the Defender of the Patria. If he would act contrarywise, he would be remembered by all men of the world as bad and perverse. And though these words of Mondragón were important and worthy of being very well considered, they stung the Prince of Orange in such a way he never again saw the colonel. Using the excuse that Mondragón heard mass in his house and had the bells sounded at his door so everybody could come and hear mass, he asked for somebody else to be sent in his place, because he, as a man born in Spain, and even in the middle of Old Castile, heard mass and invited everybody to join by sounding the bells, not withstanding the heretics and the Prince, their captain.[164]

Another discussion between the two is reflected in the letter from Requesens to Philip II, this time not taking place in a public space but during a meeting:

---

[162] Mondragón to Philip II, Breda, 6 May 1575, AGS, E. 562, 85.
[163] Soen, *Vredehandel*, 104-105; Requesens to Philip II, Antwerp, 29 June 1575, CP III, 307. He had left for Breda before 1 May 1575. Viron to Granvelle, Brussels, 1 May 1575, CG V, 306.
[164] Trillo, *Historia*, 263-264.

> Colonel Mondragón wrote to me from Dordrecht, where the Prince of Orange had invited him two or three times, and having several conversations with him. Mondragón had said to him, among other things, that he now could render such an important service to Your Majesty that it would not only make him forget all things from the past, but that he would do Your Majesty such service that he could be made Captain-general of one of his armies. He answered that he did not want this, because they committed too many brutalities in the armies, and he wanted nothing for himself, but only that Your Majesty would guard the privileges, throw out the foreigners and unite these estates, and with this everything would be finished. He also wanted to be a subject of the Estates of Holland and Zeeland, because they had received him when he was in need. And if this was a problem, he would be forced – against his will – to put his business in more powerful hands. So, Your Majesty should look quietly what is more convenient; and he complained very strongly that they had taken away his possessions and his son, and it pitied him very much that his son was now badly educated.[165]

The descriptions coincide in depicting the Mondragón's conciliatory character as he tried to convince Orange to return to the obedience of the King, promising him that he would be restored in all his possessions. The difference is that the chronicler adds a Catholic and Spanish flavour to it, and does not give any insight into Orange's reasoning, while Requesens does explain the arguments of Orange in detail and in a neutral style. The differences may be explained by the fact that one text was intended for internal use, while the other was written with the intention of attracting a wider public and, even more, written by an author with a very sharp pen.

In another situation during this period, Mondragón did not show himself as a man looking for compromises. Whilst in Breda he had an open conflict with the experienced secretary, Jacques de la Torre (c. 1513-1581), of the Secret Council in Brussels, son of an important Spanish merchant from Bruges and a woman from the Low Countries, and with important relations within both the merchant community and the Habsburg bureaucracy.[166]

---

[165] Requesens to Philip II, Antwerp, 7 April 1575, CP III, 299-300.

[166] Baelde, *Collaterale raden*, 236, 255, 318-319. His sister Magdalena/Madeleine was married to the Spanish merchant, Francisco del Río from Bruges, and their son, Luís, was a member of the Council of Troubles. Versele, *Louis del Río*, 17-19. The important functionary, Pedro del Castillo, was born of an earlier marriage of Francisco del Río.

The incident is reported by the negotiators at the peace talks.[167] Mondragón had been in his room with De la Torre, his wife and others, when he became angry and had shouted at De la Torre, "go away! (*que se vayan!*)", repeating this three or four times. The negotiators speak of "the great fury and indecency of the said Mondragón". The commander became even angrier after a polite reply from De la Torre, again shouting "*que se vayan!*". Mondragón stood up "*comme ung homme furieux*" and said they had tried before to chase him out of the country.

Mondragón might be referring here to the fact that they had tried to take Ghent castle away from him, but the document does not explicitly state this. We do not even know whether Mondragón was aware of the fact that his government of Ghent castle was at stake, as it went against the privileges to have a foreigner occupying this post. We can think his anger shows that he did know, as he was in Breda at the time the negotiations were taking place. Requesens seems to have been open to this idea as part of the negotiations, while the King and his advisors in Spain were completely against it.[168]

De la Torre then told Mondragón that he had known about the actions against him for quite some time, and then "the said Mondragón attacked him, pulling him by his ears with his two hands, as if he were some page or villain". He cried out that he wanted to know how the secretary had known this. De la Torre tried to escape from Mondragón, and two or three people got between them to prevent him from hurting De la Torre even more. The secretary now wanted to have his honour restored; after all he was a man of sixty-two with thirty-two years in the service of the King and he had done so much for these negotiations. This makes it a quarrel between two long-serving servants of the crown, as Mondragón was of more or less the same age and experience. The negotiators writing the letter to Requesens knew Mondragón had also written to Requesens, and they now awaited his decision on the matter.

A few days later, Requesens sent his very political answer to the negotiators. If the situation had been as they had written to him Mondragón would be in the wrong, but the commander had written to him with a completely different story and he could not believe Mondragón had treated a minister of His Majesty in such a way. As Mondragón was now very busy, the matter would have to be put on hold. Morillon, Granvelle's confidant, used the conflict to criticise the Spanish military in a letter

---

[167] Commissionaries of Philip II to Requesens, Breda, 26 June 1575, CP III, 757-760.
[168] Requesens to Philip II, Antwerp, 6 February 1575, CP III, 262; Idem, 286, and Philip II to Requesens, El Escorial, 26 March 1575, Idem, 287.

to Granvelle, and he introduced some extra blows (*soufletz*) to the story, adding in yet another lettter that the commander had also pulled him by the nose. The increase in the violence may have been the result of new incoming information, but also a way of turning the story into an even better one. Morillon also drew a conclusion from the conflict: "If they treat in this way those that are of the nation [the Spanish], what will they do with those whom they like very little?".[169] We see Mondragón here as the typical example of a violent and brutal Spanish commander, but we know who is saying it.

## The Red Sea opens again, and again

After the end of the negotiations at Breda, Mondragón inmediately returned to the war. The invasion of Fijnaart, back then an island in the Volkerak, started with the crossing of the sea at low tide. His spies had studied in secret the tides between the coast and the island and then they went in, as in 1572, with the old commander entering first. And again it provided wonderful material for the chroniclers:

> He ordered them to take off their leg coverings, trousers and other clothes, leaving them with only their gambesons, shirts and shoes. He gave every soldier a small sack of powder and some knapsacks for around their neck, and, to the one in front, food for two days.[170]

Biographer Salcedo Ruiz calls these pages of Mendoza's one of the best parts of his work, and even of the military literature of the whole world.[171] They arrived with only nine casualties, the enemies fled inmediately, he spared the lives of the rebels in the fortresses, left some men in garrison, and returned to Brabant with his troops. Dutch author Van Meteren also mentions Mondragón's freeing of the rebel soldiers, but does not attach any positive judgement to this behaviour.[172] In a letter to

---

[169] Requesens to the commissionaries of Philip II, Antwerp, 29 June 1575, CP III, 764; Morillon to Granvelle, Brussels, 3 July 1575 and 11 July 1575, CG V, 329, 332.
[170] Mendoza, *Comentarios*, 526-527.
[171] Salcedo Ruiz, *El coronel*, 90; Herrera y Tordesillas, *Historia*, II, 9-10.
[172] Van Meteren, *Historie*, 85r; Hooft, *Histoorien* X, 432; Ham, 'Willemstad'; Mondragón to Requesens, 28 June 1575, AGS, E. 562, 133. See also Requesens to Philip II, Antwerp, 29 June 1575, CP III, 337. He had with him 1,000 Walloons, two companies of Spaniards, two of Germans, and seven pieces of artillery. See also Morillon to Granvelle, Brussels, 11 July 1575, CG V, 332.

Requesens, Mondragón tells his own story of the crossing through the water:

> All the Spanish captains and those of Walloons have served very well and with enthusiasm. I don't know how I can praise them any more to Your Excellency. With the desire of them and that of all the soldiers, and without knowing more than seeing the enemy defences, they crossed the water… with the mud up to their waist, in such a way as to convert the sea into land, and even the sailors did not serve as usual, but under the captains that had brought them, and they did it all so fast that we arrived to the small island before the end of the low tide, from where we reached the dyke, passing through water, mud and arquebus shots that were fired against us. But with the will to serve God and Your Excellency, this was no problem, and though the enemies were with many more, they greatly feared the good order we had in attacking them.[173]

In September royal troops repeated the same trick, now going from Sint Philipsland to Duiveland, making use of the knowledge derived from Mondragón's crossing to Goes in 1572. The commander was again involved in the action, but this time he did not go into the water himself.[174] One chronicle gives Italian commander Chiappino Vitelli the honour of entering the water, but considering his famous corpulence this is not very likely. In the fighting after their arrival rebel commander Charles de Boisot was killed, probably due to fire from his own troops. Mondragón is prominently present at this dramatic scene in an eighteenth-century

---

[173] 'An servido todos los capitanes españoles y los demas de Walones tan prinçipalmente y de buena gana que no lo sabre encaresçer a vuestra excelencia, con la voluntad que ellos y todos los soldados, sin saber mas de ver la deffensa que el enemigo les hazia, passando ellos contra el agua, y el lodo hasta mas de la çinta, de manera que an hecho de la mar tierra, hasta los marineros an servido no como suelen, sino haziendo los capitanes que los an traydo a cargo, y ellos tanta diligençia que con ella antes que nos faltasse la baxa mar, nos pusieron en la isleta, de donde para llegar al dique tuvimos el agua y el lodo y muchos arcabuzazos en contra, mas con la voluntad de servir a Dios y a vuestra excelencia, todo se tuvo en nada, y aunque los enemigos fueron muchos mas tuvieron miedo y temor a la buena orden que se tuvo para combatirlas'. Mondragón to Requesens, 28 June 1575, AGS, E. 562, 133.

[174] Janssens, *Brabant*, 260-261, includes a copy of an engraving of the crossing from AGS, E. 1516, 171.

Dutch engraving.[175] Charles de Boisot was the brother of Louis de Boisot, the commander of the fleet of the Sea Beggars at the relief of Leiden in 1574 (see chapter IV).

In the last sea crossing on foot, from Duiveland to Schouwen, chronicler Mendoza again sees Mondragón taking off his clothes before entering with his troops, and he is followed by his fellow commanders, Sancho Dávila and Juan Osorio de Ulloa. It turns Mondragón into the Spanish champion in crossing the waters in Zeeland on foot and, combined with his grey hair and mature age, into the only real Spanish Moses of the Low Countries. This expedition to Zeeland was a joint command by Sancho Dávila and Mondragón, with Juan Osorio as their right hand. The idea came from Requesens, but later on he was sorry for his decision as he had to inform the King that several disagreements had occurred between the two commanders that had caused great inconvenience.[176]

A first conflict arose about the strategy on the island of Schouwen. While Mondragón preferred a direct attack on the town of Zierikzee, Dávila and Osorio decided to go first against the small fortress of Bommenede, nowadays completely disappeared under water. It shows Mondragón was not dominating the decision-making process. Sancho Dávila, former captain of the guard of the Duke of Alba, Governor of Antwerp citadel, and the hero of the Battle of Mookerheyde, demonstrated in these years that he was the most powerful Spanish commander in the Low Countries. The siege of Bommenede, also the theme of a Hogenberg engraving, is one of these smaller episodes that could do with a more complete analysis. While the royal army and the French garrison in the fortress were negotiating, some of the Spaniards attacked without permission. Then the French no longer wanted to surrender and they started a brave defence: "those that were called chickens (*gallinas*) by the Spanish, showed they had the dash of very brave cocks (*gallos*)". As in English, *gallinas* refers to cowards, while *gallos* is the nickname of the French, related to their origin as Gauls. We can find this word play, here quoted from Mendoza, with the traditional name for the French as *gallos*, in many chronicles and histories. All defenders were killed, but

---

[175] *Mémoires anonymes*, I, 175-177; De dood van Charles de Boisot. Rijksmuseum Amsterdam, RP-P-OB-79.097.

[176] Van Meteren, *Historie*, 86v-88r; Requesens to Philip II, Tholen, 15 October 1575, CP III, 375-377; Mendoza, *Comentarios*, 531-534; Hooft, *Histoorien* (1972) X, 436-451 ('s koninx volk trekt te voete, door 't waater, naa Duyvelandt en Schouwen'); 'Relación', CEF, 60, 222r-226v; Schortinghuis, 'Mondragon'.

the attack also caused many casualties among the royal troops, such as Mondragón who "received an arquebus shot and stayed in Antwerp".[177]

## The siege of Zierikzee (1575-1576)

The subsequent siege of Zierikzee would become another of the large heroic sieges in Dutch history, though it has, like the siege of Middelburg, received far less attention than similar sieges in the county of Holland, like Leiden, Haarlem or Alkmaar. During the first months Mondragón did not succeed in closing off the town's support lines and twice a large relief fleet was able to enter. He also had to close the holes in the dykes that had been dug by the town's Protestant minister and his adherents. Mondragón's very generous proposal for surrender caused a conflict in the city that was finally won by the radical Protestant forces. The Catholic regents of the city were imprisoned and taken by ship to Middelburg.[178] Though Mondragón had then wanted to attack Zierikzee directly, it was decided first to attack the small fortress of Bommenede, already discussed above. The Spanish commander did issue an order that refugees from Zierikzee would be directly sent back to the town "in order to more quickly consume the [available] food".[179] It was the same strategy Orange had used at Middelburg.

The famous Brussels archivist, Louis Prosper Gachard, included in his edition of Philip II's correspondence some seventy-eight letters from Mondragón, written between 5 March and 26 August 1576 and generally addressed to the Council of State which had taken over the government of the Low Countries after Requesens' death.[180] Gachard stated that the letters made it possible to be present at all the military encounters, offering all possible details on the negotiations. But then he almost seems to abandon the objective viewpoint of the historian: "reading them you cannot but get sympathy for the Spanish leader, maybe the only one among all those of his nation, who did not receive the public animosity of the inhabitants of the Low Countries".[181] Salcedo Ruiz confesses in his biography of Mondragón that it was by reading these same letters that he got the idea of writing a book on the commander: "these

---

[177] Hooft (1972), *Histoorien*, X, 440-441; Morillon to Granvelle, Brussels, 30 October 1575, CG V, 416-417.
[178] Pot, *Beleg*, 17-22.
[179] Pot, *Beleg*, 34.
[180] CP IV, 543-738.
[181] CP IV, xi-xii.

letters, that portray not his body, but the complete soul of Cristóbal de Mondragón".[182]

The rebels succeeded several times in getting relief fleets with supplies into the town, including on 23 October 1575 and 9 January 1576. As a solution, Mondragón closed the harbour of Zierikzee off with "certains poles connected with anchor ropes and chains", as he explained himself in a letter to the King.[183] On 11 April a rebel fleet tried in vain to break this blockade, a heroic attempt that was immortalised on one of the famous Zeeland tapestries on the Revolt, now in the Zeeuws Museum at Middelburg.[184]

Two days after these events, Mondragón wrote to the Council of State a letter from the dykes, in which he reported floating human legs in the water: "this morning, human legs have been found in the water, together with four dead bodies".[185] He also wrote a separate letter to Spanish councillor Gerónimo de Roda who in turn informed the King: "Colonel Mondragón writes that one saw a great number of arms and legs floating on the water".[186]

Roda regularly included copies of Mondragón's letters on the situation around Zierikzee in his correspondence, written in what Salcedo Ruiz calls Mondragón's 'international gibberish', as his "Castellano is as bad as his French", a fact that Mondragón himsef was also aware of.[187] Of course, most space in the letters was filled not with battlefield stories, but with logistics: he needed money as everything was twice as expensive on the dykes as in Brabant; he needed experienced artillerymen as his had been wounded; and he needed more men, as the dykes were so very long and he had not enough men to cover them all.

A next attempt to relieve the town would again turn into a huge defeat for the rebels. Louis Boisot, the hero of the relief of Leiden in 1574, had gathered an impressive fleet of more than 150 ships, with more than twenty infantry banners on board.[188] Jan Pot, who wrote his PhD thesis on the siege of Zierikzee, offers two reasons for this dramatic

---

[182] Salcedo Ruiz, *El coronel*, 94.
[183] 'Ciertas antenas incadas y por ellas tendidas gumenas y cadenas'. Mondragón to Philip II, Nieuwerkerke, 24 March 1576, AGS, E. 567, 122; Van Meteren, *Historie*, 86v-88r. Pot, *Beleg*, 47-48; Pot, 'Verhaal', 128.
[184] Heyning, *Tapijten*, 129.
[185] Mondragón to the Council of State, the dyke close to Zierikzee, 13 April 1576. CP IV, 566-567.
[186] Gerónimo de Roda to Philip II, Brussels, 14 April 1576, CP IV, 70.
[187] Salcedo Ruiz, *El coronel*, 96.
[188] Lem, 'Louis'.

defeat: a sailor from Sint Maartensdijk had betrayed the plan, and the royal army had intercepted a pigeon carrying a message with the date of the attack. Chronicler Trillo describes a battle of more than six hours with the commander all night on the dykes, resulting in more than a thousand of the enemy dead against eighty dead and wounded in the Colonel's army. Louis de Boisot died when his ship capsized, and all four hundred men on board perished.[189]

Mondragón had been very well prepared for the battle: "the infantry is fully prepared, and ready to receive them, with so much courage as I have not seen for a long time in men of war". Together with Sancho Dávila and Francisco de Valdés he had made a detailed plan describing the movements of all troops.[190] The presence of Valdés turns this confrontation into a revenge for the relief of Leiden, where Boisot had defeated Valdés. On 28 May Mondragón could inform the Council of State of their clear victory over the Beggar's fleet the evening before. The story of the pigeon messages and the account of the victory reached Philip II's desk, and Gerónimo de Roda praised both Mondragón and Sancho Dávila for having fought through the night without ever resting and for risking their lives.[191] And again, Morillon saw things otherwise, as he reported in his letter to Granvelle, once more using Mondragón as an example of all Spanish commanders:

> But nothing is sure, except that Mondragón has written much more [to Brussels] than what has really happened during the exploit. This is normal for such people, to put all good and bad things on one pile, and to entertain the world with lies they consider in the service of His Majesty, in order to have the whole country subjected in fear.[192]

The victory over the rebels did not solve all of Mondragón's problems at once. In June 1576 we find many letters from the commander lamenting the needs among his troops.[193] He also needed to protect Bergen-op-

---

[189] Pot, *Beleg*, 49-50; Trillo, *Historia*, 2800-287; Mendoza, *Comentarios*, 536-540, 542-543; Van Meteren, *Historie*, 86v-88r; Hooft, *Historien*, X, 441; Pot, 'Verhaal', 130.

[190] Mondragón to the Council of State, Ouwerkerk, 7,9,11,17 May 1576; Close to Zierikzee, 19 May 1576; Ouwerkerk, 22 May 1576, CP IV, 593-603.

[191] Council of State to Philip II, Brussels, 30 May 1576, CP IV, 177; Roda to Philip II, Brussels, 30 May 1576, CP IV, 182.

[192] Morillon to Granvelle, Brussel, 3 and 4 June 1576, CG VI, 99.

[193] Mondragón to the Council of State, Ouwerkerk and near Zierikzee, 14 letters between 20 May and 30 June 1576, CP IV, 612-645.

Zoom and the road from Bergen to Antwerp.[194] The Council of State wanted him to finish the siege as soon as possible as they needed the troops to defend the Low Countries from possible invasions from France. Possibly the high nobility of the Low Countries was more worried about the southern border than about events in the north.

When Mondragón's negotiations with Zierikzee's Governor, Arend van Dorp, started, Van Dorp called himself "vostre bien bon ami et serviteur".[195] The Council of State decided to use a strategy based on clemency and, of course, they wanted a quick surrender. Therefore they had problems with the large sum of four hundred thousand florins from the town asked for at first by Mondragón. He had to reduce the sum. Mondragón wanted to know if he was allowed to handle the negotiations and which soldiers should enter the city after capitulation. For all this, Captain Alonso de Sotomayor was used as go-between for the commander and the Council.[196]

In the Council a debate started about Mondragón's capabilities regarding the capitulation. Councilor Roda wrote to Philip II about the anti-Spanish tension in the Council and pointed to the Duke of Aarschot as its instigator: "he has accustomed himself to speaking badly about the Spaniards in our presence".[197] Aarschot wanted to replace Mondragón by somebody from the Council, and when Roda explained to him that Mondragón was just following the orders of the Council, Aarschot replied that "now it is good that those of these lands are governing". From Rome, Cardinal Granvelle joined in the debate, defending Aarschot's position, though he admitted this high nobleman was just a mediocre politician:

> Those of the town [Zierikzee] did not wish to surrender to Mondragón, because they do not trust the Spanish nation, and the examples from the past have inspired their fear. Leiden would have been taken without Valdés, because he had wanted to plunder the city and Mondragón had the same intention with Zierikzee.

---

[194] Mondragón to the Council of State, Ouwerkerk, 1, 6, 7, 10, 13, 17, 19, 23, 24, 25, 28, 30 June 1576; Close to Zierikzee, 14 and 20 May 1576, CP IV, 612-645.

[195] Van Dorp to Mondragón, Zierikzee, 9 June 1576, Gachard, CP IV, 616-617; Idem, Zierikzee, 17/19 June 1576, Gachard, CP IV, 624-625, 627-628; Mondragón to Van Dorp, Ouwerkerk, 19 June 1576, Gachard, CP IV, 627.

[196] Van Dorp to Mondragón, Zierikzee, 9 June 1576, CP IV, 616-617; Idem, Zierikzee, 17/19 June 1576, CP IV, 624-625, 627-628; Mondragón to Van Dorp, Ouwerkerk, 19 June 1576, CP IV, 627; Council of State to Mondragón, Brussels, 10 and 22 June 1576, CP, 618-619, 632-633.

[197] Roda to Philip II, Brussels, 1 July 1576, CP IV, 222.

> Acting in this manner, is fighting a war against the King himself, ruining his land… The Low Countries will never be pacified by force.[198]

Morillon, of course, agreed with his master, but as always he had his own particular view of things: Sancho Dávila and Mondragón never obeyed in any case and the Council did not go against them because it did not want to be seen as going against 'la nation', a phrase referring at the time solely to the Spanish nation.[199] Clearly, Mondragón was not liked by all Netherlanders.

On 2 July Mondragón could inform the Council of State that on that morning, at eight o' clock, Zierikzee had returned under the obedience of the King.[200] The Council had, however, two problems with the treaty Mondragón had concluded: against its wishes he had not made the rebel troops swear an oath not to take up weapons against the King in the future, and he had freed two Protestant ministers. On both points he openly responded that they were right, but continued stating that if the King was not satisfied with his decisions, "he would have good reasons not to trust in the future other important affairs to someone who knows so little as me, as seems to the *messeigneurs*".[201] Though the answer was put in seemingly humble terms, he suggested the King would support him against any criticism from the *messeigneurs* of the Council. He also showed the King his satisfaction that the siege had been relatively cheap: "if somebody else had done it, it would have cost Your Majesty twelve thousand ducats, what now has cost only two".[202] Mondragón was not only a brave soldier; he came from a merchant town.

The defenders were allowed to leave the town with their weapons, their banners furled, and with all their equipment, again much like what had happened in Middelburg. Though Protestant Dutch historian Hooft criticises Mondragón for considering the victory as a personal one, in general he is very positive about the commander, even calling him a noble man.[203] Directly after the surrender, Mondragón was already occupying

---

[198] Granvelle to Philip II, Rome, 13 July 1576, CP IV, 235.
[199] Morillon to Granvelle, Brussels, 21 May 1576, CG VI, 77-78.
[200] Mondragón to the Council of State, Zierikzee, 2 July 1576, CP IV, 646-647.
[201] Council of State to Mondragón, Brussels, 4 July 1576, CP IV, 653-654; Mondragón to the Council of State, Zierikzee, 6 July 1576, Idem, 655-657.
[202] 'Si oviera passado por otras manos costara a Vuestra Magestad doçe mill ducados lo que no cuesta dos'. Mondragón to Philip II, Zierikzee, 4 July 1576, AGS, E. 567, 126.
[203] Trillo, *Historia*, 280-287; Mendoza, *Comentarios*, 536-540, 542-543; Van Meteren, *Historie*, 86v-88r; Hooft, *Histoorien* (1972) X, 441.

himself with the continuation of the war. He needed three thousand men to safeguard Zeeland from the enemy and – following the ideas of the deceased Requesens – he wanted to attack Brielle and IJsselmonde "without losing one hour of time". However, the Council of State was not prepared to pay for an armada. Mondragón also used his moment of victory to criticise the government in the Low Countries, and, of course, to ask for permission to go to Spain:

> To reward me with a licence to go and kiss the feet of Your Majesty before the few days that are left to me for serving you have ended… of my services of forty-one years. I hope that Your Majesty is informed of them [my services] so I will not need to present more memorials.[204]

So please Philip, no more paperwork!

In the end, Mondragón had reduced the sum to be paid by Zierikzee to one hundred thousand guilders at once, and another one hundred thousand within another month, but those of the town succeeded in reducing the sum to half this amount. The Spanish commander furthermore acted in a noble manner by letting bailiff Casper van Vosbergen go free, even though he refused to return to the King's service.[205] In the end, only five Walloon banners from his own regiment entered the town, while the Spaniards and Germans had to remain outside the walls.[206] In this way Mondragón could guarantee that order in the town would be maintained. He showed himself a noble victor, which offers reason enough for the inhabitants of Zierikzee to respect him as an honourable and merciful conqueror.

However, there was another reason for his unexpected popularity in the town's history. Mondragón's opponent, Governor Arend van Dorp, was not at all the prototype of a Dutch patriotic hero. Jan Pot, who in general shows himself in his thesis of 1925 to be a true fatherlander, is quite clear about it: Van Dorp was always looking out for his own interest, he did not shoulder his responsibilities, he lacked the self-confidence and energy

---

[204] 'Sin perder una hora de tiempo'; 'Me haga merced de darme liçencia de yr a bessar los pies de Vuestra Magestad antes de acavar los pocos dias que me quedan en servir… de mis serviçios de quarenta y un años. Yo espero teniendo Vuestra Magestad como tiene notiçia dellos no tendre nesçessidad de presentar mas memoriales'. Mondragón to Philip II, Zierikzee, 4 July 1576, AGS, E. 567, 126; Mondragón to the Council of State, Zierikzee, 6 July 1576, Idem, 655-657.
[205] Hooft, *Historien*, XI, 451; Pot, *Beleg*, 65.
[206] Pot, *Beleg*, 57-59.

to act, and he was not highly regarded by the government of the town. He was even not true to his faith, as he married his daughter, Louise, in 1575 to the Calvinist admiral Louis de Boisot, while he decided that the children of another daughter had to be educated by Jesuits in Antwerp. Pot went even further in his brutal characterisation:

> He was a good friend of a good table; an incredible abundance reigned during his meals. But he was only generous for himself. For his wife and children he was miserly, even heartless. After the death of the Prince of Orange he was left aside by everyone. [207]

On the same pages Pot extensively praised Mondragón:

> Compared to him [Van Dorp] his opponent Mondragón makes a very sympathetic impression.... But above all he is honest, righteous, and a religious man of faith. He had such an authority over his soldiers, that they would always, even unpaid, continue their duties. Towards his enemies, he was generous. [208]

However, we must be cautious not to be swept away by this very positive image of the commander. When Jacques Manteau put his memories about the siege and the surrender on paper in 1630-1631, he did not even mention his name. [209] Writing after more than fifty years, this old witness of the events told the story without recalling the commander's role.

## The mutiny

After the surrender of Zierikzee, the royal troops constitued the largest problem. Being generous towards the defeated caused problems among the victorious. The collected money went almost entirely to the Walloon troops residing in the town, while the Germans and the Spaniards received hardly anything. When some Spanish soldiers went to Zierikzee to complain, the Walloons violently threw them out of the town, killing several Spaniards. [210] The dissatisfaction was enormous. The Spanish soldiers, in particular, were accustomed to being paid after victory. Otherwise they generally started to mutiny. This had happened after the surrender of Haarlem in 1573 and after the Battle of Mookerheyde in 1574.

---

[207] Pot, *Beleg*, 8-9.
[208] Idem.
[209] Manteau, 'Memorie', 115-140.
[210] Pot, *Beleg*, 60; Pot, 'Verhaal', 132.

And this is what happened in Zeeland in 1576. On 4 July Mondragón wrote for the first time about 130 Spanish arquebusiers who had started a mutiny on the island of Tholen. On 8 July Spanish soldiers from the surroundings of Zierikzee joined the mutiny. Mondragón was furious: "I have told them how much damage they are causing". And in less polite terms, "they are so mean that, if it were in my hand, I would not mind hanging half of them… they are devils". Hooft also wrote about Mondragón speaking to the mutineers, but he described a completely different and more positive tone: "he succeeded in making their rage dissappear, by proof of his brave courage and unmovable perseverance, with strong words and an honourable face, that served the man of war as his rhetoric".[211] In this sense, even the mutiny could provide an occasion to praise the commander. In a pamphlet on the mutiny of Zierikzee published that same year in Brussels in both a Dutch and a French edition, Mondragón's name does not even appear, again showing that the positive image of the commander was not damaged by the mutiny.[212]

His main objective was to stop the mutineers from crossing to the mainland. But to make matters worse, in the evening of 9 July his Walloon troops also mutinied and expelled their commanders from the army camp "under shots of arquebuses, saying that their colonel had never fulfilled his promises, reminding him of Mookerheyde, the departure from Middelburg, and other places". In a third letter to the Council on that very same day he had to report that his troops had found transport to Sint-Annaland.[213] The letters show his fears that the mutiny would leave Zeeland "to the mercy of the Prince of Orange". You can even feel the panic in his words: "God knows what we are getting ourselves into!", combined with his anger at "the way these mutinying devils are comporting themselves".[214] On 11 July 1,500 Spanish mutineers arrived at Wouw and Roosendaal, while Valdés tried to pacify those in Bergen-op-Zoom. The experienced commander was confronted with fifty soldiers shooting their arquebuses and shouting *"Buelvanse, buelvanse"* ("go away, go away") and *"Acaben ya, acaben ya"* ("finish now, finish

---

[211] Hooft, *Historien*, XI, 452.
[212] *Waerachtich verhael*; *Discours véritable*. The date of 2 July is not correct.
[213] Mondragón to the Council of State, Zierikzee, 4, 5, 8, 9 July 1576, CP IV, 659-668; Council of State to Mondragón, Brussels, 8 July 1576, Idem, 661.
[214] Mondragón to the Council of State, Zierikzee, 10 and 12 July 1576, CP IV, 668-674 (two long letters on one day). 'Diables altérez', also in Mondragón to the Council of State, Zierikzee, 18 July 1576, Idem, 694-695.

now").²¹⁵ The mutineers had reached the Duchy of Brabant and could continue in the direction of the wealthy cities of the south.

Though the Spanish chroniclers describe how Mondragón had left just in time to avoid dishonourable imprisonment by the mutineers, in reality he was effectively locked up by his own Walloons on the afternoon of 13 July: "they locked me up in my quarters... and up to this moment, eight o'clock in the morning, they have not spoken to me nor told me what they pretend or what their intentions are".²¹⁶ Two weeks later he succeeded in getting a brief letter out through a confidant, but it took him until 7 August to get a real letter to the Council of State. Now they could also start debating the reformation of the Walloon troops. The Council ordered Mondragón to convert the mutinied seventeen companies into ten new ones and he had to put in charge "capitains of their own nation who have led them before".²¹⁷ The Council sent Mondragón's letters to the King, while Roda also informed the King of the Colonel's imprisonment by his own troops and about the Council's ideas to reform Valdés' Spanish infantry tercio and to dissolve Mondragón's Walloon companies, "the best Walloon soldiers there are to be found". According to Roda, this was done intentionally so William of Orange and the Council of State could take them into their own service.²¹⁸ A few weeks later Roda heard from Mondragón that indeed his mutinied troops had threatened to go into the service of the Estates-General. They had even offered to serve for four months for free if they were just paid the wages due to them.

The Spanish troops who had mutinied would finally be allowed to enter the Antwerp citadel by its Governor, Sancho Dávila, to help him in his struggle against the troops of the Estates-General who had been gathering in the city. The attack from the citadel on 4 November would lead to the cruel sack of Antwerp, an event very soon to be known as the Spanish Fury. Mondragón's decision not to have his troops plunder Zierikzee is indirectly connected to the pillaging of Antwerp several

---

²¹⁵ Captain Claude de Vers to Champagney, Gastel [Oud Gastel?], 12 July 1576, CP IV, 674-675; secretary Baltasar López to the Council of State, Bergen-op-Zoom, 12 July 1576, Idem. 675-677.

²¹⁶ Trillo, *Historia*, 280-287, 297; Mendoza, *Comentarios*, 536-540, 542-543; Mondragón to the Council of State, Zierikzee, 14 and 22 July 1576, CP IV, 683-685, 699-700.

²¹⁷ Council of State to Mondragón, Brussels, 3 September 1576, Gachard, CP IV, 735. See also: Mondragón to the Council of State, Zierikzee, 30 July 1576, 2 and 7 August 1576, CP IV, 703-704, 710, 712-713.

²¹⁸ Council of State to Philip II, Brussels, 15 July 1576, CP IV, 248-249; Roda to Philip II, Brussels, 7 August 1576, CP IV, 290; Roda to Philip II, Antwerp, 4 September 1576, CP IV, 352.

months later. Tomorrow never comes, but in this case it did come. In a letter from 19 November, after the Spanish Fury of Antwerp, William of Orange was informed that Mondragón's own Walloon troops had indeed changed sides to the Estates-General.[219] Mondragón had lost his soldiers, and he would lose even more.

## The siege of Ghent castle

By that time Mondragón had other worries. His wife and his men in the castle of Ghent were under attack by troops from the Estates-General. It is the last important episode in Mondragón's life until 1577, and again one that has resulted in one of Hogenberg's engravings: the surrender of the castle by his wife, Madame Mondragón. According to chronicler Trillo, who was never afraid of high numbers, the defenders killed 2,500 attackers before capitulating, with only forty dead Spaniards. He also mentions that the Colonel's wife and daughter were imprisoned. However, he does not say anything about an active part played by Madame Mondragón during the siege. Mendoza paid more attention to her, and according to him she showed "the valour that her husband would have had in encouraging them".[220] Hooft and Van Meteren do not mention much resistance from the defenders of the castle, but Hooft does mention Madame Mondragón supporting them. He may have taken this from Mendoza, but also the Italian historians, Famiano Strada and Girolamo Bentivoglio, speak about Madame who "defended herself with heroic bravery, taking the place of her husband, in an extraordinary way for somebody of her sex".[221] A nineteenth-century Belgian historian describing how she took the place of her absent husband even said of her that "she had the courage enter into the soul of the besieged". His version of the story is that the women threw boiling water over the attackers and that even the children had helped out. In this sense, the role of this French-speaking noblewoman resembled the image of Dutch heroine Kenau fighting the royal army at Haarlem. When the 150 defenders had to surrender on 11 November 1576, the wounded and the sick included, they had lost six men and nine women.[222]

---

[219] Roda to Philip II, Antwerp castle, 28 September 1576, CP IV, 398, 402; Morillon to Granvelle, Saint-Amand, 3 November 1576, CG VI, 159; Jean de Croÿ (Roeulx) to Orange, Ghent, 19 November 1576, BO, 6146.
[220] Mendoza, *Comentarios*, 543, 550-551; Trillo, *Historia*, 305-308.
[221] Salcedo Ruiz, *El coronel*, 127 (quote from the French edition of Strada, 1770); Van Meteren, *Historie*, 94v, 98v-99r; Hooft, *Histoorien* (1972) XI, 458, 479.
[222] Duyse, 'Notice'.

Mondragón had not been able to cross the river Scheldt to come to his wife's aid.[223] So he had asked the Estates-General to send him his wife and his chests. Morillon thought they would let the lady go, but not the chests, as they contained Mondragón's treasure. He later stated about Mondragón that he was "as poor as Job, having lost everything he had in the world at the castle of Ghent where his wife and his daughter were taken prisoner with their possessions".[224] After the surrender, the army of the Estates took Madame Mondragón's two dinner services, in gold and silver, and they were sold at auction. When Juan of Austria became the new Governor-general of the Low Countries he made certain the services were returned to her.[225] Madame Mondragón was taken to Flushing, but Charles-Philip of Croy, Lord of Havré, asked William of Orange's permission to take her to a safer place. However, there is another story about her whereabouts after the surrender. According to the Netherlandish-Spanish chronicler, Martín Antonio del Río, she was taken on a tour: "a nobleman from Flanders, before liberating the wife of the castellan, took her through some cities, as in triumph, as symbol of their victory". Salcedo Ruiz stated it had been John of Croy, the Count of Roeulx: "the plebs celebrating her imprisonment and insulting her for her bad fortune, with the rudeness and the cruelty properly belonging to the political passions that ran so high in those terrible days of enthusiasm and hatred".[226] The year 1576 ended for Mondragón with his troops having mutinied, his wife shown off as a trophy, his treasures lost, and William of Orange triumphing over the Low Countries.

## Life and death (1577-1596)

Mondragón would still have almost twenty years ahead of him. When the Spanish troops left for Italy in 1577 because it had been agreed with the Estates-General that all foreign troops would leave the country, the Colonel most probably returned to one of his wife's possessions in Lorraine. After Governor-general Don Juan of Austria renewed the war,

---

[223] Roda to Philip II, Antwerp castle, 28 September 1576, CP IV, 402. Mondragón had arrived the afternoon of the day before in Antwerp castle; Idem, 10 October 1576, 422.

[224] Morillon to Granvelle, Saint-Amand, 26 October 1576, CG VI, 144; Idem c. 15 November 1576, 168. See also Idem, Saint-Amand, 3 November 1576, 159.

[225] Salcedo Ruiz, *El coronel*, 128.

[226] Havré to Orange, Ghent, 13 November 1576, BO, 6045; Salcedo Ruiz, *El coronel*, 127-128; Río, *Crónica*, 81.

Mondragón quickly returned and served under the Duke of Parma, and was present at the famous siege of Maastricht in 1579. According to chronicler Alonso Vázquez, Parma valued him for his age, his valour and his experience. By that time both his arms were "damaged" (*estropeados*), as Spanish sources at the time graphically expressed it.[227]

He returned once more to Spain in that same year to inform the King on Parma's behalf of the victory at Maastricht. He had to pass through Paris to visit the ambassador and then continue directly to the royal court.[228] And, of course, he used the visit to the King to plead for compensation for his own services: after so many years, he finally met the King, spoke to royal secretary Delgado, and was even invited to the table of Cardinal Granvelle, by then in Madrid.[229] However, we find an angry Mondragón, who complained that he had hurried back to Spain on horseback and that after three months of waiting they tried to give him an insufficient reward for his services. He did not accept the eight hundred escudos from the Kingdom of Naples when he had to give up the ten thousand florins promised to him for his daughter four years previously. He would prefer to send her to a convent. He then stated that Sancho Dávila and Francisco Valdés had received much greater compensation for their services:

> As they [Dávila and Valdés] had profited during sacks and in disservice, and when they had won and pillaged Antwerp and other places, he was standing in water up to his neck, fighting and serving; and he has never profited from sacks nor other things.

And then Mondragón again tried to threaten the King and his advisors that he would leave the King's service:

> that he is going to live in the lands of the Duke of Lorraine with his wife, and he will ask permission to Your Majesty to go and serve the said Duke, who has often asked him to do so.

---

[227] Vázquez, 'Sucesos', CD LXXII, 122, 195.

[228] Instruction al señor coronel Christoval de Mondragon de lo que a de hazer por serviçio de su majestad, Alexander Farnese, close to Maastricht, 25 June 1579; Memorial del coronel Mondragon, BL, Add. 28.702, f. 239r-242r.

[229] Granvelle to secretary Delgado, Madrid, 26 October 1579, CD 31, 179-180. also Idem, 181-182; Vázquez, 'Sucesos', 72, 218.

We find both Granvelle and secretary Delgado trying to calm him down. Granvelle stated that the administrators of the financial department needed documents in order to have proof of his deeds, as there were so many people asking the King for compensation. And if he were to tell the King about his plan to serve the Duke of Lorraine while residing in Madrid, the King would most certainly take this badly, while he could do so honourably once in Lorraine. But Granvelle mostly warned him not to lose the King's grace. Delgado added that Dávila and Valdés had not received the rewards Mondragón thought they had. The King himself showed no initiative, and asked Mondragón for documentation and then returned the case to his advisors. "advise me what you think would be best for him". Mondragón had to go through all the red tape again. The Habsburg bureaucracy did not make exceptions for this war hero.

The day after meeting Granvelle the commander wrote a memorial to the King stating that he was going back to the Low Countries, that he wanted payment for his services since 1577, as well as the now-promised payment from Naples and the ten thousand florins for his daughter. He wanted everything, even mentioning the three thousand florins his wife had paid for wheat in Ghent castle.[230] He most certainly was not a happy man when he returned to the north, and in Madrid he had made more enemies than friends.

Because of the treaty between Parma and the reconciled provinces, Mondragón was forced to give up his position as Governor of Limburg and the lands of Overmaas, returning to his wife and children in Lorraine.[231] From the village of Saint-Mihiel in Lorraine he wrote a letter to the King asking him for compensation or to take him back into his service after "36 years he had been doing nothing else".[232] And indeed he was taken back into the King's service.

Between 1582 and 1588 he acted as a member of the Duke of Parma's council and as a Maestre de campo of the *tercio viejo*, the tercio of the experienced veterans. He had finally become a high officer within the Spanish infantry. After the successful siege of Antwerp, he became its

---

[230] He did receive royal payments in 1583. Mondragón to Philip II, Duinkerke, 17 July 1583 and Ieper, 4 October 1583, AGS, E. 586, 11 and 17.

[231] A chronicle from Zeeland states that Mondragón married a woman from Zeeland during his years as Governor of Limburg/Overmaas (1578-1579). It concerns Magdalena van Wissekercke, the daughter of Anthonis, Lord of Couwerve and bailiff of Middelburg. Smallegange, *Cronyk*, 755. However, in 1590 Guillemette de Châtelet was still alive. Calmet, *Histoire génealogique*, ccxc. In this last book his marriage with Guillemette is problematically dated 1560. Idem, clxxvi, 158.

[232] Mondragón to Philip II, Saint-Mihiel, 20 February 1581 (or 1582), AGS, E. 582, 25.

effective governor in 1585, though he had to remind the King several times to send him the official appointment, even still in January 1587 when he bluntly opened his letter to the King with the following words:

> A soldier of fifty years of service to the Emperor of glorious memory and to Your Majesty, who finds himself with the strength and health to serve Your Royal Majesty, may well take the liberty, being my services so well known by the whole world.[233]

Under the government of the Count of Mansfelt he was nominated Captain-general of the Duchy of Brabant and Maestre de campo general of the whole royal army in the Low Countries. The soldier from Medina del Campo had finally reached the absolute top of the military hierarchy. Between 1585 and his death in 1596 Antwerp castle became his home, though it is unclear whether he remained permanently in the service of the King.[234]

During this period he also kept in contact with merchants from his home town of Medina, as is proven by the preserved letters to the rich local merchant, Simón Ruiz. [235] The main purpose of these letters was the financial organisation of his incomes and investments. Most of the money seems to have come from Naples and had to be invested in Medina.[236] He also informed the merchant about the situation in the Low Countries, for example, that Antwerp was soon to surrender. However, several months later he was still writing from outside the city walls. A Pedro de Mallea appears as his financial agent, 'mi hombre', in Madrid.[237]

---

[233] 'Un soldado de çinquenta años de serviçio al Emperador de gloriosa memoria y de Vuestra Magestad que se halla con fuerzas y salud para servir a Vuestra Real Magestad bien puede tomar liçencia siendo tan conocidos mis serviçios de todo el mundo'. Mondragón to Philip II, Antwerp, 17 January 1587, AGS, E. 593, 68. See also Mondragón to Juan de Idiáquez, Antwerp, 8 October 1586, Idem, 590, 109.

[234] Cabañas Agrela, 'Cristóbal'. Mondragón to Philip II, Antwerp, 30 November 1589, AGS, E. 596, 122.

[235] In the Museo de las Ferias of Medina del Campo some twenty letters from Mondragón dated between 1585 and 1590, and letters from family members, have been preserved.

[236] Mondragón to Simón Ruiz, Army camp before Antwerp, 10 April 1585, Vázquez de Prada, *Lettres marchandes*, IV, 16.

[237] Mondragón to Simón Ruiz, Fortress De la Cruz, outside Antwerp, 15 August 1585, Vázquez de Prada, *Lettres marchandes*, IV, 31-32. Also Idem, Antwerp, 3 October 1585, 22 November 1585, 20 February 1586, 13 May 1586 and 9 June 1586, *Idem*, 43-44, 55, 69-70, 81, 90. The letters also show a personal relationship with a certain Álvaro Verdugo and his family.

As from 1584, his nephew and son-in-law, Alonso de Mondragón, can also be found in the merchant's correspondence, busy with Cristóbal's financial transactions.[238] Notwithstanding his continuous complaints to the crown, Cristóbal was not a poor man.

There is still much to be said about this last period of almost twenty years, but this cannot be done within the scope of this book.[239] For example, there is a famous anecdote concerning the night in 1578 he stayed in a recently conquered castle in which his men went treasure hunting carrying candles. They caused an enormous explosion when eighteen barrels of ammunition exploded, completely destroying the castle. But Mondragón was not hurt and his bed survived the blast without any damage.[240] He kept functioning as an ideal protagonist for storytellers.

Mondragón produced narratives and letters until almost the final hour of his death. On 30 December 1595 he wrote a last letter to his King, who was already an old and sick man himself. Of course, the Colonel repeated his service of by now sixty continuous years, but the main goal of the letter was to ensure the government of Antwerp castle for his son-in-law and nephew, Alonso de Mondragón, and a company of lancers for his grandson, Cristóbal de Mondragón.[241] After his death on 4 January 1596 his heir Alonso also wrote a letter to royal secretary Martín de Idiáquez, but all their attempts were in vain, as Antwerp was too important a fortress to be given away so lightly.[242]

And, of course, there is an anecdote related to his death, even recently used by Spanish author Arturo Pérez-Reverte, claiming the dying Mondragón wanted to be put next to a window so his beloved soldiers could see him die. Salcedo Ruiz offers another version of the same story in which he wanted to see the war from his window, but he does not think it fits the

---

[238] Alonso de Mondragón to Simón Ruiz, Antwerp, 18 February 1586, 1 and 7 October 1587, 10 April 1588 and 31 July 1588, Vázquez de Prada, *Lettres marchandes*, IV, 69, 190-191, 193, 228, 262-263.

[239] Much can be found in Vázquez, 'Sucesos'. A short evaluation of Mondragón in which Vázquez states regarding the colonel's deeds that 'no hay para qué encarecerlos ni escribirlos', in Idem, III, 361.

[240] Brouwer, *Kronieken*, 76; Vázquez, 'Sucesos', CD 72, 127-128. On Mondragón and the command of the army in the 1590s: González de León, *Road* (2009) 100-101.

[241] Alonso was the son of his sister, Magdalena de Mondragón, and Diego González del Castillo. From his marriage to Cristóbal's daughter, Margarita, he had three children: Catalina, Juana and Cristóbal. Atienza and Barreda de Valenzuela, 'Los Mondragón', 322.

[242] Mondragón to Philip II, Antwerp castle, 30 December 1595, AGS, E. 609, 231; Alonso de Mondragón to Philip II, Antwerp castle, 21 January 1596, AGS, E. 609, 232. See also Alonso de Mondragón to Martín de Idiáquez, Idem, 233.

character, and neither do I. Dutch Calvinist historian Pieter Bor tells a completely different story in which he died "washing his hands to sit at the table".[243] Had Bor a metaphorical or moralistic intention in ascribing this peculiar way of dying to somebody who had been in the war for more than sixty years? Or is it perhaps the simple truth?

Although he was first buried in the chapel of Antwerp castle, he was later taken to be buried in the chapel of his son-in-law's family in the church of Vera Cruz in Medina del Campo. When a reburial was needed in 1674-1675, a new text was made to accompany his grave with a short – and not always accurate – biography of the commander, listing his commands and his great deeds, and finishing with a "eulogy in which he is praised, not only by the Spanish chroniclers, but also by the foreign ones".[244] This chapter serves as evidence of this rather remarkable statement from a seventeenth-century Castilian: Cristóbal de Mondragón had indeed a very good press among foreign authors.

## Mondragón on the Dutch stage

And his international fame was not to stop there. In late-eighteenth-century Dutch theatre Mondragón was turned into an important protagonist within the stories of the local, provincial and national past. Dutch historical theatre was booming between 1780 and 1800, and this also had its effect on Mondragón's image.[245] Already in 1774 one of the few female Dutch writers of the period, Lucretia Wilhelmina van Merken (1721-1789) from Amsterdam, produced a play on *Jacob Simonszoon de Ryk*, a rebel whose life was spared thanks to Mondragón.[246] This play had the honour of opening the new Amsterdam theatre on 15 September 1774, after a fire had destroyed the old building. The first public performance of Menken's play two days later sparked great interest among the public, and soldiers had to help restore order when everybody tried to rush in.[247] The play would have some thirty-nine stagings in Amsterdam until 30 November 1840, but it also had success in other cities, even as far away

---

[243] Pérez-Reverte, 'Historia'; Salcedo Ruiz, *El coronel*, 186. The anecdote probably originates from Diana, 'Cristóbal', 163-164 and 173. I thank Juan Luis Sánchez (Madrid) for this last reference; Boekelman, *Mondragón*, 61.
[244] Salcedo Ruiz, *El coronel*, 194.
[245] Jensen and Van Deinsen, 'Theater', 194.
[246] Merken, *Jacob Simonszoon*; Rijksmuseum Amsterdam, Reinier Vinkeles, engraving 1774; Merken, *Jacob Simonszoon* (2019).
[247] Jensen and Van Deinsen, 'Theater ', 193-194. Merken, *Jacob Simonszoon* (2019) 9-11.

as Batavia.²⁴⁸ Van Merken is also famous for her play on the siege of Leiden, the city she moved to after her marriage.²⁴⁹

Four years later, in 1778, prolific writer Johannes Nomsz. published his *Maria van Lalain of de verovering van Doornik* [Mary of Lalaing or the conquest of Tournai], a play in which Mondragón is one of the five main protagonists.²⁵⁰ Nomsz. (1738-1803) also wrote short biographies of Charles V and Philip II. He is famous for being an author who changed sides between the Patriots and the Orangists, the two opposite parties dominating Dutch politics during the late eighteenth century. The performance in the Amsterdam theatre on 13 December 1783 caused an enormous commotion as the public applauded when the Duke of Parma declaimed, "the Prince of Nassau, the plague of the Dutch states". ²⁵¹ The applause made continuing the performance impossible, and again soldiers had to come in to control the public. The anti-Nassau speech had sounded to the Amsterdam public as "heavenly music to their ears".²⁵² *Marie van Lalain* had thirty-nine performances in Amsterdam by 14 February 1849, making both it and Merken's play bestsellers well into the nineteenth century.²⁵³

Another ten years later, in 1788, *'t beleg en overgaan der stad Middelburg* [the siege and surrender of the city of Middelburg] was re-published. It was originally written by a seventeenth-century author from Middelburg, Joos Claerbout, and first published in 1661. The re-edition was clearly influenced by the popularity of historical theatre at the time, as can be deduced from the introduction.²⁵⁴ Another three years later, in 1791, it was followed by an anonymous play under the title *Boisot en Mondragon of de belegering en verovering der stad Middelburg* [Boisot and Mondragón or the siege and conquest of the city of Middelburg].²⁵⁵ So within seventeen years, Dutch theatre staged four different plays in which Mondragón was one of the main protagonists of the story. For Dutch theatregoers of the time he must have been a well-known character.

The 1791 anonymous play seems to be connected to the 1774 play by Van Merken. In 1791 the play is situated in a room of Mondragón's

---

²⁴⁸ Onstage, http://www.vondel.humanities.uva.nl/onstage/; Merken, *Jacob Simonszoon* (2019) 30-35.
²⁴⁹ Logchem, 'Lucretia', 677-679.
²⁵⁰ Nomsz., *Maria*.
²⁵¹ 'Nassaus prins, de pest van Nederlands staten'.
²⁵² 'Hemelmelody in de ooren'. Jensen and Van Deinsen, 'Theater', 203.
²⁵³ Onstage.
²⁵⁴ Martínez Luna, *Ondraaglijk juk*, 114; Claerbout, *'t beleg*.
²⁵⁵ Claerbout, *'t beleg*; anonymous, *Boisot en Mondragon*.

house, while in 1774 the stage had been set in Mondragón's Ghent castle. In both plays we find Francisco de Bobadilla[256] as a Spanish commander and a friend of Governor-general Luis de Requesens, and Osorio de Angulo[257] as a commander and friend of Mondragón. But the most striking similarity is the presence of Elvire de Moncada[258] as Mondragón's wife, while he was, of course, married to the noble Madame Guillemette de Châtelet. As the authors clearly used historical descriptions for their story, it was a deliberate decision to give Mondragón a Spanish noblewoman as his wife. The clear opposition in the play between Dutch and Spanish would otherwise have been blurred.

In all these plays Mondragón is in essence the only good Spaniard, the only one that could be trusted. In *Jacob Simonszoon de Ryk* the play is centred around Mondragón's promise after the surrender of Middelburg to spare some of the rebel prisoners or himself go into captivity. The author used the histories of P.C. Hooft, a relative of the title hero, and "the only one… as far as I know, who has extensively reported on the deeds that are the subject of this drama".[259] A problem was that Mondragón was a member of Alba's faction, and so Elvire explains: "As much as the Low Countries hate the cruel Alba, he did justice to my spouse, and he supported him".[260] Mondragón is the man of honour, while in general "the unfaithful Castilian does not hold his word nor his promises to be sacred".[261] Mondragón only appears relatively late on stage in order to criticise Requesens, who does not want to free De Ryk: "is this all the pay you owe me for my loyalty?…You must not regard my services very high, if they do not hold against five Beggars".[262] In the end Requesens is convinced by the commander: "I did you wrong. Please return your friendship to me".[263]

---

[256] Maestre de campo Francisco Arias Bobadilla (1537-1610), Count of Puñonrostro, Williams, 'Francisco'. His troops were saved in December 1585 from rebel forces as a result of the Miracle of Empel, near Bois-le-Duc ('s-Hertogenbosch).

[257] Captain Osorio de Angulo was a captain of the Spanish infantry, wounded at the Battle of Saint-Quentin in 1557.

[258] The surname was probably taken from Francisco de Moncada (1586-1635), a Spanish commander in the Low Countries, active since 1622. García Hernán, 'Francisco'.

[259] 'De eenige… zo verre my bekend is, die een omstandig bericht geeft van de daad, die het onderwerp van dit treurspel uitmaakt'. Merken, *Jacob Simonszoon* 1774, 119.

[260] 'Hoe zeer ook Nederland den wreeden Alva haat, hy deed myn wederhelft-recht, en was zyn toeverlaat'. *Idem* 126.

[261] 'De ontrouwe Castiljaan houd woord noch eeden heilig'. *Idem* 173.

[262] 'Is dit het loon dat ge aan myn trouw verschuldigd zyt… U ligt gewis niet veel aan mynen dienst gelegen, zo zy te ligt is om vyf Geuzen op te weegen'. *Idem* 193-194.

[263] 'Ik deed u ongelyk. Geef my ue vriendschap weder'. *Idem* 227.

*Boisot en Mondragon* is centred around the relationship between the royal Spanish commander and the rebel commander. Now Mondragón opens the play as a noble and haughty general: "How d'Alinas, do you dare speak like this to Mondragón? To Mondragón, who has never avoided the enemy? Who kept Goes by an expedition through the water, as daring a deed as ever a mortal has completed".[264] It is also explained that he was promoted by the Duke of Alba who "did feed on cruelties, though never permitted cowardice",[265] and this meant he was not favoured by Requesens. He is strong and stubborn: "I do not tolerate objections againt my orders, as long as I hold Middelburg for Spain".[266] But at the same time he does not treat his own family better than the poor. Boisot speaks of Mondragón as "this war hero" and "I call you a friend, whom I should consider an enemy".[267] He sees him as the exceptional Spaniard: "there are few of them we can trust".[268] Mondragón does not want to speak with Boisot about surrendering the city as he still hopes a relief fleet will succeed in rescuing it, but he sees the people suffering. We then re-live the disaster of the double fleet of Sancho Dávila and Julián Romero. In the end he has to surrender to Boisot, but this takes place with mutual respect. He describes himself in this play: "Am I not Mondragón, born low, who left his estate and through his bravery in war, rose above the estate of nobility by birth and blood?"[269] Exactly the same discourse on the importance of nobility versus practical qualities that we can find in the seventeenth-century Spanish plays on the habit of Julián Romero.

*Maria van Lalain* by Johannes Nomsz. has, like the other two plays, a rebel hero in the person of the heroic Maria de Lalain[g] who defended the city of Tournai during a siege by Parma in 1581.[270] She was a cousin of Count Horne, executed by Alba in 1568. The author states that he based his description of the heroine on the histories of Bentivoglio and

---

[264] 'Hoe d'Alinas durft gy tot Mondragon dus spreeken? Tot Mondragon, die nooit den vyand is ontweeken? Die Goes behouden heeft, door eenen watertogt, zoo stout als nimmermeer een sterfling heeft volbrogt' (pages 3-4).

[265] 'Wel wreedheden heeft gevoed, dog lafheid nooit gedoogd' (4).

[266] 'Ik duld geen tegenspraak op myn gedaan bevel, zoo lang ik Middelburg voor Spanjen hou' (12).

[267] 'Dien oorlogsheld' (19); 'Ik noem u vriend, wien ik als vyand moet beschouwen' (28).

[268] ''t zyn weinigen van hen die wy vertrouwen schenken' (22).

[269] 'Ben ik niet Mondragon, die laag, in stand geboren, zyn' laagen staat vertrad, en door zyn oorlogsmoed, klom boven d'eedlen rang en van geboorte en bloed!' (64).

[270] Maria Christina de Lalaing (1545-1582).

*Protagonists of War*

Le Clerq.²⁷¹ Maria (or Christina) might be seen as the rebel counterpart of Madame de Châtelet. Again the playwright explains his relationship with the Duke of Alba: "Toledo, the country's tyrant, though completely without virtues, always valued Mondragón's righteousness".²⁷² And again, he is the exceptional Spaniard, saying to Maria:

> How I would like to free you from Spain's rod of war! I hate Toledo's revenge and the anger of his executioners; you have to believe that your well-being is very dear to me... And it makes me sad, that I have to fight against such a brave people as the Dutch.²⁷³

He tries to convince Maria to surrender to Parma: "do trust Farnese's word, he is not Toledo".²⁷⁴ Alba is clearly the enemy in this play, much more anti-Spanish than the others. Parma judges Mondragón very positively: "You are not only a hero in the heat of battle, but also an honest man who tells me the truth".²⁷⁵ However, Mondragón refuses to follow Parma's orders to kill her son. In the end Parma understands Mondragón was right and praises him: "that Mondragón will remain Farnese's guide for many years".²⁷⁶ In this sense the play resembles *Jacob Simonszoon de Ryk*, with Mondragón convincing Requesens to do the noble thing.²⁷⁷

The three plays together show that Mondagón was very positively judged in Dutch theatre as the exceptional, good Spaniard, just and honest, and his relations with the rebel heroes are always positive. This was less so in Claerbout's play which was originally published in 1661. In the 1788 introduction Mondragón is called "the brave" ("*de dappere*"), but in the play itself he is much less noble and open than in the other plays, and much more Catholic, using words like "Beggar vermin" ("*Geuse ongediert*") and "the calvinist sect" ("*secte der kalvinisten*"), and

---

²⁷¹ Probably historian Jean Le Clerc (1657-1736), author of the *Histoire des Provinces Unies* (Amsterdam 1728).
²⁷² 'Toledo, 's lands tiran, hoe ook van deugd ontaart, achtte altyd Mondragons oprechtheid achting waard' (6).
²⁷³ 'Hoe gaarne ontrok ik u aan Spanjes oorlogsroede! Ik doem Toledoos wrok, en zyner beulen woede; geloof my dat uw heil my diep ter harte gaat... Intusschen smart het my, dat ik zo braaf een volk als Nederlands volk bestry' (10).
²⁷⁴ 'Vertrouw Farneses woord: hy is Toledo niet' (11).
²⁷⁵ Gy zyt niet slegts een held in 't hevigst van 't gevecht, maar ook een eerlyk man, die my de waarheid zegt' (28).
²⁷⁶ 'Dat Mondragon noch lang Farneses leidsman zy' (65).
²⁷⁷ In his *Willem de Eersten* (Amsterdam 1779), 11th zang, Nomsz. praises Mondragón as 'de dappre Mondragón' and 'de fiere Mondragón'.

offering a very negative image of William of Orange.[278] Claerbout's praise is mostly directed at his abilities: "because monseigneur Mondragón is very experienced in affairs of war".[279] Though less overtly Spanish in character than military commanders Sancho Dávila and Julián Romero, Mondragón was in 1661 not yet the noble hero in the Low Countries he would become in the late eighteenth century.

## Victory of the good

We return to the image from the beginning of this chapter. In the 1795 chronicle from Zierikzee he was the great exception, the only good Spaniard! He has maintained this fame until today. This positive image can already be found in his own time, but it has become clear that both his life and the descriptions of it during the course of the centuries offer a much richer and more diverse palette. He was not a good Spaniard in the eyes of all Netherlanders, and he certainly was not without stain or fault. However, that was to be expected from a Spanish commander during the Revolt in the Low Countries. It was the exceptional side of Mondragón, his good side, that would survive the centuries and is still alive today.

The fact that he had resided in the north for many years before the outbreak of the Revolt may explain a large part of his positive image in the Low Countries and, as a result, also the understanding he seems to have had for the land and the people. Mondragón was a completely integrated Spaniard, whose Spanish would even lose ground to his French. His friends, his relatives, his soldiers were all French-speaking. As French was the language most members of the elite in the Low Countries were able to speak, Mondragón could perfectly communicate with all the important people. There is no clue about his possible knowledge of the Dutch language, but evidence also remains unclear about the active knowledge of Dutch of even William of Orange.

His relatively lowly origins in Spain and the fact that a knighthood of one of the Spanish chivalric orders seemed out of the question, combined with the small family empire he was building in the Low Countries, also make it more than logical that a great number of his interests were vested in the Low Countries. Though we can also see that even this integrated Spaniard regularly asked to be permitted to return to Spain and also invested in his home town. In the end he would remain

---

[278] Idem, 12.
[279] 'Want Mons Dragon, die is in 't krygs-stuk wel ervaren' (24).

in the north for more than fifty years, interrupted by only a few short visits to Spain.

Also the use of his old age in many of the chronicles may have favoured his image. His grey hair may have turned him into a more respectable person, though, of course, the Duke of Alba was even older than Mondragón. Mondragón's age, combined with his experience and his sense of honour, turned him into a reliable person.

His character must indeed have been calmer than that of his close comrade-in-arms, Sancho Dávila, and his great patron, the Duke of Alba. When reading the letters from both Dávila and Mondragón, we note the differences in character, although somebody like Morillon saw the two men as one and the same. The fact that the good Spaniard of the Revolt in the Low Countries was a companion of Sancho Dávila and even a creature of the Duke of Alba shows that it is difficult to attach a certain set of values to the whole group of people around the Duke. Besides a difference in character, Dávila had hardly known the Low Countries before the outbreak of the Revolt. Dávila looked for friends among the Spaniards present in the army and among the Spanish merchant colonies of Antwerp and Bruges.

It is interesting to see how the Dutch plays make use of the fact that Mondragón was a close collaborator of the Duke of Alba. Maybe it made him even more interesting for the story. But for the Dutch, it was his connection to William of Orange that really made him special. The letters exchanged between Mondragón and Orange after the surrender of Middelburg show that already during his lifetime Mondragón was seen by the rebel leader as different from the others. The same holds for Julián Romero, when we think of their discussion of the 'bonne guerre', but this relationship was little known at the time. Besides questions of personal character, the fact that Romero, Mondragón and Orange shared a common past before the outbreak of the war may have been of great importance. They had been fighting in the same army for years.

There are also negative stories to be found about Mondragón: his behaviour in Deventer, the sack of Dendermonde, his harsh stands in Middelburg and Antwerp, and his temper and his behaviour at Breda. And then there is Maximilien Morillon, who sees him along with Sancho Dávila as the worst Spanish commanders during the Revolt. However, all these stories have been forgotten over time. This might prove that the stories that do not fit into the general idea regarding a person are more easily forgotten than the stories that do fit. In the same way, we never tell any good stories about the Duke of Alba in the Low Countries, or use his grey hair as a way to soften his image. In his case, the grey hair fits the image of the 'Iron Duke'.

The Zeeland tryptich turns Mondragón into a special hero in the Low Countries: two major sieges and the subsequent crossings through the sea have turned him into a special Spanish hero, the Moses of Zeeland. Though the history of the siege of Zierikzee still plays a prominent part in this town, the history of the siege of Middelburg seems almost completely forgotten, and even more so the role Mondragón played in it. Perhaps again the fact that a Spanish defender of a Dutch city does not fit the general idea of the Revolt may explain this situation, but, on the other hand, the surrender of Zierikzee to a noble Spaniard also makes an awkward fit. In any case, the Zeeland stories have hardly made it into the canon of the Revolt in the Low Countries, though they can easily compete in intensity and heroism with the sieges of Haarlem, Alkmaar and Leiden in the County of Holland. The story of Mondragón can be used to bring the history of the war in Zeeland during the early phase of the Revolt back to our attention.

Mondragón's image in Spain may not be as spectacular as his image in the Low Countries, but ever since the publication of his biography in 1905, Mondragón has belonged to a canon of important Spanish military heroes. However, a modern writer such as Pérez-Reverte understands that it is not good for the story to explain to a Spanish public that Mondragón was for most of the time a commander of Walloon soldiers, so the author turns him into a commander of Spanish tercios. This may be compared to the authors of the Dutch plays who changed his noble wife from Lorraine into a spouse from the Spanish nobility. In literature one is allowed to play with the historical facts, and to look for images the readers and the public will understand: a Spanish commander has to have Spanish soldiers and a Spanish wife.

Magdalena Moons begs her fiancé Francisco de Valdés to postpone the storming of Leiden another night, 1574. Painting by Simon Opzoomer (1840-1850), Rijksmuseum Amsterdam.

CHAPTER IV

# Francisco de Valdés: the exemplary soldier[1]

## A Miles Christi

Francisco de Valdés is famous within the historiography on early modern military treatises. His *Diálogo militar*, later also published under the title of *Espejo y desciplina militar*, is clearly the most important reason why Spanish historians remember this commander from the wars in the Low Countries. The 1989 edition by the Spanish defence ministry is still available in its series of military treatises. The first edition of the *Diálogo* was published in Madrid in 1578, while the author was still alive and active as a commander, followed by editions in Brussels, Antwerp and again Madrid. By the close of the century the treatise had been translated into English and Italian: enough evidence to claim that Valdés's work had become a minor early modern bestseller.[2]

Finishing his manuscript in Deventer on 20 October 1571, Valdés dedicated his work to Fadrique de Toledo, the son of the Duke of Alba, and he informs his readers that his friends had encouraged him to write a treatise on the position of the *Sargento mayor*, a function he had fulfilled within the tercio of Lombardy under Maestre de campo Sancho de Londoño. He had been in the Low Countries since arriving from Italy with the tercio in 1567. According to the first edition, Valdés had been a Maestre de campo already in 1571, but this was in fact not the case.

Valdés's treatise was published in 1589 jointly with the first edition of the *Discurso sobre la forma de reducir la disciplina militar a mejor y antiguo estado*, written by his Maestre de campo Sancho de Londoño, and signed at the beginning of April 1568. Londoño would die in office in 1569 while acting as the military governor of Maastricht. University graduate Londoño wrote his treatise during a three-month period at the end of his stay in the Brabantine city of Lier, and he did so because the

---

[1] Fagel, *Spaanse belegeraar* and Idem, 'Maestre de campo', were based on an earlier draft of this chapter.
[2] Valdés, *Espejo*; González de León, 'Doctors'.

Duke of Alba had asked him to write.³ Valdés therefore takes his place in a tradition within the Spanish army that stimulated its officers to write treatises on the military profession.

We can imagine officers like Valdés and Londoño debating their military profession during their long and probably often boring residence in the cities of the Low Countries, especially between 1569 and 1572 when little fighting was taking place. So maybe it is no coincidence that Valdés's treatise took the form of a dialogue between two officers, his Maestre de campo Londoño and another officer called Vargas. Though generally it is thought that the latter refers to cavalry general Alonso de Vargas, it is highly probable that Valdés was thinking of Alonso's brother, Sargento Francisco de Vargas, a member of the same tercio of Lombardy. Valdés and Francisco had fought together at the Battle of Dahlem in 1568 where Vargas had been severely wounded.⁴

In his treatise Valdés defends the idea of the Sargento mayor as an individual trained in both military theory (*el arte militar*) and military discipline. It is all about creating balance and harmony between theory and practical experience. In the *Diálogo* we find one of the most quoted sentences of military historiography, for example to be found in Geoffrey Parker's seminal work on the Spanish army in the Low Countries:

> El día que uno toma la pica para ser soldado, ese día, renuncia a ser Christiano.
>
> The day a man picks up his pike to become a soldier is the day he ceases to be a Christian.⁵

This quotation is generally used to demonstrate the cruelty of early modern warfare. However, when we continue reading, we find an author who is perfectly aware of the not very Christian elements of his profession, but who at the same time wants to emphasise the Sargento mayor's role as the guardian of the souls of the soldiers under his command. He has to take care that the army camp is free of any vices and he has to fight blasphemy: "que no se jure en nombre de Dios". The Sargento mayor has to prohibit concubines and punish thieves. Valdés understands perfectly

---

3   Sáenz Herrero, 'Humanismo'; Martínez, *Front lines*, 234. Martínez claims the Leiden manuscript could be the original text of Londoño's treatise: UBL, Codices Vulcanii, 92; González de León, 'Doctors'.
4   García Hernán, 'Don Sancho', 85.
5   Geoffrey Parker, *Army* 2004). 153 (translation Geoffrey Parker); Valdés, *Espejo*, 70.

that there were many soldiers who followed what he calls "the bad life" ("*mal vivir*"), but without fearing God it was completely impossible to function as a good soldier.[6] So he does not accept the violence, and instead defends a very Christian posture as the essence of his profession. Of course, this is a difficult position to hold onto in practice, as the war might ask you to go against your Christian values. But his treatise shows that he wanted to see himself, and the same holds for his fellow soldiers, as being Milites Christi, soldiers of Christ.

At this point it is instructive to contrast this idea of a Miles Christi with a quotation by Valdés that has often been used within Dutch historiography on the Revolt. We have to move on to the moment Maestre de campo Francisco de Valdés writes a letter to his Governor-general and Captain-general, Luis de Requesens. It is 21 September 1574 and Valdés writes from the small village of Zoeterwoude, just outside the city of Leiden, besieged by Valdés and his troops:

> It surely is devilish stubbornness by evil rebels who have taken such a strange resolution, not only to flood the whole country in a way that it can never be recovered, but also destroying three cities to save one; if it is relieved and Your Excellency gives me a licence to open the sluices of Maassluis I will drown these bad people, because they do not deserve less punishment than this.[7]

In another letter from a few days earlier he had already defended a similarly aggressive solution to the situation:

> It has seemed to me [important] to inform Your Excellency so he understands that if at any given time he would be served by flooding this country, it is in his hands, because they have started with it, and if they persist in their obstinate rebellion they deserve to be drowned.[8]

---

[6] Valdés, *Espejo*, 70-71.

[7] 'Y cierto es diabolica ostinacion de malvados rebeldes que ayan tomado una tan estraña resolucion como es no solo anegar todo el pays sin que jamas se pueda recuperar pero destruyr tres villas por socorrer una la qual si se socorren y vuestra excelencia me da licencia abrire las esclussas de Meslanclus y acabare de anegar tan mala gente pues no merecen menos castigo que este'. AGS, E. 560, 91-94.

[8] 'Hame parescido dar dello aviso a vuestra excelencia para que entienda que siempre que fuere servido de anegar este pays esta en su mano y pues ellos han dado principio a lo hazer si perseveran en su obstinada rebelion bien merecen ser anegados'. AGS, E. 560, 91-94.

In Dutch historiography these quotations stand to illustrate the cruel reasoning and harsh behaviour of the Spanish military during the Revolt, especially by somebody close to the much-hated Duke of Alba. The violent nature of the quotations can be compared to aggressive formulations in letters written by the Duke, for example when defending the massacre at Naarden in December 1572.[9] How can we reconcile our image of the Miles Christi of the treatise with that of the author of these unmerciful letters?

## A love story

The idea of flooding Holland is also difficult to connect to the rather positive image the inhabitants of Leiden nowadays have of their former besieger. Generally referred to as 'Francisco Valdez' his name has even been given to one of the streets in the neighbourhood dedicated to the history of the siege, albeit a rather small one. Just like Mondragón's, his fame was not so negative as to make this impossible around 1900. The reason lies in the fact that the Leiden citizens of 1900, just like the ones living in the city today, would directly connect the name of Valdés with that of Magdalena Moons, the famous local heroine of the siege.[10]

As the story goes, the Maestre de campo got involved in a sentimental relationship with a woman from The Hague. Magdalena promised to marry Francisco if he refrained from attacking the city of Leiden where part of her family was living at the time. Although we will never know for certain whether Valdés did indeed make such a far-reaching promise to his loved-one, the fact that the commander did not have the necessary artillery to storm the city would have turned it into an easy promise.

We know that a marriage between the two did indeed take place some years after the lifting of the siege, as proven by Els Kloek.[11] Around the time of the siege they were no longer young lovers. Magdalena had been born around 1541 and Valdés around 1518, making them about thirty-three and fifty-six when they met in The Hague. By the time they got married, Magdalena must already have been some thirty-seven years of age, making the marriage not so much the happy start of a young new family, but more a union of two mature individuals.

---

[9] Alba to Philip II, 19 December 1572, EA III, 261.
[10] The History department of Leiden University hosts a special chair in local history named for 'Magdalena Moons'.
[11] Kloek, *Kenau*. A laser technique was used to read the lines in the text that had been made unreadable.

Magdalena was the daughter of Pieter Moons, a lawyer working for the Court of Holland in The Hague, as had her brother, Reinier, who had recently died in 1571. It seems probable that Reinier, working for the Habsburg government, had remained loyal to Philip II. Another brother, Willem, was, however, removed as mayor of the city by Valdés when he took possession of The Hague.[12] The fact that he returned again as mayor when the royal troops left the city seems to indicate he was a supporter of the rebellion. And of course, we do not have any evidence on the political ideas of Magdalena herself.

In her work, Els Kloek has already unravelled the development of this episodic narrative through time. Calvinist historian Pieter Bor in 1624 published a story about the love between Valdés and an unknown woman from The Hague, whom he maintained. Several years later, Italian historian Famiano Strada tells how Valdés had wanted to storm the city but a dinner party with a woman from The Hague then made him change his mind.[13] But in these stories the woman still had no name. This would change only when the Leiden playwrights introduced her into their versions of the events.

The siege of Leiden, and its subsequent final lifting, may well be the single historical event sparking the largest theatrical interest in the Dutch Republic during the seventeenth and eighteenth centuries. There is an impressive number of plays, and the number of editions is overwhelming. Though perhaps secondary to Magdalena Moons and especially hero and Leiden mayor, Pieter Adriaansz. Van der Werff, Francisco de Valdés developed into one of the most represented characters in Dutch Golden Age drama. There is no doubt that he has been larger on stage than classical Spanish heroes such as Don Juan or Don Carlos, albeit nowadays he has been largely forgotten outside Leiden.[14]

Jacob Duym published a series of six plays in his *Ghedenck-boeck* of 1606. The author was a Brabantine rebel who had fled to Leiden many years before. In the introduction he directly stated that it was his intention to show the cruelties of the Spanish so people would not forget them, and he clearly sided with the House of Orange.[15] At the top of the list of characters in his Leiden play we find Baldeso (Valdés), the King's

---

[12] Kloek, *Kenau*, 244-245.
[13] Kloek, *Kenau*, 245-246.
[14] Bordewijk, *Lof*; Meijer Drees, 'Burgemeester'; Bood, 'Between Hispanophobia', 303-325.
[15] 'Duits, 'Om de eenheid', 7-8; Rodríguez Pérez, 'Leopardo', 152-154.

general, followed by two Spanish officers, Alonso and Carion.[16] Valdés opens the first act and directly threatens the inhabitants:

> The child in the cradle may shake and shiver freely:
>
> If now you do not accept the mercy of the King…
>
> In short, the city has to be destroyed[17]

The Spaniard made clear that he wanted to win the city by trickery (*soet met list*) as he did not want to lose as many soldiers as had perished in the sieges of Haarlem and Alkmaar, but he remained rather polite, ending this speech in Act Two with a mere "If they don't do it, I shall deny them all my mercy".[18] In Act Three, the threats do get stronger and the inhabitants have to fear worse treatment than that suffered by Naarden, Zutphen and Haarlem, as Valdés exclaims, "Oh Leiden, you have a knife to your throat". In the same Act Baldeso showed himself as not very cultivated because when he received a letter in Latin he stated he did not understand the language (*"twelck ick gants niet en weet"*).[19] This is clearly not the same person as the author of the *Diálogo*, but the ignorance may relate to the idea of the Spanish commanders being of low birth. In a last dramatic scene in Act Five he had to flee the city to escape the rising water after the rebels had broken the dykes. His last sentence in the play shows some comical sense of reason: "with wet feet, it is very difficult for the men to fight".[20] Of his love affair, still no trace.[21]

Jacob van Zevecote, born in Ghent (County of Flanders), was first ordained a Catholic priest, but after his arrival in Leiden in 1623 he converted to Calvinism.[22] In his *Belegh van Leyden* of 1626 the convert showed himself a great enemy of the Spanish, in language much more aggressive than that of Duym twenty years earlier.[23] This also had an enormous effect on Valdés' image and on the cruel words he spoke on stage:

---

[16] Duym, *Benoude belegheringe*.
[17] 'Het jonck kind inde wiegh' magh schudden en vrij beven: Soo ghy ons conincx gnaed' dees reys niet en neemt aen… Die stad die moeter aen, dats nu int cort gheseyt'. Duym, *Benoude belegheringe*, Act 1.
[18] 'Doen sy't niet, ick ontseg haer al mijn ghenade'. Duym, *Benoude belegheringe*, Act 2.
[19] 'O Leyden, Leyden, ghy hebt het mes op de keel'. Duym, *Benoude belegheringe*, Act 3.
[20] 'Mit natte voeten, ist voor t'volck, seer quaet om vechten'. Duym, *Benoude belegheringe*, Act 5.
[21] Bordewijk, 'Lof', 10-13.
[22] Dambre, 'Jacob'.
[23] Zevecote, *Belegh*.

> I see the city is mine, she cannot escape me any more
>
> Then I shall cut the throats of small children everywhere
>
> Play with the cut-off heads as if they were balls
>
> I shall open the bellies of the pregnant women
>
> And feed my strange lusts with the unborn child.[24]

The play is a perfect example of the aggressively anti-Spanish Black Legend that by that time dominated public discourse in the Republic, stating that all Spaniards were liars and cruel by nature: "The Spaniard who lives according to his style is the most cruel animal that ever lived".[25] But still no sign of Valdés's love affair.

The next play is that of Leiden pastry baker Reinier Bontius, and it is this work that will have an enormous impact. Researchers to date have found 111 editions of the play, published between 1645 and 1850,[26] a record in the history of Dutch Golden Age theatre. Though it was, of course, very popular in Leiden, it was also published in other cities with sixty editions issued in Amsterdam. More than three hundred performances in the Amsterdam theatre between 1645 and 1772 made it the third most popular play of the entire period.[27] And with it, Commander Baldeus became the most important Spanish character on the Dutch stage, especially every year around the beginning of October when the lifting of the siege was commemorated in the Dutch Republic.

The first edition of 1645 shows that Bontius made use of the earlier plays, and Baldeus is as aggressive as in the play by Zevecote: "I am thirsty for the blood of burghers, and long for women's shame". Also present are the officers Carion and Alonso who joined in, telling how they cut unborn babies out of their mothers' wombs and also killed all the Catholics they met.[28] And still no love story to be found. However, in the second edition of 1646 we find the mention of Amelia, "byzit van Baldeus", his concubine. On his way to storm the city Baldeus meets

---

[24] Bordewijk, 'Lof', 14. 'Ick sie de stat is myn, z'en kan my niet ontgaen; Dan sal ick overal de teere kinders kelen; Met 't afgesneden hooft gelyck met bollen spellen; Ick sal den zwangren buyck der vrouwen open doen; Met onvolmaeckte wicht myn vreemde lusten voen'. Zevecote, *Belegh*, Act 2.

[25] 'Die eenen Spaignaert is of op zijn wijse leeft, is t'wreetste dier dat oyt natuer gewonnen heeft'. Zevecote, *Belegh*, Act 3; Rodríguez Pérez, 'Leopardo'.

[26] Harmsen, 'Reynerius Bontius'; Bordewijk, 'Lof', 15-20.

[27] On stage, http://www.vondel.humanities.uva.nl/onstage/plays/200 (accessed 21-1-2019).

[28] 'Ick dorst na burgers bloet, en haeck na vrouwe schande'. Bontius, *Belegering* (1645), Act 1.

her for the first time, dressed in mourning clothes. She convinces him to stop the attack as she had family in the city. The scene ends with the following words of Baldeus: "Come, let's go to my tent and rest for the night".[29] Though not yet a romantic love affair, it is the first introduction of a female protagonist into the play.[30]

Kloek has argued that after this first appearance people started to connect the concubine in the play with Magdalena Moons, and her family then started a campaign to stop the rumours about her: a campaign that achieved important results. In 1659, after the author's death, others continued to edit revised versions of the play and Amelia was turned into M.M. This change is explained in an introduction citing the history of the Revolt by Strada, who had written that the woman in question had been a noblewoman and lawfully married to Valdés after the siege. By this time Baldeus had changed into Francisco Baldeo, but he remained the blood-thirsty Spanish commander of the first edition. The scene between the two no longer ended with a reference to the tent, but with a promise of matrimony.[31] However, it does not take the commander long to realise he has done wrong in listening to the plea of M.M. instead of to his Spanish advisors. In this sense, the anecdote serves as an alternative explanation for the fact that Leiden was never stormed by the Spanish commander.

In successive re-editions this new version with noblewoman M.M. was sometimes followed, but there also continued to reappear editions using the story of concubine Amelia, and even mixed versions with noblewoman Amelia.[32] Over the course of time, the family also convinced the people responsible for the play to use N.N. instead of M.M.[33] Though still very ambiguous, the very presence of Valdés and Magdalena Moons in this play was the beginning of the famous love story that has survived until today.

In H. Brouwer's plays on the siege and the relief, both from 1683, Valdés finally changed character. He became brave instead of cruel, and true hearted instead of treacherous. He even received his correct name of Francisco de Valdés. However, there is no Magdalena and the love story in the play takes place between other protagonists.[34] The Black Legend

---

[29] 'Com, gaen wy naer mijn tent en ruste daer de nacht'. Bontius, *Belegering* (1646), 15th sorting; Kloek, *Kenau*, 272-277.
[30] The introduction of a secondary love plot in Dutch plays was strongly influenced by the Spanish comedias that had much success in the Low Countries.
[31] Bontius, *Beleg* (1659), Act 5.
[32] Kloek, *Kenau*, 277.
[33] Harmsen, 'Reinier Bontius'.
[34] Meijer Drees, 'Burgemeester', 172; Brouwer, *Ontset* (1683).

of Spain in the Low Countries was maybe not a wholly continuous narrative from the sixteenth century onwards, right up to the modern era. It might well be that the threat of Louis XIV's France had made the old Spanish enemy less diabolical.

We have to wait until Cornelis Boon in 1711 to find the modern story with 'Magdaleene' and 'Baldes' on stage. The Spanish commander had an internal conflict between his love for Magdalena and his duties as a soldier. Though he put honour above love, in the end he decided not to storm the city.[35] The stereotype of the cruel commander of the plays by Zevecote and Bontius had finally given way to a much more humane character, though the Spanish cruelty of the Black Legend can still be found in the play, with the classical Spanish vices of infanticide, rape and murder:

> He hung the wet nurse by her breasts
>
> While the milk, mixed with blood, dripped down along them.[36]

Magdalena's sister stated to her that Baldes could never lose his Spanish character, while Magdalena thought highly of him. When they finally met in the play, it was very clear it was true love. Baldes called himself her slave, and he loved her more than he loved himself.[37]

The love story received its final shape with the play on the siege by Lucretia van Merken, who also wrote works in which we can find Cristóbal de Mondragón as their protagonist.[38] In the introduction to the 1774 edition, the history of Magdalena Moons is explained using the available historical knowledge of the time, and for the first time she appears in a play with her full name. She is even turned into the main protagonist. Magdalena stated that she trusted Valdés completely, and the author of the play introduced fellow Spanish commander Julián Romero as the one who wanted to attack the city. In this way Valdés could be described as the one who tried to stop Romero. Valdés himself wanted to negotiate a surrender in order to save Magdalena's relatives, but the city magistrates did not trust him.

---

[35] Meijer Drees, 'Burgemeester', 172; Bordewijk, 'Lof', 22; Boon, *Leiden* (1711).
[36] 'Hy hang de zoogster aan haar' volle borsten weder; Terwyl de melk, met bloedt gemengt, daar langs druipt neder'. Boon, *Leiden*, 4.
[37] Boon, *Leiden*, 50.
[38] Merken, 'Beleg' (1774).

Disguised in the clothes of a plain soldier, Valdés secretly met with Magdalena, telling her he could no longer stop Romero. He himself had, "never than through coercion, spilled the blood of burghers".[39] Though he tried to tell her he had no choice other than to attack the city, in the end he promised to refrain from storming: "if Magdalena loves me, this is enough fame for Valdés", leaving the scene with a "goodbye my bride".[40] At the end of the play, as the Spanish army left, Magdalena is celebrated as the great heroine who will be remembered forever. The love story finally softened Francisco de Valdés' memory, turning him into an example of the good Spaniard. However, in contrast to Cristóbal de Mondragón, this occurred only from the eighteenth century, and only on stage.

**What a terrible man!**

His image during his own lifetime was maybe even the very opposite. One night in March 1576, Fernando de Lannoy, the Lord of La Roche and brother-in-law of Cardinal Granvelle, was dining in the palace in Brussels with other noblemen from the Low Countries, such as the Duke of Aarschot. When they saw passing below their window Maestre de campo Francisco de Valdés, Lannoy, immediately enfuriated, uttered, "If he would meet such a mean man, he would not be able to sustain from treating him badly and beating him".[41] He took his leave of the Duke and went down to get his horse, together with all of his men. In front of a large group of people he openly stated that "If he could find the unfortunate coward Valdés, he would break his head and finish him off".

Morillon, Granvelle's confidant in the Low Countries, explained that Valdés had written very negatively to the King about Lannoy. The story continued. Lannoy told his men to mount their horses and prepare their guns. The Lord of Lalaing tried to stop them: "My cousin, do not harm him and yourself, to lead us against one who before was not more than a lackey". It was a classic argument in those days. Most of the Spanish commanders that governed the Low Countries were supposedly of very low birth, like chimney sweeps and basket makers. Drummer was another possibility. Even though this was an exaggeration, their relatively low

---

[39] 'Nimmer dan door dwang der burgrenbloed vergoten'. Van Merken, 'Beleg', 44.
[40] 'Zo Magdaleen my mint, is 't Valdez roems genoeg'; 'Vaar wel myn bruid'. Van Merken, 'Beleg', 77.
[41] Morillon to Granvelle, Brussels, 31 March 1576, CG VI (1887) 42-44.

(and non-noble) birth was taken as an enormous affront by the high nobility of the Low Countries.

When royal councillor Gerónimo de Roda appeared, Lannoy confronted him with his complaints:

> Don Fernande [Lannoy] asks Roda how it is possible that the King is using such a mean man, who had prevented the reduction of Leiden, and as a result, of the whole of Holland.

Morillon even informed Granvelle that it was said that Lannoy had opened a letter from Valdés to Luis de Requesens and that he had found "wickedness" ("*villaquerie*") in the letter. According to chronicler Everhard van Reyd, Lannoy had also complained to the court in Brussels about Valdés's behaviour.[42]

The enmity between the two men went back a long way. On 30 April 1574 Valdés had arrived near Utrecht with his troops and he had asked Lannoy, who at the time was governing the city, for permission to lodge his soldiers on the outskirts of the city, outside the city wall, "because the major part of the soldiers carried their arquebuses without the cases and their equipment badly treated".[43]

Lannoy gave permission to quarter the soldiers on the outskirts, but before he did so he had given its inhabitants the opportunity to remove all objects of worth from their houses. He also did not provide food and drink to the men. Some of Valdés's soldiers got so angry they set fire to some of the houses. The commander had them arrested directly and made them pay for the damage. At least, this is how the story is told by Valdés in his letter to Requesens.

The commander explained how the burghers had started to act against the Spaniards in the city, with their swords in their hands. Some Spaniards did not succeed in escaping and "they hurt and mistreated them and they were deadly wounded".[44] He especially mentioned the case of a wounded Spanish soldier who had been badly treated by the inhabitants:

---

[42] Álvarez Francés, 'Fabrication; Van Reyd, *Voornaemste gheschiedenissen*, 18.

[43] 'Porque la mayor parte de los soldados trayan sus arcabuzes sin caxas y sus coseletes mal tractados. Asimismo venian los mas sin zapatos y casi todos sin vaynas en las espadas'. Valdés to Requesens (copy), Utrecht, 2 May 1574, AGS, E. 557, f. 160; CP III (1851) n. 1343.

[44] 'Los hirieron y maltractaron y estan heridos de muerte'.

> They took the crutches from a disabled soldier in the middle of the street and they forced him to dance, mocking him, and they talked – not in secret but in public – in their conversation and their drunkenness about where they could attack and take the castle.[45]

It is in this letter that he accused Lannoy of defending the burghers of Utrecht better than the interests of the royal army. And he was perhaps right in saying so. In his own letter Lannoy described the tense situation in Utrecht in a completely different way. He wrote that more than two thousand people had witnessed the Spaniards burning down houses and this had caused great disorder among the inhabitants of the city. According to the governor, only a few Spanish soldiers were hurt and they had only thrown some stones and taken out some knives. Nothing about mortal injuries, and no swords drawn. Both Lannoy and Valdés were serving Philip II, but their descriptions of the situation had little in common.[46] We have seen the same conflict played out, for example, in Zeeland between the Spanish commanders and the nobility from the Low Countries, and between Champagney and Sancho Dávila in Antwerp.

A local Utrecht chronicle, very hostile to the Spanish presence, stated that Valdés possessed a "great hatred and envy against the city of Utrecht". In this story the Spaniards threatened to burn down all the suburbs of Utrecht if they were not let into the city, something Valdés had promised them, in order to receive their payment. The chronicle does not refer to violence on the part of the inhabitants, only that "there almost started a riot among the burghers". The description of the relationship between the two men is, however, very different: "Lannoy, whom he had to slightly provoke because it was a good man and committed to the Spaniards". Finally, one banner at a time was allowed to enter the city to be reviewed in front of Lannoy.[47]

---

[45] 'Quitar en medio de la calle las muletas a un soldado estropiado y haziendole por fuerça baylar escarneciendo del y hazer discursos no en secreto sino publicamente en sus conversaciones y borracherias de que parte podrian batir y tomar el castillo'. Valdés to Requesens (copy), Utrecht, 2 May 1574, AGS, E. 557, f. 160.

[46] Requesens wanted Lannoy to communicate all his letters with Valdés, 'como á persona de tanta experiencia y conianza'. Requesens to Lannoy, 4 April 1574, NCD II, 86-88.

[47] 'Groote haet ende nijdt jeghens die stadt van Utrecht'. Also: 'Uuyt ranceur van zijn eygheen giericheyt ende ambitie'; 'Bynae een oploepe onder die borgheren in die stadt gecommen soude hebben'; 'Lanoy, die hy daertoe lichtelick te induceren hadde, soe het een goet man was, den Spangaerts wel toegedaen sijnde'. 'Utrechtsche kroniek', 137-140.

Also during the siege of Leiden, Lannoy and Valdés did not collaborate at all. Lannoy left Valdés out of the negotiations with the defenders of the city.[48] It all would build up to the tense night in Brussels. Also his soldiers did not always like their Maestre de campo. During the great mutiny of 1574 they wanted to kill Valdés, "who had just arrived in Antwerp, called by the Comendador [Requesens] to receive instructions on the affairs of Holland; he was forced to hide himself to escape from their anger".[49] So, beside the image of the learned author of a military treatise and the story of Francisco and Magdalena, there has also existed a very negative image among some of the nobility from the Low Countries, and even among his own soldiers. The question is whether we can get any closer to the real Valdés.

## The unknown Valdés (and the story of his wounds)

If we try to reconstruct the facts of his life it becomes clear that we do not know much about this Spanish protagonist of the Revolt. We are unaware of his year and place of birth, we do not know who his parents were, and we hardly have a clue as to his descendants. In this sense Valdés occupies a very different position compared to the much-better-studied Romero, Dávila and Mondragón.

The origin of the Valdés family most surely must be found in Asturias, the cold and rainy mountainous region in the north of Spain, where we can find a village with this name. The Valdés family in the city of Gijón in Asturias was very important, and it owned a palace in the city. We can also find his name in local histories and genealogies of this family, but it is never clear what place the commander occupied within the family.[50] The new Spanish national biographical dictionary mentions Gijón as his place of birth, but with a question mark.[51]

---

[48] Requesens was aware of the communication problems between Valdés and Lannoy: 'estando el conde de la Roche tan cerca, y también Francisco de Valdés, es necesario irles avisando de cuando en cuando lo que se ofreciere, y que ellos hagan lo mismo, para que los unos entiendan lo que los otros hacen para tener buena correspondencia y se haga mejor el servicio de Su Magestad'. Requesens to Romero, 27 July 1574, NCD IV, 162-166.

[49] Requesens to Philip II, Antwerp, 15 May 1574, CP III (1851) n. 1348.

[50] Fernández Secades, *Valdés*. The author also confirmed personally that she had not been able to situate our Francisco; Valdés, *Memorias*. The manuscript from 1622 can be found in the BNM, ms. 11.457; Menéndez Valdés, *Avisos*, 145, 147.

[51] Sánchez Martín, 'Valdés'.

However, the fact that he cannot be traced in Asturias might indicate that Francisco belonged to another branch of the family. In the beginning of the sixteenth century we can find this last name spread all over Castile. There was a Francisco de Valdés in the times of Isabel of Castile, Governor of the castle of Zamora. Other examples show a Francisco de Valdés born in Abarca de Campos in Castile, and in the city of Segovia a certain Francisco de Valdés had brought a court case against a convent. At the moment, neither of these lines can, however, be directly connected to the commander, but it shows that there is no reason to limit the search to Asturias.[52] We must not forget that Julián Romero and Cristóbal de Mondragón had fathers with a Basque origin, but were born in Castile.

Other letters prove that the commander had a daughter, Francisca, from an earlier relationship, who lived in Spain. It was precisely during the last months of the siege of Leiden that he was occupied with this daughter. He had given orders to pay Juan de Albornoz, the Duke of Alba's secretary, by then back in Spain, the sum of one thousand ducats through a Spanish merchant in Antwerp, Juan de Cuéllar. Albornoz himself worked with the well-known merchant Juan de Curiel. It was all to help out his daughter Francisca.[53] But there were in fact two daughters, as in 1571 there was mention of one daughter who was going to marry while another one had entered a convent. Valdés had already asked permission to travel to Spain because the wedding could not go ahead without his presence.[54] What we know for sure is that in 1575 besides a daughter in a convent he still had an unmarried daughter in Madrid.[55] But it is striking that Valdés was occupied with the future of his daughters during the tense final months of the Leiden siege.

A final clue that may help to reconstruct his family is a very short memorial from García de Rojas y Valdés, Francisco's nephew, who had been active in the armies of Flanders and Portugal. In 1594 he participated in an armada sent to the French coast. This son of a sister of Valdés must have thought that he could strengthen his petition by stating he was a

---

[52] Vigil, *Asturias*. Several documents in the ARCV: Pares: http://pares.culturaydeporte.gob.es/inicio.html; Archivo General de Indias, Sevilla, Justicia 1149, N.1, R.2; Cubero Garrote, *Atar cabos*.

[53] Juan de Albornoz to Alonso Díaz de Aguilar, 22 October 1574; Albornoz to Maestre de campo Francisco de Valdés, 22 October 1574, AA, C66, 54b-54c; EA III, 600-601. The letters refer to a marriage with Antonio de Brito, someone who is said to have the Queen of Portugal on his side.

[54] Philip II to Alba, Madrid, 2 February 1571, AGS, E. 547, f.54; EA III, Alba to Philip II, Brussels, 23 March 1571.

[55] Valdés to Philip II, Antwerp, 18 April 1575, AGS, E. 563, f. 39.

nephew of the Maestre de campo, who had died in 1580: "García de Rojas y Valdés, nephew of the maestre de Campo Francisco de Valdés, states he always has had extra pay (*ventaja*) of xxx in the Low Countries and Portugal".[56]

Antwerp merchant Juan de Cuéllar, who helped Valdés transfer money to Spain, must have been an important contact of the commander. Cuéllar had come from Segovia to Antwerp where he can already be found in 1531, aged around twenty-four. It is during this period that Ignatius of Loyola, the future founder of the Jesuits, visited him in his house on the corner of the Lombaerdstreet, close to St. James Church. He was married to a local woman, Clara Pels, and would remain in the city of Antwerp until his death in 1583. His two sons traded with Germany and Spain, and we can find them later residing in Seville.[57]

In a letter dated 26 July 1574 Cuéllar wrote from Antwerp to another Spanish merchant, Simón Ruiz, in Medina del Campo, informing him that Francisco de Valdés was residing in The Hague with 2,500 Spaniards, ten banners of Germans, fifteen to twenty banners of Walloons, and eight hundred cavalrymen. To increase the value of the information, Cuéllar added on Valdés, "who generally writes me what is happening" ("*el cual me escrive de hordinario lo que pasa*").[58] In an earlier letter he explained that he had received Valdés's letters from Holland:

> To Holland, from where I have letters from Maestre de campo Francisco de Valdés, who had returned to take all the strongholds and he also took ten banners from the enemies, and he killed all the people and was lord of the countryside, and that Orange was in Rotterdam with forty banners and did not dare to go out of the town.[59]

In yet another letter he speaks about the great mutiny of 1574 in Holland, explaining why the soldiers had taken Valdés prisoner: "Maestre de campo

---

[56] The full text: 'Garçia de Rrojas y Valdes, sobrino del maestre de campo Francisco de Valdes dize que siempre a tenido ventajas de xxx en Flandes y Portugal abiendose senalado y benido con horden como compta por sus lizenzias y xxxx aunque supplica le aga merced de una bentaja para las galeras y cerca de la persona de don Diego Brochero que se le ara merced y la rreçibira en rrenumerazion de sus serbiçios y los de sus pasados'. Memorial 17 July 1594, AGS, Guerra y marina 418, f. 193.

[57] Ródenas Vilar, *Vida cotodiana*, 66; Stols, *Spaanse Brabanders* II, 23; Fagel, *Hispano-Vlaamse wereld*, 362; Vázquez de Prada, *Lettres marchandes* I, 217-218.

[58] Agellakis, Civilian lives', 55; Vázquez de Prada, *Lettres marchandes* II, 117-118.

[59] *Lettres marchandes* II, 111-112. Juan de Cuéllar to Simón Ruiz, Antwerp 16 June 1574.

Valdés tells them not to steal from the friends and for this reason they have taken him prisoner".[60] Most probably again an assumption based on first-hand information from the commander himself. Years later, in a letter of 20 April 1576, he tells the story of how Valdés was wounded in 1572:

> And a Maestre de campo, called Francisco de Valdés, was wounded before Mons in the same manner, that they had broken the joints of his elbow and he could not close or open his hand, nor bring it to his head. Afterwards he was recovering over here every summer, with the result that he now can write properly with his hand, and he can open and close it, though his fingers remain weak and he carries his sword as a left-handed man.[61]

These wounds were the reason for the Duke of Alba to propose Valdés for a place within the military bureaucracy in the Low Countries. He had written to the King that now that *veedor general* Jordán de Valdés had died, "he had laid eyes on Captain Francisco de Valdés, who is a very good man and on top of it he had ended up disabled (*estropeado*) from the wound he received before Mons".[62] In the end this important office was left vacant and Valdés had to stay in active service. The letter does not mention any family relationship between Francisco and Jordán, who did come from Gijón and was even the founder of the important Gijon branch. Jordán had died during the same siege of Mons in which Francisco had been wounded. He had been hit by a cannonball that took away his left leg and had subsequently died of his wounds.[63]

By 1572, this man from a humble background had already reached a high position in the Spanish army, but few heroic deeds can be identified with him up to that year. This might be related to the fact that his descendants (who did not have the same means as Romero, Mondragón or Dávila) and historians have not really looked for facts and stories to reconstruct his earlier life. The two most important moments up to then were the finishing of his treatise in 1571 and his severe wounds before

---

[60] *Lettres marchandes* II, 128-130.
[61] *Lettres marchandes* II, 189-190. 'Francisco de Valdes, capitan y sargento mayor del dicho terçio de Lombardía, herido sobre el dicho Mons en el braço derecho de que quedara manco', in: 'Las personas particulares y conoçidas que han muerto y sido heridos despues de este levantamiento de Flandes hasta veinte de Diziembre 1572 que se dio el primero asalto a Arlehen son los siguientes', AGS, E. 561, 170.
[62] Alba to Philip II, Nijmegen, 19 December 1572, EA III, 259-264.
[63] Fernández Secades, *Valdés*, 115-117.

Mons in 1572. Alba was even thinking about giving him a job away from the front line. Born around 1518, he must have been about fifty-four years old at the time, just a little younger than Charles V when he abdicated in 1555.

## The correspondence

Though Valdés, with the help of his secretaries, must have written thousands of letters and brief notes in his career, especially since he was away from Spain for so many years, only a small part of his correspondence has been preserved, in particular the letters from the years 1573 and 1574. Unfortunately, there are no love letters between Magdalena and Francisco. Most of the some eighty letters are to be found in the archive of the Duke of Alba in Madrid.[64] In the second part of this chapter I want to use these letters to study his experiences in the Low Countries. What was it like to be a Spanish commander during the Revolt? How did he see his job? And how did he look at the inhabitants of the Low Countries? At the same time, these letters make it possible to confront his view of these experiences with the different narratives on the commander we have seen so far.

The best introduction to his career is through a letter written by Valdés in Antwerp on 18 April 1575, asking for compensation for his services from Philip II. It is the only letter presented in full in this chapter, and it gives an example of his letter writing: [65]

---

[64] These letters are studied by Beatriz Santiago Belmonte in her forthcoming PhD thesis at Leiden University on the correspondence of the Spanish commanders during the first decade of the Revolt. This chapter owes much to her research.

[65] 'El dia que tome la pica en los exercitos de Vuestra Magestad viendome desnudo de todo favor, propuse de procurallo tener de mis obras y propia virtud y assi en treinta y ocho años que a sirvo en esta profesion a Vuestra Magestad. Los treinta y dos de los quales sin jamas salir ni me apartar de sus reales vanderas, he trabajado de no faltar punto a mi obligacion como se han hecho fee y testimonio sus generales de Vuestra Magestad y particularmente el duque de Alba y comendador mayor de Castilla. Ha veynte años que enpece a servir a vuestra magestad en la jornada de Sena en los oficios de capitan de ynfanteria comisario general de la gente darmas y cavalleria ligera y despues en Lonbardia de capitan y sargento mayor continuando otros seis años en estos estados en los mismos oficios y ultimamente el duque de Alba antes de su partida me eligio por maestro de campo general del exercito que quedo en Hollanda y al presento sirvo a vuestro magestad con el cargo de maestro de campo de ynfanteria. No quiero sacra magestad dezir particularmente los muchos y particulares servicios que en tanto tiempo he hecho a vuestra magestad sino remitirme a lo que el duque dAlba podra ynformar demas de lo que otros capitanes generales han ynformado solo dire que acabo de tantos años aviendo muchas vezes derramado mi sangre en su real servicio me hallo estropeado

The day I took up the pike in the armies of Your Majesty, I was deprived of all favour, and I decided to obtain it through my deeds and my own virtue and so for thirty-eight years I have served Your Majesty in this profession. During thirty-two of these years I have never left nor separated myself from your royal banners; I have always worked and complied with my obligations, as can be testified and sworn by the generals of Your Majesty, especially the Duke of Alba and the Comendador Mayor of Castile [Requesens].

Twenty years ago I started to serve Your Majesty in the expedition to Siena in the ranks of infantry captain, commissionary general of the infantry and the light cavalry and afterwards in Lombardy as captain and sergeant-major, continuing another six years in these states in the same ranks and finally, before his departure, the Duke of Alba choose me as Maestre de campo general of the army that remained in Holland and at present I serve Your Majesty in the office of Maestre de campo of the infantry. I do not want to tell Your Holy Majesty in particular the many and specific services I have rendered to Your Majesty over such a long period, but only to refer to the information given by the Duke of Alba and other Captains-general. I only want to say that after so many years having many times spilt my blood in Your royal service, I find myself with a ruined right arm and so poor that in order for a daughter to enter a convent I was forced to sell part of the patrimony my parents had left me, and in order to find a solution for another unmarried daughter I have in Madrid with no possibilities, I find myself only with the hope that the greatness of Your Majesty, who as a just prince I hope will not allow that only I will be left without reward. During the little time I have left of my life I remain with the desire and the obligation as a loyal vassal and debtor, to offer and sacrifice my life for the royal service of Your Majesty.

---

del braço derecho y tan pobre que para meter monja una hija me fue fuerça vender parte del patrimonio que mis padres me dexaron y para remediar otra hija donzella que tengo en Madrid con ninguna posibilidad me hallo sino solo la esperança en la grandeza de vuestra magestad que como principe tan justo espero no permitira para mi solo falte el premio, pues lo poco que de la vida me queda con la voluntad y obligacion que como fiel vasallo soy deudor me contento ofrecerla y sacrificarla en el real servicio de vuestra magestad. Guarde nuestro señor por muchos años la real persona de vuestra magestad con augmento de mayores reynos como la christiandad a menester y sus vasallos deseamos de Anveres a 18 de abril de 1575'. Valdés to Philip II, Antwerp, 18 April 1575, AGS, E. 563, f. 39.

May Our Lord guard the royal person of Your Majesty for many years, augmenting his realms and christianity, as is your vassal's wish, from Antwerp, 18 April 1575.

He had entered the army because he lacked sufficient means, somewhere around 1537, unfortunately too late to participate in the famous attack on Tunis in 1535, unlike Cristóbal de Mondragón and maybe also Julián Romero. As Francisco was born around 1518, he was probably just under twenty years of age, joining the army at a somewhat later age than Mondragón. As from around 1543 he continuously served the King in his army, and since the expedition to Siena in 1553-1554 he had been active in Italy, from 1558 as part of the tercio of Maestre de campo Sancho de Londoño, though they had already met in 1553 in Montalcino.[66] In Italy, he was first promoted to Captain and later to Sargento mayor. Philip II had started to follow his own political strategies in Italy after becoming Duke of Milan and King of Naples in July 1554, even sometimes in confrontation with his own father. In May 1555 the Duke of Alba became Philip's general and superintendent of Italy, governing both Naples and Milan.[67] At least from that time onwards, Valdés entered the world of Alba, who was to become his main protector. Just before Alba left the Low Countries at the end of 1573 he had him promoted to Maestre de campo general of the army in Holland. Afterwards, he functioned as an ordinary Maestre de campo of the Spanish tercios.

## The first years in the Low Countries (1567-1572)

Francisco de Valdés arrived in the Low Countries with the Duke of Alba's army in 1567, as Sargento mayor of the tercio of Lombardy, serving under Maestre de campo Sancho de Londoño. As far as we know, this was his first visit to the north of Europe, and certainly his first visit to the Low Countries. This makes his story again very different from those of Julián Romero and Cristóbal de Mondragón, who had spent many years in the north before the outbreak of the Revolt and who had had affectionate relations with women from the Low Countries. Valdés and Sancho Dávila did not have such a history with the Low Countries, and this has most surely influenced their ideas on the country and its inhabitants. For example, both Sancho Dávila and Valdés probably did not speak French at the time of their arrival.

---

[66] García Hernán, 'Don Sancho', 66.
[67] Rodríguez-Salgado, 'Il capo dei capi', 233-235.

Valdés participated in the Battle of Dahlem in 1568. Londoño praised his first officer's conduct in a letter: "Francisco de Valdés did very well perform the office of Sergeant major and Captain, giving his orders and fighting in a ditch".[68] With five companies he succeeded in defeating a large number of the enemy, taking the survivors prisoner together with all their belongings. He would also participate in the Battle of Jemmingen in July and the battle near the river Gete in October of that same year. In the chronicles his presence is hardly noticed. He is missing from Antonio Trillo's chronicle, and Bernardino de Mendoza related only how he left the city of Lier with several regiments of the tercio. In his descriptions of the Battle of Jemmingen and that of the almost totally forgotten battle near the river Gete, he is just one more name in the story.[69] In 1568 he was clearly not yet one of the great names of the Spanish army, and in the quiet subsequent years no opportunities arrived to establish a reputation on the battlefield.

If he resided close to his Maestre de campo, it is probable he returned to Lier after the battles of 1568. Londoño, who had signed his treatise in this small town in April 1568, could still be found there in May 1569. After that, his health deteriorated and he left for the Spa waters, in a last attempt to recover from his illnesses. As he was also Governor of Maastricht at the time, Londoño died in the castle of Severenborn, near Maastricht, on 30 May 1569. We can only guess whether Valdés was present at his funeral in the Saint Servatius Church of Maastricht, or whether it was his duty to remain with the tercio.[70]

Most likely, Valdés travelled with all ten banners of the tercio of Lombardy to the city of Utrecht, where they arrived on 21 August 1569. As Utrecht had blocked the payment of new subsidies, Alba had decided to burden them with quartering a complete tercio. Most of the tercio of the new Maestre de campo Fernando de Toledo would remain there for a longer period, but its stay was certainly not continuous. Soon two banners were sent to Waterland to fight the Sea Beggars, and two banners went to Culemborg. In August 1570 another banner left for Nijmegen, and in January 1571 six banners were sent to Arnhem. These last troops returned to Utrecht in February. In March 1571, four hundred men left to protect the coastline, and in May all remaining Spanish troops, up to six banners, left Utrecht for Amsterdam and other cities in the County of Holland. When in August 1571 Philip II ordered the retreat

---

[68] Londoño to the Duke of Alburquerque, 26 April 1568, CD XXX, 442.
[69] Sánchez Martín, 'Valdés'; Trillo, *Historia*; Mendoza, *Comentarios* (1948) 411, 425, 435.
[70] García Hernán, 'Londoño'; Ubachs and Evers, *Historische encyclopedie*, 317.

of all Spanish troops from the city, it is unclear how many troops were actually there. In any case, Alba again sent eight Spanish banners to the city on 18 November 1571, six from the tercio of Lombardy and two from the tercio of Naples.[71] By that time, Valdés had already travelled in the direction of Deventer, in the east of the Low Countries. But we may assume that Valdés had become well acquainted with Utrecht and its inhabitants before the conflict between him and Lannoy took place in 1574.

We have already seen that Valdés took up the pen during this relatively quiet period, and on 20 October 1571 he signed the manuscript of the *Diálogo militar* in the city of Deventer. Six months earlier, Alba had written on his behalf to the King:

> Captain Valdés is a good man and has served much, deserving that Your Majesty will honour and reward him, especially to solve the situation of the daughter he has; Your Majesty would be served by returning me his licence, or I shall take him with me or I shall give it to him when he wants to make use of it, because he is a man that would be very missed in his office, and it is convenient that Your Majesty rewards such men without them having to go there [to court] to ask for it.[72]

So, he had a licence finally to return home to resolve his daughter's situation, and it could be decided whether he would return with Alba or on his own account. The first letter we have from Valdés himself demonstrates that plans had changed in the meantime. On 25 June 1571 Valdés wrote from Deventer to Juan de Albornoz, Alba's secretary, expressing his dissatisfaction: "it seems that when I try to get closer to my journey to Spain, situations occur that make that I am exiled even further".[73]

Don Fadrique had ordered him to take over the government of Deventer as other captains and their companies had not performed well in this office. Though Mondragón had been governor of that city in 1569, residing there with his Walloon troops, it seems Valdés followed in the footsteps

---

[71] Struick, *Utrecht*, 157-158; 'Utrechtsche kroniek', 95-97, 104-110; ARAB, Audience 339, f. 17; 191-195.

[72] Alba to Philip II, Brussels, 23 March 1571, EA III. Also a letter from secretary Zayas with the same date about Valdés. Philip had sent this licence on 2 February 1571 from Madrid. AGS E. 547, f. 54.

[73] 'Pareçe que quando pretendo llegarme mas çerca al viaje de Spaña se ofreçen ocasiones de desterrarme mas lexos'. Valdés to Albornoz, Deventer, 25 June 1571, AA C/54, 18.

of Captain Hernando Pacheco of his own tercio of Lombardy. Pacheco had arrived in August 1570, and during his government an attempt had been made by traitors from within to hand the city over to the rebels. According to a chronicler present at the time, seventeen inhabitants were executed as a result. Pacheco was later executed in Flushing by the rebels, and his cruel behaviour in Deventer was used as an argument for his death sentence. After Valdés, the next governor would be Francisco de Vargas in 1572, another colleague from the tercio of Lombardy and perhaps even one of the protagonists of his treatise. Strangely enough, Dutch and local historiography has never acknowledged the presence of Valdés in Deventer.[74]

In his letter of 25 June, Valdés explained to Alba's secretary that he had decided to wait in order to return to Spain together with Alba, his protector. He did ask for permission to return to Brussels somewhat earlier in order to prepare for the journey, as this was impossible to organise from Deventer. The fact that he described his new office again as an exile ("*destierro*") shows he did not particularly like his new residence. In August 1571 he was still in Deventer, writing a second letter to remind Albornoz of the first one.[75] He now wanted permission to come to Brussels, and he asked the secretary for payment of his overdue wages, all in order to prepare for his journey to Spain. Finally, after years in the Low Countries and now even banishment in far-away Deventer, it was time to go home. Valdés could hardly wait, but it was not to happen. The same feeling can be found with the Duke of Alba, writing in the autumn of 1571: "I should wish to see the Duke [his replacement as Governor-general the Duke of Medinceli] here already, that I might get out of this place, be it by the window, but I shall be patient".[76]

Both Valdés and Alba were still in the Low Countries when, on 1 April 1572, the Sea Beggers gained the small city of Brielle on the coast of the County of Holland. It was the beginning of a new violent phase of the Revolt. Both men must have quickly understood that a return to Spain was out of the question for the time being. We know Valdés was back in Utrecht in February 1572, and he must have been one of the main protagonists in the suppression of an attempt to mutiny:

---

[74] Holthuis, *Frontierstad*, 27; Stein-Wilkeshuis, 'Deventer'; Moonen, *Korte chronyke*, 110, 113; Van Reyd, *Oorspronck* (1633) 9; Spanish letter from Governor Vargas to the Mayors of Deventer, Deventer, 21 September 1572. Deventer City Archives, 202722, 898-70.
[75] Valdés to Albornoz, Deventer, 12 August 1571, AA C/54, 19.
[76] Fagel, 'The Duke', 275.

> On 2 April, some Spaniards from the eight banners residing in Utrecht, started a conspiracy, and the other day, being White Thursday (while the Spaniards themselves would flag themselves in the evening, according to ancient custom) they would have violently killed all their officers, also killing all the burghers, both religious and worldly, small and important, and pillaging the city and burning it. When this information reached the colonel and the captains, they arrested that same evening many of the accomplices and immediately strangled one who would have been the most important author, and the other day his corpse was laid down on the square, with writing on his chest declaring him a traitor, as an example and mirror of such mean and murderous design and treason.[77]

Though information is scarce, we can place him during the following period in Rotterdam where he may have participated in the violence taking place in early April against its inhabitants under Fernando de Toledo, with the Count of Boussu as head of the army.[78] However, we do not have detailed information on Valdés's behaviour. In June he was invited by Alba to go to Brussels in order to prepare for a new attack, possibly directed against Enkhuizen. Alba's letter from 19 December 1572 to the King, already quoted, describes how Valdés had been wounded at the siege of Mons in Hainaut. After recovering he must have been present at the siege of Haarlem in December 1572, but as a Sargento mayor he did not make it into the chronicles as a main protagonist.[79] Until the middle of 1573 Valdés clearly was not one of the major commanders of

---

[77] 'Den 2 Aprilis hebben sommighe Spaengaerts van de 8 vendelen, binnen Utrecht leggende, zeker conspiratie gemaeckt, die des anderen daechs, wesende Witten Donredach, (terwylen die Spaengaerts haerselven in den avont naer oude gewoente geselen zouden) allen haer officiers vermoert ende doot gesmeten souden hebben, ende voirts allen den borgeren, soe gestelic als werlic, clein ende groot, vermoert, die stadt geplondert ende in brant gesteken souden hebben. Twellic tot kennisse gecommen zijnde van den colonel ende den capitainen, zijn tenselven daghe des avonts veel van de complicen geapprehendeert ende een tersont mitter coorde geworricht, die die principaelste autheur soude hebben geweest, die oic des anderen daechs doot op die Plaetze geleyt woorden, hebbend een gescryfte als een verrader op zijn borste gescreven, tot een exemple ende spigel van een alsulke lelicke mordadighe opset ende verraet'. 'Utrechtsche kroniek', 111-114. Struick dates the event on 1 April and explicitly mentions Valdés as the commander of the Spanish troops. Struick, *Utrecht*, 159.
[78] Brouwer and Vellekoop, *Spaans benauwd*, 21-25.
[79] Mendoza, 'Comentarios', 447; Albornoz to Valdés, Brussels, 17 April 1572, AA C/27, 40; EA III, 90; Alba to Philip II, Brussels, 24 June 1572 and 19 December 1572, EA III, 149 and 259; Sánchez Martín, 'Valdés', 916.

the Spanish troops in the Low Countries, but although he had not really gained a name for himself in battle, Alba was aware of the capacities of his 'creature' (*hechura*), as Valdés often signed his letters to the Duke. His main 'claim to fame' was his treatise, and though this was not published until 1578, manuscript copies must have circulated among the officers of the army of Flanders.

### From Sargento mayor to Maestre de campo

A few weeks after Haarlem finally surrendered on 12 July 1573, Captain Lope de Acuña died.[80] He had recently arrived from Italy with new enforcements: twenty-five companies with five thousand men, some eight thousand people in total with 140 carts of luggage, reaching the Low Countries from Lombardy in forty-two days, arriving on 16 May.[81] These fresh troops were then divided into two separate tercios: 'San Felipe el destacado de Lombardía' and 'Santiago el de la Liga'. Valdés was to be the new commander of these troops, albeit like Acuña without the rank of Maestre de campo.

From just before this period, June 1573, some twelve letters of Valdés have been preserved in the Alba archive.[82] In these letters we read about the difficulties in safeguarding the route between Utrecht and Amsterdam during the final phase of the siege of Haarlem, the problems he had with the water, the lack of provisions and money, and the difficult communication lines with Fadrique de Toledo. He sometimes wrote two letters a day to both the Duke and his secretary. In these letters he usually described the enemy using neutral terminology, and only once did he use the word rebels, and once the word villains (*bellacos*), also a favourite word of the Duke himself, but these words refer only to the small groups of rebels moving between the moats and marches (*fosos y pantanos*). We can understand his situation better using a quotation from a letter written by Valdés to the Duke of Alba at five o' clock in the morning:

---

[80] Lope (Valladolid 1529) died on 29 July 1573. Mazzocchi, 'Lope de Acuña', 223, puts his death in August 1573. He was married to noblewoman Isabel de Lompré, of Tournai, related to the Croy family, and he had a daughter Constanza, who married Diego Sarmiento de Acuña, the first Count of Gondomar, and a famous Spanish ambassador in England. Manso Porto, 'Diego Sarmiento'; Barrientos Grandon, 'Antonio Sarmiento', DBE, accessed 28-1-2019.
[81] Parker, *Army* (2004) 86, 88, 240.
[82] AA, C/54, 20-32.

> I have received two letters from Your Excellency of the 14th and 15th of this month, and if I have not written as often as Your Excellency has ordered me to do, the reason is that I have been working continuously, day and night, surveying all those canals, roads and throughways where the enemy can install himself to block the transport of provisions to the army camp.[83]

When the enemies conquered an important lock, Valdés tried to soften the defeat by a slightly funny decription of the situation: "a thing of which we were all very sure, as we had the passages so well protected that it was impossible to get through without having wings".[84] But then he dedicated the rest of the letter to the causes and possible solutions: the German reinforcements had been too slow so the enemy had arrived before them, but with some more men and people to work on a new fortress it would be possible to maintain their position. Valdés was, however, not just somebody who did what he had been told without offering his own opinion. In the same letter he elaborated on the situation:

> As Your Excellency knows well, many things do not prosper when many heads are governing, and when one is late in executing the decisions that have been made. I do not say this to blame anybody in particular, but as I have so much experience on these things and seeing that they do not listen to me, I am at risk of losing my reputation. But I would undergo this with patience, if it did not hurt the service of Your Majesty and Your Excellency.[85]

He also complained of the lack of money, ammunition and Spanish troops, as he could not attack with only Walloons under his command. Here we see that he was used more for his capacities as an organiser than

---

[83] 'Dos de vuestra excellencia he rreçebido juntas de 14 y 15 deste y si estos dias no he escrito tantas bezes como vuestra excellencia me tiene mandado la causa a sido que de noche ni de dia yo no he parado reconoçiendo todos estos canales, caminos y pasos adonde el enemigo se podia poner para ynpedir la vitualla al campo'. Valdés to Alba, Oudekerk, 18 June 1573, AA, C/54, 24.

[84] 'Cosa de que estabamos todos muy seguros por tener tan bien armado los pasos que hera ynposible pasar sinno con alas'. Valdés to Alba, Loenen, 18 June 1573, AA, C/54, 22.

[85] 'Bien sabe vuestra excellencia que muchas cosas no suzeden prosperamente por gobernar muchas cabezas y ser tardos en el esecutar de las rresuluçiones que se toman y no digo esto por ynculpar a ningun particular sino es a mi solo que tiniendo ya tanta esperiençia destas cosas y biendo que no me creen me pongo riesgo de perder mi rreputacion pero todo lo sufrire com paçiençia como no se herrase en el serbizio de su magestad y de vuestra excelencia'. Ibidem.

to lead his own company of Spanish infantry. We find him collaborating with the Count of Boussu, with the Lords of Hierges and Noircarmes, and with officers such as Juan Bautista de Tassis and Rodrigo Zapata. He used his mixed army of Spanish, Walloon and German troops to occupy the small fortresses they built in order to protect the important roads and canals. Valdés showed he was ready to fight:

> The goodness of God caused the fall of Babylonia, and by the love of God we should hurry in getting tight with those rebels as I have certain information from the prisoners that all these lands of Holland are unsteady.[86]

While still only a Sargento mayor, we find him discussing with Alba the strategy to follow in Holland. Both men knew that most inhabitants were loyal and that they were fighting small groups of rebels. So Alba told him to urge the local population to kill as many rebels as possible and offer them his help to do so, and Alba wanted Valdés to inform him of the whereabouts of William of Orange, preferably from hour to hour. Alba, in a letter to Valdés, laid out his policy, "We need to follow the road of softness, if they do what they have to do, but if not, we do it the hard way".[87]

By the end of July Valdés was active in the region close to Alphen aan den Rijn, where we will also find him around the siege of Leiden. In a letter he described how – with Spanish infantry and two hundred Walloons – they attacked the enemy near Nieuwerbrug aan den Rijn: "though those from inside started defending themselves bravely, pike against pike and halberd against halberd, they threw them out of the fortress, but killing fewer men than I had wanted, but I think still more than forty". By this time he already perfectly understood the importance of waterways, calling Alphen aan den Rijn "the passage way to the whole of Holland, both by water as on land".[88] In another letter he wrote

---

[86] 'Por la bondad de dios cayo la gran Babilonia por amor de dios que nos demos priesa apretar estos rebeldes que yo tengo çiertos abisos por bia de los prisioneros que todas estas tierras de Holanda andan banbaleando'. Valdés to Albornoz, Harmelen, 16 July 1573, AA, C/54, 31.

[87] 'Lo que conviene es llevarlos por el camino de la blandura, haciendo ellos lo que deben, y cuando no, por el de la fuerza'. Alba to Valdés, Utrecht, 20 July 1573, AA, C/65, 151-152.

[88] 'Aun que los de dentro se empeçaron a defender gallardamente asta benir pica com pica y alabarda con alabarda los hecharon del fuerte matando no tantos como yo quisiera pero creo pasaron de quarenta'. Valdés to Alba, Alphen aan den Rijn, 29 July 1573, AA, C/54, 33.

about the strength of the enemy's fortifications: "like most of the places in Holland, because of the great amount of water on all sides".[89] From the letters of this period we clearly get the idea of an army on the attack, building fortifications and throwing the enemy out of theirs.

But in that same letter he reports about the unexpected mutiny of the Spanish troops in Haarlem, and he immediately understood the problems this might cause, though hoping it would soon pass: "I am hurt as much as I can say by the mutiny of the Spanish infantry at Haarlem, for the anger it has given Your Excellency and for making it impossible to proceed against those rebels".[90]

And the moment was critical, as they had information that the rebels were falling apart. With an army entering Holland it could all be over soon:

> I have no information about the return of the Prince [Orange] to Dordrecht and everywhere they tell me that the heretics and the Catholics are murmuring every day amongst them. I think it certain that if they saw an army entering in these parts they would easily surrender much of the land. The reason is that everywhere you see the discord and the fact that the Prince has left Holland. As later I knew about these Spanish banners entering these lands, I hope by God that soon we shall see the decline of the very obstinate rebellion of these towns.[91]

But it was exactly the army that was failing. There was a great need for money, troops, provisions and materiel in order to be able to continue the war effort. The letters are filled with complaints, and Valdés used all the rhetoric he was capable of: "the necessity of all those Spanish and Walloon troops is so great…they leave me twenty at a time… Half of

---

[89] 'Como lo son los mas lugares de Holanda a causa de la mucha agua que por todas partes tienen'. Valdés to Alba, Oude Wetering, 3 August 1573, AA, C/54, 36.
[90] 'De la alterazion que la ymfanteria Española a hecho en Harlem me pesa quanto sabre decir por el enojo que a vuestra excelencia an dado y por el ympedimiento que sera a prozeder contra estos rebeldes'. Ibidem.
[91] 'Del Prinçipe no tengo abiso que se a tornado de Dordreq y en todas estas tierras me diçen ay cada dia rumores entre los erejes y catolicos por mui çierto tengo que si bieran entrar ejerçito por esta parte que sin mucha dificultad se rindieran hartas tierras destas, argumento dello es el ber la discordia que en todas ellas ay y aun el aberse ydo de Holanda el prinçipe luego como supo entrar estas banderas españolas en ella yo espero en dios que presto berna en declinaçion la mui obstinada rebellion destas billas'. Ibidem.

the Spaniards have fallen ill for eating cabbage and meat, and drinking water... If the remedy is delayed, I will probably find myself with only the banners".[92] The army was falling apart. Soldiers did not want to move without pay, some companies had more banners and officers than soldiers left, and he had not enough men to create a fighting force: the five companies of Spaniards he had amounted to only a mere four hundred men instead of the thousand he was supposed to have.[93] He also gives the example of Don Gabriel Niño's company, "so licentious and ill-disciplined", who had started directly after their arrival to kill the poor people's cows.[94] He wanted permission to punish at least one of them to set an example.

The next move was to get the soldiers from Egmond in the north to the southern part of Holland. Valdés shows he knew his way around Holland, as we can deduce from his very detailed advice in which he described all the possible ways to travel through Sassenheim, Noordwijk, Katwijk aan den Rijn, Valkenburg, Voorschoten, Zoeterwoude, etc., and advised where to cross the canals.[95] Valdés himself would in the meantime fortify Leiderdorp and Alphen aan den Rijn. However, one week later we find him sending Albornoz a letter in his own hand from Beverwijk, up in the north, close to Egmond. While the first troops arrived at Leiderdorp from the north, Valdés was lying ill in bed, and had time to reflect on his life:

> The many works of mind and body, accompanied by fifty-five years of age, have directed me to my bed with a serious illness and more fever than I can say, with large amounts of vomiting. For this reason I was forced to remain behind in the house of Captain Aurelio [Palermo] and I have sent a letter to Your Excellency with don Joan de Quiñones, also informing about the present state I am in. In the future I will be more compassionate with myself, finishing with my own ambitions that again have overtaken me.

---

[92] 'Es tan grande la neçesidad que toda esta gente padeze española y valona... Se me ban de veinte en veinte... Los españoles de comer berzas y carne y beber agua an caido la mitad malos... Si el remedio tarda yo creo me quedare con solas las banderas'. Valdés to Albornoz and Alba, Alphen aan den Rijn, 31 August 1573, AA, C/54, 41-42.

[93] Valdés to Albornoz and Alba, Alphen aan den Rijn, 2 September 1573, AA, C/54, 43-44; Valdés to Albornoz, Alphen aan den Rijn, 3 September 1573, AA, C/54, 45.

[94] 'Tan liçenciosa y maldeçiplinada'; 'matando las bacas de la pobre gente'. Valdés to Albornoz, Harmelen, 3 September 1573, AA, C/54, 46.

[95] Valdés to Alba, Harmelen, 4 October 1573, AA, C54, 48.

> Though I may say that in reality it is mostly out of my hands, because I so desire to obey and serve the Prince that it makes me refute my own being.[96]

And, to make matters worse, Don Fadrique had left the army camp without clearly handing over command to Valdés. So he found himself with soldiers who did not want to obey him:

> Don Fadrique did not utter a word, nor did he leave any orders for the captains and officers related to my government and there are already some who pretend and assume not to take orders from me. For this reason it is necessary that Your Excellency write to the three governors of this tercio of Italy and the same holds for the tercios of Lombardy and Naples, explaining them his wishes.[97]

He must have been very worried about the situation, as it was quite unusual directly to criticise Don Fadrique in letters to his father's secretary.[98] That very same night, at eleven o' clock, there was even an attempted mutiny by soldiers from the tercio of Naples, as he described in a postscript to the letter: "and they shot four or five arquebuses saying 'fuera vellacos' (go away villains!), but then some officers came out and it was put to rest without them having their way".[99] On 1 November Alba

---

[96] 'Los muchos travajos de espiritu y cuerpo acompañados con çincuenta y cinco años de edad me an deribado en el lecho con un muy grande acidente y callentura mayor que sabre dezir y vomito y camaras grandes y asi me fue fuerça quedarme aqui en casa del capitan Aurelio y enbiar esta mañana el despacho a su excelencia con don Joan de Quiñones haziendo asi mismo saber en el estado en que me hallo. Espero en la divina magestad que si mi mal passa adelante sera para comigo usar de mas misericordia terminando y poniendo fin a las ambiçiones en que de nuevo me via engolfar aunque puedo dezir con verdad que son bien fuera de mi voluntad pero el obedeçer a prinçipe que tanto desseo servir me hazia negar mi propio querer y asi no he querido faltar a dar aviso dello a Vuestra Merced cuya illustrissima persona y estado nuestro señor guarde y acreçiente como yo su servidor desseo de Bevervick a 11 de otubre 1573. Beso las manos a Vuestra Merced, su muy sierto servidor, Francisco de Valdés'. Valdés to Albornoz, Beverwijk, 11 October 1573, AA, C/54, 49.

[97] 'Don Fadrique no dixo palabra ni dexo orden alguna a estos capitanes ni ofiçiales en lo tocante a mi govierno i ya ay alguno o algunos que pretenden y procuran no tomar de mi la orden y asi sera menester que su excelencia escriva a los tres governadores deste terçio de Ytalia y asi mismo a los terçios de Lombardia y Napoles significandoles su voluntad'. Valdés to Albornoz, Beverwijk, 27 October 1573, AA, C/54, 51.

[98] Criticism of Don Fadrique in a letter directly to Alba: Valdés to Alba, Katwijk, 29 October 1573, AA, C/54, 52.

[99] 'Y se dispararon quatro o çinco arcabuzazos diçiendo fuera vellacos pero salieron algunos ofiçiales y luego se mitigo sin salirles su disigno'. Ibidem.

signed Valdés' promotion to the rank of Maestre de campo general "of all troops of all nations residing between Haarlem and Utrecht" ("*sobre las tropas de todas las naciones alojadas desde Haarlem hasta Utrecht*"). This man of humble background very remarkably would even receive higher wages than the other Maestres de campo.[100] This must have irritated the commanders with more experience such as Julián Romero, as well as the commanders of high noble birth. It also shows Valdés was considered the most important specialist regarding the almost amphibious warfare in the County of Holland.[101] The Duke of Alba and his son were preparing their long-awaited departure from the Low Countries, and Valdés was promoted in order to avoid the collapse of the army in the north. Alba had longed for this moment to come. In his final letter from the Low Countries he described himself as "a man fresh out of prison", a sentiment many Spanish commanders in the Low Countries at the time may very well have shared.[102]

## The first siege of Leiden

On 31 October Valdés wrote his first letters from The Hague,[103] where he and his men had arrived a day earlier. For the period up to 1 December 1573 we have fourteen letters from The Hague. It is possible that this was his first longer visit to the town, and perhaps we have to place his first encounter with Magdelena Moons during this stay in The Hague. It was to be his headquarters during the first siege of Leiden. He clearly preferred the castle of the counts, the Binnenhof, to the village of Leiderdorp where the main fortification was to be found.[104] In a long letter to Alba he told the story of his arrival, and first had to excuse himself to the Duke for going against his wishes:

> In the letter I wrote to Your Excellency yesterday, I did not explain the reason for occupying The Hague even though it went against the ideas of Your Excellency to take this place. However, I was motivated by seeing the army camp starving without any remedy of provision if I had to put them in the designated quarters, and so I felt myself forced to take them where they could eat. And for sure, I convince myself I was guided in everything by God

---

[100] Sánchez Martín, 'Francisco de Valdés'.
[101] Van Nimwegen and Sicking, 'Opstand', 66.
[102] Fagel, 'Duke', 284.
[103] Valdés to Albornoz and Alba, The Hague, 31 October 1573, AA, C/54-55.
[104] Wit, Riool and Van Doorn, *Rond de schans*, 15-16; Smit, *Den Haag*, 210.

because in all these lands we have been received with the greatest happiness of the world and every hour villagers arrive from their places, asking with much emphasis to receive soldiers that can defend them from the insolences of the rebels.[105]

He defended his disobedience to Alba by citing the great necessity of the troops, but also by emphasising the very positive welcome by the inhabitants of The Hague. Who could go against God's guidance? The letter is full of positive descriptions: "I see the villagers so full of desire to liberate themselves from the yoke and tyranny of those rebels".[106] The enemies were divided, and Valdés tried to win them over by offering them Alba's pardon, but also he let them go free so they could inform everybody about the "treatment the soldiers of this army give to the whole country".[107] He also describes how he had changed the government by appointing new mayors and aldermen, all Catholics. In this action Magdalena's brother lost his position as Mayor. Valdés would also try to get Catholic inhabitants back to The Hague, and on 1 November Catholic mass was restored. The new town government even hired an interpreter who could understand and speak Spanish.[108] The only negative remarks in the letter concerned the bad situation of the tercio of Italy which lacked clothing, and the need for ammunition. The positive welcome in The Hague can also be found in other texts, such as the chronicle of the Welsh soldier, Roger Williams: "found it a place sufficient to lodge double his troops, all in covert and most in beds. This Hague is counted the fairest village in Europe".[109]

Valdés informed Alba that the inhabitants of the region were even willing to "take up arms jointly with us, against the Beggars, the 'Guses'".[110]

---

[105] 'En la que escrevi ayer a Vuestra Excelencia no di quente de la causa que me movio a ocupar La Haya y mas sabiendo ser fuera de la opinion de vuestra excelencia el tomar este lugar pero a mi me movio el verme con el campo tan afamado y tan sin remedio de le proveher si le ponia en los alojamientos destinados que me fue fuerça traerle a donde comiese, y çierto me persuado que a sido guiado todo de Dios pues que en todo este pays nos an reçibido con la mayor alegria del mundo y cada ora llegan villanos de los lugares pidiendo con grande instançia soldados que los defiendan de las ynsolençias de los rebeldes'. Valdés to Alba, The Hague, 31 October 1573, AA, C/54, 55.

[106] 'Veo los villanos deseasisimos de librarse del jugo y tirania destos rebeldes'. Ibidem.

[107] 'Tratamiento que an entendido se haze de los soldados deste campo a todo el pays'. Ibidem.

[108] Wouter Jacobszoon, *Dagboek* I, 332; Smit, *Den Haag*, 212, 215.

[109] Williams, *Actions*, 98-101.

[110] 'Tomar las armas juntamente con nosotros contra los 'Guses'. Valdés to Alba, The Hague, 2 November 1573, AA, C/54, 56.

It was the first time in all his letters that he used this word for the rebels. In another letter he even described the possibility of organising a small army with the local population:

> As all this land is so favourable to us that I cannot explain it sufficiently, but it is proven by the fact that we receive news every hour of what they are doing in these lands and all the villagers are full of courage and good intentions to take up arms against these rebels. If I just had more men to be able to occupy the 'plat pais' (countryside) I imagine I could turn the villagers of these places into a 'petit ejerçito' (a small army).[111]

Besides the optimism about the assistance from the local population of the region, it is also remarkable that he now for the first time started to use words from French, such as 'Guses', 'plat pais', and 'petit [ejerçito]'. This seems to point to more direct contact with the local population. Taken together with the optimism in these letters, one is tempted to suggest that his positive outlook was caused by his blissful encounter with Magdalena.

There were also military encounters during this period as the rebels tried to fortify the strategically important Maassluis. After the great difficulty of getting enough men together, the attack was successful. On 4 November the rebel garrison surrendered. Marnix of Sint-Aldegonde, Orange's commander in the region and his close associate, was taken prisoner and some six hundred rebels were killed. Chronicler Trillo may be refering to Maassluis (and Vlaardingen) when simply writing that "From The Hague, Maestre de campo Valdés had taken two fortresses from the enemies".[112] Roger Williams, however, gives all the credit to his colleague, Julián Romero, with whom Valdés had co-organised the attack.[113] Again we see that Valdés does not possess great fame related to battles and actual fighting. Captain Julián was much more of a warrior. We might consider Valdés to be more of an organiser, a military manager.

---

[111] 'Pues todo este pais nos estan propiçio quanto no sabre significar y harto argumento dello es el tener cada ora abisos de quanto se haze en estas tierras y tomar todo el villanage con grandisimo animo y boluntad las armas contra estos rebeldes. Si me hallara con mas gente para poder ocupar el plat pais me persuado que pudiere hazer de los billanos destos lugares un petit ejerçito'. Valdés to Albornoz, The Hague, 8 November 1573, AA, C/54, 58.
[112] Trillo, *Historia*, 220.
[113] Williams, *Actions*, 102.

For the remainder of the month of November, Valdés was busy organising fortifications, travelling around between the Maas region and the surroundings of Leiden, asking for money to finish his own fortifications, building a canal, breaking some dykes, asking for iron cannons to put on his ships, and pleading for two armed ships to be sent to control the river Maas. It shows how Valdés was involved in the warfare in these wet parts of the country.[114] But as winter came another problem arose. Valdés warned Alba in a letter about "the time of the frost"("*el tiempo de los yelos*").[115] He had received information that the people of Leiden were making a large number of sledges (*esleides o trineos*). A day later he wrote to Albornoz asking for money to make sledges and a great number of crampons (*ramplones*) that would make it possible for the soldiers to walk on the ice.[116]

The coming of winter also caused problems regarding the soldiers. In a lettter to paymaster Alameda, Valdés explained that the banners were losing men, and that everybody was cheating: "I have tried to inform myself in particular about the people at present in the Spanish banners and it is a shame to see how much is being stolen".[117] If these banners were visited, a lot of money could be saved. Most probably, Valdés is referring to the well-known tactic of not reporting dead and deserted soldiers in order for officers to enrich themselves with their pay. A visit by the paymasters, and a mustering, could solve this problem. Also the cavalry was responsible for "grandes desordenes". The soldiers of the tercio of Italy desperately needed clothing, colourfully described by Valdés as "they look like spirits coming out of purgatory" ("parezen animas que salen del purgatorio").[118]

And there was more to complain about. He even became personal for a moment: "I find myself with more work of body and mind than I can say, because I have many who work against me and nobody who helps me carry this burden".[119] He lacked ammunition, carts, bread, diggers, cannons, armed ships, and nobody helped him out. The Lord

---

[114] Valdés to Alba and paymaster Alameda, Leiderdorp, and The Hague, 13 November 1573 to 19 November 1573, AA, C/54, 60-63.

[115] Valdés to Alba, The Hague, 19 November 1573, AA, C/54, 63.

[116] Valdés to Albornoz, The Hague, 20 November 1573, AA, C/54, 64.

[117] 'Yo e procurado ynformarme muy particularmente de la gente que ay en las banderas españolas y es berguença de ber lo mucho que se hurta'. Valdés to Alameda, The Hague, 16 November 1573, AA, C/54, 62.

[118] Valdés to Alba, The Hague, 20 November 1573, AA, C/54, 64.

[119] 'Yo me hallo con mas trabaxos de espiritu y cuerpo de lo que sabre deçir porque tengo muchos que me desayuden y ninguno que me ayude a llebar esta carga'. Ibidem.

of Noircarmes, the new stadtholder of Holland, did not even reply to his letters, and let his couriers wait a day before letting them enter the city of Utrecht.[120] Other letters took six days to receive an answer: "this is the state I am in at this moment".[121] You can feel his anger and his desperation:

> And I also don't want to be silent about the fact that there are very few captains that are actually governing their regiments, as some of them are wounded and sick and others have gone to places where they prefer not to look too much for their honour. But in this army camp there is no auditor, nor a captain or an official to perform justice. But not even for this I am giving up my spirit: quia dominus michi ad jutor.[122]

The Lord is my helper! Does it show the Latinity of the commander, or is he merely copying Philip II's motto, also to be found on coins from the royal mint?[123] Nobody helped him, and he literally had to do the work himself, "using the strength of my own arms (I may say) I have brought 350 *botas* of flour to The Hague".[124] We can imagine the commander carrying the heavy loads on his own shoulders, a perfect reflection of his everyday reality. He lacked time, "even to read the letters that arrive I have no time, moving as I do from one fortress to another".[125] He also had to use his own money to pay for the army: "until now, looking after my honour has cost me many ducats, as I [have to act] by the strength of my arms and spending my own possessions".[126]

---

[120] Philip of Sainte-Aldegonde, Lord of Noircarmes, died in Utrecht on 4 March, 1574. Soen, 'Collaborators'.

[121] 'Esto es el estado en que al presente me hallo'. Valdés to Alba, The Hague, 20 November 1573, AA, C/54, 64.

[122] 'Tampoco quiero callar que no solamente amuy pocos capitanes que gobiernen parte por estar heridos y enfermos y parte por yrse adonde les da gusto mirar poco por su onrra, pero en este campo no a quedado auditor ni capitan de campaña ni ministro con que se pueda executar la justicia, pero ni por eso me tengo de perder de animo, quia dominus michi ad jutor'. Ibidem.

[123] De Groot, *Seventh window*, 116.

[124] 'A fuerza de mis propios brazos (puedo dezir) tengo traidas a La Haya 350 botas de harina'. Valdés to Alba, The Hague, 20 November 1573, AA, C/54, 64.

[125] 'Aun para leer las lettras que me bienen me falta tiempo andando como ando de un fuerte al otro'. Ibidem.

[126] 'Hasta aora me cuesta muchos ducados el mirar por mi honrra pues a fuerça de brazos y gastando mi haçienda'. Valdés to Albornoz, The Hague, 26 November 1573, AA, C/54, 65.

His letters full of self-pity can, however, be contrasted in this case with a 'cartel' from some Spanish mutineers asking for payment: "pagas, pagas, pagas".[127] They blamed their commander for not taking care of housing and food, while they stated that food did not fail in his own household. They also accused Valdés of informing Alba that his troops did not need much payment, and then they added a still unclear accusation: "and because you understand we know of the function you had in Milan, we inform you that we cannot live the way we do now in the villages without orders for our payment. We shall ruin the country and you will be to blame".[128]

It is in this complicated situation that he reminded Alba in his letter of his loyalty: "as I am your servant (*criado*) and creature (*hechura*) and only the fervour in serving you forces me to remain engaged over here, where I hope God will make that I can serve you despite rivals and envious people".[129] However, even his patron and Albornoz seemed to have forgotten him as he had not received any letters for a long time, waiting every hour for the postman to arrive. As he knew his place within their relationship, he modestly wrote that the absence of their letters was surely the result of the unsafety of the roads. And Alba did deliver as a patron, as Valdés wrote he was very happy to receive the news of Alba's favour, brought to him personally by the Lord of La Motte:

> As much as from the greatness of the Duke my lord was to be expected and from the favour and grace that is given to me... I find myself very inferior and incapable of returning the satisfaction on equal terms. I shall do everything I can and that is a pure and very complete desire to sacrifice myself in your service until I die.[130]

---

[127] Copy of the 'cartel' of the Spanish infantry to Valdés, Holland, 19 November 1573, AGS, E. 554, f. 155. See also: Sherer, *Warriors*, 112.

[128] 'Y porque entendáis que sabemos el cargo que teniades en Milan os avisamos que no podemos vivir de la manera que estamos en los casares sin orden de pagarnos. Porque arryunaremos el país y será vuestra culpa'. Spanish soldiers to Valdés, 19 November 1573. AGS, E. 554, f. 155.

[129] 'Pues soy su criado y echura y solo el zelo de su serviçio me obligo a quedar aqui empeñado a donde spero en Dios de azertarle a serbir a pesar de emulos y embidiosos'. Valdés to Albornoz, The Hague, 26 November 1573, AA, C/54, 65.

[130] 'Tan amplio como de la grandeza del duque mi señor se podia esperar y del fabor y merced que se me de... Me hallo muy ynfirior y ymposibilitado a poder equibalentemente sastifazer ofreçere todo lo que tengo que es una pura y muy entera boluntad sacrificada hasta que muera en su serviçio'. Ibidem. Valentin Pardieu, heer van La Motte (1530-1595). Diegerick, ed., *Correspondance*; Soen, *Vredehandel*, 335.

Does this refer to the official documents of his appointment as Maestre de campo general, or is it about financial compensation for his work? Valdés, notwithstanding his positive image in Leiden nowadays, was clearly an Albista, a client of the Duke of Alba. We see his negative side when he talked in a letter to Albornoz about Philip Marnix of Sainte-Aldegonde:

> The few times I have spoken to him I have been amazed and even scandalised by him, seeing what a terrible heretic he is, and even as a prisoner he pretends that His Majesty will give freedom of conscience to these states. He certainly is of a very sound mind and a great learned man, dominating all the languages Latin, Greek, and Hebrew, but he uses all these abilities for bad purposes. Orange is very sad about his loss because, as they say, he is the one who knows everything about his council and government.[131]

On 1 December Valdés wrote a last letter from The Hague. He was examining two prisoners taken between Leiden and Delft with letters addressed to William of Orange and the Estates.[132] The letters were written by captains from Leiden urging Orange to get his soldiers out of the city, "because they can no longer suffer the dissensions they have with those from the country, and the bad will and hate they show to them as every day they tell them that they should leave and that they themselves would guard their city".[133] The conflict in Leiden could even be heard outside the city, as we can understand from Valdés' description:

> Last night alarm was given in Leiden with drums and bells, and many arquebus shots were heard for one hour. Until now I

---

[131] 'Las pocas bezes que le e ablado me tiene marabillado y aun scandalizado biendo quan maldito ereje es, y que aunque se be preso pretende que su magestad de libertad de conçiençia en estos estados y çierto es hombre de muy bibo juizio y gran letrado docto en todas lenguas Latina, Griega y Ebrea, sino que toda esta abilidad la emplea en mal. El de Orange a sentido mucho su perdida porque hera segun dizen los que le conoçen todo su consejo y gobierno'. Valdés to Albornoz, The Hague, 28 November 1573, AA, C/54, 66. See also Valdés to Alba, Maassluis, 4 December 1573, AGS, E. 554, f. 158.

[132] 'Los estados que ellos llaman'. Valdés to Alba, The Hague, 1 December 1573, AA, C/54, 67.

[133] 'Porque ya no pueden sufrir las disensiones que con los de la tierra tienen y la mala boluntad y odio que les muestran pues cada dia les dizen que se salgan fuera que ellos quardaran su villa'. Ibidem.

> have not been able to verify what it was, but it is said by these prisoners that there is a conflict between those from the city and the soldiers and they think it certain that a revolt has taken place amongst them.[134]

It is in this same letter he first used the expression "la guerra de Holanda" ("the war of Holland"), which seems to imply that in his eyes it had become more than just a struggle against a group of rebels. However, he wrote in a letter some days later that this division could be used to win the war, if only they were given the means to act.[135]

Two last letters from this period date from Warmond, near Leiden, and describe the taking of two castles.[136] It is interesting to note that Valdés used neutral words to describe these castles in his letter to Alba, but in his short letter to Albornoz he called them "*ladroneras*" ("dens of thieves"), demonstrating the perfect use of different speech registers. The defenders of the castle of Warmond escaped through the back door, and instead of criticising their cowardly behaviour he was full of praise for their abilities:

> And though they were closely watched, those of this country are so skillful and quick in walking on the ice with their skates that it is impossible to catch them, even with horses. It is pleasant to see all the villagers and the soldiers of this land going about in the said manner, not with the intention of offending our soldiers that are now without the crampons that are necessary to walk on the ice, of which many days ago I had informed monsieur de Noircarmes, but until now he has not provisioned any of these.[137]

---

[134] 'Antenoche se toco arma en Leiden con cajas y campanas y se oyeron muchos arcabucazos por espaçio de un ora, no e podido saber hasta aora que sea pero dizen estos presos que segun andan a malas los de la villa con los soldados que creen çierto que abra sido rebuelta entre ellos'. Ibidem.

[135] Valdés to Alba and Albornoz, Warmond, 7 December 1573, AA, C/54, 68-69.

[136] Ibidem.

[137] 'Y aun que estava con vigilançia son tan diestros y prestos los deste pays a caminar por el hielo con sus patines que no es posible alcançarlos ni aun con cavallos. Ya si es cosa graçiosa ver la moltitud de villanaje y soldados deste pays que caminan de la manera que digo sin que sean parte nuestros soldados a los ofender mayormente hallandose aora sin los ramplones que son neçesarios para caminar por el yelo de lo qual muchos dia a que e dado aviso a monsiur de Norcarme [Noircarmes] pero hasta aora no a hecho provision ninguna dellos'. Ibidem.

These letters also mark the end of an epoch, as Valdés thanked Albornoz for all that he had done for him, and he sent a Spanish nobleman to court to wish Alba a good journey home and to welcome the new Governor-general, Luis de Requesens. Alba was finally leaving the Low Countries, after spending more than six continuous years as its Governor and Captain-general. His departure also created a kind of radio silence in Valdés' correspondence, as his letters to Requesens are much more difficult to trace. Until 15 April 1574, we do not have letters from the commander.[138] Within this period we find the lifting of the first siege of Leiden on 21 March 1574 in order for Valdés to travel east with his army to stop another invasion from Germany by William of Orange's brothers.

He must also have participated in the large-scale attack in December in the direction of the river Maas. Only Delft, Schiedam and Rotterdam now remained in the hands of the rebels. The Hague was probably his central residence during this period, but we have only some proclamations as evidence of his presence there, besides some letters mentioning him as residing in The Hague.[139] He ordered that civilians were not allowed to buy goods from the soldiers and indicated the number of beds and other services the inhabitants had to offer to the quartered soldiers.[140]

On 14 April Sancho Dávila became the glorious hero of the Battle of the Mookerheyde, close to the eastern borders of the Low Countries. Valdés and his men came just too late to participate, but it had made them leave their positions around Leiden. The orders to travel east with his troops had already been received at least a month before, but at the time Valdés had been ill.[141] Again, Valdés did not gain honour and prestige participating in an important battle.

Valdés's arrival was also delayed because his troops had started some kind of a mutiny on their passing of Utrecht. If we believe priest refugee Wouter Jacobszoon, who was living in Amsterdam at the time:

> They were calling for money, tearing five or six banners completely into rags. And they were very bitter with their captain, named Baldeus, whom they tried to destroy, shooting heavily at him,

---

[138] Instruction Requesens to Bracamonte, Antwerp, 20 February 1574, NCD I, 218-222. Letters from Requesens to Valdés from 20 February, 11 March, and 4 April 1574, NCD I, 228-229; 347 and idem, II, 88. In these letters Requesens refers to letters from Valdés from 26, 29, and 30 January, 23 and 26 February, and 1, 4, 6, 23, and 28 March.

[139] Instruction from Requesens to Bracamonte, Antwerp, 20 February 1574, NCD I, 218-222.

[140] Brouwer and Vellekoop, *Spaans benauwd*, 46; Smit, *Den Haag*, 216.

[141] Requesens to Valdés, 11 March 1574, NCD I, 347.

so as to shock everybody, fearful of what was to become of this,
and with great fear of further devastation of the whole country.[142]

The message can be found between news from 1 and 3 April, and is repeated again on 7 April.[143] In his memoirs Jacobszoon also mentions on 19 April that he was busy making an inventory of the books the Spanish Franciscans wanted to send to Spain, given to them by 'Baldeus', who had stolen them from the house of nobleman Van Swieten. In his turn, Adriaan van Swieten had stolen them from the Franciscans of Gouda when he had pillaged that city.[144] Though the Spaniards thought they were within their right to take them as spoils of war, the King did not want church goods to be taken as prizes. Three days later, Jacobszoon heard of the royal victory against the 'Beggars' on the battlefield.[145]

The day after the Battle of the Mookerheyde Valdés wrote a letter to Alba to inform him about the events.[146] We have to realise that this letter was no longer directed to his Captain-general in the Low Countries, but to his noble patron in Spain. Sending information on current events was one of the things a client could offer to his patron in order to maintain their relationship from a distance. He had already sent him another letter three days earlier, but this letter has not been preserved.

On the way back from the east, on 30 April, Valdés and his troops again arrived in Utrecht, resulting in the events we discussed earlier, leading up to a confrontation between Valdés and Fernando de Lannoy. Jacobszoon mentions these problems in his memoirs.[147] Two weeks later Valdés had to hide from the mutineers while in Antwerp, in order to save his own life. Like Romero and Mondragón, Valdés was not always loved by his soldiers.

## The second siege of Leiden (1574)

Another two weeks later, the second siege of Leiden had started. It is perhaps Valdés's biggest accomplishment of his career that he succeeded so quickly in converting a large band of mutineers into an organised army that was able to return to the attack.[148] It demonstrates again his skills

---

[142] Jacobszoon, *Memoriën*, I, 389.
[143] Ibidem, 391.
[144] Adriaan van Swieten (1532-1584), a nobleman and follower of William of Orange.
[145] Ibidem, 395-396.
[146] Valdés to Alba, Nijmegen, 15 April 1574, AA, C/54, 70.
[147] Jacobszoon, *Memoriën*, 400.
[148] Fagel, *Leids beleg*.

as an organiser. On 28 May he was back in The Hague, now writing to his new Captain-general, Luis de Requesens.[149] After leaving Utrecht on May 24, they had first reached Alphen aan den Rijn, the strategic crossroads he knew so well, and where he had been fighting in July 1573. Again it turned into a violent confrontation with the enemy, and again it was one of the few moments we find actual fighting described in his correspondence, calling it "a very good and very bloody skirmish" ("*una muy buena scaramuça y bien sangrienta*"). The enemy resisted for more than an hour, but when Valdés's men finally entered the fortification they killed many of them, and afterwards chased the enemy for one and a half miles, killing as many as possible, while others drowned. Valdés speaks of some three hundred dead on the side of the rebels against five or six Spaniards and an equal number of Walloons. His final judgement of the fighting was very positive:

> I am more delighted than I can say to have seen the spirit and valour of this infantry when attacking the fortress. I promise Your Excellency that during all the time of the fighting, and that was more than one hour, I have never in my career as a soldier seen anything more persistent or done with more endeavour.[150]

Four regiments of English troops fighting with the rebels quickly surrendered to the Lord of Licques, who immediately sent them off to prison in Haarlem.[151] Valdés was not amused as it was his district, and it had been his decision to make. However, "I did not want to irritate any more those Burgundians in hating the Spanish nation".[152] Again, the distrust between Spanish commanders and Netherlandish nobles divided the royal army, and clearly this must be considered an important factor in explaining its failure to defeat the rebels.

Valdés knew that both Delft and Leiden lacked garrisons, and so he tried to convince them to open their gates, using Hollanders to speak

---

[149] These first letters are preserved only as copies: Valdés to Requesens, The Hague, 28 May 1574, AGS, E. 558, f.36-37. See also CD LXXV, 258-262, where the first letter is incorrectly dated 18 May 1574. Valdés left Utrecht on 25 May. 'Utrechtsche kroniek', 141.

[150] 'He holgado mas que sabre dezir de aver visto quan animosamente y con quanto valor acometio el fuerte esta infanteria que prometo a vuestra excelencia que despues que soy soldado del tiempo que duro el combatir que como he dicho, fue mas de un ora, no he visto cosa mas bien porfiada ni con mas esfuerço hecha'. Ibidem.

[151] Philip of Récourt, Lord of Licques (1534-1588), a captain of Walloon troops.

[152] 'No quisse yrritar mas estos Borgoñones a odio contra la nacion Spañola'. Ibidem.

to their fellow 'landsmen', but without any success.¹⁵³ In July, Valdés remained hopeful that Leiden would surrender, and Requesens informed the King of that very same hope.¹⁵⁴

Regarding his attempts to gain the city of Delft we know much less, though we are informed through another letter of 19 August from Requesens to the King that Valdés had tried to get into this city with the help of some Frenchmen from within. However, the secret signals went amiss, and they arrived at the gates too early.¹⁵⁵ In his own letters from 14 August, Valdés wrote about going on a campaign with one thousand infantry and three hundred cavalry, to position themselves between Leiden and Delft.¹⁵⁶ These unsuccessful attempts to take over Delft have not been studied in depth. However, especially within English literature we find references to what some authors call 'the Battle of Delft'.¹⁵⁷ Though, as we saw above, at least some of the events relate to 1574, the whole story is generally situated in October 1573. This mix-up may find its origin in the main source, the chronicle of Roger Williams, who was a member of the English forces involved in fighting around Delft in support of the rebels:

> Valdéz practised all he could with Leiden and Delft, once by treachery of some who kept the town port toward Utrecht, Valdéz prepared sundry turf boats in which he lodged good troops of soldiers. Once being entered the ports, with the resolution of the garrison and the good conduct of Poyet, they were repulsed, where Valdéz lost many of his men. Another time he had intelligence with some in Delft, but being discovered to the townsmen and garrison, divers of our bands which lodged hard by entered in the night, but either some of the townsmen or Valdéz' guards

---

¹⁵³ There is mention of Johan van Matenesse and Jan de Huyter. Koppenol, *Leids Onzet*. 17.

¹⁵⁴ Requesens to Philip II, Brussels, 25 July 1574, AGS, E. 560; CP III, n. 1371; Idem, NCD IV, 105-110; Requesens to Lannoy, 20 July 1574, NCD IV, 50-52.

¹⁵⁵ Requesens to Philip II, Antwerp, 19 August 1574, CP III, n. 1382; NCD V, 62-81. See also Mendoza, 'Comentarios', 519; Requesens to Valdés, 14 August 1574, NCD IV, 343-345.

¹⁵⁶ At the same time he sent Requesens a plan of how Waterland, in the north of Holland, could be controlled by nine strongholds, four hundred men, and three hundred horse. Requesens to Lannoy, 14 August 1574, NCD IV, 339-342.

¹⁵⁷ https://en.wikipedia.org/wiki/Battle_of_Delft_(1573), accessed 30 January 2019. The Dutch Wikipedia page seems to be an abbreviation of the English page without the annotation, showing the lack of interest in the Netherlands for this subject: https://nl.wikipedia.org/wiki/Slag_bij_Delft. Van Nierop, *Verraad*, 114.

discovered our arming, so as he gave over his enterprise, when he was ready to attempt, in the like order as he did at Leiden.[158]

The 'Battle of Delft' is essentially a heroic English story in which Valdés is supposed to have lost some seven hundred men, and in which the Spaniards had in vain attempted to gain Delft by tricks and treason. The Spanish trick of using peat boats with hidden troops in order secretly to enter a city will much later be repeated by the rebels. The story of their successful capture of Breda in 1590, using this very same method of a peat boat (*turfschip*), is one of the most famous events within Dutch historiography on the Revolt, as the Dutch version of the Trojan horse. Valdés apparently showed them the way.

In August, Valdés again wrote letters to the Duke of Alba and Albornoz, telling the Duke about his successful second entry into Holland, even when he now did not have any regiment of old Spanish tercios (*Spañoles de los biejos*) at his disposal, but only the fresh and inexperienced Spanish troops from the tercio of Italy, and furthermore only German and Walloon soldiers. We get a detailed account of the companies involved. He offered his judgement on the actual state of affairs:

> I have Leiden caught in extreme necessity and their obstinance is such that even without having soldiers in the city and with the people dying of hunger, they still do not want to surrender. Already for many days they receive a portion of half a pound of bread, and this only for the rich, as the major part of the population lives off eating carrots and other vegetables and fruit. And so many people die of hunger and plague. I have constructed fortresses on all sides at the distance of an arquebus shot, to make sure that they cannot take their cows to pasture and to prevent them from harvesting the vegetables. I think it cannot take long before they surrender.[159]

---

[158] Williams, *Actions*, 100.

[159] 'Tengo a Leiden en estrema neçesidad y es tanta su obstinación que con no tener gente de guerra dentro moriendo de hambre no se quieren rindir pues ha muchos dias que se les de media libra de pan de raçion y esto a los ricos porque la mayor parte del pueblo biven de comer çanahorias y otras ortalizas y frutas y asi muere mucha gente de hambre y peste. He le hecho por todas partes fuertes a tiro de arcabuz para quitarles que no se saquen a paçer las vacas y ympedirles el coger de la ortaliza, creo no podia durar muchos dias que no se rinda'. Valdés to Alba, The Hague, 9 August 1574, AA, C/54, 72; Mendoza, *Comentarios*, 519. The obstinacy of the Leideners can also be found in newsletters; Lamal, 'Orecchie'; Lamal, *News*; Lamal, 'Internationale berichtgeving'.

He wrote to Alba that he still had not received any letters from him, and he even did not know whether the Duke had received his letters. Of course, he remained very polite in his expression, as a loyal servant ought to be. Correspondence between client and patron had a tendency to be unequal, not only in content, but also in quantity, as the patron often did not respond to the letters.

In his letter to secretary Albornoz his tone was different: "I do not know the reason for His Excellency having erased me from his memory".[160] He for his part would remain their loyal servant until death. But there was another side to the relationship between a client and a patron. He was in great need of favours from the Duke, and through Sancho Dávila he knew the Duke had arrived at court. As his client, he had always remained in the Low Countries, "in this banishment" ("*en este destierro*"), as he repeats the expression he had used back in 1571, but this had been bad for his honour. The situation in the Low Countries was terrible:

> I (praise the Lord) am healthy, but with more work than ever, of both body and mind, because the necessities are without any comparison larger than when Your Grace was over here, because in more than two months there still has not been sent one complete payment to this infantry, and winter is coming, with the rains having started already with great fury.[161]

After the reformation of the Spanish tercios, the old infantry had been divided between Fernando de Toledo and Julián Romero, while Valdés had become the commander of the tercio of Italy. But he clearly had enough of the war and uttered a heartfelt wish: "that they let me go to Spain and lay the pike aside".[162] When we think of the most quoted phrase from his treatise: "El día que uno toma la pica para ser soldado, ese día, renuncia a ser christiano" ("The day a man picks up his pike to become a soldier is the day he ceases to be a Christian"), we might conclude he wanted to become Christian again.[163]

---

[160] 'No se qual sea la causa de que su excelencia [Alba] me aya borrado de su memoria'. Valdés to Albornoz, The Hague, 9 August 1574, AA, C/54, 73.

[161] 'Yo (loado Dios) quedo con salud, pero mas cargado de travajos que nunca, asi de cuerpo como de spiritu, porque las neçesidades son sin comparaçion mayores que quando vuestra merced aca stava, pues en dos meses y dias mas aun no se ha embiado a esta ynfanteria un socorro entero y el ynbierno viene abiendo ya aqui empeçado las aguas a gran furia'. Ibidem.

[162] 'A que dexe de yrme en España y arrimar la pica'. Ibidem.

[163] Parker, *Army* (2004) 153.

These letters demonstrate that Valdés needed favours, but the type of rewards was left open. Already five days later, Valdés wrote another set of letters to Albornoz and Alba, in which he did make clear what he expected from the Duke:

> My daughter writes to me about an affair of honour and convenience of hers and mine, for which she needs to have some letters from His Majesty, that she pretends to have through the favour of Your Excellency. I humbly request that Your Excellency can favour this affair of such a servant and creation of yours.[164]

The letter to Albornoz again was more direct, reflecting correspondents writing on a more equal level. He was very happy that he had just received a letter from Albornoz written on 3 August, but he still wondered why they had not received his other letters as he had always sent them with Requesens' official post. He was also grateful for the fact that Albornoz had visited his daughter. By way of thanking the secretary he filled the letter with news of the war. Within this letter there was another one in which he discussed the matter of his daughter. For her 'affair' she needed a thousand ducats, and it was necessary that Albornoz give her the money, and then Valdés would pay him back through merchant Juan de Cuéllar. That he speaks about 'dressing her' ('*vestirla*') is the only reference to the character of this 'affair'. In the middle of the siege of Leiden, Valdés was busy with family matters in Madrid. Besides being a (good) lover, he was clearly trying to be a good (though very absent) father.

It may also have been a good diversion from his professional activities, as things were not going well around Leiden for the besiegers. We have already seen the conflict between Fernando de Lannoy and Valdés, as a result of which Valdés was in the end kept out of the negotiations with the city government. There may also have been a conflict between Valdés and Julián Romero when this last commander came to help Valdés out with his siege. Both Trillo and Mendoza criticise Valdés for not listening to Romero, and Trillo, in particular, shows him as somebody who "wanted to be alone and not to share the honour and effort with anybody else".[165]

---

[164] 'Escriveme mi hija que para un negoçio de honrra y comodo suyo y mio tiene neçesidad de algunas letras de su magestad las quales pretende haver mediante el favor de vuestra excelencia. Suplico humilmente quanto puedo a vuestra excelencia favorezca este particular como negoçio de un tan su criado y hechura'. Valdés to Alba and Albornoz, Wilsveen, 14 August 1574, AA, 4, 74-75.

[165] 'Quisiera ser solo y que no huviera con quién partir de la honra ni del trabajo'. Álvarez Francés, 'Fabrication'; Mendoza, *Comentarios* (2008) 498-500; Trillo, *Historia*, 254.

However, he had sent messages to the city government, trying to convince the city to surrender.[166] These letters even play a prominent role in the discourse on the siege of Leiden, and can also be found in the theatre plays. As the story goes, the city government around the end of May responded in a letter to Valdés with only the following words: "Fistula dulce canit volucrem dum decipit auceps". Leiden city historian Orlers tells the story that went with it:

> In our language this is rendered as: "if the bird catcher sees the little bird flying freely, he whistles very sweetly to fool the little bird". The letter that had been sent to commander Baldeo was elegantly closed and sealed with the city seal, in the inside, there was a subtle circle drawn in the middle, in which the foresaid sentence had been written. When Baldeus opened the foresaid letter, he thought it was not written at all, and out of anger he threw it from him with several swear words: but when he looked closer, he saw the said answer, saying that he would make the writers pay.[167]

This story seems to imply he did read Latin. In Orlers's work we can also find another letter of 30 July from Valdés to the city, politely opening with "honourable good friends, again I hope that you have always remained in favour of the Royal Majesty, your natural hereditary lord, and that you do not desire to ruin your fatherland…", and ending with "Your good friend".[168]

His letter of 4 September was written in Spanish, and the tone had changed completely, though negotiations and surrender still remained his main intention.[169] He starting by calling them "obstinate Leideners against God, and against your King and Lord", but then returns to invite them to come and negotiate with him, offering them safe-conducts. At the end of the letter the tone gets stricter again: "that you do not fool yourselves with vain hopes of relief… If you accept my offer, you will find a good friend in me, but if you hold on to you ruinous plans, believe me, you will experience the sword of justice".[170]

---

[166] Valdés to Leiden, 17 June 1574 and 4 September 1574, UBL, Vulcanius 53.
[167] Orlers, *Beschrijvinge*, 459.
[168] Orlers, *Beschrijvinge*, 482-483.
[169] Orlers, *Beschrijvinge*, 497-498.
[170] The complete text of this letter: 'Para el magistrado y pueblo de Leyden, Obstinados Leidenses contra Dios, y contra vuestro Rey y Sennor. Aunqui no es digna de misericordia buestro grande obstinacion, pero siendo la voluntad de Su Magestad clementissima de

Again four days later, Valdés wrote another letter in Spanish to the city leaders of Leiden about the delegates and a few days later the passports followed. They could also bring open letters for Fernando de Lannoy and for Leideners living at present in Haarlem or Utrecht.[171]

In a letter from Requesens to the King dated 1 September we find news that the rebels had broken several dykes and were on their way with three hundred small boats. Valdés still thought he could stop them.[172] History would prove him wrong. King Philip II received one document with the

acceptar os con clemencia, si connoceis buestra culpa, no he querido faltar de scrivir os estos ringlones para haser os la ultima protestation (como por esto os hago) de que rindays la tierra a Su Magestad y yo en su nombre os prometo la fee de Christiano, y de cavallero, que todos sereis per donados generalmente vidas y haziendas sin excepcion ninguna, y aunque sean monsr. De Nortvick el commissario Brunchorst, y Piter Ariars burgomaestre, consiguiran esta gratia infaliblemente. Y para que meior podays considerar y determinar loque mas os conviene, os doy de termino por todo el lunes que viene seis deste mes, en el qual tiempo podreis libremente embiar una, dos, o mas personas a tractar con migo sobre este particular, embiando adelante un tambor, que por la presente concedo salbo conducto para venir, y tornar, libremente a las personas que embiaredes, y no os dexeis enganar de vanas esperancas de succorro, pues lo que mas os conviene es la gratia de Su Magestad, que se os offrece, y sed ciertos (que si aceptais lo que os affresco) en mi terneis un buen amigo. Pero si per severays en vuestro ruyn proposito, creed me, que pasareys por el cuchillo de iustitia, Dat. en Leyderdorp, 4 de Septiembre 1574. Francisco de Valdés'. Valdés to Leiden, Leiderdorp, 4-9-1574, UBL, Vulcanius 53; Fruin, 'Beleg', 427.

[171] The complete text: 'A los señores burgomaestros y magistrado de la villa de Leyden, Sennores burgomaestros, he recevido su letra y perque en ella ay algunos particulares, a los quales no se puedo responder, ni satisfaser enteramente por letra holgaro mucho que embien los quatro diputados que dizen con los quales yo pretendo communicar algunas cosas del servicio de Su Magestad y bien de sa villa, lo qual hecho si me pareciere comvenir y ser necessario que pasen al Principe de Oranie yo lohare y en caso que no comviniere yo prometo mi paalabra de dexair los tornar libremente a la villa luego, a la ora que quisieren sinque se les de ympedimento ni ngunoo y bien sera que los quatro deputados que venieren trayan comission del magistrado y gobierno des sa villa, para responder me a algunos cosas que pretendo tractar con ellos del servicio de Su Magestad. Datum en Leyderdorp, 6 de Septiembre 1574. Francisco de Valdés'. Orlers, *Beschrijvinge*, 501; 'Francisco de Valdés, maestro del campo general del exercito de Su Magestad en Hollanda, por la presente conzedemos salbo conducto y licentia, a una o a dos personas de la villa de Leyden para que puedan veir a Leyderdorp a tratar comigo algunas cosas del servicio de Su Magestad y que puedan traer las letras que quisieren abiertas para el sr. Conde de La Rocha [Fernando de Lannoy], y para quales quiera otros burgeses de Leyden de los que al presente est an en Vtrecht, o Harlem, y para que azi mismo puedan tornar se libremente a su villa, quado quisieren. Dada en Leyderdorp a 9 de Septiembre 1574. Valga este pasaporte por dos dias. Ibidem, 501-502.

[172] Requesens to Philip II, Antwerp, 1 September 1574, CP III, n. 1388 (AGS, E. 560); Requesens to Juan de Zúñiga, 7 September 1574, NCD V, 184-186.

most important points of Valdés's letters from 15, 17, and 18 September. His letters from 21 and 23 September would reach the King by way of complete copies. It shows the importance of the siege of Leiden, but it also indicates how well the Spanish bureaucracy functioned. The King could follow the events at his desk through the letters of the commander leading the siege. These documents also give us the opportunity to feel what it must have been like for Valdés, when the water slowly flowed in the direction of Leiden.

As the salty water from the sea could reach Leiden only if all the dykes between the river Maas and Leiden were broken, it was up to Valdés to defend the dykes. If the boats could pass over the fields, Leiden would be lost. Standing on the dykes near Zoetermeer, Valdés was very surprised at this new situation in which he had to defend them with his troops: "as it had never been seen in Holland that dykes were broken to flood the land, instead of making them stronger to defend themselves from the water".[173] He did what he could, but "if the heavens are against me, I will have to be defeated by the flood, as you can call it, but not by the enemy".[174] In a letter written by William of Orange he had intercepted in 1573, he had read that breaking the locks would flood the lands, never to be recovered. If that is what the rebels wanted, the Spanish commander stated, he was ready to do it himself:

> It has seemed to me [important] to inform Your Excellency so he understands that if at any given time he would be served by flooding this country, it is in his hands, because they have started with it, and if they persist in their obstinate rebellion they deserve to be drowned.[175]

---

[173] 'Pues jamas en Holanda se ha visto romper los diques para anegarla, sino crecerlos siempre para defenderse del agua'. Letters from Requesens to Valdés, 15, 17 and 18 September 1574, Zoeterwoude, 21 and 23 September 1574, Zoeterwoude and Leiden, copies, AGS, E. 560, 68, 91-94. The letters from Zoeterwoude also in IVDJ; CP III, n. 1394, 1399, 1400.

[174] 'Si el cielo me fuere contrario vencerme ha el diluvio que tal se puede llamar, pero no el enemigo'. Ibidem.

[175] 'Hame parescido dar dello aviso a vuestra excelencia para que entienda que siempre que fuere servido de anegar este pays esta en su mano y pues ellos han dado principio a lo hazer si perseveran en su obstinada rebelion bien merecen ser anegados'. Idem, 17 September 1574.

It is one of the quotations from the beginning of this chapter. It was a very aggressive proposition, but born out of anger for the new self-destructive policy of the rebels, who wanted to destroy their own country. Before reaching this point he had gone through a whole series of views on the conflict, starting from a distant professional military view, to even a positive belief in the good inhabitants of the Low Countries fighting against the rebels. His disappointment cannot be separated from his earlier optimism. It was not caused by some kind of natural Spanish cruelty, as the Black Legend would like to make us believe.

On 21 September Valdés had to leave the dykes because of the water; ships were already sailing over the fields: "with more reason you can now better call it an ocean".[176] Also because of the high winds he feared that soon the ships could sail everywhere. Most of the houses in Delft, Rotterdam and Gouda had already been flooded, and he did not understand why the rebels flooded three cities in order to save one. He called this the work of the "diabolical obstinacy of wicked rebels" ("*diabolica ostinacion de malvados rebeldes*"). And again, he offered to Requesens that he would open the dykes himself: "if it is relieved and Your Excellency gives me a licence to open the sluices of Maassluis I will drown these bad people, because they do not deserve less punishment than this".[177]

By this time Valdés was completely left out of the negotiations between Lannoy and the Leiden Mayors. He realised that now that the rescue fleet was on its way the inhabitants of Leiden would certainly not surrender. Meanwhile his Spanish soldiers were standing up to their knees in water and becoming ill, his Germans refused to move unless they were paid, and the Walloons had started plundering. However, in his letters he kept faith with the situation, or perhaps we should say that he did his best to give that impression to Requesens: "the difficulties at any given time are so many and so enormous, but they do not make me lose my spirit".[178]

This is the last we hear from Valdés before the end of the siege some ten days later. There are still two more letters from Requesens to Philip II.[179] In one of them the Governor-general expressed his doubts about a pardon for the inhabitants of Leiden. As there were no soldiers in the

---

[176] 'Con mas razon se puede agora llamar mar oceano'. Ibidem, 21 September 1574.

[177] 'si se socorren y vuestra excelencia me da licencia abrire las esclussas de Meslanclus [Maassluis] y acabare de anegar tan mala gente pues no merecen menos castigo que este'. AGS, E. 560, 91-94.

[178] 'Las difficultades tantas que a un tiempo se offrecen, son muchas y muy grandes, las quales no me han de hazer perder de animo'. Ibidem, 23 September 1574.

[179] Requesens to Philip II, Antwerp, 25 and 27 September 1574, AGS, E. 560, f. 41, 73; CP III, n. 1406, 1408.

city, the burghers had made the decision to resist. Maybe it would be better to kill them all as a lesson to the other cities, demonstrating that they could not continue to resist and hope they could still be pardoned. These words are not from the feared Duke of Alba, but from Requesens, who had started his government following a reconciliation policy. It shows again how opinions could change dramatically over time as a result of events. Requesens also feared that even if there was a treaty, he probably could not stop his men from sacking the city, as they had held on for so long only in the hope of pillage. On 27 September Requesens advised the King to start fighting the rebels with water and fire.

The first letter on the lifting of the siege on 3 October was written by paymaster Alameda in Utrecht, who had heard the bad news from a Spanish captain. Requesens heard about the lifting on 7 October through a courier of Lannoy's. A day before he had still written a long letter to the King about the siege, not knowing that it had already been ended. He waited until 10 October to send a letter to the King with the bad news. By then, still no direct letter from Valdés had arrived. His first letter to Requesens was written on 17 October, but it was all about actual problems, without any comments on the events in Leiden.[180] In this case the rhetoric of silence was well used by Valdés.

King Philip wrote a letter from Madrid on 22 October, answering Requesens on the change of policy in the Low Countries.[181] It is a beautifully elaborated policy letter that shows how the royal government was weighing the different possibilities. There should be severe punishment, but at the same time the King wanted to treat his subjects as mildly as possible. Flooding everything would also damage other regions, so burning the villages would be better, to leave the rebels without food in order to force them to leave. The end of the letter is remarkable: after discussing all possibilities, the King left the decision to Requesens to do as the situation called for. Though Philip II has often been seen as incapable of delegating, at this crucial point he left the decision to his representative in the Low Countries.[182]

---

[180] Alameda to Requesens, Utrecht, 5 October 1574, AGS E. 560; Requesens to Philip II, Antwerp, 10 October 1574, Idem, CP III, n. 1410 and 1414; Valdés to Requesens, The Hague, 17 October 1574; Idem, Haarlem, 22 October 1574, AGS, E. 560, f. 2-3; Requesens to Philip II, 6 October 1574, NCD V, 361-368.
[181] Philip II to Requesens, Madrid, 22 October 1574, AGS E. 561; CP III, n. 1415.
[182] Parker, *Felipe II*, 582-589.

When writing the letter the King still did not know that the siege of Leiden had already been lifted.[183] On 6 November Requesens would inform the King that he had given orders to Valdés and the stadtholder of Holland to break several dykes in Holland, but without damaging Haarlem and Amsterdam. However, Hierges had informed Requesens that this would not get all the cities of Holland and Zeeland out of rebel hands, and that from Zeeland the enemy could also flood parts of Flanders causing much damage to the surroundings of Antwerp.[184] And first the royal troops had to leave Holland.[185] The implementation of the new policy had to be postponed.

Leonor Álvarez Francés has extensively studied the portrayal of Valdés in chronicles and histories from Spain and the Low Countries, concluding that authors created their own Valdés depending on the purpose of their text: "a fabricated character with a rhetorical function". If a text wanted to highlight the unity and other positive qualities of the defenders, then the image of Valdés became more negative, while more neutral texts also offered a more neutral description of the Spanish commander. In the first text printed during the siege, *Een waerachtig verhael*, Valdés was even completely missing. Jan Fruytiers's *Corte beschrijvinghe*, published shortly after the lifting of the siege, used Valdés as protagonist in a comparison between the siege of Leiden and the sieges of Jerusalem, Samaria and Bethulia in the Bible. The Spaniards in 1574 played the part of the Assyrians; Valdés is portrayed as the rabshakeh, the commander of the Assyrian army, who in vain tried to convince the King of Judah to surrender with his 'beautiful promises'.[186]

## Mutiny

Several months later, Valdés wrote a long letter to the Duke of Alba in Spain, in which he said he had already sent him a report on "the strange manner of how Leiden was relieved" ("*la estraña manera como se socorrio Leiden*"), unfortunately lost.[187] However he did summarise the events again:

---

[183] On 26 October, the King received a letter from Requesens dated 6 October in which the news of the lifting of the siege was not yet included, NCD V, 361.
[184] Gilles of Berlaymont, Baron of Hierges, died 18 June 1579.
[185] Requesens to Philip II, Brussels, 6 November 1574, AGS E. 560, CP III, n. 1421.
[186] Álvarez Francés, 'Fabrication'; 'Waerachtig verhael'; Fruytiers, 'Corte beschryvinghe'.
[187] Valdés to Alba, Amersfoort, 28 December 1574, AA, C/54, 76.

> Breaking the dykes in twenty-five places and turning the land into an ocean, and travelling over the fields as if it were the sea, with eighty rowing ships, smaller ships and more than three hundred boats. But what they did in order to save one city meant a knife for all the villages of the countryside (*plat pais*) that were completely drowned.[188]

In the letter he explained to the Duke that even after the lifting of the siege on 3 October he had still been in control of the situation. He had let in a large quantity of salty water that would force the cities "to return to the obedience of His Majesty or leave the lands".[189] According to the commander, the real origin of the defeat in Holland was the mutiny:

> Being in such a state, they were favoured by the devil, as God permitted it because of our sins, because the Spaniards of my tercio mutinied and not satisfied with their payments they did such an infamous thing as to leave Holland and taking me with them as their prisoner, and because of their example the Germans and Walloons also left.[190]

Is Valdés speaking the truth to his patron, or was he trying to clear himself of any culpability for the loss of control in Holland? The chronicler from Utrecht on the contrary blames the whole mutiny on Valdés himself. The soldiers wanted payment out of the "large robbery he had received in Holland from ransomming (*brandschatten*), compositions, passports, licences and other means of extraction".[191]

The correspondence between the commander and the mutineers shows that Valdés did everything possible to continue the struggle against the rebels, and he tried to control the dykes and fortresses in the region, though the mutiny made it almost impossible to function properly.[192] This very

---

[188] 'Abriendo en veynte y cinco partes los diques y haziendo de la tierra mar oceano y caminando con ochenta navios de remo y muchas charruas y mas de trezientas barcas otras por los prados como pudiera por la mar. Pero lo que hizieron para remedio de una villa fue cuchillo para todas las villas del plat pais porque quedaron anegadas totalmente'. Ibidem.

[189] 'Reduzirse a la obedientia de Su Magestad o dexar las tierras'. Ibidem.

[190] 'Estando en este estado les favorecio el diablo permitiendolo Dios por nuestros pecados porque se amotinaron los españoles de mi tercio y no contentos con pedir sus pagas hizieron una cosa tan ynfame como fue salirse de Holanda llevandome preso y al explo suyo se salieron los Alemanes y Balones'. Ibidem.

[191] 'Utrechtsche kroniek', 162.

[192] The study of these letters is also part of Beatriz Santiago Belmonte's research.

special correspondence between a commander and his mutineers consists of some thirty letters dated between 6 November 1574 and 18 February 1575. Until 27 November he was still in The Hague, but afterwards we find him in Beverwijk, Muiden, Utrecht, Amersfoort and Maastricht. At first he was held in detention at his home, but in the end he successfully escaped. The letters show how Valdés was caught between the service of his King, the protection of the population of the Low Countries, and the interests of his troops. There was no easy solution for the Spanish commander.

Already in the first letter we find a typical aspect of Spanish military correspondence between a commander and his mutineers. As the mutiny had frozen the hierarchical relationship between the officer and his soldiers, Valdés addressed the letter at the top of the paper to the 'muy magníficos señores'.[193] This does not imply that he was not critical of their behaviour: "I am not surprised that the other nations do it [not listening] but we give them the example of disobedience".[194] We witness how the mutineers crossed the usual boundaries between soldiers and officers, and how Valdés tried to maintain his position: "when they want to ask me something, the letter has to be signed, as it is not reasonable that I answer to something that may have been written by whatever soldier that has its mind to it".[195] In another letter he also stated that "it was never done, nor was it normal, that the minsters of His Majesty that govern these soldiers should respond to what is asked of them by way of placards, because often such placards are posted by people with bad intentions, even villainous ones".[196] He only wanted to talk to the official representatives of the mutineers and react only to their letters. In another letter he stated that they had to respect him as he was still their Maestre de campo and otherwise it would damage his reputation.[197] In

---

[193] Valdés to the *Electo* and the soldiers of the tercio of Italy, The Hague, 6 November 1574, BZ 106D2. Comparable to the 'muy nobles señores' used during Spanish mutinies in Italy under Charles V. Sherer, 'All of us', 911.

[194] 'Yo no me maravillo que las demas naçiones lo hagan [not listening] pues nosotros les damos exemplo de poca obidientia'. Valdés to the *Electo* and the soldiers of the tercio of Italy, The Hague, 6 November 1574, BZ 106D2.

[195] 'Quando me pidieren alguna cosa venga firmada la letra, que no es razon que responda yo a lo que podria escrevir qualquier soldado que se le antojase'. Ibidem.

[196] 'Nunca fue ni es costumbre que los ministros de Su Magestad que goviernan gente de guerra respondan a lo que por via de carteles se les pide, pues muchas vezes los tales son puestos por personas mal yntencionadas y aun facinorosas'. Valdés to the *Electo* and the soldiers of the tercio of Italy, The Hague, 18 November 1574, BZ 106D6.

[197] Valdés to the *Electo* and the soldiers of the tercio of Italy, The Hague, 19 November 1574, BZ 106D7.

a letter to Requesens his tone was both negative and comprehensive: "It hurts my soul to see all those people so in need and unhappy…the ruin actions of these mutineers".[198]

As the mutineers threatened to leave the County of Holland, he put his main arguments to the fore: "I convince myself that such honourable and valiant soldiers will not do such an ugly thing against their honour as to leave the fortresses without orders from Your Excellency".[199] Honour became the key argument at a time when the normal hierarchical structure had stopped functioning. The mutineers now also had to take him at his word. As from 18 November he was confined to his room by *electo* Marcos Naranjo, who put double guards in front of his door and ordered them to let nobody through, not even the representatives of the other nations.[200]

He tried to remain reasonable: "If I am not mistaken there are two main reasons that have caused this mutiny", referring to the payments and the housing for the coming winter.[201] He tried to convince them that money was on its way, and he suggested besides Haarlem and The Hague several rich villages in Holland for their winter quarters. If necessary, also the village of Wassenaar, which until then had been housing a cavalry unit, might be used.

In this situation of crisis Valdés maintained his vengeful tone about the punishment of the inhabitants: "if I could throw a pike height of water on Holland, I would do so voluntarily".[202] As a pike could easily measure more than five metres, this was a very harsh way of expressing himself, but it is difficult to know whether he was maybe thinking this

---

[198] 'En el alma siento el ver toda esta gente tan necesitada y descontenta… el ruyn proceder destos alterados'. Valdés and Pedro de Paz to Requesens (copy), The Hague, 10 to 22 November 1574, AGS, E. 560, f. 39.

[199] 'Me persuado que soldados tan honrrados y valerosos no haran cosa tan fea a sus honrras como seria abandonar los fuertes sin orden de su excelencia'. Valdés to the *Electo* and the soldiers of the tercio of Italy, The Hague, 18 November 1574, BZ 106D6.

[200] Valdés to the *Electo* and the soldiers of the tercio of Italy, The Hague, 19 November 1574, BZ 106D7.

[201] 'Si no me engaño dos causas principales han sido las que han causado este alteracion'. Valdés to the *Electo* and the soldiers of the tercio of Italy, The Hague, 23 November 1574, BZ 106D8.

[202] 'Si pudiese echar una pica de agua en alto en Hollanda que lo haria de voluntad'. Valdés to the *Electo* and the soldiers of the tercio of Italy, The Hague, 24 November 1574, BZ 106D9. A whole set of document copies from 24-26 November 1574, including letters from Valdés to Requesens and from the mutineers and their *electo* to Valdés, can be found in AGS, E. 560, f. 40-42. The mentioned *electo* in these letters was still Diego Sánchez de Bahamonde, who was followed as *electo* by Marcos Naranjo.

phrase would be positively received by the mutineers. In the same letter he showed his desperation: "I do not see the hour we can leave this purgatory" ("*no veo la ora que salir deste purgatorio*").

One day later, Valdés wrote a letter to Requesens in which he described the dire circumstances:

> This morning at dawn their Sergeant-major came with a lantern and followed by musketeers. They entered my room shooting as they usually do, putting their arquebuses to my breast and demanding the letter I had from Your Excellency'.[203]

The devilish (*endemoniados*) mutineers threatened to go to serve the Prince of Orange, or to go to Ghent until they were paid and then leave for France. The threat to join the rebels must have been meant to frighten the commander, but it did happen that Spanish mutineers joined the rebel army.[204] The origin of the mutiny could be found in the behaviour of many officials who had at first supported the mutiny. They behaved in a terrible manner: "their insolences and shameless deeds are so numerous that it is impossible to describe them successfully".[205]

As he could not stand the situation any longer, he decided to escape: "the shameless Naranjo has forced me to separate myself from this tercio, as he has so much power and evilness, as a very low person, telling me in my presence that he is going to hang me".[206] However, at the same time, Valdés introduced a new way of connecting to the mutineers: "I advise them as a father" ("*yo les aconsejo como padre*"). In the next letter the addressees were even described as "very magnificent lords and children of mine" ("*muy magníficos señores y hijos míos*") and the letter is signed "your father who loves and serves you" ("*su padre que los ama y*

---

[203] 'Esta mañana al amaneçer vino su sargento mayor con la laterna que tras de moxqueteros y entraron en mi camara dando bozes como suelen poniendose los arcabuzes a los pechos que les diesse la letra que tenia de vuestra excelencia'. Valdés to Requesens, The Hague, 25 November 1574, BZ 96D27.

[204] Fagel, 'Orange's Spanish mulatto', 107.

[205] 'Son tantas sus ynsolencias y desverguenças que no es posible acertarlas a escivir'. Valdés to Requesens, 25 November 1575, BZ 96D27.

[206] 'La desverguença de Naranjo me ha obligado a que me aparte deste tercio, pues tanto poder tiene avra la maldad que ose y un tal omo vil como ese a dezirme en mi presencia que me ahorcara''la desverguença de Naranjo me ha obligado a que me aparte deste tercio, pues tanto poder tiene avra la maldad que ose y un tal omo vil como ese a dezirme en mi presencia que me ahorcara'. Valdés to the *Electo* and the soldiers of the tercio of Italy, Beverwijk, 1 December 1574, BZ 106D10.

*servira*").²⁰⁷. All through the rest of the mutiny, this wording of a loving father and his children would be continued. It clearly does not imply an improvement of their mutual relationship, but it is a way of maintaining some kind of power over the mutineers. During the Spanish mutinies in Italy under Charles V the mutineers were addressed in a comparable way as "brothers" ("*hermanos*").²⁰⁸

Around Muiden and Weesp some of the mutineers were clearly harassing the population: putting bounties on the local population and in Weesp it even led to the death of many inhabitants:²⁰⁹

> By such evil deeds we make ourselves hated by God and the whole world, and we cause the revolt of the whole country against us. For the love of God, this has to be remedied, and those who do such things must be punished severely, as to prove that this mutiny is not done in order to perpetrate and perform villainous acts, but to request what is rightly owed to them.²¹⁰

He refers to the honour of the tercio and their reputation, calling the violent acts very ugly: "your graces have to promise me that there will be no disorders in this tercio, but that they [the soldiers] live with modesty and look for the service of God and King".²¹¹ During these moments of crisis the author of the *Espejo y disciplina militar* was putting sentences on paper that could easily have been taken from his own treatise. In another part of the letter he also used his personal history with the soldiers as an argument for them to listen to him:

> By the love of God, you have the whole country revolted, and close to taking up arms against us. I beg you not to let yourself be guided by your desires, because in this tercio there are valient soldiers who have the discretion and the prudence to govern

---

²⁰⁷ Valdés to the Señores mis hijos electo y soldados de mi tercio, Muiden, 8 December 1574, BZ 106D12.
²⁰⁸ Sherer, 'All of us', 911; Sherer, *Warriors*, 124-125.
²⁰⁹ Valdés to the Señores mis hijos electo y soldados de mi tercio, Muiden, 10 December 1574, BZ 106D13; Idem, 'de casa', 16 December 1574, BZ 106D15A.
²¹⁰ 'Con semejantes maldades nos hazemos a Dios y al mundo odiosos, y damos causa a que todo el pais se levante contra nosotros, por amor de Dios que se ponga en ello remedio, y que se castiguen con rigor los que tales cosas hazen y no parezca que esta alteracion sea hecho para perpetrar y hazer vellaquerias y no para pedir lo que justamente se les debe'. Ibidem.
²¹¹ 'Prometerme vuestras mercedes por ella que no se haria desorden en ese tercio sino que se viviria con mucho recato mirando por el servicio de Dios y del Rey'. Ibidem.

armies. Please return to your senses and I promise as Christian and hidalgo to be a very good intermediary with Your Excellency, and a true father who will satisfy you completely, in paying all that is owed and that you are lodged to your satisfaction. I ask you to trust me, as your graces know that I have never fooled you, and less concerning fraud. For this reason and other motivations, it would be better to speak in person than communicate in writing. I would be very served if you would receive me and listen to me.[212]

The violent killing of the population by the mutineers was "in disservice of God and King, and so damaging the honour of the whole Spanish nation, and it is true that this was an enormous (*bastantissima*) reason for all the states rising against us".[213] He had already used the pronoun 'we' (*nosotros*) in the meaning of all Spaniards, but now he clearly referred to the Spanish nation as an entity.

However, at this point he saw new possibilities for overcoming the mutiny. He connected the last quotation with a call to forget about the past and think about the future:

> I think your graces remember how many times in meetings with me and in letters I have written to you, I have foreseen the evil deeds that have occured. However, we cannot remedy these solely by recalling them, and it is better that we forget about them to prevent them from hindering us in the things we have to remedy in the future.[214]

---

[212] 'Por amor de Dios que tienen ya todo el pais alterado, y muy çerca de tomar todos las armas contra nosotros, no se dexen, les suplico, guiar de sus apetitos pues ay en ese tercio tan valerosos soldados y que tienen discrecion y prudencia para governar exercitos, alleguense a la razon que yo les prometo como christiano y hijo dalgo de serles muy buen yntercesor con su excelencia, y verdadero padre para que se les de todo contentamiento assi en pagarles todo lo que se les deve como en que sean alojados a su contento, fien les suplico esto de mi, pues saben vuestras mercedes que nunca les engañe, ni menos en cosa alguna de lo que les a tocado de fraude, y por que estos y otros particulares se tratan mejor a boca que no por escrito recibire mucha merced en que me quieran oyr y dar audiencia'. Ibidem.

[213] 'En deservicio de Dios y del Rey, y tan en perjuyzio de la honrra de toda la nacion Española y es cierto que fuera bastantissima causa para que todos los estados se levantaran contra nosotros'. Valdés to the 'Señores mis hijos electo y soldados de mi tercio', Utrecht, 18 December 1574, BZ 106D14.

[214] 'Bien creo se acordaron vuestras mercedes quantas vezes en parlamentos que les he hecho y en cartas que les he escrito, he ante visto estos males que an suçedido los quales pues no se pueden remediar por traerlos a la memoria, mejor es que los olvidemos para que mas no nos lastimen y que en lo por venir se ponga remedio'. Ibidem.

He praised all the good men in the tercio, "people with a clear mind and full of discretion" ("*personas de tan claro juyzio y de tanta discrecion*"), but they had been led by "ignorant men, ruinous and with bad intentions" ("*hombres ignorantes, precipitosos y de malas yntenciones*"). Valdés suggested that every company name two deputies to work together with the *electo* and his council.

By this time the mutineers had arrived around Utrecht, the city where they had been badly treated after returning from the east in April. In a letter to the Duke of Alba Valdés tells the story of what happened in Utrecht:

> They arrived at the quarter of Utrecht situated outside the Amsterdam gate, that has walls and a moat, and guarded by three companies of Germans. They attacked it and six of them were killed, with ten more wounded. Their foolishness grew even greater and four days later, on the seventeenth of this month, they attacked the city through a gate next to the citadel [Vredenburg] and they put up their ladders and climbed the wall. Ten men entered with their Sergeant-major and they made the burghers that were guarding this part of the wall flee. And certainly, they would have succeeded with their plan had not a piece of artillery broken six supports of the ladder, breaking their connection. The soldiers from the citadel fought against them as if they were enemies and they killed up to forty, and wounded an equal number. They retreated from the outside quarters of the city and that night they went to some hamlets on the road to Rhenen with the intention of continuing in the direction of Brabant. But as they did not find boats on the riverside, they changed direction and went to two hamlets in the Duchy of Guelders.[215]

---

[215] 'Vinieron al burgo de Utrecht que sta a la puerta de Amsterdam que tiene muro y foso y estavan a la guardia del tres compañias de Alemanes y le assaltaron a do murieron seis dellos y fueron heridos hasta diez. Paso adelante su desatino y quatro dias despues a dezisiete deste dieron el asalto a la tierra por una puerta que sta junto al castillo y arrimaron sus escalas y subieron en el muro y entraron dentro diez con su sargento mayor y hizieron huyr los burgeses que stavan a la guardia de aquella parte del muro y cierto ellos salieron con su yntento si una pieça de artilleria no les derribara seis escalas por donde se les rompio el hilo y los soldados del castillo pelearon contra ellos como contra enemigos y assi les mataron hasta quarenta y fueron heridos otros tantos. Retitaronse luego de los burgos y fueronse aquella noche a unos casares de buelta de Renen [Rhenen] con determinacion de pasar en Brabante, pero como no hallaron barcas en toda la ribera torzieron el camino y vinieron a dos casares del ducado de Gueldres'. Valdés to Alba, Amersfoort, 28 December 1574, AA, C/54, 76, 80.

We can find an extensive description of the events in an Utrecht chronicle, but there Valdés does not play a specific role. We find, however, the story of the good Spaniard, Francisco Fernández Dávila, the governor of the castle who chose the side of the inhabitants of the city against his fellow Spaniards, using his sword to force his soldiers to fire their guns and even threatening to use the cannons of the citadel against the mutineers.[216]

In a letter from 19 December to Requesens he informed his Captain-general that the mutineers seemed to be pacified, most probably because of the fatal events in Utrecht: "begging me for pardon and promising that they would follow orders".[217] However, they still did not listen to Valdés's orders so he kept fearing the worst:

> But the whole country has revolted against the Spanish name, and it was not considered good that these mutineers travelled across these states. If the mutineers persevere in their evil plans, they will become the cause of great scandals and revolts in all these estates. Because though we have defended the entrance to the city [of Utrecht] with so many deaths of men from our nation, they criticise us and say that we do not kill these Spaniards. The villagers walk around hunting to find them [the Spanish mutineers] on the roads, and with good reason, as these devilish men act in such a manner'.[218]

By the end of December Valdés had arrived in Maastricht and the whole episode was finally coming to a close.[219] By that time, the tone was back to normal again, leaving out the references to fathers and children, and Valdés ended his last letter from this period with a formal "in the service of your graces" ("*al servicio de vuestras mercedes*").[220] The unsuccessful siege of Leiden was dominated by two successive mutinies in the Spanish army

---

[216] 'Utrechtsche kroniek', 164-185.
[217] 'Pidiéndome perdón y prometiendo que harian lo que les mandasse'. Valdés to Requesens, 19 December 1574, AGS, E. 559, f. 116.
[218] 'Pero esta todo este país tan alterado contra el nombre español que no le parescio era bien atravessassen estados hasta ver ado para esta gente amotinada, la qual si persevera en su malvado propósito temo sea causa de grandes escándalos y alteraciones en todos los estados pues con aver nosotros defendido la entrada de la tierra con muerte de tantos de nuestra nación nos escapen las casas y dizen que hazemos que no matamos a estos españoles y el villanaje anda a caza de los que topa por los caminos y a todos les sobra razón pues estos endemoniados proceden de tal manera'. Ibidem.
[219] Valdés to Albornoz, Maastricht, 16 January 1575, AA, C/54, 78.
[220] Valdés to the 'muy magnificos señores, electo y soldados del tercio de Ytalia', Maastricht, 18 February 1575, BZ 106D19.

that – as Valdés explains – were a main cause of the revolt of the people against the Spaniards. The mutiny had not only made it impossible to beat the rebels, but it also turned the whole country against the Spanish soldiers.[221] Though Valdés had tried to minimise the violence of the mutineers against the population, a subsequent mutiny in 1576 would definitively turn the Spanish soldiers into hated men in the eyes of a large part of the population of the Low Countries.

## Final years

In June 1575 Valdés was successfully besieging the castle of Buren, originally a possession of William of Orange. In a letter he complained about "being again very tired by the pains in my stomach. Too much exercise of the campaign and too much calmness in the trenches, have broken me again and put me in great danger".[222] His health clearly was a problem now; at around fifty-seven years of age, he was an old and tired officer, already having lived continuously in the Low Countries for almost eight years. In 1575 he also participated with his tercio in the siege of the small Holland town of Oudewater, ending with the terrible sack of that town on 7 August. He was however not the chief commander of the royal army that fought under command of the Lord of Hierges.[223] Again, Valdés did not receive the honour of a victory. At the same time, his personal image was also not stained by the consequent brutal sack, though the Spanish soldiers involved in it were most certainly men from his own tercio.

For these last years of his life we have only a few letters from Valdés to Alba and his secretary, demonstrating a very irregular correspondence between the Duke and his client. On 2 July 1575 he was answering a letter from Albornoz dated 12 March and, as before, the letter is about the situation of his daughter, Francisca, and about payments. The marriage between his daughter and the Portuguese Antonio Brito was still not resolved, and a payment by the Duke to Valdés of 1,500 ducats lacked the official paperwork, and "it is a matter of honour that they cannot charge me with having taken anything without the order of the

---

[221] Parker, *Felipe II*, 586-587.
[222] 'Estar otra vez muy fatigado de mis dolores destomago que con el demasiado exercitio de la campaña y el sereno de la trinchea me a deribado otra vez y puesto en harto peligro'. Valdés and the captains Pedro de Paz and Diego de Felices to Requesens (copies), Buren, 26 and 27 June 1575, AGS, E. 562, f. 138.
[223] Boon, *Oudewater*; Kuijpers, 'Creation'; Pollmann and Kuijpers, 'Why remember terror?'.

Captain-general".²²⁴ The marriage affair was still playing out in 1578. It seems that De Brito was disinherited by his father, and both the Spanish ambassador and the chaplain of the Portuguese queen became involved in the affair, "one of the strangest you have ever seen".²²⁵

When Captain Diego de Felices went to Spain in April 1576, Valdés gave him a letter for the Duke about the situation in the Low Countries, as well as a letter directed to Philip II. In the short note to the King he informed him that he was now staying in Brussels "where I went from Holland because of my bad health" ("*ado por mi poca salud vine de Hollanda*"), again showing that he suffered from health problems. The lettter to Alba was more informative:

> The dangerous state in which the things from here are is caused by the length of time it is already in ruins (because of the great necessities that they suffer), and also because of the unexpected death of the Comendador Mayor [Requesens], leaving everything abandoned.²²⁶

Valdés also realised the importance of the pamphlet campaigns by the rebels and the fact that he used the word 'yoke' (*jugo*) in his letter shows he was perfectly aware of the language of rebellion that could be found in the pamphlets:

> This caused the declaration of ruinous intentions and evil desires by some particulars, and especially by the people (*populo*), not only for the great number of publications (*beletines*) they have produced, in which they threaten that if they do not sign the

---

²²⁴ 'Es caso de honrra de que no me puedan ymputar que yo tome cosa alguna sin orden del Capitan-general'. Valdés to Albornoz, Culemborg, 2 July 1575, AA, C/54, 79.

²²⁵ 'Que es de los mas estraños que has visto', Francisco Cano to Secretary Zayas, Xabregas, 8 August 1578, AGS, E. 395, 136; Juan de Silva to Zayas, Lisbon, 9 May 1578, CD XL (1862) 5-6. I thank Adalid Nievas Rojas (Universidad de Girona) for the reference to Cano's letter and for providing me with a copy. Antonio's father, Ambrosio de Brito, came from Madeira, and he is probably the same person as Ambrosio de Brito Pestana who married Ines de Bettencourt. His sister Maria was a lady to Queen Mary of Portugal and married Aleixo de Abreu. In earlier publications I have assumed that the letter from Juan de Silva concerned the commander's marriage to Magdalena Moons, but it most certainly refers to the marriage affairs of his daughter.

²²⁶ 'Del peligroso estado en que se hallan las cosas de aqui asi por estar ellas mucho ha (a causa de las grandes neçesidades que se padezen) en rruin termino como por que la ynpensada muerte del comendador mayor, dexando todo esto desamparado'. Valdés to Alba, Brussels, 14 April 1576, AA, C/54, 81.

peace there will soon be large movements to be seen, and that they will not give more money, but in their discussions they speak with more and more freedom… It all breathes towards throwing us out of here and getting rid of the yoke, and this design, I do not know to whom of the natives of these states this looks bad. I, my lord, see everything much in need of the appointment of a new governor by His Majesty, because otherwise, I am afraid this building will not fall down in one blow.[227]

Just as Valdés was writing this letter, news arrived from Spain stating that the Council of State was to govern until the arrival of the new Governor-general:

This has given great satisfaction to the whole country. By God I hope that the spirits of the people will quiet down, although (as Your Excellency knows very well) there is little to trust from a people that so easily changes its opinions (*moverse*).[228]

His undersigning as the Duke's servant and creature indicates that Valdés was still thinking in terms of patronage. The same tone can be found in a letter to the Duke from 17 August 1576 from Antwerp, largely written in cipher.[229] He had already written some ten days earlier, but though some people thought things were going better now, he remained very worried: "the people are as armed and agitated as the first day, and the universal voice of the whole country says the Spaniards have to leave".[230] The Duke of Aarschot in particular was described as the enemy, exchanging letters with William of Orange. The Duke had used scandalous words, stating for example that "if he [the new Governor-general] came armed,

---

[227] 'A dado lugar para que las ruines yntençiones y malos deseos de algunos particulares se declaren, y prinçipalmente del populo, que no solo por muchos beletines que an hechado, por los quales amenazan que sino hazen las pazes que veran presto grandes movimientos y que no haran mas serviçio de dinero, pero en sus platicas dizen cada dia grandes libertades… todo aspira a hecharnos de aqui y a quitarse el jugo y este disigno, no se quien aya en estos estados de los naturales dellos que les parezca mal, yo señor veo esto muy neçesitado de que su magestad proveha con toda brebedad de governador, porque de otra manera, temo no caya de golpe este edifiçio'. Ibidem.

[228] 'Lo qual ha dado gran contentamiento a todo el pais, spero en Dios que se aquietaran mucho los animos del pueblo aunque (como vuestra excelencia mejor sabe) ay poco que fiar del populo que tan facil es ense mover'. Ibidem.

[229] Valdés to Alba, Antwerp, 17 August 1576, AGS E. 567, f. 69.

[230] 'Esta el pueblo tan armado y alborotado como el primer dia y la boz universal de todo el pays es que salgan los españoles'. Ibidem.

they would not let him enter because they did not want to suffer any longer what they have suffered until now and they would rather die".[231] Aarschot had also affirmed that though the German colonels supported the Spanish, he knew that paying the soldiers would bring them to their side. Closing his letter, after affirming that he had just received one from Alba of 31 July, he still hoped he would get his rewards in the end "if these things quiet down" ("*si estas cosas se aquietan*"), he being a servant of the Duke of Alba. The hopeful parenthetical expression demonstrates that he had not yet given up all dreams of a peaceful ending of the revolt.

Valdés finally left the Low Countries in 1577, to return quickly when Juan de Austria asked for the support of Spanish soldiers.[232] He would serve as Maestre de campo of the tercio of Sicily under Alexander Farnese, and as such he was involved in the siege and victory of Maastricht in 1579. His career did end with a victory, although not as commander in charge as in Leiden. Lope de Vega's *El asalto de Mastrique por el Príncipe de Parma* mentions Valdés several times as an experienced commander: "Francisco de Valdés, *anima, enseña, aconseja*" ("Francisco de Valdés gives spirit, teaches and gives council"). The old commander, ruined by the war, clearly was in no conditions to fight any more. According to chronicler Alonso Vázquez, during the siege of Maastricht the Duke of Parma got angry with Valdés for leaving his post to have his meal. Valdés replied, "when the King, our lord, sent him to serve under his hand, he perfectly well knew that he could not fight, as he saw him with both arms ruined". In 1580, he returned to Italy with his tercio, where he died that very same year.[233]

## An exemplary soldier

The character of this chapter is different from that of the three others, as Francisco de Valdés was not as famous in his own day as Julián, Sancho or Cristóbal, perhaps with the sole exception of the period of the siege of Leiden. Valdés also did not have descendants who would occupy themselves with the preservation of the memory of their family hero, except for a nephew who tried to increase his pay by referring to his

---

[231] 'Que si venia armado [the new Governor-general] que no la dexarian entrar porque ya no querian sufrir lo que hasta alli avian sufrido sino morir todos antes'. Ibidem.

[232] A short letter from Valdés to Juan de Austria, Antwerp, 13 December 1576, AGS, E. 569, f. 191.

[233] Sánchez Martín, 'Valdés'; Lope de Vega, 'Famosa tragicomedia', 439, 441, 465, 469; Vosters, *Nederlanden*, 214-215; Vázquez, 'Sucesos', I, 195.

famous uncle. This means that there are fewer comments on Valdés to be found in the chronicles of the time, and also that much less is known about his life. Fortunately we do have information on Valdés as the author of a military treatise, and the important memory culture of the siege of Leiden has offered the opportunity to describe the fame of this commander in his own time. As Leonor Álvarez Francés has shown, the rather meagre image of the commander could be filled in by different authors depending on the purpose of their own story.

For this reason, the emphasis has been put on Valdés' experience as reflected through his own letters, and contrasting this image with those that have survived of this commander: on one side, very positive as the husband of Magdalena Moons and the author of the treatise, but we also have the negative portrait of someone who was hated by the nobility of the Low Countries and who wrote that Holland should be flooded.

The first letters that are preserved show a rather ordinary military commander who was fulfilling his job in the Low Countries, seemingly rather bored and describing his long residence in these territories as a banishment. The enemy at first was a military one, a group of rebels that had to be defeated. He made a clear distinction between these rebels and the general population of the Low Countries. After he became involved in the conflict, we can see him even creating a positive image of the good Netherlanders, who also wanted to free themselves of the rebels. It will never be clarified whether his amorous relationship with Magdalena Moons had any influence in this respect, but it is, of course, tempting to draw this conclusion, or at least hint at the possibility. Anyway, he seems to have got closer to the local population because of his direct involvement with them as a Spanish commander on the ground who greatly depended on local support.

When it became evident that the siege of Leiden would not produce the success he must have craved, his positive image of the population diametrically reversed, and he became very negative about the Dutch population. The aggressive tone of this later period was not caused by a natural hatred of the Dutch and/or of Protestants, which is generally used as an explanation for the Spanish policy in the Low Countries. In this sense, Valdés is very different from Sancho Dávila, who did have a negative image of Protestants from the very beginning of the rebellion. Francisco de Valdés had tried to behave as a good Christian soldier, and again during the mutiny of his men he tried to reconcile the mutineers and limit their use of violence against the population. It is in this sense that the chapter is headed 'the exemplary soldier', as through his treatise he tried to show how a good soldier should behave, and during his lifetime he actually tried to live up to his standards.

However, this lived experience has little to do with the image of Valdés that was created in Leiden, especially beginning in the eighteenth century. Valdés was then turned into an extra, a walk-on, quietly standing next to Magdalena Moons as the real protagonist of the story. There he loses all colour and becomes the stereotype of a good person. However, this is not at all comparable to the positive image of Cristóbal de Mondragón, who was already seen as remarkably good during his own lifetime, both by other Spaniards and by Netherlanders.

Valdés' life and letters bring us closer to the lives of many of the other Spanish soldiers in the Low Countries, who were not great and famous commanders like Julián, Sancho and Mondragón, but who mostly did their job as well as possible, but were caught up in a difficult conflict with no easy soultion. They continued because they needed to be rewarded, but they kept on begging for a return to Spain. Also in this sense we may call Valdés 'an exemplary soldier'.

# General conclusion
# Episodic war narratives in comparison

## Chronicles, pamphlets and *relaciones*

In the preceding chapters on the episodic narratives related to four Spanish commanders, use has been made of a wide spectrum of different sources that sometimes agree, but often do not. In this general conclusion some comparisons regarding these different war narratives will be drawn, and the descriptions of the individual commanders will be placed in a broader perspective.

As was to be expected, there are differences to be found in the treatment of the events of the war between Spanish and Dutch chronicles. Spanish chroniclers often tried to conceal errors committed by the Spanish commanders, going so far as to convert an obvious defeat into a victory. Antonio Trillo, in particular, has a preference for this technique, as in the case of Julián's famous naval defeat at Reimerswaal in 1574, or when he turned Sancho's defeat near Maastricht in that same year into a victory.[1]

Our sources have also proved that not all stories existed in both cultures. The famous Dutch story of the dog saving William of Orange's life during the *camisada* by Julián never made it into the Spanish chronicles. This absence also seems to indicate that the Spaniards were never aware of the fact that they had nearly captured – or killed – the rebel leader. The same can be said about commander Gaspar de Robles, who possessed – and still possesses – a very particular fame in the Low Countries as the protagonist of positive stories that are not at all known in Spain.[2]

More in general, something similar can also be argued with regard to famous battles and sieges.[3] The Battle of Heiligerlee (May 1568), won by the rebels, figures prominently in Dutch history books, counting as the beginning of the Eighty Years' War, while Spanish authors pay much more attention to the subsequent Battle of Jemmingen (July 1568), won by the royal army.[4] The same process is visible regarding sieges, as

---

[1] For a comparable example see Thomas, 'How a defeat became a victory'.
[2] Fagel, 'Imagen'.
[3] Lamal, *News*; Lamal, 'Orecchie', Lamal, 'Internationale berichtgeving'.
[4] Fagel, Santiago Belmonte and Álvarez Francés, 'Eer en schuld'.

the sieges of Alkmaar and Leiden – both rebel victories – hardly figure in Spanish sources, while the siege of Haarlem appears prominently in Spanish historiographical works but has received much less attention in the history of the Low Countries. Interestingly, this focus on certain events can be found both in early modern chronicles and in more recent history works. It reveals one of the main weapons of historians: to decide what to include and what stories to omit, or occlude, contributing in this manner to the continuation of certain narratives. It also means that even the most factual descriptions possess a subjective character that is often overlooked, as is the case with the Spanish *relaciones* of the sixteenth century.

Another example that illustrates this dynamic is the story of the betrayal around the cruel punishment of Naarden. In Spanish sources there is no discussion of a possible false oath by Julián, while most of the local Dutch sources speak of a deceitful Spanish commander. However, all the first-hand texts by the Dutch were written by authors directly or indirectly involved in the negotiations. It would be very hard for a 'truth commission' to decide on the 'real facts'.

Historian P.C. Hooft, who made ample use of Bernardino de Mendoza's chronicle, more than once quoted the Spanish author more or less literally, but tended to alter Mendoza's line of argument, excluding or adding part of the story, for example around Julián's defeat at Reimerswaal. Where Mendoza described the mutual respect between the commander and the Governor-general, Hooft used the quotation to turn Romero into a typically arrogant Spaniard. However, to complicate matters, we also have a Spanish letter written on the capture of the Count of Egmont that perfectly coincides with the description given by Hooft.

Differences in episodic narratives do not involve just the different national traditions, since there were also clear differences between the individual Spanish and Dutch chronicles. Stories in Van Meteren often do not coincide with Hooft's descriptions, and we also encounter different anecdotes in the chronicles of Mendoza and Trillo, although both authors published in the same year and came from the same city. More interesting and less predictable is the evidence that a simple dichotomy between Spanish authors praising Spaniards and Dutch authors praising Dutchmen did not exist. Mendoza openly praised the rebel commanders during the Battle of Mookerheyde, completely unlike the image we receive from Trillo's text.

Spanish chronicles describe Sancho Dávila's participation in a series of battles in 1568 in various ways, connecting him with a specific battle or omitting him from the story of another. It is remarkable that Sancho is praised much more in letters and newsletters of the period itself, written directly at the time. This means that there is a clear difference in his protagonism between contemporary unpublished sources and the narrative sources by Trillo and Mendoza published much later. This difference is most certainly connected to the fact that, as an Albista, Sancho was greatly praised in texts written in the vicinity of the Duke.

A story about Dávila's burned hands and face could be found only in a Spanish manuscript chronicle and not in the published ones. It is possible that these kinds of stories may have been cut at the moment of publication by either the author or the editor as not being sufficiently heroic. Though we have letters from Mondragón describing his imprisonment by the mutineers in Zierikzee, in the Spanish chronicles we are told that he had just managed to flee in time, saving his honour.

The Spanish chronicles also differ again in dealing with Sancho's attack on Middelburg. In the letters and *relaciones* Sancho was described as a much more cunning and intelligent commander than in the chronicles that were meant for publication, such as the one by Trillo, where he is depicted as much more brutal. In this case Trillo seems badly informed on the events, decorating his text with stereotypical elements. However, at other moments we have a martial letter by Sancho that is perfectly reflected in Trillo's chronicle, as can be seen just before the Battle of Mookerheyde. A similar difference can be found in descriptions of the encounter between Mondragón and William of Orange in Breda (1575). The letter that survives is much more rational – even explaining Orange's point of view without any judgement – than the aggressive tone in Trillo's chronicle which turns Orange into a vile and mean enemy.

Different stories can also be found about the subsequent attack on Arnemuiden. While in English sources it is said that children and women were also killed, there are Spanish sources that explicitly state that women and children were spared. This may imply that the Spanish text served as a defence against the accusation of Spanish violence towards the innocent that was circulating publicly. Also the French ambassador wrote to his King using newsletters and other sources, clearly trying to offer a negative view of the Spanish commanders.

These examples confirm that it is important to compare the episodic narratives directly created after a battle and sent as *relaciones* and letters, and almost immediately turned into pamphlets. On the Battle of Mookerheyde there are three different narratives to be found in the pamphlets: a military story, a religious one and one defending the rebels. This implies that a pamphlet written in Brussels on 17 April could have a completely different narrative from another written in Antwerp a day later, though both authors clearly belonged to the royal camp.

The same narrative variations can be found around the Battle of Jemmingen.[5] Even before the end of the actual battle, the Duke of Alba had already sent his version to the King, while in another parallel Spanish version the Duke's importance was largely downplayed. The chronicle by Alonso de Ulloa, published in Venice in 1569, describes in detail how the Duke spread his version around, sending letters with the news of his victory to the Emperor, to the Spanish ambassador in Rome, the viceroys of Naples and Sicily, and the Spanish consul at Venice, who used Alba's letter to inform the Venetian Senate.[6] Alba created his own fame as a military hero, and he knew Italy was the centre of all international news.[7] However, Cees Reijner has recently proven that seventeenth-century Italian historiography on the Revolt in the Low Countries was greatly influenced by both the Farnese family and the desire to differentiate between the Spanish and the Italians in the royal army, leading in both cases to a negative view of the Duke of Alba.[8]

Chronicles, newsletters and *relaciones* seem factual at first, but when one compares them and reads them against the backdrop of the contemporary situation, they reveal how some figures are singled out and turned into protagonists while others are not. No single Spanish national story exists as different groups were trying to shape the narratives to influence opinions, ranging from the royal court to a much more general public. Ulloa, for example, always puts emphasis on the heroism of the Duke of Alba, his family and his followers, like Sancho Dávila.

After his famous crossing to Goes in 1572, Mondragón took care to inform everybody about the outcome of the expedition, and he even sent a painting of the story to the Duke of Alba, who was so impressed by this heroic deed that he wanted to order a larger painting of it. The Duke considered Mondragón to be 'his' man, and thus the victory was almost his own.

---

[5] Idem.
[6] Ulloa, *Comentarios*, 34r; Rodríguez-Salgado, 'Do not reveal…', 18-19.
[7] His letters were read out in public in Ypres. Stensland, *Habsburg communication*, 35; Lamal, *News*; Lamal, 'Orecchie'; Lamal, 'Internationale berichtgeving'.
[8] Reijner, *Italiaanse geschiedschrijvers*, 244; Stensland, *Habsburg communication*, 159.

The Spanish Fury of Antwerp in 1576 is another famous moment that can be followed through time. This episode is particularly relevant because, by tracing the different narratives, we can illustrate how one of them would become the canonical interpretation. At first it seems that both Dutch and Spanish stories agreed on the fact that it was a military confrontation that subsequently led to the brutal sack of the city. Even the local pamphlet written in 1576 against the Spanish military mostly dealt with the military facts and even praised their military worth, but over time international historiography directed the description towards the sack, converting it more and more into the result of the mutiny of the Spanish soldiers, and therefore gradually omitting the military confrontation from the stories. In this way this narrative gradually became the historical episode *par excellence* that illustrated the stereotypical Spanish cruelty of the Black Legend.

## Friends and foes

This research has also exposed how fruitful the use of merchants' letters can be in the study of the Revolt and, more generally, in discovering narratives on war written by civilians who were not directly involved in the conflict. We have seen that Sancho, Valdés and Mondragón maintained contact with Spanish merchants from Bruges and Antwerp. In the case of Sancho these were also close friendships, but these contacts were also needed to send money home, as in the cases of Valdés and Mondragón. The fact that Mondragón originally came from the Castilian merchant town of Medina del Campo made it much easier for him to connect to the commercial world.

For Sancho these contacts were of vital importance. As one of the commanders who had little previous knowledge of the Low Countries, it was easier to get in contact with fellow Spaniards. As governor of Antwerp citadel, he was also in a very good position to maintain these contacts with the Spanish merchant community. His friends are mentioned in his letters in opposition to his enemies, and accordingly described as 'amigos'. He is the only commander often using the word 'heretics' (*herejes*) to label the enemy, while others like Valdés tended to employ much more general terminology.[9] This could partly be motivated by Sancho's more religious outlook, but it also illustrates the black-and-white manner in

---

[9] The expression 'Luteranos' for all Protestants is not found in the correspondence of the four commanders, though in general it is considered to be the normal word used by Spaniards to refer to all Protestants. Van Campene, *Dagboek*, I, 132.

which he divided the world into friends and foes. One could image him as being a very good friend, but he surely was a terrible enemy to have. His descendants in later centuries continued propagating this image of a Catholic crusader against Protestantism.

It has also become clear that the image of the commanders could vary greatly, even within the reports of the same author. Morillon, Cardinal Granvelle's confidant, had faith in the Spanish military commanders during the first period around 1568, but after 1572 his image of them completely changed, and they became the worst enemies of the country. By that time his beloved Mechelen had been plundered by the royal army. At first he spoke positively about both Sancho Dávila and Julián, but he ended up especially loathing Sancho Dávila, and almost to the same degree the generally less outspoken and less criticised Mondragón. Targeting the Spanish commanders and the Spanish soldiers may have been a much more generalised way for Catholics and royalists in the Low Countries to position themselves during the conflict.[10] This shows that it was not only Protestant rebels who made use of anti-Hispanic propaganda, but that royalist Netherlanders did the same as a strategy to distance themselves from the Spaniards present in the Low Countries. However, they mostly refrained from expressing this criticism in print.

These war narratives also demonstrate that the commanders were hated and feared by both the enemy and their own soldiers. The image of Julián, Valdés and Mondragón as commanders loved by their men, as projected in later texts, is clearly not valid, though it can even be found in Hooft's work. The common soldiers' interests and opinions certainly were not the same as those of their commanders. There is evidence enough to state that all these three commanders were at some point hated by their own soldiers. Romero seems to have been both feared and ridiculed by his own men, at least if we are to believe Requesens's words. Julián was a real war hero, but with an apparently complicated character. We can also detect this element in the writings of Trillo, who sided with the common soldier much more than did his learned colleague, Mendoza. For example, when discussing the mutiny in Haarlem, Trillo described the events from the viewpoint of the mutineers, praising the organised and pacific behaviour of the Spanish troops.[11]

Some of the Spanish commanders were also really hated by the high nobility from the Low Countries, not only by political opponents, but also by those on the same royal side. The Lord of Champagney hated

---

[10] Stensland, *Habsburg communication*, 69.
[11] Trillo, *Historia*, 207-211. See also Martínez, 'Narrating mutiny'.

Sancho Dávila, Fernando de Lannoy despised Valdés and even wanted to kill him, while Mondragón violently attacked government official Jacques de la Torre at Breda. The policy makers at Brussels and Madrid had to cope with these personal conflicts between their commanders, as in the case of the very different letters Requesens received describing the violence at Utrecht in 1574. Valdés was himself well aware of the hatred the 'Burgundians' felt towards the Spanish commanders. Around 1576 this mutual distrust became the leading idea among both the Spanish commanders and the nobility from the Low Countries, creating a completely chaotic situation there. Though in Belgium this French-speaking nobility has been amply studied, its role in the conflict deserves more attention from Dutch scholars.[12]

Friction was also to be found among the Spaniards: Romero (not an Albista) did not like Fernando de Toledo (the Maestre de campo) or Sancho Dávila (both Albistas). Sancho seems to have been very attached to Prior Fernando de Toledo, Alba's natural son, and though there is not enough evidence yet, there are indications that this meant he did not belong to the camp of Alba's heir, Don Fadrique de Toledo.[13] Though Mondragón seemed to have been considered the friendliest Spaniard and Sancho Dávila as maybe the most aggressive one, which at first might be seen as clear opposites, the sources describe them in general as very good colleagues and friends, showing that even among Albistas there were differences in opinion on the policy towards the inhabitants. There is even a letter from Albista Valdés openly criticising Don Fadrique.

## Before the outbreak of the Revolt

The early careers of these commanders were mostly fabricated after they had reached certain fame. As there are hardly any reliable data for their early careers, the room for free invention is ample. It was especially rewarding for eulogists and biographers to place them at the scene of important battles and victories, such as the attack on Tunis in 1535, the Battle of Mühlberg in 1547 or the Battle of Saint-Quentin in 1557. There is even a document stating that the Duke of Alba himself was present at Saint-Quentin, while historical documents prove he was at the time residing in Italy.[14] Also Philip II's journey to England in 1554 in order to marry Mary Tudor holds special interest, for example in the

---

[12] The loyal nobility has been recently studied by Soen, *Vredehandel*.
[13] Kamen, *Duke*, 77.
[14] Fagel, 'Duke of Alba', 264.

case of the play on Julián Romero attributed to Lope de Vega, and in the life story of Sancho Dávila. The most revealing example, however, is the fact that Sancho Dávila's and Mondragón's heroism at Mühlberg (swimming across the river with their swords in their mouths) seems to be a story fabricated a posteriori. It is telling that a modern writer such as Pérez-Reverte uses precisely this anecdote in his work. Modern historical novels also have the ability to choose between turning Julián into a hero at Saint-Quentin or – on the contrary – downplaying him and his historical contribution completely.

The stories of this earlier period are particularly indicative since they make tangible the fact that many facets of the revolt were already present during the earlier wars against the French, the Duke of Guelders and the Scots. For example, the harsh punishment of Düren during the earlier wars, the punishment of towns in the war between England and Scotland in which Julián was active, and the life of the Spanish soldiers in the north during the wars with the French already offer an image of cruel sieges, overdue wages, mutinies and plundering. This proves that the events during the early phase of the Revolt were in part a continuation of earlier practices, albeit perhaps with less intensity and not directed against the subjects of the same prince. Julián Romero and William of Orange agreed that the Revolt was much crueler compared to the 'bonne guerre' of earlier times in which they had fought together on the same side.

The narratives also reveal that the last experience of many of the commanders immediately before the Revolt was related to the famous Ottoman siege of Malta in 1565. Commanders like Julián also worked as governors of fortresses in the Mediterranean, organising the defence against the Ottoman threat. Many of the Spanish troops that came to the Low Countries under the Duke of Alba in 1567 had been involved in this war against the Ottomans. King Philip II also had to shift his attention directly after Malta to the chaotic situation in the Low Countries. The history of the war in the Mediterranean is closely connected to the beginning of the Revolt in the Low Countries.

Also worth mentioning is the fact that there was a direct link between William of Orange and several of the Spanish commanders. Both Julián and Mondragón had had a prior relationship as comrades-in-arms that was used during the Revolt: think of the letters between Orange and Julián during Marnix of Sint-Aldegonde's captivity in 1573, the letters and agreement between Orange and Mondragón after the siege of Middelburg in 1574, and the meetings between the two men around the peace negotiations at Breda in 1575. Valdés and Sancho Dávila did not have such a shared past with the high nobility of the Low Countries, and this certainly influenced their outlook on the events.

## A life in letters

There was a tradition in the Low Countries to describe the Spanish commanders condescendingly as people of very low birth, such as basket makers, chimney sweeps and drummers.[15] The story seems most strongly related to former drummer Sancho Dávila, who was, however, probably the commander of highest birth among the four examples in this book. Also interesting is the story of how a Dutch nobleman derogatorily described Valdés as somebody who had not been more than a lackey. On the other hand, a Spanish play on Romero framed his humble starting point in life as a drummer's helper as a telling example of how you could start from scratch and end up a general. This narrative of professional self-made men could be used in the seventeenth century to criticise the members of the high nobility.

These illustrious and famous ancestors could prove of great relevance for the commanders' descendants, since the descendants could draw on their forebears' records to improve their own progress in life. The most remarkable example is that of Sancho Dávila, as already in the seventeenth century his direct descendants were using his fame and figure by publishing memorials and history works, quoting letters Sancho had received from the royal government and even from King Philip II himself, preserved in the family archive. For one of those descendants it meant obtaining high office in America, while for another it was a means of attracting the favour of the new Bourbon King in the early eighteenth century.

The fact that Sancho and Mondragón did not succeed in receiving the habit of one of the religious military orders in Spain – because of possible Jewish ancestors – did not stop their descendants from continuously attempting to secure a habit using the fame of their ancestors. In the end, perhaps simply because the passing of time, both commanders were successfully used to obtain the much-desired honours.

This news would certainly have given much joy and pride to these commanders, as the letters written by all four commanders show the importance they gave to the future of their offspring. They always pointed out that they themselves were willing to die poor, but that they needed to be rewarded to help out their children. Of course, this continuous lament of not being rewarded enough seems to have been part of a narrative style

[15] Horst, *Opstand*, 64-65.

as a sort of topos, since at least Mondragón and Sancho Dávila earned a large income during their lifetimes. In Julián's case, it was clearly after his death that his wife and daughter were rewarded. The royal secretary understood that this was necessary as evidence of the King's goodwill towards all other men at arms.

The commanders' letters offer a complete range of tone, from very polite letters to the King and the high nobility when they had to thank them for rewards given, up to very unfriendly letters when they had to complain about the complete lack of attention. Especially when writing to Alba's secretary, Albornoz, the commanders were not afraid to use a harsh tone in their letters. Often, when they wrote a letter the same day to the Duke of Alba you can distinguish the difference in tone between the two letters. Requesens was very polite when writing about Julián Romero's capabilities to the King or other high officials, but in a letter to his brother – in cipher – he insulted him as a worthless commander.

But all of the commanders had their critical moments when they no longer took no for an answer. Accordingly, Mondragón and Romero even threatened the royal government with leaving the Low Countries without royal permission in order to get things moving, whereas Sancho could not accept the fact that the King was not capable of procuring for him his promised Spanish knighthood. Such a moment of anger can also be found with the Duke of Alba when he discovered in 1570 that he was not returning to Spain with the future Queen Anne.[16] Valdés was maybe a little less outspoken in the expression of his feelings, but he used the word 'banishment' to describe his difficult and boring stay in the Low Countries.

Valdés seemed to have felt that way during the quiet years from 1569 up to 1 April 1572. We have only a very few letters concerning this period, and this means we cannot use them to fill the void during these years to be found in the chronicles, which tend to go almost directly from 1568 to 1572. The fact that letters in this period are also scarce may be caused by the fact that the commanders had more personal encounters with their frequent correspondents, like the Duke of Alba, but also that during this period there was simply less to write about. Commanders tended to write when a problem needed to be solved, which implies that we are still not well equipped to reconstruct the lives of the commanders during those quiet years. Nonetheless, Sancho's letters in particular show how his life could be filled with his own glorious wedding (including tournaments)

---

[16] Fagel, 'Duke of Alba', 271.

and with parties, gambling and other forms of entertainment. On the other hand, commanders like Valdés and Londoño spent their free time writing military treatises.

Often the commanders' negative tone was related to the omnipresent problem of communication. They lived far from court and had difficulty in making their needs known to the King. They asked permission to go to Spain for several months, but often this permission was not given. It was obvious that they could not be spared from the war, and Philip II preferred to read memorials to meeting these commanders in person. The idea of Philip II as a paper king is perfectly reflected in their letters.[17] Mondragón was explicitly prohibited from visiting the King during his stay in Spain and the commander – grumbling – had to continue sending memorials to try to obtain his rewards.

Another major communication problem was the fact that Alba often did not respond to their letters after his return to Spain at the end of 1573. Sancho, Valdés and Mondragón were true Albistas and they always turned to the Duke for their advancement and rewards, signing their letters as 'creatures' of the Duke. The fact that he often did not answer them was not understood at all. They saw him as their defender at court, their alarm clock. It must have been difficult for them to understand that the Duke had fallen into disgrace with the King. Then they had to switch and look for support from the new Governor-general, Requesens, but he was much less inclined to support these Albistas. It also became clear that their heroic deeds under Alba had lost much of their brilliance. They felt completely lost in a war that was no longer theirs.

When they wanted to please their patron, they sent information on the war to the Duke of Alba in Spain, but during one of the cooler moments in their relationship, Mondragón even refused to continue this practice. If his patron did not help him out, then the client would not comply with his implicit part of the deal. In the same way, we have letters from Romero to Alba only when he needed personal favours, directly offering information on the war in return.

Sometimes we also find sadness in their letters, but generally the commanders were sparing with words. After losing his wife and shortly afterwards his father-in-law, Sancho strongly desired to return home, revealing his emotions by adding three small words: 'y ahora mas': and now more than ever. Julián, too, after the death of his natural son, simply described his son as somebody he had vested his hopes in,

---

[17] Parker, *Felipe II*, 167.

showing implicitly the sadness of the mourning father. Mondragón had a melancholic moment after the death of a fellow commander whom he could not honour by attending his funeral. He then also reflected on his own mortality.

Completely at the other end of the spectrum we find Valdés' letters after arriving at The Hague, where he probably met the Dutch woman he would marry years later. These letters are in a much more positive tone than his normal letters, also using words in French, something he had not done before. Especially telling is his constructive idea of forming 'a *petit ejército*' with the loyal farmers.

We cannot omit the fact that in their letters the commanders used all the rhetoric they could handle to defend their actions. Valdés tried to cover critical situations with a small joke, as when he suggested the successful enemy attackers must have possessed wings, or the pitiful image he offered when he thought himself to be without men and left behind alone between the banners, or when he compared the poor soldiers to souls leaving purgatory. His most famous description compares the floodwater around Leiden to an ocean. For his part, the Duke of Alba in his own letters often made use of his image as an old grey-haired man.[18] Julián Romero, of course, was greatly praised by Brantôme for his eloquent soldiers' rhetoric.

The commanders and the chroniclers were also well aware of the hatred of some of the inhabitants towards the Spaniards as a group, as in Valdés's letters where he even used the word 'yoke' which stems directly from anti-Hispanic rebel propaganda and their much exploited image of the so-called Spanish yoke. In his letters to the mutineers Valdés tried to stop the mutineers from further blackening the image of the Spanish nation. Interestingly, the word nation, implicitly connected to the Spaniards, is also used by the noble opponents of the Spanish commanders with a clearly negative connotation. Chroniclers like Pedro Cornejo and Alonso de Ulloa were well informed about the Spaniards' negative image among the inhabitants of the Low Countries.[19] Others, like Romero, mostly hinted at the very negative image of the Duke of Alba, again revealing that he could not be seen as an Albista.

Regarding their vision of the conflict in general, we find the commanders expressing the idea that the rebels could be beaten, often even in a short time, if only they would be given the means to continue the war. However,

---

[18] Fagel, 'Duke of Alba', 278.
[19] Rodríguez Pérez, Sánchez Jiménez and Den Boer, *España*; Cornejo, *Sumario*, 224, 263; Ulloa, *Comentarios*, 18v.

we also find the voice of defeat when Valdés wrote that he continued struggling against all odds, and we see how even the martial Sancho was at some point considering the possibility that the rebels were going to win the war. The Catholic war hero was imagining defeat by the heretics. Opinion could clearly change over time. Valdés, and also Requesens, started off as rather optimistic about the possibility of coming to an agreement with the Dutch, but both men in the end were so infuriated by the stubborn resistance from the inhabitants of the Low Countries that they advocated the flooding of the whole of Holland.[20] These harsh views on the war were not the result of a previously negative view of the inhabitants or of an innately cruel Spanish nature, but much more the result of their destroyed confidence in the inhabitants of the Low Countries and their lost hope in a good end for their cause.

Both in eighteenth-century Dutch plays and in the texts by modern author Arturo Pérez-Reverte the commanders were turned into much more Spanish heroes than they actually were. In fictional re-elaborations of the events, Mondragón was granted a Spanish wife despite the facts of his life, and his Walloon soldiers were turned into Spanish tercios. Some literary sources reveal a tendency to create clear-cut opposites that do not fit the complicated lives of these commanders and the multinational – or pre-national – character of early modern society. Figures like Mondragón had been in the north for such a long period that he was unable to write letters in correct Spanish. He was indeed born a Spaniard, but with possessions and family in the border region between France, the Roman Empire and the Low Countries.

When modern Dutch authors converted Mondragón into a positive hero in the Low Countries, his negative image was completely overshadowed. All elements that did not fit the description were left out of the narrative. In this way we have forgotten about his violent activities at Dendermonde and Deventer, and we do not remember the – hopefully fictitious – story of Mondragón's soldiers eating children during his harsh defence of Middelburg. As early as in the seventeenth century his descendants knew that Mondragón had a positive press among the foreign chroniclers, and this would be continued by eighteenth-century Dutchmen.

The same happened regarding Valdés's narrative; he would be turned from a normal Spanish commander into a good man through the story of Magdalena Moons. However, unlike Mondragón, Valdés did not possess a good reputation with the inhabitants of the Low Countries in

---

[20] Van der Essen, *Ejército*, 195-196.

his lifetime. His positive image is purely a later fabrication as the husband of a Dutch national heroine.

This last aspect addresses the importance of local memory cultures. Without the stories from Zeeland (Middelburg and Zierikzee) Mondragón would not have become such an outstanding figure; without the Leiden stories Valdés would hardly have been known; and Gaspar de Robles owes his positive fame mostly to authors from Frisia. The stories of these men now overshadow Julián's great deeds and the swift actions taken by Sancho, the two commanders who have a strong foothold in Spanish collective memory. Perhaps only Mondragón has the honour of being remembered as a relevant war hero in both cultures.

Warrior Julián, Catholic crusader Sancho, the good Mondragón and the exemplary Valdés are all part of the shared past between Spain and the Low Countries. More than war heroes or war criminals, they were professional soldiers involved in a very intricate conflict in which they had to survive for years.[21] I hope this study of these protagonists of war and the related episodic narratives can serve as a bridge between Dutch and Spanish historiography.

---

[21] On the complexities of the conflict see;: Van Nierop, *Verraad*.

# Bibliography

Aa, van der, A.J., *Biographisch woordenboek der Nederlanden*, 21 vols. (Haarlem 1852-1878).

Aertsz, Pieter, 'Cort verhael van de moort ende destructie der stadt Naarden', in: Johannes Gysius, ed., *Oorspronck ende voortgang der Nederlantscher beroerten* (Delft 1626).

Agarge, Gasparus de L', *De blokkade van Zult-Dommel. Dagverhaal van Gasparus de L'Agarge*, H.F.M. Huybers and J. Kleyntjens, eds. (Arnhem 1925).

Agellakis, Nikos, 'Civilian lives in wartime: Spanish merchants in Antwerp during the Dutch Revolt' (unpublished MA thesis, Leiden University 2017).

Álvarez Francés, Leonor, 'Soldado sanguinario o heroic adalid? Gaspar de Robles en las crónicas de Groninga', in: Enrique García Hernán and Davide Maffi, eds., *Estudios sobre guerra y sociedad en la Monarquía Hispánica. Guerra marítima, estrategia, organización y cultura militar (1500-1700)* (Madrid 2017) 769-784.

Álvarez Francés, Leonor, 'The fabrication of Francisco de Valdés. Episodic narratives in Spanish and Dutch chronicles on the siege of Leiden 1573-1574', in: Raymond Fagel, Leonor Álvarez Francés and Beatriz Santiago Belmonte, eds., *Early modern war narratives and the Revolt in the Low Countries* (Manchester 2020) 36-55.

*An historical discourse or rather a tragicall historie of the citie of Antwerpe*, in: William Scott Lancaster, 'A Larum for London. A critical edition of the performative text' (PhD thesis, Texas A&M University-Commerce, 2011) 461-462.

*Archives ou correspondance inédite de la maison d'Orange-Nassau*, 26 vols., G. Groen van Prinsterer ed. (Leiden and The Hague 1835-1915).

Arellano, Ignacio, *Historia del teatro español del siglo XVII* (Madrid 1995).

Arnade, Peter, *Beggars, iconoclasts and civic patriots. The political culture of the Dutch Revolt* (Ithaca and London 2008).

Arquellada, Juan de, *Sumario de prohezas y casos de guerra*, Enrique Toral y Peñaranda, ed. (Jaén 1999).

Atienza, Julio de, and Adolfo Barredo de Valenzuela, 'Los Mondragón de Medina del Campo. Una familia vallisoletana, radicada en Medina por siglos', *Hidalguía* 1976, 321-337.

Aubery du Maurier, Louis, *Mémoires pour servir à l'histoire de Hollande et des autres Provinces-Unies* (1680).

Azevedo Coutinho, G.D., *Korte chronycke der stad ende provincie van Mechelen*, 3 vols. (Leuven 1747-1779).

Baelde, M., *De collaterale raden onder Karel V en Filips II (1531-1578). Bijdrage tot de geschiedenis van de centrale instellingen in de zestiende eeuw* (Brussels 1965).

Baes, Christian, 'Une épisode de la querelle Habsbourg-Valois. La campagne de Henri II aux Pays-Bas en 1554', *Belgisch Tijdschrift voor Filologie en Geschiedenis* 73 (1995) 319-341.

Baes, Christian, 'La Guerre au XVIe siècle: un vecteur de destruction', in: *Verwoesting en wederopbouw van steden, van de Middeleeuwen tot heden* (Brussels 1999) 185-206.

Balbi di Correggio, Francisco, *The siege of Malta 1565*, English translation by Ernle Bradford (Woodbridge 2005).

Barrientos Grandon, Javier, 'Antonio Sarmiento de Acuña', DBE.

'Battle of Delft', https://en.wikipedia.org/wiki/Battle_of_Delft_(1573) (accessed 30 January 2019).

'Battle of Le Quesnoy', https://en.wikipedia.org/wiki/Battle_of_Le_Quesnoy_(1568) (accessed 11 April 2019).

Baumgartner, Frederic J., *Henry II, King of France 1547-1559* (Durham and London 1988).

Belloso Martín, Carlos, *La antemuralla de la monarquía. Los tercios españoles en el reino de Sicilia en el siglo XVI* (Madrid 2010).

Bermúdez de Castro, General, 'El tercio viejo y su mejor soldado', *Blanco y negro* 19-7-1936, 58-61.

Blok, P.J., 'De slag op de Mookerheide, 14 april 1574', in: P.J. Blok, *Verspreide studiën op het gebied der geschiedenis* (Groningen 1903) 154-171.

Blokker, Jan, *Waar is de Tachtigjarige Oorlog gebleven?* (Amsterdam 2006).

Boekelman, A., *Mondragón, Spaans kolonel tijdens de Tachtigjarige Oorlog* (Den Helder 1997).

*Boisot en Mondragon of de belegering en verovering der stad Middelburg*, anonymous (Middelburg 1791).

Bontius, Reinier, *Belegering ende het ontset der stadt Leyden* (Leiden 1645).

Bontius, Reinier, *Belegering ende ontsetting der statd Leyden* (Leiden 1659).

Bood, Rena, 'Between Hispanophobia and Hispanophilia. The Spanish fascination in English and Dutch 17th-century literature' (PhD thesis, Universiteit van Amsterdam, 2020).

Boomsma, Peter, 'Beeldenstorm. Een onderzoek naar de beeldvorming rond de plundering van Zutphen en Naarden door de koninklijke troepen in 1572', (MA diss., Universiteit Leiden, April 2008).

Boon, Cornelis, *Leiden verlost* (Rotterdam 1711).

Boon, J.G.M., ed., *1570-1580: Oudewater. Vrijheid en gezag* (Oudewater 1975).

Boone, Marc and Martha C. Howell (eds.), *The power of space in late medieval and early modern Europe: the cities of Italy, Northern France and the Low Countries* (Turnhout 2013).

Boone, Marc, 'From cuckoo's egg to "sedem tyranni" – the princely citadels in the cities of the Low Countries, or the city's spatial integrity hijacked (15th-early 16th centuries)', in: Marc Boone and Martha C. Howell, eds., *The power of space in late medieval and early modern Europe. The cities of Italy, Northern France and the Low Countries* (Turnhout 2013) 77-95.

Bor, Pieter Christiaensz, *Vande Nederlantsche oorloghen, beroerten ende borgerlijcke oneenicheyden, gheduerende den gouvernemente vanden hertoghe van Alba inde selve landen* (Utrecht 1601).

Bordewijk, Coby, *Lof zij den helden. Vier eeuwen Leidse stedentrots op het toneel* (The Hague 2005).

Boutens, R.C., and others, *Middelburg's overgang in 1574, openluchtspel* (Middelburg 1924).

Brantôme, Pierre de Bourdeille, Lord of, *Never before translated Spanish rhodomontades* (London 1741).

Brantôme, Pierre de Bourdeille, Lord of, 'Rodomontades et gentilles rencontres espagnoles', in: *Oeuvres du seigneur de Brantome* XIII (London 1779) 1-225.

Brantôme, Pierre de Bourdeille, Lord of, *Œuvres complètes de Pierre de Bourdeille*, I, Vies des grands capitaines, J.A.C. Buchon, ed. (Paris 1839).

Brésin, L., *Chroniques de Flandre et d'Artois*, E. Mannier, ed. (Paris 1880).

Briones Moreno, Mariano, *Julián Romero de Ibarrola. Un Conquense en Flandes* (Cuenca 2007).

Broek, Jan van den, *Voor God en mijn koning. Het verslag van kolonel Francisco Verdugo over zijn jaren als legerleider en gouverneur namens Filips II in Stad en Lande van Groningen, Drenthe, Friesland, Overijssel en Lingen (1581-1595)* (Groningen 2009).

Brouwer, Albert, and Ingena Vellekoop, *Spaans benauwd. Strijdende Geuzen en Spanjaarden in het Maasmondgebied 1568-1575* (Vlaardingen 1984).

Brouwer, H., *Het ontset van Leyden* (Amsterdam 1683).

Brouwer, Johan, *Kronieken van Spaansche soldaten uit het begin van den Tachtigjarigen Oorlog* (Zutphen 1933).

Brouwer, Judith, and Michael Limberger, *Hedendaagse biografieën over vroegmoderne lieden* (Leuven, 2018), *Nieuwe Tijdingen. Over vroegmoderne geschiedenis* 2018, 5-18.

Brulez, Wilfrid, 'Het gewicht van de oorlog in de nieuwe tijden. Enkele aspecten', *Tijdschrift voor Geschiedenis* 91 (1978) 386-406.

Buisman, J., *Duizend jaar weer, wind en water in de Lage Landen*, III (Franeker 1998)

Busto, Bernabé de, 'Quadernos de historia de Carlo V en Alemania alta y baxa', Real Biblioteca del monasterio de El Escorial, Manuscript L.I.6.

Busto, Bernabé de, *Geschichte des Schmalkaldischen Krieges* (Burg 1910).

Cabañas Agrela, José Miguel, 'Cristóbal de Mondragón', DBE.

Cabañas Agrela, José Miguel, 'Fadrique Álvarez de Toledo Enríquez', DBE.

Cabañas Agrela, José Miguel, 'Alonso de Vargas', DBE.

Cabañas Agrela, José Miguel, *Don Bernardino de Mendoza. Un escritor-soldado al servicio de la Monarquía Católica (1540-1604)* (Guadalajara 2001).

Cabañas Agrela, José Miguel, 'Los agentes de Alba en Flandes: El caso de Don Bernardino de Mendoza', in: Gregorio del Ser Quijano, ed., *Congreso V centenario del nacimiento del III duque de Alba, Fernando Álvarez de Toledo, actas* (Ávila and Salamanca 2008) 483-497.

Cabrera de Córdoba, Luis, *Historia de Felipe II, rey de España*, José Martínez Millán and Carlos Javier de Carlos Morales, eds., 3 vols. (Valladolid 1998).

*Calendar of letters and papers, foreign and domestic, of the reign of Henry VIII*, 21 vols., J.S. Brewer, James Gairdner and R. Brodie, eds. (London 1862-1932).

*Calendar of State papers and manuscripts, relating to English affairs existing in the archives and collections of Venice*, 38 vols., Rawdon Lubbock Brown et al., eds. (London 1864-1907).

*Calendar of state papers, foreign, Elizabeth*, 23 vols., Joseph Stevenson, Allan James Crosby and Arthur John Butler, eds. (London 1863-1950).

*Calendar of the Acts of the Privy Council of England, A.D. 1542-[June 1631]*, 46 vols., J.R. Dasent, et al., eds. (London 1890-1964).

Calmet, Augustin, *Histoire généalogique de la maison du Chastelet, branche puînée de la maison* (Nancy 1741).

Campene, Cornelis and Philip van, *Dagboek behelzende het verhaal der merkwaardigste gebeurtenissen, voorgevallen te Gent sedert het begin der godsdienstberoerten tot den 5en april 1571*, F de Potter, ed. (Ghent 1870).

Cañizares, José de, *Comedia famosa. Ponerse avito sin pruebas, y guapo Julian Romero* (Valencia 1768).

Carlos Morales, Carlos Javier de, *Felipe II: el imperio en bancarrota. La hacienda real de Castilla y los negocios financieros del Rey prudente* (Madrid 2008).

Casey, James, *Family and community in early Modern Spain: the citizens of Granada, 1570-1739* (Cambridge 2007).

Caunedo del Potro, Betsabé, 'La disgregación de una rica hacienda: el ocaso mercantil de los descendientes de Diego de Soria. ¿Un problema politico?', *Espacio, tiempo y forma. Historia medieval* 19 (2007) 77-97.

Cervera, César, 'Sir Julián de Romero. El temido "mediohombre" de los tercios de Flandes', *ABC*, 18 December 2015: https://www.abc.es/historia/abci-julian-romero-temido-mediohombre-tercios-flandes-201512180143_noticia.html (accessed 7 July 2019).

Cervera, César, 'El viejo coronel de los tercios de Flandes que atrevesaba ríos helados para arrasar herejes', *ABC*, 24 November 2016, https://www.abc.es/historia/abci-cristobal-mondragon-viejo-coronel-tercios-flandes-atravesaba-rios-helados-para-arrasar-herejes-201611240259_noticia.html (accessed 29 November 2018).

Charles, Jean-Léon, 'Le sac des villes dans les Pays-Bas au XVIe siècle. Etude critique des règles de guerre', *Revue Internationale d'histoire militaire* 24 (1965) 288-301.

*Chronica de los Descalzos de la santíssima Trinidad, redentores de cautivos*, D. de la Madre de Dios (Madrid 1662).

*Chroniques de Douai, recueillis et mise en ordre*, Eugène François Joseph Tailliar, ed. (Douai 1875).

*Chroniques Liégeoises*, II, S. Balau and E. Fairon, eds. (Brussels 1931).

*Chronologische lijsten van de Geëxtendeerde Sententiën berustende in het archief van de Grote Raad van Mechelen*, VI, J. Th. de Smidt, ed. (Brussels 1988).

Cianca, Antonio de, *Historia de la vida, invención, milagros y translación de S. Segundo, primero obispo de Avila [...]* (Madrid 1595).

Claerbout, Joos, *'t beleg en overgaan der stad Middelburg onder het doorluchtige beleid van Willem den Eersten* (3d edition Flushing/ Vlissingen 1788).

Cloulas, Ivan, *Henri II* (Paris 1985).

*Colección de Documentos Inéditos para la Historia de España*, 112 vols. (Madrid 1842-1895).

Cornejo, Pedro, *Sumario de las guerras civiles, y causas de la rebellion de Flandres* (Lyon 1577).

*Correspondance de Guillaume le Taciturne*, III [CT] L.P. Gachard, ed. (Brussels, Leipzig and Ghent 1851).

*Correspondance de Marguérite d'Autriche, duchesse de Parme, avec Philippe II*, I [CM] L.P. Gachard, ed. (Brussels 1867).

*Correspondance de Philippe II*, [CP] 2nd series, Joseph Lefèvre, ed. (Brussels 1960).

*Correspondance de Philippe II*, II-V [CP] L.P. Gachard, ed. (Brussels, Ghent and Leipzig 1851-1879).

*Correspondance du cardinal de Granvelle 1565-1586*, 12 vols. [CG] E. Poullet and C. Piot, eds. (Brussels 1877-1896).

*Correspondance française de Marguérite d'Autriche, duchesse de Parme, avec Philippe II*, III, J.S. Theissen, ed. (Utrecht 1942).

Correspondence of William of Orange, Instituut voor Nederlandse Geschiedenis: http://www.inghist.nl/Onderzoek/Projecten/WVO/ [BO]

Cotereau, Alycex de, 'Voyage de la reine Anne en Espagne, en 1570', in: L.P. Gachard and C. Piot, eds., *Collection des Voyages des souverains des Pays-Bas*, III (Brussels 1881) 573-596.

Cristóbal de Mondragón', Wikipedia.org (accessed 26 October 2018).

*Crónica del Rey Enrico octavo de Inglaterra*, Marqués de Molins, ed. (Madrid 1874).

Crowley, Roger, *Empires of the sea. The final battle for the Mediterranean 1521-1580* (London 2008).

Cubero Garrote, José, *Atar cabos en Villafrechós* (Madrid 2012).

Dambre, O., 'Jacob van Zevecote', in: *Nationaal Biografisch Woordenboek* IV (Brussels 1970), 987-996.

Dávila Jalón, Valentín, *Nobiliario de la ciudad de Burgos* (Madrid 1995).

Dávila y Guevara, Sancho, *Memorial de los servicios del General Sancho Davila por don Sancho Davila y Guevara su nieto, cavallero de la Orden de Alcantara*, 20 June 1629, RAH, Legajo 1, carpeta 8.

Dávila y San-Vitores, Gerónimo Manuel, *El rayo de la guerra. Hechos de Sancho Dávila: successos de aquellos tiempos, llenos de admiración* (Valladolid 1713).

Dehaisnes, C., ed., *Inventaire sommaire des archives départementales antérieur à 1790, Archives départementales du Nord*, III (Lille 1877).

Delmaire, Bernard, 'Thérouanne et Hesdin: deux destructions (1553), une reconstruction', in: *Verwoesting en wederopbouw van steden, van de Middeleeuwen tot heden* (Brussels 1999) 127-153.

Derks, Sebastiaan, 'Madama's minister: Tomás de Armenteros at the court of Margarita of Austria', in: René Vermeir, Maurits Ebben and Raymond Fagel, eds., *Agentes e identidades en movimiento. España y los Países Bajos, siglos XV-XVIII* (Madrid 2011) 49-69.

Diana, Manuel J., 'Cristóbal de Mondragón', *Semanario Pintoresco Español* 1849, 163-164, 173.

Díaz, Concha, 'Julián Romero de Ibarrola pintado por El Greco', *Cuaderno de Sofonisba*, 2 October 2015, http://cuadernodesofonisba.blogspot.com (accessed 3 July 2019).

Diegerick, J.L.A., ed., *Correspondance de Valentin de Pardieu, seigneur de la Motte, gouverneur de Gravelines, 1574-1594* (Bruges 1857).

Dijk, Teun van, 'Episodes as units of discourse analysis', in: Deborah Tannen, ed., *Analyzing discourse: text and talk* (Georgetown 1982) 177-195.

*Discours de la victoire qu'il a pelu à Dieu donner au Roy Catholique, par le bon conseil & vertueuse conduite de Don Sancho d'Avilà, capitaine de la citadelle d'Anvers, à l'encontre du Comte Ludovic frere du Prince d'Orenge, le mercredy 14. iour d'avril 1574, extraict d'une lettre envoyee par un gentil-homme flamand* (Lyon 1574).

*Discours véritable sur ce qui est advenu, touchant l'alborote et esmotion des Espaignolz mutinéz es isles de Zelande incontinent apres la prinse de Ziericzee, le second de Juillet 1576* (Brussels 1576).

'Documents inédits sur la prise de Dinant par les Français', *Annales de la Société Archéologique de Namur* 3 (1853) 193-241.

Doran, Susan, *Elizabeth and her circle* (Oxford 2015).

Doren, P.J. van, *Inventaire des archives de la ville de Malines*, IV (Mechelen 1866).

Drelichman, Mauricio, and Hans-Joachim Voth, *Lending to the borrower from hell. Debt, taxes and default in the age of Philip II* (Princeton 2014).

Duits, H., 'Om de eenheid en vrijheid van de gehele Nederlanden: Jacob Duyms Ghedenck-boeck (1606) als politiek manifest', *Voortgang* 20 (2001) 7-45.

Duym, Jacob, *Benoude belegheringe der stad Leyden, uyt bevel des machtighen conincx van Hispaingnen, in den Iaere 1574 haer aen-ghedaen, ende het wonderbaerlijck ontset daer op den derden dagh Octobris 1574 ghevolght* (Leiden 1606).

Duyse, van, Prudens, 'Notice sur la défense soutenue au château de Gand para Madame de Mondragon (Guillemette de Chastellet), *Bulletin de l'Académie Royale des Sciences, des Lettres et des Beayx-Arts de Belgique* 23 (1856) 173-179.

*Epistolario del III duque de Alba, don Fernando Álvarez de Toledo* [EA], Duque de Alba, ed., 3 vols. (Madrid 1952).

Ercilla, Alonso de, *La Araucana*, Isaías Lerner, ed. (Madrid 1993).

Escudero Baztán, Juan Manuel, 'La construcción del mito del buen militar: historia y funcionalidad dramática en Don Lope de Figueroa', *Neophilologus* 98 (2014) 259-274.

Eembd, Goverd van der, *Haerlemse belegeringhs treur-bly-eynde spel* (The Hague 1619).

Esparza, José Javier, *Memorias del Maestre de campo de los tercios Julián Romero. San Quintín* (Madrid 2019).

Essen, Léon van der, 'Kritisch onderzoek betreffende de oorlogvoering, v.h. Spaans leger in de Nederlanden in de XVIe eeuw, nl. de bestraffing van opstandige steden, I, Tijdens het bewind van Alva', *Mededelingen van de Koninklijke Vlaamse Academie voor Wetenschappen, Letteren en Schone Kunsten van België, Klasse der Letteren* 12, 1 (1950) 3-36.

Essen, Léon van der, 'Kritische studie over de oorlogvoering, van het Spaanse leger in de Nederlanden tijdens de zestiende eeuw, nl. de bestraffing van opstandige steden, II, Onder Requesens', *Mededelingen van de Koninklijke Vlaamse Academie voor Wetenschappen, Letteren en Schone Kunsten van België, Klasse der Letteren* 14, 1 (1952) 3-26.

Essen, Léon van der, 'Croisade contre les hérétiques ou guerre contre des rebelles?', *Revue d'Histoire Ecclésiastique* 51 (1956) 42-78.

Essen, Léon van der, *El ejército español en Flandes 1567-1584*, Gustaaf Janssens, ed. (Cuacos de Yuste 2008).

Fagel, Raymond, *De Hispano-Vlaamse wereld. De contacten tussen Spanjaarden en Nederlanders 1496-1555* (Brussels and Nijmegen 1996).

Fagel, Raymond, *Leids beleg en ontzet in Spaanse ogen* (The Hague 1998).

Fagel, Raymond, 'Es buen católico y sabe escribir los cuatro idiomas. Una nueva generación mixta entre españoles y flamencos ante la revuelta de España', in: Bartolomé Yun Casalilla ed., *Las redes del imperio. Élites sociales en la articulación de la Monarquía Hispánica 1492-1714* (Madrid 2009) 289-312.

Fagel, Raymond, 'El esplendor de los Tercios españoles en el siglo XVI. Los héroes de San Quintín: defensores de los Países Bajos', in: Francisco José Galante Gómez, ed., *Caminos legendarios. Los tercios y el regimiento Soria en la historia y la cultura* (Madrid 2009) 143-154.

Fagel, Raymond, 'La imagen de dos militares españoles decentes en el ejécito del Duque de Alba en Flandes: Cristóbal de Mondragón y Gaspar de Robles', in: Patrick Collard, Miguel Norbert Ubarri and Yolanda Rodríguez Pérez, eds., *Encuentros de ayer, reencuentros de hoy* (Ghent 2009) 73-91.

Fagel, Raymond, *Kapitein Julián. De Spaanse held van de Nederlandse Opstand* (Hilversum 2011).

Fagel, Raymond, 'The Duke of Alba and the Netherlands, 1520-1573', in: Maurits Ebben, Margriet Lacy-Bruijn and Rolof van Hövell tot Westerflier, eds., *Alba, general and servant to the crown* (Rotterdam 2011) 256-287.

Fagel, Raymond, 'Julián. Un héroe español en Flandes entre el Príncipe de Orange y el Duque de Alba', in: René Vermeir, Maurits Ebben and Raymond Fagel, eds., *Agentes e identidades en movimiento. España y los Países Bajos, siglos XV-XVIII* (Madrid 2011) 271-288.

Fagel, Raymond, 'La furia española (1576) en el teatro. ¿Un trágico accidente de la guerra o una agresión premeditada', in: Yolanda Rodríguez Pérez and Antonio Sánchez Jiménez, eds., *La Leyenda Negra en el crisol de la comedia. El teatro del Siglo de Oro frente a los estereotipos antihispánicos* (Madrid and Frankfurt am Main 2016) 51-66.

Fagel, Raymond, 'Alexander Farnese and Francisco Verdugo; the war in the North east', *Tiempos modernos* 35,2 (2017) 14-29.

Fagel, Raymond, 'Describir la guerra. Narrativas de la primera década de las guerras de Flandes (1567-1577)', in: Enrique García Hernán and Davide Maffi, eds., *Estudios sobre guerra y sociedad en la Monarquía Hispánica. Guerra marítima, estrategia, organización y cultura militar (1500-1700)* (Madrid 2017) 507-518.

Fagel, Raymond, *De Spaanse belegeraar van Leiden. Het eigen verhaal van Francisco de Valdés* (Leiden 2017).

Fagel, Raymond, 'Gascoigne's *The Spoyle of Antwerpe* (1576) as an Anglo-Dutch text', *Dutch Crossing* 20 (March 2017) 1-10.

Fagel, Raymond, 'El mejor soldado español en Flandes: Sancho o Julián?, in: Magdalena de Pazzis Pi Corrales and José Cepeda Gómez, eds., *Aspectos de la historiografía moderna. Milicia, iglesia y seguridad. Homenaje al profesor Enrique Martínez Ruiz* (Madrid 2018) 469-483.

Fagel, Raymond, 'La imagen de la Furia española de Amberes (1576)', in: José I. Fortea Pérez, Juan E. Gelabert Gonzalez, Roberto López Vela and Elena Postigo Castellanos, eds., *Monarquías en conflicto. Linajes y nobleza en la articulación de la Monarquía Hispánica* (Madrid and Santander 2018); http://hmoderna.cchs.csic.es/webfehm/, 51-63.

Fagel, Raymond, 'Maestre de campo Francisco de Valdés. ¿Un soldado ejemplar en Flandes?', in: Magdalena de Pazzis Pi Corrales and Ana Sanz de Bremond Mayáns, eds., *Los Habsburgo y Europa: soldados y ejércitos (siglos XVI y XVII)* (Madrid 2019) 71-88.

Fagel, Raymond 'Introduction', in: Raymond Fagel, Leonor Álvarez Francés and Beatriz Santiago Belmonte, eds., *Early modern war narratives and the Revolt in the Low Countries* (Manchester 2020) 1-17.

Fagel, Raymond, 'Orange's Spanish mulatto and other side-changers: narratives on Spanish defection during the Revolt in the Low Countries', in: Raymond Fagel, Leonor Álvarez Francés and Beatriz Santiago Belmonte, eds., *Early modern war narratives and the Revolt in the Low Countries* (Manchester 2020) 107-124.

Fagel, Raymond, 'The origins of the Spanish Fury at Antwerp (1576): a battle within city walls', *Early Modern Low Countries* 4 (2020) 102-123.

Fagel, Raymond, *Cristóbal de Mondragón. De goede Spanjaard uit de Opstand* (Zierikzee 2020).

Fagel, Raymond, 'Cardinal Granvelle and the Revolt in the Low Countries: long distance communication and information 1567-1577' (in publication).

Fagel, Raymond, Beatriz Santiago Belmonte and Leonor Álvarez Francés, 'Eer en schuld. Heiligerlee en Jemmingen in Spaanse ogen', in: Inge Dekker and Sietse van der Hoek, eds., *Heiligerlee. Strijd in een landschap.van glorie en nederlaag* (Gorredijk 2021) 79-89.

Fernández Álvarez, Manuel, 'La cuestión de Flandes en la retina de la España de la época', in: J. Craeybeckx, F. Daelemans and F.G. Scheelings, eds., *1585. Op gescheiden wegen* (Leuven 1988) 107-120.

Fernández Conti, Santiago, and Félix Labrador Arroyo, '"Entre Douro e Minho". El prior don Hernando de Toledo y Portugal', in: Francisco Ruiz Gómez and Jesús M. Molero García, eds, *La orden de San Juan entre el Mediterráneo y La Mancha* (Alcázar de San Juan 2009) 367-383.

Fernández Gómez, Juan, 'Sobre la comedia El guapo Julián Romero de José de Cañizares', in: *Estudios ofrecidos a Emilio Alarcos Llorach, con motivo de sus xxv años de docencia en la Universidad de Oviedo* (Oviedo 1979) 407-417.

Fernández Izquierdo, Francisco, *La orden militar de Calatrava en el siglo XVI. Infraestructura institucional, sociología y prosopografía de sus caballeros* (Madrid 1992).

Fernández Izquierdo, Francisco, 'Las órdenes de caballería hispánicas y su proyección militar en los siglos XVI y XVII. Una aproximación a la orden de Santiago', in: Enrique García Hernán and Davide Maffi, eds., *Guerra y sociedad en la Monarquía Hispánica*, II (Madrid 2006) 861-883.

Fernández Secades, Lucía, *Los Valdés. Una casa nobiliaria en el Gijón de los siglos XVI y XVII* (Oviedo 2009).

Fineman, Joel, 'The history of the anecdote: fiction and fiction', in: H. Aram Veeser, ed., *The new historicism* (New York and London 1989) 49-76.

Fludernik, Monika, *Towards a 'natural' narratology* (London and New York 1996).

Fludernik, Monika, 'Letters and chronicles: How narrative are they?', in: Göran Rossholm, ed., *Essays on fiction and perspective* (Bern and Oxford 2004) 129-153.

Fonvieille, René, *La Seigneurie et la Ville de Hesdin-le-Vieux depuis le XIIme siècle jusqu'à la destruction de la ville, 1553* (Lille 1938).
Foreest, Nanning van, *Kort verhaal van het beleg van Alkmaar. Een ooggetuigenverslag*, H.F.K van Nierop and M. Joustra, eds. (Alkmaar 2000).
France, Renon de, *Histoire des troubles des Pays-Bas*, I, Charles Piot, ed. (Brussels 1886).
'Francisco de Carvajal', https://es.wikipedia.org/wiki/Francisco_de_Carvajal (accessed 5 December 2018).
Fruin, Robert, 'Prins Willem in onderhandeling met den vijand over vrede', in: *Verspreide geschriften*, II (The Hague 1900) 336-384.
Fruin, Robert, 'Het beleg en ontzet der stad Leiden in 1574', *Verspreide geschriften* II (The Hague 1900), 385-490.
Fruytiers, J., 'Corte beschryvinghe vande strenghe belegheringe ende wonderbaerlicke verlossinghe der stadt Leyden in Hollandt (Delft 1574)', in: R.J. Fruin, J.E.H. Hooft van Iddekinge and W.J.C. Rammelman Elsevier, eds., *De oude verhalen van het beleg en ontzet van Leiden bij gelegenheid van het derde eeuwgetijde in hun oorspronkelijken vorm herdrukt* (The Hague 1874).
Fuente, Manuel de la, 'Cristóbal de Mondragón, un héroe vasco en los tercios', *ABC*, 2 November 2013, https://www.abc.es/cultura/libros/20131005/abci-cristobal-mondragon-heroe-tercios-201310031211.html (accessed 30 June 2020).
Gachard, L.P., and J. Lefèvre, eds., *Correspondance de Philippe II* [CP] (Brussels, Ghent and Leipzig, 1851-1960).
Gachard, L.P., ed., *Correspondance de Guillaume le Taciturne*, [CT] III (Brussels, Leipzig and Ghent 1851).
Gachard, L.P., ed., *Correspondance de Marguérite d'Autriche, duchesse de Parme, avec Philippe II* [CM] (Brussels 1867).
García Cárcel, Ricardo, *La Leyenda negra. Historia y opinión* (Madrid 1998).
García Hernán, David, *La cultura de la guerra y el teatro del Siglo de Oro* (Madrid 2006).
García Hernán, Enrique, 'Francisco de Moncada y Moncada', DBE.
García Hernán, Enrique, 'Sancho de Londoño', DBE.
García Hernán, Enrique, 'Don Sancho de Londoño, perfil biográfico', *Revista de Historia Moderna* 22 (2004) 61-86.
García Hernán Enrique, *Ireland and Spain in the reign of Philip II* (Dublin 2009).
Gayangos, Pacual de, ed., *Catalogue of the manuscripts in the Spanish language in the British Library*, I (London 1875).
Geevers, Liesbeth, 'Hoe toegankelijk was de "papieren koning"? Een informeel communicatiekanaal tussen Lamoraal van Egmont en Willem van Oranje en de Spaanse centrale besluitvorming in de jaren 1559-1564', *TSEG. Low Countries Journal of Social and Economic History* 4,1 (2007) 39-60.

Geevers, Liesbeth, *Gevallen vazallen. De integratie van Oranje, Egmont en Horn in de Spaans-Habsburgse monarchie 1559-1567* (Amsterdam 2008).

Gelder, Esther van, *Tussen hof en keizerskroon. Carolus Clusius en de ontwikkeling van de botanie aan Midden-Europese hoven, 1573-1593* (Leiden 2011).

Génard, P., ed., 'La furie espagnole. Documents pour servir à l'histoire de Sac d'Anvers en 1576', *Annales de l'Académie d'Archéologie de Belgique* 32 (1876) 5-728.

González Dávila, Gil, *Teatro de las grandezas de la villa de Madrid, corte de los Reyes Católicos de España* (Madrid 1623).

González Dávila, Gil, *Teatro ecclesiastico de las iglesias metropolitanas y catedrales* (Madrid 1647).

González de León, Fernando, *The road to Rocroi: The Duke of Alba, the Count Duke of Olivares and the high command of the Spanish army of Flanders in the Eighty Years War 1567-1659,* (PhD thesis, Johns Hopkins University, Baltimore 1991).

González de León, Fernando, 'Doctors of the military discipline: Technical expertise and the paradigm of the Spanish soldier in the Early Modern period', *Sixteenth Century Journal* 27 (1996) 61-85.

González de León, Fernando, *The road to Rocroi. Class, culture and command in the Spanish army of Flanders 1567-1659* (Leiden and Boston 2009).

Goris, Jan-Albert, 'Alva en de Jesuïeten te Antwerpen', *Bijdragen tot de Geschiedenis* 17 (1926) 290-301.

Graaf, Ronald de, *Oorlog, mijn arme schapen. Een andere kijk op de Tachtigjarige Oorlog, 1565-1648* (Franeker 2004).

Greg, W.W., ed., *A Larum for London, 1602* (Oxford 1913).

Groenveld, Simon, *Hooft als historieschrijver* (Weesp 1981).

Groot, Wim de, *The seventh window. The King's window donated by Philip II and Mary Tudor to Sint Janskerk in Gouda (1557)* (Hilversum 2005).

Gysius, Johannes, *Oorspronck ende voortgang der Nederlandscher beroerten* (Delft 1626).

Haecht, Godevaert van, *Kroniek over de troebelen van 1565 tot 1574 te Antwerpen en elders*, R. van Roosbroeck, ed., 2 vols. (Antwerp 1929).

Ham, Gijs van der, *80 jaar oorlog* (Amsterdam 2018).

Ham, Willem van, 'Willemstad', www.Dutchrevolt (accessed 14 November 2018).

Harari, Yuval Noah, *Renaissance military memoirs. War, history, and identity, 1450-1600* (Woodbridge 2004).

Harmsen, Ton, 'Reynerius Bontius', Ceneton (Census Nederlands Toneel), www.let.leidenuniv.nl/Dutch/Ceneton/Bontius/index.html (accessed 21 January 2019).

Harmsen, Ton, 'Reinier Bontius en zijn toneelstuk over het *Beleg van Leiden* (1646)', *Omslag* 2 (2005) 12.

Hart, Kees 't, 'De slag op de Mokerheide. "Daer geschiede groote moort", *De groene Amsterdammer* 16 (17 April 2004), https://www.groene.nl/artikel/daer-geschiede-groote-moort (accessed 19 April 2019).

Heras, Jesús de las, *Julián Romero, él de las hazañas. De mozo de tambor a maestre de campo general 1518-2018* (Madrid 2018).

Herrera y Tordesillas, Antonio de, *Historia general del mundo*, 3 vols. (Madrid 1601-1612).

Herwerden, P.J. van, *Lodewijk van Nassau. Een leven gewijd aan de Nederlanden* (Assen 1939).

Hessen, Willem, *Beleegering van Haarlem* (Haarlem 1739).

Heyning, Katie, *De tapijten van Zeeland* (Middelburg 2007).

Hillgarth, J.H., *The mirror of Spain, 1500-1700. The formation of a myth* (Ann Arbor 2000).

Holthuis, Paul, *Frontierstad bij het scheiden van de markt. Deventer, militair, demografisch, economisch 1578-1648* (Groningen 1993).

Hooft, P.C., *Nederlandsche historien*, W.G. Hellinga and P. Tuynman, eds., editie 1642-1647; www.dbnl.org (Amsterdam 1972).

Hooft, P.C., *Nederlandse historiën. Een keuze uit het grote verhaal van de Nederlandse Opstand*, Frank van Gestel, Eddy Grootes and Jan de Jongste, eds. (Amsterdam 2007).

Horst, Daniel R., *De Opstand in zwart-wit. Propagandaprenten uit de Nederlandse Opstand 1566-1584* (Zutphen 2003).

Horst, Daniël R., 'The Duke of Alba: the ideal enemy', *Arte nuevo. Revista de estudios áureos* 1 (2014) 130-154.

Hortal Muñoz, José Eloy, *Los asuntos de Flandes. Las relaciones entre las Cortes de la Monarquía Hispánica y de los Países Bajos durante el siglo XVI* (Saarbrücken 2011).

Hortensius, Lambertus, 'Over de opkomst en den ondergang van Naarden', in: Petrus Hofman Peerlkamp, ed., *Werken uitgegeven door het Historisch Genootschap gevestigd te Utrecht*, nieuwe reeks 5 (Utrecht 1866) 55-187.

Hugo, Victor, *Oeuvres complètes de Victor Hugo, en voyage*, II, G. Simon, ed. (Paris 1910).

Huguerye, Michel de la *Mémoires*, Baron A. de Ruble, ed., I (Paris 1876).

Huisman, Anneke, 'Serviele secretaris of kleurrijke klerk? Een studie naar de politieke invloed van Juan de Albornoz, privé-secretaris van de derde hertog van Alva, tijdens diens verblijf in de Nederlanden 1567-1573', (MA thesis, Leiden University 1990).

Hume, A.S., 'Julian Romero – swashbuckler', in: *The year after the Armada and other historical studies* (London 1896) 75-121.

Hume, A.S., 'Los mercenarios españoles', in: *Españoles é ingleses en el siglo XVI* (Madrid and London 1903) 1-79.

Huussen, A.H., *Het leven van Ogier Ghislain de Busbecq en het verhaal van zijn avonturen als keizerlijk gezant in Turkije (1554-1562)* (Leiden 1949).

Janssens, Gustaaf, *'Brabant in het verweer'. Loyale oppositie tegen Spanje's bewind in de Nederlanden van Alva tot Farnese, 1567-1578* (Kortrijk-Heule 1989).

Jensen, Lotte and Lieke van Deinsen, Het theater van de herinnering. Vaderlandshistorisch toneel in de achttiende eeuw', *Spiegel der Letteren* 54,2 (2012) 193-225.

Jong, J.D. de, 'Culemborg onder Spaanse bezetting 1567-1577', *Bijdragen en Mededelingen Gelre* 57 (1958) 191-200.

Kagan, Richard L., *Clio & the crown. The politics of history in medieval and early modern Spain* (Baltimore 2009).

Kamen, Henry, *The Duke of Alba* (New Haven and London 2004).

Kanter, Johan de, *Chronijk van Zierikzee* (2$^{nd}$ edition: Zierikzee 1795).

Kiernan, V.G., *The duel in European history. Honour and the reign of aristocracy* (Oxford 1988).

Kloek, Els, *Kenau en Magdalena. Vrouwen in de Tachtigjarige Oorlog* (Nijmegen 2014).

Kooij, Barbara, *Spaanse ooggetuigen over het beleg van Haarlem, 1572-1573* (Hilversum 2018).

Koppenol, Johan, *Het Leids Ontzet. 3 oktober 1574 door de ogen van tijdgenoten* (Amsterdam 2002).

Krusenstjern, Benigna von, *Selbstzeugnisse der Zeit des Dreissigjährigen Krieges. Beschreibendes Verzeichnis* (Berlin 1997).

Kuijpers, Erika, et al., eds. *Memory before modernity. Practices of memory in early Modern Europe* (Leiden and Boston 2013).

Kuijpers, Erika, 'The creation and development of social memories of traumatic events: the Oudewater massacre of 1575', in: Michael Linden and Krysztof Rutkowski, eds., *Hunting memories and beneficial forgetting. Posttraumatic stress disorders, biographical developments, and social conflicts* (Amsterdam, etc. 2013) 191-201.

Kuin, Roger, ed., *The correspondence of Philip Sidney*, I (Oxford 2012).

Lamal, Nina. 'Le orecchie si piene di Fiandra. Italian news and histories on the revolt in the Netherlands (1566-1648)', (PhD thesis, KU Leuven and University of Saint Andrews, 2014).

Lamal, Nina, 'Internationale berichtgeving over de opstand in de Nederlanden', lecture at the symposium entitled 'Berichten over tachtig jaar oorlog. De Nederlandse Opstand tussen feit en fictie, Royal Library, The Hague, 22 November 2018, https://www.youtube.com/watch?reload=9&v=BslCmOkRu6U (accessed 8 April 2020).

Lamal, Nina, *News from Antwerp. Italian communication on the Dutch Revolt* (Leiden, forthcoming).

Lammers, C.J., *Vreemde overheersing. Bezetten en bezetting in sociologisch perspectief* (Amsterdam 2005).

Lancaster, William Scott, 'A Larum for London. A critical edition of the performative text', (PhD thesis., Texas A&M University-Commerce, 2011).

Landía Pacual, Carmen M., 'Hernando de Toledo', DBE.

Le Clerc, Jean, *Histoire des Provinces Unies* (Amsterdam 1728).

Le Petit, Jean François, *La grande chronique ancienne et moderne de Hollande, Zelande, etc.*, II (Dordrecht 1610).

Lem, Anton van der, 'Louis de Boisot', www.Dutchrevolt.edu (accessed 26 November 2018).

Lem, Anton van der, 'Sancho Dávila', www.Dutchrevolt.edu (accessed 8 April 2020).

Lem, Anton van der, *De Opstand in de Nederlanden, 1568-1648. De Tachtigjarige Oorlog in woord en beeld* (Nijmegen 2018).

Lem, Anton van der, *Revolt in the Netherlands. The Eighty years War, 1568-1648* (London 2019).

León Pinelo, Antonio de, *Anales de Madrid*, Pedro Fernández Martín, ed. (Madrid 1971).

*Lettres et négociations de Claude de Mondoucet, résident de France aux Pays-Bas 1571-1574*, L. Didier, ed., 2 vols. (Paris and Reims 1891-1892).

'Lespakket Slag op de Mookerheide', https://www.huystemoock.nl/nl/verhalen-2/lespakket-slag-op-de-mookerheide (accessed 16 April 2019).

'Libro de las cosas que succedieron en Flandes', Jacome Fernández?, Bibliothèque Nationale de France, Paris, Ms. Español 182.

Logchem, Elly van, 'Lucretia Wilhelmina van Merken', *1001 vrouwen uit de Nederlandse geschiedenis*, Els Kloek ed. (Nijmegen 2013) 677-679.

Lom, C., *Beschryving der stad Lier in Brabant* (The Hague 1740).

Lorenz de Rada, Francisco, *Libro segundo. Arte del instrumento armigero. Espada* (Madrid 1705).

Losada, Juan Carlos, *San Quintín. El relato vivo y vibrante de las campañas del conde de Egmont en la convulsa Europa de Felipe II* (Madrid 2005).

Losada, Juan Carlos, 'Julián Romero. Una leyenda', *La aventura de la historia* 90 (2006) 82-87.

Lottin, Alain, 'Nobles, Calvinistes et Gueux en 1566. trois figures de la révolte: Escobecques, Longastre, Hannescamps', *Revue du Nord* 395 (2012) 307-325.

Mackenzie, Ann L., 'A study in dramatic contrasts. The Siege of Antwerp in *A larum for London* and *El saco de Amberes*', *Bulletin of Hispanic Studies* 59, 4 (1982) 283-300.

Mackenzie, Ann L., 'El saco de Amberes. Comedia falsamente atribuida a Calderón. ¿Es de Rojas Zorrilla?', in: Hans Flasche, ed., *Hacia Calderón. Sexto coloquio Anglo-germano* (Wiesbaden 1983) 151-168.

Manso Porto, Carmen, 'Diego Sarmiento de Acuña', DBE.

Manteau, Jacques, 'Memorie of histories verhaal van het geen staande de belegering der stad is voorgevallen', in: *Tweehonderd-jarig jubelfeest, ter gedagtenisse der verlossinge van de stad Zierikzee uit de Spaansche dwwingelandy, plegtig geviert op den zevenden november 1776* (Zierikzee 1777).

Maréchal, Dominique, 'De portretten van Juan Lopez Gallo, zijn echtgenote Catharina Pardo en hun kinderen, door Pieter Pourbus, 1561-1568. Onbekende documentaire foto's van hun eind 19de eeuwse toestand', *Handelingen van het Genootschap voor Geschiedenis te Brugge* 149 (2012) 233-238.

Mariana. Juan de, 'Historia general de España', in: Francisco Pi y Margall, ed. *Obras completas*, II (Madrid 1854).

Marichalar, Antonio, 'Muerte de Julián Romero', *Cuadernos Hispanoamericanos* 35 (1952) 3-19.

Marichalar, Antonio, *Julián Romero* (Madrid 1952).

*Marnixi epistulae. De briefwisseling van Marnix van Sint-Aldegonde. Een kritische uitgave, pars I, 1558-1576*, Aloïs Gerlo and Rudolf de Smet, eds. (Brussels 1990).

Martels, Z.R.W.M. von, *Augerius Gislenius Busbequius* (Groningen 1989).

Martín García, Gonzalo, *Sancho Dávila, soldado del Rey* (Ávila 2010).

Martínez, Miguel, *Front lines. Soldiers' writing in the Early Modern Hispanic world* (Philadelphia 2016).

Martínez, Miguel, 'Narrating mutiny in the army of Flanders: Cristóbal Rodríguez Alva's *La inquieta Flandes* (1594)', in: Raymond Fagel, Leonor Álvarez Francés and Beatriz Santiago Belmonte, eds., *Early modern war narratives and the Revolt in the Low Countries* (Manchester 2020) 89-106.

Martínez Hernández, Santiago, 'El desafío de la casa de Toledo: Felipe II y el proceso contra Don Fadrique de Toledo, IV Duque de Alba (1566-1585)', *Mediterranea, richerche storiche* 10 (2013) 473-512.

Martínez Laínez, Fernando, *El ocaso de los héroes I, Aceros rotos* (Madrid 2013).

Martínez Laínez, Fernando, *Roncos tambores, el ocaso de los heroes* II (Madrid 2015).

Martínez Luna, Fernando, *Een ondraaglijk juk. Nederlandse beeldvorming van Spanje en de Spanjaarden* (Hilversum 2018).

Martínez Ruiz, Enrique, 'Sancho Dávila', DBE.

Martínez Ruiz, Enrique, 'Sancho Dávila y la anexión de Portugal', *Chronica Nova. Revista de Historia moderna de la Universidad de Granada* 2 (1968) 5-35.

Martínez Ruiz, Enrique, 'El gran motín de 1574 y la coyuntura flamenca', *Miscelánea de estudios dedicados al profesor Antonio Marín Ocete*, II (Granada 1974) 637-659.

Martínez Ruiz, Enrique, 'Sancho Dávila en las campañas del duque de Alba en Flandes', *Anuario de Historia Moderna y Contemporánea* 2-3 (1975-1976) 105-142.

Martínez Ruiz, Enrique, *El Castellano de Flandes. El hombre que mantuvo en pie el imperio de Felipe II* (Madrid 2007).

Martínez Ruiz, Enrique, *Los soldados del rey. Los ejércitos de la Monarquía Hispánica 1480-1700* (Madrid 2008).

Más Chao, Andrés, 'El soldado español de los tercios. Dos tipos determinantes: el profesional y el aventurero. Las vidas contrapuestas de Julián Romero y Alfonso de Contreras', in: *El ejército y la armada de Felipe II, ante el IV centenario de su muerte* (Madrid 1997) 39-56.

Mayalde, Condesa de, 'Antonio Marichalar: Julián Romero', *Revista de estudios políticos* 46, n. 46, (November-December 1952) 179.

Mazzocchi, Giuseppe, 'Un governatore spagnolo di Mortara: Lope de Acuña y Avellaneda', *Anali di storia pavese* 16-17 (1988) 221-225.

Meij, J.C.A. de, *De watergeuzen en de Nederlanden 1568-1572* (Amsterdam and London 1972).

Meijer Drees, Marijke, 'Burgemeester Van der Werf als vaderlandse toneelheld; een politieke autoriteit in belegeringsdrama's', *De zeventiende eeuw* 8 (1992) 167-176.

Meijer-Drees, Marijke, 'Vaderlandse heldinnen in belegeringstoneelstukken', *De Nieuwe Taalgids* 85 (1993) 71-82.

*Mémoires anonymes sur les troubles des Pays-Bas 1565-1580*, Alexandre Henne and J.B. Blaes, eds., 5 vols. (Brussels and The Hague 1859-1866).

*Mémoires de Fréderic Perrenot, sieur de Champagney 1573-1590*, A.L.P Robaulx de Soumoy, ed. (Brussels and The Hague 1860).

Mendoza, Bernardino de, *Comentarios de las guerras de los Países Bajos*, in Biblioteca de autores españoles XXVIII, *Historiadores de sucesos particulares* II (Madrid 1948).

Mendoza, Bernardino de, *Comentarios de lo sucedido en las guerras de los Países Bajos*, Antonio Cortijo Ocaña and Angel Gómez Moreno, eds. (Madrid 2008).

Menéndez Valdés, Gregorio, *Avisos históricos y políticos*, I (Madrid 1774).

Merken, Lucretia Wilhelmina van, 'Het beleg der stad Leyden', in: Nicolaas Simon van Winter and Lucretia Wilhelmina van Merken, *Tooneelpoëzy* (Amsterdam 1774) 1-115.

Merken, Lucretia Wilhelmina van, *Jacob Simonszoon de Ryk* (Amsterdam 1774).

Merken, Lucretia Wilhelmina van, *Jacob Simonszoon de Rijk*, Lotte Jensen and Tommie van Wanrooij, eds. (Nijmegen 2019).

Merriman, Marcus, and John Summerson, 'The Scottish border', in: H.M. Colvin, ed., *The history of the King's works*, IV-2 (London 1982) 607-726.

Mesa, Eduardo de, and Ángel García Pinto, *La batalla de San Quentín, 1557* (Madrid 2004).

Meteren, Emanuel van, *Belgische oft Nederlandsche historie van onsen tijden* (Delft 1599).

Meteren, Emanuel van, *Historien der Nederlanden, en haar naburen oorlogen tot het iaar 1612* (Dordrecht 1646).

Meulleners, J.L., 'De slag van Mook, 1 april 1574', *Publications de la Société historique et archéologique dans le Limbourg* 30 (1893) 171-196.

Millar, Gilbert John, *Tudor mercenaries and auxiliaries 1485-1547* (Charlottesville 1980).

Montaigne, Michel de, 'L'heure des parlements dangereuses', *Essais* I, 6 (Paris 1595).

Moonen, Arnold, *Korte chronyke der stadt Deventer van de oudste geheugenisse af tot het vredejaer van 1648* (3d edition, Deventer 1714).

*Moort-dadich verhael vande gheschiedenissen, moort ende destructie vande stede van Naerden*, pamphlet collection Van Someren 53, University Library Utrecht, (published after 6 November 1573).

Morand, Paul, *Monplaisir… en littérature* (Paris 1967).

Moréri, Louis, *Le grand dictionnaire historique ou le mélange curieux de l'histoire sacrée et profane*, 6 vols. (Amsterdam 1740).

Morgan, Walter, *The expedition in Holland, 1572-1574*, Duncan Caldecott-Baird, ed. (Slough 1976).

Morley, S. Griswold, and Courtney Bruerton, *Cronología de las comedias de Lope de Vega, con un examen de las atribuciones dudosas, basado todo ello en un estudio de su versificación estrófica* (Madrid 1968).

Mosmuller, Jos, 'Tachtigjarige Oorlog is niet alleen van de Hollanders', *De Volkskrant*, 22 January 2019.

Motley, John Lothrop, *The rise of the Dutch republic*, I (London 1929).

Mulcahy, Rosemarie 'The manifestation of his magnificence: the third Duke of Alba and the arts', in: Maurits Ebben, Margriet Lacy-Bruijn and Rolof van Hövell tot Westerflier, eds., *Alba, general and servant to the crown* (Rotterdam 2011) 137-167.

Muñoz Altea, Fernando, *Blasones y apellidos* (México D.F. 2002).

Murrin, Michael, *History and warfare in renaissance epic* (Chicago 1994).

*Nederlandsche geschiedzangen*, J. van Vloten, ed., II (Amsterdam 1864).

*Newe Zeitung von dem Scharmutzel, so geschehen auff der Mouckerheid, bij Nemwegen gelegen. Und von den Spanischen, wie sie, nach dem diese slacht gehalten und die uberhand bekommen, mit grosser gewalte nach Andtorff gezogen und mit list darinn gekommen sein. Auch wie schrecklich sie allda wuten, rasen und toben. Geschehen im Monat Maij* (1574), published in: Gasparus de l'Agarge, *De blokkade van Zalt-Bommel. Dagverhaal van Gasparus de L'Agarge*, H.F.M. Huybers and J. Kleyntjens, eds. (Arnhem 1925) 25-27.

Nicolasen, Lidy, *De geuzendochter* (Amsterdam 2017).

Nierop, Henk van, *Het verraad van het Noorderkwartier. Oorlog, terreur en recht in de Nederlandse Opstand* (Amsterdam 1999).

Nievas Rojas, Adalid, 'Nuevos datos para la biografía de Francisco de Aldana (II). Primera etapa en Flandes, 1567-1571', *Boletín de la Real Academia Española* 100, 321 (2020) 147-206.

Nimwegen, Olaf van, and Louis Sicking, 'De Opstand', in: Petra Groen, ed., *De Tachtigjarige Oorlog. Van opstand naar geregelde oorlog, 1568-1648* (The Hague 2013) 37-110.

Nomsz., Johannes, *Maria van Lalain of de verovering van Doornik* (Amsterdam 1778).

Nomsz., Johannes, *Willem de Eersten* (Amsterdam 1779).

Noordervliet, Nelleke, *Door met de strijd* (Amsterdam 2018).

*Nueva Colección de Documentos Inéditos para la Historia de España*, 6 vols. [NCD] (Madrid 1892-1896).

Nuyens, W.J.F., *Geschiedenis van den Opstand in de Nederlanden, van de komst van Alva tot aan de bevrediging van Gend, 1567-1576*, II (Amsterdam 1867).

Ocampo, Florián de, 'Sucesos de los años 1548 a 1558', Biblioteca Nacional Madrid, Mss. 9937.

On stage, http://www.vondel.humanities.uva.nl/onstage/ (accessed 27 November 2018).

Orlers, J.J., *Beschrijvinge der stadt Leyden*, 2nd edition (Leiden 1641).

'Overste Sancho d'Avila', http://www.marceltettero.nl/Spanje/Avila/Avila.htm (accessed 11 April 2019).

Padilla, Pedro de, *Romancero* (Madrid 1583).

Padilla, Pedro de, *Romancero*, Marqués de la Fuensanta del Valle, ed. (Madrid 1880).

Pando Fernández de Pinedo, Manuel, Marqués de Miraflores, *Vida del general español D. Sancho Dávila y Daza, conocido en el siglo XVI con el nombre de El Rayo de la Guerra* (Madrid 1857).

Pando y Fernández de Pinedo, Manuel, *Vida política* (Madrid 1865).

Paradin, Guillaume, *Histoire de notre tems* (Lyon 1558).

Parker, Geoffrey, *The army of Flanders and the Spanish Road, 1567-1659* (Cambridge 1972).

Parker, Geoffrey, *The Dutch Revolt* (London 1977).

Parker, Geoffrey, 'Mutiny and discontent in the Spanish army of Flanders, 1572-1607', in: *Spain and the Netherlands 1559-1659. Ten studies* (London 1979) 106-121.

Parker, Geoffrey, 'Corruption and imperialism in the Spanish Netherlands: the case of Francisco de Lixalde, 1567-1613', in: *Spain and the Netherlands 1559-1659. Ten studies* (London 1979) 152-163.

Parker, Geoffrey, *Spain and the Netherlands 1559-1659. Ten studies* (London 1979).

Parker, Geoffrey, 'The etiquette of atrocity: the laws of war in Early Modern Europe', in: *Empire, war and faith in Early Modern Europe* (London 2002) 143-168.

Parker, Geoffrey, *The army of Flanders and the Spanish Road, 1567-1659* (2nd edition, Cambridge 2004).

Parker, Geoffrey, *Felipe II, La biografía definitiva* (Madrid 2010).
Parker, Geoffrey, *Emperor. A new life of Charles V* (New Haven and London 2019).
Pérez de Montalbán, Juan, *El segundo Séneca de España y príncipe Don Carlos*, Federico Carlos Sainz de Robles, ed., in: *Teatro español* IV (Madrid 1943)
Pérez-Reverte, Arturo, 'Una historia de violencia', *XLSemanal*, 25-9-2011. www.perezreverte.com/articulo/patentes-corso/626/una-historia-de-violencia, (accessed 6 November 2018).
Pérez Reverte, Arturo, 'Cuartos de final en Goes', *XLSemanal*, 7-10-2012. Web official de Arturo Pérez-Reverte www.perezreverte.com/articulo/patentes-corso/706/cuartos-de-final-en-goes/ (accessed 6 November 2018).
Perrenot, Frédéric, *Mémoires de Frédéric Perrenot, sieur de Champagney, 1573-1590*, A.L.P. Robaulx de Soumoy, ed. (Brussels and The Hague 1860).
Phillips, Gervase, *The Anglo-Scots wars 1513-1550. A military history* (Woodbridge and Rochester 1999).
Phillips, William D. and Carla Rahn Phillips, 'Spanish wool and Dutch rebels: the Middelburg incident of 1574', *American Historical Review* 82 (1977) 312-330.
Pí Corrales, Magdalena de Pazzis, *España y las potencias nórdicas. La otra invencible, 1574* (Madrid 1983).
'Plundering van de stad Mechelen door de Spanjaarden (2 oktober 1572)', in: *Mengelingen van historisch-vaderlandschen inhoud,* J.F. Willems, ed. (Antwerp 1827-1830) 390-422.
Pollmann, Judith, 'Eine natürliche Feindschaft: Ursprung und Funktion der Schwarzen Legende über Spanien in den Niederlanden, 1560-1581', in: *Feindbilder. Die Darstellung des Gegners in der politischen Publizistik des Mittelalters und der Neuzeit,* Franz Bosbach, ed. (Cologne and Weimar 1992) 73-93.
Pollmann, Judith, *Memory in Early Modern Europe, 1500-1800* (Oxford 2017).
Pollmann, Judith and Erika Kuijpers. 'Why remember terror? Memories of violence in the Dutch Revolt', in: Jane Ohlmeyer and Micheál Ó Siochrí, eds., *Ireland 1641. Contexts and reactions* (Manchester 2013) 176-196
Pollmann, Judith, and Monica Stensland, 'Alba's reputation in the early modern Low Countries', in: Maurits Ebben, Margriet Lacy-Bruijn and Rolof van Hövell tot Westerflier, eds., *Alba, general and servant to the crown* (Rotterdam 2011) 309-325.
Porreño, Baltasar, *Dichos y hechos del señor rey don Felipe Segundo*, Antonio Álvarez-Ossorio Alvariño and Paloma Cuenca, eds. (Madrid 2001).
Postma, Folkert, *Viglius van Aytta. De jaren met Granvelle 1549-1564* (Zutphen 2000).
Pot, Jan, *Het beleg van Zierikzee* (Leiden 1925).
Pot, J., 'Verhaal van het beleg voor Zierikzee (1575-1576) door Cornelis Claes', *Bijdragen en Mededeelingen van het Historisch Genootschap* 50 (1929) 107-140.

Poullet, E., and C. Piot, eds., *Correspondance du cardinal de Granvelle 1565-1586, 12 vols.* [CG] (Brussels 1877-1896).

Puddu, Raffaele, *Il soldato gentiluomo. Autoritratto d'una società guerriera: la Spagna del Cinquecento* (Bologna 1982).

Punt, Jeroen, and Louis Ph. Sloos, *Willem van Oranje. De jonge prins van Oranje als edelman en militair* (Zutphen 2018).

Quatrefages, René, *Los tercios españoles 1567-1577* (Madrid 1979).

Quatrefages, René, *Los tercios* (Madrid 1983).

Quevedo, Francisco de, *El Buscón*, Pablo Jauralde Pou, ed. (Madrid 1990).

Regt, W.M.C. 'Jan van Hangest-Genlis, gezegd d'Yvoy', in; *Nieuw Nederlandsch Biografisch Woordenboek* VII (Leiden 1927).

Reitsma, R., *Centrifugal and centripetal forces in the Early Dutch Republic. The States of Overyssel, 1566-1600* (Amsterdam 1982).

Reijner, Cees, *Italiaanse geschiedschrijvers over de Nederlandse Opstand, 1585-1650. Een transnationale geschiedenis* (PhD thesis, University of Leiden, 2020).

Reijner, Cees, '"Lode della nazione italiana": Italian historians on the Spanish soldiers', in: Raymond Fagel, Leonor Álvarez Francés and Beatriz Santiago Belmonte, eds., *Early modern war narratives and the Revolt in the Low Countries* (Manchester 2020) 74-88.

*Relación de la rota que se dio al conde Ludovico de Nasao y a los que le seguían a 14 de abril de 1574.* AGS E. 557.

'Relación de la toma y combate del castillo de Dinant', Biblioteca de El Escorial, Manuscritos españoles V, II, 3, f. 370.

*Relations politiques des Pays-Bas et de l'Angleterre sous le règne de Philippe II*, 10 vols., Joseph Kervyn de Lettenhove, ed. (Brussels 1882-1892).

Remón, Alonso, 'La famosa comedia de Don Juan de Austria en Flandes', *Obras de Lope de Vega* XII (Madrid 1901) 399-433.

Rennert, Hugo Albert, *The life of Lope de Vega 1562-1635* (New York 1968).

Reyd, Everhard van, *Voornaemste gheschiedenissen inde Nederlanden ende elders beschreven* (Arnhem 1626).

Reyd, Everhard van, *Oorspronck ende voortganck vande Nederlantsche oorloghen* (Arnhem 1633).

Rijkse, Ronald, 'Marnix van Sint Aldegonde: God, Nederland en Oranje', in: *Philips van Marnix van Sint Aldegonde,* Inge Schoeps and Arnold Wiggers, eds. (Antwerp 1998) 163-204.

Río, Martin Antonio del, *La crónica sobre Don Juan de Austria*, Miguel Ángel Echevarría Bacigalupe, ed. (Vienna and Munich 2003).

Risco, Alberto, *The apostle of the Marianas: the life, labors and martyrdom of ven. Diego Luis de San Vitores, 1627-1672* (Guam 1970).

Rittersma, Rengenier C., *Mytho-poetics at work. A study of the figure of Egmont, the Dutch Revolt and its influence in Europe* (Leiden and Boston 2018).

Rivarola y Pineda, Juan Féliz Francisco de, *Monarquía española, Blasón de su nobleza*, II (Madrid 1736).

Ródenas de Moya, Domingo, 'Presentación', in: Antonio Marichalar, *Riesgo y ventura del Duque de Osuna* (Madrid 1998) 7-11.

Ródenas de Moya, Domingo, 'Antonio Marichalar. El embajador europeo del generación del 27', in:Antonio de Marichalar, *Ensayos literarios* (Santander 2002) ix-liv.

Ródenas Vilar, Rafael, *Vida cotodiana y negocio en la Segovia del Siglo de oro. El mercader Juan de Cuéllar* (Valladolid 1990).

Rodríguez Hernández, Antonio José, *Los tercios de Flandes* (Madrid 2015).

Rodríguez Pérez, Yolanda, *De Tachtigjarige Oorlog in Spaanse ogen. De Nederlanden in Spaanse historische en literaire teksten, circa 1548-1673* (Nijmegen 2003).

Rodríguez Pérez, Yolanda, *The Dutch Revolt through Spanish eyes. Self and other in historical and literary texts of Golden Age Spain, c. 1548-1673* (Oxford and Bern 2008).

Rodríguez Pérez, Yolanda, 'El amotinado como español ejemplar. Apuntes sobre *El Saco de Amberes* de Rojas Zorrilla *y Los amotinados en Flandes* de Vélez de Guevara', in: *Alianzas entre historia y ficción. Homenaje a Patrcik Collard,* Eugenia Houvenaghel and Ilse Logie, eds. (Geneva 2009) 237-248.

Rodríguez Pérez, Yolanda, 'Muiters op het toneel van de Spaanse Gouden Eeuw. Van verraders tot oorlogshelden', in: *Oorlogsliteratuur in de Vroegmoderne tijd. Vorm, identiteit en herinnering,* Lotte Jensen and Nina Geerdink, eds. (Hilversum 2013) 71-86.

Rodríguez Pérez, Yolanda, 'Un leopardo no puede cambiar sus manchas. La leyenda negra en Los Países Bajos', in: *La sombra de la leyenda negra,* María José Villaverde Rico and Francisco Castilla Urbano, eds. (Madrid 2016) 140-172.

Rodríguez Pérez, Yolanda, ed., *Literary Hispanophobia and Hispanophilia in Britain and the Low Countries (1550-1850)* (Amsterdam 2020).

Rodríguez Pérez, Yolanda, Antonio Sánchez Jiménez and Harm den Boer, eds., *España ante sus críticos: las claves de la Leyenda Negra* (Frankfurt am Main and Madrid 2015).

Rodríguez, Pedro, and Justina Rodríguez, eds., *Don Francés de Alava y Beamonte. Correspondencia inédita de Felipe II con su embajador en París, 1564-1570* (San Sebastián 1991).

Rodríguez-Salgado, M.J., *The Changing face of empire. Charles V, Philip II and Habsburg authority, 1551-1559* (Cambridge 1988).

Rodríguez-Salgado, M.J., 'Il capo dei capi: The Duke of Alba in Italy, in: *Alba. General and servant,* Maurits Ebben, Margriet Lacy-Bruijn and Rolof van Hövell tot Westerflier, ed. (Rotterdam 2013) 227-255.

Rodríguez-Salgado, M.J., '"Do not reveal that I wrote this". Diplomatic correspondence, news and narratives in the early years of the civil war in the Low Countries', in: *Early modern war narratives and the Revolt in the Low Countries,* Raymond Fagel, Leonor Álvarez Francés and Beatriz Santiago Belmonte, eds. (Manchester 2020) 18-35.

Rojo Vega, Anastasio, '1572. Testamento e inventario de Hernando del Castillo, regidor de Medina del Campo': https://investigadoresrb.patrimonionacional.es/uploads/2013/07/1572-CASTILLO.pdf (accessed 30 October 2018).

Romero, Julián, *El barba azul de los reyes* (Paris; year of publication unknown).

Rooms, Etienne, 'Een nieuwe visie op de gebeurtenissen die geleid hebben tot de Spaanse Furie te Antwerpen op 4 november 1576', *Bijdragen tot de Geschiedenis* 54 (1971) 31-55.

Rooze-Stouthamer, Clazina, *De opmaat tot de Opstand. Zeeland en het centraal gezag, 1566-1572* (Hilversum 2009).

Roquefort, Jean Baptiste Bonaventure de, *Glossaire de la langue romane, rédigé d'après les manuscrits* (Paris 1820).

Rozas, Juan Manuel, 'La obra dramática de Lope de Vega', in: *Estudios sobre Lope de Vega* (Madrid 1990) 37-68.

Rozet, Albin, *L'invasion de la France et le siège de Saint-Dizier par Charles-Quint en 1544* (Paris 1910).

Sáenz Herrero, Jorge, 'Humanismo militar en el siglo XVI: Sancho de Londoño y su Discurso sobre la forma de reducir la disciplina militar a mejor y antiguo estado', *Berceo* 163 (2012) 59-82

Salcedo Ruiz, Ángel, *El coronel Cristóbal de Mondragón. Apuntes para su biografía* (Madrid 1905).

Saltillo, Marqués del, 'Servidores del rey Don Felipe', *Hispania* 1,4 (1941) 120-122.

Sánchez Jiménez, Antonio, *El Sansón de Extremadura: Diego García de Paredes en la literatura española del siglo XVI* (Newark 2006).

Sánchez Jiménez, Antonio, 'Las comedias del capitán Julián Romero, héroe de Flandes', in: Julio Vélez Sainz and Antonio Sánchez Jiménez, eds., *El teatro soldadesco y la cultura militar en la España imperial* (Madrid 2015) 105-130.

Sánchez Martín, Juan Luis, 'Valdés, Francisco de', in: *Diccionario Biográfico Español* 48 (Madrid 2013) 914-920; DBE.

Sandoval, Prudencio de, *Historia de la vida y hechos del emperador Carlos V*, III, Carlos Seco Serrano, ed. (Madrid 1956).

Santiago Belmonte, Beatriz, 'The year of the furies. Military correspondence around the Sack of Antwerp (1576)', in: Raymond Fagel, Leonor Álvarez Francés and Beatriz Santiago Belmonte, eds., *Early modern war narratives and the Revolt in the Low Countries* (Manchester 2020) 56-73.

Schelven, A.A. van, *Marnix van Sint Aldegonde* (Utrecht 1939).

Schepper, Hugo de, 'de markies van Havré, vredemaker en adellijk bueaucraat 1549-1613' in: *Bestuurders en geleerden. Opstellen over onderwerpen uit de Nederlandse geschiedenis van de zestiende, zeventiende en achttiende eeuw, aangeboden aan Prof. Dr. J.J. Woltjer bij zijn afscheid als hoogleraar van de Rijksuniversiteit te Leiden,* S. Groenveld, M.E.H.N. Mout and I. Schöffer, eds. (Amsterdam and Dieren 1985) 33-43.

Schepper, Hugo de, 'La "Guerra de Flandes". Una sinopsis de su leyenda negra 1550-1650', *Foro Hispánico* 3 (1992) 67-86; special issue: http://dbe.rah.es/ Contactos entre los Países Bajos y el mundo ibérico, Jan Lechner, ed. (Amsterdam and Atlanta 1992).

Schepper, Hugo de, 'Frederik Perrenot van Champagney (1536 1602), het "enfant terrible" van de familie Granvelle', in: *Les Granvelle et les anciens Pays-Bas,* Krista de Jonge and Gustaaf Janssens, eds. (Leuven 2000) 233-244.

Schortinghuis, D.H., 'Mondragon. De wad-lopende Spaanse kolonel, *Ons leger* 48,9 (1964) 22-26

Schulten, C.M., 'Het beleg van Alkmaar', in: *Alkmaar ontzet 1573-1973* I. Schöffer et al. (Alkmaar 1973) 61-82.

Sevenster, J., *De stenen man. Caspar de Robles, stadhouder van Friesland, Groningen en Ommelanden van 1572-1576* (Leeuwarden 1985).

Sherer, Idan, '"All of us, in one voice, demand what's owed us". Mutiny in the Spanish infantry during the Italian Wars, 1525-1538', *Journal of Military History* 78 (2014) 893-926.

Sherer, Idan, *Warriors for a living. The experience of the Spanish infantry in the Italian Wars, 1494-1559* (Leiden and Boston 2017).

Siebelink, Jan, 'Ik bleef krabben tot hij eindelijk wakker werd', *NRC Handelsblad,* 30 juli 2007, 16.

Simonneau, H., 'Antoine Olivier, officier d'armes et agent double au sein de la Toison d'Or, 1567-1573, *Publication du Centre européen d'études bourguignonnes* 48 (2008), 291-305.

Simons, Adam, *Over 't kasteel van Antwerpen*, I (Utrecht 1831).

'Slag bij Delft', https://nl.wikipedia.org/wiki/Slag_bij_Delft (accessed 30 January 2019).

Smallegange, M., *Cronyk van Zeeland*, I (Middelburg 1696 [1700]).

Smit, J., *Den Haag in den geuzentijd* (The Hague 1922).

Smith, Leonard V., *The embattled self. French soldiers' testimony of the Great War* (Ithaca and London 2007).

Smolderen, L., 'La statue du duc d'Albe a-t-elle été mise en pièces par la population anversoise en 1577?', *Jaarboek Koninklijk Museum voor Schone Kunsten* (1980) 113-136.

Soen, Violet, *Geen pardon zonder paus! Studie over de complementariteit van het koninklijk en pauselijk generaal pardon (1570-1574) en over inquisiteur-generaal Michael Baius, 1560-1576* (Brussels 2007).

Soen, Violet, ¿Mas allá de la leyenda negra? Léon van der Essen y la historiografía reciente en torno al castigo de las ciudades rebeldes en los Países Bajos (siglos XIV a XVI)', in: Léon van der Essen, *El ejército español en Flandes 1567-1584*, Gustaaf Janssens, ed. (Cuacos de Yuste 2008) 45-72.

Soen, Violet, 'Collaborators and parvenus? Berlaymont and Noircarmes, loyal noblemen in the Dutch Revolt', *Dutch Crossing* 35,1 (2011) 20-38.

Soen, Violet, *Vredehandel. Adelijke en Habsburgse verzoeningspogingen tijdens de Nederlandse Opstand* (Amsterdam 2012).

Soest, Juan van, 'Un español en Holanda: el capitán Gaspar de Robles'. *Hispania* 15 (1955) 110-116.

Soly, Hugo, 'De bouw van de Antwerpse citadel (1567-1571), sociaal-economische aspecten', *Belgisch tijdschrift voor militaire geschiedenis* 21 (1976) 549-578.

*Souvenirs de la Flandre wallone, recherches historiques et choix de documents relatifs à Douai et aux anciennes provinces du nord de la France* 19 (1879).

'Spotsagen en spotnamen. Middelburg', http://www.verhalenbank.nl/items/show/39216 (accessed 29 November 2018).

Steegmans, Martin, 'Erfenis van een vriendelijke vijand', *Acta* 1,2 (2012) 12-16. http://actahistorica.nl/publication/view/2012-0-2 (accessed 22 October 2018).

Steen, Jasper van der, *Memory wars in the Low Countries, 1566-1700*, (PhD thesis, University of Leiden, 2014).

Steen, Jasper van der, 'North and south: a comparison of episodic war narratives during the Revolt in the Low Countries, in: Raymond Fagel, Leonor Álvarez Francés and Beatriz Santiago Belmonte, eds., *Early modern war narratives and the Revolt in the Low Countries* (Manchester 2020) 146-166.

Stein-Wilkeshuis, M.W., 'Deventer en het Spaans bewind 1528-1591', *Deventer jaarboek* 23 (2009), 33-46.

Stensland, Monica, *Habsburg communication in the Dutch Revolt* (Amsterdam 2012).

Stols, Eddy, *De Spaanse Brabanders of de handelsbetrekkingen der Zuidelijke Nederlanden met de Iberische wereld*, 2 vols. (Brussels 1971).

Strada, Famiano, *De thien eerste boecken der Nederlandtsche Oorloge* (Rotterdam 1655).

Struick, J.E.A.l. *Utrecht door de eeuwen heen* (Utrecht and Antwerp 1968).

Swart, Koenraad Wolter, 'The Black Legend during the Eighty Years War', in: *Some political mythologies. Papers delivered to the fifth Anglo-Dutch historical conference,* John S. Bromley and Ernst H. Kossmann, eds. (Britain and the Netherlands V; The Hague 1975), 36-57.

Swigchem, C.A. van, and G. Ploos van Amstel, *Zes unieke wandtapijten: strijd op de Zeeuwse stromen 1572-1576* (Zwolle 1991).

'Tercio Cristóbal de Mondragón', https://terciocristobaldemondragon.wordpress.com/ (accessed 22 October 2018).

Theissen, J.S., ed., *Correspondance française de Marguérite d'Autriche, duchesse de Parme, avec Philippe II* [CM] (Utrecht 1942).

Thomas, Werner, 'How a defeat became a victory: the siege of Ostend in contemporary Dutch war coverage and post-war chronicles', in: *Early modern war narratives and the Revolt in the Low Countries,* Raymond Fagel, Leonor Álvarez Francés and Beatriz Santiago Belmonte, eds. (Manchester 2020) 125-145.

Thou, Jacques-Auguste de, *Histoire universelle despuis 1543 jusqu'en 1607* (London 1734).

*Tractaet van accoordt, ghemaect ende ghesloten tusschen den doorluchtighen ende hooghgheboren vorst ende prince mijn heere, alle prince van Orangien, grave van Nassau, etc., gouverneur van Hollandt, Zeelandt, Westvrieslant ende Utrecht, ende den coronnel Mondragon op het overleveren vande steden van Middelburch ende Arnemuyden* (Delft 1574).

Trillo, Antonio, *Historia de la rebelión y guerras de Flandes*, Miguel Ángel Echvarría Bacigalupe, ed. (Vienna and Munich 2008).

Trim, D.J.B., 'The Huguenots and the European wars of religion, c. 1560-1697, soldiering in national and transnational context', in *The Huguenots: History and memory in transnational context*, David J.B. Trim, ed. (Leiden 2011) 153-192.

Truan, Elena, *El Saco de Amberes by Pedro* Calderón, (MA dissertation, University of Leiden, 2018), https://openaccess.leidenuniv.nl/handle/1887/65007 (accessed 20 May 2019).

Ubachs, Pierre, and Ingrid Evers, *Historische encyclopedie Maastricht* (Zutphen 2005).

Uil, Huib, 'De degen van Mondragón', *Zeeuwse ankers*, https://www.zeeuwseankers.nl/verhaal/de-degen-van-mondragon (accessed 20 May 2019).

Ulloa, Alonso de, *Comentarios de la guerra que el illustrissimo y valerosissimo Príncipe don Hernando Alvarez de Toledo, Duque de Alva, y Capitan General del Rey don Felippe nuestro señor ha hecho contra Guillermo de Nausau, Príncipe de Oranges...* (Venice 1569).

'Utrechtsche kroniek over 1566-1576', H. Brugmans, ed., *Bijdragen en Mededeelingen van het Historisch Genootschap* 25 (1904) 1-258.

Vaernewijck, M. van, *Van die beroerlicke tijden in die Nederlanden en voornamelijk in Ghendt 1566-1568*, Ferdinand Vander Haeghen, ed., 5 vols. (Ghent 1872-1881).

Valdés, Francisco de, *Espejo y disciplina militar* (Madrid 1989).

Valdés, Luis, *Memorias de Asturias*, José María Patac de las Traviesas, ed. (Gijón 1978).

Valladares, Rafael, 'Alba in Portugal: conquest and government 1580-1582', in: Maurits Ebben, Margriet Lacy-Bruijn and Rolof van Hövell tot Westerflier, eds., *Alba, general and servant to the crown* (Rotterdam 2011) 289-305.

Valle de Juan, María Ángeles, 'Manuel Pando y Fernández de Pinedo', DBE.

Vandormael, Herman and Aline Goosens, *Slachtoffer van verraad en intrige. Graaf Lamoraal van Egmond 1522-1568* (Leuven 2007).

Vargas, Baltasar de, *Breve relación en octava rima de la jornada que ha hecho el Duque de Alba desde España hasta Flandes,* Duque de Alba and José López de Toro, eds. (Madrid 1952).

Vázquez de Ávila, Cristóbal, 'Nuevas de la guerra. Traslado de una carta que Christoval Vasques de Avila embio del campo de su magestad al illustrissimo y muy excelente señor duque de Medina Sidonia, en que le da relación de la victoria que su majestad ha avido contra sus enemigos' (1553). Biblioteca Nacional Madrid, Ms. R 29839.

Vázquez de Prada, Valentín, ed., *Lettres marchandes d'Anvers*, 4 vols. (Paris 1960).

Vázquez, Alonso, 'Los sucesos de Flandes en tiempo de Alejando Farnese 1577-1592', CD LXXII-LXXIV (Madrid 1879).

Vega y Carpio, Lope Félix de, *La defensa en la Verdad. Comedia famosa* (Madrid 1700?).

Vega y Carpio, Félix Lope de, 'La famosa tragicomedia de el asalto de Mastrique por el Príncipe de Parma', *Obras de Lope de Vega* XII (Madrid 1901) 437-475.

Vega y Carpio, Félix Lope de, 'Comedia famosa de Julian Romero', in: *Obras de Lope de Vega, obras dramáticas* VII (Madrid 1930) 31-69.

Vega y Carpio, Félix Lope de, 'El valiente Céspedes', *Obras de Lope de Vega* XXVI (Madrid 1969) 51-112.

Vega y Carpio, Félix Lope de, *La aldehuela y el gran prior de Castilla*, Ricardo Serrano Deza, ed. (Ávila 2007).

Velasco Sánchez, José Tomás, 'Ángel Salcedo y Ruiz', DBE.

*Vera realtione dell rota, che e stata data in Fiandra al Conte Lodovico di Nansao, con molti altri signori che lo seguivano nel giorno 14. D'aprile, con il numero de prigioni, e della gente morta, e sbarattata, & altri assai particolari notabili* (Milan 1574).

'Verdwijning van zwaard Mondragon is stunt', https://www.pzc.nl/schouwen-duiveland/verdwijning-van-zwaard-mondragon-is-stunt-a8b54ab1 (accessed 22 October 2018).

Verduyn, Wouter Dirk, *Emanuel van Meteren* (The Hague 1926; Middelburg 2008)

Verhofstad, K., *De regering der Nederlanden in de jaren 1555-1559* (Nijmegen 1937).

Vermaseren, B.A., *De Katholieke Nederlandse geschiedschrijving in de 16e en 17e eeuw over de Opstand* (Leeuwarden 1981).

Versele, Julie, 'Jerónimo de Roda', http://dutchrevolt.leidenuniv.nl/Nederlands/personen/r/roda.htm (accessed 30 June 2020).

Versele, Julie, *Louis del Río (1537-15780. Reflets d'une période troublée* (Brussels 2004).

Verwer, Willem Jansz., *Memoriaelboeck. Dagboek van gebeurtenissen van 1572-1581*, J.J. Temminck, ed. (Haarlem 1973).

Vigil, Ciriaco Miguel, *Asturias monumental* (Valladolid 2003).

Villalobos y Benavides, Diego de, 'Comentarios de las cosas sucedidas en los Países Baxos de Flandes', *Libros de antaño* VI, Alejandro Llorente, ed. (Madrid 1876).

Visser, J. and J.G. Hoogenraad, *Mondragónpad. In de voetsporen van Mondragón. Met route en kaartje* (Zierikzee 2002).

Vloten, J. van, *Middelburgs beleg en overgang, 1572-1574* (Middelburg 1874).

Vosters, Simon A., *De Nederlanden in de Spaanse literatuur (van 1200 tot 1700)* (Breda 2014).

*Waerachtich verhael van tgene dwelck aengaet die rebellie ende oprueficheyt vande gemutineerde Spaignaerden in Zeelant, terstont nae dinnamen van Ziricxzee, den tweeden van julio anno 1576* (Brussels 1576).

'Waerachtig verhael van schermutsinghe by die van Leyden opten 29 julij 1574 jeghen den viandt ghehouden', in: R.J. Fruin, J.E.H. Hooft van Iddekinge and W.J.C. Rammelman Elsevier, eds., *De oude verhalen van het beleg en ontzet van Leiden bij gelegenheid van het derde eeuwgetijde in hun oorspronkelijken vorm herdrukt* (The Hague 1874).

'Waerachtige beschryvinge van de destructie geschiedt binnen der stad Mechelen, gedaen bij den Spaigniaerden', in: *Byvoegsel van authentyke stukken die in de historie van Pieter Bor Christiaensz. slechts sommierlijk en stuksgewijs of in 't geheel niet gevonden worden* (Amsterdam 1679) 140-145.

Wal, Jaap van de, *In naam van Oranje* (Zutphen 2013).

Walsh, William Thomas, *Philip II* (London and New York 1937).

*Warachtige beschrijvinghe van het innemen van Antwerpen ende vande onmenschelijcke ende gants grouwelicke moort, brandt, plonderinge, ongehoorde vrouwen cracht ende maechden schenderye by den Spaniaerden ende haren aenhanck den 4. Novembris anno 1576, ende eenige dagen daerna, aldaer bedreven, ghestelt door een die daer selfs teghenwoordich gheweest is*, Leiden University Library, Manuscripts, Thyspf. 258.

Wegg, Jervis, *The decline of Antwerp under Philip of Spain* (London 1924/ Westport 1979).

Weiss, Ch., ed., *Papiers d'état du cardinal de Granvelle*, IV (Paris 1843), VIII (Paris 1850).

Wernham, R.B. *The making of Elizabethan foreign policy, 1558-1603* (Berkeley, Los Angeles and London 1980).

White, Hayden, *Metahistory. The historical imagination in nineteenth-century Europe* (Baltimore and London 1973).

White, Hayden, 'Value of narrativity in the representation of reality', in: *On narrative*, W.J.T. Mitchell, ed. (Chicago and London 1981) 1-23.

Williams, Patrick, 'Francisco Arias de Bobadilla', DBE.

Williams, Patrick, 'Philip III and the restoration of Spanish government 1598-1603', *English Historical Review* 88 (1973) 751-769.

Williams, Roger, *Memoriën*, J.T. Bodel Nyenhuis, ed. (Utrecht 1864).

Williams, Roger, *The actions of the Low Countries*, D.W. Davies, ed. (Ithaca 1964).

Wit, Arjaan, Marleen Riool and René van Doorn, *Rond de schans van Valdez* (Leiderdorp 2004).

Wolf, J.G.C. de, 'Burocracia y tiempo como actores en el proceso de decisión. La sucesión del gran duque de Alba en el gobierno de los Países Bajos', *Cuadernos de Historia Moderna* 28 (2003) 99-124.

Wortel, T.P.H., 'De vesting Alkmaar anno 1573', in: I. Schöffer et al., *Alkmaar ontzet 1573-1973* (Alkmaar 1973) 41-60.

Wouters, H.H.E, 'Beschouwingen rond de slag bij Mook', *De Maasgouw* 93, 5/6 (1974) 129-164.

Wriothesley, Charles, *A chronicle of England during the reigns of the Tudors, from A.D. 1485 to 1559*, William Douglas Hamilton, ed., 2 vols. (London 1875-1877).

Wyts, Lambert, 'Itinera in Hispania, Viennam et Constantinopolim', Österreichissche Nationalbibliothek, Wien, Cod. 3325, f. 2r-3r (accessed online 28 April 2020).

Wyts, Lambert, 'Voyages de Lambert Wyts', *Handelingen van de Koninklijke Commisie voor Geschiedenis* 5 (1863) 310-325.

Ximénez de Ayllón, Diego, *Sonetos a illustres varones de este felicísimo y catolico ejército y corte* (Antwerp 1569).

Zeller, Gaston, *Le siège de Metz par Charles-Quint* (Nancy 1943).

Zevecote, Jacob van, *Belegh van Leyden* (Leiden 1626).

'Zwaard van Mondragon moet zo snel mogelijk terug', https://www.pzc.nl/schouwen-duiveland/zwaard-van-mondragon-moet-zo-snel-mogelijk-terug~af327400 (accessed 22 October 2018).

'Zwaard van Mondragón op Havenpoort', https://www.omroepzeeland.nl/nieuws/76666/Het-zwaard-van-Mondragon-op-havenpoort (22 October 2018).

# Index

## A

Aa, Van der, A.J. 116, 228
Aalst 84, 177, 180-181, 186
Aarschot, Philip of Croy, Duke of 41-42, 84, 177, 181, 188, 250, 280, 331-332
Abarca de Campos 284
Acuña, Fernando de 105
Acuña, Lope de, captain 20, 294
Aertsz., Pieter 63-64
Agarge, Gasparus L' 162
Aguilar, Marquis of 190
Alameda, paymaster 303, 319
Alamos, Antonio de 203, 226
Alamos, Juan de 203
Alba de Tormes 170, 208
Alba, Fernando Álvarez de Toledo, Duke of, passim
Albania, 14
Albert of Austria, Archduke 101
Albornoz, Juan de 31, 51, 69, 80, 87, 115, 133, 135, 141, 143, 146, 148-149, 152-158, 166, 172, 174, 213, 216, 221, 225-226, 236, 239-240, 284, 291-292, 298, 303, 305-308, 312-314, 344
Albornoz, Juana 153-154
Alcalá de Henares 103
Alessandria della Paglia 95, 99-100, 189
Algiers 122
Alkmaar 70-71, 247, 269, 276, 336
Alphen aan den Rijn 296, 298, 310
Altemps, Count Jacob Hannibal of 181
Alternach 46
Álvarez de Toledo, Marquis Alonso 195
Álvarez Francés, Leonor 19, 320, 333
Allaumont 210
Ambly 211
America (see also Indies) 343
Amersfoort 322
Amiens 214
Amsterdam 23, 69, 154, 262-263, 294, 308, 320
Anne of Austria, Queen of Spain 54, 56, 213, 217, 344
Antequera 110
Antwerp (Spanish Fury) 15, 19, 22, 77, 80, 81, 85-88, 99-101, 116, 118, 127, 133-141, 143-144, 146, 148-149, 152, 154-157, 160-161, 164-165, 167-171, 174, 176, 178-182, 184-188, 192, 195, 202, 209, 215-216, 219, 222, 233, 235, 237, 240, 246-247, 250, 253, 255-256, 258-262, 268, 271, 282-285, 287, 289, 309, 320, 331, 338-339
Aragon 141
Arco, Francisco del, captain 103
Arias Montano, Benito 154
Armenteros, Tomás de 211
Arnemuiden (Ramua) 144-146, 191, 222, 337
Arnhem 290
Arras 45
Arrieta, captain/ colonel 147, 151, 213
Artois 38-39, 213, 216-217
Aspremont, Anne d' 136
Aspremont, Gerard d', Lord of Marchéville 210
Asti 51
Asturias 283-284
Augsburg 229
Aulnou 210
Austria, George of, Prince Bishop of Liège 39
Avalos y Guzmán, Alonso de 101
Ávila 122, 136, 161, 173, 194-195
Ayamonte, Antonio de Zúñiga, Marquis of 189

## B

Barbarossa 32, 105, 203
Barrera y Mondragón, Juan de la 218
Barrientos, Luis de 194, 196
Batavia 263
Bayern, Sabine of 52

Baza 102
Beamonte, Martín de 202
Belpois, Aymot 210
Beauvoir, Lord of, see Philip of Lannoy
Benazuza 48, 94
Bentivoglio, Girolamo 145, 189, 256, 265
Bergen-op-Zoom 74, 143, 147, 156-157, 174, 222, 224, 237, 249, 254
Berlaymont, Charles, Count of 86
Berlo, Lord of 54
Bermúdez, general 205
Bernia 125
Beverwijk 32, 298, 322
Binche 37, 131
Biscay 31, 55, 93, 105
Bisselt 163
Blok, P.J. 162
Blomberg, Barbara 83
Boesbeeck 119
Bois-le-Duc (Den Bosch) 79
Boisot, Charles de 245-246
Boisot, Louis de 246, 248-249, 253, 263, 265
Bommenede 174-175, 195, 246-247
Bontius, Reinier 277
Boon, Cornelis 279
Bor, Pieter 63, 70, 262, 275
Borja 103
Borja, Juan de 58
Boulogne-sur-Mer 33, 36-37
Boussu, Maximilien de Hennin, Count of 72, 293, 296
Boutens, P.C. 227, 234
Bouvignes 37, 41
Brabant 60, 71, 76, 84, 169-170, 177, 179, 211, 219, 244, 248, 255, 260, 327
Bracamonte Dávila Gonzalo de, maestre de campo 19, 48, 50, 66, 87, 159
Brançion, Jan van 61
Brantôme, Pierre de Bourdeille, Lord of 28, 30, 34, 49, 51, 53, 111-112, 126, 346
Breda 79, 154, 216, 222, 237, 241-244, 268, 312, 337, 341-342
Brenner Pass 37
Brésin, Louis 38
Brielle 13, 56, 143, 216, 252, 292
Brito, Antonio 284, 329
Brouwer, H. 278

Brouwer, Johan 14, 34, 202
Bruges 135-136, 138, 140, 142-143, 152, 210, 242, 339
Brussels 13, 15, 32, 38, 41, 44, 47, 50-52, 57, 75, 77, 79, 84, 88, 92, 100, 102, 112, 127, 129, 131, 166, 177-179, 183-184, 195, 206, 209, 214, 237-238, 242, 254, 271, 281, 283, 292-293, 330, 338, 341
Bulgnéville 210
Buren 329
Burghley, Lord 176
Burgos 118, 136
Busto, Bernabé del 204

## C

Cabrera de Córdoba, Luis 93, 188
Cáceres, maestre de campo 108
Cádiz 47
Calais 33
Calderón de la Barca, Pedro 184
Calfven 219
Cambrai 37
Cambrésis 132
Canary Islands 208
Cañizares, José de 93, 109-110
Caraballo, Sebastián de 218
Cárdenas, Teresa de 203
Carreño Maldonado, Diego 230
Carvajal, captain 44
Carvajal, Francisco de 171, 230
Castellanos, paymaster 129
Castile and León 122, 284
Castillo, Pedro del 175, 242
Catalonia 162
Câteau-Cambrésis (Peace of) 37, 45, 207
Catherine de Medici, Queen of France 78
Cervantes, Miguel de 85
Cianca, Antonio de 123
Claerbout, Joos 263, 266
Cobejo de la Sagra 102
Coligny, Gaspar de, French admiral 43-44, 106-108
Cornejo, Pedro 74, 130-131, 144, 346
Cremona 99-100
Cuéllar, Juan de 284, 285, 314
Cuenca 29, 31, 48, 93
Culemborg 19, 136, 290
Curiel, Juan de 284

Champagney, Fréderic Perrenot, Lord of 79, 86, 99, 165-168, 170, 179, 181, 183-184, 196, 222, 282, 340
Charles II, King of Spain 116, 118
Charles IX, King of France 68
Charles V, Emperor, passim
Châtelet, Claude de, Lord of Bulgnéville 210
Châtelet, Guillemette de 210, 256-257, 264, 266

### D
Dahlem, battle of 15, 128-131, 142, 151, 156, 191, 194-195, 272, 290
Damvillers 46, 95, 207-211, 213-216
Dávalos, César 132
Dávila, Beatriz 122
Dávila, Fernando 140, 142, 173, 194
Dávila, Tomás 122
Dávila y Daza, Sancho, chapter II passim, 15, 18-23, 30-31, 50, 74-77, 79-80, 83, 86-89, 92, 99-101, 201, 205, 210, 218-219, 223, 226-227, 237, 240, 246, 249, 251, 255, 258-259, 265, 267-268, 282-283, 286, 289, 308, 313, 332-335, 337-345, 347-348
Dávila y Guevara, Sancho 118, 120, 191
Dávila y San Vitores, Gerónimo Manuel 115-125, 192
Daza, Ana 117-118, 121, 192
Daza, Pedro 122
Dehesa de Villagarcía 173
Delft 68, 72, 201, 235, 306, 308, 310-312, 318
Delgado, secretary 258-259
Dendermonde 216, 268, 347
Deventer 212-213, 268, 271, 291-292, 347
Diest 51
Dinant 16, 37, 39-42, 44, 106-107, 206
Djerba 119, 124
Dordrecht 80-82, 241-242, 297
Dorp, Arend van 221, 250, 252-253
Douai 16, 43, 46, 95, 106-107, 205, 207, 209
Dourlens 214
Duiveland 192, 245-246
Düren 32, 36, 342
Duym, Jacob 275

### E
East Frisia 53
Eberstain, Otto, Count of 180
Edward VI, King of England 35
Egmond 298
Egmont, Lamoral, Count of 15, 44-45, 52-53, 85, 88, 108, 112, 127-128, 191, 195, 336
Egmont, Philip, Count of 88
Elbe 118, 122, 203-204, 207
El Greco 18, 29, 97, 102-103, 110
Eleonor, Queen of France 35
Eliot, T.S. 29
Elizabeth I, Queen of England 82
Enghien 51
England 14, 16, 32, 35, 37, 50, 105-106, 119-120, 123-124, 128, 184, 224, 226, 341-342
Enkhuizen 293
Eraso, Francisco de, royal secretary 45
Ercilla, Alonso de 27
Escobedo, Juan de, 90
Escorial, San Lorenzo de El 43, 108
Esparza, José Javier 44
Espinar, Andresa del 192
Estrée, Jean d' 41
Eyemouth 36
Eynde, Cornelius van 185

### F
Farnese, Alexander, Prince of Parma 200, 258-259, 263, 265-266, 332
Felices, Diego de, captain 86, 330
Ferdinand I, Emperor 119
Fernández Dávila, Francisco 328
Fernández de Pineda, Manuel Pando, Marquis of Miraflores 115, 120-121, 131, 161, 192
Figueroa, Lope de, captain 20-21, 94, 129
Fijnaart 244
Flanders 84, 143, 169, 320
Floyon, Florent, Lord of 86
Flushing (Vlissingen) 56, 143-144, 157, 212, 257, 292
Fontainebleau 27, 33, 35, 37, 50, 92
Foreest, Nanning van 70
France 16, 32, 38, 43, 50, 77, 121, 131, 171, 206-207, 210-211, 214, 216, 224, 226, 250, 279, 324, 347

Francis I, King of France 33-35, 92
Franco Bahamonde, Francisco 200
Frías, Hernando de 136-137, 152, 171, 173, 196
Frisia (Friesland) 19, 58, 80, 211, 348
Fruin, Robert 162
Fruytiers, Jan 320
Fuenterrabia 121

## G

Gachard, Louis Prosper 247
Gallo, Barbara 136
Gallo, Catalina 118, 136, 142, 195
Gamboa, Pedro 32-33, 36, 48
Gascoigne, George 181
Gaytán, María 48, 93-94, 100, 103
Gaytán, Pedro, captain 33, 48, 93
Geertruidenberg 76, 154, 156, 222, 235
Gelderland (see also Guelders) 162
Génard, P. 182
Geraardsbergen 181
Germany 44, 51, 57, 86, 88-89, 180, 182, 226, 239-240, 243, 256, 259, 276, 324
Gete, battle of the river 15, 128, 130-131, 156, 290
Ghent 44, 51, 57, 86, 89, 180, 182, 226, 239-240, 243, 256, 259, 276, 324
Gijón 283, 286
Goes 147-148, 219-222, 227, 245, 338
González Dávila, Gil 119, 125
González de León, Fernando 14, 87, 92
González del Castillo, Diego 202
Gorinchem (Gorcum) 223
Gouda 309, 318
Granada 97, 110, 190
Granvelle, Antoine Perrenot de, Cardinal 27, 39, 47, 53, 62, 65, 75, 80, 92, 112, 133, 165, 169, 177, 179, 181, 207-208, 233, 235, 243-244, 249-250, 258-259, 280-281, 340
Gravelines, battle of 45
Groenlo 200
Groningen 213
Guam 118
Guelders 32, 50, 80, 327
Guevara, Luisa de 118
Guijosa, Jerónimo de, captain 203

Guînes 45
Gussainville 210
Guzmán de Silva, Diego 209
Gysius 63

## H

Haarlem (siege of) 15, 21, 36, 61, 66-70, 73, 94, 99, 154, 199, 216, 233, 247, 253, 256, 269, 276, 293-294, 297, 300, 310, 316, 320, 323, 336, 340
Haecht, Godevaert van 133-134, 137, 165, 167, 216, 233
Ham 45
Hangest, Jean de, Lord of Genlis 148-149
Harari, Yuval 12
Haro, captain 224
Hatton, Christopher 88
Haussy, Jeanne de 209
Havré, Charles-Philip of Croy, Marquis of 181, 257
Heiligerlee, battle of 15, 335
Helfault, Antoine de 95
Hem, Catherine du 209
Hem, Robert du, Lord of Auby 209
Henry II, King of France 33-35, 41, 205
Henry VIII, King of England 32-33, 35, 92
Herrera Daza, Francisco de 202
Herrera y Tordesillas, Antonio de 180
Hesdin 16, 37, 39, 95-96
Heumen 162
Hierges, Giles of Berlaymont, Lord of 81, 162, 296, 320, 329
Hoefnagel, Jacob 77
Hogenberg, Frans 127, 181-182, 246, 256
Holland 58, 66, 76-77, 80-82, 144, 154, 179, 226, 233, 242, 247, 269, 274, 281, 283, 285, 288-290, 292, 296-298, 300, 307, 312, 317, 320-321, 323, 330, 333, 347
Hooft, P.C. 16, 28, 30, 50, 52-53, 58-59, 61-64, 66, 70, 74-75, 85, 90, 110, 128, 131, 187, 220, 251, 254, 256, 264, 336, 340
Horne, Philip of Montmorency, Count of 15, 53, 85, 127, 265
Hortensius, Lambertus 63-65
Hoyo, Martín del 188
Huélamo 31, 93

Hugo, Victor 200
Hulst 102
Hume, A.S. 30, 35-36
Huy 212
Huy, Philip of Namur, Lord of 131

## I

Ibarra, Esteban de 87
Ibarrola, Pedro de, Julián Romero's father 31, 97
Ibarrola, Pedro de, Julián Romero's son 103
Ibiza 48, 95, 125
Idiáquez, Martín de 261
IJsselmonde 81-82, 252
Illán, Esteban, captain 69, 95
Indies (see also America) 208
Ireland 36-37, 55, 101
Isabel of Austria, Princess of Spain 101
Isabel, Queen of Castile 284
Istanbul 119
Italy 14, 16, 28, 36, 89-91, 94, 103, 105, 119, 125-127, 169, 189, 257, 271, 289, 294, 325, 332, 338, 341
Italy, tercio of 299, 301, 303, 312, 313

## J

Jacobszoon, Wouter 308-309
Jedburgh 37
Jemappes 147
Jemmingen (Jemgum), battle of 15, 53, 94, 128-131, 135, 144, 156, 191, 290, 335, 338
Jerez de los Caballeros 45, 92
Juan (don) de Austria 83, 86-87, 89-90, 99, 110, 178, 182-183, 188, 257, 332

## K

Katwijk (aan den Rijn) 71, 298
Kenau 21, 70, 256
Kloek, Els 274-275
Krimpen aan de IJssel 81

## L

La Abadía 170
La Goleta 47, 95, 173
La Mancha 90
La Motte, Valentin Pardieu, Lord of 305
Ladron, Albrecht, Count 138
Lagrange 210

Lalaing, Mary of 265-266
Lalaing, Philip, Count of 177, 280
Laleu 42
Langstraat 76
Lannoy, Fernando de, Lord of La Roche, 280-283, 291, 309, 314, 316, 318-319, 341
Lannoy, Philip of, Lord of Beauvoir 146, 227-228
Laon 41
Laredo 55, 60
Le Clerc, Jean 266
Le Quesnoy, battle of 131
Leiden (siege of) 15, 21-22, 71, 78, 159, 227, 233, 246-250, 269, 273-278, 281, 283-284, 296, 300, 303, 306-312, 314-318, 320, 328, 333-334, 336, 346
Leiderdorp 298, 300
Leith 36
Lens 16, 43, 206, 214
Leuven 84-85, 237
Licques, Philip of Récourt, Lord of 310
Liège 39
Lier 51, 86, 89, 219, 271, 290
Limburg (and Overmaas) 162, 259
Lipsius, Justus 153
Lisbon 47
Livorno 51
Lodeña, Juan de 94
Loevestein 77
Lombardy 51, 120, 123, 288, 294; tercio of 48, 50-51, 79, 124, 203, 271-272, 289-292, 299
London 35, 47, 92, 120
Londoño, Sancho de 19, 30, 48, 50, 124, 129, 271, 289-290, 345
Longastre, Charles de Houchin, Monsieur de 214
López de Ávalos, Ruy 132
López Gallo Vega, Luis 136
López Gallo, Alonso 19, 136, 142, 194, 210
López Gallo, Juan, Lord of Male 118, 136, 142
López Gallo, Juan, son of Juan López Gallo 136, 210
López Osorio, Juan 206
López, Josine 136

Lorraine 28, 51, 210, 225-226, 257-259, 269
Losado, Juan Carlos 44
Low Countries, passim
Loyola, Ignatius of 285
Lus (Luz) 210
Luxembourg 83, 87, 127, 200, 210

# M

Maas 159, 223, 303 308, 317
Maassluis 72, 273, 302, 318
Maastricht 19, 53, 89, 129, 158, 162, 189, 193, 200, 258, 271, 290, 322, 328, 332, 335
Mackenzie, Ann 184
Madrid 15, 17, 23, 47-48, 50, 55, 73, 75, 93-94, 99, 101, 103, 125, 148, 183, 238, 258-260, 271, 284, 287, 314, 319, 341
Mahdia (África) 119-120, 123-124
Malaga 47
Malta 28, 48-49, 342
Mallea, Pedro de 260
Manpad, battle at the 69
Mansfelt, Peter-Ernst, Count of 84, 189, 260
Manteau, Jacques 253
Marchéville 210
Marchiennes 205
Margaret of Parma 27, 46, 136, 207
Mariana, Juan de 124
Marichalar, Antonio 29, 81, 88, 91, 104
Mariembourg 215
Mariemont 37
Marnix of Sint-Aldegonde, Philip 15, 72, 234-236, 302, 306
Martín García, Gonzalo 115, 124-125, 192
Martínez Ruiz, Enrique 115, 119, 195
Mary Tudor, Queen of England 106, 119, 128, 341
Mary, Princess of Scotland 35
Mary of Austria, Princess of Spain 213
Maximilian I, Emperor 39
Maximilian II, Emperor 54, 213
Mechelen (sack of) 15, 52, 54, 60-62, 94, 340
Medina del Campo 136, 201-202, 205, 208, 217-218, 260, 262, 285, 339

Medinaceli, Juan de la Cerda, Duke of 55-57, 60, 141-142, 292
Medrazo y Garreta, Ricardo 201
Meerssen 158
Megen, Charles of Brimeu, Count of 81-82
Méndez, Luisa 94
Mendoza, Bernardino de 16, 20, 30, 53, 59, 61-62, 67, 74-75, 80, 86, 127, 130-132, 145, 159-161, 164, 187, 219-220, 229, 232, 234, 244, 246, 256, 290, 314, 336-337, 340
Mendoza, Gabriel de 225-226
Mendoza Sarmiento, Juan de, cavalry general 19
Mendoza, Pedro de, captain 45
Mercado, Mencía de 202
Merken, Lucretia Wilhelmina van 262, 279
Messina 28, 49, 118
Meteren, Emanuel van 16, 52, 61-63, 74, 130, 132, 220, 244, 256, 336
Metz (siege of) 37, 216
Meulleners, J.L. 162
Mewtys, Peter 36
Middelburg (siege of) 15, 74, 144-145, 156, 191, 217, 223, 227-231, 233-234, 236-237, 247-248, 251, 254, 263-265, 268-269, 337, 342, 347-348
Milan 100, 134, 155, 305
Miota Romero, Julián de 97
Miota Romero, Pedro Melchor de, Marquis of Lugros 97
Miota, Pedro 97
Mol 83
Molve, Monsieur de 119
Moncalvo 191
Mondragón, Alonso de 203
Mondragón, Alonso de, Mondragón's son-in-law 209, 217, 261
Mondragón, Catalina de 202, 205-206
Mondragón y Mercado, Cristóbal de, chapter III passim, 15-16, 18-23, 30, 48, 50, 72, 75, 80, 84-85, 87, 92-93, 99, 118, 122, 136, 142, 146-148, 150, 152-153, 157, 159, 161, 168-169, 174-175, 177, 180, 189, 192, 274, 279-280, 283-284, 286, 289, 291, 309, 332, 334, 337-340, 342-348

Mondragón, Cristóbal de, Mondragón's grandchild 261
Mondragón, Juan de 203
Mondragón, Magdalena de 202
Mondrágon, Margarita de 209
Mondragón, María de 203
Mondragón, Martín de 202
Mons (Hainaut; siege of) 15, 57-58, 60, 93, 147, 156, 226, 286-287, 293
Montalcino 289
Montesdoca, Francisco de 19, 180
Montmorency, Anne de, connétable de France 40-42, 44, 106-108
Mook 162
Mookerheyde, battle of 15, 77, 116, 159-166, 169-170, 184, 193-195, 237-238, 246, 253-254, 308-309, 336-338
Moons, Magdalena 274-275, 278-280, 283, 287, 300-302, 333-334, 347
Moons, Pieter 275
Moons, Reinier 275
Moons, Willem 275, 301
Mora, Cristóbal de 33-34
Morales, Damián de, captain 80, 85, 102
More, Thomas 121
Morgan, Thomas 59, 229
Morillon, Maximilien 53, 62, 65-66, 75, 80-81, 112, 133, 165, 167, 169, 171, 174-177, 179-181, 233-235, 237, 243-244, 249, 251, 257, 268, 280-281, 340
Mühlberg, battle of 118, 120, 123-124, 203, 205, 341
Muiden 322, 325
Murélaga 93
Mures 48, 94

# N
Naarden (sack of) 15, 22, 36, 60-66, 73, 110, 274, 276, 336
Namur 155-156
Naples 105, 120, 124, 258-260, 338; tercio of 51, 291, 299
Naranjo, Marcos 323-324
Nassau, Louis of 60, 70, 130, 147, 159-161, 163, 194
Nassau, Maurice of 200
Navarrete, *electo* 186-187
Navarrete, maestre de campo 108
Navarro, captain 205
New-Biscay 120
Newcastle 32-33
Nieuwerbrug aan den Rijn 296
Nijmegen 62, 77, 290
Niño, Gabriel 298
Noircarmes, Philip of Sainte-Aldegonde, Lord of 296, 304, 307
Nomsz., Johannes 263, 265
Noordwijk 71, 298
Noyelles, Georges de Montigny, Monsieur de 213-214

# O
Olivares, Count Duke of 97
Olivier, Antoine 226
Oostende 103, 193
Oosterhout 154, 156
Opzoomer, Simon 23
Orange, William of 15, 17, 20, 29, 45-47, 53, 58-59, 61, 68, 70, 72-73, 75, 79-80, 82, 88, 108, 111-112, 129, 131-132, 148, 160-161, 166, 179-180, 183-185, 191, 194, 227, 230, 232-238, 241-242, 247, 253-257, 267-268, 285, 296-297, 302, 306, 308, 317, 324, 329, 331, 335, 337, 342
Orange, Philip William of 73
Orejón, Rodrigo, Dávila's cousin 125, 154, 158, 180
Orejón, Rodrigo. Dávila's grandfather 192
Orlers, J.J. 315
Ortega y Gasset, José 29
Osorio de Ulloa, Juan, captain 54, 175, 246
Oss, Adrian van, Lord of Heembeke 81
Oudewater 81, 329
Oudorp 70
Overijssel 80

# P
Pacheco, Hernando, captain 20, 143, 212, 292
Padilla, Pedro de 85, 126, 145, 148, 222
Palermo, Aurelio, captain 298
Pannemaker, Willem de 32
Paracuellos de Jarama 98
Pardo, Jerónimo 143

Pardo, Juan, Lord of Frémicourt 136, 142-143
Pardo, Silvester 136
Pardo Garrido, Catalina 118, 136
Paredes, García de 109
Parfonru 210
Paris 58, 120-121, 134, 206-207, 214, 258
Parker, Geoffrey 14, 30, 272
Parma, Prince of, see Farnese
Pavia 119, 125, 133
Pels, Clara 285
Pembroke, Count 59
Peñausende 94, 98
Pérez de Goitia Jubero, Juan 94
Pérez de Montalbán, Juan 109
Pérez de Vargas, Luis, Maestre de campo 203
Pérez-Reverte, Arturo 204, 220, 261, 269, 342, 347
Perrenot, Fréderic, see Champagney
Peru 230
Peso y Guevara, Francisca del 118
Philip II, King of Spain, passim
Philip IV, King of Spain 118
Philip V, King of Spain 116
Piedmont 32, 120, 123
Pinkie, battle of 36
Poitiers 29
Plymouth 32
Pollmann, Judith 12
Ponce, Andrés 194
Ponce, Luis 194
Portugal 14, 191-194, 284
Pot, Jan 248, 252-253
Poyates 31
Poyet 311
Puddu, Raffaele 18, 110
Porto Ercole (Puerto Herculis) 127

# Q

Quatrefages, René 14
Quevedo, Francisco de 28, 109
Quiévrain, battle of 15, 57-58, 148
Quiñones, Juan de 298

# R

Rabelais, François 128
Rabuecourt 210
Rabutin, François de 41
Reimerswaal 74, 174, 222, 335-336
Remerchicourt (Remicourt) 210
Remón, Alonso 20
Renard, Simon 41-42
Requesens, Luis de, passim
Reyd, Everhard van 281
Rhenen 327
Ridderkerk 81
Río, Antonio del, Lord of Cleydael 152-153, 194
Río, Francisco del 242
Río, Martin Antonio del 92, 153, 257
Ríos, Martín Alonso de los 208
Robles, Gaspar de 19, 89, 168, 209, 213, 240, 335, 348
Robles, Melchor de, maestre de campo 48
Rocroi 43
Roda, Gerónimo de 53, 83-86, 88-89, 157, 177-180, 182-183, 248-250, 255, 281
Rodríguez Hernández, Antonio José 14
Roermond 129, 192
Roeulx, John of Croy, Count of 257
Rojas y Valdés, García de 284-285
Rojas Zorrilla, Francisco 184
Rome 118, 120, 122, 250, 338
Romero de Villalba, Julián 102
Romero, Francisca 94, 100-104, 111
Romero, Julián, chapter I, passim, 118, 125, 129, 131, 133, 136, 156-157, 167, 174, 177, 180-181, 183-184, 189, 195, 202, 206-207, 218, 231, 234, 240-241, 265, 167-268, 279-280, 283-284, 286, 289, 300, 302, 309, 313-314, 332, 334-336, 340-346, 348
Romero, Juliana 31, 80. 100, 102-103
Roosendaal 83, 254
Rooze-Stouthamer, Clasien 143
Rotterdam 81-82, 285, 293, 308, 318
Roucy, Hélène de 210
Ruiz, Simón 260, 285

# S

Saeftinghe 150
Saint-Aignan 210
Saint-Amand 181
Saint-Dizier 16, 203
Saint-Mihiel (Lorraine) 259
Saint-Omer 39, 95

Saint-Quentin (battle of) 16, 27, 43-45, 50, 52, 59, 88, 93, 107-108, 111-112, 206, 341
Salamanca 192
Salazar, Juan de, captain 54
Salcedo Ruiz, Ángel 201-202, 217, 244, 247-248, 257, 261
Salinas, Catalina de 20
Salinas, Jerónimo de, captain 19, 52, 127, 239
Salvatierra, Francisco de, sargento mayor 147
San Cugat 161
San Vitores, Diego Luís 118
San Vitores, Francisca de 118
Sánchez de Bahamonde, Diego 323
Sande, Álvaro de 119
Sandoval, Prudencio de 42
Santana, Francisco de 94
Santander 56
Santiago Belmonte, Beatriz 19, 178
Sardinia, tercio of 48, 51
Sassenheim 298
Savoy 51
Savoy, Philibert, Duke of 41, 43, 102
Scheldt 257
Scotland 14, 32, 35-37, 342
Schiedam 308
Schoonhoven 81
Schouwen 246
Segovia 192, 284-285
Sepúlveda, Juan Ginés de 38
Severenborn 290
Sevilla, Fernando de 153
Seville 285
Sicily 34, 48, 112, 338; tercio of 27-28, 48, 50-51, 54, 56, 94, 100, 105, 332
Siena 288-289
Sint-Annaland 254
Sint Maartensdijk 249
Sint Philipsland 192, 245
Sint-Truiden 53
Somerset, Edward Seymour, Duke of 35-37
Soria, Diego de 20
Sotomayor, Alonso de, captain 98, 250
Spa 290
Spaarndam 66-67
Spain, passim

Steen, Jasper van der 12
Strada, Famiano 132, 204, 256, 275, 278
Stukeley, Thomas 55
Suárez de Figueroa, Gómez, Count of Feria 207
Swieten, Adriaan van 309
Syracuse 48

# T

Tännisberg 205
Tassis, Juan Bautista de 296
Teresa of Ávila 117, 121
Terneuzen 234
The Hague 71-72, 274-275, 285, 300-302, 304, 306, 308, 310, 322-323, 346
Thérouanne 37-38
Thionville 51, 127, 215
Tholen 83, 223, 237, 254
Thornton 36
Tienen 85, 191, 237
Tigeville 210
Tisnacq, Charles de 46
Titian 203
Toledo 46, 93, 101-102, 201
Toledo y Enríquez, Fernando de, maestre de campo 19, 78-79, 81, 111, 159, 290, 293, 313, 341
Toledo, Fadrique de 20, 61-63, 65-66, 68-69, 87, 143-144, 146, 212, 225, 238, 271, 294, 299, 341
Toledo, Fernando de, cavalry general 20, 51, 79, 127-128, 135, 137-138, 140, 143, 146, 191, 193, 196, 201, 341
Toledo, Francisco de 132
Toledo, García de, Viceroy of Sicily 48, 50, 100, 105
Toledo, Pedro de 100, 105-106
Toledo, Rodrigo de 19
Toledo, Teresa de 118
Torre, Jacques de la 242-243, 341
Torrejoncillo del Rey 31, 34, 44, 93
Tournai 213, 265
Trillo, Antonio de 16, 61-62, 71, 130-131, 145, 147, 151, 158-160, 183, 220, 228, 234, 237, 241, 249, 256, 290, 302, 314, 335-337, 340
Tunis 32, 47, 105, 203, 214, 289, 341

## U

Ulloa, Alonso de, chronicler 13, 338, 346
Ulloa, Alonso de, Maestre de campo 19, 51-52
Unamuno, Miguel de 29
Utrecht 72, 80, 82, 154, 215, 281-282, 290-294, 300, 308-311, 316, 319, 321-322, 327-328, 341

## V

Valdés, Francisca 284, 329
Valdés, Francisco de, chapter IV passim, 15, 19, 21-23, 30, 50, 71, 78-79, 90, 118, 129, 146, 159, 167, 183, 189, 249-250, 254-255, 258-259, 339-348
Valdés, Jordán de 286
Valencia 119, 125
Valenciennes 154, 158, 180, 182
Valkenburg 298
Valladolid 41
Vallecas 94
Van der Essen, Léon 14, 65
Vargas, Alonso de, cavalry general 19, 84-85, 88-90, 99, 168, 177, 189, 272
Vargas, Baltasar 126
Vargas, Francisco de, sargento 272, 292
Vatronville 210
Vaucelles, Truce of 41, 43
Vázquez de Ávila, Cristóbal 38
Vázquez, Alonso 258, 332
Vázquez, Antón 117-118, 122
Vázquez, Mateo 100
Veere 143
Vega, Lope de 18, 21, 28, 30-31, 94, 102, 104, 108-110, 136, 193, 332, 342
Venice 338
Verdugo, Francisco 19, 30
Vermeyen, Jan Cornelisz. 32
Vienna 201
Vilvoorde 65, 98, 149
Villalar, battle of 122
Villalba, Pedro de, captain 100, 102
Villers, Jean de Montigny, Lord of 131
Vincennes 42
Violente 172-173, 175
Vissenaken 85
Vitelli, Giovanluigi (Chiappino) 51, 79, 89, 245

Vitoria y Zárate, Catalina de 48, 93
Vitoria, Francisco de 61
Vlaardingen 302
Volkerak 244
Voorschoten 298
Vosbergen, Casper van 252
Vrouwenpolder 227

## W

Walcheren 145, 149, 156, 219, 223, 227-228, 239
Walem 85
Walsh, W.T. 30
Warmond 307
Wassenaar 323
Waterland 290
Weert 222
Weesp 325
Werff, Pieter Adriaansz. Van der 275
White, Hayden 11
Williams, Roger 57, 59, 62, 74, 301-302, 311
Wissekercke, Magdalena van 259
Worms 117
Wou, Hendrik 63-64
Woudrichem 222-223
Wouters, H.H.E. 162
Wouw 254

## Y

Yeste 107
Yuste 220

## Z

Zacatecas 118, 120
Zalamea 217-218
Zaltbommel 77
Zamora 39, 284
Zapata, Rodrigo, captain 20, 296
Zayas, Gabriel de, royal secretary 56, 58, 164, 221
Zeeland 46, 54, 58, 74, 82-83, 144, 146, 149, 152, 156, 171, 174-175, 179, 219, 223, 227-229, 233, 237-238, 242, 246, 252, 254, 269, 282, 320, 348
Zevecote, Jacob van 276-277
Zevenbergen 76, 216

Zierikzee (siege of) 15, 22, 81-82, 84, 87, 172, 175-177, 192, 199-201, 221, 227, 246-248, 250-255, 267, 269, 337, 348
Zoetermeer 317
Zoeterwoude 273, 298
Zuid-Beveland 219, 237
Zúñiga, Juan de, brother of Luis de Requesens 75, 168, 240
Zúñiga, Juan de, father of Luis de Requesens 155
Zutphen 15, 32, 60, 62, 276

www.ingramcontent.com/pod-product-compliance
Ingram Content Group UK Ltd.
Pitfield, Milton Keynes, MK11 3LW, UK
UKHW050457150426
5217IPUK00025B/1727